Praise for

International Libel and Privacy Handbook

*A Global Reference for Journalists, Publishers,
Webmasters, and Lawyers*

Edited by Charles J. Glasser Jr.

"For many years, attorneys have awaited publication of a single volume summarizing libel and privacy law throughout the world. At long last, we can now compare on a nation-by-nation basis how countries in the Americas, Asia, and Europe deal with libel and privacy issues and how that treatment differs from that in the United States. **This book offers a sophisticated and reader-friendly response to the core questions that any practitioner frequently must consider.**"

Floyd Abrams

"Charles Glasser's impressive book could not have come at a better time. We've entered the post–*Gutnick v. Dow Jones* era, where the protection of geographical borders is history and where the online media face exposure to liability in every corner of the globe. **This welcome volume offers practical guidance about the legal environment in many jurisdictions abroad. Mr. Glasser, a former journalist and now the media law counsel for Bloomberg worldwide, is ideally suited to the challenge this eminently useful work meets.**"

Richard N. Winfield
International Senior Lawyers Project
Clifford Chance US LLP

"For thirty-five years, the Reporters Committee has helped journalists navigate American laws regarding their rights to publish. **But in the Internet Age, we increasingly are required to know media laws around the world. Charles Glasser's *International Libel and Privacy Handbook* is an indispensable addition to our law library.**"

LUCY DALGLISH
Executive Director, Reporters Committee for Freedom of the Press

"Bloomberg's *International Libel and Privacy Handbook* is a highly readable guide to the legal standards that affect media reporting and publishing in a selection of countries in the Americas, Europe, and Asia. Today's journalists inevitably speak to the entire world no matter where they may be based. Prudence dictates that they recognize the differing legal rules and norms they will encounter beyond their own borders. **Charles Glasser has assembled a blue-ribbon panel of legal experts who provide essential information in a series of accessible outlines that make quick checks of specific issues easy. Additional essays on special topics such as book publishing, Internet and copyright issues, and enforcement of foreign judgments will be particularly useful for media attorneys.** But anyone who speaks or writes for a living—or who advises those who do—will benefit from consulting this handbook."

JANE E. KIRTLEY
Silha Professor of Media Ethics and Law
Director, Silha Center for the Study of Media Ethics and Law
School of Journalism and Mass Communication
University of Minnesota

International Libel and Privacy Handbook

International Libel and Privacy Handbook

A Global Reference for Journalists,
Publishers, Webmasters, and Lawyers

Edited by

CHARLES J. GLASSER JR.
MEDIA COUNSEL, BLOOMBERG NEWS®

With a Foreword by MATTHEW WINKLER

BLOOMBERG PRESS
NEW YORK

First edition published 2006
1 3 5 7 9 10 8 6 4 2

Library of Congress Cataloging-in-Publication Data

International libel and privacy handbook : a global reference for journalists, publishers, webmasters, and lawyers / edited by Charles J. Glasser, Jr. -- 1st ed.
     p. cm.
   Includes bibliographical references and index.
   ISBN 1-57660-188-9 (alk. paper)
 1. Libel and slander 2. Privacy, Right of. 3. Freedom of speech. 4. Mass media--Law and legislation.
I. Glasser, Charles J., Jr.

K930.I58 2006
346.03'4--dc22
                                                                 2005033618

CONTENTS

PART ONE | AMERICAS

PART TWO | ASIA

PART FOUR | ISSUES OF GLOBAL INTEREST

FOREWORD

I'LL NEVER FORGET the day in 1982 when a London-based colleague realized as we were opening our mail that he was reading something destined to become a front-page scoop. Inside a manila envelope with no return address was a half-inch-thick document prepared by one of the four largest clearing banks in the U.K. The text was riveting. A country-by-country breakdown of each South American nation's nonperforming indebtedness to the British bank leapt off each page. Almost every major American and European bank was having difficulty reducing bad debts to Latin American countries. The U.K. bank's shareholders and competitors would be eager to learn the extent of the bank's bad loans derived from South America. Here at last was the answer.

As the document was sent anonymously, we had to determine its authenticity. Within thirty minutes, my colleague confirmed that someone unknown to us, or to the bank, had obtained something prepared by bank employees and that we were the recipients. He told his editors that we had an exclusive. When he called bank officials for comment, they inadvertently revealed the authenticity of the document by asserting that we couldn't publish something that was "stolen."

Publishing our discovery suddenly became a race against legal jeopardy: Before the bank could get a restraining order from a London judge, we needed to get the story outside of the country, where U.K. law wouldn't apply. Seconds before we received a hand-delivered writ forbidding us from publishing our story about the document, my colleague pressed the "send" button on his video display terminal, delivering it to New York and ensuring that our newspaper could publish the piece in the United States the next day. British newspapers and magazines, prevented from publishing anything derived from the original document, printed dozens of stories citing our scoop.

Since that episode more than twenty years ago, the challenges of reporting amid diverging and idiosyncratic press laws worldwide are more intimidating than ever.

That's why every serious journalist, publisher, lawyer, and webmaster should embrace the *International Libel and Privacy Handbook*, edited by Charles J. Glasser Jr., the media counsel to Bloomberg News. The most important issues in media law are explained in this global reference manual consisting of specific entries from thirty-seven experts in eighteen countries. At Bloomberg, no one has safeguarded the process of editorial integrity better than Charles Glasser. So we are delighted that his experience can now be shared with the widest possible audience of professionals committed to getting the facts legally, without fear or favor.

—MATTHEW WINKLER
Editor in Chief
BLOOMBERG NEWS®

ACKNOWLEDGMENTS

MANY PEOPLE DESERVE a public "thank you" for the help they have given me, as professionals and as friends. Many in the legal and academic worlds were kind enough to nurture my passion for media law, and deserve my thanks: Sandra Baron, executive director of the Media Law Resource Center, who gave me my first legal job and taught me how to really read cases; Professors Burt Neuborne and Dianne Zimmerman of New York University School of Law, who were so generous with their knowledge and experience; Judge Harry T. Edwards of the U.S. Court of Appeals for the District of Columbia, who taught me to trust myself to argue persuasively; Judge Robert D. Sack of the U.S. Court of Appeals for the Second Circuit, who in writing *Sack on Defamation* inspired me to try to contribute to the literature of media law; and John Piper and Michael Kaplan of Preti Flaherty Beliveau Pachios & Haley in Portland, Maine, who gave me the opportunity to prove myself as a lawyer on the briefs and in the courtroom. The attorneys at Willkie Farr & Gallagher are due thanks not only for their contributions to this book, but for my relying on them day in and day out for so much hard work and commonsense advice. I cannot overstate the quality and quantity of learning I received working under the late Rick Klein. In particular, Willkie's Tom Golden deserves credit for being the best sounding board, reality check, and consultant that an in-house lawyer could have.

Matthew Winkler, editor in chief of Bloomberg News, is central to why I believe I have the best job in the best news organization in the world. When there is the slightest question about a story, Matt's default query is always "what is the right thing to do?" Matt puts clarity, fairness, and accuracy ahead of legal defenses, making my job all that much easier. He has given me the moral and intellectual breathing room to be a lawyer, ombudsman, journalist, researcher, psychologist, advocate, and ethics coach to a great newsroom, and I am deeply in his debt. Likewise, many wonderful people at Bloomberg are owed thanks, including John McCorry, William Ahearn, Fred Wiegold, JoAnne Kanaval, and Jared Kieling.

On a personal level, I owe some friends and family my thanks: Cyndi Johnson, who has had to put up with so many dinners interrupted by urgent phone calls from reporters in trouble; Sean and Barbara Brogan, Chris Otazo, the Pascotto family, and Jean Marie Bonthous, friends in the deepest sense of the word; and most of all Prem Rawat, known to millions as Maharaji, who taught me that life's greatest gift is a joy to be found inside of each of us.

Understanding Media Law in the Global Context

THERE IS NO single body of "international law" that explains the risks a reporter, editor, or webmaster faces. There is no such unified theory of law in securities litigation or in environmental or health care law, so why should there be one in publishing?

Spend five minutes at the United Nations or any international congress—where arguing about the shape of a meeting table can go on for a day—and it will come as no surprise that media law around the world is a crazy patchwork quilt of laws, with each square reflecting a nation's cultural biases, political history, and economic structure. Most of us in the mass media—and especially in newsrooms—believe that free speech isn't merely an economic or political activity, but is one rooted in basic and transnational human rights. The desire to express oneself is a part of who we are. Indeed, many jurisdictions recognize this by making free expression a constitutionally protected right.

In the United States, those of us who practice journalism or media law often echo the language of Supreme Court Justice William O. Douglas, who referred to the "preferred position" of the First Amendment in order to "bring fulfillment to the public's right to know."[1]

Americans tend to believe that it is the *First* Amendment, because the right to speak freely is the right from which all other freedoms flow. One can't make informed decisions about the virtues of legalizing marijuana, the right or wrong of abortion, the illegal activities of Wall Street CEOs, or the wanton sex lives of movie stars without the right to speak openly. Free speech is part of—and maybe even responsible for—the American culture.

For better or worse, "everyone has a right to their opinion" is a concept Americans learn at an early age. As thick-skinned as we are, we also learn on the playground that "sticks and stones may break my bones, but names will never hurt me." In short, it takes a lot in America to say something so hurtful, in such a context, and with such loudness that the law will punish it.

But punishment does occur, even in the home of free speech. Libel cases, even those in which the press is victorious, are long, expensive, and often emotionally painful experiences. Susan Antilla, now an award-winning columnist for Bloomberg News, was sued by businessman Robert Howard over a 1994 story Antilla wrote when she was a reporter for the *New York Times*.[2] Howard was the chairman of two publicly traded companies whose stock price had been fluctuating enough to draw Antilla's attention. After extensive investigation and research, Antilla determined that the market might have been reacting to rumors that Howard may have had a dual identity, the "other" identity being Howard Finklestein, a convicted felon.

Antilla, after interviewing more than thirty people during the course of a month, wrote an article that didn't adopt as "fact" that Howard had a dual identity. Instead, it simply reported that the rumor was being passed around Wall Street and that it may have had an impact on the companies' share prices. The article also contained Robert Howard's unequivocal denial.

In 1997, three years after the publication, Howard brought a libel and privacy suit, not against the *Times,* but against Antilla. Although the eventual outcome—at the appellate level—vindicated Antilla's reporting on First Amendment grounds, the trial was a grueling and abusive experience for Antilla.

Antilla tried to be fair and clear in her story, which she knew was reported thoroughly, but the experience of being sued scared her and shook her confidence, and it took a long time for her to recover from it.

"From the very beginning, the plaintiff did everything to grind me down. He wanted revenge," says Antilla. Even before Howard filed his suit, a burly private investigator showed up at her house and questioned her about her sources and the way she reported the story.

Things didn't improve. The trial process, including two days of depositions and six days of trial, made her feel "picked apart." "They had looked at everything I had ever written, even going back to where I grew up," says Antilla. "They questioned my competence and training as a reporter. In the end you feel so naked and like there's nothing that's safe to write… you lose your confidence. It's the worst thing I've ever gone through."

Afraid that the jury might sympathize with Antilla, Howard's lawyer began his arguments by saying, "Sometimes good people can do bad things." The jury believed him.

Even though Antilla and her reporting were eventually vindicated on appeal, the experience took its toll not just on Antilla's confidence, but on the way she felt back in the newsroom. "After the trial, I went back to writing and having tremendous complications working with an editor again because I was quadruple reporting everything," she says. "The way journalists look at you after being sued is never the same. Even though fifteen people approved the story, the shame really hung around my neck. You don't end up being a hero: everyone runs for the hills and you have a sense of it being your fault. My lawyers were great, very supportive, but you're the one holding the bag. I still get defensive about it."

The financial consequences of being sued for libel can be more devastating than the emotional toll. Newspapers have been put out of business by the cost of libel litigation and the subsequent monetary judgments.

In the late 1990s, Barricade Books, a division of Lyle Stuart, published *Running Scared,* a book about Steven Wynn, one of the best-known and most highly regarded casino operators in the world. The book and its advertisements alleged that Wynn had improper connections to the Genovese crime family, and ostensibly based some of that writing on reports from England's Scotland Yard, generated when Wynn applied for a casino license in London.

Long and arduous litigation followed. In 1997, a jury found those allegations false and defamatory, and awarded Wynn $3.2 million. That judgment was litigated throughout Nevada's legal system. The Nevada Supreme Court eventually overturned the judgment and ordered a new trial. Wynn declined to prosecute his case further, saying through his lawyers that he felt vindicated. By that time, the damage had been done, and not just to Wynn's reputation. The libel suit forced Lyle Stuart into bankruptcy.

There may be good reason to argue that the damage to Lyle Stuart was self-inflicted. The case raised questions of whether a UK police report qualified to be protected under Nevada law or if UK law regarding police reports could, or should, be applied in Nevada. It seems that this international aspect was never fully examined.

Even discounting these episodes as aberrant, there is no doubt that being sued for libel is something to avoid. When questions of international law appear, it raises the stakes even higher.

The threat of libel litigation is now exacerbated by the reach of the Internet. Today, bloggers are breaking news that is chased down by mainstream media. They are now credentialed at national political conventions and even at the White House. Acting as self-appointed mass-media watchdogs, bloggers have claimed credit in ending the careers of a famous television news commentator and various news executives.

More news media are distributing their content across borders. Bloomberg, the news provider for whom I am fortunate to work, is American-owned, but its success is built on global reach. In more than 100 newsrooms around the globe, headlines and stories are flashed on desktops at the speed of light.

There is no telling where the next story will come from or what it will say. A reporter in Milan is working on a story about a deal between an Italian bank, a Spanish executive, and a Japanese bond issuer. A New York-based reporter is moving a story about a Russian oil company headed by a British resident and his battles in a U.S. bankruptcy court with French investors. These stories will be read in Hong Kong, London, Kansas City, and places the reporter may not even be able to locate on a map.

Given that libel suits are often ruinous, if not emotionally grueling, given that words are sent instantly around the world and archived forever, are there guidelines that reporters and editors should use? What is needed is a global approach requiring that reporters and editors review their practices and philosophy toward global newsgathering, and that they develop an understanding for the basic moral engine that drives each nation's media laws.

American editors and their lawyers generally review news stories from a solely U.S. perspective, publish stories conforming to a level of risk under U.S. law, and hope that either the facts are good enough to win a libel suit, or, in the alternative, that either their publisher has no assets to attach in a foreign country or that an adverse judgment won't be enforced in the United States.

In essence, the U.S. model is based on the press-friendly moral engine that drives American media law. As a democracy, constitutionally derived rights (like the right to speak freely) transcend other rights rooted in common law or statute. As mentioned previously, the right to publish is embedded in the First Amendment of the U.S. Constitution and is considered paramount. The "personal" rights of privacy, to enjoy a good reputation, to be free from defamation or other assault on personal identity, aren't constitutionally protected in the U.S. Thus, under U.S. law, the press's rights trump these "personal" rights.

I once attended a libel law conference where I sat next to the general counsel of a large media conglomerate. The panel was discussing a libel case in Europe where the press had enormous burdens to meet in court.

"Haven't they ever heard of the First Amendment?" asked this American lawyer.

The answer is that they may have heard of it, but don't give it any weight. In many nations, there is no constitutional right to press freedom, but the constitution does recognize the personal rights (also called "dignitary rights" in some jurisdictions). In many of these nations, there simply is no "First Amendment" that trumps other rights. Yet other nations' press law represents a balance of the two: a constitutional right of a free press is on an equal footing with personal rights. In balancing the two, courts weigh the rights of the press against the responsibilities to avoid harming dignitary interests.

The danger of taking a strictly American approach is highlighted by the British case of *Berezovsky v. Michaels and Others (Forbes)*.[3] From an American perspective, everything seemed right about this hard-hitting story. In December 1996, a *Forbes* magazine story about Boris Berezovsky retold stories about the Russian media, oil, and finance oligarch's rise to riches.[4] Introduced with a headline that read *"Power, Politics, and Murder. Boris Berezovsky can teach the guys in Sicily a thing or two,"* the story was the result of months of reporting by a team of some of the most experienced journalists in the world. They spoke to dozens of first-hand witnesses who alleged that they knew that Berezovsky left behind "a trail of corpses, uncollectible debts and competitors terrified for their lives."

The article called Berezovsky a "powerful gangland boss," and basing their reporting on police reports, corporate documents, and interviews, the reporters strongly suggested that Berezovsky was behind the murder of Vladislav Listyev, a popular television host and top official at Russian Public Television.

In the United States, such reporting would be protected by a plethora of privileges, and *Forbes*'s editors didn't expect that a libel case would be brought, let alone brought in the United Kingdom. Berezovsky filed a libel claim in Britain, where few privileges protect the press and sued-upon stories are assumed by the court to be false. Since Russian prosecutors never charged Berezovsky for Listyev's murder, how could a magazine on the other side of the world conduct a criminal investigation to convict Berezovsky of murder?

Forbes fought the case the best way they knew how: challenge the location of the suit in London. The House of Lords disagreed with their American cousins and allowed the case to continue, because Berezovsky convinced the court that even though the story was published by an American newsroom, and was about a Russian citizen, enough Britons had read the article (published simultaneously on *Forbes*'s Web site) to damage Berezovsky's reputation in England.[5]

The case dragged on, and millions of dollars later, *Forbes* was finally forced to relent, reading a statement in open court that apologized to Berezovsky and issuing a detailed retraction.[6]

Following the American model may place reporters and news organizations at risk in other ways. For example, American reporters are often shocked to learn that the UK (and most of Europe) often places considerable restriction on the ability to quote arguments and documents from court cases.

Where American law presupposes the right of access to court proceedings, the United Kingdom and many other nations use "publication bans" to restrict the ability of the press to publish many parts of court proceedings. Following the theory that juries might be unfairly persuaded by "evidence" they read in the newspapers but do not examine in court, these jurisdictions set out strict limits as to what can and cannot be published.

This problem was underscored in 2005 when a publication ban was issued in a trial about corruption in Canada's Liberal Party. The court banned publication of testimony on the Internet. American webmasters, especially those with nothing to lose and no assets at risk in Canada, began to publish articles about the trial. Canadian news organizations then linked their Web sites to the U.S.-based Web sites. Although some of those Canadian news organizations later removed the links for fear of contempt of court prosecution, the court did not try to punish the U.S. webmasters.[7]

Although the American webmasters may have struck a blow for Canadians' right to know, the problem remains and looms large for bona fide news organizations, especially those who do business or maintain offices in Canada. Although the webmasters might have been too small for the courts to go after, it is by no means certain that large, well established news organizations will not come within the courts' crosshairs.

The global model suggests that the right guidelines might satisfy some of the international constants. In other words, if the highest standards of accuracy, clarity, and fairness are met, then a story should be suitable for publication anywhere. Distilling those universal constants to a few principles, global publishers should consider the following:

Put Accuracy Ahead of Style and Speed. Unlike U.S. law, the laws of many nations assume that a sued-upon story is false, and places the burden of proof on the publisher. This means that every fact should withstand close scrutiny prior to publication and should be subject to exacting proof with notes, interviews, documents, and other primary source material prior to publication. It is also worth noting that some nations, like France, do not allow reporters to prove the truth of their stories with information gathered in the course of a lawsuit. If the reporter did not have it to rely upon while writing the story, then the reporter may not rely upon it at trial. There's a world of difference between a story that you *know* is correct and one you can *prove* is correct.

Publishers should also be aware that "the rush to publish" is a nearly fatal accusation in many nations. In those countries without a First Amendment analogue, courts give less weight to the "public's need to know" than to a person's dignitary right, especially in light of an error committed because the reporter did not have time—or take the time—to adequately research a story and seek comment. Many of these same nations do not recognize competitive pressures and deadlines as reasons that justify an allegedly damaging and inaccurate story.

Make Fairness an Obvious and Primary Element of All News Stories. Failure to provide a meaningful opportunity to comment is often the most damaging element of a libel claim in Europe. In a recent English case, George Galloway, a politician known for pro-Arab views and opposition to the Iraq War, won a libel judgment of almost $300,000, plus attorney's fees, against the *Daily Telegraph* after the paper published an article the court found fundamentally unfair.[8]

The paper's reporter, who was in Iraq after the 2003 invasion, claimed to have found a set of documents showing that Galloway had been receiving illicit payments from Saddam Hussein and had meetings with Iraqi intelligence officers. The reporter telephoned Galloway on the evening of April 21, and in that conversation, Galloway denied the allegations and told the reporter he had never seen the documents in question.

The next morning, the *Telegraph* published a five-page spread with the headline "SADDAM'S LITTLE HELPER" and a story that began: "George Galloway, the Labour backbencher received money from Saddam Hussein's regime, taking a slice of oil earnings worth at least £375,000 a year, according to Iraqi intelligence documents found by the Daily Telegraph in Baghdad."

Under English law, the seriousness of the allegations has to be met with an equal zeal to allow a meaningful opportunity to respond. This was the failure that may have most damaged the *Telegraph*'s case. Reviewing the facts of the case, Justice Eady pointed out that the *Telegraph* admitted it did not have the documents examined for authenticity prior to publication, and did not read the documents to Galloway when asking him for comment.

The reporter did not tell Galloway that the story would be published the next morning, nor that it would be featured in a five-page spread. The reporter refused to tell Galloway where and how the damning documents were obtained. Instead of presenting Galloway with the specific allegations that he would surely have to answer later, the reporter merely told Galloway that the documents had "come to light." Given that Galloway was accused of nearly treasonous acts that would surely damage his career, the court found that Galloway was not given a reasonable and meaningful attempt to comment.

Although as of this writing the case is on appeal, the lesson should not be lost from whatever outcome occurs: *the more serious the allegation, the more detailed must be the attempt to reach the subject.*[9] One phone call may not be enough, and asking people to comment on documents they have never seen is even more troublesome. Consider follow-up e-mails, faxes, and, if necessary, hand-delivered letters setting out the details of what a subject is going to be accused of, and asking for comment.

More often than not, doing less simply looks unfair. In nations without a rich tradition of a First Amendment, facts that look like a "cheap shot" usually work against the press.

Serve the Public Interest. In many nations, especially those without a constitutional counterweight to dignitary rights, even truth is not an absolute defense to libel claims. These courts require that such intrusions serve the public interest. American law is on the whole very generous to the media in determining what is and isn't in the public interest. Guided by the First Amendment's "marketplace of ideas" theory, American law generally defers to that marketplace.[10] Editors, after all, know what interests the public and they try to provide that kind of story. If the story isn't of interest to the public, then readership and circulation decline. This free market approach assumes that the public interest is indicated by what the public consumes.

But in most of the world, courts don't grant such deference to journalists, and what is of interest "*to*" the public is not the same thing as what is "*in*" their interest. For example, Italian courts ask whether journalists are "fulfilling their mission to inform the public about news it needs to protect itself."

Bloomberg's editor in chief Matt Winkler says that a fundamental element in all news stories is "what's at stake." In his handbook, *The Bloomberg Way,* Winkler explains that "people need a sense of what's at stake in order to know why they ought to care about an event."

When reporting a story, the "what's at stake" underscores the public interest by asking and answering the same questions: Is there an effect on public health? Is there a risk of harm to a nation's economic or physical security? Is there a chance that an act of wrongdoing might go unpunished and repeated? Are society's more vulnerable members likely to become victims?

Reporters and editors should be encouraged to find the angle in each story where society can be said to benefit from publication of information that can be used to protect itself. The merely prurient and prying—although popular—may not meet the court's standards of public interest.

Cultural Sensitivity Counts. Phrases that may be innocuous in one culture are often offensive—and even libelous—in others. For example, in the United States, to say that someone was "fired" is not by itself defamatory. Yet the same statement in France or Japan will almost always raise eyebrows and get the libel lawyers' sabers rattling. Why the difference? The answer is cultural.

In the United States, people are used to the notion of an unfair dismissal. People can be fired in many states for no reason at all, or for reasons that people think are unfair. In isolation, it doesn't imply that the former employee did something wrong. By contrast, French unions and employment law make it next to impossible to "fire" people without a strong showing that the employee violated some duty. Thus, if a person was "fired" he must have done something wrong, or at best been incompetent.

Similarly, in Japan, where people are expected to work for one company their entire adult lives, being fired is a shameful event. This is why Asian and European publishers often use the phrase "made redundant" to describe persons who are laid off for economic savings reasons.

Assuming the public interest, one can report that an executive was fired, but the publisher of that statement had better be prepared to prove it with direct quotes or documentary evidence.

Cultural differences are reflected in the varying definitions of defamatory meaning. What is offensive or worthy of ridicule in one place might make no difference in another. To be called "gay" in San Francisco would not raise contempt, hatred, or scorn, while using the same term in Hong Kong may cause an uproar.

It's not just rude or imperialistic to assume that your nation's moral values are the appropriate yardstick; it may be considered intrusive or libelous.

Similarly, iconographic figures or political doctrines may be so ingrained in the culture that the laws specifically proscribe attacks upon them. Statements that question the integrity and political wisdom of Chairman Mao will almost certainly set alarms ringing in China, and endorsement of an independent Taiwan are expressly criminalized.

In the United States, some might characterize Singapore's Lee Kuan Yew as a plutocrat. Yet in that nation, he is genuinely revered by most of the populace as a founding father and strong, benevolent leader. Reporters and editors should at the very least be aware of these potential pitfalls.

Translation in reporting from various languages also raises problems. In reviewing a story about warring Mexican shareholders in a takeover bid, I noticed the original draft had one side accusing the other of actions that were "illegal." Although I'm not a Mexican securities lawyer, it seemed far fetched to say that offering a certain price for stock was a criminal act, so I asked the reporter to check back and see if the sources meant against the law ("*contrario a la ley*") or instead merely not legally binding ("*sin precedente vinculante*"). It turned out to be the latter, not the former, and we accurately described ordinary business litigation, rather than accusing someone of committing a crime.

Don't Confuse the Right to Publish With What's Right to Publish. Common sense and good taste will almost never steer you wrong. Reporters' competitive nature leads them to use facts that are "exclusive" without asking if any of those facts move the story forward. But should we?

A reporter's job is not to gratuitously inflict damage. Nor is it to be "hard-hitting." It is to "seek truth and report it." In order to do that, the truth has to be contextualized, and presented in a fair manner. The fact that some detail may be true is not always by itself an ethical justification for publishing it. The more sensitive the fact, the closer reporters and editors must look at whether the public truly needs to know that fact. Asking whether the fact is gratuitous or if it answers a question the public needs answered is a good start. These are not often easy or pleasant choices, yet asking these questions helps guide us to a more ethical outcome that also serves the public interest.

In the early days of the Enron collapse and scandal, Bloomberg News obtained through entirely legal and ethical means a copy of a suicide note left by an executive who had taken his own life. The note was addressed to his wife, and did not discuss Enron. Should we publish the contents of the note?

We had to ask ourselves the same questions outlined above. Sure, it was interesting, even sensational, made more so by the fact that we had it exclusively. But did it move the story forward? Did it answer a question that the public needed to know, or was it voyeurism?

After a close look and a lot of discussion, we realized that the larger public debate was whether the executive had actually committed suicide or was instead killed by people afraid he would disclose damaging information. Publishing the note helped answer that question. But our inquiry could not end there. Did the note disclose personal details about the surviving family? Would disclosing those details move the story forward, or merely subject the family to intrusive examination? Fortunately, the note did not contain that kind of detail.

We believed that our decision to publish the suicide note helped answer the debate about the executive's death. But this kind of inquiry is exhaustive and soul-searching.

In conclusion, we do well to avoid terse justifications for publishing sensitive material. "He deserves it" or "that's his tough luck" are not substitutes for thoughtful analysis. Putting ourselves in the position of the subject, and asking ourselves if we are really being fair—how we would like it if the roles were reversed—goes a long way to answering these questions.

There's often no single "right" answer, but we have an ethical obligation, as well as a legal one, to ask the right questions.

—CHARLES J. GLASSER JR.
January 2006

Chapter Notes

1. *Branzburg v. Hayes,* 408 U. S. 665, 721 (1972).

2. *Howard v. Antilla,* 294 F.3d 244 (1st Cir. 2002).

3. *Berezovsky v. Micheals and Others,* http://www.parliament.the-stationery-office.co.uk/pa/ld199900/ldjudgmt/jd000511/bere-1.htm

4. http://www.forbes.com/forbes/1996/1230/5815090a_print.html.

5. Since the Berezovsky case, British courts have become less of the libel tourist's destination. See Laura Handman and Robert Balin, "It's a Small World After All: Emerging Protections for the U.S. Media Sued in England," available online at http://www.dwt.com/related_links/adv_bulletins/CMITFall1998USMedia.htm.

6. http://www.carter-ruck.com/articles/200306-Berezovsky.html.

7. The problems of publication bans are explored at http://www.dcexaminer.com/articles/2005/04/20/opinion/op-ed/10oped19adamson.txt.

8. *Galloway v. Telegraph Group Limited* [2004] EWHC 2786 (QB); Case No. HO03X02026 (appeal pending).

9. It is worth noting that the *Galloway* court took a dim view of the publisher's argument that time constraints justified the meager opportunity to respond, and when pressed, the publisher admitted that it was not so much the public's need to know that drove the rush to publish, as it was a sense of competitive pressure for fear of losing a big scoop. The court found that this hurt rather than helped the *Telegraph*.

10. See, e.g., *Huggins v. Moore,* 94 N.Y.2d 296, 303 (1999). ("Absent clear abuse, the courts will not second-guess editorial decisions as to what constitutes matters of genuine public concern.")

ABOUT THE EDITOR

Charles J. Glasser Jr. is media counsel to Bloomberg News. Prior to joining Bloomberg, he represented a wide range of broadcasters, magazines, and newspaper publishers. A former daily newspaper and wire service journalist, he has litigated many of the issues covered in this book. Mr. Glasser collects vintage sports cars, is an accomplished classical guitarist, and resides in the New York metropolitan area.

Nellie Alexandrova of Denton Wilde Sapte has been practicing for fifteen years as a Russian-qualified lawyer, much of that time in international legal practice. She has extensive experience in corporate and commercial matters with an international element (including acquisitions and joint ventures) and cross-border financial and securities matters (including project and trade finance, and financial markets). She also has substantial intellectual property experience and has advised a variety of clients on transactions involving licensing, copyright, trademarks, software imports, service agreements, and customs duties. Alexandrova is a graduate of Moscow State University, where she holds a degree in law (with distinction) and a doctorate degree in international law. She has also completed a special program at Cambridge University. She regularly speaks at various high-profile forums and contributes to Western and Russian business publications such as *Eastern European Forum Newsletter* and BNA's *Eastern Europe Reporter*. Alexandrova is a member of the Moscow City Bar and sits on the editorial board of *Kollegia,* the first Russian professional journal for practicing lawyers.

Almudena Arpón de Mendívil is head of the telecommunications and audiovisual department at Gómez-Acebo & Pombo (Spain). She has extensive experience advising corporations with business in the communications area, which includes telecommunications, media, and IT. Ms. Arpón de Mendívil is a council member of the IBA Legal Practice Division, immediate past co-chair of the IBA Committee on Communications (Cm), and chair of the Regulatory Commission of the Spanish Association of Corporate Communications Users. She is also a member of the Telecommunications and IT Commission of the ICC and of the European Space Law Centre. She has been designated by the Spanish Regulator as independent arbitrator at the Spanish Arbitration Court for telecommunications conflicts. She has published widely and is a correspondent for several specialized international publications. She is author of *International Joint Ventures in Spain* (Butterworths, 1992 and 1997). In Spain, she directed *Comments to the General Telecommunications Law* (Aranzadi, 1999), is co-author of *Legal Regime of Acquisitions of Companies* (Aranzadi, 2001 and 2004), of *Regulation and Competition in Telecommunications* (Dykinson, S.L. 2003), and of *Electronic Communications and Competition* (Bosch, 2004). Her department's leadership in the telecommunications and media sectors has been recognized most recently by, among others, the rankings *Chambers & Partners* (2004), *European Legal 500* (2004), *PLC Which lawyer?, Practical Law Company* (2004/2005), and *Euromoney's Best of the Best Telecom Media and IT* (2004).

Rolf Auf der Maur is a partner at VISCHER, one of the leading Swiss law firms with offices in the main commercial centers of Zurich and Basel. He is head of the IP/IT practice group. He studied at Zurich University and University of California, Los Angeles, and published his thesis in the area of copyright law. Before beginning his career as a lawyer in 1991, he was an entrepreneur in the IT and media sector and a journalist. As early as 1994, he began advising clients on Internet-related legal matters. The global communication network and the converging industries (IT, media, and telecommunications) remain his core interests and practice areas.

Auf der Maur advises leading international and Swiss corporations in the media, telecommunications, and IT sectors in litigious and nonlitigious matters as well as in regulatory affairs. Auf der Maur is vice president of the executive board of the Simsa Swiss Interactive Media and Software Association (the Swiss Internet industry organization) and a member of the board of the International Association of Entertainment Lawyers. He also serves as a vice chair of the Technology Law Committee of the International Bar Association. He speaks and publishes regularly on IT and media-related legal issues and takes part actively in the further development of the Swiss regulatory environment for the converging industries.

Barbosa, Müssnich & Aragão is one of the top ten business law firms in Brazil with important practices in almost all areas of business law, including the intellectual property area. The practice of law at Barbosa, Müssnich & Aragão is characterized by rigorous legal analysis, coupled with creative solutions that maximize clients' business opportunities. In relation to intellectual property, Barbosa, Müssnich & Aragão provides services in matters involving trademarks, copyrights, and entertainment law, which covers, among other areas: cinema, television, music, theater, literature, print and electronic media, art exhibition, and advertising. The firm works with specialized lawyers in this area, such as Laura Fragomeni, coordinator and professor at the IP Post Graduation Course of Getulio Vargas Foundation, with a LL.M. degree from Harvard Law School, an M.B.A. in Law and Economics at Getulio Vargas Foundation, and a LL.B. at Catholic University—RJ; and Paula Mena Barreto Pinheiro, teaching assistant at the IP Post Graduation Course of Getulio Vargas Foundation, with a postgraduate degree in Intellectual Property Law and a LL.B. at Catholic University—RJ.

Peter Bartlett is chairman of Minter Ellison, the largest law firm in Australia in terms of number of lawyers, and ranked the largest legal group in the Asia Pacific (according to *Asian Legal Business*). He is national head of the Minter Ellison Media and Communication Group. Bartlett has over twenty years' experience in media and telecommunications and a comprehensive knowledge of media-related issues, including defamation, prepublication advice, contempt, suppression orders, legislative restrictions on publications and advertising codes, together with e-commerce (content) and privacy issues.

Minter Ellison has acted for *The Age* newspaper since 1863 and Bartlett is its chief legal adviser. He has worked on behalf of an extensive range of media-related clients, including Fairfax in Victoria, *Business Review Weekly*, SBS Television, Simon & Schuster Australia, and Pan Macmillan Australia. He has also acted for QANTAS airlines on various matters, including the recent high-profile deep vein thrombosis litigation. Bartlett is also chair of the Media Committee and coordinator of the Intellectual Property, Communications and Technology Section of the International Bar Association.

The highly respected "Asia Pacific Legal 500 2003/2004" ranked Bartlett as a "leading individual" lawyer in media and named Minter Ellison as a "leading technology, media and telecommunications firm."

Jill Cottrell teaches law on a part-time basis at the University of Hong Kong, where she was a Senior Lecturer from 1990 until her formal retirement in 2003. She previously taught at Ahmadu Bello University and what is now known as Obafemi Awolowo University in Nigeria (from 1965 to 1976), and at the University of Warwick in England. Cottrell obtained her law degrees from the University of London (LL.B. and LL.M.) and Yale Law School (LL.M.). She has written on the law of torts (particularly defamation), environmental law, and on various topics in Indian law, Hong Kong law, Nigerian law, and the law of the Pacific Islands states. For many years, Cottrell taught torts, environmental law, and human rights law. She has also taught courses on legal research and legal method for undergraduate and postgraduate students. Since her formal retirement, Cottrell has worked as a consultant on issues of constitutional law in societies emerging from conflict.

Edward J. Davis is a partner in the New York office of Davis Wright Tremaine LLP. He specializes in representing media organizations, especially in matters of libel, privacy, press access, reporter's privilege, copyright, and trademark. His clients include leading magazines, newspapers, book publishers, television and electronic news organizations, entertainment companies, and nonprofit institutions, as well as authors and artists (or their estates). He has represented coalitions of publishers, authors, museums, and advocacy groups in landmark cases to protect freedom of expression. He provides prepublication and prebroadcast advice for clients and often represents them in business litigation as well as cases where First Amendment freedoms may be at stake. Davis has served as vice-chair of the American Bar Association's Committee on Media Law and Defamation Torts, chair of the Committee on Copyright and Literary Property of the Association of the Bar of the City of New York, and a member of the latter Association's committees on the Judiciary, Communications and Media Law, Civil Rights, and Drugs and the Law. He graduated magna cum laude from Harvard Law School and Harvard College and received master's degrees in economics and in Chinese studies from the London School of Economics and the School of Oriental and African Studies of the University of London, where he studied as a Marshall Scholar.

Evaristo de Moraes law firm has a long tradition in Brazil. Founded in 1894 by Antonio Evaristo de Moraes, the firm presently is run by Antonio Eduardo de Moraes and Renato de Moraes (grandsons of the deceased Evaristo) who, with the support of experienced lawyers, continue the tradition initiated by their ancestors.

Steven De Schrijver, a partner at Van Bael & Bellis, an international law firm with over sixty lawyers based in Brussels (www.vanbaelbellis.com), has concentrated his practice on corporate transactions and information technology. De Schrijver advises Belgian and foreign companies, banks, and investment funds on mergers and acquisitions, joint ventures, corporate restructuring, financing of acquisitions, private equity, and venture capital. His work in the area of corporate transactions has involved him in several national and cross-border transactions in the telecom, IT, biotech, petrochemical, and cement sectors. In addition, De Schrijver has handled numerous complex commercial agreements and projects dealing with new technologies (e-commerce, software licensing, Web site development and hosting, privacy law, technology transfers, digital signatures, IT-outsourcing). For instance, he has coordinated several pan-European data protection compliance programs. De Schrijver received his J.D. (magna cum laude) from the University of Antwerp (Belgium) in 1992 and received an LL.M. from the University of Virginia School of Law in 1993.

Mario Gallavotti (Gallavotti Honorati & Pascotto) has been practicing law in Rome since 1973. He is also admitted to the Italian Supreme Court and is a Certified Auditor. He served as assistant professor of Civil Law at the Faculty of Political Sciences of University of Rome and has served as secretary of the Conference of Young Lawyers of the Rome Bar, and as president and national secretary of A.I.G.A.—Italian Young Lawyers Association—of Rome. He is a frequent lecturer in various areas of entertainment, media, and sport law.

In 1976, Gallavotti was visiting lawyer with the U.S. law firm Kutak, Rock & Huie, and had extensive work experience abroad. In 1982, he opened an office in Los Angeles, where he acquired experience working within the American judicial and legal systems.

Gallavotti specializes in entertainment, media and technology, and sport law. He represents several Italian and international large corporations focused in these areas.

Thomas H. Golden and **Stephen B. Vogel** are attorneys in the litigation department of Willkie Farr & Gallagher LLP, which serves as primary outside counsel to Bloomberg News. Golden received his bachelor's degree cum laude in 1988 from the College of the Holy Cross and his law degree magna cum laude in 1991 from New York University School of Law, where he was awarded membership in the Order of the Coif. Vogel received his bachelor's degree cum laude in 1998 from Dartmouth College and his law degree in 2003 from Columbia University. Willkie Farr & Gallagher LLP is an international law firm of over 600 attorneys with offices in New York, Washington, D.C., Paris, London, Milan, Rome, Frankfurt, and Brussels. The firm is headquartered in New York City.

Jonathan D. Hart is a member of the law firm of Dow, Lohnes & Albertson PLLC, Washington, D.C., where he specializes in the representation of media and technology companies on a broad range of commercial, transactional, operational, and content matters. His clients include dozens of web publishers, software and technology companies, newspapers, magazines, and broadcasters.

Hart is on the faculty of the Stanford Professional Publishing Courses and is the author of *Web Law: A Field Guide to Internet Publishing* (Bradford Publishing, 2005). He speaks frequently on media law and the Internet and has written extensively on media and technology law, particularly for WSJ.com, the online edition of the *Wall Street Journal.*

Before entering private practice, Hart clerked for U.S. Circuit Judge Jerome Farris and U.S. District Judge Almeric L. Christian. He is a graduate of Middlebury College (B.A., English and music, 1978) and Stanford Law School (J.D., 1983).

Prof. Dr. Jan Hegemann is a partner in the Munich office of Hogan & Hartson Raue LLP and is a member of the Intellectual Property, Litigation, Corporate, Securities and Finance Groups. His practice focuses on intellectual property, information technology, press and media, the arts, and entertainment. His clients include numerous publishing companies, theaters, universities, and several internationally known artists and authors. Hegemann represents major newspaper publishers and advises politicians and artists with regard to press and media law. In addition, he provides advice for German literature publishers and represents several information technology companies, with a particular emphasis on intellectual property protection and software rights.

Prior to joining Hogan & Hartson Raue, Hegemann was a partner in the Berlin office of a leading German law firm. He studied law and philosophy at the Universities of Bonn and Munich and passed his First State Exam. He served as a judicial clerk in Berlin and Tokyo and passed the Second State Exam. In 1995, he received his doctorate, magna cum laude, from Humboldt University in Berlin. Since 1996, Hegemann has been an associate lecturer for culture and media law at the Academy of Music "Hanns Eisler" in Berlin and obtained the title of professor in 2002.

Fluent in English and German, Hegemann is an active member of the German Association for Intellectual Property and Copyrights (GRUR) and the German-Japanese Law Association.

Peter Karanjia is an associate in the New York office of Davis Wright Tremaine LLP. He represents U.S. and foreign broadcasters, book publishers, magazines, newspapers, and individual authors in the areas of libel, privacy, copyright, trademark, misappropriation of ideas, newsgathering, and other aspects of First Amendment and publishing law. He has represented several publishing clients in libel cases, including a recent case in which he successfully argued an appeal before a New York appellate court, resulting in a decision affirming the trial court's dismissal of the plaintiff's claims for libel. Karanjia is a member of the Committee on Entertainment Law of the Association of the Bar of the City of New York, for which he has organized a number of presentations by guest speakers; the Forum on Communications Law of the American Bar Association; and the New York State Bar Association. He received his M.A. in English law from Oxford University, with First Class Honors, and his LL.M. from Harvard Law School, where he was a Kennedy Scholar and an editor of the *Harvard International Law Journal.*

Kim & Chang, founded in 1972, is the largest and the most specialized law firm in Korea. It is a full-service law firm based in Seoul with approximately 400 professionals including lawyers, tax lawyers and accountants, and patent and trademark attorneys.

The expertise and multicultural background of Kim & Chang's professionals make the firm the recognized leader in providing specialized legal services for cross-border transactions and uniquely qualified to address the legal needs of international companies doing business in Korea. The firm is active in practically all areas of commercial practice. Its practice groups include securities, capital markets and banking, mergers and acquisitions, privatization, foreign investment, bankruptcy/corporate restructuring, human resources, antitrust and fair trade, international trade, product liability, real property/construction, environment, telecommunications, health care, intellectual property, litigation and arbitration, tax and maritime. Kim & Chang handles legal matters in English, German, French, Japanese, Chinese, and Swedish as well as Korean. Whether career attorneys, former judges, prosecutors, or regulators, Kim & Chang's professionals are committed to the firm's philosophy of providing clients with custom-tailored legal services of the highest quality. Kim & Chang's professionals and staff are taught to meet the needs of clients by finding creative solutions to help them succeed in Korea. It is due to this underlying philosophy that the firm has established its present status and reputation around the world within thirty years.

Elena Kirillova has been advising multinational companies investing in the former Soviet Union since 1990. She has been lead counsel in relation to numerous major transactions in Russia and Central Asia throughout this period.

She was a visiting lecturer on Russian law at the University of Surrey, Guildford, from 1992 to 2000. She holds a Bachelor of Laws degree from the University of Sydney (1985) and a Masters of Jurisprudence from the Institute of State and Law of the Russian Academy of Sciences (2000), where her thesis topic was "Foreign Investment Law in the Russian Federation."

She is a board member of the Russo-British Chamber of Commerce, chair of the CIS Advisory Panel of International Financial Services, London, and a director of the Mariinsky Theatre Trust. She is bilingual in Russian and English and is a regular speaker on Russian and CIS legal issues.

Kochhar & Co. is one of the leading and largest corporate/commercial law firms in India with full-service offices in Bangalore, Chennai (Madras), Mumbai (Bombay), and New Delhi with resident partners in each of these offices.

Kochhar & Co. offers a wide range of legal services in the areas of corporate and commercial law and specializes in representing foreign corporations in connection with their business interests in India. The firm represents some of the largest multinational corporations from North America, Europe, and Japan (including many Fortune 500 companies). Kochhar's major practice areas include antitrust, unfair trade practices, arbitration, banking and finance, bankruptcy and reorganization, commercial contracts, corporate and securities laws, e-commerce transactions, environmental law, foreign investment, information technology, infrastructure projects, insurance, intellectual property, international trade and customs, joint ventures and technical collaborations, labor law, litigation, media and entertainment, mergers and acquisitions, privatization and disinvestment, real estate, regulatory approvals, shipping, taxation—international and local, and telecommunications.

Janmejay Rai and Barunesh Chandra are senior associates with the New Delhi office.

Amber Melville-Brown is an English solicitor specializing in media law advice as a consultant at niche London media law firm David Price Solicitors & Advocates from where she runs her own media law practice. Her expertise is in defamation, privacy, and media litigation and media and crisis management. Prior to becoming a consultant, she was a partner at London media specialist law firm Schillings, where her client base included claimants seeking advice in defamation, privacy, and other media litigation matters. Before that she was head of defamation practice at London-based Finers Stephens Innocent, acting mainly for major U.S. media defendants, including CNN, the *New York Times,* and *Time Magazine.*

Melville-Brown provides crisis and media management advice and assistance to both claimants and defendants in relation to various media issues. Her clients include celebrities, television presenters, entertainers, and other individuals and national and international corporations including those involved in health care, diamond-mining, and construction. She advises UK and U.S. photographic agencies on privacy issues in connection with publications in the UK.

Melville-Brown is the media columnist for the biggest circulation news magazine for lawyers in Europe, the *Law Gazette,* in which she writes a regular legal update column in addition to features and reviews. She also writes and contributes on legal issues to national newspapers, including the *Times* and the *Independent.* In 2005, she was asked to write, present, and co-produce a training program for lawyers for Legal Network Television on "Knowing the Media," with an audience of lawyers nationwide including at least half of the top 100 legal firms and in-house practitioners in the UK. Melville-Brown is also the external examiner for media for the College of Law, the largest post-graduate law school in Europe.

Slade R. Metcalf, a partner in the New York office of Hogan & Hartson LLP, focuses his practice on media law and litigation for various media and entertainment companies. He counsels newspapers, television stations, syndicated television programs, magazines, and book publishers on pre-publication and prebroadcast issues. He also represents media companies, reporters, authors, and photographers in litigations regarding issues of libel, invasion of privacy, copyright, and trademark. His practice is nationwide, with many of his cases outside the state of New York.

Metcalf is a member of the Forum on Communications Law of the American Bar Association, a member and past chair of the Committee on Media Law of the New York State Bar Association, and a member of the Association of the Bar of the City of New York.

Metcalf has been a partner at Hogan & Hartson since March 2002. Prior to joining Hogan & Hartson, he was a partner at Squadron Ellenoff Plesent & Sheinfeld LLP (which merged with Hogan & Hartson in 2002) from 1981 to 2002, and prior to that an associate at the Squadron firm from 1977 to 1981. Metcalf was an associate at Townley Updike Carter & Rodgers from 1973 to 1977. He is a former chairman of the Legal Affairs Committee of the Magazine Publishers of America, and has participated in numerous bar association committees regarding media, communications, art, copyright, and literary property. He has lectured extensively on media law at forums including conferences of the Media Law Resource Center, Practicing Law Institute, the Magazine Publishers of America, and the American Society of Magazine Editors.

Metcalf is the author of a legal treatise entitled *Rights and Liabilities of Publishers, Broadcasters and Reporters,* which is updated annually and has been a leading media law resource book since 1981. He is also the founder of the "Media Law Update," a quarterly Hogan & Hartson publication. He received his J.D. from New York University School of Law in 1973 and his A.B. from Princeton University in 1968. He is admitted to the New York Bar as well as to several federal courts.

Dominique Mondoloni, a practicing Avocat admitted to the Paris Bar, is a partner in the Litigation Department of Willkie Farr & Gallagher LLP and a member of the Paris Bar Council. He has significant experience as a civil and commercial litigator. He has handled, notably for U.S. and European clients, matters involving French civil, commercial, and criminal law. He has developed an extensive experience in corporate-related disputes. He has acted for plaintiffs in a number of libel cases and regularly assists a U.S.-based media firm in relation to French press law issues. He has authored a number of articles on issues involving French private international law, civil law, and bankruptcy law.

Mori Hamada & Matsumoto is a full-service international law firm based in Tokyo, with offices in Beijing and Shanghai. The firm has over 200 attorneys and a support staff of over 250, including legal assistants, translators, and secretaries. It is one of the largest full-service firms based in Japan and is particularly well-known for its work in the areas of mergers and acquisitions, finance, litigation, insolvency, and intellectual property. The firm was formed through the merger on December 1, 2002, of Mori Sogo and Hamada & Matsumoto, two well-established Tokyo-based firms. On July 1, 2005, the firm merged with Max Law Offices, a Tokyo-based firm with highly regarded expertise in the areas of copyrights, trademarks, and patents, as well as information technology, the Internet, media, and entertainment law. The firm's senior lawyers include a number of highly respected practitioners and leaders in the Japanese and international legal community, including the current president of the Daini-Tokyo Bar Association, the former president of the Japan Federation of Bar Associations, the former president of the Tokyo Bar Association, the former secretary general of the Inter-Pacific Bar Association, and a prominent professor of law at the University of Tokyo. In addition, a former senior partner of the firm now sits on the Japanese Supreme Court. The firm has lawyers with primary legal qualification in Japan, the United States, the People's Republic of China, and the Philippines.

Anna Otkina is based in the Moscow offices of the international law firm Denton Wilde Sapte, where she has been advising foreign investors on international corporate and financial projects. She graduated from MGIMO Ministry of Foreign Affairs of the Russian Federation with distinction. She also holds an LL.M. in International Trade Law from the University of Georgia School of Law, USA, and a Master of International and Comparative Law/European Studies from Vrije Universiteit Brussels, Belgium.

Otkina regularly advises on corporate as well as regulatory issues involved in transfer and registration of rights to issued share capital in international transactions, telecommunications, as well as aviation law matters.

Brian MacLeod Rogers of Toronto, Canada, practices media law and litigation, with an emphasis on libel, privacy, copyright, freedom of expression, and Internet-related issues. He represents writers, newspapers, magazines, book publishers, producers, broadcasters, and electronic media and has an extensive practice of prepublication/broadcast review. He has conducted hundreds of freedom of expression and libel cases and has appeared before all levels of courts, including the Supreme Court of Canada. He is currently acting as counsel for a coalition of fifty-one international, U.S., and Canadian media-related organizations intervening in the Ontario Court of Appeal in *Bangoura v. Washington Post* on the issue of jurisdiction and Internet publication. He was founding president of Advocates In Defence of Expression in the Media (Ad IDEM, the Canadian media lawyers association) and the first Canadian member of the Defense Counsel Section, Media Law Resource Center, for which he co-authors annual surveys on Canadian libel and privacy laws. Rogers has authored and edited articles and books on media law, constitutional law, and civil litigation and co-founded the media law course at Ryerson University's School of Journalism. He has been peer-rated as "AV" by Martindale-Hubbell and "most frequently recommended" by Lexpert. He was graduated from Queen's University (Hons. B.A.) and University of Toronto (LL.B.) and was admitted to the Ontario Bar in 1979. He is located in the offices of Stockwoods, Barristers, a litigation boutique firm in Toronto.

Mark Stephens has been described by the *Law Society Gazette* as "the patron solicitor of previously lost causes." It is this reputation for creativity with law that leads international publishers and broadcasters to his door. He has created a niche in international comparative media law and regulation. His practice takes him to Africa, the Commonwealth, Europe, and the United States. Stephens was appointed by the foreign secretary to the Foreign and Commonwealth Office free-expression advisory panel and is chair of the management board of the postgraduate Program in Comparative Media Law and Social Policy at Wolfson College, Oxford University. He is regularly asked to litigate privacy, free speech, and public interest issues before domestic and international courts (including the European Court of Human Rights and the Privy Council) and has given expert evidence before courts in three jurisdictions. In 2005, Stephens was asked to draft a new EU- and NATO-compliant freedom-of-information law for

Romania. He is a trustee of *Index on Censorship* and sits on the editorial boards of *Communications Lawyer, Copyright World,* and *EIPR.* He has litigated points arising from libel tourists visiting London and founding claims merely on the basis of Internet publication. As founding chair of the Internet Watch Foundation, Stephens has lectured for the Foreign and Commonwealth Office and the Department of Trade and Industry on Internet content control and regulation and has run courses and tutorials on media law and policy for the Commonwealth Parliamentary Association and World Bank Institute. He is also a regular commentator on legal matters in both print and electronic media.

Tay Peng Cheng is a partner in Wong Partnership. He has extensive experience in litigation and arbitration, encompassing corporate and commercial disputes, construction and civil engineering matters, insolvency, receivership and judicial management, and libel. Tay has acted for a division of a U.S.-based publishing house in a defamation suit commenced in Singapore pertaining to the publication of allegedly defamatory words in an online real-time electronic publication.

Wong Partnership, a full-service law firm, is one of the largest firms in Singapore with over 120 fee earners. In addition to its very highly regarded Litigation & Dispute Resolution Practice, Capital Markets, and Corporate departments, the firm offers specialized practices in China, India, Competition, and Intellectual Property. The firm has a Shanghai representative office, through which it has advised on a number of cross-border corporate and M&A transactions and represented parties in arbitrations held in China and Singapore. Wong Partnership also has a joint law venture in Singapore with Clifford Chance LLP, known as Clifford Chance Wong.

Jens P. van den Brink, associate at Kennedy Van der Laan attorneys in Amsterdam, the Netherlands, specializes in intellectual property and media law. Apart from the more classical intellectual property rights, his practice concentrates on unlawful publications, media law, the law pertaining to counterfeit, as well as the gaming industry. Van den Brink acts for several major players in the Dutch media industry, including both conventional (newspapers, broadcasters, publishers) and new media (Internet, mobile telephony). He regularly publishes on these subjects. Van den Brink studied French at the University of Nice, France, and international and Dutch commercial law (specializing in intellectual property law) at the University of Amsterdam and Columbia University in New York. He also obtained a Master of Laws (LL.M.) at King's College London, United Kingdom.

Vincent Wang is a legal consultant in the Shanghai office of Davis Wright Tremaine LLP. He represents and counsels clients on a wide range of activities in China, including media and Internet issues, intellectual property, telecommunications, foreign direct investment, corporate structure, commercial transactions, customs, land use, engineering, and dispute resolution. He received his B.S. and LL.B. degrees from Shanghai Jiao Tong University, where he chaired the Legal Forum. He is fluent in Mandarin, English, and the Shanghai dialect and has published articles in English and Chinese concerning legal issues on the Internet, e-commerce, intellectual property, employment, and contract law in China.

Kurt Wimmer is a partner concentrating in media law in the Washington, D.C., office of Covington & Burling, a 550-lawyer international law firm, and is co-chair of its technology, media, and communications group. From 2000 to 2003, he was managing partner of the firm's London office. He advises media companies on libel, privacy, newsgathering, and other content issues in the United States and abroad. Representative clients include the Washington Post Company, *Newsweek, National Geographic,* Raycom Media, The New York Times Broadcast Group, and others. He also has advised journalists and legislators in more than twenty emerging democracies on proposed laws concerning media, access to information, and protection of journalists, and he was named by the OSCE and UN to the Advisory Group on Defamation and Freedom of Information Legislation for Bosnia and Herzegovina. He is the president of the Defense Council Section of the Media Law Resource Center; chair of the First Amendment Advisory Counsel of the Media Institute and a member of the Institute's Board of Trustees; and chairman of the board of the International Research Exchanges Board, the major nongovernmental organization supporting independent media internationally.

Nancy E. Wolff is the managing partner of Wolff & Godin, LLP located in New York, where she specializes in intellectual property law and new media law. The firm represents both media companies and individual clients. Clients include the Picture Archive Counsel of America, the trade association of stock photo libraries, as well as many other stock photo libraries, individual photographers, authors, illustrators, designers, and publishers. The firm counsels clients in copyright, trademarks, licensing, contracts, rights of publicity and privacy and libel. In addition to transactional work, the firm appears in arbitration hearings as well as state and federal court civil actions.

Wolff is a member and former trustee of the Copyright Society of U.S.A., was co-chair of the Entertainment Law Committee—New York

County Lawyers Association (NYCLA), and named a rising star by NYCLA in 1999. She was on the Steering Committee for the Copyright Society of U.S.A.'s FA©E initiative to encourage copyright education. She has been a frequent speaker throughout the United States and Europe on copyright, new technology, and licensing for many organizations including the AIPLA (American Intellectual Property Law Association), PACA (Picture Archive Council of America), CEPIC International Conference (Coordination of European Picture Agencies, Press and Stock), The Copyright Society, Art Buyers Club, Graphic Artists Guild, International Center of Photography, Practicing Law Institute in New York (Advanced Licensing), New York County Lawyers Association, Graphic Artist Professionals, Agricultural Publishers, Viscom, and PhotoPlus West and East. She has been an adjunct professor at Benjamin N. Cardozo School of Law teaching Mass Media and Entertainment Law.

Wolff graduated magna cum laude from the University of Maryland in 1978 and holds a B.S. degree in Business Management. She received her law degree from Rutgers School of Law in Newark, New Jersey, in 1981 where she was the business manager and editor of the *Rutgers Law Review.*

How to Use this Book

IN PREPARING THIS BOOK, we submitted a list of the most commonly troublesome libel issues to lawyers around the world with expertise in media and privacy law. The questions are not exhaustive, and of course, no book or outline is a substitute for careful editing and legal review.

The best way for journalists and other publishers to avoid legal problems is to understand those problems *before* setting pen to paper. For that reason, the material presented here is designed for use by journalists to help *avoid* libel suits; it is not oriented toward tactics and defenses in litigation *after* a suit is filed. If you are not a lawyer experienced in the language of media law, I strongly recommend that before consulting the nation-specific chapters in this book, you read this section to familiarize yourself with the concepts explained. They are:

1. What is the locally accepted definition of libel?
2. Is libel-by-implication recognized, or, in the alternative, must the complained-of words alone defame the plaintiff?
3. May corporations sue for libel?
4. Is product disparagement recognized, and if so, how does that differ from libel?
5. Must an individual be clearly identified (by name or photograph) to sue for libel? Can a group of persons sue for libel, even though not named?
6. What is the fault standard(s) applied to libel?
   a. Does the fault standard depend on the fame or notoriety of the plaintiff?
   b. Is there a heightened fault standard or privilege for reporting on matters of public concern or public interest?
7. Is financial news about publicly traded companies, or companies involved with a government contract, considered a matter of public interest or otherwise privileged?

8. Is there a recognized protection for opinion or "fair comment" on matters of public concern?

9. Are there any requirements upon a plaintiff, such as demand for retraction or right of reply, and if so, what impact do they have?

10. Is there a privilege for quoting or reporting on papers filed in court, government-issued documents, or quasi-governmental proceedings?

11. Is there a privilege for republishing statements made earlier by other, bona fide, reliable publications or wire services?

12. Are there any restrictions regarding reporting on ongoing criminal investigations, criminal prosecutions, regulatory investigations, civil litigation, or other judicial proceedings?

13. Are prior restraints or other prepublication injunctions available on the basis of libel or privacy, and if so, what are the standards for obtaining such relief?

14. Is a right of privacy recognized (either civilly or criminally)?
    a. What is the definition of "private fact"?
    b. Is there a public interest or newsworthiness exception?
    c. Is the right of privacy based in common law, statute, or constitution?

15. May reporters tape-record their own telephone conversations for note-taking purposes (not rebroadcast) without the consent of the other party?

16. If permissible to record such tapes, may they be broadcast without permission?

17. Is there a recognized evidentiary privilege preventing the disclosure of confidential sources relied upon by reporters?

18. In the event that legal papers are served upon the newsroom (such as a civil complaint), are there any particular warnings about accepting service of which we should be aware?

19. Has your jurisdiction applied established media law to Internet publishers?

20. If established media law has been applied to Internet publishers, are there any ways in which Internet publishers (including chat room operators) have to meet different standards?

21. Are there any cases where the courts enforced a judgment in libel from another jurisdiction against a publisher in your jurisdiction?

Note: Introductions to each country's legal system at the beginnings of the chapters were written by the chapter authors or by Charles J. Glasser Jr.

The Key Questions Explained

1. What is the locally accepted definition of libel?

In the broadest terms, a libel claim usually requires that a publisher:

1. makes a statement to a third party;
2. that is false; and
3. defamatory, meaning that it exposes a subject's reputation to harm.

This third element—"defamatory meaning"—is central to most libel issues. If a statement is false but not defamatory, in most nations there is no libel. For example, if a statement that a cabinet minister drives a blue car turns out to be false, and his car is in fact green, it would take an unreasonable stretch to attribute reputational harm to the error: no one would think less of him for driving a blue car instead of a green one.

In many countries, to be considered defamatory, a statement must expose the subject to "hate, ridicule, contempt, or scorn" or to "lower the subject's reputation in the eyes of right-thinking members of society." Generally, defamatory words are those that would damage reputation, and would reasonably cause people to stop associating or doing business with the subject. Typically, these are statements of criminal or ethical wrongdoing, professional incompetence, lack of integrity, impending financial insolvency, loathsome disease, or immorality.

Each jurisdiction has different limits regarding what is and isn't considered defamatory, and these standards are reflective of the societal norms of that culture. Of course, some statements would put the subject's reputation into disrepute globally: an accusation of thievery or violent crime is universally condemned. However, less obvious issues require looking at the society in which the subject would complain. For example, in cosmopolitan cities such as New York and San Francisco, being called homosexual is not considered defamatory, because the society does not assume that it is something of which one should be ashamed. By contrast, in rural Georgia, being called "gay" is actionable, because that society considers homosexuality as a moral wrong.

Some jurisdictions allow a libel claim to be brought on seemingly innocent statements that would injure reputation if the reader happens to be aware of certain undisclosed facts. The law calls this *libel per quod*. For example, consider the statement: "Mr. Smith was seen kissing a blonde-haired woman in a restaurant last night." This in and of itself shouldn't expose his reputation to harm—unless the reader knew that Mr. Smith was in fact married to a dark-haired woman!

One common mistake journalists and publishers make here is to confuse "falsity" with "defamatory meaning." In most jurisdictions, even if a statement exposes a person to reputational damage, if it is true, it may not be the basis of a libel suit. But conflating truth with defamatory meaning leads to problems. With the exception of the United States, if sued upon, the publisher or journalist carries the burden of proving the truth of the statement in court, which is not as easy as it sounds. The proof must be hard, documented, and reliable enough to stand up in court. (See the discussion of fault standards in Question 6 below.) The safest, most responsible approach for any journalist or publisher is, as a first rule, determine whether the statement at issue is capable of defamatory meaning: will it harm the subject's reputation? If so, the next step is to determine how much solid, incontrovertible proof you can offer that the statement is indeed true.

There are certain circumstances when the statement is considered "privileged." This is when the subject matter is considered by law to be so important to society that a publisher is relieved of the duty to determine the truth of defamatory allegations. These "privileged" circumstances are usually found in situations where *the fact that the statement was made* is in itself newsworthy. For example, allegations made in court pleadings, police reports, government agencies' reports, or legislative debates are important because society needs to be informed about what transpires in courts and government. Thus, many nations treat these circumstances as "privileged," and provided they are accurately and fairly reported, the press may republish these statements without liability. (See the discussion of privilege in Question 10 below.)

In many nations, truth is not always an absolute defense, and if the statement at issue exposes the subject to reputational injury, it need not be false to be actionable: In these nations, a true statement that exposes a person to reputational damage may still be sued upon if the court finds that the statement does not serve the public interest. Mere curiosity or gossip may not satisfy the court that the public "needed to know" the damaging facts, despite their truth, or that telling these facts was an example of fulfilling a journalist's mission. (See the discussion of fault standards in Question 6 below.)

2. Is libel-by-implication recognized, or, in the alternative, must the complained-of words alone defame the plaintiff?

Some statements are defamatory "on their face," meaning that by themselves, they may defame the subject, for example, "X is a murderer." By contrast, libel-by-implication can occur either by arranging innocent facts in a way that suggests wrongdoing, or by leaving out information that the reader ought to know to have a less damaging view of the subject.

In the first instance, a common occurrence in libel analysis is the juxtaposition of a series of facts: "A is a child-care specialist. The government is investigating child-care specialists for evidence of child abuse." Put together, a reader could reasonably infer that "A" might be under investigation for child abuse. *This is true even though there is no specific statement that "A" is under investigation.* Courts often allow a hypothetical reader to make reasonable inferences, even though such implications were not necessarily the intent of the writer. Avoiding this problem requires clarity and precision of language.

Similarly, leaving out facts that clarify a story can also create the impression that someone has committed wrongdoing or is subject to other defamatory meaning. For example, to say that "University Professor X failed to report to the school that he made extra money tutoring students at his home" implies that he had a duty to report his extra income, and may have committed a wrongful act. But something is omitted here: is the professor actually *obligated* to make this disclosure? If the story omitted that fact, the reasonable reader might assume that the professor violated some trust or even a legal obligation. Did he really *fail* to do something he should have?

It is also worth noting that in many jurisdictions, raising hypothetical questions may be a form of libel-by-implication. To ask: "Is X wanted by government investigators?" raises the question that he *might* be a wanted criminal.

3. May corporations sue for libel?

The question of whether a company has the right to sue for libel comes up frequently in the areas of consumer reporting, financial news, and product reviews. Some jurisdictions severely limit the ability of companies to sue for libel, and other jurisdictions do not allow companies (as corporate entities) a right of privacy. Individual executives, of course, may still bring libel claims subject to the laws of the applicable jurisdiction.

The question also comes up when a story or publication targets an individual who may be closely associated with a particular company.

4. Is product disparagement recognized, and if so, how does that differ from libel?

Product disparagement (sometimes called "trade libel") issues arise when a product or brand of goods is held in disrepute. This occurs often in product reviews, consumer reporting, and comparative advertising. Some jurisdictions apply the same substantive standards as a libel claim, while others allow these kinds of claims to apply only when competitors make statements that might be construed as unfair competition or deceptive trade practices.

5. Must an individual be clearly identified (by name or photograph) to sue for libel? Can a group of persons sue for libel, even though not named?

Also referred to as the "of and concerning" doctrine in libel, jurisdictions have differing degrees of specificity with which the subject of a story is described. Usually, the law does not require that a subject be named: if he or she is reasonably identifiable from the details provided, that will suffice for a libel claim. Other jurisdictions, such as France, however, adopt a "libel par ricochet" doctrine, through which not only the subject, but people with whom the subject is normally associated by the public, may also have a libel claim.

6. What is the fault standard(s) applied to libel?

Misapprehension of the "fault standard" is probably responsible for more sloppy journalism—and libel suits—than any other doctrine in law. Moreover, the plain fact of the matter is that reporters, writers, and editors do sometimes get their facts wrong.

Too many publishers overlook the fact that the fault standard is essentially a legal excuse for making a mistake: "the right to get it wrong." In many nations, courts and legislators have realized that the public would be shortchanged if the press were strictly liable for every mistake. This is because the press would be forced to "self-censor" and cut off the flow of information, lest it face a bankrupting libel claim for any mistake. The fault standard seeks to strike a balance between the public's need for important news and the right that citizens have in being free from libelous statements. Without some leeway for good faith error, the chilling effect of libel suits would prevent most publishers from taking the financial risk of publishing important news, especially about the powerful and well-funded. Publishers must recognize that in most jurisdictions, the complained-of story is assumed to be false as a starting point for most courts.

Fault standards generous to the press have in some cases been relied upon by unscrupulous journalists who see it as a license to print whatever they want without due care for whether the material they publish is accurate. On the other hand, thoughtful publishers and journalists see the fault standards as a guidepost of due care, a minimum standard of professional responsibility and behavior.

a. Does the fault standard depend on the fame or notoriety of the plaintiff?

In some nations, courts differentiate libel plaintiffs in varying degrees as "public" or "private" figures, and may apply a more stringent set of hurdles for a "public figure" to overcome as a plaintiff in a libel suit. This is not, as some journalists think, rooted in a theory that public figures are "asking for it." Instead, the law in nations applying a "public figure" test assumes that public figures have the ability to command attention and can easily dispel false stories by issuing a press release or holding a press conference to challenge stories. Their fame or notoriety will help ensure that their side of a story is heard. In these cases, public figure plaintiffs will have to show more than mere falsity or defamatory meaning: they usually have to show that the reporter breached all standards of ethical or professional duty in making the mistake.

In some jurisdictions, such as the United States, the plaintiff will have to prove that the reporter knew his or her story was incorrect or entertained serious doubt about its falsity but chose to publish anyway. This is often referred to as *actual malice*. By contrast, in nations with heightened fault standards, private figures, or persons involved in a matter not deemed of public importance, do not have to meet such a difficult task. They often need only prove negligence on the part of the journalist. *That comes down to a court asking in sometimes detailed terms if the reporter did that which a reasonable reporter should have done.* In journalism, this commonly includes:

- Extensive fact-checking and note-taking;
- Exhaustive documentary research and personal interviews;
- Clear and precise writing without a malicious tone;
- Providing an opportunity to fairly and fully respond; and
- Asking yourself whether the story was so important to the public interest that it could not wait for further research or fact-checking.

It is important to recognize that in most jurisdictions the fact the reporter simply *believed* in good faith that the material was accurate is not enough to satisfy the test.

b. Is there a heightened fault standard or privilege for reporting on matters of public concern or public interest?

In jurisdictions where the story is assumed to be in error, or where there is in fact a defamatory inaccuracy, some courts allow this error to go unpunished if it is made in "good faith" *and* the matter is one of public concern. The definition of "public concern" is informed by each jurisdiction's approach to excusing error. In other words, in nations such as the United States where adherence to the First Amendment is seen as a primary goal, and protection for the press is at its greatest, courts will generally allow editors—not lawyers—to determine what is and isn't in the public interest. Some U.S. courts have gone as far as saying that if an editor chose to publish the story, it must be, by definition, a matter of interest to the public.

By contrast, courts in most other jurisdictions take a very close look at the question of "public concern" and ask actively whether the story at issue was something that served the public welfare, not the public's idle curiosity or appetite for gossip.

7. Is financial news about publicly traded companies, or companies involved with a government contract, considered a matter of public interest or otherwise privileged?

In some jurisdictions, the courts recognize that the press is the "watchdog" of the activities of publicly traded companies. Thus, reports on their activities may be "privileged" to one extent or another, heightening the legal protections. When companies or their products are the subject of reporting, one important risk publishers should take into account is the varying degree of damages that companies may be able to claim are the result of an inaccurate and defamatory story. Companies can in some cases claim that lost sales, lost value of assets, failed transactions, and even a drop in stock price are recoverable.

Although not generally recognized in the United States, some nations recognize a cause of action for "negligent publication," which some academics describe as a "libel claim without the libel." In essence, these are claims where the false statement does not necessarily expose the subject to reputational damages, but is somehow relied upon by readers to the subject's detriment. For example, if a news story inaccurately describes a company losing a big contract, and based on that story the company has trouble borrowing money, they may claim that the higher cost of financing is attributable to the erroneous story. Similarly, under this theory claims have been brought on the publications of faulty recipes that made people sick, product reviews that "encouraged" people to buy defective products, or instructions for mechanical engineering procedures that resulted in personal injury.

8. Is there a recognized protection for opinion or "fair comment" on matters of public concern?

Most jurisdictions allow some leeway for the expression of opinion on matters of public concern, subject to varying restrictions. Intellectually, the defense is based on the following syllogism: If libel claims require a false fact; and opinions are not capable of being proven true or false; then opinions are not subject to libel claims.

On a more practical level, opinions can be the subject of a libel claim if they are not "pure" opinion (e.g., "I don't like Mercedes-Benz automobiles") but are instead opinions that imply undisclosed fact (e.g., "I don't think Mercedes-Benz automobiles are safe"). The second example implies to the reader that there is something *factually provable* about the Mercedes that serves as a basis for the opinion. In many jurisdictions, unless the writer disclosed to the reader *why* she thinks the Mercedes is unsafe, a libel claim might arise. Note that those facts have to be accurate, of course. Despite this framework, a surprisingly high number of editors and commentators are subjected to libel claims because of the false comfort to be had from couching otherwise defamatory statements in the language of opinion, such as "I think" or "it is believed that..."

Many jurisdictions also place restrictions on the "tone" of the opinion. In the United States, the more vitriolic, or at least hyperbolic the language, the closer to "pure" opinion the article will be found, on the theory that "heated rhetoric" is patently obvious as a writer's opinion, rather than stating actual facts. Thus, American defendants have been able to call subjects "nazis," "pigs," "butchers," and in one case, "a chicken butt." Many nations are not as generous with wild language, and may hold publishers liable for the use of "uncivil" or "ridiculing" language.

9. Are there any requirements upon a plaintiff, such as demand for retraction or right of reply, and if so, what impact do they have?
The "right of reply" is grounded in two different theories, each of which should be understood by publishers. Some jurisdictions, particularly those that have a generous press-friendly body of law, are driven by the belief that "more speech is better," in other words, that the public interest is best served by having opposing sides of a story brought into the open. These jurisdictions usually reward publishers who publish replies from story subjects by limiting the amount of damages that may be awarded at trial. Other pro-press jurisdictions even deny libel plaintiffs the right to sue at all if they do not make specific written demands for retraction within certain time periods.

By contrast, some jurisdictions approach the right of reply from a "press responsibility" theory, namely, that because publishers control access to the press, fairness requires that people who take issue with stories have a right to be heard. These jurisdictions place a serious requirement on publishers who do receive such demands from libel plaintiffs, and publishers who fail to publish responses in a specified manner may be subjected to civil fine.

10. Is there a privilege for quoting or reporting on:

a. Papers filed in court?

Variants on the "fair and true report" privilege essentially allow reporters to reproduce potentially defamatory statements made in court without independently verifying those facts. This is because courts often accept that the reporting is about what transpires in civil or criminal proceedings, and accordingly, the public has a need to be informed about the administration of justice. That said, great care should be taken when reproducing the allegations made in court. First, because court cases (whether civil or criminal) usually involve some degree of wrongdoing, the odds are high that a potentially defamatory statement will arise.

Second, very few jurisdictions allow the press absolute, unfettered ability to publish defamatory statements plucked from courtrooms or court papers. This second caveat is the heart of the "fair and true" doctrine: the report must be fair to the subject of the allegations, and true, meaning it must accurately describe the legal argument or court document at issue. Although by no means exhaustive, reporters should consider the following guidelines:

"Fair" generally means:

- Reporting not just the damaging facts or allegations, but including the counterarguments or defenses raised by the subject;
- Making clear the distinction between unproven allegations and an actual finding of fact;
- Providing an opportunity to respond.

"True" generally means:

- Accurately describing the legal argument or allegation made;
- Refraining from adding conjecture about innocence and guilt;
- Quoting from the documents or statements when possible, instead of paraphrasing.

b. Government-issued documents?

Jurisdictions have differing views on what kind of government papers may or may not be subject to the fair and true report privilege. In most areas, public statements, reports, fact-finding papers, and statements made by government agencies are privileged to one degree or another, as are usually legislative or parliamentary debates.

Not all jurisdictions allow defamatory allegations contained in documents or statements made by a government agency to be quoted without some limitations. Jurisdictions also vary widely in defining what a "government document" is: for example, in some places police reports are privileged, in others they are not. As a general rule, an "official" statement will be one that is: (i) made by a government employee authorized to speak on behalf of his or her agency; and (ii) made in a situation or occasion expressly convened for the purpose of disseminating information to the public at large, such as press conferences, press releases, public meetings, or e-mailed statements to the press.

c. Quasi-governmental proceedings, such as those issued by professional associations (for example, disciplinary proceedings)?

As described above, jurisdictions have varying definitions of what is and isn't a government agency for purposes of applying a privilege to reporting defamatory allegations contained in their documents. Many jurisdictions apply this privilege to the statements, reports, findings, and hearings of "quasi"-government agencies. These may be loosely defined as bodies that have been given a degree of authority to make decisions on behalf of the public, or of bodies that have the authority to discipline specific industries on behalf of the public interest, such as medical or bar associations, or self-regulating bodies such as those that oversee stock brokers and traders.

11. Is there a privilege for republishing statements made earlier by other, bona fide, reliable publications or wire services?

As a basic rule, those who repeat a libel are as responsible as those who first published it. Nonetheless, some jurisdictions allow publishers to rely on the reporting of bona fide, reputable news agencies in certain circumstances, particularly in jurisdictions that require a plaintiff to show more than mere negligence to recover libel damages. The application of this privilege varies, but courts generally require that the "republisher" did not alter the language of the original report, did not excise any exculpatory information from the original report, and did not have specific knowledge or reason to believe that the original report was wrong.

Publishers find themselves in a quandary when the fact of the original report is *in itself* newsworthy. There are often instances when the fact that a major publication or broadcaster publishes a groundbreaking and important story has an effect on the marketplace or the political dialogue. Courts that recognize this privilege often require that those republishing allegations made by other publishers should try to craft their story in a manner that does not adopt those allegations as a fact, but rather sets forth the controversy in an even-handed manner.

12. Are there any restrictions regarding:

a. Reporting on ongoing criminal investigations?

Few areas are as fraught with landmines as reporting ongoing criminal investigations. Aside from the libel issues (see Questions 10a. and b. above), non-U.S. courts generally take a dim view of publishers perceived as "interfering" with law enforcement or regulatory activities. This is because of the argument that the publication may be inadvertently "tipping off" suspected individuals and allowing them to escape detection or to destroy evidence.

b. Reporting on ongoing criminal prosecutions?

Several nations place restrictions on reporting ongoing investigations because the law is concerned with publications that might taint the public's perception of a case from which a jury pool might be selected. In these cases, reporters and publishers who reveal details about criminal proceedings may be charged with Contempt of Court, and be subject to fines or imprisonment.

Restrictions on the reporting of criminal proceedings include, variously, "blackout" periods of publishing between the time of arrest and verdict; names and identifying information about suspects and witnesses, details about the crime, and speculation about guilt or innocence. Contempt of Court in many of these nations is a "strict liability" crime, meaning that there is no justification defense available: if the forbidden material is published, the reporter or publisher faces charges.

c. Reporting on ongoing regulatory investigations?

Reporters may face the same difficulties reporting on regulatory investigations as they might in criminal cases.

d. Reporting on ongoing civil litigation or other judicial proceedings?

Although civil cases are usually subject to fewer restrictions, reporters should be advised that courts may declare certain types of material "off limits" depending on what kind of civil case is being litigated. For example, the publication of proprietary trade information, personal private data, identities of minors, material in family court such as paternity issues, and other sensitive material may be proscribed.

13. Are prior restraints or other prepublication injunctions available on the basis of libel or privacy, and if so, what are the standards for obtaining such relief?

"Prior restraints" are judicial actions whereby the court forbids a publisher from disclosing or reporting certain information before it is published. The United States is one of the few jurisdictions that bans "prior restraints" under its Constitution.

Prior restraints are generally granted when the subject of the story has a reasonable basis for believing that the material is about to be published, and can convince the court ahead of time that the story is false and damaging. Publishers or webmasters served with notice of a hearing for a prior restraint should consult local counsel immediately, and should never ignore such a notice.

Even if the publisher believes that the story is accurate under the local law, failure to obey the prior restraint without attending the hearing may subject the publisher to criminal charges. The bad news is that attending such a hearing may delay publication, or even ruin the exclusivity of the story. The good news is that in most nations that allow prior restraints, the person requesting relief will have to put up a bond and bear the publisher's legal costs if the restraint is not granted.

14. Is a right of privacy recognized (either civilly or criminally)?

The right of privacy should be understood as separate and distinct from defamation. Where defamation addresses the reputation of entities impacted by false speech, "privacy" addresses not damage to reputation (what others think of the subject) but instead the damage to the subject's *feelings*. The truth or falsity of the statement at issue is rarely germane to privacy claims.

At its core, privacy claims center on the offensiveness of having material published about a person that (the plaintiff claims) has no business being disclosed to the public at large. Although corporations can bring claims based on the disclosure of private data or trade secrets, they usually do not have standing to bring "invasion of privacy" claims because these claims are designed to repair "hurt feelings" or "emotional damage," both injuries that corporations (as opposed to human individuals) do not have the ability to suffer.

a. What is the definition of "private fact"?

In those nations that recognize a right of privacy, the central question is whether the sued-upon story discloses a fact that is generally personal and private, and the disclosure of which is highly offensive. Defining a "private" fact is not an easy task for plaintiffs. The fact at issue may not be known, but if it is *knowable* to the public (for example, through easily accessed public records), it may not be considered "private."

Even if the fact at issue is secret, mere secrecy is not enough to make a claim. Courts will examine the nature of the fact itself, and its inherent "offensiveness." Courts will generally find "privacy" to have been violated when a fact discloses something of an *intimate* nature. Medical information, information about sexual preferences or behavior, information about children, marital matters, and the like are more likely to be actionable. Publishers should also be aware of restrictions in the European Union and elsewhere about disclosure of data that is considered private under Data Protection Laws.

b. Is there a public interest or newsworthiness exception?

Some jurisdictions that recognize a right of privacy still protect publishers if the fact at issue is "rationally related" to a public controversy. This usually becomes a very fact-specific examination. Broadly speaking, media superstars such as notoriously misbehaving pop singers are often deemed to have almost no right to privacy at all, while other celebrities, although famous, may be allowed to pursue claims of privacy *when the private fact at issue is not rationally related to the reason he or she is famous.* Superstar fashion model Naomi Campbell was allowed to pursue privacy claims in the United Kingdom when a tabloid showed photographs of her leaving a drug rehabilitation clinic. Campbell argued that the disclosure of her medical condition was private and not in the public interest. The UK courts and the EU Court of Human Rights agreed.

c. Is the right of privacy based in common law, statute, or constitution?

Several jurisdictions also have statutes addressing a form of privacy claim called "misappropriation of likeness." This claim is similar to a false endorsement, trademark, or unfair competition claim, wherein people— usually celebrities—who have a value in their image, claim that it is being misused for the purpose of profit. Some celebrities have tried to use this claim as an end run around substantive defamation laws, arguing that because newspapers or broadcasters are in the business of making a profit, their image shouldn't be used in newspaper stories without their consent. Courts have almost universally rejected this approach, and apply a "newsworthiness" exemption to this claim as well. This protection has also been extended to unauthorized biographies, movies, posters, and even artwork. It should be noted that there have been several cases where the claim was allowed to proceed because the story underlying the unconsented use of the photo was erroneous, or, in the words of one judge, "so infected with substantial falsity" that the judge said it would be illogical to allow a newsworthiness defense to a story that was clearly not news.

15. May reporters tape-record their own telephone conversations for note-taking purposes (not rebroadcast) without the consent of the other party?

Many jurisdictions forbid the recording of telephone conversations without the consent of all parties to the phone call (also called "two-party" consent). In these places, the mere act of making the recording itself may be a crime, and it does not matter whether the tape is disclosed to a third party or not. In some of these jurisdictions, such an improperly made tape might not be admissible as evidence in a libel trial in the event that the recording is needed for the reporter to prove that something in particular was said.

16. If permissible to record such tapes, may they be broadcast without permission?

Even in areas where it is permissible for reporters to tape-record their telephone interviews without the other person's consent, that is not a guarantee that such tapes may be broadcast without consent. The act of making the tape is separate from disclosing the tape (or its contents), which might be a violation under statutory privacy laws, or broadcasting regulations.

17. Is there a recognized evidentiary privilege preventing the disclosure of confidential sources relied upon by reporters?

Using confidential sources is something that reporters should never take lightly. A "shield law" or "reporters' privilege" is a doctrine that protects reporters from having to disclose their confidential sources. This comes up in a variety of ways:

1. when parties are in litigation and seek to obtain reporters' notes or outtakes to prove their case (usually through a subpoena);
2. when law enforcement agencies want to investigate or prosecute someone who may have been interviewed by the reporter (also demanded through a subpoena); and
3. when the reporter or publisher is sued for libel in a story that uses confidential sources (usually demanded in discovery or disclosure).

Nations that do have shield laws are usually protective to the press in the first instance when civil litigants seek to use a reporter's notes, especially when those notes might reveal the identity of a confidential source. The second instance, however, is not as clear-cut, and generally, law enforcement agencies have been successful in convincing courts that reporters should disclose their confidential sources. Judges in these matters are generally required to balance the harms at issue. On the media's side, forcing disclosure makes the press an official "arm" of law enforcement, and erodes the press's independence. Press freedom advocates add that this has a "chilling effect" on sources who want to tell the press important information but are afraid of being targeted for retribution. On the other hand, law enforcement agencies have been able in some cases to convince courts that reporters have no higher standing or more rights than "ordinary" citizens, and, like "ordinary" citizens, must come forward and testify as to facts they have that the government might need to protect the public.

Shield laws may not apply to the third situation, when the press is sued and the plaintiff seeks the identity of the confidential source. Because plaintiffs in most cases have a right to attack the credibility of a reporter or his source, the press is often barred from relying on confidential sources to defend a libel claim unless it is willing to disclose the identity of the source. This puts the press in a difficult position, because sources who are promised confidentiality by the press have been allowed to sue the press for breach of contract when their identity is disclosed without consent. Moreover, some European jurisdictions make it a criminal act for reporters to disclose the identity of confidential sources.

18. In the event that legal papers are served upon the newsroom (such as a civil complaint), are there any particular warnings about accepting service of which we should be aware?

Each nation has its own set of procedural laws regarding the manner in which legal papers such as subpoenas and complaints (and sometimes demands for retraction) must be delivered. Failure to respond properly to such papers might result in a default judgment against the publisher or reporter, and local counsel should be consulted immediately in all cases.

19. Has your jurisdiction applied established media law to Internet publishers?

It should not be assumed that all established media law and case decisions will be applied the same way. For example, the archival aspect of the Internet has established different rules for statutes of limitations, whereby claims can "expire" if not acted upon within a certain date of the publication. Where stories published on paper might not be sued upon after a set period (say three years after the first publication in any medium), many courts outside the United States have said that on the Internet, each day that the offending web page is available brings a new publication, and the claim renews. Thus, Internet publishers might face "infinite" exposure for their stories.

20. If established media law has been applied to Internet publishers, are there any ways in which Internet publishers (including chat room operators) have to meet different standards?

Federal communications law in the United States provides a "safe harbor" for most operators of ISPs, chat rooms, and electronic bulletin boards, protecting them from liability for the defamatory statements made by others without the operator's prior knowledge. However, many non-U.S. jurisdictions apply a strict liability rule, making the operators of Web sites and the like responsible for defamatory statements, whether they are aware of the falsity of the statement or not.

Web site operators outside the United States have also been held accountable for the unknowing use of their Web sites for the improper posting of copyrighted material and materials that violate the EU Data Privacy Act.

21. Are there any cases where the courts enforced a judgment in libel from another jurisdiction against a publisher in your jurisdiction?
A judgment in one nation against a publisher or reporter might not be enforceable in others. The enforcement of judgments is determined by a patchwork of statutes, treaties, and common law. Although judgments issued outside of the United States rooted in non-U.S. libel law might not be enforceable in the United States, the same is not necessarily so for entities who have employees or assets elsewhere. (See Chapter 22, "Enforcing Foreign Judgments in the United States and Europe.")

PART ONE

Americas

Brazil

Canada

United States

CHAPTER 1

Brazil

LAURA FRAGOMENI, PAULA MENA BARRETO,
Barbosa, Müssnich & Aragão

AND EDUARDO DE MORAES
Evaristo de Moraes

Barbosa, Müssnich & Aragão
Av. Almirante Barroso, n0 52, 32 Floor
Rio de Janeiro/RJ/Brazil 20031-00
Phone: (55 21) 3825-6001
Fax: (55 21) 3824-6069
www.bmalaw.com.br
lfo@bmalaw.com.br
pmb@bmalaw.com.br

Evaristo de Moraes
Rua México, n0 90 sala 402
Rio de Janeiro/RJ/Brazil 20031-141
Phone: (55 21) 2240-6128
Fax: (55 21) 2240-6128
evaristomoraes@uol.com.br
edumoraeseva@uol.com.br

Introduction to the Brazilian Legal System

The Brazilian legal system is derived from traditional civil law theories and is guided by the Brazilian Federal Constitution, which was drafted in 1988. The "new" system has significantly streamlined a Brazilian system that was infamous for having an excessive number of laws.

The current judicial system has two branches, a federal branch and a state branch. There are two levels of federal courts in Brazil. Federal districts, composed of states and municipalities, each have their own court, called the Federal District Court. The second level of the federal branch is the Supreme Court of Justice, the highest federal court in the country. The state system is composed of states and municipalities within each state. Each state has its own uniquely organized judicial system, and each state's courts, judges, and jurisdiction are determined by a state constitution. State legal powers are limited by the federal constitution, but are otherwise unhindered. Municipalities have constitutional equivalents, called organic law, but no court system, and must obey all federal constitutional laws.

Brazilian Civil Code and Media Law

Persons producing content subject to Brazilian law are advised to familiarize themselves briefly with the structural framework of Brazil's legal system and its approach to media law. Article 5 of the Constitution of Brazil (CB, in force since 1988) and Brazil place a high value on freedom of the press;[1] however, the CB also provides citizens with the inviolability of privacy and private life. Therefore, the various constitutional guaranties must be weighed against each other in any given case. In addition, certain restrictions on press freedom have been established via legislative means.

The Brazilian Civil Code (BCC), which was passed in 2002, introduced changes in the area of personality rights, including the right to private life. The BCC provides that the private life of natural persons is inviolable and that the courts, on application by an interested party, may adopt such measures as may be necessary to prevent any act contrary to the inviolability of private life or to cause such acts to cease.

1. What is the locally accepted definition of libel?

The CB guarantees both freedom of the press and the right to privacy. Provision is made for the freedom of artistic and scientific expression and communication which is free from censorship or restriction. On the other hand, the CB also states that "honor, dignity, image, and the right to privacy are all inviolable rights," breach of which gives rise to an entitlement to damages. Libel is both a criminal offense and a civil wrong in Brazil.

Chapter 3 (Capítulo III) of the Press Law[2] sets out the offenses arising from abuse of the right to freedom of thought and information using communication/information media. The term media, in this context, covers newspapers and periodical publications, radio transmission, and other news services.

Media crimes are divided into two classes: on the one hand, public order offenses or the divulging of state secrets, and on the other, defamation ("crimes against reputation"). Depending on the conduct of the agent, libel (in a broad definition) can take, according to Brazilian law, three different forms: *calumny* (calúnia), *defamation* (difamação), and *injury to dignity* or decorum (injúria). These three crimes are defined as follows:

Calumny: To falsely accuse someone of committing a criminal act (punishable by 6 months' to 3 years' imprisonment plus a fine ranging from 1 to 20 minimum salaries).[3]

In the offenses of calumny (art. 20) and defamation (art. 21), the publisher alleges a provable fact. In the former (calumny), the publisher must have knowledge of the falsity prior to publication. It is important to note, however, that in certain circumstances the defendant accused of the crime of calumny or defamation may rely on the defense of truth. This defense is generally available in calumny (art. 20) but only in limited circumstances in defamation (art. 21), and not at all for injury to dignity (art. 22). The defense of truth, where applicable, is an absolute defense, whereby the defendant avoids conviction.

Examples of calumny include the following: The unproven allegation that a judge, in the city of Canoinhas, had committed the offense of threatening behavior (which constitutes a crime) against the owners of a publishing company, saying that if the editor in chief did not stop writing about the mayor of the city, he would be severely punished, with payment of fines and, additionally, imprisonment. The publisher published such threats. The truth of the allegedly calumnious statement was not proved and, for this reason, the owners of the company were convicted.[4] In a city in the State of São Paulo, a public agent was accused of manipulating the results of a public contest and making false representations. The court decided that such a statement would constitute a crime of calumny.[5]

The following statements were found not to constitute calumny: A news report was published of a charge of manslaughter filed against a medical practitioner. Because the charges had in fact been brought, the court found the statement justified by truth and held there was no crime of calumny.[6] A journalist authored an article in which he referred to the plaintiff as a drug dealer, for being criminally convicted and currently on conditional release. However, the court decided that libel was not present, once the defendant had established his fact-finding on the *animus narrandi* ("willing to tell").[7]

Defamation: To allege that someone has performed a disreputable act (punishable by 3 to 18 months' imprisonment plus a fine of between 2 and 10 minimum salaries).[8]

In the lower-level offense of defamation, the act which the victim is stated to have performed is not a criminal act, but is nonetheless conduct that is detrimental to the victim's reputation (*disreputable*). An individual's reputation is the person's "standing in society." The law seeks to uphold and protect the esteem in which a person is held by society—*objective dignity.*

Examples of defamation include: Blaming the mayor of a municipality for improper accounting procedures at City Hall, saying he had "never been transparent" in his accounting and that the "public authorities were reluctant to publish the accounts" because of fear of reprisals.[9] In another case, an article referred to the mayor of a certain city as "mentally disordered." The court understood this conduct as defamatory, and no public interest was present in the context of this statement. For this reason, the statement was not supported by the principle of freedom of speech in the Brazilian Constitution.[10]

The following statements were found not to constitute defamation: A newspaper reported the filing of administrative proceedings against an educational institution. The court held that the aim of the report was to inform the community of an issue of public interest. The journalist's intention was not to defame the legal entity referred to or its partners.[11] In another case, a journalist published a satire *animus jocandi* ("willing to make fun") that alleged provable facts. Because they were true, the way they were published was considered a legal form of expression by the journalist.[12]

Injury: To offend someone's dignity or decorum (punishable by 1 to 12 months' imprisonment or a fine of between 1 and 10 minimum salaries).[13] The offense of injury (art. 22) involves making statements which simply offend the subjects' "decorum and dignity." Decorum (in Portuguese *dignidade*) refers to a person's moral attributes, whereas dignity (in Portuguese *decoro*)[14] refers to the individual's physical and intellectual attributes. The mere use, to describe a person, of words which express a negative concept or image and which offend "subjective" honor (the victim's self-image, as opposed to that person's image in society) constitutes grounds for prosecution for this offense.

Examples of injury include: An article describing one of the candidates standing for presidency of a municipal legislative assembly (City Hall) as a "hypocrite," "false moralist," and "a man of limited cultural resources" was held to show a clear intention of offending the individual's dignity and decorum rather than making a criticism based on public interest.[15] In another instance, a newspaper published an article stating that the mayor of a city in the State of Rio de Janeiro was a "scoundrel" and his behavior was harmful for the poor population. The court understood that the use of the word "scoundrel" constituted a violation of the subjective honor of the mayor and the newspaper was convicted.[16]

The following examples found that injurious publications had not been committed: A politician was called "selfish" and a "political opportunist" by his political opponent. The court decided that such conduct did not characterize injury because it constitutes (legitimate) criticism.[17] The case of a person named to a public function and who was called "incompetent" and "unable to exercise such function" was adjudicated not injurious because the court held that the expressions were used not to offend the individual but in order to instigate the public opinion against the politician's appointment.[18]

2. Is libel-by-implication recognized, or, in the alternative, must the complained-of words alone defame the plaintiff?

Most expressions need to be interpreted in the context in which they are written in order to determine whether or not one of the three crimes referred to above (calumny, defamation, or injury) has been committed. Expressions which in isolation are not offensive may be held by the judge to be so following examination of the circumstances and manner in which they were used.

3. May corporations sue for libel?

Although there is a divergence in both the precedent and authorities on this question, the dominant position in the Brazilian Superior Court of Justice (Superior Tribunal de Justiça—STJ) is that crimes against honor (which include calumny, defamation, and injury) can only be committed against natural persons. Therefore, corporations could not sue third parties based on libel for criminal purposes. However, legal persons can bring a civil action for damages if they believe they have been defamed.

4. Is product disparagement recognized, and if so, how does that differ from libel?

The mere allegation that a product is unequal (inferior or superior) to another does not constitute a crime against reputation. Neither the Brazilian legislature nor the courts therefore consider the affirmation made in the media that a given brand is better than its competitor to be a criminal offense (crime against reputation).

Denigration of a competitor's product, in the guise of promoting a given trademark, could constitute the crime of defamation and could amount to contravention of other provisions relating to crimes against industrial property (Law no. 9.279/96, Industrial Property Law—IPL). In this sense, and according to article 195 of IPL, the publication of false information or false statements about a competitor in order to obtain any advantage is considered to be a crime.[19]

5. Must an individual be clearly identified (by name or photograph) to sue for libel? Can a group of persons sue for libel, even though not named?

In order to bring an action, the plaintiff must be identified (by any means, such as name, photograph) or at least identifiable (as in the case where reference to a position or function allows the individual to be identified). The same rule applies to a group of persons that can be identified by reason of the function they exercise, even if they have not been referred to by name and their image has not been published.

6. What is the fault standard(s) applied to libel?

a. Does the fault standard depend on the fame or notoriety of the plaintiff?

The fame or notoriety of the plaintiff is not relevant to the question of whether defamation has occurred, although the dominant position among the authorities is that public personalities generally enjoy less protection with respect to their private life.

b. Is there a heightened fault standard or privilege for reporting on matters of public concern or public interest?

The general rule in Brazilian law is that there are no aggravating or attenuating factors in crimes against honor in connection with reporting on matters of public concern, although the circumstances mentioned in the paragraph below should be observed. Nonetheless, courts will allow a limited "public interest" defense in civil cases.

With respect to the public interest in reporting criminal matters, and specifically in connection with the crime of calumny, the CC provides for truth as a defense. However, by statute, truth is not a defense when calumny is committed against the president of the Republic, the head of a foreign state, the president of the Senate, the president of the Chamber of Deputies, or the ministers of the Supreme Federal Court (Supremo Tribunal Federal—STF). However, it is important to mention that the CC was passed when Brazil was under a dictatorship, and the same can be stated with regard to the LP. For this reason, both laws are strict in relation to this matter, but their application is doubtful. Nowadays, in cases of publication considered to be calumnious against any of the public persons mentioned above, the public interest may be invoked (and used as a defense) in order to justify such publication.

In cases of defamation, proof of truth of the statement will be admitted as a defense if the subject is a public servant and the offense is related to the exercise of his office.

Under civil law, the public interest may prevail over the principle of inviolability of a person's honor, private life, and privacy, if the facts reported are true. Thus, even if the plaintiff's honor has been affected by the report, if the facts reported are true and there is a relevant public interest in the report, the plaintiff has no right of redress. The same principle applies in conflicts between the right to inform and the right to preservation of an individual's image or an individual's right to private life, provided, here again, that the facts reported are true.

In contrast, in cases where there is no relevant public interest in the facts, they should not be reported, regardless of their truth. It should be borne in mind that a crime may be committed even when the aim of the reporting is based upon the exercise of the right to serve the public interest, but such right is exercised with malice—a clear intent to damage the reputation of a subject.

7. Is financial news about publicly traded companies, or companies involved with a government contract, considered a matter of public interest or otherwise privileged?

The CB provides that the public administration must comply with the principles of legality, impersonality, morality, efficiency, and publicity, among others. Likewise, Law 8666, which governs government contracting, provides for the publicity of acts and contracts entered into with the public administration. Accordingly, all contracts entered into with the government are public, unless they contain a confidentiality clause. In relation to the financial news of publicly traded companies, they are required by law to publish their financial information periodically, in the form of quarterly reports and annual reports. Therefore, all information published in this manner can be relied upon by a journalist to show relevant public interest.

8. Is there a recognized protection for opinion or "fair comment" on matters of public concern?

The LP sets out in two provisions (art. 21, paragraph 2 and art. 27, section VII), that criticism made on the grounds of public interest does not constitute an abuse of the exercise of freedom of thought and information.

In addition to the grounds of public interest, the specific legislation further excludes *inter alia* from the roll of crimes committed via abuse of the exercise of the freedom of expression and information the following (save where there is manifest intention to prejudice the third party):

1. adverse literary, artistic, scientific, or sporting criticism or commentary (art. 27, subsection I);
2. the reproduction of reports, expert opinions, decisions, or other acts performed by the relevant organs of the legislature, save where such information is confidential (art. 27, subsection II);
3. the reproduction of written or oral debate/argument in court, as well as the reporting of court orders and decisions and such other orders or communications as may be made by the judiciary (art. 27, subsection IV);
4. the reporting of statements or allegations made during court hearings by the parties to the proceedings or their representatives (art. 27, subsection V).

Thus, critical commentary, irritating though it may be, provided it falls within the limits referred to, does not in itself amount to media crime.

9. Are there any requirements upon a plaintiff, such as demand for retraction or right of reply, and if so, what impact do they have?

Yes. The LP provides for a right of reply, in the following terms: any natural or legal person which is accused in, or offended by, a report published in a newspaper or periodical, or in a broadcast, or about whom an untrue or incorrect fact is published through the information media, has the right of reply or rectification. The reply or rectification must be submitted in writing within a period of sixty days from the date of the publication or transmission.

Under the Brazilian CC, the right of reply consists of:

1. publication of the response or rectification of the offended party, in the same newspaper or periodical, with the same characteristics as the original report;
2. transmission of the written reply or rectification of the offended party, by the same broadcaster and on the same program and at the same time as the original report; or
3. transmission of the reply or rectification of the offended party, by the news agency, to all media to which the original report was transmitted.

The broadcaster, newspaper, or news agency must comply with the demand for reply or rectification within twenty-four hours. If the twenty-four hour time limit is not met, the offended party may bring a judicial proceeding to enforce the right of reply. It should be noted that publication or transmission of a reply or rectification does not affect the offended party's right to seek redress through criminal and civil actions. Under the Brazilian CC, if the accused retracts the calumnious or defamatory statement in an appropriate manner at any time prior to judgment, the accused is exempted from criminal liability.

10. Is there a privilege for quoting or reporting on:

a. Papers filed in court?

Yes. The LP authorizes, in whole or in part, the reproduction of news, reports, or transcriptions of oral or written debate before judges or courts, and the publication of orders and judgments and all other communications and orders by judicial authorities. The privilege is absolute: even if the reproduction or report contains calumny, defamation, or injury to dignity and decorum, it will not constitute an abuse of the freedom of information if it is accurate and is not disclosed in a manner that shows bad faith.

b. Government-issued documents?

Yes. The LP authorizes reproduction in whole or in part of reports, opinions, decisions, or acts performed by agencies or departments of the Legislative Houses, unless they contain reserved or secret material; and reports and comments on bills and acts of the legislative branch of government, and related debates and criticism.

c. Quasi-governmental proceedings?

Yes, although the extension of immunity to quasi-governmental proceedings is a closer question, depending on the specific legislation governing the various professional associations at issue. Because the publication of administrative acts of this nature has the potential to violate the members' right to privacy, the legality of such publication will depend on the public interest in the published information and, of course, on the truth of the information reported. In the case of attorneys, for example, who are members of the Order of Attorneys of Brazil, disciplinary proceedings are secret and only the parties, their attorneys, and the directors and other officers of the OAB are allowed to be present. In any event, the question of whether the proceedings of a given professional association are public can only be answered on a case-by-case analysis.

11. Is there a privilege for republishing statements made earlier by other, bona fide, reliable publications or wire services?

Yes. The Brazilian legislature provides for the imposition of a penalty for calumny only for circumstances in which the defendant publishes or transmits allegations of criminal conduct, which the individual knew to be false (i.e., the reporting of an allegation which amounts to calumny, and which the reporter knows to be false) (art. 20, paragraph 1).

In relation to the crime of defamation, the courts have consistently held that the reporting of facts previously published in other newspapers, when the intention is merely to divulge the information and there is no bad faith or wish to prejudice a third party, is not a crime. It is important to state that if, in the opinion of the judge, the person who retransmitted or republished the offending item acted in good faith, that individual should be acquitted.

12. Are there any restrictions regarding reporting on:

a. Ongoing criminal investigations?

Generally, there are no restrictions in this regard, and Brazilian law recognizes the freedom of expression and information in relation to reporting ongoing criminal investigations. Liability may attach only in cases where there is malice—an "unmistakable intent"—on the part of the reporter to defame the person who is the subject of the report. A newspaper report that a certain individual is being investigated for involvement in a criminal organization, for example, is not a crime against reputation or an abuse of the exercise of freedom of information, provided the report is not malicious or in bad faith.

b. Ongoing criminal prosecutions?

As has been set out above, Brazilian law expressly states that the whole, partial, or summarized reproduction, publication, or outline of a written or oral argument before courts or tribunals, and the reporting of court orders and sentences and any other measures taken by the judiciary, shall not be deemed an abuse of the freedom of expression and information (art. 27, subsection IV). The same applies to "articulation, citations (references/quotations) or allegations made in court by the parties or their representatives" (subsection V).

Brazilian law also recognizes a "presumption of rehabilitation." The law prohibits the reporting of an individual's completed prison sentence, unless there are public interest grounds for the publication.

c. Ongoing regulatory investigations?
No.

d. Ongoing civil litigation, or other judicial proceedings?

No; however, in some legal proceedings, either criminal or civil, e.g., those relating to child-care issues or where sensitive issues of state security are involved, the court may order that the proceedings be heard in private (on camera). Any breach of such order, for example by reporting on any aspect of the case, is a serious criminal offense.

13. Are prior restraints or other prepublication injunctions available on the basis of libel or privacy, and if so, what are the standards for obtaining such relief?

No. There is no provision for preemptive censorship of information, even with a view to protecting privacy. There are no means within the criminal law with which to prohibit the publication of news/journalistic material. Specific legislation provides for seizure of printed material which contains war propaganda, discriminatory material relating to race or social class, incitement to subversion of the social and political order, or offense to public decency or values.[20]

14. Is a right of privacy recognized (either civilly or criminally)?

As mentioned in the introduction to this memorandum, the right of privacy is recognized in the CB (art. 5, subsection X), the BCC (art. 21), and the CC (crimes against the inviolability of correspondence and secrets).

a. What is the definition of "private fact"?

There is no definition of private fact in the law of privacy. It can be said that "the right to private life can be defined as the right to live one's own life in isolation, without being subjected to publicity that one neither asked for nor wanted."[21] Privacy interests often outweigh priority over the right to inform, which may prevail only if the necessary public interest in disclosure exists.

b. Is there a public interest or newsworthiness exception?

As mentioned above, the constitutional protection of privacy may give way in the face of public interest. However, such cases are exceptional and must usually be authorized by a court order. A typical example would be access to confidential banking information (which falls within the sphere of privacy), when authorized by a court to serve an overriding public interest.

c. Is the right of privacy based in common law, statute, or constitution?

As mentioned above, the right of privacy is provided for in the CB (art. 5, subsection X). The BCC, which came into effect in January 2003, deals expressly with personality rights, including the right of privacy (art. 21).

15. May reporters tape-record their own telephone conversations for note-taking purposes (not rebroadcast) without the consent of the other party?

Although the courts and the scholars are not unanimous on this point, the dominant opinion is that it is legal to record one's own telephone conversation without the consent of the other party. The Court of Justice of São Paulo, for example, decided that recording a conversation on an answering machine is not illegal, even though the recording was made by only one of the participants in the conversation. The court found that "what the Constitution forbids is the interference of third parties in the dialog, without the consent of the speaker or the listener: that which is referred interception, resulting in clandestine recording. But it is permissible for one of the parties to make a recording of an ordinary conversation between people who accept each other as speaker and listener, in the free expression of their thoughts, just as it would be possible to record the content of direct conversations, carried on without the use of the telephone."

16. If permissible to record such tapes, may they be broadcast without permission?

No. Because publication or broadcasting of telephone conversations represents, in principle, a violation of the privacy or private life of another, the other party's consent is required. Disclosure of the contents may result in a civil action.

If the conversation contains confidential information, disclosure of such information can constitute the crime of breach of confidentiality provided for under the CC, unless there is just cause for disclosure.

17. Is there a recognized evidentiary privilege preventing the disclosure of confidential sources relied upon by reporters?

Yes. The CB guarantees reporters confidentiality of the source of information, whenever necessary to the exercise of a profession (art. 5, item XIV). Article 7 of the LP also provides for confidentiality of the source or origin of information received from or collected by journalists.

In addition, journalists who disclose such information may themselves be subjected to civil liability under the LP, which treats such dissemination as a violation of professional confidentiality. It is also a crime under the CC.

18. In the event that legal papers are served upon the newsroom (such as a civil complaint), are there any particular warnings about accepting service of which we should be aware?

Criminal liability is successive. In other words, primary liability for a media crime lies with the author of the published or transmitted material, and, should the author not be identifiable, the material shall be deemed to have been reprinted by the editor of the section in which it was published or by the director or by the editor in chief or the manager.

A criminal summons must be served personally on the person named in it. The Court Official (Process Server) cannot, in criminal proceedings, effect service by leaving the document at the company office (e.g., with a secretary). In the case of civil litigation, however, depending on the nature of the claim, service may be effected on any company employee, so that for example the Court Official can in theory effect service by leaving the documents with the receptionist. It is therefore advisable to provide training to certain "key" employees (e.g., receptionists, door staff) so that they are aware that any formal legal document of this nature must be immediately forwarded to the responsible manager/editor or other such designated person.

All other staff should be instructed to refer the Court Official to the identified "key" staff, so that if, for example, the Court Official attempts to effect service on the trainee, the employee knows that the correct procedure is to direct the official to reception, where the citation will be appropriately dealt with. Given that court deadlines in Brazil are frequently very tight, all official legal documents should be referred to the company's attorneys at the earliest possible moment, if necessary by means of fax or electronic communication, and the legal advisers should be alerted immediately by telephone or personally that an official court document has been received.

19. Has your jurisdiction applied established media law to Internet publishers?

Brazilian law is not clear on this issue. Because the LP dates from 1967, it does not contemplate Internet publishing. However, the trend among the scholarly authorities and the courts is to accept application of the LP to publication on Web sites. The Superior Court of Justice (STJ), in a case concerning publication on a Web site of a letter containing accusations against an elected representative, admitted a criminal complaint against the author of the document, based on the provisions of the LP. In another case, a São Paulo court found that the commission of crimes against honor on Web sites dedicated to journalistic activities in general should be subject to the LP.

20. If established media law has been applied to Internet publishers, are there any ways in which Internet publishers (including chat room operators) have to meet different standards?

Depending on the structure and content of the Web site, it can be very difficult for publishers to have complete control over all the published content, since part of the content is created by third parties without the express authorization of the publisher, as in the case of chat rooms and bulletin boards.

For this reason, some specialists in the field believe that the LP should not apply where end users supply content, such as chat rooms and blogs. Even if the Web site has mechanisms to filter out undesired messages, it would be impossible to review and, if necessary, block information that is automatically inserted or updated.

However, in cases where the Web site has journalistic content, the application of the LP would be appropriate. In certain cases, the Internet service provider could also be held jointly liable for defamatory postings. However, the ISP would not have any liability if its only function was to publish content inserted by third parties who are identifiable and therefore liable for the publication of the information.

21. Are there any cases where the courts enforced a judgment in libel from another jurisdiction against a publisher in your jurisdiction?

It should be borne in mind that, as we have stated above, libel in Brazil takes the form of three crimes (calumny, defamation, and injury). Jurisdiction lies with the court where the offending matter was printed, or the location of the studio of the radio transmission service and/or head office of a news agency. If in a jurisdiction where defamation (libel or slander) is a tort, the court makes a civil law order; such order may be enforced in Brazil by means of an application to the Brazilian Superior Court.

Chapter Notes

1. Federal Law 5250 of 1967, known as the "Law of the Press" (LP).

2. *Id.*

3. Art. 20 (LP).

4. TJSC, ap. n. 97.005781/4, 1998.

5. TACRIM SP, p. 723.743/1, 1993.

6. TACRIM SP, ap. n. 348.899.

7. TJRJ, p. n. 2002.051.00404, 2003.

8. Art. 21 (LP).

9. TJRJ, 1999.

10. TJRJ, 1999.050.05049, 2001.

11. TACRIM SP, ap. n. 775847/9, 1993.

12. TACRIM SP, p. n. 348.879/2, 1984.

13. Art. 22 (LP).

14. Please note that the terms are false cognates.

15. TACRIM SP, p. 838.797/7.

16. TJRJ, p. 2002.050.05.477, 2002.

17. TACRIM SP, p. 221443, 1980.

18. TACRIM SP, p. n. 401.059/1, 1985.

19. Furthermore, note that comparative advertising is acceptable, but the Code issued by the National Agency of Publicity Regulation (Conselho Nacional de Auto-Regulamentação Publicitária) must be observed. Some of its principles, in relation to comparative publicity, are (i) the clarification and defense of consumers, (ii) objectiveness in the comparison, and (iii) the possibility of proving such

comparison, among others. Please note that general statements, such as "the best," and subjective information, such as "the most beautiful," are not considered to be offensive to competitors, nor have to be proved.

20. Art. 61, subsections I and II.

21. William Swindler, cited by Enéas CostaGarcia, in "Responsabilidade Civil dos Meios de Comunicação." Juarez de Oliveira, ed. São Paulo, 2002.

CHAPTER 2

Canada

BRIAN MacLEOD ROGERS

Brian MacLeod Rogers
150 King Street West, Suite 2512
Toronto, Ontario Canada M5H1J9
Phone: 416-593-2486
Fax: 416-593-8494
brian@bmrlaw.ca

Introduction to the Canadian Legal System

Every province in Canada uses a common law system except Quebec, which uses civil law. Quebec's civil law system is based on a Civil Code enacted in 1991. There are four basic levels to the Canadian common law court system: the first level is the provincial courts; the second level includes the provincial and territorial superior courts and the federal court, trial division; the third level is the provincial courts of appeal and the federal court of appeal; and the highest level is the Supreme Court of Canada.

Provincial courts are located in each province throughout Canada. The Provincial Court is the court of first resort for most criminal offenses, claims over smaller amounts of money (limit varies in the various provinces), family court issues, and other small offenses. There are also several provincial courts designated for specific types of crimes—domestic violence, for example. The most serious criminal offenses and many appeals from provincial courts are heard in the Provincial Superior Court. The superior court has jurisdiction over every legal matter in its province except those specifically reserved for provincial courts and handles most serious civil cases. Some provinces organize superior courts by subject—family law, property claims, and so on. Appeals from the superior courts are heard in the courts of appeal. This court generally sits in panels of three judges who will hear and adjudicate cases. Provincial Superior Courts have inherent jurisdiction over all matters except those specifically banned by statute. Conversely, the Federal Court of Canada (FCC) only has jurisdiction over claims against the federal government and others specified in federal statutes.

The FCC is similar in hierarchy to a superior court, but with solely civil jurisdiction. The FCC is divided into a trial division and an appeal division; it shares jurisdiction with superior courts.

1. What is the locally accepted definition of libel?

Libel is defamation in written or other material form, including a broadcast (as confirmed by statute). A defamatory statement "tends to lower a person in the estimation of right-thinking members of society" and should be judged from the perspective of a "reasonably thoughtful and well-informed person who has a degree of common sense."

Examples of defamatory statements are: taxi driver and owner alleged to be "trafficking in licenses";[1] lawyer acting for a real estate developer said to have engaged in a "serious breach of faith" and to have been "practicing deception";[2] lawyer said to have improperly paid himself legal fees from funds belonging to a community organization;[3] politician said to be part of "the Jewish Mafia";[4] politician said to be racist;[5] engineer said to be lacking integrity and not competent to design certain facilities;[6] doctor on a government-appointed committee said to have been in a conflict of interest.[7]

2. Is libel-by-implication recognized, or, in the alternative, must the complained-of words alone defame the plaintiff?

Libel may arise by implication. This may occur by an inference drawn from the published words alone or by "legal innuendo," based on unpublished facts that would be known to some readers.

3. May corporations sue for libel?

Corporations may sue for libel but will generally only recover "nominal damages" unless they can prove economic injury.

4. Is product disparagement recognized, and if so, how does that differ from libel?

A separate tort for malicious falsehood exists and deals with disparagement of a product. It requires the plaintiff to prove that the defendant published a false statement about the product with malice, or the intention to cause injury, and that actual financial injury occurred as a consequence. Therefore, the plaintiff must prove falsity, malice, and actual injury flowing from the statement in question. A libel claim may be included where the disparagement reflects on the individuals or company producing, distributing, or selling the product.

5. Must an individual be clearly identified (by name or photograph) to sue for libel? Can a group of persons sue for libel, even though not named?

An individual must be identifiable, but need not be named or have his photograph published, in order to sue for libel. In these cases, the issue will be whether the published information serves to identify the plaintiff.

An unnamed group of persons cannot sue for libel as a group. However, insofar as individual members of the group are identifiable and have personally been defamed by what was published, each such individual has a cause of action in libel. This approach generally imposes a limit on the size of groups that may be involved, but no clear line has been drawn on what size is too large.

6. What is the fault standard(s) applied to libel?

a. Does the fault standard depend on the fame or notoriety of the plaintiff?

In general, libel is a strict liability tort and does not require the plaintiff to prove any degree of fault on the part of the defendants. The standard does not depend on the position, fame, or notoriety of the plaintiff. The plaintiff need only show that a defamatory statement that is identifiably about him or her has been published by the defendant, and falsity and malice are presumed. The defendant then must establish one or more defenses, and defenses of truth and consent are the only ones that cannot be defeated by a plaintiff who can show that the defendant acted with malice.

b. Is there a heightened fault standard or privilege for reporting on matters of public concern or public interest?

Apart from certain report privileges for newspapers and broadcasters protected by statute, the common law defense of qualified privilege may be available for media reporting on matters of public interest. This would require overruling earlier Supreme Court of Canada decisions which held that any publication in the media amounted to "publication to the world" and put it beyond the scope of a privilege defense, but some trial and appeal decisions, as well as recent English cases, give some hope.

In *Hill v. Scientology,*[8] the Supreme Court of Canada explicitly rejected a *New York Times v. Sullivan* defense on the facts of that case. However, the more recent UK House of Lords decision in *Reynolds v. Times Newspapers,*[9] acknowledges a common law defense of qualified privilege for media on the basis of public interest; it has not yet been specifically ruled on by any senior Canadian court. However, references to that decision in appeal decisions appear to treat it as a persuasive authority, and it may lead to a broader qualified privilege defense at common law along the lines proposed in that decision.

7. Is financial news about publicly traded companies, or companies involved with a government contract, considered a matter of public interest or otherwise privileged?

No statute or case law has established that financial news about public companies or companies with government contracts amounts to a matter of public interest or would be automatically protected by a defense of qualified privilege. If the publication was based on information contained in a report or other document released to the public by government or a related agency, a statutory qualified privilege would be available.

8. Is there a recognized protection for opinion or "fair comment" on matters of public concern?

Yes, the common law defense of fair comment protects statements of opinion on matters of public interest, provided the plaintiff cannot establish that they were published with malice. The dividing line between statements of fact and opinion can be difficult to draw, and the facts upon which the opinion is based must be contained in the article in question or be generally known, and must be proven true by the defendant. A recent case, *Leenan v. CBC,*[10] suggests that an objective test of fairness should be applied in light of all the facts available to the defendant at the time. Traditionally, the defense only required that the opinion be honestly held by the defendant. Almost all provincial statutes protect defendants when they publish the opinions of others which they do not share. The defense of fair comment will not fail simply because the defendants (or even the person who expressed the opinion) did not hold the opinion as long as "a person could honestly hold the opinion."[11] This overcomes a Supreme Court of Canada decision, *Chernesky v. Armadale Publishers Ltd.,*[12] which held that an honest belief in the opinion was essential for a newspaper defendant even for letters to the editor published by it.

9. Are there any requirements upon a plaintiff, such as demand for retraction or right of reply, and if so, what impact do they have?

The rules vary among provinces. For a libel published or broadcast by a publisher or broadcaster in Ontario, a plaintiff must serve written notice of libel specifying the matter complained of within six weeks of the alleged libel coming to his or her attention. This has recently been extended to cover online versions as well. A failure to give the required notice is an absolute bar to bringing an action. (There is also a three-month limitation period in Ontario.) Further, the notice triggers a period of time (three days in Ontario) within which the defendant can publish a "full and fair retraction in as conspicuous a place and type as the alleged libel" in order to limit the plaintiff to recovering only actual damages (actual, provable losses directly attributable to the libel). Other provinces require written notice to be given at least seven days before the commencement of an action so that a retraction can be published before an action is started, and most provinces have a six-month limitation period. However, British Columbia has no notice requirement, and it, Alberta, and Manitoba have a two-year limitation period. In the event that a demand for retraction is received, publishers are advised to contact local counsel immediately.

10. Is there a privilege for quoting or reporting on:

a. Papers filed in court?

A common law qualified privilege is available for fair and accurate reports of documents and records in court files that are publicly available, as established by *Hill v. Scientology, supra.*

b. Government-issued documents?

As long as the documents were issued by the government for the public, a statutory qualified privilege is available for any fair and accurate report of all or part of such a document, or a synopsis of it. This defense is established by provincial defamation legislation and varies to some extent among jurisdictions. Arguably, there would also be a common law qualified privilege for fair and accurate reports of such publicly available information, issued for the public's benefit.

c. Quasi-governmental proceedings?

There is a qualified privilege available for fair and accurate reports of public proceedings of administrative tribunals. In Ontario, disciplinary proceedings for legal and health professionals are governed by legislation, and fair and accurate reports of their proceedings are protected by statutory qualified privilege as they are in other provinces. Such a privilege also applies to other nonstatutory bodies that govern their members, such as "an association formed in Canada for the purpose of promoting or safeguarding the interests of any trade, business, industry or profession, or persons carrying on or engaged in them" (or "any game, sport or pastime open to the public") where its constitution provides such disciplinary powers. Fair and accurate reports of their disciplinary decisions (or findings) are protected by statutory qualified privilege.

In all cases, the statutory privilege can be lost if the defendant refuses to publish a "reasonable statement of explanation or contradiction" on behalf of the plaintiff. This may be considered a modified right of reply but can often be provided by inviting a response from the person affected for the initial publication or publishing one in a follow-up article.

11. Is there a privilege for republishing statements made earlier by other, bona fide, reliable publications or wire services?

There is no such privilege. Each republisher is liable for whatever is published and must prove at least one of the available defenses.

12. Are there any restrictions regarding reporting on:

a. Ongoing criminal investigations?

Apart from the general law of libel, there is no restriction on reporting on ongoing criminal investigations. Insofar as an article reports on an investigation, without imputing guilt, it can be defended as true merely by proving the fact of the police investigation. However, if serious criminal charges already exist against those being investigated, attention should be paid to (b) below.

b. Ongoing criminal prosecutions?

The traditional common law of contempt of court continues to apply in Canada. A publication that causes a serious risk of prejudice to the fair trial of an action can lead to a contempt citation against the publisher and all those involved. This is a criminal proceeding. Over the past ten to fifteen years, strict enforcement of law of contempt has waned, and a more considered approach is taken as to whether the publication actually poses a serious risk of prejudice. Previously, any publication of an accused's prior criminal record or bad character would be strictly prohibited after arrest. This is no longer the case, but enforcement varies from province to province; Alberta is the strictest, and Ontario, British Columbia, and Quebec are the most lenient. As a result, a precise test can no longer be given. A number of factors need to be considered, such as the time intervening before trial, the size of the community involved, the potential impact of the information, and the public interest being served by publishing it now. At all times, disclosing a confession or other admission by an accused is the most risky since it is highly prejudicial and yet may not be admissible at trial.

However, it has been deemed almost impossible to prejudice a judge sitting alone in a criminal case, and even in jury trials, publication well in advance of trial, depending on all of the circumstances, should not give rise to a real risk of prejudice. Change of venue, challenges for cause, and strict jury instructions can be used to minimize any such risk. In addition, a respected appeals judge in Alberta recently proposed a defense of public interest in contempt cases. Simply put, this is a gray area of the law, and it requires close judgment calls based on the facts at hand.

In addition to the law of contempt, the Criminal Code provides for various statutory publication bans, so that reports of bail hearings and preliminary inquiries are severely restricted, and bans on identifying sexual complainants and certain other witnesses can be obtained as a matter of course. There is also a discretionary right for the court to impose broader publication bans on identifying witnesses, but normally notice must be given to the media when such orders are being sought.

During jury trials, nothing can be reported about what occurs when the jury is not present since they are not sequestered. Such information can only be published when the jury retires to render its verdict. In general terms, such statutory publication bans are purportedly intended to protect the fair trial process, acting as a specific means of enforcing the more general law of contempt. Anonymity orders are based on the risk of possible harm to the person in question and the societal interest of encouraging victims and witnesses to come forward, especially in underreported crimes such as sexual assault.

c. Ongoing regulatory investigations?

No, other than the general law of libel.

d. Ongoing civil litigation, or other judicial proceedings?

The law of contempt may be applied where a civil jury trial is being conducted, and nothing should be published during a trial about what occurs in the jury's absence. In particular, publication of the damages being sought in a statement of claim can lead to a mistrial since jurors are not advised of these amounts. There can also be specific publication bans (including anonymity orders) in civil proceedings, but they are more unusual than in criminal cases. Otherwise, there are no restrictions on reporting on publicly conducted proceedings, and the defense of qualified privilege is available for fair and accurate reports of them.

13. Are prior restraints or other prepublication injunctions available on the basis of libel or privacy, and if so, what are the standards for obtaining such relief?

No prepublication injunctions have been awarded in the last fifteen years on the basis of allegations of libel alone. To succeed, the plaintiff would first have to meet the usual requirements for an interlocutory injunction in these circumstances; in essence, that there is a serious (or arguable) issue to be tried and a real risk of irreparable harm. The plaintiff would also have to counter any defenses that might be raised by the defendants. Essentially, any bona fide defendant should be able to defeat a motion for such an injunction by asserting a willingness to defend on the basis of a legally permissible defense.

Certain provinces (British Columbia, Saskatchewan, Manitoba, Quebec, and Newfoundland) have privacy statutes which create statutory torts for invasion of privacy. With the exception of Quebec, these have been very little used against the media. Other provinces have not recognized such a tort, but as in England, the tort of breach of confidence has been used against the media to obtain prepublication injunctions with some success.

In these cases, the traditional test for injunctions (as set out above) is applied, and the plaintiff need only show that confidential information might be published, causing irreparable harm. The media have usually been successful in subsequently setting aside these preliminary injunctions, and the significant additional publicity garnered for the broadcast or publication in question has made plaintiff counsel more wary of using such tactics.

14. Is a right of privacy recognized (either civilly or criminally)?

Apart from provincial privacy legislation (British Columbia, Saskatchewan, Manitoba, Quebec, and Newfoundland), there is federal legislation that restricts the use by private organizations of third party information, Personal Information Protection and Electronic Documents Act.[13] It now applies not only within the federal jurisdiction but also provincially, where a province does not have its own legislation. All privacy legislation has an exception for newsworthiness or for journalists, as set out below.

In Quebec, privacy rights are much more established and are even given specific protection in its provincial *Charter of Human Rights and Freedoms*. For example, publication of a photograph should not take place without the subject's permission unless he or she is simply part of some public event.[14] However, evidence must be given of damage. At common law, no tort of invasion of privacy has been recognized with the exception of commercial misappropriation of personality, which generally requires some unauthorized suggestion that a known personality endorses a particular product or company.

a. What is the definition of "private fact"?

There is no definition of "private fact" at present that has any broad application. Generally, the courts have focused on whether there was a reasonable expectation of privacy in the information involved.

Examples include: publishing the identity of a complainant in a criminal sexual assault case where her identity was protected by court-ordered publication ban;[15] broadcasting without consent a videotape of hair transplant surgery;[16] concealed videotaping by a landlord of a woman using a washroom;[17] and in Quebec, publishing without consent a photograph of a young woman sitting in a doorway by a sidewalk on a public thoroughfare.[18]

b. Is there a public interest or newsworthiness exception?

Provincial privacy legislation recognizes a form of newsworthiness exemption where the matter published was of public interest, was fair comment on a matter of public interest, or would be protected by privilege under defamation law (with some variation among provinces). In Quebec, public interest is also cited as a defense, recognizing newsworthiness in articles about public issues and public figures. The federal Personal Information Protection and Electronic Documents Act[19] specifically exempts organizations collecting, using, and disclosing personal information for "journalistic, artistic or literary purposes."

c. Is the right of privacy based in common law, statute, or constitution?

Privacy rights are defined by provincial and federal statutes, discussed above.

15. May reporters tape-record their own telephone conversations for note-taking purposes (not rebroadcast) without the consent of the other party?

Yes.

16. If permissible to record such tapes, may they be broadcast without permission?

No. By Canadian Radio-television and Telecommunications Commission regulations, such interviews cannot be broadcast without consent.

17. Is there a recognized evidentiary privilege preventing the disclosure of confidential sources relied upon by reporters?

No. However, at a minimum there is judicial discretion to require such disclosure only in limited circumstances, essentially where the evidence is truly necessary because it is relevant and not available by other means and where the value of requiring the evidence outweighs the potential harm of disclosure. The Supreme Court of Canada refused to rule on this issue under the *Canadian Charter of Rights and Freedoms* in *Moysa v. Alberta Labour Relations Board*[20] on the facts of that case, but it also cast doubt on whether protection of confidential sources even amounted to an element of free expression protected by section 2(b) of the *Charter.*

A recent case in Ontario ruled in favor of a "qualified" privilege, on a case-by-case basis, for protection of a journalist's confidential sources relying on the *Charter* and common law; it is under appeal.[21] Such an approach to journalists' sources was specifically cited in obiter by the Supreme Court of Canada in *R. v. McClure.*[22] In Ontario, the "newspaper rule" developed in England applies in libel cases to prevent disclosure of journalists' confidential sources at the discovery stage of litigation. This rule does not apply in British Columbia and a number of other provinces.

18. In the event that legal papers are served upon the newsroom (such as a civil complaint), are there any particular warnings about accepting service of which we should be aware?

No. However, the very short time periods for responding to libel notices (which need not follow any particular form) mean that a lawyer should be immediately advised if anyone on staff receives a document complaining of damage to reputation.

19. Has your jurisdiction applied established media law to Internet publishers?

In general, the existing common law of libel and privacy applies to all communications media, including the Internet in its various forms. However, thus far there have been few cases to reach trial involving Internet libel or privacy concerns.

The Ontario Court of Appeal has pointed to the "ubiquity, universality, and utility" of the Internet and its potential as "a medium of virtually limitless international defamation."[23] This breadth of potential dissemination has an impact on defenses such as common law qualified privilege, as well as on damages, unless Web site access has been limited to those to whom publication is properly directed.[24]

20. If established media law has been applied to Internet publishers, are there any ways in which Internet publishers (including chat room operators) have to meet different standards?

To date, neither the courts nor the legislatures have developed special standards or laws for Internet publishers in these areas. However, the defense of "innocent dissemination" may be available to bulletin board or chat room operators where they had no knowledge, nor ought to have had knowledge, of the alleged libel.[25] This is beneficial to these operators and ISPs generally where no attempt is made to monitor postings. However, once notice is received of an alleged libel, a decision will have to be made whether to remove the offending posting, and the operator can no longer rely on its "innocence." As a result, it is useful to publish on the Web site clear notice that the chat room is not being monitored but the operator will respond to complaints that are made in a prescribed fashion.

There also remains an issue as to whether a Web site or online publication qualifies for the special provisions for newspapers and broadcasters under provincial legislation (see above, Question 9). It has, however, been ruled that the online version of a magazine otherwise qualifying as a "newspaper" does not lose that benefit.[26] However, one appeal court has rejected a "single publication" rule with respect to Internet publication, and subsequent accessibility may extend limitation periods.[27] Differences in legislative definitions from province to province could well produce different results.

21. Are there any cases where the courts enforced a judgment in libel from another jurisdiction against a publisher in your jurisdiction?

The leading case on this issue is a British Columbia case: *Braintech Inc. v. Kostiuk*.[28] The court refused to enforce a default judgment obtained in Texas under its long-arm rules over bulletin board postings by a B.C. resident concerning a company with principal operations in British Columbia. As stated by the court:

> It would create a crippling effect on freedom of expression if, in every jurisdiction the world over in which access to the Internet could be achieved, a person who posts fair comment on a bulletin board could be hauled before the courts of each of those countries where access to the bulletin could be obtained.

In a recent case with profound implications for the application of Canadian jurisdiction against foreign publishers, the Court of Appeal for Ontario recently found that the *Washington Post* was not subject to Canadian process based upon the libel claims of former U.N. diplomat Cheickh Bangoura. In 1997, at the time of the alleged libel appearing in the *Washington Post*, only seven subscribers in Ontario received the paper physically, although its online edition was theoretically available to many Canadians. The plaintiff had not moved to Ontario until 2000. The court found that it was not reasonably foreseeable that the *Post* would have been sued in Ontario, and it was unfair to assume that a newspaper can be sued anywhere in the world by virtue of its publication on the Internet. "To hold otherwise would mean that a defendant could be sued almost anywhere in the world based upon where a plaintiff may decide to establish his or her residence long after publication of the defamation."[29] The court added that the Internet publication involved did not create a substantial connection between the *Post* and the forum. A contrary holding would result in "Ontario publishers and broadcasters being sued anywhere in the world with the prospect that the Ontario courts would be obligated to enforce foreign judgments filed against them."

Chapter Notes

1. *Ross v. Lamport* (1956), 2 D.L.R. (2d) 225 (S.C.C.).

2. *Sykes v. Fraser* (1973), 39 D.L.R. (3d) 321 (S.C.C.).

3. *Botiuk v. Toronto Free Press Publication Ltd.* (1995), 126 D.L.R. (4th) 609 (S.C.C.).

4. *Snyder v. Montreal Gazette Ltd.* (1982), 49 D.L.R. (4th) 17 (S.C.C.).

5. *Chernesky v. Armadale Publishers Ltd.* (1979), 90 D.L.R. (3d) 321 (S.C.C.).

6. *Hiltz and Seamone Co. v. Nova Scotia* (Attorney General), [1997] N.S.J. No. 530 (S.C.); [1999] N.S.J. No. 47, 172 D.L.R. (4th) 488 (N.S.C.A.).

7. *Leenan v. C.B.C.*, [2000] O.J. No. 1359; aff'd [2001] O.J. No. 2229 (C.A.); leave denied [2002] S.C.C.A. 432.

8. [1995] 2 S.C.R. 1130.

9. [1999] H.L.J. No. 45.

10. [2001] O.J. No. 2229; 54 O.R. (3d) 612 (C.A.) (leave to SCC denied).

11. s. 24, Libel and Slander Act, R.S.O. 1990, c.L.12.

12. [1979] 1 S.C.R. 1067.

13. S.C. 2000, c. 5.

14. *Aubry v. Editions Vice-Versa Inc.*, [1998] 1 S.C.R. 591.

15. *J.M.F. v. Chappel and News Publishing Company Ltd.*, [1995] B.C.J. No. 1438 (B.C.S.C.), varied (1998), 158 D.L.R. (4th) 430 (B.C.C.A.), leave dismissed [1998] S.C.C.A. No. 154.

16. *Hollinsworth v. BCTV,* [1996] B.C.J. No. 2638 (B.C.S.C.); [1998] B.C.J. No. 2451 [1999] 6 W.W.R. 54 (B.C.C.A.).

17. *Malcolm v. Fleming,* [2000] B.C.J. No. 2400 (S.C.).

18. *Aubry v. Editions Vice Versa Inc.,* [1998] 1 S.C.R. 591.

19. S.C. 2000, c. 5, s. 4(2)(c).

20. [1989] 1 S.C.R. 1572.

21. *R. v. National Post,* [2004] O.J. No. 178 (S.C.).

22. [2001] 1 S.C.R. 445.

23. *Barrick Gold Corp. v. Lopehandia,* [2004] O.J. No. 2329 (C.A.); (undefended claim over web postings).

24. *Christian Labour Association of Canada v. Retail Wholesale Union,* [2003] B.C.J. No. 3100 (S.C.) (union Web site available to public).

25. *Carter v. B.C. Federation of Foster Parents Assoc.,* [2004] B.C.J. No. 192 (S.C.), but on appeal, this defense was ruled to be not available where the operator was negligent in leaving the offending posting on the Web site long after receiving notice: [2005] B.C.J. No. 1720 (C.A.).

26. *Weiss v. Sawyer,* [2002] O.J. No. 3570, 61 O.R. (3d) 256 (C.A.).

27. *Carter v. B.C. Federation of Foster Parents Assoc.,* [2005] B.C.J. No. 1720 (C.A.).

28. [1999] B.C.J. No. 622, 171 D.L.R. (4th) 46 (C.A.); leave denied, [1999] S.C.C.A. No. 236.

29. Decision available at http://www.ontariocourts.on.ca/decisions/2005/september/C41379.htm; [2005] O.J. No. 3849 (C.A.).

CHAPTER 3

United States

THOMAS H. GOLDEN AND
STEPHEN B. VOGEL

Willkie Farr & Gallagher LLP

Willkie Farr & Gallagher LLP
787 Seventh Avenue
New York, NY 10019-6099 USA
Phone: 212-728-8000
Fax: 212-728-8111
www.willkie.com
tgolden@willkie.com
svogel@willkie.com

Introduction to the U.S. Legal System

The U.S. legal system is a common law system modeled after the British common law system. There are two distinct court systems in the U.S. judiciary: the state systems of each of the fifty states and the federal system. Each state has at least one Federal District Court, which, with the exceptions of bankruptcy, tax, and other specialized matters, is the federal court of first instance. Judges in the federal system serve life terms: state judges may serve life terms or be elected by the citizenry.

Each system is governed by its respective constitution, the federal constitution, and each individual state constitution; however, the federal constitution is considered the "supreme law of the land" and trumps any conflict between state and federal constitutions. The federal constitution reserves certain powers for the federal government and reserves the rest for the states.

The progression of a case is similar in both court systems. A jury composed of citizens often decides verdicts. Appeals courts and specialized courts do not have juries, but have panels of judges. The courts of first instance hear both civil and criminal cases.

The judge determines the issues of law at hand and the jury, or judge sitting without a jury, will determine findings of fact. The trial court is the only court in which new facts can be presented and considered in a given case. In the federal system, cases are appealed to a geographically determined appellate court organized by "circuits." Some states have intermediate appellate courts, while others have appeals heard directly by the State Supreme Court.

Appeals in the federal system are made thereafter to the Supreme Court of the United States, and the hearing of such cases is granted at the discretion of the Supreme Court. State supreme courts can recommend cases to the federal Supreme Court, too; however, since the federal Supreme Court has the ability to choose which cases it hears, most recommended cases are never accepted. The U.S. Supreme Court is composed of nine justices appointed for life by the president and approved by Congress.

1. What is the locally accepted definition of libel?

Although the definition varies significantly by state, a cause of action for libel often includes the following elements: (a) a statement of fact; (b) that is false; (c) and defamatory; (d) of and concerning the plaintiff; (e) that is published to a third party (in written or otherwise tangible form); (f) that is not absolutely or conditionally privileged; (g) that causes actual injury (unless obviated by the presence of presumed harm); (h) that is the result of fault by the defendant (usually); (i) that causes special (pecuniary) harm in addition to generalized reputational history (on occasion).[1]

Libel claims rise and fall on defamatory meaning. There are many definitions of "defamatory" and these are reflective of the cultural constraints embedded in the common law of the states. What is defamatory in Georgia may not be so in New York. The RESTATEMENT (SECOND) OF TORTS § 559 (1997) defines defamatory communications as those that tend "to harm the reputation of another so as to lower him in the esteem of the community or to deter third persons from association or dealing with him." Similarly, other treatises define a defamatory statement as that which "tends to injure 'reputation' in the popular sense, to diminish the esteem, respect, good-will, or confidence in which the plaintiff is held, or to excite adverse, derogatory or unpleasant feelings or opinions against him."[2]

In essence, to "defame" means to damage one's reputation, usually by the assertion (or implication) of something shameful or worthy of scorn. Defamatory meaning may vary from state to state, and is largely dependent on context.

Some examples of statements found to be defamatory are: playing a role in an alleged kidnapping and murder;[3] incompetence of a professional;[4] being a communist;[5] or being a "liar and a fraud."[6] The following are examples of nondefamatory statements: calling someone "a bum";[7] calling a college basketball player a disgrace;[8] or referring to someone as "short, ugly and stupid."[9]

2. Is libel-by-implication recognized, or, in the alternative, must the complained-of words alone defame the plaintiff?

Courts generally agree that libel by implication is allowed in the United States: "Falsity can be either express or implied.... A story that contains only truthful statements may nonetheless be false and defamatory as it relates to the plaintiff if it omits material facts.... It is not enough to get the details right if you fail to put them in the proper context."[10] Thus, courts generally consider the challenged statement in the context in which it was used and examine the totality of the circumstances.[11] Some states, however, are more demanding in the requirements that must be met in order to plead libel by implication.[12]

3. May corporations sue for libel?

Yes. Generally, a corporation has reputational interests and is protected against false and malicious statements affecting its credit or property, and against statements impugning corporate honesty, efficiency, or matters of business performance.[13] It is worth noting that in several states, corporations are deemed public figures, which are required to meet a higher standard in order for a libel claim to succeed.

4. Is product disparagement recognized, and if so, how does that differ from libel?

Most U.S. jurisdictions recognize "product disparagement," also known as "trade libel," as a cause of action. This tort is generally defined as a false communication that damages the reputation of a company's goods or services. The same requirements that govern defamation appear to govern claims for product disparagement, and the same First Amendment protections that apply to libel also apply to trade libel.[14]

This tort differs from traditional libel in that it is primarily a business tort designed to protect economic interests, and therefore requires a specific showing of special harm in the form of actual pecuniary damages (usually a demonstrable loss of sales, customers, or contracts).[15] Also, it is more likely that punitive or injunctive relief may be available in a product disparagement claim.[16]

5. Must an individual be clearly identified (by name or photograph) to sue for libel? Can a group of persons sue for libel, even though not named?

To be actionable, the defamatory statement must be "of and concerning" the plaintiff, and the hypothetical average reader would have to understand who is being referenced. It is incumbent on the plaintiff to demonstrate that in "some definite and direct sense, the plaintiff was the person against whom the defamatory statements were directed, and by whom the reputational damage was suffered."[17] It is not necessary that every recipient of the communication identify the plaintiff, so long as there are at least some who reasonably do.[18]

Most American law rejects "group libel." The Supreme Court has also held that it is constitutionally insufficient to equate statements defaming a government agency with statements defaming the head of the group merely on the presumption that to libel one is to libel the other.[19] This has been extended to protect criticism of other groups and businesses.[20] To the extent that actions by a member of a group are allowed, a plaintiff would need to show that the statement about a group is "of and concerning" the particular individual. Factors to be considered include: (1) the size of the group; (2) the degree of organization of the group (is the composition definite and its size fixed?); and (3) the prominence of the group and its individual members.[21]

6. What is the fault standard(s) applied to libel?

The U.S. Supreme Court, in *New York Times Co. v. Sullivan*, 376 U.S. 254 (1964), and *Gertz v. Robert Welch Inc.*, 418 U.S. 323 (1974), has established minimum constitutional fault levels that must be met before recovery is possible in an action for defamation. Individual states are free to adopt higher standards.

a. Does the fault standard depend on the fame or notoriety of the plaintiff?

Yes. A central distinction in libel law is the distinction between public and private figures.[22] A plaintiff who is a public figure must prove, by clear and convincing evidence, that the defendant made a defamatory statement with actual malice, which is defined as "knowledge that [the statement] was false or ... reckless disregard of whether it was false or not."[23] By contrast, a plaintiff who is a private figure must merely prove the defendant's negligence,[24] though it is possible that the Supreme Court would allow for a strict liability standard where the plaintiff is a private figure and the defamatory statement does not concern a matter of public interest.[25]

The majority of states have adopted a negligence standard for private figure cases, though a number of states have adopted a standard that requires actual malice in cases involving private plaintiffs in matters of public concern.[26] The plaintiff, as part of his *prima facie* case, carries the burden of proof in establishing the requisite fault standard. In short, the difference is that whereas "actual malice" requires "knowing falsity" or, at best, "purposeful avoidance of the truth," defendants adjudged by the negligence standard may face liability if they did not report the news in a manner which any "reasonable" reporter would have followed. The former is difficult to prove because it requires the subjective knowledge of the reporter be shown. The negligence standard is subjective, and expert witnesses (such as journalism professors or retired journalists) may give testimony as to the reportorial shortcomings of the defendant.

b. Is there a heightened fault standard or privilege for reporting on matters of public concern or public interest?

Yes. In matters of public concern, plaintiffs may not recover presumed or punitive damages absent actual malice, without regard to whether the plaintiff is a public or private figure.[27] American publishers generally enjoy great latitude as to what constitutes "public concern": "[a]bsent clear abuse, the courts will not second-guess editorial decisions as to what constitutes matters of genuine public concern."[28]

7. Is financial news about publicly traded companies, or companies involved with a government contract, considered a matter of public interest or otherwise privileged?

Many jurisdictions employ a case-by-case methodology to determine whether a company is a public or private figure, and assume that if it is a public figure, the matter is one of public concern. The Fifth Circuit identified two factors that were important in differentiating between public and private figures: (1) public figures are better able to counteract false statements because of their access to channels of effective communication; and (2) public figures "invite attention and comment" and, thus, assume the risk of greater scrutiny.[29] In order to apply these factors, there must be a case-by-case assessment of the extent to which they are implicated by the circumstances giving rise to the alleged defamation.[30] Some courts have applied the pre-*Gertz* test and attempted to determine whether the defamatory statement concerned a topic of public interest either "because of the nature of the business conducted or because the public has an especially strong interest in the investigation or disclosure of the commercial information at issue."[31]

To make this assessment, courts will often consider the notoriety of the corporation in the relevant geographical area, the nature of the corporation's business, and the frequency and intensity of media scrutiny that the company receives.[32]

8. Is there a recognized protection for opinion or "fair comment" on matters of public concern?

Yes; however, only "pure" opinion—that which does not imply a discernable fact—enjoys complete First Amendment protection. The Supreme Court in *Milkovich v. Lorain Journal Co.*, 497 U.S. 1 (1990), refused to recognize a blanket First Amendment privilege for opinion. In that case, students were being interrogated under oath in a high school athletics scandal. When discrepancies among the students' stories were discovered, the local newspaper opined that they had changed their stories at the behest of the wrestling coach, and ran a headline that said: "Milkovich Teaches the Big Lie." Although the newspaper asserted that it was merely their opinion, Milkovich argued that this headline reasonably implied that he had encouraged the youngsters to commit perjury: a crime. The Court agreed, holding that defamation actions can be based on statements of opinion that imply undisclosed defamatory facts.

The dispositive inquiry is whether a reasonable reader would view the statement in question as conveying defamatory facts about the plaintiff and, if so, whether these statements can be proved false.[33] Defamation suits cannot be based upon "imaginative expression," "rhetorical hyperbole," or "loose, figurative, or hyperbolic language" that would signal to the reasonable reader that what is being said is opinion, and not an assertion of fact.[34]

9. Are there any requirements upon a plaintiff, such as demand for retraction or right of reply, and if so, what impact do they have?

Over half of the states have statutes covering retraction. A number of states require a plaintiff to demand a retraction in writing, and failure to do so often limits recovery to actual damages.[35] Florida, for example, requires the plaintiff to serve a retraction demand before a suit can be filed.[36] States that do not have a retraction requirement often allow a retraction to be used as evidence of lack of malice or for mitigation of damages.

10. Is there a privilege for quoting or reporting on:

a. Papers filed in court?

There is a well-recognized privilege to publish fair and accurate reports of certain judicial, legislative, and executive proceedings, commonly known as the "fair report" privilege. This privilege exists in common law, but has been codified in many jurisdictions. The latitude varies from state to state. In some jurisdictions, reporters may only be immune for the near-verbatim reporting of the court documents: in other states, almost any statement reasonably related to the court proceedings will be privileged.

The "fair report" privilege allows reporters to republish or report on documents filed in court without liability so long as the report itself is accurate and fair.[37] "The accuracy of the summary, not the truth or falsity of the information being summarized, is the 'benchmark of the privilege.'"[38] There is often an exception, however, for defamatory statements made by the person who files defamatory statements in a pleading and then reports to others what he has said (or forms a collusive arrangement with the person who reports on the contents of the filing).[39] Also, some jurisdictions have held that a complaint is not a public document until there has been some official action in the proceeding.[40]

b. Government-issued documents?

Generally, yes.[41] The scope of this privilege varies by jurisdiction.[42]

c. Quasi-governmental proceedings?

Many jurisdictions include the "reports of bodies which are by law authorized to perform public duties (e.g., bar association disciplinary proceedings, findings of blue-ribbon panels)" in their definition of an official proceeding.[43]

11. Is there a privilege for republishing statements made earlier by other, bona fide, reliable publications or wire services?

Some jurisdictions recognize a "wire service" defense for republication of materials, provided that there was no substantial reason to question the accuracy of the material or the reputation of the original reporter.[44] Many other jurisdictions appear to provide a narrower defense where a local media organization republishes a release from a reputable news agency without substantial change and without actually knowing that the article is false.[45] Regardless of whether a particular jurisdiction recognizes this defense, the plaintiff must still prove the requisite level of fault.

12. Are there any restrictions regarding reporting on:

a. Ongoing criminal investigations?

In order to determine whether there is a right of access to records and proceedings, a court must determine whether: "the place and process have historically been open to the press and general public" and "public access plays a significant positive role in the functioning of the particular process in question."[46] There is a split of authority as to the right of the news media to gain access to pre-indictment access to search warrant affidavits. Some courts have held that there is no right of access,[47] while others have held that there is a right of access.[48] A third group has held that, while there is no First Amendment right of access, there is a "common law qualified right of access ... committed to the sound discretion of the judicial officer who issued the warrant."[49] The judicial officer may deny access when sealing is essential to preserve higher values and is narrowly tailored to serve that interest.[50]

b. Ongoing criminal prosecutions?

Open trials are a fundamental feature of the American system of justice. The Supreme Court has held that open access is fundamental to both pretrial hearings[51] and trials and thus, there is a qualified First Amendment right of access to criminal proceedings.[52] It stated that a trial can be closed "only if specific findings are made demonstrating that, first, there is a substantial probability that the defendant's right to a fair trial will be prejudiced by publicity that closure would prevent and, second, reasonable alternatives to closure cannot adequately protect the defendant's fair trial rights."[53] Many states do restrict the distribution of certain information in special cases, such as juvenile matters, sex crimes, and other sensitive matters.

The Supreme Court has struck down a number of laws that prohibited press access to criminal proceedings and public records relevant to them. Specifically, the Court has held that: (1) there can be no tort liability for the publication of facts obtained from public records—more specifically, from judicial records which are maintained in connection with a public prosecution which themselves are open to public inspection;[54] and (2) a statute which absolutely bars access to rape trials where the victim is a minor is unconstitutional.[55]

c. Ongoing regulatory investigations?

There is no fundamental right of access to administrative proceedings. Many courts have analogized this situation to that of the right to attend civil proceedings and have employed the *Richmond Newspapers, Inc. v. Virginia*, 448 U.S. 555 (1980), "experience and logic" test.[56] In determining whether there is a right of access, a court must consider: whether there is a tradition of accessibility for the proceeding and whether the Supreme Court has traditionally considered whether public access plays a significant positive role in the functioning of the proceeding.[57]

d. Ongoing civil litigation, or other judicial proceedings?

Generally, there are few restrictions,[58] although the Supreme Court has never decided whether the public has a First Amendment right to attend civil proceedings. However, several federal appeals courts and state courts have held that civil cases are presumed to be public under the First

Amendment,[59] and it has been generally accepted that there is a common law right of press access. In certain circumstances certain pleadings may be filed under seal. The Sixth Circuit has stated that "while District Courts have the discretion to issue protective orders, that discretion is limited by the careful dictates of Fed. R. Civ. P. 26" and "is circumscribed by a long-established legal tradition" which values public access to court proceedings. Rule 26(c) allows the sealing of court papers only "for good cause shown" to the court that the particular documents justify court-imposed secrecy.[60]

13. Are prior restraints or other prepublication injunctions available on the basis of libel or privacy, and if so, what are the standards for obtaining such relief?

Aside from restricting the ability to report on criminal cases, prior restraints are presumptively invalid. "In addition to the First Amendment's heavy presumption against prior restraints, courts have long held that equity will not enjoin a libel."[61] In its nearly two centuries of existence, the Supreme Court has never upheld a prior restraint on pure speech.[62] The First Circuit has stated: "as the Supreme Court made clear in *Nebraska Press Association,* a party seeking a prior restraint against the press must show not only that publication will result in damage to a near sacred right, but also that the prior restraint will be effective and that no less extreme measures are available."[63] It added that although the Supreme Court has "implied that such a restraint might be appropriate in a very narrow range of cases, when either national security or an individual's right to a fair trial is at stake. An individual's right to protect his privacy from damage by private parties, although meriting great protection, is simply not of the same magnitude."[64]

The Supreme Court has established a three-part test to determine whether a trial court can issue a prior restraint, which prohibits the media from reporting information that imperils a defendant's right to a fair trial. Courts must consider: (a) "the nature and extent of pretrial news coverage"; (b) "whether other measures would be likely to mitigate the effects of unrestrained pretrial publicity"; and (c) "how effectively a restraining order would operate to prevent the threatened danger."[65] These orders face a very high presumption of their invalidity; in fact, Justice White in his concurring opinion expressed "grave doubt" that any prior restraint in the area would "ever be justifiable."[66]

14. Is a right of privacy recognized (either civilly or criminally)?

Yes, a right of privacy is civilly recognized in certain jurisdictions in the United States.

a. What is the definition of "private fact"?

A "private fact" is a fact concerning a truly intimate or private matter such as one's private sexual affairs or the health of one's self or one's family, which is not already known to the public, and the disclosure of which is offensive to a reasonable person.[67]

b. Is there a public interest or newsworthiness exception?

Yes. Statements "of legitimate concern to the public" are not actionable. This privilege is broader than the one associated with defamation and, thus, a factually accurate statement is not tortious when newsworthy even though "offensive to ordinary sensibilities."[68] This privilege encompasses such matters as births, deaths, marriages, divorces, crimes, accidents, arrests, personal tragedies, and the activities of celebrities and other prominent individuals.[69]

c. Is the right of privacy based in common law, statute, or constitution?

The right of privacy is primarily based in common law, although the First, Fourth, Fifth, and Fourteenth Amendments to the Constitution have been read to protect a number of privacy rights. Also, there are a number of state and federal statutes that protect various privacy interests.

15. May reporters tape-record their own telephone conversations for note-taking purposes (not rebroadcast) without the consent of the other party?

The majority of states and the federal government allow reporters to record telephone conversations without the consent of all parties.[70] A number of states, however, have enacted criminal and/or civil penalties for the recording of telephone conversations without the consent of all parties (commonly called "two-party" states).[71] In general, state statutes apply to conversations that take place within a single state, while federal law applies to conversations between states. However, an individual state may attempt to enforce its laws and it is unclear whether the federal law, which allows one-party-consent recording of conversations, will preempt a conflicting state law.

16. If permissible to record such tapes, may they be broadcast without permission?

The FCC has adopted a rule that requires a reporter, before recording a telephone conversation, to inform the other party of her intentions to broadcast the conversation unless it is "obvious that it is in connection with a program in which the station customarily broadcasts telephone conversations"[72] (such as call-in shows or contests).

17. Is there a recognized evidentiary privilege preventing the disclosure of confidential sources relied upon by reporters?

Yes. The Supreme Court has recognized a limited qualified privilege wherein the asserted privilege should be judged on its facts by striking a balance between freedom of the press and the obligation of all citizens to give relevant testimony.[73] Many states have enacted shield laws, or constitutional amendments, which give journalists varying degrees of protection against the compelled production of confidential sources.[74]

18. In the event that legal papers are served upon the newsroom (such as a civil complaint), are there any particular warnings about accepting service of which we should be aware?

In the United States, the time within which a defendant is obligated to respond to legal papers typically begins to run on the date it is served with those papers. Consequently, news employees should bring such papers—including all enclosures, attachments, and the envelope in which they were contained—to their legal advisers immediately. They should also make note of the date and time at which such papers were received.

In addition, most U.S. jurisdictions provide that only limited categories of employees are authorized to accept service on behalf of their employer. Employees should not assume that they have such authority, and should not indicate that they are authorized to accept service unless they are certain that they have such authority.

19. Has your jurisdiction applied established media law to Internet publishers?

A number of cases have applied libel law to the Internet, and Congress has acted in this area, as discussed below.

20. If established media law has been applied to Internet publishers, are there any ways in which Internet publishers (including chat room operators) have to meet different standards?

The most significant substantive development related to libel law on the Internet is the "safe harbor" portion of the Communications Decency Act of 1996, which protects "provider[s] or user[s] of an interactive computer service" by providing that they shall not be treated as the "publisher or speaker of any information provided by another information content provider."[75]

Also, some courts have applied the single-publication rule (there may be only one cause of action by a plaintiff for any edition of a written publication) to libel cases involving Internet publications in the same manner as they do to traditional materials.[76] These courts found that failure to apply this rule would subject Web publishers to almost perpetual liability and would seriously inhibit the exchange of free ideas on the Internet. The Firth court also stated that the addition of other, unrelated information to the Web site containing the defamatory statement is not a republication.[77]

Finally, there are important issues relating to personal jurisdiction for Internet publications. Two federal appellate courts have considered whether a court has jurisdiction over defendants from outside the court's jurisdiction. In one, two Connecticut newspapers published articles criticizing the state of Connecticut for housing some of its prisoners in Virginia facilities. A warden of one Virginia facility sued the newspapers in federal district court in Virginia. The court found that there was no personal jurisdiction as the newspapers directed their activities to Connecticut readers, had no connection to readers in Virginia (even though the articles could be read online in Virginia), and did not intend or attempt to serve a Virginia audience.[78]

21. Are there any cases where the courts enforced a judgment in libel from another jurisdiction against a publisher in your jurisdiction?

Generally, the U.S. courts have not been receptive to libel judgments from jurisdictions outside of the country, as they often do not meet First Amendment requirements. For instance, courts have declined to enforce judgments from the United Kingdom.[79] A U.S. court would be more likely to enforce a judgment from a foreign jurisdiction that complied with the requirements of the U.S. Constitution. (See Chapter 22, "Enforcing Foreign Judgments in the United States and Europe: When Publishers Should Defend.")

Chapter Notes

1. Rodney A. Smolla, *Law of Defamation* § 1:34 (2d ed. 2004).

2. W. Page Keeton, *Prosser & Keeton on Torts* § 111 (5th ed. 1984); *Prosser & Keeton on the Law of Torts* § 111 at p. 773.

3. *Condit v. Dunne,* 317 F. Supp. 2d 344 (S.D.N.Y. 2004).

4. *Scripps Texas Newspapers v. Belalcazar,* 99 S.W.3d 829 (Tex. 2003).

5. *MacLeod v. Tribune Pub'lg Co., Inc.,* 52 Cal 2nd 536 (Cal. 1959).

6. *Raymond U v. Duke University,* 91 N.C. App. 171 (N.C. 1988).

7. *Kilcoyne v. Plain Dealer Publ'g Co.,* 112 Ohio App. 3d 229 (Ohio 1996).

8. *Bauer v. Murphy,* 191 Wis. 2d 518 (Wis. 2002).

9. *Grillo v. John Alden Life Ins. Co.*, 939 F. Supp. 1685 (D. Minn. 1996).

10. See, e.g., *Mohr v. Grant* (Wash. Ct. App. 2003); *Turner v. KTRK TV, Inc.*, 38 S.W.3d 103 (Tex. 2000); *Memphis Publ'g Co. v. Nichols*, 569 S.W.2d 412 (Tenn. 1978).

11. See *Boule v. Hutton*, 138 F. Supp. 2d 491 (S.D.N.Y. 2001); *Smith v. Cuban Am. Nat'l Found.*, 731 So. 2d 702 (Fla. Dist. Ct. App. 1999).

12. See, e.g., CAL. CIV. CODE § 45a (West. 2004) (plaintiff must allege and prove special damages to recover for defamation not libelous on its face).

13. Smolla, *Law of Defamation* § 4:75.

14. See *Nat'l Life Ins. Co. v. Phillips Publ'g, Inc.*, 793 F. Supp. 627 (D. Md. 1992); *Suzuki Motor Corp. v. Consumers Union of U.S., Inc.*, 292 F.3d 1192 (9th Cir. 2002); but see *Procter & Gamble Co. v. Amway Corp.*, 242 F.3d 539 (5th Cir. 2001); *World Wrestling Fed'n Entm't, Inc. v. Bozell*, 142 F. Supp. 2d 514 (S.D.N.Y. 2001).

15. See Smolla, *Law of Defamation* § 11:45.

16. *Id.* §§ 11:46, 11:47.

17. See Smolla, *Law of Defamation* § 4:40.50 (citing, *inter alia*, *Serv. Parking Corp. v. Wash. Times Co.*, 92 F.2d 502 (D.C. Cir. 1937)); *Michigan United Conservation Clubs v. CBS News*, 485 F. Supp. 893 (W.D. Mich. 1980), *judgment aff'd*, 665 F.2d 110 (6th Cir. 1981); *Blatty v. N.Y. Times Co.*, 728 P. 2d 1177 (Cal. 1986).

18. Smolla, *Law of Defamation* § 4:44 (citing, *inter alia*, *Geisler v. Petrocelli*, 616 F.2d 636 (2d Cir. 1980); *Bindrim v. Mitchell*, 155 Cal. Rptr. 29 (Cal. App. 1979); Prosser & Keeton § 111).

19. *Rosenblatt v. Baer*, 383 U.S. 75 (1966).

20. See *QSP, Inc. v. Aetna Cas. & Sur. Co.*, 773 A.2d 906 (Conn. 2001); *Auvil v. CBS "60 Minutes,"* 800 F. Supp. 928 (E.D. Wash. 1992); *Isuzu Motors Ltd v. Consumers Union of U.S., Inc.*, 12 F. Supp. 2d 1035 (C.D. Cal. 1998).

21. *Brady v. Ottaway Newspapers, Inc.*, 445 N.Y.S.2d 786 (2d Dep't. 1981).

22. In *Gertz*, 418 U.S. 323 (1974), the Supreme Court identified two classes of public figures. An individual may have such "pervasive fame or notoriety" so that he is a public figure for "all purposes and in all contexts," a general-purpose public figure (*Gertz*, 418 U.S. at 345). Or, more commonly, an individual "voluntarily injects himself into" a particular public controversy and thereby becomes a public figure with respect to the limited range of issues surrounding the controversy, a limited-purpose public figure. *Id.*

23. *New York Times Co.*, 376 U.S. at 280.

24. *Gertz*, 418 U.S. at 347.

25. *Dun & Bradstreet, Inc. v. Greenmoss Builders, Inc.,* 472 U.S. 749 (1985).

26. New York has adopted a "gross irresponsibility" standard which compares the defendant's conduct to the "standards of information gathering and dissemination ordinarily followed by responsible parties." *Chapadeau v. Utica Observer-Dispatch, Inc.,* 379 N.Y.S.2d 61, 64–65 (1975).

27. See, e.g., *Dun & Bradstreet, Inc. v. Greenmoss Builders, Inc.,* 472 U.S. 749 (1985); *Levinsky's, Inc. v. Wal-Mart Stores, Inc.,* 999 F. Supp. 137 (D.Me. 1998).

28. *Huggins v. Moore,* 704 N.Y.S.2d 904, 908 (1999).

29. *Snead v. Redland Aggregates Ltd.,* 998 F.2d 1325 (5th Cir. 1993).

30. Smolla, *Law of Defamation* § 2:98.

31. *Jadwin v. Minneapolis Star & Tribune Co.,* 367 N.W.2d 476, 487–88 (Minn. 1985); see also *Martin Marietta Corp. v. Evening Star Newspaper Co.,* 417 F. Supp. 947 (D.D.C. 1976); *Dairy Stores, Inc. v. Sentinel Publ'g Co.,* 465 A.2d 953 (N.J. Super. Ct. Law Div. 1983).

32. *Snead,* 998 F.2d at 1329; see also *Reliance Ins. Co. v. Barron's,* 442 F. Supp. 1341, 1348 (S.D.N.Y. 1977) (company found to be public figure because it was a large, publicly traded company, had been the subject of great public interest, was in a heavily regulated industry, filed financial reports, and was in the process of offering its stock to the public); *Global Telemedia Int'l, Inc. v. Doe 1,* 132 F. Supp. 2d 1261 (C.D. Cal. 2001) (company is a matter of public interest because it has 18,000 public investors and is the topic of thousands of Internet postings); but see *Blue Ridge Bank v. Veribanc, Inc.,* 866 F.2d 681(4th Cir. 1989) (extensive government regulation not sufficient to make company a public figure).

33. See *Levin v. McPhee,* 119 F.3d 189 (2d Cir. 1997).

34. *Cochran v. NYP Holdings, Inc.,* 58 F. Supp. 2d 1113 (C.D. Cal. 1998).

35. See, e.g., Cal. Civ. Code § 48(a) (West 2004); Ga. Code Ann. § 51-5-11.

36. Fla. Stat. Ann. § 770.01-02 (2004).

37. See, e.g., Mich. Comp. Laws § 600.2911(3) (2004) (privilege for reporting on "matters of public record, a public and official proceeding, or of a governmental notice, announcement, written or recorded report or record generally available to the public, or act or action of a public body…"); N.Y. Civ. Rights Law § 74 (2004) ("a civil action cannot be maintained against any person, firm or corporation, for the publication of a fair and true report of any judicial proceeding, legislative proceeding or other official proceeding"); Cal. Civ. Code § 47(d) (West 2004) (applying to judicial, legislative, or other public official proceeding); *Langston v. Eagle Publ'g Co.,* 719 S.W.2d 612 (Tex. Ct. App. 1986) (applying Tex. Civ. Pract. & Rem. Code § 73.002).

38. *Myers v. The Telegraph,* 773 N.E.2d 192, 198 (Ill. App. Ct. 2002).

39. See RESTATEMENT (SECOND) OF TORTS § 611 cmt. c (1997); *Amway Corp. v. Procter & Gamble Co.,* 346 F.3d 180 (6th Cir. 2003).

40. See *Amway,* 346 F.3d at 186 (citing RESTATEMENT (SECOND) OF TORTS § 611 cmt. e (1997)); but see *First Lehigh Bank v. Cowen,* 700 A.2d 498 (Pa. Super. Ct. 1997).

41. See *Stewart v. Sun Sentinel Co.,* 695 So. 2d 360 (Fla. Dist. Ct. App., 1997) (qualified privilege to accurately report on the information received from government officials, including broadcast of contents "of an official document"); MICH. COMP. LAWS § 600.2911(3) (2004); N.Y. CIV. RIGHTS LAW § 74 (2004); CAL. CIV. CODE § 47(d) (West 2004).

42. See, e.g., *Wilson v. Slatalla,* 970 F. Supp. 405 (E.D. Pa. 1997) (presentence reports and letters from an A.U.S.A. to a judge conditionally privileged); *Bowers v. Loveland Publ'g Co.,* 773 P.2d 595 (Colo. Ct. App. 1988) (report of police reports was a matter of public concern subject to constitutional protection); *White v. Fraternal Order of Police,* 909 F.2d 512 (D.C. Cir. 1990) (ad hoc investigatory police department committee with no adjudicatory powers was a governmental proceeding); *Edwards v. Paddock Publ'ns, Inc.,* 763 N.E.2d 328 (Ill. App. Ct. 2001) (privilege protects news accounts based upon the written and verbal statements of governmental agencies and officials made in their official capacities).

43. See, e.g., RESTATEMENT (SECOND) OF TORTS, § 611 cmt. d (1977) (the privilege ... is also applicable to public proceedings and actions of other bodies or organizations that are by law authorized to perform public duties, such as a medical or bar association charged with authority to examine or license or discipline practitioners); *Harper v. Walters,* 822 F. Supp. 817 (D. D.C. 1993).

44. *Jewell v. NYP Holdings, Inc.,* 23 F. Supp. 2d 348, 371 (S.D.N.Y. 1998); see also *Karaduman v. Newsday, Inc.,* 435 N.Y.S.2d 556, 565–66 (1980).

45. *Brown v. Courier Herald Publ'g Co.,* 700 F. Supp. 534, 537–38 (S.D. Ga. 1988); see also *Nelson v. Associated Press, Inc.,* 667 F. Supp. 1468, 1478–80 (S.D. Fla. 1987); *Appleby v. Daily Hampshire Gazette,* 478 N.E.2d 721 (Mass. 1985); *Howe v. Detroit Free Press,* 555 N.W.2d 738 (Mich. Ct. App. 1996); but see *Friedman v. Israel Labour Party,* 957 F. Supp. 701 (E.D. Pa. 1997) (wire service defense not available in Pennsylvania).

46. *Press-Enterprise Co. v. Superior Court of California,* 464 U.S. 501, 505 (1984); *Press-Enterprise Co. v. Superior Court of California,* 478 U.S. 1 (1986).

47. *Times Mirror Co. v. United States,* 873 F.2d 1210 (9th Cir. 1989).

48. *In re Search Warrant for Secretarial Area, Outside Office of Gunn,* 855 F.2d 569 (8th Cir. 1988).

49. *Baltimore Sun Co. v. Goetz,* 886 F.2d 60 (4th Cir. 1989).

50. *Id.* at 65–66.

51. But there is no right of access to grand jury proceedings. See *Douglas Oil Co. v. Petrol Stops Northwest*, 441 U.S. 211, 219 (1979); but see *Butterworth v. Smith*, 494 U.S. 624 (1990) (state statute that banned witnesses from disclosing own grand jury testimony was unconstitutional).

52. *Press-Enterprise Co. v. Superior Court of California*, 478 U.S. 1 (1986).

53. *Id.*

54. *Cox Broad. Corp. v. Cohn*, 420 U.S. 469 (1975); see also *Smith v. Daily Mail Publ'g Co.*, 443 U.S. 97 (1979) (challenge to application of W.Va. law making it illegal to publish name of child prosecuted in a criminal proceeding).

55. *Globe Newspaper Co. v. Superior Court*, 457 U.S. 596 (1982).

56. See *North Jersey Media Group, Inc. v. Ashcroft*, 308 F.3d 198 (3d Cir. 2002) (immigration hearing); *Detroit Free Press v. Ashcroft*, 303 F.3d 681 (6th Cir. 2002) (same); *United States v. Miami Univ.*, 294 F.3d 797, 824 (6th Cir. 2002) (university's student disciplinary board proceedings); *First Amendment Coalition v. Judicial Inquiry & Review Bd.*, 784 F.2d 467 (3d Cir. 1986) (access to records of disciplinary measures against a judge); *Soc'y of Prof'l Journalists v. Sec'y of Labor*, 616 F. Supp. 569, 574 (D. Utah 1985) (administrative hearing), vacated as moot, 832 F.2d 1180 (10th Cir. 1987).

57. *Press-Enterprise Co. v. Superior Court of California*, 478 U.S. 1, 8 (1986).

58. See, e.g., *Tex. Civ. Prac. & Rem.* § 73.002 (2004) (allowing fair comment on judicial proceedings, other proceedings to administer the law, executive or legislative proceedings, proceedings of a public meeting, or comment on or criticism of an official act of a public official or other matter of public concern).

59. *Publicker Indus., Inc. v. Cohen*, 733 F.2d 1059 (3d Cir. 1984) (preliminary injunction hearing); *In re Cont'l Ill. Sec. Litig.*, 732 F.2d 1302 (7th Cir. 1984) (hearing on motion to dismiss); *In re Iowa Freedom of Info. Council*, 724 F.2d 658 (8th Cir. 1984) (contempt hearing); *Newman v. Graddick*, 696 F.2d 796 (11th Cir. 1983) (pre- and post-trial hearings); *NBC Subsidiary (KNBC-TV), Inc. v. Superior Court*, 980 P.2d 337, 353 (Cal. 1999) (presumptive right to access to civil trial unless court expressly finds: (i) an overriding interest supporting closure and/or sealing; (ii) a substantial probability that the interest will be prejudiced absent closure and/or sealing; (iii) the proposed closure and/or sealing is narrowly tailored; and (iv) there is no less restrictive means of achieving the overriding interest).

60. *Proctor & Gamble v. Bankers Trust Co.*, 78 F.3d 219 (6th Cir. 1996) (citations omitted).

61. *Metro. Opera Ass'n v. Local 100*, 239 F.3d 172, 177 (2d Cir. 2001).

62. *In re Providence Journal Co.*, 820 F.2d 1342 (1st Cir. 1986).

63. *Id.* at 1351.

64. *Id.* at 1350.

65. *Nebraska Press Ass'n v. Stuart,* 427 U.S. 539, 562 (1976).

66. *Id.* at 570.

67. See Smolla, *Law of Defamation* §§ 10:39, 10:42.

68. RESTATEMENT (SECOND) OF TORTS, § 652D (1977); see also Smolla, *Law of Defamation* §§ 10:49, 10:50.

69. See Smolla, *Law of Defamation* § 10:50.

70. See, e.g., 18 U.S.C. § 2511(2)(d) (West 2004).

71. See, e.g., CAL. PENAL CODE §§ 631, 632 (West 2004); FLA. STATE ANN. § 934.03 (West 2004); MICH. COMP. LAWS § 750.539c (2004).

72. 47 C.F.R. § 73.1206 (2005).

73. *Branzburg v. Hayes,* 408 U.S. 665, 710–11 (1972).

74. See, e.g., N.Y. CIV. RIGHTS LAW § 79-h (2004) (providing unqualified protection for journalists' confidential sources and materials); CAL. CONST. ART. 1 § 2(b) (reporters may not be held in contempt for refusing to disclose sources or unpublished information obtained during news gathering); FLA. STATE ANN. § 90.5015 (West 2004) ("professional journalists" cannot be compelled to be witnesses or disclose information that they have obtained while actively gathering news, but which may be overcome by a "clear and specific" showing that: (a) the information is "relevant and material," (b) the information cannot be obtained elsewhere, and (c) a compelling interest exists for requiring disclosure).

75. 47 U.S.C. § 230 (West 2004); see also *Batzel v. Smith,* 333 F.3d 1018 (9th Cir. 2003) (providers of interactive computer services not liable for publishing or distributing defamatory material written or prepared by others); *Doe v. GTE Corp.,* 347 F.3d 655 (7th Cir. 2003); *Zeran v. Am. Online, Inc.,* 129 F.3d 327 (4th Cir. 1997); *Ben Ezra, Weinstein, & Co. v. Am. Online, Inc.,* 206 F.3d 980 (10th Cir. 2000); *Green v. Am. Online, Inc.,* 318 F.3d 465 (3d Cir. 2003).

76. *Firth v. State,* 747 N.Y.S.2d 69 (2002); *Traditional Cat Ass'n v. Gilbreath,* 13 Cal. Rptr. 3d (Ct. App. 2004); *Van Buskirk v. N.Y. Times Co.,* No. 99 Civ. 4265 (MBM) 2000 WL 1206732 (S.D.N.Y. Aug. 24, 2000).

77. *Firth,* 98 N.Y.2d at 372.

78. *Young v. New Haven Advocate,* 315 F.3d 256 (4th Cir. 2002); see also *Revell v. Lidov,* 317 F.3d 467 (5th Cir. 2002) (plaintiff could not gain personal jurisdiction in Texas over a defendant located in Massachusetts posting to a Columbia University Web site); but see *Bochan v. La Fontaine,* 68 F. Supp. 2d 692 (E.D. Va. 1999) (Virginia court had personal jurisdiction over out-of-state defendant who posted his message through a Virginia-based ISP, but not over a different out-of-state defendant who posted through a California or New Mexico ISP (but the

court had jurisdiction over this defendant because he regularly solicited business in Virginia)).

79. *Bachchan v. India Abroad Publ'ns, Inc.*, 585 N.Y.S.2d 661 (Sup. Ct. 1992) (declined to enforce because English courts do not adhere to First Amendment standards); *Matusevich v. Telnikoff,* 877 F. Supp. 1 (D.D.C. 1995) (same).

PART TWO

ASIA

Australia

China

Hong Kong

India

Japan

Korea

Singapore

CHAPTER 4

Australia

PETER BARTLETT

Minter Ellison

Minter Ellison
Rialto Towers, 525 Collins Street
Melbourne, VIC 3000
Phone: +61 3 8608 2677
Fax: +61 3 9620 5185
www.minterellison.com
peter.bartlett@minterellison.com

Introduction to Australian Media Law

There are currently eight sets of defamation laws across the Australian States and Territories; the following outline is designed to inform journalists on the general scope of Australian law. The States and Territories are in the process of enacting a model uniform defamation law which is likely to be in force in early 2006. While not all jurisdictions have released their proposed laws, uniformity looks likely. Where the proposed uniform laws differ from the common law, this has been identified below.

1. What is the locally accepted definition of libel?

The classic definition is found in *Parmiter v. Coupland:*[1]

> Matter ... calculated to injure the reputation of another, by exposing him to hatred, contempt and ridicule.

A more modern test is found in *Mirror Newspapers v. World Hosts:*[2]

[A] statement about the plaintiff of a kind likely to lead the recipient as an ordinary person to think less of him.

In reality, material is defamatory if it lowers the reputation of someone in the eyes of others. Defamatory material can be expressed in any mode of communication capable of being comprehended visually. Libel is defamatory material in permanent form. The new uniform defamation proposals all remove the distinction between libel and slander. Television and radio broadcasts are deemed to be broadcast in permanent form.[3]

Australian law has a fairly broad interpretation of what statements subject a person to defamatory meaning. For example, statements that a restaurant owner was going bankrupt,[4] or that a minister in the Australian government was an adulterer, were held to be defamatory.[5] The courts have also found that publications that, while not accusing the subject of wrongdoing but nonetheless holding him up to ridicule, could be actionable. In one case, a professional football player stated a claim for libel after a newspaper published a photograph of him in the shower.[6] The court found that his reputation was tarnished because it made him look "ridiculous" and the public may have believed that the athlete intentionally posed for the photograph.

In rare cases, criminal liability will attach to the unlawful publication of defamatory material in certain, limited circumstances. As the offense has been codified, its exact terms differ across the states and territories, and there are often a number of defenses available.

2. Is libel-by-implication recognized, or, in the alternative, must the complained-of words alone defame the plaintiff?

Defamation can arise either from the ordinary and natural meaning of the words published, or from the imputations the words carry. This may be determined by examining the context and tone of the statement at issue. It is worth noting that the intention of the publisher is irrelevant. The question is whether a defamatory meaning is capable of arising and then whether it in fact arises.

3. May corporations sue for libel?

Currently, a corporation may sue for damage to its trading or business reputation except in the state of New South Wales (Sydney). Unlike an individual, a corporation cannot sue for damage to feelings. Government bodies cannot sue for defamation, as political discussion is seen as a crucial element of freedom of speech.

Under the proposed uniform defamation laws, only corporations with fewer than ten employees and not-for-profit entities will be able to sue for defamation. Otherwise, corporations will be prohibited from commencing defamation proceedings. Employees will retain the right to sue for defamation where identifiable.

4. Is product disparagement recognized, and if so, how does that differ from libel?

In Australia an action lies for "injurious falsehood" where a false and malicious statement against a person's business, property, or goods causes provable economic loss.

An action for injurious falsehood is separate from an action for defamation, although both actions can be run in conjunction. The difference between the two is that an action for injurious falsehood protects a person's business, while an action for defamation protects a person's reputation.

A publication need not be defamatory to ground an action in injurious falsehood. In other words, it need not subject the target to reputational damage, but need only be false and reasonably linked to damages suffered by the business. For example, an inaccurate story that says that "Company X has lost its key employees in the widget-making department" might be actionable if Company X could show that the statement is false, and that contracts to sell widgets were canceled by buyers because they believed that X could not produce the sought-after widgets.

An action may also lie under Section 52 of the Trade Practices Act 1974 (Cth), which prohibits conduct that is misleading and deceptive.

5. Must an individual be clearly identified (by name or photograph) to sue for libel? Can a group of persons sue for libel, even though not named?

A person needs to show that the material complained of identified him as the subject of the defamatory imputations contained in the article. The person does not need to be named in the material published, rather only be identifiable by other persons acquainted with him. Basically, any connection that one can reasonably make between the material published and the person will identify the person.

Group libel is possible in limited circumstances. Defamatory statements about a group of unnamed persons are actionable by one of those persons if the statement is shown to be referring to individual members of the group. The members of the group can only sue if they can show that the statement refers particularly to them.

This is usually the case where the group is so small as to make members easily identifiable. You can potentially defame each member of a group because it is small enough to allow the defamatory meaning to apply to each member of that group.

6. What is the fault standard(s) applied to libel?

There are a number of defenses that provide protection from liability for otherwise defamatory statements. The main defenses are:

- Truth is a complete defense at common law and in some Australian jurisdictions where statute has been introduced. Some jurisdictions also require a public interest or benefit in the publication. All uniform defamation proposals will make substantial truth alone a complete defense to a defamation claim;
- Fair comment and honest opinion (see discussion in Question 8 below);
- Specified "privileges," including fair and accurate reporting of certain government and judicial proceedings and documents; and
- "Public interest" privilege relevant to government and political matters.

Absolute privilege. This defense protects statements made in the course of parliamentary or judicial proceedings. Journalists and webmasters should note that this defense is not available for anyone but the participants in the proceedings (i.e., parliamentarians, lawyers who are taking part, the judges, and the witnesses giving evidence). Under the uniform defamation law proposals, the situations where this defense arises will be extended.

Qualified privilege. This is the defense relied upon by publishers producing reports of parliamentary proceedings and judicial proceedings. It is available to the media as long as the material published is in the public interest, is not founded on malice, and is fair and accurate. Currently the interpretation of standards that govern qualified privilege vary from state to state in Australia. Common to all of these interpretations is the requirement that the publication be made in furtherance of a public interest. Journalists should note that "public interest" is not defined as material that is "of interest" to the public, but rather whether the material in question serves "the common convenience and welfare of society."[7] (See discussion in Question 6b. below.)

The uniform defamation proposals will extend the range of matters falling within the scope of this defense to include a fair copy or summary of a public document and reports of particular bodies and tribunals. The defense will only be defeated where the matter was not published honestly for the information of the public or the advancement of education.

a. Does the fault standard depend on the fame or notoriety of the plaintiff?

There is no differing fault standard in the case of the fame or notoriety of the plaintiff except where qualified privilege is claimed for publication of a matter of public interest or concern, or the publication concerns government and political matter. The fame or notoriety of the plaintiff may be relevant in calculating damages.

b. Is there a heightened fault standard or privilege for reporting on matters of public concern or public interest?

1. To succeed in a qualified privilege defense, other than a report of parliamentary or judicial proceedings, it is necessary to show that:
   - Recipients had an interest in receiving the information;
   - The reporter had a duty to publish the material; and
   - The conduct of the publisher in publishing the matter was reasonable and there was no malice.

2. The "subject" must necessarily be of public interest. The defamation will occur as an unavoidable incidental to giving information on that subject. The defense of qualified privilege is extremely difficult for the media to establish. To prove reasonableness at common law, a journalist researching a story must at least:
   - Contact, or attempt to contact, the person or company referred to in any story to provide them with the opportunity to comment on the allegations made in the story;
   - Include their comments (if any) in the publication;
   - Take care to use reliable sources and verify each available source of information; and
   - Check the accuracy and authenticity of any material contained in the report.[8]

3. There is a separate qualified privilege to response to attacks published elsewhere.

4. A publisher will have a qualified "public interest" defense to a defamation action where the material published discusses government or political matters and publication of the material was reasonable in the circumstances. These are subject to the limitations enumerated in section (2) above.

Australia has not yet moved as far as the UK decision in *Reynolds v. Times Newspapers*.

The statutory qualified-privilege defense under the uniform defamation law proposals will provide a broader basis than the common law for finding that a recipient had the necessary interest in receiving the defamatory information. However, courts have interpreted reasonableness under statute narrowly, making it more difficult than at common law for publishers to prove that publication was reasonable in the circumstances. The defense will still be defeated by the plaintiff proving that publication was actuated by malice.

7. Is financial news about publicly traded companies, or companies involved with a government contract, considered a matter of public interest or otherwise privileged?

There would be a strong argument to suggest that "financial news about publicly traded companies, or companies involved with government contracts," is a matter of public interest and privileged, but it is still necessary to satisfy the test that:

- The recipients had an interest in receiving the information;
- The reporter had a duty to publish the material; and
- The publisher's conduct in publishing the material was reasonable and not actuated by malice.

This defense will be harder to invoke when the uniform defamation proposals become law, due to the statutory requirement of reasonableness.

8. Is there a recognized protection for opinion or "fair comment" on matters of public concern?

Fair comment is a defense that protects the public interest in freedom of discussion. It enables publishers to publish reviews of theater, music, literary works, and restaurants. It also allows journalists to make comments on almost any issue.[9]

A "comment" is an honestly expressed point of view. To be considered "fair," the comment at issue must be:

- On a matter of public interest;
- Based on facts stated in the report which are substantially true, or are common knowledge, or privileged; and
- Honestly held not being actuated by malice.

The philosophy behind the defense is that if the facts are stated accurately, then the viewers/readers can form their own view as to whether they agree with the publisher's comment. This defense encourages the publisher to focus on the material rather than statements about the individual. For instance, reporters should consider saying that the painting is bad, not that the painter is clearly cross-eyed and color-blind.

9. Are there any requirements upon a plaintiff, such as demand for retraction or right of reply, and if so, what impact do they have?

There are no requirements in Australia upon a plaintiff to demand a retraction or a right of reply. An apology is relevant on the question of damages, but is not a defense.[10]

The proposed uniform defamation legislation will enact a codified offer-of-amends procedure similar to that in the United Kingdom. Rejection of a publisher's reasonable offer of amends, made in accordance with the legislation, can provide a full defense to a defamation claim. In considering the reasonableness of an offer, the court must consider any correction or apology published before trial and its prominence compared with the matter in question, and the time elapsed between publication of the matter in question and the apology.

10. Is there a privilege for quoting or reporting on:

a. Papers filed in court?

Papers filed with the Court Registry in most states are not protected by privilege until they have been accepted into evidence by the judge. Affidavits which have not been read out in open court or taken as read by the judge are not protected.

The proposed uniform defamation legislation would provide a privilege for a fair quoting or summary of any document filed or lodged with a court that is open to inspection by the public.

b. Government-issued documents?

Depending on the content of the documents, there may be an argument for qualified privilege, subject to a "fair and accurate" reporting or other requirement.

The uniform defamation laws will generally provide a defense for publication of a fair copy or summary of a public or government document.

c. Quasi-governmental proceedings?

Again, depending on the circumstances, findings, or decisions of an association, a committee of an association or the governing body of an association relating to a member or to a person subject to the association's control may in some circumstances be covered by a defense of qualified privilege.

The subject matter must be one in which the public has a genuine interest in the outcome of the proceedings, which generally embraces associations:

- for the advancement of learning;

- for the promotion or protection of the interests of a trade, business, profession, or industry; or
- for the promotion of a public spectator sport, pastime, or game and the promotion or protection of the interests of persons in connection with the sport, pastime, or game.

Any such reports must be accurate and balanced and published in good faith for public information. It must be a precis of what happened in the proceedings. In some states and territories, such reports have specific statutory protection.

The range of proceedings to which this defense applies will be codified and extended under the uniform defamation reforms.

11. Is there a privilege for republishing statements made earlier by other, bona fide, reliable publications or wire services?

There is no privilege for republishing such material except where an innocent dissemination defense may apply (see discussion in Question 20, below). The publisher is deemed to have published that republished material and, if defamatory, is liable in damages.

12. Are there any restrictions regarding reporting on:

a. Ongoing criminal investigations?

Clearly it can be defamatory to report ongoing criminal investigations to the extent that the report suggests that the person or persons being investigated are guilty or even that there is sufficient evidence available to justify the continuing investigation.

There are statutory restrictions on areas such as identifying the victim of sexual assault, or minors. A publication that has a real and definite tendency to prejudice a pending trial could be held in Contempt of Court.[11]

b. Ongoing criminal prosecutions?

Certain restrictions are placed upon reporting of ongoing criminal prosecutions, such as:

- where the matter involves children;
- where it involves a sexual offense; or
- where a court order suppressing publication is in place.

The publisher does not have a potential problem with Contempt of Court until charges are laid. It would be a Contempt of Court to publish material that would prejudice the fair trial of the matter. The publisher should be particularly careful where the matter is being heard by a jury, and avoid publishing facts not heard by the jury.

Generally, reporters may repeat any evidence given in civil or criminal proceedings so long as it is a fair and accurate report of the matter and is not in Contempt of Court, such as being the subject of a nonpublication order.

c. Ongoing regulatory investigations?

There are various statutory restrictions on reporting some ongoing regulatory investigations and prosecutions, and journalists should consult local counsel prior to publishing such reports or investigatory material.

d. Ongoing civil litigation, or other judicial proceedings?

Certain restrictions are placed upon the reporting of civil litigation where:

- The matter is before the Family Court or the Children's Court;
- A court order suppressing publication is in place; or
- The civil litigation involves evidence of sexual offenses.

Unless the report is a fair and accurate account of the proceeding, the normal rules relating to defamation and contempt apply.

13. Are prior restraints or other prepublication injunctions available on the basis of libel or privacy, and if so, what are the standards for obtaining such relief?

It is generally considered that injunctions will rarely be granted in Australia to prevent the publication of defamatory material, as courts are reluctant to prevent freedom of speech on matters of public interest and there is always the right to sue for damages after publication if a person has been defamed.

An injunction could be granted if monetary damages are not an adequate remedy. That would be very rare. An injunction can be obtained to prevent the publication of confidential material, in some circumstances.

14. Is a right of privacy recognized (either civilly or criminally)?

There is no general right of privacy in Australia, but the civil laws against breach of confidentiality and trespass, and the criminal laws against secretly recording private conversations, are important privacy protections.

a. What is the definition of "private fact"?

To the extent that a privacy claim would be recognized, the Privacy Act 1988 (Cth) is concerned with the protection of personal information of individuals (being information from which a person's identity is reasonably ascertainable) that is handled by organizations, especially the protection of the collection and distribution of such information without that person's consent, i.e., how that information is disclosed.

b. Is there a public interest or newsworthiness exception?

The Privacy Act affords exemptions to journalists.[12] Acts engaged in by a media organization which are *in the course of journalism* will be exempt. The easiest way to ensure this applies is, when collecting information about an individual, make sure that it is used for the purposes of writing the story and not for some other sideline purpose, such as advertising.

c. Is the right of privacy based in common law, statute, or constitution?

The Privacy Act is statutory in nature, and the causes of action sounding in breach of confidence are rooted in common law.

15. May reporters tape-record their own telephone conversations for note-taking purposes (not rebroadcast) without the consent of the other party?

Tape-recording your own telephone conversation by placing a tape recorder next to the telephone's speaker or mouthpiece is permitted. It is preferable to obtain the consent of the other party to the conversation, but not required.

Putting in place special technology which intercepts a telephone conversation over the line, even internally in your receiver, is illegal in Australia, unless all parties to the conversation are aware that tape-recording is taking place and consent to the conversation being recorded.

16. If permissible to record such tapes, may they be broadcast without permission?

Illegal tape recordings are inadmissible in court cases; thus, interviews that may be challenged in libel cases later should be made with an eye toward admissibility, and local counsel should be consulted during the preparation of such material.

Legislation in many states and territories means tape recordings obtained by recorders external to the phone cannot be broadcast without the permission of all parties to the conversation, subject to limited exceptions such as when used in legal proceedings, or where its use would be in the public interest.

17. Is there a recognized evidentiary privilege preventing the disclosure of confidential sources relied upon by reporters?

No. Currently, journalists have no legal right to withhold their source of confidential information, although journalists in Australia do maintain and uphold an ethical right not to reveal sources. Journalists who refuse to reveal the sources of confidential information before the court will be held in contempt. They can be penalized by fine or imprisonment, or both. There is a current push for enactment of "shield laws" to protect journalists in such circumstances, but it is unclear whether this will occur.

Judges would normally only order a journalist to disclose a source where the judge takes the view that it is essential for the fair determination of the case for the identity to be disclosed. That is rare.

18. In the event that legal papers are served upon the newsroom (such as a civil complaint), are there any particular warnings about accepting service of which we should be aware?

There are no particular warnings about accepting service of process in Australia, other than that the documents served should be forwarded to the publisher's lawyers as soon as possible to ensure the proper response is made to the service and that any action is defended appropriately.

Normally, documents would be served on the registered office of the publisher's company.

19. Has your jurisdiction applied established media law to Internet publishers?

Defamation law has been applied to Internet publishers. In *Dow Jones & Company Inc. v. Gutnick*[13] it was held that defamation on the Internet occurs in the jurisdiction where the material is downloaded (i.e., read or heard).

20. If established media law has been applied to Internet publishers, are there any ways in which Internet publishers (including chat room operators) have to meet different standards?

1. *"Primary" Publishers*

   For primary publishers (i.e., online newspapers) there are no different standards for defamation. They are liable for defamatory material published on their site.

2. *Internet Intermediaries (Web Hosts)*

   The Broadcasting Services Act 1992 provides a statutory defense to defamatory "internet content" carried, hosted, or cached by Internet content hosts and Internet service providers where they are not aware of the nature of the material.

This defense extends to material held on a data storage device (i.e., server or hard drive), a posting to a newsgroup, and postings to a chat room, but does not protect defamatory ordinary e-mail messages, instantaneous chat services, or information transmitted in the form of a broadcasting service, i.e., streaming television or radio programs.

The proposed uniform defamation laws contain a defense of "innocent dissemination" meaning most Internet intermediaries would not be liable for defamatory matter they republish so long as they are not the author of the material and do not exercise any editorial control over the content of the matter.

21. Are there any cases where the courts enforced a judgment in libel from another jurisdiction against a publisher in your jurisdiction?

We are not aware of any such cases. It is likely that Australia would enforce a judgment from a common law country. It would be unlikely to enforce an award from a country with more restrictive libel laws than Australia.

Chapter Notes

1. *Parmiter v. Coupland* (1840) 6 M&W 105 at 108; 151 ER 340 at 342, per Parke B.

2. *Mirror Newspapers v. World Hosts* (1979) 141 CLR 632, at 638 per Mason and Jacobs JJ.

3. Broadcasting Services Act 1992, section 206.

4. *Id.*

5. *Morosi v. Mirror Newspapers* (1972) 2 NSWLR 749.

6. *Ettinghausen v. Australian Consolidated Press Ltd.* (1991) 1 NSWLR 443.

7. *Andreyevich v. Kosovich* (1947) SR (NSW) 357.

8. See *Lange v. Australian Broadcasting Corporation* (1997) 198 CLR 520.

9. See, e.g., *Gardiner v. Fairfax* (1942) 42 SR (NSW) 125.

10. *Carson v. John Fairfax* (1993) 178 CLR 44, at 66. The Australian Press Council (APC) provides a forum for complaints about and against the press based on a "Statement of Principles." In considering complaints, the APC will consider whether the publication has made amends "for publishing information that is found to be harmfully inaccurate by printing, promptly and with appropriate prominence, such retraction, correction, explanation or apology as will neutralise the damage so far as possible." The APC cannot impose sanctions or remedies.

11. See, e.g., *Hinch v. Attorney General (Vic)* (No. 2) 164 CLR 15 and *Attorney General (NSW) v. TCN Channel Nine Pty Ltd* (1990) 20 NSWLR 368.

12. Privacy Act 1988 (Cth), section 7B(4).

13. *Dow Jones & Company Inc. v. Gutnick* (2002) 210 CLR 575.

CHAPTER 5

China

VINCENT WANG AND EDWARD J. DAVIS

Davis Wright Tremaine LLP

Davis Wright Tremaine LLP	Davis Wright Tremaine LLP
Suite 640 East Tower	1633 Broadway
1376 Nanjing Xi Road, Shanghai	New York, NY 10019
200040	Phone: 212-489-8230
Phone: 011-86-21-6279-8560	Fax: 212-489-8340
Fax: 011-86-21-6279-8547	www.dwt.com
www.dwt.com	eddavis@dwt.com
vincentwang@dwt.com	

Defamation and Chinese Law

There is no specific law governing defamation or mass communication in China. Rather, the legal rights of parties to defamation cases are governed by general laws such as the Constitution of the People's Republic of China, the Criminal Law of China, and the General Principles of Civil Law of China, as well as "judicial interpretations" issued by the Supreme Court of China. The Supreme Court's judicial interpretations explain and clarify the application of broadly worded statutes to specific situations—often based on the facts of actual cases—to provide guidance for lower courts. They are viewed as definitive. In 1993 and 1998, the Supreme Court issued judicial interpretations that addressed questions regarding defamation. In addition, the Supreme Court has issued "replies" in response to questions presented by lower courts regarding particular defamation cases. Decisions in defamation cases by courts at various levels have been reported, but, because China does not employ the common law system, the decisions in individual cases serve as references rather than binding precedents.

The media in China are closely controlled and regulated by the government. Thus, the private law of defamation is not as extensively developed in China as in some other countries. Many issues remain unresolved as yet.

1. What is the locally accepted definition of libel?

Chinese law protects the right to reputation more broadly than does U.S. law. The Chinese Constitution provides that "[t]he personal dignity of citizens of the People's Republic of China is inviolable. Insult, libel, false accusation or false incrimination directed against citizens by any means is prohibited."[1] To be sure, legal action may be taken based on acts that most courts worldwide would recognize as defamation: denigrating the character of another by publishing false statements of fact.

Going further, however, Chinese law punishes speech that is often not actionable in many Western nations: tarnishing the image of another with malice, or harming someone's reputation by way of insult.[2] Insulting statements may be found actionable even if they do not contain false statements of fact. Derogatory words such as "bastard," "shameless," "monster," "hooligan," "presumptuous," "rotten," and "human scum" have been cited as examples of actionable insults.[3]

Public insults and defamation based on the knowing publication of false statements of fact may be the subject of criminal proceedings for libel, with penalties of up to three years in prison, surveillance, and loss of political rights, but the State prosecution department generally will not initiate prosecution for such a crime unless the victim requests it.

The Supreme Court has directed judges to consider the following issues before a finding of defamation may be made:

1. whether the reputation of the plaintiff has been harmed;
2. whether the activities of the defendant were in violation of the law;
3. whether the illegal activities caused damage to the plaintiff's reputation; and
4. whether the defendant was at fault.[4]

2. Is libel-by-implication recognized, or, in the alternative, must the complained-of words alone defame the plaintiff?

Chinese courts have not readily recognized libel-by-implication. A good illustration of the difficulty for plaintiffs came in a case decided in 2000.[5] Two newspapers published a news story praising a young man for the life-saving support he provided for an elderly lady. The article stated that all the woman's children had died and that she was living in misery and distress before the young man began supporting her. In fact, the woman had two daughters who were alive. One of her daughters was living in another city and could not conveniently visit and take care of her mother on a regular basis. The other daughter was living in the same city as her mother, but she was living in poverty herself and could visit her mother only on national holidays and at times when her mother was ill. When the two daughters read the news story, they thought it implied that they were bad daughters who did not treat their own mother well, in addition to stating falsely that they had died. They filed suits against the newspapers for defamation, but judgment was rendered in favor of the newspapers. Although the court agreed that some part of the news story was untrue (the statement that the children had all died), it held for the defendant on the ground that the plaintiffs failed to prove that their reputation was harmed in any way by the untrue statement in the story. The court's decision emphasized that the article focused on the young man who was being praised and that readers would interpret it to be intended to praise him rather than to criticize the woman's daughters. They were not even named and were in fact asserted to be dead.

The possibility that a court may entertain claims based on libel by implication cannot be ruled out, however. Another instance, unreported in the law journals, involved the author Yang Mo. An article was published which reported that Yang had said in an interview that he met George Bush in 1989 when Bush visited China as president of the United States. Yang alleged that the article defamed him because, although it would be an honor to meet the U.S. president, in fact Yang had not met him, had not been interviewed for the article, and had never said he met President Bush. The article, therefore, made him look like a boastful liar. Yang won the lawsuit.[6] His victory indicates that courts may be open to libel by implication if plaintiffs can provide evidence of extrinsic facts that will render words defamatory in the minds of certain readers even though such words look innocuous on their own.

3. May corporations sue for libel?

Yes. Publicly traded companies, limited liability companies, governmental agencies, nonprofit institutions, associations, and schools may all sue for libel. Common instances are suits over reports that a company's products are of inferior quality, unfairly high in price, or so poorly made that they compromise the quality of other products into which they are incorporated.

4. Is product disparagement recognized, and if so, how does that differ from libel?

Yes, product disparagement is recognized. The same fundamental legal principles apply to product disparagement and defamation, but additional procedural options under administrative law are available for product disparagement claims.

Product disparagement claims are governed by the Anti-Unfair Competition Law. A victim of product disparagement may file a complaint in court or submit a complaint to the relevant administrative agency, usually the State Administration of Industry and Commerce, which polices commercial markets in China. The SAIC conducts an investigation and, if product disparagement is determined to have occurred, may impose fines. In addition to assessing fines to be paid to the government, the SAIC may also require payment of damages to the complainant, including costs incurred in investigating the unfair business practice. Either side may appeal the administrative determination to court.

Administrative complaints are ordinarily submitted by business competitors. In the event that a media defendant—not a competitor—is alleged to have defamed a product, a civil action for damages would be appropriate. Such a suit would not be likely to differ from a suit for defamation. In fact, the Supreme Court of China recognized, in its 1998 interpretation, that defamation law may be used appropriately to address losses suffered in manufacturing, distribution, and other business operations if the content of criticisms or comments in the media regarding the quality of products or service is not "basically true."[7] The interpretation specifies that such losses may be measured by the value of product returns, canceled contracts, or other pertinent evidence showing profit, loss, and so on.

5. Must an individual be clearly identified (by name or photograph) to sue for libel? Can a group of persons sue for libel, even though not named?

It is not necessary for an individual to be identified by name or photograph, and a group of persons can sue for libel although their names are not used in the allegedly defamatory documents. Such questions arise regularly in China, perhaps because of the prevalent habit of indirectly expressing social and political criticism through ostensibly fictional stories and historical allegories in reaction to an environment of censorship. Pursuant to the Supreme Court's judicial interpretation of 1993, content that is insulting, defamatory, or revealing of private facts may be actionable even if the real name and identity of the person referred to are not given out, so long as readers can determine that the person referred to is based on a specific person readily identifiable and the reputation of that person is harmed by the reference.[8]

The defendant in one case in the 1990s did not have a good relationship with three of his colleagues. He wrote a novel set at a time before the Chinese Revolution (1949), and the novel was published in a newspaper as a serial. In the novel, the physical characteristics of a drug dealer, a brothel boss, and a hooligan matched those of his three colleagues, but the author did not use his colleagues' names and he made their social backgrounds different. He did everything, in the novel, however, to insult and denigrate the three characters. When the three colleagues read part of the novel, they recognized their portrayals and asked the newspaper not to continue publishing the story, but the newspaper refused. Afterward, they filed a lawsuit against the author and the newspaper, and the plaintiffs won.[9] According to the judgment, although the three characters and the novel were made up, the descriptions of the three characters were so detailed that it was easy for people who knew the plaintiffs to recognize that the three characters were meant to represent the plaintiffs, and they had been shown in a false and insulting light. Therefore, the author was found liable for defamation. As to the newspaper, although the newspaper did not know that there would be a dispute about the novel when it started to publish the installments, it was held liable because it continued publishing the novel after being informed by the plaintiffs that the story contained defamatory depictions of them.

On the other hand, if a character is not based on a real person but just happens to have some similarity to that person, no defamation shall be found. In another case of alleged libel in fiction, an author, after gathering information from several hospitals, created a novel about a story of malpractice in a hospital.[10] All the names, including the names of the hospital and all the characters in the novel, were fictitious. After publication of the novel, the director of one of the hospitals the author had visited to gather information for his novel filed a lawsuit against the author for defamation, claiming that the character of the director of the fictitious hospital was meant to represent him. The court held for the defendant. According to the judgment, the descriptions of the hospital and the director were too general, and there were apparent differences between the real and fictional hospital and director. After reading the novel, the court held that it would be impossible for anyone, even someone who knew the plaintiff well, to think that he was the hospital director portrayed in the novel.

In another case, an article reported erroneously that human flesh was used as a filling for buns in an unnamed restaurant.[11] Because the article did not refer to any identifiable person or restaurant, it could not amount to defamation.

6. What is the fault standard(s) applied to libel?

a. Does the fault standard depend on the fame or notoriety of the plaintiff?

In China, whether the defendant in a libel case is at fault is judged by an objective negligence standard: whether the defendant has exercised the due care that would be exercised by someone in the same profession or someone who has comparable knowledge or experience, acting in good faith.

Regardless of whether the defendant actually anticipated the consequences of publishing the defamatory statements or not (i.e., whether the defendant knew something was false and defamatory or knew it might be false and defamatory), the defendant is deemed to have the capability to anticipate the consequences if others in the same profession would anticipate the same.

b. Is there a heightened fault standard or privilege for reporting on matters of public concern or public interest?

The fault standard does not depend on the fame or notoriety of the plaintiff, nor is there a heightened standard or privilege for reporting on matters of public concern or public interest. However, commentators have noted an unresolved tension between the constitutional protection for reputation, on the one hand, and the constitutional guarantees of freedom of speech, freedom of the press, and freedom to criticize any State organ or State official, on the other.[12]

A good example of the application of the negligence standard comes from a commentary on a case in 1988 provided by a judge of the Supreme Court of China in a treatise he authored.[13] A newspaper published an article about a fire in an apartment next door to the apartment of the vice secretary of the Politics and Law Commission of the county. (The Politics and Law Commission department ensures that the Chinese Communist Party's policies are fully implemented in the law enforcement departments in the government.) The article said that, at the time of the fire, the vice secretary kept his door closed and neither helped the others to fight the fire nor allowed them to take water from his home. The vice secretary sued for defamation. In his complaint, he claimed that the story was not true and explained that he was doing carpentry work at the time of the fire and did not know there was a fire in the neighborhood. He closed his door to prevent the wind from blowing the sawdust everywhere in his home. The judge of the Supreme Court commented that, although the criticism in the article was not well founded, at the time the article was written it was impossible for the author and the newspaper to guess what the vice secretary was doing at home when there was a fire next door. Therefore, neither of them knew or should have known that the article would defame the vice secretary. As a result, the author and the newspaper were not at fault, and no liability for defamation could be found in the case.

Another example is the 1994 case of Song Jianping.[14] Police authorities informed a newspaper that they had detained Ms. Song and her husband for scalping tickets. The newspaper printed a front-page story about them, without contacting Ms. Song. It turned out that Ms. Song was a telephone operator, not a ticket scalper, and was not married. A ticket scalper had used Ms. Song's name when the police held her. The newspaper and the police were found negligent and held liable for defamation.

The facts that led to the finding of negligence in the *Song* case were not fully explained, beyond the fact that the newspaper had not contacted Ms. Song. It should be possible to introduce evidence of standard journalistic practices in defamation cases where fault is in question. It has been reported that professional journalists have sometimes been added to judicial panels in defamation cases in Hefei, Anhui Province, presumably to reflect the standards of the profession and help inform the judges as they determine what may constitute negligence.

7. Is financial news about publicly traded companies, or companies involved with a government contract, considered a matter of public interest or otherwise privileged?

Financial news is protected if it (1) is based upon true statements which do not constitute private facts or State secrets; (2) accurately reflects statements made by the publicly traded companies concerned; (3) is a republication of news reported by the Xinhua News Agency; (4) is based on official documents released by government agencies that have not been amended or rescinded; or (5) qualifies as "fair comment" as elaborated below.

There have not been many court decisions to illuminate the boundaries between the confidential information of private businesses or government agencies and information that may be freely published because it is of legitimate interest to the public. Chinese enterprises fall into several categories along a spectrum from completely private to completely State-owned. Information concerning particular enterprises may be protected from disclosure as a trade secret or a State secret (both of which are protected by separate laws), but more and more information is becoming routinely available to the public, especially regarding publicly traded companies. An archive of information about all companies in China is kept by the SAIC, which maintains a publicly available database. The operations of private and State-owned enterprises and the prices they charge for their products and services are regularly reported on in the media, but the fear of lawsuits for defamation prompts most news organizations to ask all businesses involved in a news story to confirm the facts in a news report before it is published. The news organizations usually will not publish if the company denies the facts.

State secrets are serious issues for publishers sending news to or from China. Information about State-owned or private companies providing products or services for the military or State security is likely to be highly protected. The legal definition of State secrets in China is broad enough to encompass information that would be considered of legitimate public concern elsewhere in the world. Publishers and broadcasters in China have historically been careful, therefore, especially in reporting on sensitive information about State-owned enterprises, even outside the military/security sphere. For example, employees who reveal the nature of a project on which a defense contractor is working may be arrested, and individuals have been prosecuted for disseminating State secrets in such cases.

Pursuant to the China Law on Maintaining State Secrets and its related regulations and rules, the following matters are regarded as State secrets:

1. matters kept secret in decision-making in State affairs;
2. secret matters pertaining to activities of defense and the military forces;
3. secret matters concerning diplomatic activities, foreign affairs, and matters on which the State undertakes an obligation of confidentiality to another country;
4. secret matters pertaining to the economy and social development;
5. secret matters in scientific technologies;
6. secret matters pertaining to State security activities and the investigation of crime; and
7. secret matters as determined by the governmental agencies dealing with State secrets (internal reviewers employed by newspapers may bring questions to the attention of authorities prior to publication for such determinations).

The definition of "secret" matters is broad. Information may be "secret" if its release or dissemination would:

1. undermine the strength and defense capacity of the State;
2. affect the unity of the State, the unity between ethnic groups, and social stability;
3. damage the political and economic interests of the State in its external activities;
4. affect the security of State leaders or important officials of foreign countries;
5. hinder major State safety and security work;
6. reduce the reliability of, or render ineffective, measures for the maintenance of State secrets;
7. weaken the economic, scientific, or technological strength of the State; or

8. deprive State agencies of the safeguards necessary for the exercise of their lawful power.

Some documents containing State secrets are marked with a "secret" or "super-secret" chop, but others are not, and their status is subject to the determination of relevant governmental authorities. Journalists practicing in China watch one another and develop a feeling for whether the State will object to disclosure in certain circumstances. The one foolproof clue that a document has been classified as containing State secrets is the mark of a chop with the characters "confidential" or "super-confidential" on it. Disclosure of the confidential content is not permitted, and it is doubtful that the fact that another party has already disclosed such material may be relied upon in defense.

There is no established procedure for requesting that certain materials be declassified for release to the public. Nor is there a Chinese equivalent to freedom-of-information laws that permit citizens to compel the government to release unclassified information.

8. Is there a recognized protection for opinion or "fair comment" on matters of public concern?

There is no specific provision of Chinese law to protect opinion or "fair comment." The recognition of protection for opinion or "fair comment" is subject to the discretion of judges, as there is no statute or judicial interpretation specifically addressing it.

A judge of the Supreme Court who is responsible for trials of civil cases has written, in a treatise on media torts, that, to be protected, an expression of opinion or "fair comment" must be a matter of public concern and must be fair.[15] Generally, the following could be held to be matters of public concern, depending on the precise circumstances: (1) the policies and measures of the State and of local governments and legislative and judicial bodies; (2) the decisions and activities of enterprises, companies, institutions, and associations, which relate to the public interest; (3) artistic performances or works (such as books); (4) public figures and newsworthy events (there is no definition of public figures and newsworthy events, so the determination is subject to the discretion of the court); and (5) major events such as natural disasters, major accidents, or serious crimes that attract public attention and therefore merit analysis.

In order for the expression of opinion or the comment to be deemed fair, the following requirements should be satisfied: (1) the comment must be made in good faith, which means that the opinion is honestly held by the commentator, whose standing is impartial and fair; (2) the facts on which the opinion and comment are based are true; and (3) opinion and commentary on artworks and academic works should be purely discussions and debates of their artistic or scholarly value, and not defamation in disguise.

The facts on which critical comments are based need not be literally true, only substantially accurate. In one case, three party officials were criticized for spending RMB117 of public money on a private feast, when it was actually a group of four officials who had spent RMB112 on the feast.[16] The court held that the inaccuracy was not significant enough to render the criticism actionable. In another case, officials in a municipality in Hunan Province sued a newspaper for reporting that they had spurned requests for help after a murder took place, by sticking their heads out the window of a building and saying no one was in their office.[17] The windows were built in a way that would have prevented anyone from putting a head out, but the officials did not prevail, presumably because the gist of the claim was that they were actually in the office and did not respond to the requests for help, which was apparently true.

In addition to the two cases cited above, the *Beijing Evening News,* for instance, was sued by a soft-drink factory that had been fined by the government for poor sanitary maintenance. The article said the factory was "full of flies," while the government report had referred to only "a few flies."[18] The suit failed, despite the exaggeration, but the court warned the newspaper about reckless use of words.

Most press entities in China are arms of the government. They are often shielded from liability for critical statements they publish, particularly if such statements serve as an expression of certain public policies of the State.

9. Are there any requirements upon a plaintiff, such as demand for retraction or right of reply, and if so, what impact do they have?

There are no such requirements in Chinese law.

10. Is there a privilege for quoting or reporting on:

a. Papers filed in court?

Yes. Pursuant to the Supreme Court's 1998 judicial interpretation on the trial of defamation cases, there is a privilege for reporting on official court documents and public actions of government agencies so long as such reporting is "objective and accurate" and does not reveal State secrets.[19]

However, if a court decision is later reversed or the court paper quoted is subsequently corrected, the quoting or reporting party must report such reversal or correction in later editions. Otherwise, if the original report damages the reputation of the parties concerned, and the additional information goes unreported, the privilege will be lost.

A decision in 1996 illustrates this principle. An official in the prosecutor's office of Guangxi Province issued a press release to a newspaper based upon documents prepared by the prosecutor regarding the arrest of two judges who were alleged to have committed the crime of official malpractice.[20] Afterward, however, the two judges were found not guilty and their exoneration was officially recorded by the court. The official and the newspaper did not update or correct the previous press release. The two judges sued the official and the newspaper, and won. The court's reasoning was that there was no wrong when the official and the newspaper first reported that the two judges were arrested based on papers filed in court. However, the official and the newspaper were held to be at fault for not correcting their previous damaging reports when the judges were exonerated and such exoneration had been recorded by the court.

b. Government-issued documents?

Yes. Newspapers need not report on governmental documents or decisions with absolute accuracy, as noted above with respect to opinion and fair comment. Official newspapers, at least, have been granted some latitude, at least in reporting on behavior that the government seeks to curb. The *Liberation Army Daily,* for example, won a lawsuit over an article that claimed a young man had changed his identity to hide prior crimes of gang rape and theft.[21] Police records revealed that he had been involved in theft and hooliganism, which the court held were close enough to gang rape and theft, considering that the point of the story was that he had changed his identity to hide his police record.

Similarly, the *Wenzhou Daily* prevailed in a suit brought by a singer whom the paper had called a convicted rapist.[22] He had actually been convicted of hooliganism, not rape, but the court found that the two crimes were equally serious in the public eye. (His additional argument that he had served his sentence and should no longer be identified as an ex-convict was also rejected.) Another PRC newspaper won a case brought by a Hong Kong businessman in 1988 over an article that criticized him for "zhapian" (a criminal offense of deception or fraud) when he had in fact been held liable for "qipian" (misrepresentation, which is not a criminal offense).[23] It remains to be seen whether foreign or nonofficial news outlets and individual defamation defendants would benefit from the same degree of latitude these newspapers have enjoyed, with their official sanction and supervision.

c. Quasi-governmental proceedings?

Government agencies, social organizations (such as the branches of the China Youth League or Women's Protection Association), enterprises (including businesses), and other institutions may not be held liable for defamation for decisions made about their internal operations. For instance, the Hunan Institute of Foreign Language and Foreign Trade disciplined six students for drunkenness and sexual conduct and announced that disciplinary decision to all of its students. The court of first instance accepted the defamation case the six students filed, ruled in favor of them, and awarded them more than RMB200,000 for the harm to their reputations. An appellate court reversed, holding that the case should never have been accepted in the first place because it challenged an internal decision of the Institute. (The Case Receipt Office of a Chinese court screens all cases submitted and is responsible for rejecting cases that do not assert legitimate causes of action, before any further proceedings take place.) If a business or institution disseminates false statements about disciplinary proceedings to outsiders, however, it may be sued. Whether newspapers that correctly report those statements may be held liable remains an open question, but would probably depend on the degree of care shown by the publisher.

11. Is there a privilege for republishing statements made earlier by other, bona fide, reliable publications or wire services?

No. Under Chinese law, not only publishers but also republishers have the obligation to examine the truth of the articles they publish or republish. Therefore, if a republisher does not independently examine the truth of statements or otherwise republishes them with some fault, the republisher may be held liable. However, due to the special position of the government-run Xinhua News Agency in China, the republication of statements issued by the Xinhua News Agency may be redistributed without liability.

A 1985 case illustrates this rule. A journal called *Women's Literature* first published a news story. Later, three other journals republished the same story. An individual filed suit for defamation against the author of the news story, *Women's Literature,* and the three other journals.[24] The court determined that the article defamed the plaintiff and that all four journals had committed defamation by publishing or republishing the article without adequately examining the truth of the story.

12. Are there any restrictions regarding reporting on:

a. Ongoing criminal investigations?

There is no specific provision in China prohibiting or imposing restrictions upon reporting on ongoing criminal investigations, except to the extent that such reporting may reveal State secrets. And, the information about criminal investigations must come directly from a police official authorized to share it with reporters.

b. Ongoing criminal prosecutions?

Access to courtrooms is not specifically guaranteed to reporters. The public has a right of access to judicial proceedings, except in cases involving State secrets, trade secrets, divorce, individual privacy, or crimes committed by minors, but reporters are required to request permission, in writing, to attend public court proceedings. If they are discovered taking notes or making recordings without permission, reporters may be removed from courtrooms and their notebooks, tape recorders, and video cameras may be confiscated.

Reporters often do not attend court proceedings because the courts have public relations departments that issue summaries of proceedings for the purpose of public education. If a reporter requests permission to attend a trial and report on it, permission may be granted (on the condition that the reporter report without bias and not tendentiously), but the court may also have one of its own reporters prepare a summary. Newspapers may reprint the official summaries, but any revisions the newspaper may make to that summary should be approved by the court.

c. Ongoing regulatory investigations?

None, with the exception that reporting on matters involving State secrets is strongly proscribed.

d. Ongoing civil litigation, or other judicial proceedings?

None, although it may be helpful for reporters seeking access to courts to know that news reports of criminal or civil cases involving foreign individuals or companies, or foreign subject matter, must not be published before the embassy or consulate of the foreign country has been informed of the case. The court or government agency should notify the embassy or consulate.

13. Are prior restraints or other prepublication injunctions available on the basis of libel or privacy, and if so, what are the standards for obtaining such relief?

There is no provision of law that specifically addresses this issue. However, injunctions to cease publication of material that has been found to be defamatory are available, and it seems reasonable to anticipate that a court may grant a prior restraint if the plaintiff proves before publication that the material is defamatory. Oftentimes, internal control exercised by press entities helps to prevent such cases from reaching the courts.

Some other possible remedies for defamation in China are noted below, as are administratively enforced restrictions on publishing materials on certain sensitive topics or expressing certain views.

14. Is a right of privacy recognized (either civilly or criminally)?

a. What is the definition of "private fact"?

The term "private fact" has not been defined by the law in China. Judges and lawyers identify private facts by applying the common meaning of the words in light of prevailing concepts of morality as endorsed and accepted by society at large. The most widely accepted definition of "private facts" in China is facts of private life that a person is not willing to have disclosed and that have nothing to do with the person's public social life. It appears to be not too different from the concept of a "reasonable person" standard. Generally, an individual's health status, disease, disability, family life, private diary, private letters, and the like are regarded as private facts.

One category of private facts that the Supreme Court has specifically addressed resembles the old *per se* libel category of "loathsome disease." Medical and health care institutions violate the law protecting reputation if they disclose that a person suffers from gonorrhea, syphilis, AIDS, or Hansen's disease (leprosy), but they may notify relatives of such illnesses.

b. Is there a public interest or newsworthiness exception?

No public interest or newsworthiness exception is recognized. In China, unlike many Western legal systems, the right of privacy is included within the right of reputation. It is unlawful to publicly disclose private facts about an individual in oral or written form, or to publish private materials without permission, where such disclosure and publication do harm to the reputation of the concerned party. If the reputation of the concerned party is not harmed, the right of privacy will not be found to have been violated, even though private information was published.

In a 1998 case, a transsexual individual accepted a visit by a news reporter and provided certain information about why he chose transsexuality.[25] However, during the visit, the individual repeatedly told the reporter that he could write a news story about him, but that the report should not disclose his real name and photo. The news reporter ignored those requests and published a report in a newspaper with the individual's real name and photo. The individual filed and won a lawsuit against the reporter and the newspaper that published the article.

Businesses do not have privacy rights but may be able to protect confidential information as trade secrets. Information about executive compensation, for instance, may be published if it is available from public filings. If the information comes from a source with a duty to keep it confidential, however, some form of trade secret protection may apply. A publisher may face liability for publishing a trade secret if the publisher knew, before publishing it, that the information was obtained by theft, threat, promise of gain, or some other unlawful or inappropriate means. As a matter of practice, when publishers receive documents disclosed without authorization, they generally contact the business entity involved and do not publish the information without its consent.

c. Is the right of privacy based in common law, statute, or constitution?

The right to privacy is based upon statutes and the Constitution. China employs the civil law system and does not recognize the concept of common law.

15. May reporters tape-record their own telephone conversations for note-taking purposes (not rebroadcast) without the consent of the other party?

There is no prohibition of such taping in Chinese law.

16. If permissible to record such tapes, may they be broadcast without permission?

There is no prohibition of broadcasting secretly recorded tapes, but the content of tapes may raise defamation issues. If nothing on the tapes will harm the reputation or character of any individual, and the statements on the tapes record the truth, there should be no liability. But both the taper and the broadcaster may be liable if material that is broadcast is found to be defamatory. A legal interpretation issued by the Supreme Court provides that, if a news source actively provides news material or expressly permits the publication of it, the source will be deemed to have defamed the concerned party if the material is defamatory.

17. Is there a recognized evidentiary privilege preventing the disclosure of confidential sources relied upon by reporters?

There is no such provision in Chinese law.

18. In the event that legal papers are served upon the newsroom (such as a civil complaint), are there any particular warnings about accepting service of which we should be aware?

In the event that a civil complaint is served, the newsroom may accept it or refuse it. If the newsroom wishes to accept it, the chairman, legal representative, or other person authorized to receive external documents on behalf of the newsroom must sign the receipt in his or her name and record the date of service. If it does not want to accept service, it may tell the delivery person so. However, the documents will still be deemed to have been served, so long as the delivery person records the refusal and leaves the complaint at the newsroom's registered business address before a witness who signs the service sheet to attest that service was made.

If the complaint names the news organization, not accepting service will probably be useless. If, on the other hand, the complaint names only an individual employee or independent contractor, it is not necessary for the news organization to accept service on the individual's behalf. Accepting service for the employee or independent contractor will not make the organization a defendant, but there is usually no reason for an organization to accept service on an employee's or contractor's behalf, especially if the organization itself is not a party. As in the newsroom situation, an individual employee may also refuse to accept service. However, a complaint will be deemed to have been served if the refusal is properly witnessed and documented.

In the event that a request for cooperation in an administrative or criminal investigation is served, you should make sure that there are two investigators on site. You should also check their identity certificates to see whether the certificates and the investigators sent are consistent and whether the identity certificates are properly sealed. You should also check whether the legal request is properly signed and chopped. If you have any questions, you may make a call to the investigators' bureau chief for confirmation. If everything is real, you must to cooperate with the investigation.

19. Has your jurisdiction applied established media law to Internet publishers?

Yes, the same rules are applied to Internet publishers, as a 2001 case illustrates.[26] The plaintiff was one of the administrators of a chat room, using a screen name. The defendant was a registered user of the same chat room and another chat room of the same Web site, using two different screen names. The plaintiff and the defendant met each other at a party held by the users of the chat rooms. Afterward, the defendant began to post articles in the chat room to insult and defame the plaintiff, using the screen name of the plaintiff, and the plaintiff sued. The court held that, although the space on the Internet is virtual, the actions taken by people on the Internet are real. The acts of the defendant resulted in damage to the plaintiff's reputation in the chat room and among people the plaintiff and defendant knew, who knew their real names. The defendant was held liable for defamation and was ordered to post an apology in the chat room and on the Web site and to pay RMB1,000 for the plaintiff's mental anguish, as well as court costs.

20. If established media law has been applied to Internet publishers, are there any ways in which Internet publishers (including chat room operators) have to meet different standards?

Different standards have not been developed at this time. No cases filed against ISPs or chat room or bulletin board operators have been found.

21. Are there any cases where the courts enforced a judgment in libel from another jurisdiction against a publisher in your jurisdiction?

None have been found. Chinese courts may enforce judgments rendered in jurisdictions with which China has entered into treaties providing for the enforcement of judgments on a reciprocal basis.

APPENDIX

Navigating Media Law in China

Because the Chinese media and legal systems are so different from the media and legal systems elsewhere, many basic principles and practices in Chinese journalism differ significantly from those of the rest of the world. The following are some differences worth keeping in mind.

1. Parties

In China, defamation claims may be asserted on behalf of individuals who are deceased. Suits may be filed by lineal relations, namely spouses, parents, children, siblings, grandparents, or grandchildren.

In media cases, both author and publisher may be sued, unless the author is employed by or is under the administrative control of the publisher, in which case the Supreme Court has indicated that only the publisher may be named as a defendant. News sources may be sued as well as media outlets, but only if the sources have authorized the media to publish the news the sources provide.

2. Remedies

In addition to awards of damages and injunctions to cease publication, courts may order defendants to apologize and to publish retractions, clarifications, and apologies to the same extent that the original statements were published, in order to restore the reputation of the defamed party. Pursuant to the 1998 interpretation of the Supreme Court, courts will examine and approve retractions, clarifications, and apologies before they are published. If a defendant fails or refuses to print a correction or clarification, the court may publicly announce its decision to help remedy the damage the defamation caused.

3. Sensitive Topics

The media in China are subject to direct government controls, but many news organizations are able to operate without day-to-day supervision because the government has established lists of "restricted" and "prohibited" topics to guide their treatment of sensitive issues.

The list of outright prohibitions, summarized below, is directed generally at preventing the expression of particular views. Editors in chief are responsible for ensuring that "prohibited" articles are not published. The penalties for publishing prohibited items may include large fines, suspension or revocation of the license to publish, and criminal prosecution.

"Restricted" topics, also outlined below, are general subjects on which views the government considers as dangerous could be expressed. Articles about such subjects are not banned outright, but publishers are required to submit the articles to be reviewed and "recorded" through the local branch of the China News and Publications Administration prior to publication. The approval and "recording" of an article protects the publisher from punishment for statements made on a potentially perilous topic, while serving as surveillance radar for the government and the Communist Party. Publishers make their own decisions about which articles to submit for review and recording, but the rule requires approval and recording before publishing on one of the restricted topics.

a. Prohibited articles

The State Council of the PRC, in its Regulation on the Administration of Publications (2002), has listed the following types of articles that may not be published:

- Articles that oppose basic principles set out in the Constitution of the PRC. An example might be an article asserting that men are superior to women and therefore should have greater rights. Equal rights and status are guaranteed by the Constitution.
- Articles that may do harm to the integrity, sovereignty, and completeness of the dominion of the PRC. Calling for the independence of Taiwan, for instance, is forbidden. Articles about the debate over independence for Taiwan may be published, but they may not reach the conclusion that independence for Taiwan is appropriate.
- Articles that disclose State secrets or harm the safety of the PRC (see above).
- Articles that may do harm to the glory and interests of the PRC. Insulting generalizations about the Chinese people, government, and military are prohibited. However, criticism of particular people or institutions with regard to particular matters is not precluded.
- Articles that promote divisions between peoples in China, destroy

solidarity, and harm the customs of minority groups. China has many ethnic minority groups, including Tibetan, Uigher, and Miao peoples. Criticisms of minority groups are not permitted, nor is the advocacy of independence or greater autonomy for them.

- Articles that promote sex, superstition, false science, murder, or violence.
- Articles that harm the morality of society and negate or erode respected cultural traditions. For instance, an article exhorting young people not to feel obligated to take care of elderly parents would not be permitted.
- Articles that defame or insult anyone (see above).
- Articles that deny the need for society to be guided by Marxism, Leninism, the system of thought of Mao Zedong, and the theories of Deng Xiaoping.
- Articles that depart from the strategies and policies of the Chinese Communist Party.
- Articles that conflict with official policy on religions in a way that affects social stability. The Chinese government is officially neutral on religion, and articles that discriminate against particular religions are not allowed. On the other hand, religion may not be exalted as a source of authority superior to the Communist Party.
- Articles that promote vulgarity, base tastes, or incorrect political views. For the most part, this prohibition concerns promoting sex, drug use, drinking, and Western democracy.
- Articles that spread rumors or false news and interfere with the work of the Communist Party and the government. This prohibition could be broadly applied.

b. Restricted topics

The China News and Publications Administration, in its Rules on Recording of Sensitive Subjects Selected for Books, Journals, Videotapes and Electronic Publications (1997), set out the following list of "restricted" topics on which official approval should be sought for publication:

- The important documents of the Communist Party and the State.
- The work and life of current and former important leaders of the Communist Party and the government.
- State secrets and confidential information of the Communist Party.
- The structure of the government and its Communist Party and administrative leadership.
- The various peoples and religions of China.
- National defense and the campaigns, battles, lives, and important figures of the People's Liberation Army in every historical period.

- The Cultural Revolution.
- Important events and figures in the history of the Chinese Communist Party.
- Figures at high levels of the Kuomintang (the Nationalist Chinese Party, which established the current government on Taiwan) and other parties defeated by the Communist Party in China. Chiang Kai-shek is the most prominent example. One or more recent articles reflecting somewhat favorably on his patriotism have probably been officially vetted.
- Important events and leaders of the former Soviet Union, Eastern Europe, communist parties, and other friendly parties in other countries.
- Maps of the territory of China.
- Books published in the Hong Kong Special Administrative Region, Macao, and Taiwan.
- Translations of ancient novels into contemporary language.
- Imported comic books or videotapes.
- Lists containing contact information for individual enterprises.

Although articles on such topics are not forbidden, the government has put publishers on notice that they should be submitted for review. Publishers therefore proceed at some risk, but guidance can be drawn from precedents established by other publishers.

Chapter Notes

1. China Const. Art. 38.

2. Opinions of the People's Supreme Court of China on Several Issues in Implementing the General Principles of Civil Law of China (1990), Art. 140.

3. See cases collected at H.L. Fu & Richard Cullen, *Media Law in the PRC* (1996), 193.

4. Replies of the People's Supreme Court of China to Several Questions in Hearing Defamation Cases (1993), Reply 7.

5. *Li Guzhen v. Tuan Jie News Press for Defamation,* Ref. No. 115212000014, Intermediate People's Court of Miao Autonomous Prefecture (September 11, 2000), Laws and Regulations of China (CD available from China National Information Center).

6. Chen Xiaoyan, *China Journalist,* June 2000.

7. Interpretations of the People's Supreme Court of China on Several Questions in Hearing Defamation Cases (1998), Reply 9.

8. Replies of the People's Supreme Court of China to Several Questions in Hearing Defamation Cases (1993), Reply 9.

9. *Hu Jichao, Zhou Kongzhao and Shi Shucheng v. Liu Shouzhong and Zunyi Evening News for Defamation,* Ref. No. 113216199202, Intermediate People's Court of Zunyi (June 20, 1992), Laws and Regulations of China (CD published by China National Information Center).

10. *News and Media Torts* (Cao Ruilin, ed.), in *Theory and Legal Practice of Compensation for Damages* (Zhu Mingshan, gen. ed.) (Publishing House of the People's Court, 2000).

11. Cited in Fu & Cullen, *supra,* at 199.

12. See, e.g., Fu & Cullen, *supra,* at 200–201, 204–07.

13. *News and Media Torts, supra,* at 113.

14. China Trial Review (1994), cited in Fu & Cullen, *supra,* at 200.

15. *News and Media Torts, supra,* at 146.

16. Wei Yongzhen, *Bei Gao Xi Shang de Ji Zhe* (Reporter as Defendant) 52 (Shanghai People's Publishing House, 1994).

17. *Id.*

18. Wei, *supra,* at 14.

19. Interpretations of the People's Supreme Court of China on Several Questions in Hearing Defamation Cases (1998), Reply 6.

20. *Huang Shiguan and Huang Xinde v. Guangxi Legal News Press and Fan Baozhong for Defamation* (Guangxi High Court 2001), in *Disputes on Defamation* (Zhu Mingshan, ed.), 219 (China Legal Publishing House, 2003).

21. Hu & Cullen, *supra,* at 202.

22. Wei, *supra,* at 52.

23. *Id.* at 61–62.

24. *Wang Faying v. Liu Zhen, Women's Literature (and three other magazines) for Defamation,* Ref. No. 113216198901, Hebei High Court (July 5, 1989), Laws and Regulations of China, *supra.*

25. *Li X (anonymous) v. Hao Dongbai for Defamation,* Ref. No. 115211999067, Lanzhou Intermediate People's Court (November 17, 1999), Laws and Regulations of China, *supra.*

26. *Zhang Jing v. Yu Lingfeng for Defamation on the Internet,* Ref. No. 113216200103, Nanjing Gulou District Court (July 16, 2001), Laws and Regulations of China, *supra.*

CHAPTER 6

Hong Kong

PETER KARANJIA AND EDWARD J. DAVIS

Davis Wright Tremaine LLP

WITH JILL COTTRELL

University of Hong Kong

Davis Wright Tremaine LLP
1633 Broadway
New York, NY 10019 USA
Phone: 212-489-8230
Fax: 212-489-8340
www.dwt.com
peterkaranjia@dwt.com
eddavis@dwt.com

Introduction to the Hong Kong Legal System

As a consequence of its historical status as a British colony, Hong Kong relies heavily on English cases as a source of law and a touchstone for the development of legal principles in the area of tort law. Decisions of courts in other Commonwealth common law jurisdictions, such as Australia, are also influential, and the Hong Kong Constitution, the Basic Law, provides that the decisions of "other common law jurisdictions" may be relied on as precedents. According to Hong Kong practitioners, there is not a great body of defamation law in Hong Kong. Many of the cases are not extensively argued, and some decisions seem to have been reached without full appreciation of their implications.

This is the only area of civil law in which there may be trial by jury in Hong Kong; in fact there have been a handful of such trials over the last ten years.

1. What is the locally accepted definition of libel?

Courts in Hong Kong generally look to English sources for the basic concepts of libel and its general elements and defenses. For example, referring to the English text, *Gatley on Libel and Slander* ("*Gatley*"), as the "leading textbook," one Hong Kong court applied the following "working definition of defamation": "Defamation is committed when the defendant publishes to a third person words or matter containing an untrue imputation against the reputation of the plaintiff."[1]

Citing various English authorities, a textbook on Hong Kong tort law explains that words may be considered to have a defamatory meaning not only if they expose the plaintiff to "hatred, ridicule or contempt," but also if they "tend [...] to lower the plaintiff in the estimation of right-thinking members of society generally" or have the effect of causing members of society to shun the plaintiff.[2] Allegedly libelous words are considered in their "ordinary and natural meaning."[3]

When ridicule can amount to defamation is a controversial issue in most legal systems, but ridicule has been successfully relied on in Hong Kong, notably in the case of *Li Yau-wai, Eric v. Genesis Films Ltd.* [1987] HKLR 711, where the plaintiff's photograph had been used in a bawdy movie to represent a deceased fictional character. The picture was used as a focus for entreaties by another character to send his mother (the deceased's wife) erotic dreams. This elicited mirth from the audience, teasing from the plaintiff's friends, and embarrassment for him. Without extensive analysis, the court held that this exposed the plaintiff to ridicule "of such a nature as to amount to defamation."

Hong Kong courts have generally followed English cases in treating defamatory statements as libel (as opposed to slander) when they are published in permanent form (for example, in books and newspapers). Section 22 of Hong Kong's Defamation Ordinance clarifies that "[f]or the purposes of the law of libel and slander, the broadcasting of words shall be treated as publication in permanent form." Accordingly, radio and television broadcasts containing defamatory statements would be considered libelous.

2. Is libel-by-implication recognized, or, in the alternative, must the complained-of words alone defame the plaintiff?

Hong Kong courts effectively recognize the concept of libel-by-implication. However, they generally distinguish between two types of innuendo: "popular" innuendo and "true" or "legal" innuendo.

The first refers to secondary meanings of words that require no special knowledge to perceive; the second requires that the audience for the allegedly libelous statement know of some circumstances that make superficially innocent words defamatory or add a further defamatory meaning to words that are defamatory in their natural meaning. As explained below, the distinction between the two categories has ramifications for the pleading requirements imposed on the plaintiff:

> First, the cause of action based on popular innuendo. If the plaintiff relies on the natural meaning of the words ... he must, in his statement of claim, specify the person or persons to whom they were published; save in the case of a newspaper or periodical which is published to the world at large, when the persons are so numerous as to go without saying—or book, I would add.
>
> Secondly, the cause of action based on a legal innuendo. If the plaintiff relies on some special circumstances which convey (to some particular person or persons knowing these circumstances) a special defamatory meaning other than the natural and ordinary meaning of the words ..., then he must in his statement of claim specify the particular person or persons to whom they were published and the special circumstances known to that person or persons.... In the second cause of action there is no exception in the case of a newspaper: because the words would not be so understood by the world at large; but only by the particular person or persons who know the special circumstances.[4]

In *Beijing Television,* the plaintiff television company sued for libel over a statement that it had "met with bad luck .... [T]he Television's popular lady program-in-charge [sic] Du Yu and the Deputy Minister of Broadcast ... had their adulterous affair exposed, and they were caught at the scene during their adulterous acts in bed. This scandal caught the leaders of Beijing Television with great embarrassment." The plaintiff pleaded as "special circumstances" supporting a defamatory innuendo (*inter alia*) the "type of the programme, the expected clean image of Du Yu in a programme for personal, family emotional life and relationships, the PRC audience it catered for, ... [and] the expectation of its audience and advertisers and the stricter moral and social standards observed in the Mainland." Based on these facts, the court declined to dismiss the action at the pleading stage. However, this is an imperfect example of innuendo—the facts relied on, such as the type of program and its audience, do not add a hidden meaning to the statement complained of; they pertain to how a particular audience would judge the plaintiff rather than what that audience would take the particular words about the plaintiff to mean.

Consistent with English cases, Hong Kong courts have also held that, in determining the meaning of the words, the court must view the statements as would the "hypothetical reasonable reader" who is "not naïve but ... is [also] not unduly suspicious."[5] According to these courts, this "reasonable reader" can:

read between the lines. He can read in an implication more readily than a lawyer, and may indulge in a certain amount of loose thinking. But he must be treated as being a man who is not avid for scandal and someone who does not, and should not, select one bad meaning where other non-defamatory meanings are available.[6]

3. May corporations sue for libel?

Yes. It is well established that corporations may sue for libel, and media companies have also sued each other for libel. Nonbusiness entities may also sue.[7] A university has also been found to have standing to sue.[8]

4. Is product disparagement recognized, and if so, how does that differ from libel?

Yes. This tort differs from libel in various ways. The plaintiff must prove that the statement was untrue, that it was primarily motivated by malice—that is, by a desire to injure the plaintiff—and unless one of two conditions applies, that actual, provable damage resulted. Under the common law, actual damage always had to be proved, but the common law has been changed to some extent by Section 24(1) of the Defamation Ordinance, which created two exceptions to the need to establish actual damage: if either (a) the statement was "calculated" (which means likely) to cause pecuniary damage and was published in written or permanent form; or (b) the statement complained of was "calculated" to cause such damage to the plaintiff in connection with any office, profession, calling, trade, or business.

5. Must an individual be clearly identified (by name or photograph) to sue for libel? Can a group of persons sue for libel, even though not named?

No. To be sued upon, a statement need not explicitly identify the plaintiff by name or image. Hong Kong courts have held that veiled references to plaintiffs in fictional works and newspapers (even using a fictitious name or nickname) may be sufficient to identify the plaintiff.[9]

Hong Kong courts also recognize some forms of "group libel" if the words complained of can be reasonably understood to refer to the plaintiff(s). For example, in *Sin Cho Chiu v. Tin Tin Publication Development Ltd. & Another,*[10] the defendant newspaper reported that a "delegation of elders of the securities industry" (including the plaintiff, who was named in the article in question) had gone to Beijing and added—without referring specifically to the plaintiff—that "most of the members of the delegation are 'tainted elements.'" The court held that since the "ordinary reader" would naturally look elsewhere in the article to discover the identity of the "tainted" members and would have little difficulty in concluding that the plaintiff was one of them, based on various references to the plaintiff, the plaintiff could sue.

6. What is the fault standard(s) applied to libel?

a. Does the fault standard depend on the fame or notoriety of the plaintiff?

No. Consistent with its roots in the English common law, libel is a strict liability tort and once the plaintiff has proved that a defamatory statement was made about him or her, the burden shifts to the defendant to prove that one of the applicable defenses applies.

b. Is there a heightened fault standard or privilege for reporting on matters of public concern or public interest?

A heightened fault standard may apply if any of the several defenses listed below, which take into account the degree of the defendant's fault, can be invoked.

1. *"Innocent Dissemination."* This can be viewed as a defense or as a plea of "not published." The principle can be relied on by booksellers, libraries, and distributors, but not by printers or publishers, who can be presumed to have the opportunity to read what is being disseminated. It amounts to saying that the defendant played a part in disseminating the publication but without actual knowledge of the defamatory nature of any of the published material and without being negligent as to whether it contained defamatory matter.[11]

2. *Lack of Malice.* Although it is not an element of the plaintiff's cause of action, the absence of malice is a common element of several defenses at common law. If a defendant has successfully invoked a defense that is vitiated by a showing of malice, malice must generally be provoked by the plaintiff.[12]

3. *The Qualified Privilege.* The qualified privilege long recognized by the common law in England is commonly said to arise where the defendant is under a duty or has an interest in communicating the allegedly defamatory statement to the recipient of the statement and the latter also has a reciprocal duty or interest in receiving it. It is well established that certain reports are privileged at common law.

The qualified privilege is defeated where the defendant has acted with "malice"—i.e., either what U.S. lawyers would call "common law malice" ("ill will or spite") or something closely approximating *"New York Times"* or "constitutional" malice (in the sense of reckless disregard for truth or falsity). Malice has also been described in somewhat amorphous terms as a defendant's misuse of the privilege. For purposes of defeating the quali-fied privilege, it makes no difference whether the plaintiff is a public or otherwise well known figure.

The House of Lords in *Reynolds v. Times Newspapers Ltd.*[13] declined to follow the alternative approach taken by the High Court of Austra-lia in *Lange v. Australian Broadcasting Corporation.*[14] In *Lange,* the court held that a qualified privilege protects the publication of information, opinions, and arguments concerning governmental and political matters, subject to the publisher proving the reasonableness of its conduct. Lord Nicholls, in *Reynolds,* insisted that there be no special rule for political and governmental matters, but that the privilege be available, more broadly, for statements on matters of serious public concern. According to Hong Kong practitioners, thus far, neither the *Reynolds* nor the *Lange* privilege has been argued in the Hong Kong courts.

Whether or not this privilege can be successfully invoked depends on a number of nonexclusive factors identified by Lord Nicholls in *Reynolds,* including:

1. The seriousness of the allegation. The more serious the charge, the more the public is misinformed and the individual harmed, if the allegation is not true.
2. The nature of the information and the extent to which the subject-matter is a matter of public concern.
3. The source of the information. Some informants have no direct knowledge of the events. Some have their own axes to grind, or are being paid for their stories.
4. The steps taken to verify the information.
5. The status of the information. The allegation may have already been the subject of an investigation which commands respect.
6. The urgency of the matter. News is often a perishable commodity.
7. Whether comment was sought from the plaintiff. He may have in-formation others do not possess or have not disclosed. An approach to the plaintiff will not always be necessary, but it will almost always help.
8. Whether the article contained the gist of the plaintiff's side of the story.
9. The tone of the article. A newspaper can raise queries or call for an investigation. It need not adopt allegations as statements of fact.
10. The circumstances of the publication, including the timing.[15]

4. *Fair Comment.* The defense of fair comment (see Question 8 be-low) is available in Hong Kong and is likewise defeated by a finding of

malice, although the inquiry is framed in a distinctive manner and, in this context, malice has a restricted meaning. Here, malice means that the defendant did not have an honest belief in the truth of the statement he or she made. As Lord Nicholls explained in the Hong Kong case *Cheng & Another v. Tse Wai Chun*,[16] one of the four elements of the defense is that "the comment must be one which could have been made by an honest person, however prejudiced he may be, and however exaggerated or obstinate his views." While the *Cheng* court, following the English cases, emphasized that "a critic need not be mealy-mouthed in denouncing what he disagrees with," many of the English authorities (including the *Reynolds* case), support the principle that the privilege "cannot be used as a cloak for mere invective."

5. **Statutory Defenses.** Under Section 4 of the Hong Kong Defamation Ordinance (C. 21), which has been relied upon in a few cases, a newspaper can plead as a defense to libel that:

> The libel was inserted in the newspaper without actual malice and without gross negligence, and that before the commencement of the action, or at the earliest opportunity afterwards, [the defendant] inserted in the newspaper a full apology for the libel, or if the newspaper in which the libel appeared is ordinarily published at intervals exceeding 1 week, had offered to publish the said apology in any newspaper to be selected by the plaintiff in the action ....
>
> Provided that it shall not be competent to any defendant in such action to set up any defence without at the same time making a payment of money into court by way of amends, and every such defence so filed without such payment into court shall be deemed a nullity and may be treated as such by the plaintiff in the action.

A newspaper defendant unsuccessfully invoked Section 4 in *Chu Siu Kuk Yuen, Jessie v. Apple Daily Ltd.*[17] The paper mistakenly identified the plaintiff solicitor (attorney) in a report about a solicitor in the same building who disappeared with a large quantity of money. Because the newspaper had failed to perform simple fact-checking, it was unable to establish the absence of gross negligence, though it was not guilty of actual malice or defamation by deliberate intention. (The decision provides no detailed discussion of these concepts.)

Section 25 of the Defamation Ordinance provides a further statutory defense for "[u]nintentional defamation" and, like the Section 4 defense, calls for "an offer of amends." According to Hong Kong practitioners, it has not yet been relied upon. Section 25 states:

(1) A person who has published words alleged to be defamatory of another person may, if he claims that the words were published by him innocently in relation to that other person, make an offer of amends under this section; and in any such case–

    (a) if the offer is accepted by the party aggrieved and is duly performed, no proceedings for libel or slander shall be taken or continued by that party against the person making the offer ... (but without prejudice to any cause of action against any other person jointly responsible for that publication);

    (b) if the offer is not accepted by the party aggrieved, then, except as otherwise provided by this section, it shall be a defence, in any proceedings by him for libel or slander against the person making the offer ..., to prove that the words complained of were published by the defendant innocently in relation to the plaintiff and that the offer was made as soon as practicable after the defendant received notice that they were or might be defamatory of the plaintiff, and has not been withdrawn.

(2) An offer of amends under this section must be expressed to be made for the purposes of this section, and must be accompanied by an affidavit specifying the facts relied upon by the person making it to show that the words in question were published by him innocently in relation to the party aggrieved; and for the purposes of a defence under Subsection (1)(b) no evidence, other than evidence of facts specified in the affidavit, shall be admissible on behalf of that person to prove that the words were so published.

(3) An offer of amends under this section shall be understood to mean an offer–

    (a) in any case, to publish or join in the publication of a suitable correction of the words complained of, and a sufficient apology to the party aggrieved in respect of those words;

    (b) where copies of a document or record containing the said words have been distributed by or with the knowledge of the person making the offer, to take such steps as are reasonably practicable on his part for notifying persons to whom copies have been so distributed that the words are alleged to be defamatory of the party aggrieved.

"Malice" also enters the analysis if an offer of amends is rejected. The publisher may not then rely on a defense of innocent publication unless the publisher can prove that the author acted without malice:

(6) Subsection (1)(b) shall not apply in relation to the publication by any person of words of which he is not the author unless he proves that the words were written by the author without malice.

7. Is financial news about publicly traded companies, or companies involved with a government contract, considered a matter of public interest or otherwise privileged?

Yes. Reports about such companies would fall within the general heading of matters of public interest, and their affairs would generally be appropriate subjects for the defense of fair comment. But there is no blanket restriction that would prevent such companies from suing.

8. Is there a recognized protection for opinion or "fair comment" on matters of public concern?

Yes. As mentioned above, the well-established qualified privilege for fair comment under the English common law has been largely followed by Hong Kong courts. In the *Cheng* case, Lord Nicholls identified the following "non-controversial" principles governing the privilege for fair comment:

1. "the comment must be on a matter of public interest" [which is] "not to be confined within narrow limits."

2. "the comment must be recognisable as comment, as distinct from an imputation of fact. If the imputation is one of fact, a ground of defence must be sought elsewhere, for example justification [i.e., the defense of truth]."

3. "the comment must be based on facts which are true or protected by privilege …. If the facts on which the comment purports to be founded are not proved to be true or published on a privileged occasion, the defence of fair comment is not available."

4. "the comment must explicitly or implicitly indicate, at least in general terms, what are the facts on which the comment is being made. The reader or hearer should be in a position to judge for himself how far the comment was well founded."

5. "the comment must be one which could have been made by an honest person, however prejudiced he might be, and however exaggerated or obstinate his views."

Despite Lord Nicholls' instruction that matters of public interest should not be narrowly construed, the concept of public interest applied by courts in Hong Kong may be surprisingly narrow.

In *Li Ching v. Koo Too Shing*,[18] the court held that the affairs of a 200-odd clansmen's organization in Yuen Long were "of supreme indifference to outsiders" and were therefore not a matter of public interest. However, a more recent decision held that the behavior of a major shareholder in a publicly listed company in selling his shares was a matter of public interest. In that case, the judge found that a prominent figure in the business community, vice chairman of a public company which owned a daily newspaper with a very wide circulation in Hong Kong, who was selling his entire shareholding in the company over a period of barely one week, for approximately $143 million, was "plainly a matter of public interest, and worthy of comment by persons involved in the media."[19]

9. Are there any requirements upon a plaintiff, such as demand for retraction or right of reply, and if so, what impact do they have?

No. There are no provisions requiring a plaintiff to seek a retraction. If a defendant wishes to rely on the statutory defense contained in Section 4 of the Hong Kong Defamation Ordinance, which protects publishers who act without actual malice or gross negligence, the defendant must publish "a full apology for the libel" before an action is commenced or at the earliest opportunity thereafter, or, "if the newspaper in which the libel appeared is ordinarily published at intervals exceeding 1 week, [the defendant must offer] to publish the ... apology in any newspaper to be selected by the plaintiff in the action ..." and must satisfy the other conditions contained in Section 4, including the payment of amends into court. Similarly, the statutory defense of Section 25 of the Defamation Ordinance for "[u]nintentional defamation" requires an "offer of amends" as described in the response to Question 6 above.

A form of right of reply is included in the requirements for qualified privileges for fair and accurate reports of certain official or public proceedings. (See, e.g., response to Question 10a. below.)

10. Is there a privilege for quoting or reporting on:

a. Papers filed in court?

Reports of court proceedings are subject to a qualified privilege at common law, if the proceedings themselves are in public. Section 13 of the Hong Kong Defamation Ordinance contains a broad and presumably absolute privilege for the press in covering litigation. This is based on English legislation and in England the privilege is treated as absolute. Hong Kong courts should follow suit:

> (1) A fair and accurate report in any newspaper or broadcast of proceedings publicly heard before any court shall, if published contemporaneously with such proceedings, be privileged: Provided that nothing in this section shall authorize the publication of any blasphemous or indecent matter.[20]

Section 14 of the Defamation Ordinance also provides a statutory qualified privilege, which may be defeated by a showing of malice, for certain specifically enumerated types of "fair and accurate" reports (including reports of quasi-governmental bodies as well as many government tribunals and commissions). Certain fair and accurate proceedings in this category are privileged unless they are published with "malice" or published without providing a sufficient "explanation or contradiction," if the plaintiff has requested one, i.e., "if it is proved that the defendant has been requested by the plaintiff to publish in the manner in which the original publication was made a reasonable letter or statement by way of explanation or contradiction, and has refused or neglected to do so, or has done so in a manner not adequate or not reasonable having regard to all the circumstances" (Defamation Ordinance § 14(2)).

Further, pursuant to Section 14(3) of the Defamation Ordinance, such statements are *not* protected if the publication is otherwise "prohibited by law" or is not regarding a matter that is "of public concern and the publication ... is not for the public benefit." English courts have held that these last two requirements—"public concern" and "public benefit"—are separate and both necessary.

b. Government-issued documents?

Yes. A copy or fair and accurate report or summary of any notice or other matter issued for the information of the public by or on behalf of any government department, or by or on behalf of the Commissioner of Police, is privileged. There is also protection for publication of an extract or abstract of a document published by order of the Legislative Council, under Defamation Ordinance Section 12.

c. Quasi-governmental proceedings?

Yes, a fair and accurate report of the findings or decision of any of the following associations may be privileged:

1. an association formed in Hong Kong for the purpose of promoting or encouraging the exercise of or interest in any art, science, religion or learning, and empowered by its constitution to exercise control over or adjudicate upon matters of interest or concern to the association;

2. an association formed in Hong Kong for the purpose of promoting or safeguarding the interests of any trade, business, industry or profession, or of the persons carrying on or engaged in any trade, business, industry or profession, and empowered by its constitution to exercise control over or adjudicate upon matters connected with the trade, business, industry or profession, or the actions or conduct of those persons;

3. an association formed in Hong Kong for the purpose of promoting or safeguarding the interests of any game, sport or pastime to the

playing or exercise of which members of the public are invited or admitted;

4. any public meeting held in Hong Kong, that is to say, a meeting bona fide and lawfully held for a lawful purpose and for the furtherance or discussion of any matter of public concern, whether the admission to the meeting is general or restricted;

5. a report of the proceedings at a general meeting of any company or association constituted, registered or certified by or under any Ordinance or Act of Parliament or incorporated by Royal Charter, not being a private company within the meaning of the Companies Ordinance, Chapter 32;

6. a copy or fair and accurate report or summary of any notice or other matter issued for the information of the public by or on behalf of the Consumer Council;

7. a copy or fair and accurate report or summary of any report made or published under Section 16 or 16A of The Ombudsman Ordinance (C. 397);

8. a copy or fair and accurate report or summary of any report prepared and supplied for the purposes of Section 30 of the Mandatory Provident Fund Schemes Ordinance (C. 485) or prepared and published under Section 32 of that Ordinance. The privilege also extends to findings of international courts, public registers, and any notices published pursuant to court order.

11. Is there a privilege for republishing statements made earlier by other, bona fide, reliable publications or wire services?

No. Hong Kong courts follow the common law rule that the republication of a libel gives rise to liability in the same way as publication of the original libel: "a person who publishes a rumor by repeating it, albeit stating it to be a rumor, cannot justify the libel contained in that rumor by proving the existence of the rumor."[21]

12. Are there any restrictions regarding reporting on:

a. Ongoing criminal investigations?

Yes. There are various statutory restrictions on reports of criminal investigations, including investigations for bribery and drug trafficking. Under the Prevention of Bribery Ordinance Section 30, reports that could tip off targets are prohibited. Penalties for violations include a fine of up to $20,000 and imprisonment for up to one year.

This statute was unsuccessfully challenged in *Ming Pao Newspapers Limited And Others v. Attorney General Of Hong Kong*[22] as contrary to the freedom of expression secured by Article 16 of the Bill of Rights. There is also a provision in the Drug Trafficking (Recovery of Proceeds) Ordinance, Section 24, criminalizing any disclosure likely to prejudice an investigation.

b. Ongoing criminal prosecutions?

Yes, there are a number of express statutory restrictions on reporting court proceedings, contained in Hong Kong's Magistrates Ordinance (C. 227). Committal proceedings are those in which a magistrate decides whether there is sufficient evidence for a person to be sent for trial by indictment, by a higher court.

Section 87A of the Ordinance contains the general rule that written reports or broadcasts of "committal proceedings" in Hong Kong are only allowed to give certain narrowly defined details, such as the name of the court and identities of the parties and witnesses:

(a) the identity of the court and the name of the magistrate;
(b) the names, addresses, occupations and ages of the parties and witnesses;
(c) the offence, or a summary thereof, with which the accused is charged;
(d) the names of counsel and solicitors engaged in the proceedings;
(e) any decision of the magistrate to commit the accused for trial, and any decision of the magistrate on the disposal of the case of any defendants not committed;
(f) where the magistrate commits the accused for trial,
(g) the charge, or a summary thereof, on which he is committed and the court to which he is committed;
(h) where the committal proceedings are adjourned, the date and places to which they are adjourned; and
(i) whether legal aid was granted to the accused.

Those who may be held liable for violating these provisions include, among others, the owner, editor, publisher, or distributor of any newspaper containing a written report that violates the above provisions. Those responsible for violation of these provisions may be found guilty of an offense and may be held liable on conviction to a fine of $10,000 and to imprisonment for six months. There are similar restrictions on the reporting of bail applications under the Criminal Procedure Ordinance Section 9P(1) and restrictions on reporting the identity of complainants in connection with certain sexual offenses under the Crimes Ordinance Section 156. Finally, there are further limits on the publication of details of matrimonial cases under the Judicial Proceedings (Regulations of Reports) Ordinance 5 Section 3.

c. Ongoing regulatory investigations?

None.

d. Ongoing civil litigation, or other judicial proceedings?

There are rather convoluted provisions about publication of reports of court proceedings held in private. Generally, if the court orders that information shall not be published, it is the offense of Contempt of Court to do so. Otherwise it is an offense to publish in certain situations (such as proceedings involving persons with mental disability), or if publication is likely to prejudice the proceedings of the court (there is an exception for innocent publication).

13. Are prior restraints or other prepublication injunctions available on the basis of libel or privacy, and if so, what are the standards for obtaining such relief?

Yes. For libel, *Glofcheski* explains:

> [i]f there is a real possibility of the defendant repeating the defamatory statement, the court may be prepared to grant an injunction. There is a greater reluctance on the part of the courts to grant an interim or interlocutory injunctions [sic]–to restrain the publication of a defamation which has not yet taken place. This is considered to be a very serious infringement of freedom of speech. A recent Hong Kong case applied the usual principles, saying that an interlocutory injunction will only be granted if it is clear that the statement is defamatory, that if the defendant intends to plead justification, the plaintiff must show that the words are untrue (this may be done on the basis of affidavits), and that there is no reason to take the view that prima facie the occasion of publication is or will be privileged. (*Chan Shui Shing Andrew & Others v. Ironwing Holdings Ltd* [2001] 2 HKC 376)

14. Is a right of privacy recognized (either civilly or criminally)?

a. What is the definition of "private fact"?

In line with the historical approach of the United Kingdom courts, those of Hong Kong have held that there is no common law tort of invasion of privacy. There is a tort of breach of confidence, which has been used to protect certain sorts of communications and which the Court of Appeal has recognized in Hong Kong.

There is also legislative protection of privacy. To some extent this is based on the United Kingdom legislation protecting electronically held data, but in Hong Kong the law protects personal data held in other forms. The legislation is the Data Protection (Privacy) Ordinance. It essentially provides that data is to be used only for the purposes for which it is collected. The persons to whom the data pertains have a right of access to it and a right to compensation for improper use.

b. Is there a public interest or newsworthiness exception?

Section 61 of the Ordinance provides certain exemptions for the collection and disclosure of data in the course of "news activity," which includes "any journalistic activity" and the gathering, preparation, and dissemination of news or articles, programs, or observations on news or current affairs, including exemptions for dissemination of data "in the public interest."

c. Is the right of privacy based in common law, statute, or constitution?

Apart from the limited common law tort of breach of confidence, privacy rights are generally set forth in Section 61 of the Ordinance.

15. May reporters tape-record their own telephone conversations for note-taking purposes (not rebroadcast) without the consent of the other party?

Yes. There appear to be no such restrictions on recording.

16. If permissible to record such tapes, may they be broadcast without permission?

Yes; however, in certain circumstances such a broadcast could be challenged as an example of the tort of breach of confidence.

17. Is there a recognized evidentiary privilege preventing the disclosure of confidential sources relied upon by reporters?

Yes. There is a recognized common law rule—known as the "newspaper rule"—that acts as a limitation on the normal principles permitting discovery of the identity of other participants in tort. In the public interest (in the protection of sources, etc.), the identity of the author of an item or the source of information will not be ordered to be revealed. This rule has been applied in at least one Hong Kong case.

18. In the event that legal papers are served upon the newsroom (such as a civil complaint), are there any particular warnings about accepting service of which we should be aware?

No, except that anyone who receives legal papers should know how and when they were received and should contact counsel promptly.

19. Has your jurisdiction applied established media law to Internet publishers?

There are a small number of cases in which ISPs or the publishers of material on the Internet have been sued in the Hong Kong courts. We can break the cases down into four categories:

1. ***Cases where a paper publication that also appears on the Internet has been the subject of litigation.*** In *Chu Siu Kuk Yuen v. Apple Daily Ltd. & Others,* a newspaper was sued for its online publication.[23] The court noted that because the circulation of the newspaper exceeded 415,000, the possible additional effect of the Internet publication was not relevant to either liability or damages.

2. ***Cases where the fact of publication on the Internet—and thus in Hong Kong—has been the basis for bringing an action in Hong Kong, even though the parties are not actually resident in Hong Kong.*** This was the situation in *Investasia Ltd. and Another v. Kodansha Co. Ltd. and Another.*[24] It was held that the plaintiff had established a sufficient connection with Hong Kong to be able to bring an action in Hong Kong; the main authority was the English case of *Berezovsky v. Michaels and Others (Forbes).*[25]

3. ***Cases where the subject of the litigation has been an e-mail.*** In *Drummond v. Atuahene-Gima,*[26] the subject matter of the action was an e-mail—but only the author was sued and the form of the communication made no difference to the legal analysis.

4. ***Cases where a Web site operator has been sued for chat room publications.*** Several actions have been commenced against the Web site IceRed.com. None of these has gone to trial. The issue appears to be whether the operator can be required to disclose names, addresses, and IP addresses of those who have posted messages. Thus far, following English authority, the answer has been positive.

20. If established media law has been applied to Internet publishers, are there any ways in which Internet publishers (including chat room operators) have to meet different standards?

Hong Kong law does not provide a statutory immunity for ISPs or webmasters. Although the normal practice in Hong Kong courts is to follow U.K. cases quite closely, there is no equivalent in Hong Kong to the U.K. 1996 Defamation Act, including its special protection for ISPs.

21. Are there any cases where the courts enforced a judgment in libel from another jurisdiction against a publisher in your jurisdiction?

The general principles and rules of enforcement of foreign judgments in Hong Kong are that:

1. Under the common law, an action may be brought for enforcement of a foreign court judgment. This procedure will not apply where there is a statutory procedure. The common law rules are the same as those of England, and would include the rule that a foreign judgment is not enforceable if it is impeachable on grounds such as having been obtained by fraud, or amounting to the enforcement of foreign penal or tax law.[27]

2. There is a statutory procedure for registration and enforcement of foreign judgments. The main legislation is the Foreign Judgments (Reciprocal Enforcement) Ordinance Cap. 319, which provides that a judgment may be registered in the Court of First Instance (that is the main court of unlimited jurisdiction in Hong Kong) within six years of the date of delivery of the judgment (§ 4). Under Section 6 a registration may be set aside on the grounds, *inter alia,* "(v) that the enforcement of the judgment shall be contrary to public policy in the country of the registering court."

With respect to the specific issue of defamation cases, in no reported Hong Kong case has any issue been raised about the enforceability of a foreign defamation judgment. In view of the fact that Hong Kong tends to fall into that group of countries with a more generous (pro-plaintiff) view of liability and quantum of damages, it is unlikely that a Hong Kong court would refuse to enforce a judgment on grounds that some U.S. courts have declined to recognize awards from countries with less forceful constitutional protection for freedom of speech.

Chapter Notes

1. *Ling Ham Herbalist Koon v. Radio Television Hong Kong* [1998] HKEC 67 (High Ct. of HK Special Admin. Region) (quoting Gatley).

2. Glofcheski, *Tort Law in Hong Kong* (Sweet & Maxwell, Asia 2002) (chapter on defamation by Jill Cottrell) (hereafter, *Glofcheski*) at 566 (citing, *inter alia, Sim v. Stretch* [1936] 2 All ER 1237 (HL) and *Youssoupoff v. Metro-Goldwyn-Mayer Pictures Ltd.* [1934] 50 Times Law Report 581).

3. See, e.g., *Glofcheski* at 572 (citing *Next Magazine Publishing Ltd. & Others v. Oriental Daily Publisher Ltd.* [2000] 2 HKLRD 333).

4. *Beijing Television v. Brightec Ltd. & Others* [1999] 2 HKC 665 (quoting, in part, *Fullam v. Newcastle Chronicle and Journal Ltd.* [1977] 1 WLR 651 at 654H-655D (*per* Lord Denning MR)) (internal quotation marks omitted).

5. See, e.g., *Peregrine Investments Holdings Ltd. v. The Associated Press* [1997] HKLRD 1073 (quoting *Skuse v. Granada, The Independent,* April 2, 1993 [1996] *Entertainment and Media Law Reports* 278).

6. *Id.*

7. See, e.g., *China Youth Development Ltd. v. Next Magazine Publishing Ltd.* (2000) HCA 6206 of 1994.

8. *Hong Kong Polytechnic University v. Next Publishing Ltd.* [1997] 7 *Hong Kong Public Law Reports* 286.

9. *Glofcheski* at 574.

10. [2002] 1 HKLRD A21. The court also cited and applied a potentially far-reaching statement of principle by Lord Atkin in the English case, *Knuppfer v. London Express Newspaper Ltd.* [1944] AC 116 at 121–22.

11. As discussed in subsection (5) of Question 6 b. ("Statutory Defenses"), Section 25 of the Defamation Ordinance provides a distinct statutory defense for "[u]nintentional defamation" if an "offer of amends" (defined in the statute) is made by the defendant and rejected by the plaintiff.

12. Since actual malice is not an element of libel, it need only be proved by the plaintiff if it is an element of a defense that the defendant has otherwise successfully raised.

13. [2001] AC 127.

14. [1997] 189 C.L.R. 520.

15. *Reynolds,* 2 AC at 205.

16. [2000] 3 HKLRD 418.

17. [2002] 1 HKLRD 1.

18. [1946–1972] HKC 414.

19. *Oriental Press Group v. Next* [2003] 1 HKLRD 751.

20. Gatley has suggested that "contemporaneous" should be taken to mean "as nearly at the same time as the proceedings as is reasonably possible, having regard to the opportunities for preparation of the report and the time of going to press or making the broadcast."

21. See, e.g., *Oriental Press Group Ltd. & Others v. Ted Thomas* (1995) HCA 5217 of 1995.

22. [1996] 2 HKLR 239.

23. [2002] 1 *Hong Kong Law Reports and Digest* 1.

24. [1999] 3 *Hong Kong Cases* 515.

25. [1999] E.M.L.R. 278.

26. (2000) 1055 HKCU 1 (reported as *Drummond v. Kwaku* [2000] 1 HKLRD 604).

27. *Korea Data Systems Co Ltd v. Chiang Jay Tien* [2001] 3 HKC 239.

CHAPTER 7

India

JANMEJAY RAI AND BARUNESH CHANDRA

Kochhar & Co.

Kochhar & Co.
S-454, Greater Kailash Part-II
New Delhi – 110-048
Phone: 91 11 2921 1606, 2921 5477
Fax: 91 11 2921 9656, 2921-4932
www.kocchar.com
delhi@kochhar.com

Introduction to the Indian Legal System

India's legal system is based on a Constitution that came into force in 1950, and largely based upon English common law. India's judiciary is often receptive to important U.S. court decisions. The Constitution guarantees equal rights to all citizens and prohibits discrimination on the basis of race, gender, caste, ethnicity, and religion. The Constitution also states that "All citizens shall have the right (a) to freedom of speech and expression. Nothing […] shall affect the operation of any existing law, or prevent the State from making any law, in so far as such law imposes reasonable restrictions on the exercise of the right conferred by the said sub-clause in the interest of the security of the State, friendly relations with Foreign States, public order, decency or morality…."[1]

Although politically arranged on a federal system and maintaining delineated central and state laws, India has a unified court system that administers both federal and state laws. A criminal case is heard first by the court of a Judicial Magistrate or District and Sessions Judge depending upon the gravity of the offense and the punishment prescribed for the same. The court of first instance for a civil case is the court of a Munsif or Civil Judge depending upon the monetary value of the subject matter under dispute. Both trial courts are divided into judicial districts, and these courts' decisions are appealed to a High Court in each state or group of states. The Supreme Court of India hears final appeals. The twenty-one High Courts and the Supreme Court are charged with protecting fundamental rights and constitutional interpretation. Supreme Court decisions are binding precedent on all courts in India.

1. What is the locally accepted definition of libel?

Indian law treats libel in both criminal and civil form. The most widely and commonly accepted definition of defamation, which takes within its sweep both libel (defamation in some permanent form) and slander (defamation in a transient form), is "a false statement about a man to his discredit." Section 499 of the Indian Penal Code, 1860 ("IPC") provides the following definition of defamation:

> Whoever, by words, either spoken or intended to be read, or by signs or by visible representation, makes or publishes any imputation concerning any person intending to harm, or knowing or having reason to believe that such imputation will harm, the reputation of such person, is said, except in the cases hereinafter excepted, to defame that person.

The IPC goes on to provide no less than ten exceptions to the above definition. However, broadly speaking, in order to maintain a criminal action for libel, the following ingredients must be present:

1. The imputation must be published;
2. The imputation must have been made by words intended to be read or by other visible representations in permanent form; and
3. The imputation must have been made with the intention to harm or with the knowledge or having reason to believe that it will harm the reputation of the person concerned.

Under the Indian civil law of torts (based on various decided cases), a defamatory statement is one that:

> Directly or indirectly, in the estimation of others, lowers the moral or intellectual character of that person, or lowers the character of that person in respect of his caste or of his calling, or lowers the credit of that person, or causes it to be believed that the body of that person is in a loathsome state, or in a state generally considered as disgraceful.

It may be pertinent to note that law of torts is neither codified nor a very well-developed branch of law in India, and most of its principles emanate from common law (decided English cases). Some illustrations with respect to a tortious view of defamation are as follows: To say that a person built his fortune on the backs of the uneducated masses is not defamatory, but to refer to a person as a "Godse" (Gandhi's assassin) was held to be defamatory because it asserted that the subject would resort to murder.[2] To say that a person is the type who would commit a crime has also been found to be defamatory.[3]

2. Is libel-by-implication recognized, or, in the alternative, must the complained-of words alone defame the plaintiff?

Libel-by-implication is recognized under Indian law. However, words which are *prima facie* innocent would not be actionable unless the plaintiff proves their secondary or latent defamatory meaning. Where the words alleged to be defamatory do not appear to be such on their face, the plaintiff is required to make out the circumstances which made such words actionable by innuendo. Courts recognize that a defamatory innuendo may be put forward by way of a question, exclamation, conjecture, or irony.

3. May corporations sue for libel?

Yes, corporations have standing to sue for libel.

4. Is product disparagement recognized, and if so, how does that differ from libel?

Product disparagement is recognized under Indian law and it is illegal for a tradesman in India to disparage the products of a rival.[4] Courts in India have also found generic disparagement of rival products, without direct reference to the competitor, objectionable and have passed orders restraining such disparagement.

The essential difference between libel and product disparagement is that libel must contain an element of malice whereas there is no such requirement in the case of product disparagement.

5. Must an individual be clearly identified (by name or photograph) to sue for libel? Can a group of persons sue for libel, even though not named?

In order to sue for libel under Indian law, it is not necessary that an individual be clearly identified by way of name or photograph. If the plaintiff can show that he was specially referred to, it is immaterial whether the words complained of described the plaintiff by his own name or initial letters or by a fictitious name or even by somebody else's name. Further, it is also immaterial whether or not the defendant intended the defamatory statement to apply to the plaintiff or knew of the plaintiff's existence (if the statement might reasonably be understood by those who knew the plaintiff to refer to him).

Indian law has rejected a "group libel" approach. The relevant rule in this regard is that for an imputation to be held as defamatory for a group of persons, it must be directed against a definite and specified group of persons.[5]

It may amount to defamation to impute anything to a deceased person, if the imputation would harm the reputation of that person if living, *and* is intended to be hurtful to the feelings of his family or other near relatives.

6. What is the fault standard(s) applied to libel?

a. Does the fault standard depend on the fame or notoriety of the plaintiff?

To a certain degree, yes. Under Indian law, the following elements are weighed in a finding of liability: (1) the nature and character of the libel; (2) the extent of circulation of the libelous imputation; (3) the position in life of the parties; and (4) the other surrounding circumstances of the case.

b. Is there a heightened fault standard or privilege for reporting on matters of public concern or public interest?

Indian libel law is dotted with a number of substantive defenses and privileges. Courts have also applied a broadly read public interest privilege, which protects a good faith opinion respecting the conduct of a public servant in the discharge of his public functions, or respecting his character, so far as his character appears in that conduct, and no further.[6]

The public interest privilege has also been read to immunize speech addressing the conduct of any person touching any public question. Again, the opprobrium must be limited to the subjects' character in direct relationship to the public issue conduct in question. The Supreme Court of India has to a considerable extent adopted the "actual malice" standard as elucidated in the U.S. case of *New York Times v. Sullivan,* and suits brought by public officials must show that at least with regard to statements confined to that person's public conduct, a claim cannot succeed absent the plaintiff establishing that the statement was made with "reckless disregard for the truth."[7]

Truth is an absolute defense in civil claims,[8] but criminal defense in libel must include a showing that the statement at issue serves the public interest.

7. Is financial news about publicly traded companies, or companies involved with a government contract, considered a matter of public interest or otherwise privileged?

Financial news about publicly traded companies or companies involved with government contracts per se may not be considered a matter of public interest and consequently may not be privileged. However, there may be cases where news regarding publicly traded companies or companies involved with government may be considered to be in the realm of public interest but at the same time would depend upon the peculiar facts and circumstances of each case.[9]

8. Is there a recognized protection for opinion or "fair comment" on matters of public concern?

Yes. Under Indian law, a qualified privilege exists for "fair and bona fide comment on a matter of public interest."[10] However, the word "fair" embraces the meaning of honest and also of relevancy to the matter of public interest. Courts will reject this defense if there is a credible allegation that the reporter's error was not in good faith, as malice (knowing falsity) will defeat the privilege. Under Indian law, a statement is said to have a qualified privilege when no action lies for it, even though it is false and defamatory, unless the plaintiff proves malice.

The following matters have been found to be considered in the "public interest": affairs of the state; public acts of ministers and officers of the state; the administration of justice; public institutions and local authorities; ecclesiastical matters; books, pictures, and works of art; theaters, concerts, and other public entertainment; and appeals to the public, e.g., a medical man bringing forward some new method of treatment and advertising it or a man appealing to the public by writing letters to a newspaper.

Indian law has also broadly interpreted a "common interest" privilege, wherein "It is not defamation to convey a caution, in good faith, to one person against another, provided that such caution be intended for the good of the person to whom it is conveyed, or of some person in whom that person is interested, or for the public good."

For purposes of criminal defamation, a mere belief in the statement made will not suffice to establish a "good faith" privilege. Under courts' reading of the IPC, "the accused must show that he had a rational basis, had acted with due care, and was satisfied that the imputation was true."[11]

9. Are there any requirements upon a plaintiff, such as demand for retraction or right of reply, and if so, what impact do they have?

No. Indian law does not require that a plaintiff demand retraction prior to proceeding with a libel claim. However, if the defendant tenders an apology, which is accepted by the plaintiff, the defendant can resist the plaintiff's action for damages for defamation in the court of law. There is no statutory right of reply under Indian law.

10. Is there a privilege for quoting or reporting on:

a. Papers filed in court?

Yes. Quoting or reporting of a true, accurate, and bona fide account of papers (pleadings, applications, and affidavits) filed in court may be privileged if they relate to matters of public interest. Papers filed in court enjoy an absolute privilege whereby no action lies even though they are false and defamatory or made falsely and maliciously or made without any reasonable or probable excuse. A statement is absolutely privileged when no action lies for it, even though it contains false or defamatory allegations, without regard to whether the reporter has knowledge of its falsity.

b. Government-issued documents?

Under the Indian law of torts, quoting or reporting of a true, accurate, and bona fide account of any governmental/official documents or publications is also absolutely privileged, provided that the documents contain matters of public interest. Because the Indian definition of "public interest" includes governmental affairs and the administration of justice, the privilege is widely construed.

Statements made during parliamentary proceedings, judicial proceedings, or state proceedings are also protected by absolute privilege.

c. Quasi-governmental proceedings?

Yes. Disciplinary proceedings are generally deemed to be in the nature of quasi-judicial proceedings in India, and thus privileged. Also, quoting or reporting of true, accurate, and bona fide accounts of the same may be privileged if they contain matters of public interest.

11. Is there a privilege for republishing statements made earlier by other, bona fide, reliable publications or wire services?

No. Although such reports may be subject to a public interest defense, there is no specific immunity for the republication of defamatory material from other publications or wire services. For this reason, when defamatory material is considered for republication, reporters and editors should make some bona fide effort to ascertain the truth of the matter reported, and determine whether the article serves the public interest.

12. Are there any restrictions regarding reporting on:

a. Ongoing criminal investigations?

Yes. Reporting of an ongoing criminal investigation should be such that the report should not malign the character and conduct of the person or body of persons being investigated without sufficient or reasonable excuse. Further, the report should not be judgmental so as to create a prejudice in the minds of the general public and also the investigating agency.

b. Ongoing criminal prosecutions?

Reporting on ongoing criminal prosecutions is allowed subject to the restriction that such report is impartial, bona fide, and gives a fair and substantially accurate account of such proceedings. Indian law also imposes certain restrictions on reporting criminal investigations, such as where: (1) the reporting or publication is contrary to the provisions of any statute in force; (2) the court has expressly prohibited reporting or publication of all information relating to the proceeding; (3) the court sits in camera for reason connected with public order or the security of the state; or (4) the information relating to a secret process, discovery, or invention is an issue before the court.

Indian law also proscribes violation of reporting restrictions above with punishment under the Contempt of Courts Act, 1971.[12] Reporters should be aware that courts can, by application or on their own initiative, institute publication bans without notice to the press.

c. Ongoing regulatory investigations?

The same restrictions would apply as for ongoing criminal investigations (in Question 12a. above).

d. Ongoing civil litigation, or other judicial proceedings?

The same restrictions would apply as for ongoing criminal prosecutions (in Question 12b. above).

13. Are prior restraints or other prepublication injunctions available on the basis of libel or privacy, and if so, what are the standards for obtaining such relief?

Yes. Prepublication injunctions are available on the basis of libel or invasion of privacy. However, the court will only interfere if the plaintiff satisfies the court that: (1) the statement about to be published is demonstrably false; and (2) there is some likelihood of immediate and pressing injury to person or property or trade of the plaintiff.[13]

Further, prepublication restraint on a publication may also be obtained by demonstrating to the court that the publication is being made for the sole purpose of harming the plaintiff. An injunction could also be obtained by establishing that the intention behind the publication is to blackmail the plaintiff.

14. Is a right of privacy recognized (either civilly or criminally)?

Yes. The right to privacy is recognized in India under the Supreme Court of India's reading of Article 21 of the Constitution, which guarantees "the right to life and personal liberty."

a. What is the definition of "private fact"?

There is no statutory definition of "private fact." However, it is surmised that a private fact must include all aspects of personal intimacies of the home, the family, marriage, motherhood, procreation, religion, health, sexuality, etc. A private fact can, at best, have an inclusive definition and cannot be defined with a catalog approach.

b. Is there a public interest or newsworthiness exception?

The Press Council of India has framed "Norms for Journalistic Conduct" which lay down general rules to be followed by all journalists. The Norms categorically provide that the press shall not intrude or invade the privacy of an individual unless outweighed and warranted by larger public interest. Provision 13 of the Norms states that:

> The Press shall not intrude or invade the privacy of an individual unless outweighed by genuine overriding public interest, not being a prurient or morbid curiosity. So, however, that once a matter becomes a matter of public record, the right to privacy no longer subsists and it becomes a legitimate subject for comment by Press and media among others.

India has recognized a newsworthiness exception to privacy claims. In the case of Auto Shankar, a convicted felon who brought claims in privacy after newspapers published details from his life available from public records, the court held that even without authorization, such use was permitted.[14] It is generally held that persons who voluntarily thrust themselves into the public light or raise a controversy may not have a cause of action for privacy, at least as far as such private facts related to the controversy being reported upon.

c. Is the right of privacy based in common law, statute, or constitution?

The right to privacy as an independent and distinctive concept originated under common law and the law of torts, under which a new cause of action for damages resulting from unlawful invasion of privacy was recognized. In recent times, however, the said right has acquired a constitutional status by virtue of a galaxy of Supreme Court judgments which have held that the right to privacy is implicit in the right to life and personal liberty enshrined under Article 21 of the Constitution of India.

It may also be noted that India is a signatory to the International Covenant on Civil and Political Rights, 1966 ("the Covenant"). Article 17 of the Covenant provides for the "right to privacy." India is also a signatory to the Universal Declaration of Human Rights, 1948 ("the Declaration"). Article 12 of the Declaration is almost similar in terms to Article 17 of the Covenant.

15. May reporters tape-record their own telephone conversations for note-taking purposes (not rebroadcast) without the consent of the other party?

Persons are generally not permitted to tape-record their telephone conversations with anyone, without the knowledge or consent of all parties to the call. However, Provision 16 of the Norms states that tape-recording a telephone conversation may be allowed where such recording is "necessitated for protecting the journalist in a legal action or for other compellingly good reasons."

16. If permissible to record such tapes, may they be broadcast without permission?

No. Even if a compellingly good reason exists for recording such, the same may not be broadcast without the permission of the other party.

17. Is there a recognized evidentiary privilege preventing the disclosure of confidential sources relied upon by reporters?

Yes. Known as the "newspaper rule," reporters may not be compelled to disclose the confidential source of their information at an interim stage in a court proceeding.[15] However, there is no privilege protecting reporters from disclosing their source of information, if the court requires such a disclosure in the interest of justice, such as the prevention of a crime or a threat to public health or safety.

18. In the event that legal papers are served upon the newsroom (such as a civil complaint), are there any particular warnings about accepting service of which we should be aware?

In case of a civil action, if service of summons is rejected by a reporter (the defendant) at his workplace (the newsroom) and if the process server affixes such summons at a conspicuous place in or outside the newsroom, the service would be deemed to have been effected.[16] If the defendant does not appear before the court after such deemed service, the court would proceed to hear the matter *ex parte*.

In case of a criminal proceeding for defamation, if a reporter (the accused) rejects the service of summons, he can have an arrest warrant issued against him.

19. Has your jurisdiction applied established media law to Internet publishers?

There have been no reported judgments thus far wherein an Internet publisher has been held liable for defamation, libel, or violation of the right to privacy. However, under the IPC's statutory definition of defamation, it would appear that the Indian law of torts is broad enough to include Internet publishers within its sweep for purposes of defamation and privacy actions.

20. If established media law has been applied to Internet publishers, are there any ways in which Internet publishers (including chat room operators) have to meet different standards?

There are no substantive differences. Internet publishers (including chat room operators) have to comply with all the aforesaid prescribed standards.

The only exception to the aforesaid has been provided in Section 79 of the Information Technology Act, 2000 ("IT Act"). Under Section 79 of the IT Act, an Internet publisher including a chat room operator (both of which fall within the definition of an "intermediary" under the IT Act) is not liable for an offense under or contravention of the IT Act in respect of any third party information or data made available by him if he proves that (a) the offense or contravention was committed without his knowledge; and (b) he had exercised all due diligence to prevent the commission of such offense or contravention.[17]

21. Are there any cases where the courts enforced a judgment in libel from another jurisdiction against a publisher in your jurisdiction?

There are no reported cases where a court in India has enforced a foreign judgment for libel against a publisher in India.

Chapter Notes

1. Article 19(1)(a) and 19(2) of the Constitution of India.

2. *Purshottam Sayal v. Prem Shanker* AIR 1966 All. 377 (1519).

3. *S.M. Narayanan v. S.R. Narayana Iyer,* AIR 1961 Mad. 254 (257).

4. *Dabur India Limited v. Emami Limited 2004 (29) PTC1 (Del); Pepsi Co. Inc. and Ors v. Hindustan Coca Cola Limited and Anr (2003 (27) PTC 305 (Del) (DB); Hindustan Lever v. Colgate Palmolive (I) Limited, 1998 (1) SCC 720).*

5. *G. Narasimhan, G. Kasturi & K. Gopalan -Vs.- T.V. Chokkappa: (1972) 2 Supreme Court Cases 680.*

6. *Sewakram Sobhani v. R.K. Karanjiya* AIR 1981 SC 1514 (1519).

7. *R. Rajgopal v. State of Tamil Nadu* (1994) 6 SCC 632.

8. *Nellikka Achuthan v. Deshabimani Printing and Publishing House Ltd.*, AIR 1986 Ker. 41 (43).

9. For example, substantiated reports alleging financial mismanagement in a publicly traded company or corruption in the award of a government contract to a particular company may fall within the realm of public interest.

10. *Dainik Bhaskar v. Madhusudan Bhargava,* AIR 1991 MP 162 (166).

11. *Sukra Mahto v. Basudeo Kumar Mahto,* AIR 1971 SC 1567 (1569).

12. Section 12 of the Contempt of Courts Act, 1971 provides that a Contempt of Court may be punished with simple imprisonment for a term which may extend to six (6) months or with a fine which may extend to Rupees Two Thousand (Rs. 2000/-) or with both. However, the accused may be discharged or the punishment awarded may be remitted on an apology being made to the satisfaction of the court.

13. *Reliance Petrochemicals Ltd. v. Indian Express Newspapers Bombay Pvt. Ltd.,* AIR 1989 SC 190 (195).

14. *R. Rajgopal v. State of Tamil Nadu* (1994) 6 SCC 632.

15. *Nishi Prem v. Javed Akhtar* AIR 199 Bom. 222.

16. Order V Rule17 of the Code of Civil Procedure, 1908 (as amended till date) lays down the procedure for service of summons when defendant refuses to accept service or cannot be found.

17. The Ministry of Information Technology is contemplating issuing a model "Code of Conduct and Practices to be adopted for the functioning of Cyber Cafes/Chat Room Centers." In this regard, a draft code is being prepared by the Asian School of Cyber Laws (ASCL) under the supervision of the Ministry of Information Technology. http://www.financialexpress.com/fe_archive_full_story .php?content_id=42771, *Financial Express* dated September 26, 2003.

CHAPTER 8

Japan

YOSHIO ITEYA, TOMOYA FUJIMOTO,
AND AKIRA MARUMO

Mori Hamada & Matsumoto

Mori Hamada & Matsumoto
Marunouchi Kitaguchi Building
1-6-5 Marunouchi, Chiyoda-ku
Tokyo 100-8222, Japan
Phone: (81) (3) 5223-7777
Fax: (81) (3) 5223-7666
www.mhmjapan.com
yoshio.iteya@mhmjapan.com

Introduction to the Japanese Legal System

The Japanese system is a nonfederalist organization with four court levels: Summary courts, district and family courts, high courts, and the Supreme Court. The Japanese system was reconstructed in 1946, at the end of World War II. The Japanese Bill of Rights (1946), with thirty-one articles related to human rights and many other laws emphasizing human rights, is modeled after the U.S. legal system. It is considered a civil law system with customary differences.

The decision-making process in Japan is unique. The Japanese legal system is divided among six codes: the Constitution, the civil code, the code of civil procedure, the penal code, the code of criminal procedure, and the commercial code. Japanese courts examine and consider both Japanese laws and international laws to determine what a fair resolution might be. The system includes a single Supreme Court, eight high courts, fifty district and family courts, and forty-eight summary courts for small criminal and small civil actions. With easily accessible court records, out-of-court settlements are very common in the Japanese system.

1. What is the locally accepted definition of libel?

In Japan, there is both civil and criminal liability for libel and related offenses. Libel (*meiyo-kison*) under the Civil Code (Articles 709 and 710) constitutes a tort, and has been interpreted to mean a statement that injures "the social reputation that a person enjoys due to his or her personal merits such as personality, character, fame and credibility."[1] The standard applied in determining whether a statement has damaged a person's social reputation is that of the average reader, giving a normal reading and attention to the statement.[2]

Under the Criminal Code, there are three offenses that are relevant to libel:

1. damage to honor (*meiyo-kison*), which is defined as the injuring of a person's social position or reputation through publicly alleging facts (Article 230);
2. insult (*bujoku*), which is defined as the injuring of a person's reputation in public without alleging facts (Article 231); and
3. damage to credit (*shinyo-kison*), which is defined as the injuring of a person's credit by delivering false rumors or employing deceptive measures (Article 233).

The definition of libel under the Civil Code includes the three offenses under the Criminal Code.

The criminal penalty for both damage to honor (*meiyo-kison*) and damage to credit (*shinyo-kison*) is imprisonment for as long as three years and/or a fine of up to 500,000 yen. The penalty for insult (*bujoku*) is imprisonment of up to thirty days and/or a minor fine (1,000 yen to 10,000 yen). Imprisonment is rarely ordered, and fines are the customary punishment.

A defendant who is found to have committed libel under the Civil Code would be liable to pay damages to the plaintiff. The amount of these damages, of course, will depend upon the circumstances of each case and the severity of the defamation. The amount of damages awarded by the court in the case of newspaper and news reports is mostly in the range of 10,000 yen to 500,000 yen, with a small number of awards in egregious cases on the order of 2–4 million yen. The courts have the authority to also demand that the publisher place a notice of apology or revocation, and in very rare cases, to delete the report altogether.

2. Is libel-by-implication recognized, or, in the alternative, must the complained-of words alone defame the plaintiff?

Under Japanese law, libel-by-implication is not recognized as a separate legal concept, but given Japan's very broad interpretation of defamatory meaning, libel may occur in a statement that does not allege any false facts. Given the central role of "face" or "honor" in Japanese culture, the test applied is whether the average person would consider that the reputation of the plaintiff has been damaged. Therefore, if the average person would consider a statement that is defamatory only by implication to have injured the plaintiff's reputation, then the statement will fall within the definition of libel, despite the fact that no direct statement has been made.

3. May corporations sue for libel?

Yes. Corporations are also recognized as having reputations of their own that can be injured. The Supreme Court has held that political parties, companies, and other legal entities may also have social reputations that can be injured.[3]

4. Is product disparagement recognized, and if so, how does that differ from libel?

Under Japanese law, product disparagement is not recognized as a separate legal concept. However, to the extent that any product disparagement falls within the above definition of libel, it would be actionable in Japan. One such example is a case where false statements made in respect of a dictionary sold by the plaintiff company were held to constitute libel.[4]

5. Must an individual be clearly identified (by name or photograph) to sue for libel? Can a group of persons sue for libel, even though not named?

In principle, an individual must be clearly identified to be able to sue for libel. It is not necessary that the statement actually name the plaintiff, rather that the plaintiff be sufficiently identifiable as a result of the report. Therefore, defamatory reports in respect of a large class of people (e.g., residents of Tokyo, members of a business community) will not constitute libel. However, in the event the class is sufficiently small, and the members of that class are specified or identifiable, a report may constitute libel of the members of that class, but not of the class itself.

6. What is the fault standard(s) applied to libel?

a. Does the fault standard depend on the fame or notoriety of the plaintiff?

No. The fame or notoriety of the plaintiff is not considered in applying the test for determining whether libel has been constituted, which is whether the plaintiff's reputation in society has been injured. However, as mentioned below, there is a defense available to a defendant in Japan that the report was a matter of public concern or in the public interest. The fame or notoriety of the plaintiff will only be a factor taken into consideration when determining whether or not a report constitutes an invasion of privacy.

b. Is there a heightened fault standard or privilege for reporting on matters of public concern or public interest?

In Japan there is only one fault standard that is applied in libel cases. This analysis is generally described as:

1. whether the report relates to a matter in the public interest (including a benefit or loss to the public's understanding of an important issue);
2. whether the report is made mainly to promote that public interest; and
3. whether the report is true or the reporter had adequate basis to believe that the report is true.[5]

Unlike law in certain U.S. cases, the fact that the reporter may have believed that the report was true is not sufficient to mount the defense. All three of the above criteria must be met. The defendant must present to the court evidence upon which the report was based, and it will be adjudged on an objective standard.

7. Is financial news about publicly traded companies, or companies involved with a government contract, considered a matter of public interest or otherwise privileged?

There is no case law in Japan that has held, as a general principle, that financial news in relation to a public company is a matter of public interest. Whether financial news about publicly traded companies is in fact in the public interest will depend on the coverage of the report and the facts of each case. For example, a report about companies involved in a government contract may be considered to be in the public interest, provided that the coverage of that report is relevant to the government contract.

8. Is there a recognized protection for opinion or "fair comment" on matters of public concern?

Yes, a protection for "fair comment" will be available where:

1. the opinion or comment is relevant to matters of public concern;
2. it is made mainly to promote the public interest;
3. a substantial portion of the facts upon which the opinion or comment is made are true or the reporter had adequate basis to believe that the facts are true; and

4. the report is not an extreme personal attack.[6] However, that opinion or comment cannot be beyond what is a reasonable opinion or comment in tone or tenor, and may constitute actionable insult (*bujoku*).[7]

9. Are there any requirements upon a plaintiff, such as demand for retraction or right of reply, and if so, what impact do they have?

Under Japanese law, the plaintiff does not have any statutory right of reply, such as the right to require the defendant to place a counterargument. However, under Article 723 of the Civil Code, a plaintiff can ask the court to require a defendant to take measures to remedy the damage to the plaintiff's reputation, such as placing a notice of apology or a notice of retraction in the defendant's publication. In very rare cases the defendant has been ordered to delete the defamatory report altogether. An order to place such a notice is usually made where the court regards the payment of damages alone as insufficient to remedy the damage to the plaintiff's reputation or honor.

Westerners are reminded here that apologies have a special meaning in Japanese culture, and in the event that a publication is inaccurate or otherwise potentially actionable, the offer of a very prominent and sincere public apology may resolve impending litigation.

10. Is there a privilege for quoting or reporting on:

a. Papers filed in court?

There is no special privilege for reporting on court documents under Japanese law. The fact that a statement was made in court papers does not relieve reporters of their responsibility regarding the accuracy of that statement. The fact that the relied upon papers come from the court may go a long way in convincing a judge that the reporter had a good faith basis upon which to base the statement; however, journalists should be cautioned that there is no "absolute" privilege. Thus, reporters have the burden of seeking out and reporting information that might be contrary to the assertions made in court papers.

Article 230-2(2) of the Criminal Code gives some assistance to a defendant in strictly deeming (i.e., there can be no exceptions or rebuttal) that reporting on criminal actions before public prosecution is in the public interest.

b. Government-issued documents?

The same will apply for government-issued documents and quasi-governmental proceedings. Provided that papers filed in court are a matter of public record (some courts may be closed), there will be no problem with respect to breach of privacy in disclosing the content of the papers.

c. Quasi-governmental proceedings?

There is no particular privilege for this type of material.

11. Is there a privilege for republishing statements made earlier by other, bona fide, reliable publications or wire services?

No. In Japan, the republishing of statements subjects the repeating party to claims of libel. However, the fact that the republishing is based on the report of a bona fide, reliable publication or wire service will be regarded as one factor in favor of the defendant's determination or belief that the facts alleged in the report are true, which is one of the elements of the defense to libel outlined in 6b. above.

Reporters and editors must be judicious in their reliance upon other publications and wire services. The fact that it was published elsewhere is not enough: the court will examine the general reliability and expertise of the first publisher. In this regard, there is at least one Supreme Court case holding that a newspaper publisher did not have a reasonable basis to believe the truth of news it sourced from a news agency the court found lacking in such reliability.[8] "Gossip" or "rumor" web pages popular throughout Asia should not be blindly relied upon.

12. Are there any restrictions regarding reporting on:

a. Ongoing criminal investigations?

There are no particular restrictions on reporting any of the matters above in addition to the general principles of libel already mentioned.

Article 230-2 (3) of the Criminal Code provides a defense to any libel claim pursuant to that Code where (1) the defendant was reporting in respect of a public official or a candidate for public office; and (2) the report was true. Please note, however, that any comments should be made carefully in accordance with the principles of "fair comment" mentioned above.

b. Ongoing criminal prosecutions?

None.

c. Ongoing regulatory investigations?

None.

d. Ongoing civil litigation, or other judicial proceedings?

None.

13. Are prior restraints or other prepublication injunctions available on the basis of libel or privacy, and if so, what are the standards for obtaining such relief?

Prior restraints and prepublication injunctions are available under Japanese law on the basis of libel and breach of privacy. The standard to obtain such relief in respect of libel is as follows:

1. the matters alleged in the report are not true or the report is clearly not made in the public interest; and
2. there is a risk that the victim will incur serious damage that cannot be remedied.

The standard to obtain such relief in respect of breach of privacy is as follows:

1. the report is clearly not in the public interest; and
2. there is a risk that the victim will incur serious damage that cannot be remedied.

14. Is a right of privacy recognized (either civilly or criminally)?

a. What is the definition of "private fact"?

Violation of the right of privacy can be the basis for civil action in tort under the Civil Code. A "private fact" is a fact that:

1. concerns the private life of a person or matters deemed to relate to the private life of a person;
2. the person would not want to have disclosed, judged on the standard of the average person; and
3. has not yet been disclosed.

b. Is there a public interest or newsworthiness exception?

Yes. As mentioned in our response to 6a. above, the privacy of celebrities or people in the public eye, such as politicians and well-known entertainers, is acknowledged by the courts to be more limited than the average "person in the street."[9] The extent to which the privacy of such people is limited will depend on the extent of their fame and the nature of their activities in society.

c. Is the right of privacy based in common law, statute, or constitution?

There is a right of privacy that is recognized under both the Japanese Constitution and the Civil Code. Under the Constitution, a right of privacy is derived from a general right to the pursuit of happiness under Article 13. The Supreme Court has generally defined this right as one that precludes the reckless or arbitrary disclosure of information about an individual's private life.

This right has been further construed by scholars to include a right to control one's personal information, although the Supreme Court has not specifically elaborated further on the definition of the constitutional "right to privacy." Article 709 of the Civil Code also provides for a tort action in connection with a breach of a right of privacy, as discussed in 14a. above.

The discussion of privacy rights has most recently been focused on protection of personal information in connection with the maintenance and use of information databases. Under the Law Concerning Protection of Private Information, "Private Information" is defined as information relating to a living individual's name, date of birth, and other matters that could identify specific individuals (including items of information that may be easily collated with other information to identify specific individuals). Private Information Handling Entities (i.e., entities who maintain databases of Private Information) are under certain obligations with respect to the use and protection of Private Information in their possession.

15. May reporters tape-record their own telephone conversations for note-taking purposes (not rebroadcast) without the consent of the other party?

This area of the law is unclear in Japan, and there are several different views as to whether reporters can tape-record their telephone conversations with another party without the consent of that party.

One view is that this action would be immoral but not illegal, as the other party has the ability to control his or her side of the conversation. A second view is that the recording could be illegal as a violation of the party's reasonable expectation of privacy. The third view attempts to resolve the two by reasoning that the legality of the action will depend on a fact-based analysis of whether the complaining party should reasonably have expected the privacy of the conversation to be maintained in the circumstances. Generally, if a person clearly identifies herself on the telephone as a journalist or reporter to the person, then it could be reasonable to assume that the conversation will be "on the record."

16. If permissible to record such tapes, may they be broadcast without permission?

The legality of broadcasting a tape-recorded conversation without explicit consent is unclear under Japanese law. Although not statutorily proscribed, there is some scholarly consensus that broadcasting the visual image of an individual requires the individual's consent, as this entails issues involving an individual's "right of portrait." While it is possible that a voice recording may not rise to the same level of legal protection as a visual image, we believe that, in the absence of legal precedent, the prudent course would be to obtain explicit consent prior to broadcasting a tape-recorded conversation.

17. Is there a recognized evidentiary privilege preventing the disclosure of confidential sources relied upon by reporters?

No. There is no statutory or common law "shield law" and confidential sources relied upon by reporters must be disclosed in legal proceedings. A reporter is not under any obligation to disclose a source prior to the proceedings.[10]

18. In the event that legal papers are served upon the newsroom (such as a civil complaint), are there any particular warnings about accepting service of which we should be aware?

If legal papers are sent to you in respect of proceedings in Japan, the papers will be served by a court-appointed agent, and no issue can be taken regarding the validity of the service. In this case, therefore, we recommend that you accept service of the documents and contact your legal advisers immediately.

19. Has your jurisdiction applied established media law to Internet publishers?

As discussed in Question 20 below, Japanese libel law has been applied to statements published on the Internet. There is, however, no case testing the jurisdictional limits of Japanese libel law in connection with Internet publications. Thus, there remains a question as to whether Japanese courts would apply its law to statements published on a server located outside of Japan. It is likely that Japanese libel law would apply in such case if, at a minimum, the libelous statement was published in Japanese and reasonably directed at an audience in Japan.

20. If established media law has been applied to Internet publishers, are there any ways in which Internet publishers (including chat room operators) have to meet different standards?

In a case involving libelous statements published on an Internet bulletin board, the Tokyo High Court has held that the system operator operating the bulletin board is under a duty to delete the libelous statements where:

1. the system operator knows about the libelous statements; and
2. the system operator has necessary authority to delete the statements.[11]

Internet service providers enjoy a "safe harbor" from liability for defamatory or infringing material under the "Law concerning Limitation of Damages to Specific Telecommunications service providers and disclosure of Sender Information," which provides that liability is limited to cases where (1) it is technologically possible for the ISP to prevent the distribution of the defamatory or infringing material, and (2) either the ISP knows that the material is defamatory or infringing or had reasonable cause to know that the material is defamatory or infringing. No case law has yet tested the meaning of "reasonable cause" in this context.

21. Are there any cases where the courts enforced a judgment in libel from another jurisdiction against a publisher in your jurisdiction?

There is no reported case of a foreign libel judgment being enforced in Japan. However, there is no reason to believe that the general principles for enforcement of foreign civil judgments in Japan should not be applied the same for a judgment in a libel case as for a case based on any other cause of action.

In general, the requirements for enforcement of a foreign civil judgment without reconsideration of the merits are as follows:

1. the foreign judgment concerned is duly obtained and is final and conclusive;
2. the jurisdiction of the foreign court is recognized under Japanese law or international treaty;
3. service of process has been duly effected other than by public notice or the defendant has appeared in the relevant proceedings without receiving service thereof;
4. the foreign judgment (including the court procedure leading to such judgment) is not contrary to public policy or good morals doctrine in Japan; and
5. judgments of Japanese courts receive reciprocal treatment in the courts of the foreign jurisdiction concerned.

Chapter Notes

1. Supreme Court, May 27, 1997, Minshu 51-5-2024.

2. Supreme Court, July 20, 1956, Minshu 10-8-1059.

3. Supreme Court, January 28, 1954, Minshu 18-1-136.

4. Tokyo High Court, October 2, 1996.

5. Supreme Court, June 23, 1966, Minshu 20-5-1118.

6. Supreme Court, April 24, 1987, Minshu 41-3-490.

7. Supreme Court, September 9, 1997.

8. Supreme Court, March 8, 2002.

9. Tokyo High Court, December 25, 2000; Tokyo District Court, February 29, 2000.

10. Supreme Court, March 6, 1980.

11. Supreme Court, September 5, 2001 (*Nifty Serve* Case).

CHAPTER 9

Korea

D.S. CHOI AND S.C. PARK

Kim & Chang

Kim & Chang
Seyang Building, 223 Naeja-dong, Jongno-gu
Seoul 110-720, Korea
Phone: (822) 3703-1114
Fax: (822) 737-9091/3
www.kimchang.com
lawkim@kimchang.com

Introduction to the Korean Legal System

The Korean legal system is a civil law system derived procedurally from the European civil law system and substantively from the Japanese legal system. After the Republic of Korea was formed in 1948, many Japanese laws remained, and much American jurisprudence was imported during the U.S. military occupation of 1945–1948. The democratization movement by the Korean public brought significant changes to the Constitution in 1987, and with the first civilian government in 1993, the legislative reform activity continued to adopt more democratic reform and to improve the legal system.

The Korean Constitution is the founding document, and it defines the government as a democratic republic, with three branches; the executive, the legislative, and the judiciary. All laws are weighed against constitutional principles. Laws are enacted by the legislative branch. The executive branch also has the authority to issue laws, as well as to submit bills to the National Assembly. The Constitution also allows the president to make emergency orders in time of internal turmoil, external menace, natural calamity, or a grave financial or economic crisis. The National Assembly, the Supreme Court, and the Constitutional Court have authority to enact regulations relating to proceedings and internal rules and the conduct of business. The Constitution provides legislative procedures during times of national emergency.

Also, "customary law" is to be relied upon as the basis for deciding civil cases. The Korean judiciary system is three-tiered: the Supreme Court, the highest court; the High Courts, the intermediate appellate courts; and the trial courts (District Courts) which include the specialized Patent Court, Family Court, and Administrative Courts. There are five High Courts and thirteen District Courts, divided into geographic districts. The chief justice of the Supreme Court is appointed by the president with the consent of the National Assembly, for a single six-year term of office. The Supreme Court justices are appointed by the president on the recommendation of the chief justice with the consent of the National Assembly. Their term of office is six years, and they may be reappointed. All other judges are appointed by the chief justice with the consent of the Conference of Supreme Court Justices. Their term of office is ten years, and they may be reappointed.

In addition, Korea maintains a Constitutional Court, formed in September, 1988. This Court is not part of the regular judicial structure. It has jurisdiction over the following areas: (1) The constitutionality of an act upon the request of the courts; (2) Impeachment; (3) Dissolution of a political party; (4) Disputes about the jurisdictions between state agencies, between state agencies and local governments, and between local governments; and (5) Petitions relating to the Constitution as prescribed by an act. The Constitutional Court consists of nine justices qualified to be court judges. They are appointed by the president for a six-year term and may be reappointed. For matters involving impeachment, three judges are appointed from persons selected by the National Assembly, and three are appointed from persons nominated by the chief justice of the Supreme Court.

Supreme Court decisions are important in interpreting the contents of the relevant acts and subordinate statutes. Article 8 of the Court Organization Act states that a judgment rendered in the judicial proceedings of a superior court shall take precedence over the judgment of a lower court with respect to a particular case, thereby denying the generally recognized doctrine of *stare decisis* and demonstrating a significant difference between the Korean legal system and Anglo–American legal systems. There is no American-style system of judicial precedent, and a decision of the Supreme Court does not have the binding force of precedent in subsequent cases of a similar nature. It merely has a persuasive effect. The interpretation of a law rendered in a particular case by the Supreme Court, however, does have a binding effect on the lower courts when the case is remanded.

1. What is the locally accepted definition of libel?

Generally speaking, libel may be described as public disclosure of information resulting in injury to another's reputation. The information may be true or false. If, however, (1) the information is proven to be true, or (2) the defendant exercised due care and had good reason to believe that the information was true (although it is later proven to be false), liability may be avoided if the intention behind the disclosure was solely to benefit the general public. If the information is proven to be false and the defendant fails to make a showing that upon exercise of due care, there would have been good reason to believe that the information was not true, more severe sanctions may be imposed.[1]

The following are examples of statements that have been found to be defamatory:

- *Hanguk Nondan*[2] published a report that citizen movement groups threatened conservative groups with violence and threatened to blackmail *chaebols* or other companies. Four citizen movement groups initiated a damages suit, and the Korea Supreme Court held that, although the report dealt with a matter of public interest, it severely harmed the social status of the victims and appeared to have been motivated by a sense of vengeance or the purpose of slander.[3]
- MBC[4] aired a false news report that public prosecutors in Daejeon received bribes from attorneys.[5]
- *Hanguk Nondan* reported that a producer of KBS,[6] who produced a documentary titled *Who Caused the Korean War,* is a follower of Kim Il Sung, the former leader of North Korea.[7]
- MBC aired a news report that an attorney's malpractice resulted in a court decision disadvantageous to his client, describing the attorney as "a man not worthy to be called a man" and "disheartening and vexing." The Supreme Court held that the news was based on truth, but the above expressions are tortious personal attacks beyond the limitation of freedom of expression of opinion.[8]

The following statements have been found to be not defamatory:

- The Supreme Court held that the sentence "The Jeju Resistance Movement of April 3, 1948 was suppressed with relentless slaughter under an illegal declaration of martial law, which was directed by ex-President Syngman Rhee" is not defamatory regarding Syngman Rhee.[9]

- An editorial cartoon depicted people who were blamed for the 1997 financial crisis purchasing airplane tickets and discussing how to fly to foreign countries. The court held that the cartoon should not be interpreted to specifically confirm that the plaintiffs are actually committing or planning a flight to foreign countries.[10]

2. Is libel-by-implication recognized, or, in the alternative, must the complained-of words alone defame the plaintiff?

Indirect, implied libel is possible, even if the complained-of words, in and of themselves, do not defame the plaintiff. Even if the plaintiff is not specifically named, and even if the injurious information is not specifically attributed to the plaintiff, if the disclosure can reasonably be deemed to be injurious to the plaintiff's reputation, libel may be implied.[11]

3. May corporations sue for libel?

Yes, any natural person or corporate or other entity may sue for libel. The infringement on the social status of an entity, in case such infringement has a detrimental effect on the accomplishment of the entity's objectives, constitutes a tort.[12]

4. Is product disparagement recognized, and if so, how does that differ from libel?

Yes, product disparagement is recognized, and there appears to be no requirement that the parties be competitors. This cause of action was allowed to proceed in a case where a TV news channel reported that automobile mileage enhancement devices do not actually work and that the producer of such devices made an exaggerated advertisement.[13] In the advertisements of a powdered milk maker, the milk maker called competitors' milk products "pus milk."[14]

Product disparagement that deceives or misleads consumers, and therefore possibly frustrates fair competition, may also be subject to administrative sanctions (corrective measures or surcharge fines) by the Fair Trade Commission or to criminal sanctions under the Act on Fair Labeling and Advertisement.

5. Must an individual be clearly identified (by name or photograph) to sue for libel? Can a group of persons sue for libel, even though not named?

As indicated above, an individual need not be specifically identified in order to sue for libel, since implied libel is possible. Group libel is recognized, even if the individual persons are not specifically named in the complained-of words. The plaintiffs to the lawsuit must be specifically identified in pleadings.

6. What is the fault standard(s) applied to libel?

a. Does the fault standard depend on the fame or notoriety of the plaintiff?

The law does not provide any detailed guidance as to the fault standard applicable to libel, and in theory, the fault standard should not change depending on the fame or notoriety of the plaintiff.

It should be noted that the heightened public status of the plaintiff may actually result in higher-than-ordinary damages: the fame or notoriety of the plaintiff will naturally have some bearing on the determination of the degree of injury suffered by such plaintiff. Since the injury to reputation may become more serious in the case of famous persons (e.g., public figures), extra care may need to be taken when dealing with information pertaining to such persons.

b. Is there a heightened fault standard or privilege for reporting on matters of public concern or public interest?

Yes. If due care is taken and there is good reason to believe that the information being disclosed is true, the defendant may be protected from liability for libel on the grounds that disclosure benefits the general public.[15] For example, MBC aired a news report that a public prosecutor mistakenly filed a double indictment for one wrongdoing, describing such action as "illegal imprisonment," "unprecedented in the history of the Korean judiciary system" and with a caption "shameful public prosecutor." The Supreme Court held that on the facts presented, even if the above information were not true, MBC exercised due care and had good reason to believe that the information was true.[16]

7. Is financial news about publicly traded companies, or companies involved with a government contract, considered a matter of public interest or otherwise privileged?

No special privilege is granted to financial news reporting about publicly traded companies or companies involved with government contracts. Absent other circumstances, such reporting may not necessarily be considered a matter of public interest.

8. Is there a recognized protection for opinion or "fair comment" on matters of public concern?

There is no statutory protection for opinion or "fair comment" on matters of public concern. In practice, however, Korean courts generally recognize protection for fair comments on matters of public concern based on the freedom of the press principle under the Constitution. The Supreme

Court has held that expression or disclosure of matters that have "public or social value (especially with regard to the morality or integrity of public officials) must be more highly protected in light of freedom of speech rights."[17] At the same time, note that extra care may need to be taken when reporting on matters of public concern or public interest (e.g., public figures), because the injury may be more severe.

9. Are there any requirements upon a plaintiff, such as demand for retraction or right of reply, and if so, what impact do they have?

Yes. Article 764 of the Korean Civil Code provides that a victim of libel may demand that "relevant measures" be taken as necessary for the restoration (to the best extent possible) of such victim's reputation. Such relevant measures would include correction or retraction of the report.

In order to exercise one's right of reply, the claimant must undergo an arbitration procedure and obtain a ruling pursuant to the Periodicals Registration Act or the Act on Promotion of News Communication or the Broadcasting Act. However, under the pending Act on Press Arbitration and Damages Remedy that went into effect on July 28, 2005, one may directly file a claim for the right of reply without undergoing the press arbitration procedure. The exercise of such rights does not preclude the victim's separate right to sue for damages.

10. Is there a privilege for quoting or reporting on:

a. Papers filed in court?

As a general matter, there is no special privilege for quoting or reporting on such material. To the extent the aforementioned documents are intended for public disclosure, accurate quotes with proper attributions and reports prepared with due care will likely benefit from the privilege afforded to disclosure of true information, because the substance of the report will likely be deemed to benefit the general public.

b. Government-issued documents?

Similarly, although there is no stated privilege, the exercise of due care in reporting a matter of public concern will in most cases avoid liability. Reporters are advised to provide an opportunity for a subject to respond to potentially defamatory allegations, and to carefully consider the authenticity of any relied-upon documents.

c. Quasi-governmental proceedings?

No reported case law speaks to this specific issue. However, the greatest degree of protection will depend on the degree to which the public interest is served by the reporting on any such material.

11. Is there a privilege for republishing statements made earlier by other, bona fide, reliable publications or wire services?

No. For instance, if the daily press uses an inadequate method to contact the persons concerned, and in reliance upon other press reports, makes a report without any further effort to verify the facts, such press cannot be exempted from damages liability.[18]

12. Are there any restrictions regarding reporting on:

a. Ongoing criminal investigations?

There are restrictions regarding the publication of the identity of persons under investigation. The Supreme Court has held that, for the report of ongoing criminal investigations: (1) the press must adequately and sufficiently collect news materials supporting the authenticity of the investigated facts; (2) the content of the report must be objective and just; (3) the report may not use such terms or expressions that may give readers an impression that the concerned person is guilty; and (4) the reporter must use anonyms as far as possible, if the concerned person is not a public figure, and must take other necessary measures not to disclose the identity of the concerned person.[19]

In one case, a daily press reporter made a false report of an ongoing criminal case, and he based his report only on other news reports and a copy of the writ of arrest. The Supreme Court held that the reporter did not pay sufficient attention to verifying the content to be reported.[20]

Since the Constitution embodies the concept of "innocent until proven guilty" (Article 27(4)), due care should be exercised when reporting on any criminal investigations or prosecutions so as not to inadvertently injure another's reputation by implying guilt.

b. Ongoing criminal prosecutions?

There are no express statutory restrictions regarding reporting on ongoing criminal prosecutions.

c. Ongoing regulatory investigations?

There are no express statutory restrictions regarding reporting on ongoing regulatory investigations.

d. Ongoing civil litigation, or other judicial proceedings?

There are no express statutory restrictions regarding reporting on civil litigation or other judicial proceedings.

13. Are prior restraints or other prepublication injunctions available on the basis of libel or privacy, and if so, what are the standards for obtaining such relief?

Yes. If the requesting party is able to make a *prima facie* showing of: (1) its right to be protected (e.g., that the information in question is of a private nature which should not be disclosed), and (2) the urgent need for the preliminary injunction (e.g., that there will result immediate and irreparable damage once such information is disclosed), preliminary injunction may be obtainable under Korean Civil Enforcement Procedure Law, Article 300(2).

14. Is a right of privacy recognized (either civilly or criminally)?

a. What is the definition of "private fact"?

The concept of "private fact" is not expressly defined in any statute, but the right of privacy is legally recognized and entitled to protection under both the Constitution and the Korean Criminal Code. Although various provisions of the laws do not provide a simple definition of what constitutes a "private fact," a person's personal life, including any and all information not generally known to the public, would be deemed to be included within the concept of "privacy."[21]

In one case, a TV program aired the silhouette of the face of a victim of failed plastic surgery on her breast, and the voice of the victim was aired without any computer alteration, which would have masked the identity of the victim. The Supreme Court held that this was an infringement of privacy beyond the scope of approval originally given by the victim, and therefore triggered damages liability.[22]

b. Is there a public interest or newsworthiness exception?

In contrast to the public interest exception in libel, newsworthiness alone would not entitle the defendant to take such an exception.[23] As discussed above, if (1) the disclosed information is proven to be true, or (2) the defendant exercised due care and had good reason to believe that the information was true (although it is later proven to be false), it may be possible to avoid liability if the defendant is able to demonstrate that the intention behind the disclosure was solely to benefit the general public.

c. Is the right of privacy based in common law, statute, or constitution?

This right is based in the Constitution.

15. May reporters tape-record their own telephone conversations for note-taking purposes (not rebroadcast) without the consent of the other party?

Yes. Tape-recording a telephone conversation by a party to the conversation is not illegal even if it is done without the consent of the other party. Please note, however, that tape-recording a telephone conversation between two parties without the consent of both parties may be a breach of the Act on Protection of Communications Secrets and may trigger criminal punishment.[24]

16. If permissible to record such tapes, may they be broadcast without permission?

Even though there is no court precedent on this point, we believe that broadcasting the recording without permission in the case above would not breach the Act on Protection of Communications Secrets.

17. Is there a recognized evidentiary privilege preventing the disclosure of confidential sources relied upon by reporters?

There is no statutory "Shield Law," and to date, there have been no court precedents granting such evidentiary privilege to reporters. We note, however, the Civil Procedure Law provides for some basis for a reporter's refusal to disclose its sources as "professional secrets" entitled to protection, in cases where the reporter is called to testify as a third-party witness.[25]

18. In the event that legal papers are served upon the newsroom (such as a civil complaint), are there any particular warnings about accepting service of which we should be aware?

In Korea, service of process will be made through the relevant court office, and not directly on the defendant(s). The defendant(s) would receive notice from the court, and as such, there should be no particular procedural concerns relating to the service of process issue.

19. Has your jurisdiction applied established media law to Internet publishers?

Yes. On November 12, 2003, the Seoul District Court handed down a decision finding the president and reporters of an Internet newspaper, *OhMyNews,* liable for defamation and holding that they must compensate victims for damages.

20. If established media law has been applied to Internet publishers, are there any ways in which Internet publishers (including chat room operators) have to meet different standards?

Not in particular. However, please note that under Article 61 of the Act on Promotion of Use of Information Network and Information Protection, the maximum sanction is increased for defamation through the Internet.

21. Are there any cases where the courts enforced a judgment in libel from another jurisdiction against a publisher in your jurisdiction?
There are no such cases to the best of our knowledge.

Chapter Notes

1. Korean Civil Code, Articles 751(1), 764; Korean Criminal Code, Articles 305(1) and 309(2).

2. A conservative Korean periodical.

3. Supreme Court Decision dated January 24, 2003, 2000 *Da* 37647.

4. Munhwa Broadcasting Corporation, a Korean broadcaster.

5. Supreme Court Decision dated September 2, 2003, 2002 *Da* 63558.

6. Korea Broadcasting System, a Korean broadcaster.

7. Supreme Court Decision dated December 24, 2002, 2000 *Da* 14613.

8. Supreme Court Decision dated March 25, 2003, 2001 *Da* 84480.

9. Supreme Court Decision dated January 19, 2001, 2000 *Da* 10208.

10. Supreme Court Decision dated July 28, 2000, 99 *Da* 6203.

11. Supreme Court Decision dated May 14, 1991, 91 *Do* 420; Supreme Court Decision dated April 12, 1994, 93 *Do* 3535; Supreme Court Decision dated November 9, 1982, 82 *Do* 1256; and Supreme Court Decision dated November 14, 1989, 89 *Do* 1744.

12. Supreme Court Decision dated October 22, 1999, 98 *Da* 6381.

13. Supreme Court Decision dated October 8, 1999, 98 *Da* 40077.

14. Supreme Court Decision dated April 12, 1996, 93 *Da* 40614, 40621.

15. Supreme Court Decision dated October 11, 1988, 85 *Da Ka* 29.

16. Supreme Court Decision dated February 27, 2004, 2001 *Da* 53387.

17. Supreme Court Decision dated February 27, 2004, 2001 *Da* 53387.

18. Supreme Court Decision dated May 28, 1996, 94 *Da* 33828.

19. Supreme Court Decision dated January 26, 1999, 97 *Da* 10215, 10222.

20. Supreme Court Decision dated May 10, 2002, 2000 *Da* 50213.

21. Constitution, Article 17; Korean Criminal Code, Article 316; Supreme Court Decision dated September 4, 1998, 96 *Da* 11327.

22. Supreme Court Decision dated September 4, 1998, 96 *Da* 11327.

23. Supreme Court Decision dated September 4, 1998, 96 *Da* 1132.

24. Supreme Court Decision dated October 8, 2002, 2002 *Do* 123.

25. Korean Civil Procedure Law, Article 315(1).

CHAPTER 10

Singapore

TAY PENG CHENG

Wong Partnership

Wong Partnership
One George Street #20-01
Singapore 049145
Phone: (65) 6416 8000
Fax: (65) 6532 5722
www.wongpartnership.com.sg
pengcheng.tay@wongpartnership.com.sg

Introduction to the Singapore Legal System

The Singapore legal system has evolved since the attainment of independence from the Federation of Malaysia in 1965. Although there are areas of Singapore law with roots in Indian, Australian, and New Zealand legislation, the foundation of the Singapore legal system is largely English in origin. In the early days, during the evolution of the Singapore legal system, the principles and rules of English common law and equity were applied in Singapore by way of general reception. There was also specific reception of English law when a local statute or provision thereof provided for such application.

The Application of English Law Act, which was enacted in 1993, clarified the application of English law in Singapore. Under this Act, English enactments after November 12, 1993 do not form part of Singapore law, except those specifically set out in the First Schedule of the Act and any other English enactment which applies to or is in force in Singapore by virtue of any written law. English enactments listed in the First Schedule of the Act (which also provides for the extent of application of each enactment) include the Partnership Act, the Misrepresentation Act, the Sale of Goods Act, and the Unfair Contract Terms Act.

The Singapore judiciary system is broadly divided into two levels: The upper tier comprises the Supreme Court, which consists of the Court of Appeal and the High Court. The Subordinate Courts follow, which comprise the District and Magistrate Courts (with a civil jurisdictional limit of S$250,000 and S$60,000, respectively) and other specialist courts including the Juvenile Court, Coroner's Courts, and the Small Claims Tribunal (with a civil jurisdictional limit of S$10,000). The structure of the Supreme Court is governed by the Supreme Court of Judicature Act and that of the Subordinate Courts by the Subordinate Courts Act. All proceedings are tried before a judge (or a panel of judges, in the Court of Appeal). There are no juries in the Singapore legal system, and fact-finding in both civil and criminal matters is undertaken by the judge.

The Court of Appeal is the highest appellate court in Singapore and hears both civil and criminal appeals. The High Court exercises both original as well as appellate civil and criminal jurisdiction. The Subordinate Courts exercise both civil and criminal jurisdiction.

1. What is the locally accepted definition of libel?

There is no exhaustive definition of what constitutes defamation in Singapore. A statement is defamatory of the person about whom it is published if it:

1. tends to lower him in the estimation of right-thinking members of society generally;[1]
2. exposes him to public hatred, contempt, or ridicule;[2] or
3. causes him to be shunned or avoided.[3]

There are two categories of defamation—libel and slander. For there to be libel, the statement must be made in writing or some other permanent form. Where the words are published orally or in some other transient form, it is termed slander.

Examples of statements that have been found to be defamatory include allegations that a politician is spreading lies and defaming the defendant and that a police report will be lodged against the politician for a criminal offense.[4] An advertisement asserting that a competitive retailer is lying to the public as to the source of parts used in his products,[5] and allegations that a company has a "poor credit rating,"[6] are further examples.

2. Is libel-by-implication recognized, or, in the alternative, must the complained-of words alone defame the plaintiff?

Yes, it is possible to defame a person by implication. When the court determines the meaning of the words, it seeks to ascertain what reasonable persons would collectively understand as the natural or ordinary meaning of the words. Such a meaning is not confined to the literal or strict meaning of the words but includes any inferences which can reasonably be drawn by such persons.[7]

Even if the ordinary meaning of the words is not defamatory, it may become so when the words are coupled with special facts that the readers know.[8]

3. May corporations sue for libel?

Yes, a corporation, as a legal entity, is entitled to mount a claim for libel. In this regard, section 19(5) of the Companies Act[9] provides that a corporation shall be capable of suing and being sued.

4. Is product disparagement recognized, and if so, how does that differ from libel?

A cause of action is available for a statement disparaging property or goods, under the separate tort of "malicious falsehood."[10] If, however, a statement disparaging property also implies some defamatory meaning about the owner and is made in writing or some other permanent form, an action for libel may be possible (although the law will ensure that a plaintiff does not recover damages twice for the same loss).

The primary difference between the tort of malicious falsehood and libel is that an essential ingredient of the former is proof of special damage.[11] Hence, if there is loss of reputation but no pecuniary loss, an action for malicious falsehood will not succeed. This is subject to the exception in section 6(1) of the Defamation Act[12] which states that:

> In any action for slander of title, slander of goods or other malicious falsehood, it shall not be necessary to allege or prove special damage:
> (a) if the words upon which the action is founded are calculated to cause pecuniary damage to the plaintiff and are published in writing or other permanent form; or
> (b) if the said words are calculated to cause pecuniary damage to the plaintiff in respect of any office, profession, calling, trade or business held or carried on by him at the time of the publication.

In libel, there is no need to show special damage before the statement becomes actionable.

Another difference is that for malicious falsehood, the words must be published maliciously. There is no such requirement for libel. Further, for malicious falsehood, it is not necessary for the statement to injure the reputation of the plaintiff, which is a requirement for libel.

5. Must an individual be clearly identified (by name or photograph) to sue for libel? Can a group of persons sue for libel, even though not named?

There is no requirement that the subject of a story be expressly named. Even if an individual is not expressly named or identified, an action may proceed if ordinary, sensible readers with their general knowledge and common sense could and did understand them to refer to the plaintiff.[13]

A class of persons cannot generally be defamed as a class, nor can an individual be defamed by a general reference to the class to which he belongs.[14] However, if the words, combined with the relevant circumstances, refer to some persons individually, those who were referred to can sue.[15]

6. What is the fault standard(s) applied to libel?

a. Does the fault standard depend on the fame or notoriety of the plaintiff?

The fame or notoriety of the plaintiff does not affect the actionability of the words, although it would have an impact on the damages recoverable. However, it may be more difficult for the plaintiff to prove that the words were defamatory (in that they caused others to think lowly of him), if he already has a poor reputation to begin with.

b. Is there a heightened fault standard or privilege for reporting on matters of public concern or public interest?

There is no higher fault standard when reporting matters of public interest. There are, however, more defenses available to the defendant if he is reporting a matter of public interest. A subject is considered a matter of public interest if it is such as to affect people at large, so that they may be interested in, or concerned with, what is going on or what may happen to them or others.

Some examples of matters of public interest include political or state matters, church and religious matters, the management of public institutions and public performances. Matters of public interest are not privileged solely for that reason, but may form the basis of two defenses—qualified privilege and fair comment. It is important to note that both defenses are defeated if the plaintiff can show that the publication was done maliciously.

A privileged occasion is an occasion where the person who makes a communication has an interest or a legal, social, or moral duty, to make such communication to the person to whom it is made, and the person to whom the communication is so made has a corresponding interest or duty to receive it.[16]

Having said that, there is no general "media privilege" at common law—the law does not recognize an interest in the public strong enough to give rise generally to a duty to communicate in the press; such a duty may only exist on special facts.[17] Along with the duty to communicate is a corresponding interest to receive such information on the part of the public.[18] In addition, the duty must be a duty to publish to the public at large and an interest must exist in the public at large to receive the publication—it is insufficient if only a segment of the public is concerned with the subject matter of the publication.[19]

Section 12 of the Defamation Act also provides for specific occasions when the defense of qualified privilege is available to a newspaper. These provisions, however, do not limit or abridge any privilege subsisting at common law before the commencement of the Defamation Act.[20]

7. Is financial news about publicly traded companies, or companies involved with a government contract, considered a matter of public interest or otherwise privileged?

In the same context, financial news about publicly listed companies would be a matter of public interest. There may be greater difficulty in making the same contention for private companies involved with a government contract.

8. Is there a recognized protection for opinion or "fair comment" on matters of public concern?

There is a defense of fair comment available under Singapore law. In order to succeed in the defense, the defendant needs to establish the following four elements:[21]

1. the words complained of are comments, though they may consist of or include inference of facts;
2. the comment is on a matter of public interest;
3. the comment is based on facts; and
4. the comment is one which a fair-minded person can honestly make on the facts proved.

The defense is only available if the statement was not published maliciously.

9. Are there any requirements upon a plaintiff, such as demand for retraction or right of reply, and if so, what impact do they have?

There is no requirement that the plaintiff must first demand a retraction or a right of reply before a suit is filed. A right of reply, commonly offered by a newspaper to an allegedly defamed person, is not necessarily of legal significance, since it does not show that the newspaper accepts that the earlier statement was in fact defamatory.

Section 7 of the Defamation Act provides that a person who claims to have published the libel innocently may make an Offer of Amends. If such an offer is accepted by the plaintiff, section 7(1)(a) provides that he may not sue for libel after that. If such an offer is rejected, section 7(1)(b) provides that it may be a defense for the defendant to show that he had published the information innocently, that the offer was made as soon as practicable, and that the offer has not been withdrawn.

Section 10 of the Defamation Act also provides that a defendant may, in mitigation of damages, provide evidence that he had made or offered an apology to the plaintiff, as soon as he had an opportunity to do so.

10. Is there a privilege for quoting or reporting on:

a. Papers filed in court?

There is qualified privilege attaching to such reports, under item 2 of Part I of the Schedule to the Defamation Act, read with section 12 of the Defamation Act. The copy or extract must be fair and accurate and the publication must be made without malice.

As for reports of judicial proceedings, under section 11(1) of the Defamation Act, "a fair and accurate and contemporaneous report of proceedings publicly heard before any court lawfully exercising judicial authority within Singapore and of the judgment, sentence or finding of any such court shall be absolutely privileged, and any fair and bona fide comment thereon shall be protected, although such judgment, sentence or finding be subsequently reversed, quashed or varied, unless at the time of the publication of such report or comment the defendant who claims the protection afforded by this section knew or ought to have known of such reversal, quashing or variation."

However, section 11(2) states the qualification that nothing in section 11 shall authorize the publication of any "blasphemous, seditious or indecent matter or of any matter the publication of which is prohibited by law."

b. Government-issued documents?

This depends on the nature of the document, and the circumstances under which it was issued. Qualified privilege will attach to documents issued in accordance with or under the circumstances contemplated in the Schedule to the Defamation Act, e.g., a notice, advertisement, or report issued by a public officer in accordance with the requirements of any written law (item 3 of Part I), or a copy of a fair and accurate report or summary of any notice issued for the information of the public by or on behalf of the government (item 5 of Part II).

Under section 7 of the Parliament (Privileges, Immunities and Powers) Act,[22] reports, papers, and journals which are published directly under the authority of Parliament are protected by absolute privilege and any person who is subject to any civil or criminal proceedings on account of the publication by such person or his employee, by order or under the authority of Parliament or any committee, of any reports, papers, or journals, has the statutory protection of a summary stay of proceedings. By comparison, those who publish extracts from or abstracts of any such parliamentary report, paper, or journal are given only a qualified privilege under section 8 of the Parliament (Privileges, Immunities and Powers) Act, and they have to prove that the extract or abstract was printed or published bona fide and without malice. Part II of the Act also enumerates a wide range of circumstances subject to a qualified privilege.

c. Quasi-governmental proceedings?

Possibly, provided it satisfies the requirements of item 3 of Part II of the Schedule to the Defamation Act, e.g., that it must be a fair and accurate report of proceedings at a meeting of a commission, tribunal committee, or board appointed for the purpose of an inquiry, being a meeting to which admission is not denied to representatives of newspapers or other members of the public.

11. Is there a privilege for republishing statements made earlier by other, bona fide, reliable publications or wire services?

Under common law, every republication of a libel is a new libel and each publisher is answerable as if it originated with him.[23] Thus, it is no defense to claim that the defendant's publication was based on a previously published statement.

12. Are there any restrictions regarding reporting on:

a. Ongoing criminal investigations?

As for ongoing criminal investigations, if information on such investigations is released by the investigating agency, these can be published. (See answers to Question 10b. above.) Restrictions may, however, be placed on the publication of information which is protected by the Official Secrets Act (OSA).[24]

It would be a contravention of the OSA for a person to receive information knowing, or having reasonable grounds to believe, that such information was, at the time of receipt, communicated to him in contravention of the OSA.[25]

b. Ongoing criminal prosecutions?

The Judicial Proceedings (Regulation of Reports) Act[26] (JPA) places some restrictions on the reporting of judicial proceedings. Under section 2 of the JPA, it is unlawful to print or publish:

(a) in relation to any judicial proceedings any indecent matter or indecent medical, surgical or physiological details being matter or details the publication of which would be calculated to injure public morals; or

(b) in relation to any judicial proceedings for divorce, dissolution of marriage, nullity of marriage, judicial separation or restitution of conjugal rights, any particulars other than the following:

(i) the names, addresses and occupations of the parties and witnesses;

(ii) a concise statement of the charges, the defences and countercharges in support of which evidence has been given;

(iii) submissions on any point of law arising in the course of the proceedings and the decision of the court thereon; and

(iv) the decision of the court and any observations made by the court in giving it.

Provided that nothing in this paragraph shall be held to permit the publication of anything contrary to paragraph (a).

The Children and Young Persons Act[27] (CYPA) also places restrictions on the publication of information relating to court proceedings. Sections 35(1) and (2) of the CYPA state as follows:

(1) Subject to subsection (2), no person shall—

(a) publish or broadcast any information relating to any proceedings in any court or on appeal from any court that reveals the name, address or school or that includes any particulars that are calculated to lead to the identification of any child or young person concerned in the proceedings, either as being the person against or in respect of whom the proceedings are taken or as being a witness therein; or

(b) publish or broadcast any picture as being or including a picture of any child or young person so concerned in any such proceedings.

(2) The court or the Minister may, if satisfied that it is in the interests of justice so to do, by order dispense with the requirements of subsection (1) to such extent as may be specified in the order.

There may also be restrictions dictated by the Court in respect of a particular matter.

c. Ongoing regulatory investigations?
Generally, the prohibitions on material prescribed in Questions 12a. and b. above.

d. Ongoing civil litigation, or other judicial proceedings?
Generally, the prohibitions on material prescribed in Questions 12a. and b. above.

13. Are prior restraints or other prepublication injunctions available on the basis of libel or privacy, and if so, what are the standards for obtaining such relief?
The Court has the power to grant interlocutory injunctions to restrain the publication or repetition of defamatory statements.[28] However, as freedom of speech is a constitutional liberty,[29] the jurisdiction will be exercised sparingly and only in clear cases.[30]

The cases show that the Court may grant such an interlocutory injunction where:
1. the statement is unarguably defamatory;
2. there are no grounds for concluding the statement may be true;
3. there is no other defense which might succeed; and
4. there is evidence of an intention to repeat or publish the defamatory statement.

14. Is a right of privacy recognized (either civilly or criminally)?

a. What is the definition of "private fact"?
There is no general right of privacy under Singapore law. There is also no specific legislative protection in Singapore with regard to privacy.

b. Is there a public interest or newsworthiness exception?
Not applicable.

c. Is the right of privacy based in common law, statute, or constitution?
Not applicable.

15. May reporters tape-record their own telephone conversations for note-taking purposes (not rebroadcast) without the consent of the other party?

There are no restrictions against the taping of conversations in such context. However, in the defense of a libel suit, the probative value of such taped conversations may be challenged if the publisher seeks to rely on the tape in evidence.

16. If permissible to record such tapes, may they be broadcast without permission?

As there is no general right of privacy in Singapore, there is no restriction on the grounds of privacy against broadcasting such tapes without permission. However, there may be restrictions on other grounds—for example, that the broadcast may be a breach of confidence. If the tape contains defamatory remarks, such broadcast may result in publication of the remarks.

17. Is there a recognized evidentiary privilege preventing the disclosure of confidential sources relied upon by reporters?

There are no such special privileges accorded to confidential sources under Singapore law.

Where a report is published based on information obtained from unnamed or confidential sources, and justification is pleaded as a defense, the publisher must be prepared to call those sources as witnesses in trial. This creates difficulties for a publisher, as it involves balancing the successful defense of a claim against journalistic principles. Ultimately, a commercial decision will have to be made as to whether a defense can be mounted without the necessity of calling such witnesses.

18. In the event that legal papers are served upon the newsroom (such as a civil complaint), are there any particular warnings about accepting service of which we should be aware?

Legal process (e.g., a Writ of Summons) has to be served personally in Singapore. Hence, if the defendant is a Singapore company, the legal process has to be served personally[31] on the registered office address of the company.

Likewise, if the defendant is a reporter, the legal process has to be served on the reporter personally (whether at home, in the office, or at any other place), unless an order for substituted service[32] is obtained. In that case, the legal process may be served through an advertisement in the newspapers, or be posted at the last known address of the reporter.

The defendant will have eight days after service to file a memorandum of appearance with the Court if he wishes to defend the claim brought against him.[33] It is important that this deadline be adhered to, as the plaintiff will be entitled to enter judgment in default of appearance if the defendant does not take the necessary steps within the stipulated time frame.[34]

19. Has your jurisdiction applied established media law to Internet publishers?

There have been cases where one of the forms of publication of the defamatory statement was publication on the Internet.[35] However, to the best of our knowledge, in these cases, the publication on the Internet was not an issue.

20. If established media law has been applied to Internet publishers, are there any ways in which Internet publishers (including chat room operators) have to meet different standards?

The cases so far have not dealt with Internet publication in detail.

21. Are there any cases where the courts enforced a judgment in libel from another jurisdiction against a publisher in your jurisdiction?

To the best of our knowledge, there have been no such cases as yet.

Chapter Notes

1. *Sim v. Stretch* [1936] 2 All ER 1237 followed in *Aaron v. Cheong Yip Seng* [1996] 1 SLR 623 and *Oei Hong Leong v. Ban Song Long David and Others* [2005] 1 SLR 277.

2. *Sim v. Stretch* [1936] 2 All ER 1237; *Lee Kuan Yew v. Davies* [1989] 1 SLR 1063.

3. *Youssoupoff v. Metro-Goldwyn-Mayer Pictures Ltd* (1934) 50 TLR 581, as accepted locally in *Oei Hong Leong v. Ban Song Long David and Others, supra,* note 1.

4. *Tang Liang Hong v. Lee Kuan Yew and Another and Other Appeals* [1998] 1 SLR 97.

5. *Cristofori Music Pte Ltd v. Robert Piano Co Pte Ltd* [2000] 3 SLR 503.

6. *L.K. Ang Construction Pte Ltd v. Chubb Singapore Private Limited* [2003] 1 SLR 635.

7. *Aaron v. Cheong Yip Seng* [1996] 1 SLR 623.

8. *Rubber Improvement Ltd v. Daily Telegraph Ltd* [1964] AC 234; *DHKW Marketing & Anor v. Nature's Farm Pte Ltd* [1999] 2 SLR 400.

9. Cap. 50.

10. *Kaye v. Robertson* [1991] FSR 62, followed in *Challenger Technologies v. Dennison Transoceanic Corporation* [1997] 3 SLR 582.

11. *Joyce v. Sengupta* [1993] 1 WLR 337, which was cited with approval in *Integrated Information Pte Ltd v. CD-Biz Directories Pte Ltd & Ors* [2000] 3 SLR 457.

12. Cap. 75.

13. *Lee Kuan Yew v. Davies, supra,* note 2.

14. *DKHW Marketing & Anor v. Nature's Farm Pte Ltd, supra,* note 7.

15. *Knupffer v. London Express Newspaper Ltd* [1944] AC 116.

16. *Supra,* note 5.

17. *Supra,* note 7.

18. Ibid.

19. Ibid.

20. *Supra,* note 12, section 12(4).

21. *Chen Cheng v. Central Christian Church* [1999] 1 SLR 94.

22. Cap. 217.

23. *Supra,* note 6; *Lee Kuan Yew v. Chee Soon Juan* [2003] 3 SLR 8.

24. Cap. 213.

25. Ibid., section 5(2).

26. Cap. 149.

27. Cap. 38.

28. In the exercise of its equitable jurisdiction under section 3(a) of the Civil Law Act (Cap. 43) and section 18(2) of the Supreme Court of Judicature Act (Cap. 322) read with para. 14 of the First Schedule thereto. The District Courts have the power to grant injunctions under section 31(2) of the Subordinate Courts Act (Cap. 321).

29. Article 14, Constitution of the Republic of Singapore.

30. *Kwek Juan Bok Lawrence v. Lim Han Yong* [1989] 1 SLR 655.

31. Rules of Court, O 10 r 1.

32. Rules of Court, O 62 r 5.

33. Rules of Court, O 12 r 2 read with O 12 r 4.

34. Rules of Court, O 13 rr 1 and 2.

35. For example, *Tang Liang Hong v. Lee Kuan Yew and Another and Other Appeals, supra,* note 4.

Europe

CHAPTER 11

Belgium

STEVEN DE SCHRIJVER

Van Bael & Bellis

Van Bael & Bellis
Louizalaan 165 Avenue Louise
B-1050 Brussels, Belgium
Phone: 32-2-647-73-50
Fax: 32-2-640-64-99
www.vanbaelbellis.com
sdeschrijver@vanbaelbellis.com

Introduction to the Belgian Legal System

The Belgian judicial system resembles the civil law system of its neighbor, France. There are two court branches within the Belgian system: the administrative courts and the ordinary courts. The administrative courts deal with matters relating to administrative law, i.e., the organization, the functioning, and the control of the executive. The ordinary courts have jurisdiction over civil and criminal actions. In view of the territorial organization of its court system, Belgium is divided into more than 200 counties (*kantons/cantons*), 26 districts (*arrondissementen/arrondissements*), and 5 judicial areas (*rechtsgebieden/ressorts*).

At the county level, which is the lowest level, a distinction must be made between the Police Court (*Politierechtbank/Tribunal de police*) and the Justice of the Peace (*Vredegerecht/Justice de paix*). A Justice of the Peace is, in general, empowered to hear all cases involving claims of up to €1,860. In addition to his general competence, a Justice of the Peace has exclusive jurisdiction over certain specific claims regardless of the amount involved in the claim (e.g., real property leases). Appeals against judgments of the Justice of the Peace are, depending on the subject matter, heard by the Court of First Instance or the Commercial Court of the district in which the Justice of the Peace is located. The Police Courts are empowered to hear all cases involving civil consequences of road accidents and cases involving misdemeanors (*overtredingen/contraventions*) (these are mostly minor traffic offenses). Appeals against judgments of the Police Court are heard by the Criminal Court (*Correctionele Rechtbank/Tribunal correctionnel*), which is a division of the Court of First Instance.

At the district level, each of Belgium's 26 judicial districts has three different courts resolving different matters. There is a Court of First Instance composed of three divisions: one dealing with civil law (Civil Court—*Burgerlijke Rechtbank/Tribunal civil*), one dealing with criminal law (Criminal Court—*Correctionele Rechtbank/Tribunal correctionnel*), and one dealing with juvenile matters (Juvenile Court—*Jeugdrechtbank/ Tribunal de la jeunesse*). Furthermore, there is a Commercial Court (*Rechtbank Van Koophandel/Tribunal de commerce*) empowered to hear commercial cases. Finally, the Labor Court (*Arbeidsrechtbank/Tribunal du travail*) specializes in labor matters.

At the judicial level, Belgium has five Courts of Appeal and five Labor Courts of Appeal. Appeals against judgments rendered by the Courts of First Instance and the Commercial Courts are brought before the Court of Appeal (*Hof van Beroep/Cour d'appel*). Appeals against judgments rendered by the Labor Courts are brought before the Labor Court of Appeal (*Arbeidshof/Cour du travail*) of the judicial area in which the Labor Court is located. In the area of criminal law, the Assize Courts (*Hoven van Assisen/ Cours d'assises*) and the military courts should also be cited.

Belgium has one Supreme Court (*Hof van Cassatie/Cour de cassation*), which is located in Brussels. The principal task of the Supreme Court is to review judgments that can no longer be appealed on the merits. The review by the Supreme Court is limited to issues of law. The Supreme Court will only verify whether the judgment which is being reviewed has applied the law correctly and has respected mandatory procedural rules.

Finally, Belgium also has a Court of Arbitration (*Arbitragehof/Cour d'arbitrage*) and a Council of State (*Raad van State/Conseil d'Etat*). Both courts have constitutional and administrative law competences.

1. What is the locally accepted definition of libel?

Criminal Libel

Law recognizes libel in both criminal and civil jurisprudential spheres. Under Articles 443 *et seq.* of the Belgian Criminal Code, libel consists of "viciously and publicly attributing to a given person a fact, the legal proof of which may not or cannot be established and which is likely to harm that person's honor or to expose that person to public contempt."

The Belgian Criminal Code distinguishes between cases where the author of the allegations is not able to prove the veracity of the allegations, even though he or she was allowed to do so[1] (*laster/calomnie*), and cases where the law does not allow the author of the allegations to bring such proof or where such proof is impossible (*eeroof/diffamation*). Criminal liability requires the satisfaction of various conditions.

First, there must be intent to harm the person who is the subject of the allegations (*animus iurandi*).[2] The intent to harm is not presumed and must be duly demonstrated by the public prosecutor. The intent to harm can simply be inferred, however, from the statement at issue.[3] Criminal libel is not simply constituted by the false facts put forth in the complained-of statement, but rather by the purely subjective and particularly insulting quality attributed by the author of the allegations to the acts of the article's subject.[4] In this regard, it does not matter whether the author of the allegations knew, at the time of making the allegations, that the allegations were false.[5]

Second, the complained-of statement must be sufficiently precise for criminal liability to lie. Indeed, Articles 443 *et seq.* of the Belgian Criminal Code require the imputation of a precise fact about the subject, i.e., not merely a general character failing about the subject.[6]

Third, the allegation must be the object of a real and actual publication. Pursuant to Article 444 of the Belgian Criminal Code, the allegations must have been made: (1) in public meetings or public places; or (2) in the presence of several individuals in a place open to a certain number of persons; or (3) in any place, in the presence of the offended person and in front of witnesses; or (4) on written documents or images which have been distributed, sold, or exposed to the public; or (5) on written documents which have not been publicized but which have been addressed to several persons.

Libel committed by journalists in the printed press is adjudicated in accordance with the laws governing the press. Pursuant to Article 150 of the Belgian Constitution, violations of the laws governing the press (*persmisdrijf/délit de presse*) must be prosecuted before the Assize Court[7] (Hof van Assisen/Cour d'assises). There is an exception for complaints about articles motivated by racism and xenophobia. In those instances, the criminal court (Correctionele Rechtbank/Tribunal correctionnel) has jurisdiction under the Law of 7 May 1999.[8]

The Belgian Supreme Court has held that four elements must be present for there to be a violation of the laws governing the press:[9] (1) a criminal offense; (2) an abuse in the expression of one's opinions (in this regard, "opinion" must be construed broadly and includes any thought); (3) the use of printed material (i.e., the laws governing the press can only be violated when the author has manifested his or her opinion in the printed press); and (4) publicity (i.e., the litigious statement must have been really and effectively publicized).[10]

In practice, prosecution before the Assize Court for violations of the laws governing the press is rare,[11] because the procedure is costly, requires a jury, and usually gives the sued-upon statements further publicity.

It should finally be noted that the Belgian Supreme Court has held that libel broadcast via radio or on television is not covered by Article 150 of the Belgian Constitution and must therefore be prosecuted before lower criminal courts (Correctionele Rechtbank/Tribunal correctionnel).[12] In one case, the Belgian Supreme Court applied Article 150 of the Belgian Constitution to the broadcasting of a television show because it was accompanied by the publication of a book on the same subject matter, thus considering that the defamatory statements were associated.[13] The question of whether libel committed on the Internet is a violation of the laws governing the press has not yet been addressed by the Belgian Supreme Court.

Civil Libel

Pursuant to Articles 1382 *et seq.* of the Belgian Civil Code, libel plaintiffs can seek vindication in tort, without regard to whether the conditions set out by Articles 443 *et seq.* of the Belgian Criminal Code are not fulfilled.[14] This is the case where, for instance, there is no *animus iurandi.*[15]

Under Belgian law, the civil libel plaintiff is required to establish the existence of the following three elements: (1) a negligent act or omission (a fault);[16] (2) an injury which he or she has sustained; and (3) a causal relationship between the negligent act or omission and the injury.

The fault standard in libel is no different from that in other torts. A fault may have been committed by a journalist where he or she has breached a legal provision or where he or she has not acted as a reasonably prudent journalist would have, if placed in similar circumstances. A breach of the provisions of the Belgian Criminal Code on libel is considered a *per se* fault for the application of Article 1382 *et seq.* of the Belgian Civil Code.

Belgian courts have found the following statements to be defamatory: allegations that the manager of a co-ownership had been previously laid off from his activities as manager of another enterprise and that his mistakes in the management of the joint ownership had cost 100,000 Belgian francs to the joint owners;[17] precise allegations that a journalist is a member of the Israeli secret service, thus casting doubt as to his objectivity;[18] allegations that sexual abuses are statistically more often committed by Catholic priests than by "normal" persons and statements that the number of Catholic priests which have been prosecuted are just the "visible part of the iceberg";[19] allegations that a security company did not have the required special license from the Council of Ministers and that the company was in fact a private militia;[20] the publication of pictures with provoking or catchy titles in order to discredit a person;[21] defamation of former NATO secretary-general Mr. W. Claes in relation to his involvement in the Agusta helicopter scandal;[22] false allegations that Finance Minister D. Reynders possesses a secret bank account in Luxembourg.[23]

Belgian law is unique insofar as it has a strict specificity requirement, and statements of a vague or generalized nature are generally rejected as the basis for a libel claim. Belgian courts have found the following statements not to be defamatory: vague allegations relating to the bad management of a co-ownership;[24] allegations that a person shows a lack of civic spirit;[25] allegations that a person is crazy;[26] allegations that a person is a racist or a fascist.[27]

2. Is libel-by-implication recognized, or, in the alternative, must the complained-of words alone defame the plaintiff?

Libel-by-implication is not expressly recognized by the Belgian Criminal Code as a separate offense. Nonetheless, if an implied statement fulfills the conditions set out by the Belgian Criminal Code or if an implied statement fulfills the conditions set out by Articles 1382 *et seq.* of the Belgian Civil Code, it will trigger the application of the aforementioned provisions. In this respect, it does not matter that the allegations are formulated in the form of insinuations or requests for explanations.[28]

For instance, the Court of First Instance of Brussels ordered a Belgian newspaper to pay damages to a plaintiff for having published, under catchy and provocative headlines, statements that a reasonable reader would interpret as the plaintiff's involvement in a widely covered pedophilia and murder case.[29] It was held that journalists must only use data which they have controlled, to the reasonable extent of their means, and that the use of smart quotes or the conditional tense does not exempt them from liability in this respect.[30]

In another case, the Court of First Instance of Brussels held that the statement, made at a conference, that a journalist is a member of the Israeli secret service, without providing any proof thereof, must be considered to be defamatory. Although there is nothing defamatory on its face about being a member of this unit, the court found that such a statement could engender, in the minds of both the employer of the journalist and his or her readers, doubts as to the objectivity of that journalist's information.[31]

In a judgment of March 10, 1998, the Court of First Instance of Brussels considered that a press article creating confusion in the minds of the readers between two series of house searches, leading the general public to believe that the two series of searches related to the same individuals and the same companies, were defamatory. The Court of First Instance considered that those insinuations harmed the reputation of the companies, even though the conditional tense had been used in the article, as the plaintiffs were still considered, in the minds of the readers, to have participated in the illegal activities described in the article.[32]

3. May corporations sue for libel?

Yes, both civilly and criminally. Pursuant to Article 443 *et seq.* of the Belgian Criminal Code, any corporation can file a complaint with the public prosecutor if it considers that a person viciously and publicly attributed a fact to the corporation, likely to harm that corporation's honor or reputation or to expose that corporation to public contempt. Indeed, the victim of any allegation may be a natural person or a legal entity,[33] whether private or public.

As a criminal procedure is not likely to bring relief to a corporation which has been the victim of libelous allegations, the corporation will usually sue the author of the allegations for libel before the civil courts on the basis of the legal provisions governing tort liability. As mentioned above, the corporation will have to demonstrate fault on the part of the author of the allegations, an actual damage it has suffered, and a causal link between the fault and the damage.[34]

4. Is product disparagement recognized, and if so, how does that differ from libel?

Disparagement is recognized under Belgian law and consists in making a declaration that contains an element or an allegation likely to harm, in the minds of third parties, the creditworthiness or the reputation of an economic operator, or the products or services it offers, or its activities.[35] Under Belgian law, disparagement is thus considered to be a very prejudicial attack on a trader, which harms that trader's reputation, by means of a libelous act or simply by means of a critique which enables third parties to identify that trader.[36] It is an allegation likely to discredit the trader.[37]

Pursuant to the Law of 14 July 1991 on Unfair Trade Practices and the Information and the Protection of the Consumer (the Law on Unfair Trade Practices),[38] any advertising that contains elements which are disparaging about another trader, his products, its services, or its activities, is prohibited.[39] Product disparagement is thus considered, under Belgian law, to be an unfair trade practice, even if it only takes place by allusions or insinuations.[40] It does not matter whether the declaration is true or false or whether the declaration was made in good or bad faith.[41]

It should furthermore be noted that any advertising which contains misleading or disparaging comparisons or comparisons which unnecessarily allow the possibility of identifying one or more other traders, is also prohibited.[42] Finally, any comparative advertising which disparages or discredits trademarks, commercial names, other distinctive signs, products, services, or activities of a competitor is forbidden.[43] For instance, a trader may not give the impression that the producer or the importer of products is guilty of counterfeiting products and selling counterfeited products, absent a judicial ruling on the matter.[44]

For a disparaging statement to be contrary to the Law on Unfair Trade Practices, some publicity must be given to the statement. A written statement which has only been sent to a small number of recipients will therefore not be considered to constitute disparagement, even if it contains, for instance, a tendentious description of legal proceedings against another trader.[45]

It should finally be noted that a critique in which a trader may be identified may constitute disparagement.[46]

5. Must an individual be clearly identified (by name or photograph) to sue for libel? Can a group of persons sue for libel, even though not named?

In order to sue for libel, a natural person or a legal entity must be clearly designated and, if the person is not named, should at least be identifiable. Any attack on a group of people or on a legal entity that does not have legal personality (such as a family)[47] does not constitute a violation of the law. Nonetheless, in such a case, any identifiable member of such entity could sue for libel if his honor has been harmed or if he or she has been subjected to public contempt.[48]

Criminal law contains exceptions allowing some form of group libel. Under Articles 446 and 447 of the Belgian Criminal Code, libel toward constituted bodies (such as, for example, legislative chambers, universities, certain religious communities) is punished in the same way as libel toward individuals. Similarly, there is specific legislation which authorizes certain associations to file claims to defend their members or certain interests they promote. For example, the Law of 30 July 1991 on the Repression of Acts Inspired by Racism or Xenophobia[49] provides, in its Article 5, that human rights associations may go to court to defend the rights of their members or the interests which they protect.

6. What is the fault standard(s) applied to libel?

As mentioned above, in order for Articles 1382 *et seq.* to apply, any injured person must establish the existence of the following three elements: (1) a negligent act or omission (a fault); (2) an injury which he or she has sustained; and (3) a causal relationship between the negligent act or omission and the injury.

There is a fault on the part of the journalist where the journalist has breached a legal provision or where he or she has not acted as a reasonably prudent journalist should have, in similar circumstances. In this regard, if a journalist breaches the provisions on libel contained in the Belgian Criminal Code or if he breaches Article 10 of the European Convention for the Protection of Human Rights and Fundamental Freedoms of the Council of Europe (the "Convention"), he will also be considered to have committed a fault for tort liability purposes. It should be noted that if criminal proceedings are pending, the outcome of which is likely to contradict the judgment of the civil court or to have an influence on the outcome of the case, the civil judge must postpone its decision until the criminal judge has rendered his or her judgment.[50]

The appreciation of the fault must be made *in concreto,* i.e., the judge must consider the alleged fault of the journalist in its context.[51] This implies that the judge must balance the appreciation of the fault with the conditions of dissemination of the sued-upon statements, in particular the particularities of the media used and the possibilities of a plaintiff's reply which were available on such a media.[52]

In his or her balancing, the judge must take into account the behavior of a reasonably competent and diligent journalist.[53] The judge must also take account of the behavior of the average reader, listener, or viewer, i.e., a reasonably intelligent and attentive public.[54] Regard must also be given to the type of media and the nature of the information.[55]

Belgian case law has established the following practical guidelines that journalists should keep in mind at all times:

1. A journalist should behave as a "normal, careful and circumspect journalist." It is not required that the information published has a scientific accuracy or absolute reliability. However, a journalist's publication cannot be based on rumors or unreliable information. Journalists are not entitled to publish articles that are manifestly incorrect or not supported by any evidence;[56]

2. A journalist's publication should be based on verified sources to the extent that this is reasonably possible. Absolute objectivity is however not required;[57]

3. A journalist should act carefully and his information should be reliable and verified;[58]

4. A journalist should prove his or her allegations.[59] It is not sufficient to publish defamatory allegations in a conditional manner or to

place them between quotation marks[60] or to formulate them as a question.[61] A journalist cannot hide behind the confidentiality of his sources to avoid the obligation to prove his allegations.[62] However, if certain allegations are based on rumors, publication may not be illegal to the extent that the requisite reservations have been made;[63]

5. In satiric press articles, allegations may be formulated more sharply or critically.[64]

a. Does the fault standard depend on the fame or notoriety of the plaintiff?

Yes. Belgian case law considers that the fault standard varies with the fame or the notoriety of the plaintiff. In this regard, it has been held that a politician, artist, or litigant must be able to withstand more severe criticism than a mere citizen.[65] The limits of the criticism must therefore be considered more loosely for a politician in his capacity of politician, than for a private person, because those who decide to publicly lead a political action must accept that their speeches, statements, and actions might be the object of controversies, during which the usual means of communication may lead to the use of an aggressive or excessive language.[66] This view is supported by the European Court of Human Rights (ECHR). According to the ECHR, public figures must endure more criticism than private persons in order for political debate, essential in democracy, to properly function. Libel laws must honor this distinction. Therefore, a person's right to protection against defamatory or slanderous speech should be analyzed in relation to his societal duties.[67]

Nonetheless, those extended boundaries are not limitless. The press is not entitled to harm the honor and reputation of a person by creating, in the minds of the general public, "malevolent suspicions or unjust assumptions."[68] There are restrictions, among which stands an obligation of strict veracity regarding the facts,[69] the interdiction of libelous or injurious statements[70] or the imputation of facts, decisions, or statements that are not accurate or not established.[71] A journalist therefore commits a serious offense when accusing a person without seeking confirmation from that person[72] or where the journalist only has weak information.[73]

b. Is there a heightened fault standard or privilege for reporting on matters of public concern or public interest?

Although there is no express privilege granted to journalists for reporting on matters of public concern, journalists nonetheless benefit from a certain heightened fault standard in reporting on matters of public interest. When ruling upon a case, Belgian courts and tribunals usually balance, on the one hand, the interests of the press and, on the other hand, the rights of the individual concerned. Nonetheless, Belgian law requires that publications must be accurate, complete, and objective. The fault standard is addressed in the following spheres.

Political sphere.[74] As mentioned above, it is accepted that speeches, statements, and actions in the political sphere may be the justifiable object of controversies.[75]

Judicial sphere. It is also judicially recognized that the press is entitled to report on the functioning of justice or the work of judges, which includes reporting on sentences pronounced in public. It is usually considered that the fact that a case is definitively ruled upon does not imply that the case may not be the object of future criticism.[76] Moreover, even though the Belgian Criminal Procedure Code provides for the secrecy of criminal investigations, it was likewise considered that the publishing of a book on a case which had not yet been ruled upon by the Assize Court could not be forbidden. In this case, the judge considered that he could see no reason why jurors would be influenced by the sued-upon book rather than by the precise and detailed information which they would obtain during the trial.[77]

Economic sphere. Considerable latitude is also given to reports of economic activities.[78] Nonetheless, when reporting on such matters, one must have recourse to serious methods of investigation and only use information, the accurateness of which has been duly verified.[79] It was thus held that consumer protection reporting must be neutral, objective, and conducted by qualified persons. The information must be collected with prudence and must be scrupulously controlled with the most serious methods of investigation.[80] The rights of the producer whose products are the subject matter of the study must be safeguarded.[81]

The public interest is addressed in other areas from time to time. In three cases regarding an information campaign organized by public authorities to warn the general public about the danger of sects, it was considered that the public authority had an obligation to provide information which is accurate, as complete as possible, and objective.[82]

7. Is financial news about publicly traded companies, or companies involved with a government contract, considered a matter of public interest or otherwise privileged?

Financial news about publicly traded companies or companies involved with government contracts is not specifically considered as a matter of public interest or otherwise privileged. There are no specific rules or privileges with regard to the protection of financial information of publicly traded companies or companies involved with government contracts. Therefore, journalists are in principle free to publish financial news about publicly traded companies as long as that information is gathered and published in a legally acceptable manner.

Pursuant to Article 6 of Directive 2003/6/EC of the European Parliament and of the Council of 28 January 2003 on Insider Dealing and Market Manipulation ("Market Abuse"),[83] EU Member States should ensure that there are appropriate regulations in place to ensure that persons who produce or disseminate research concerning financial instruments or issuers of financial instruments and persons who produce or disseminate other information recommending or suggesting investment strategy, intended for distribution channels or for the public, take reasonable care to ensure that such information is fairly presented and disclose their interests or indicate conflicts of interest concerning the financial instruments to which that information relates. Similar provisions are contained in the Law of 2 August 2002 on the Supervision of the Financial Sector and Financial Services.[84]

8. Is there a recognized protection for opinion or "fair comment" on matters of public concern?

Yes. Opinions or fair comment on matters of public concern are legally protected in Belgium. This protection is based on Article 19 of the Belgian Constitution[85] as well as Article 10 of the Convention, both dealing with the freedom of expression. The Convention, which constitutes a minimum level of protection in addition to the protection granted by the Belgian Constitution (see Article 53 of the Convention), has a direct effect in the legal system (i.e., it can be invoked in legal proceedings before a Belgian court).[86] As a result, the Convention and the case law of the ECHR are particularly important in Belgium.

ECHR Case Law and Fair Comment

The ECHR has interpreted the freedom of expression in Article 10 of the Convention in a broad way. The following examples demonstrate what may fall within the scope of protection in Article 10 of the Convention:

1. *Reporting on pending litigation*—The *Sunday Times* (1979): The *Sunday Times* published an article in relation to the thalidomide disaster that formed the background to pending litigation (parents of children who were victims of the drug thalidomide sued Distillers, the manufacturers of the drug, for negligence).[87]

2. *Criticism of politicians*—*Lingens* (1986): The ECHR held that a government official accused of holding an "accommodating attitude" toward the Nazis had to endure more criticism as a result of his public position.[88]

3. *Criticism of the government*—*Castells* (1992): Spain sued Sena-

tor Castells for insulting the government in a magazine article about violence in the Basque Country. According to the Spanish Criminal Code, insulting, falsely accusing, or threatening the government is punishable by imprisonment from six months to twelve years. Finding for Castells, the ECHR ruled that a democratic government should accept more criticism than private individuals and politicians.[89]

4. *Nonpolitical issues of public interest*—*Thorgeirson* (1992): Iceland had charged writer Thorgeirson with defamation of unspecified police officers after he published two articles about police brutality. Iceland's Criminal Code called for punishing anyone who "vituperates or otherwise insults a civil servant" with fines or up to three years' imprisonment. The government argued that such defamatory expression should not be protected because it did not relate to the democratic political process. The ECHR however ruled that there is no warrant in its case law for distinguishing between political discussion and discussion of other matters of public concern. The ECHR also discussed the value of the press as a provider of information and a "public watchdog."[90] See also: *De Haes and Gijsels v. Belgium*[91] (defamation of judges); *Thoma v. Luxembourg*[92] (criticism on civil servants); *Colombani and Others v. France*[93] (insulting a foreign head of state); *Amihalachioaie v. Moldavia*[94] (criticism on judges); *Yasar Kemal Gökçeli v. Turkey*[95] (criticism on government policy).

Significantly, the ECHR also acknowledged in *Handyside v. UK* (1976) that the freedom of expression applies not only to information or ideas that are favorably received or regarded as inoffensive or as a matter of indifference, but also to those that offend, shock, or disturb the state or any part of the population.[96]

The case law of the ECHR and the principles developed by the ECHR are equally applied in cases involving the freedom of expression decided by the Belgian courts. According to the Belgian courts, a wider degree of criticism, that could otherwise possibly be considered as defamatory, is accepted when:

(i) the criticism or polemic in the press concerns matters of public concern or facts which are the object of public debate or actual public discussion;

(ii) the criticism or defamatory allegations are directed against a politician or a publicly known person or their public function.

The following examples demonstrate what has been accepted as an opinion or fair comment on a matter of public concern:[97] criticism on a local politician;[98] a press article on certain share transactions by former president Mobutu of the Congo;[99] criticism of well-known politician S. Moureaux in relation to the Dutroux case;[100] a critical biography of a well-known person;[101] a press article on the relationship and contacts between politicians and persons convicted or suspected of certain crimes;[102] criticisms of a well-known Belgian politician named Jean Gol;[103] criticism on police and civil servants;[104] and criticism of a governmental institution.[105]

In some cases it has been decided that criticism of politicians may go further than criticism of judges.[106] Furthermore, case law demonstrates that Belgian courts are more flexible if the defamatory allegations or criticisms are expressed by means of a moderated use of language or nonexcessive use of language.[107] The same applies if the defamatory allegations or critical judgments are based on reliable and carefully collected factual material.[108] Belgian case law also acknowledges that journalists are not only entitled to be critical, but also even provocative and that the press should be regarded as a "public watchdog" of the democracy.[109]

Both Article 19 of the Belgian Constitution and Article 10 of the Convention provide that freedom of expression may be limited. Pursuant to the second paragraph of Article 10 of the Convention, the right to freedom of expression may be subject to restrictions and conditions in accordance with the following threefold test: an interference has to (1) be prescribed by law (i.e., statutory law or case law, in general law which is accessible and foreseeable); (2) have a legitimate aim (e.g., the territorial integrity, the impartiality of the judiciary, and the reputation or rights of others); and (3) be necessary in a democratic society (i.e., there has to be a pressing social need; it is not sufficient to be merely indispensable, desirable, or useful). In Belgium, these limitations are to be found in criminal as well as civil law.

Belgian Criminal Libel Law and Fair Comment

Examples of criminal laws that constitute limitations to opinions or fair comment on matters of public concern are contained in specific legislation in relation to the press (e.g., Press Decree of 20 July 1831); Criminal Code: e.g., provisions on libel and slander (Article 443 *et seq.* of the Belgian Criminal Code); offenses against the public order and public decency (Article 383 *et seq.* of the Criminal Code), etc. There is also specific criminal legislation that may restrict comment: e.g., limitations in relation to racism and xenophobia (Law of 30 July 1981 in relation to Racism and Xenophobia;[110] Law of 23 March 1995 in relation to the World War II Genocide,[111] etc.); specific limitations contained in, e.g., the Law of 8 April 1965 on the Protection of the Youth.[112]

"Fair Comment" Under Belgian Civil Libel Law

Civil law restrictions on opinions or fair comment on matters of public concern are based upon Articles 1382 *et seq.* of the Belgian Civil Code, which are the core provisions of Belgian tort law. Under Articles 1382 *et seq.* of the Belgian Civil Code, "a person who causes injury to the interests of another person must compensate that other person."

As mentioned above, Belgian law limits fair comment to avoid what it deems "unnecessarily offensive language" or "excessively critical or defamatory" allegations, solely aimed at causing damage. The following examples can be found in Belgian case law in relation to allegations and criticism that were considered to be unnecessarily offensive or excessively critical:[113] allegations against former Belgian prime minister P. Van Den Boeynants in relation to drug traffic, murder, and crime against the security of the State;[114] defamation of former NATO secretary-general W. Claes in relation to his involvement in the Agusta helicopter scandal;[115] criticism based on inaccurate facts about Finance Minister D. Reynders in relation to the possession of a secret bank account in Luxembourg.[116]

9. Are there any requirements upon a plaintiff, such as demand for retraction or right of reply, and if so, what impact do they have?

Yes. Pursuant to Article 1 *et seq.* of the Law of 23 June 1961 on the Right of Reply[117] (the Law of 23 June 1961), any person has the right to request a reply if quoted by name or implicitly indicated in a "periodic writing." Articles 7 to 15 of the Law of 23 June 1961 also provide for a right of reply in broadcast or "periodic audio-visual programs," but this system differs in many aspects, in particular with regard to the conditions of admissibility and the recourse envisaged in the event of refusal of the insertion of the right of reply. For example, for the audiovisual press, contrary to the newspaper industry, the procedure is dealt with by the civil courts (which in a preliminary injunction procedure is ruled on the substance of the case) whose judgment cannot be appealed.[118]

Significantly, Articles 1 and 7 of the Law of 23 June 1961 explicitly provide that the right of reply does not deprive the person concerned of his or her right to initiate legal proceedings. Legal scholars generally accept that the person concerned is not obliged to make use of his or her right of reply prior to commencing legal proceedings. Similarly, to the extent a right for retraction exists, it does not prevent the person concerned from initiating legal proceedings. Finally, it should be noted that although there are no specific requirements upon a plaintiff, such individual is, in accordance with the general principles of tort law, nevertheless obliged to limit his own damage.

10. Is there a privilege for quoting or reporting on:

a. Papers filed in court?

Private persons are in principle free to provide information on legal proceedings in which they are involved. An important exception, however, applies in the framework of criminal investigations. Pursuant to Article 460*ter* of the Belgian Criminal Code, the use by a suspected party or a plaintiff claiming damages (*burgerlijke partij/partie civile*) of information obtained in the framework of an access to a (criminal) file is illegal and gives rise to criminal sanctions if that use hampers the investigation or violates the privacy rights, the physical or moral integrity, or the property of a person mentioned in the file.

For example, in June 2003, the Ghent Court of First Instance condemned a journalist of a Belgian newspaper for complicity in an abuse of access to file in accordance with Article 460*ter* of the Belgian Criminal Code.[119] The journalist published excerpts of a statement made by a suspect in a pedophilia case. The journalist received these documents from the plaintiff claiming damages. The Court ruled that the journalist violated the privacy rights and moral integrity of the defendant, some minors, as well as the husband of the suspect. The judgment of the Ghent Court of First Instance was confirmed by the Ghent Court of Appeal.[120] An appeal lodged by the journalist with the Belgian Supreme Court was unsuccessful.[121]

b. Government-issued documents?

We are not aware of any specific rules or restrictions in this respect. The restrictions set out in Question 10a. equally apply. Some government-issued documents may not be copyright protected.

c. Quasi-governmental proceedings?

We are not aware of any specific rules or restrictions in this respect. Some Belgian case law indicates that the rules applicable to criminal investigations also apply to disciplinary proceedings.[122]

11. Is there a privilege for republishing statements made earlier by other, bona fide, reliable publications or wire services?

Yes. In principle, journalists are entitled to republish statements made earlier by other, bona fide, reliable publications or wire services. The ECHR ruled in its *Thoma v. Luxembourg* judgment[123] that a radio journalist was allowed to refer to an article concerning a scandal that was published earlier in a newspaper. The ECHR stated that punishing a journalist for assisting in the dissemination of statements made by another person would seriously hamper the contribution of the press to the discussion of matters of public interest and should not be envisaged unless there were particularly strong reasons for doing so. In the case at hand, the Luxembourg appellate court had explained that a journalist who merely quoted from an article that had already been published would only escape liability if he formally distanced himself from the article and its content. The ECHR went further and explained that a general requirement for journalists to distance themselves from a libelous quotation was not reconcilable with the press's role of providing information on current events, opinions, and ideas. In the case at hand, the summary of the program showed that in any event the applicant had consistently taken the precaution of mentioning that he was beginning a quotation and of citing the author, and that in addition he had described the entire article by his fellow journalist as "strongly worded" when commenting on it. He had also asked a third party whether he thought what the author of the newspaper article had written was true.

Nonetheless, journalists in Belgium should be careful if they republish defamatory statements. Pursuant to Article 451 of the Belgian Criminal Code, a journalist cannot avoid a conviction for libel by arguing that he or she simply reiterates what another person previously said. The case law on this issue is ambiguous and any factual situation should therefore be assessed on a case-by-case basis. Indeed, some courts decided that the fact that an analogue defamatory allegation has been published in other publications against which no complaint has been filed, does not deprive the republication of its tortious character.[124] In other cases, however, the Belgian courts have taken into account the fact that the same allegations had been previously published in other media channels.[125]

In light of the above, when republishing statements made earlier by other persons or publishers, journalists may wish to take some precautions such as clearly mentioning the source, using conditional language, and consulting with local counsel.

12. Are there any restrictions regarding reporting on:

a. Ongoing criminal investigations?

There are no specific rules with respect to civil proceedings. Journalists do not have a presumptive right to access papers filed in court. However, parties are in principle free to provide information in relation to civil proceedings to the press. If journalists use this information, they should comply with the generally applicable limits to the freedom of expression as described above. Particularly, they should not (1) infringe the provisions on libel and slander; (2) violate the principles of public order or public decency; (3) publish incorrect or careless allegations; (4) use unnecessary offensive language or excessively critical or defamatory allegations, solely aimed at causing damage; or (5) violate a person's privacy rights. In addition, journalists should be aware that the rules on copyright may apply.

Reporting on ongoing criminal investigations is restricted by the principle of secrecy. Article 28 *quinquies,* §1 *juncto* Article 57, §1 of the Belgian Criminal Procedure Code provides that, except for the exceptions provided for by law, [criminal] investigations are secret. Any person who is obliged, for professional reasons, to cooperate with such an investigation (such as civil servants employed by the Ministry of Justice, judges, police officers, judicial personnel, etc.) is bound by this principle of secrecy. Persons violating this obligation shall be punished with criminal sanctions (Article 458 of the Belgian Criminal Code).

Notwithstanding this general rule, information may sometimes be provided "in the public interest." Article 28 *quinquies,* §3 *juncto* Article 57, §3 of the Belgian Criminal Procedure Code state that a designated member of the court may provide information on ongoing criminal investigations to journalists if such is "in the public interest."

Any articles published in reliance thereupon should pay particular attention to the principles of the presumption of innocence, the rights of defense of the suspect, the sensitivities of the victim and third parties, as well as the privacy rights and dignity of all persons involved. In addition, the identity of the persons involved in the case should be kept secret to the extent that this is possible. This exception is further clarified in a circular letter of the Minister of Justice of April 30, 1999. For example, if information on ongoing criminal investigations is provided, this may occur under the following conditions set by the court officer acting as a source:

1. ***provision of information "on the record":*** the court member may be cited officially;

2. ***provision of information "off the record":*** the information provided by the court member may be used, but the court member may not be cited. Such information should enable journalists to publish "on the record" information correctly;

3. ***provision of "background information":*** this information may not be published by the journalist, but should allow the journalist to expand his knowledge and understand the framework;

4. ***"embargo":*** agreement between the member of the court and the journalists that the journalists keep the information silent for a while (delay of publication);

5. ***"information stop" or "black-out":*** this is a temporary refusal to communicate information to the press.

Some specific provisions apply to trials of members of the police,[126] on reporting on minors (Article 80 of the Law of 8 April 1965 on the Protection of the Youth[127]), and on victims of sexual violence (Article 378*bis* of the Belgian Criminal Code).

A journalist who publishes information of which he or she knows that it is provided by a person committing a violation of his or her confidentiality and professional secrecy obligations may be subject to criminal prosecutions (e.g., complicity in violation of professional secrecy obligations) or deontological sanctions (by the Algemene Vereniging van Beroepsjournalisten in België [AVBB]/Association Générale des Journalistes Professionnels Belges [AGJPB]).

Aside from obtaining information from the court or law enforcement officers, the press may reasonably rely upon counsel for litigants. An attorney-at-law is entitled to provide information to the press if this is in the interest of his or her client. He or she should, however, take into account the presumption of innocence and the rights of defense of all parties involved, their privacy and dignity rights, as well as some professional rules. To the extent that this is possible, an attorney-at-law should keep secret the identity of the persons involved in the case (Article 28 *quinquies,* §4 *juncto* Article 57, §4 of the Belgian Criminal Procedure Code).

b. Ongoing criminal prosecutions?

Both the Belgian Constitution and the Convention allow reporting on ongoing civil and criminal litigation. For example, Article 148 of the Belgian Constitution as well as Article 6 of the Convention guarantee the right of public access to court hearings. Article 149 of the Belgian Constitution and Article 6 of the Belgian Convention include the obligation to publicly pronounce court decisions. Articles 19 and 25 of the Belgian Constitution as well as Article 10 of the Convention include the right of the press to report on ongoing court cases and other court-related matters.

These principles are limited, however, by the existence of other fundamental Belgian law rules, such as the protection of public policy, public order, and public decency. Rights of defense, the right to privacy, and the proper functioning of the judicial system may also impose restrictions on the basic principles set out above.

In addition, specific limitations apply with regard to:

1. ***divorces:*** the publication of the judicial debate in relation to divorces is prohibited (Articles 1270, 1306, and 1309 of the Belgian Judicial Code);

2. ***the protection of minors:*** reporting on the judicial debate in youth courts as well as publishing pictures or other images allowing third parties to identify the prosecuted minor is prohibited (Article 80 of the Law of 8 April 1965 on the Protection of the Youth);

3. *victims of sexual offenses:* the publication of information, without the consent of the victim of sexual offenses or the judicial authorities, allowing third parties to identify the victims is prohibited (Article 378*bis* of the Belgian Criminal Code).

c. Ongoing regulatory investigations?

We are not aware of any specific rules in relation to reporting on ongoing regulatory investigations. However, regulatory investigations by public authorities (e.g., antitrust) will often involve the collection of confidential data. The civil servants are in principle subject to a duty of secrecy and discretion in respect of such information. The publication or release of such confidential data may constitute a fault under civil law that may create a claim for compensation. In addition, the general restrictions to the freedom of expression and fair comments apply.

d. Ongoing civil litigation, or other judicial proceedings?

Both the Belgian Constitution and the Convention allow reporting on ongoing civil litigation (see, *inter alia,* Articles 19, 25, 148, and 149 of the Belgian Constitution as well as Articles 6 and 10 of the Convention). However, as mentioned above, journalists should comply with the generally applicable restrictions on freedom of expression. Particularly, they should not: (1) infringe the provisions on libel and slander; (2) violate the principles of public order or public decency; (3) publish incorrect or careless allegations; (4) use unnecessary offensive language or excessive critical or defamatory allegations, solely aimed at causing damage; or (5) violate someone's privacy rights. In addition, other rules such as copyright may apply to briefs filed by parties.

13. Are prior restraints or other prepublication injunctions available on the basis of libel or privacy, and if so, what are the standards for obtaining such relie?

Yes, but although legally possible, it is rarely granted. Prepublication restraints are, in principle, available under Belgian law on the basis of libel or privacy. The president of the Court of First Instance may, pursuant to Articles 584 and 1039 of the Belgian Judicial Code, hear cases in summary proceedings (*kortgeding/référé*) and order interim measures in all matters which he or she deems to be urgent. Urgency is usually defined as a situation where an immediate decision is desirable in order to avoid damage of some magnitude or serious inconvenience.[128] With respect to the press in particular, account must be taken of the impact on the general public of messages disseminated on the radio or on television. The president of the Court of First Instance has substantial discretion when deciding whether a given matter is urgent. Summary proceedings are handled in an expedited way and orders given by the president of the Court of First Instance in such cases may be appealed before the Court of Appeal.

Pursuant to Article 25 of the Belgian Constitution, the press is free and censorship may never be established. Moreover, Article 10 of the Convention guarantees freedom of expression, the exercise of which may only be subject to restrictions as are prescribed by law and are necessary in a democratic society. In this regard, the ECHR states that "the dangers inherent in prior restraint are such that they call for the most careful scrutiny on the part of the Court. This is especially so as far as the press is concerned, for news is a perishable commodity and to delay its publication, even for a short period, may well deprive it of all its value and interest."[129]

In Belgium, some courts held that Article 25 of the Belgian Constitution precluded the prohibition of the publication of information relating to comparative tests carried out by a consumer protection association,[130] the publication of information relating to criminal investigations,[131] the announced publication of a book on sects in Belgium and Luxembourg,[132] or the publication of a book on Flemish misses and models.[133] However, despite the constitutional prohibition, some judges increasingly imposed prepublication restraints, as is evidenced by the number of cases where cease-and-desist orders have been issued,[134] which have usually been confirmed by appeal courts.[135] For example, it was held that the publication of notes taken by an examining judge (*onderzoeksrechter/juge d'instruction*), i.e., the magistrate examining a criminal case, which had been released following the violation of the secrecy of a parliamentary investigation, could be forbidden.[136] It was also held that a temporary prohibition to broadcast a television show where the television show appears to harm manifestly and unnecessarily the honor and the reputation of a plaintiff was justified.[137]

The Belgian Supreme Court partly settled the controversy in the *Leempoel* case[138] and considered that the prohibition of censorship only applies to judicial interventions prior to any diffusion of a written media but does not encompass interim judicial measures which occur after this diffusion, which restrict the *prima facie* abusive use of the freedom of expression. In this case, the issue of the magazine in question had already been widely distributed.

It should finally be noted that some of the case law considers that since, according to the Belgian Supreme Court, Article 25 of the Belgian Constitution does not apply to audiovisual media, nothing prevents the adoption of provisional measures preventing the broadcasting of television programs.[139]

14. Is a right of privacy recognized (either civilly or criminally)?

The Belgian Supreme Court explicitly ruled that the protection of privacy is a legitimate restriction to the freedom of the press.[140] Importantly, case law also confirms that public persons also have a right to the protection of their privacy.[141] However, a critical biography of a public person is not on its face unlawful if the privacy rights of the person concerned are not violated.[142] On the contrary, revealing the sexual orientation of the members of a music band without their consent constitutes a violation of their privacy rights.[143]

a. What is the definition of "private fact"?

There is no generally accepted definition of what constitutes a "private fact." As Article 8 of the Convention, protecting a person's private life, has direct effect in Belgium, the interpretation of this provision by the ECHR is crucial to determine what constitutes a "private fact" under Belgian law. The ECHR has not formulated an exhaustive definition of "private life."[144]

However, it is clear that the concept of private life goes further than the mere right to privacy in the sense of seclusion. It concerns a sphere within which everyone can freely pursue the development and fulfillment of his or her personality. It follows from extensive case law of the ECHR that the following elements, activities, or measures *inter alia* concern a person's private life:[145] a person's name[146] and forename(s);[147] a person's picture;[148] a person's physical and moral integrity, including his or her sexual life;[149] a person's right to develop relationships with other persons and the outside world;[150] a person's sexual life[151] and relationships between homosexuals and their partners with or without children;[152] compulsory medical treatment, including blood and urine tests imposed on prisoners to check for drugs,[153] compulsory vaccination, dental treatment, TB tests or X-rays for children,[154] compulsory administering of food;[155] a person's social life: the effective enjoyment of a social life which involves the capacity by reason of cultural and linguistic familiarity to enter into social relationships with others;[156] a person's personal relationships in business contexts;[157] the use of covert technological devices to intercept private communications; business or private conversations by telephone as well as the use of an office telephone;[158] and the collection of information by officials of the State about a person without his consent (e.g., the recording of fingerprinting, photography, and other personal information by the police even if the police register is secret).

Belgian legal scholars and case law often refer to the case law of the ECHR in order to determine what constitutes a "private fact." In any event, in Belgium, a private fact is a very broad concept. Some legal scholars include the following elements in their list of private facts: sex life, marriage and divorce, friendship, illness, religion, health, pregnancy, and political preferences. Other legal scholars also mention a person's physical and psychological integrity; moral and intellectual freedom; the right to be protected against defamation and the use of one's name, identity, or picture; the right to be protected against taking pictures, recording, taping and tape recordings, and the violation of professional secrecy.[159]

Finally, reference should be made to the Belgian Law of 8 December 1992 on the Protection of Privacy with regard to the Processing of Personal Data on the Protection of Data[160] (the "Data Protection Law") that regulates the "processing of personal data." Under the Data Protection Law, "personal data" are defined as any information relating to an identified or identifiable natural person. A person will be identifiable as soon as there is an objective possibility of identifying him or her directly or indirectly by any reasonable means (e.g., through a third person, a social security number, etc.), be it by the holder of the data or by any other person. Conversely, data that do not make the identification of the natural person possible (i.e., anonymous data) will fall outside the scope of the Data Protection Law. The notion of "processing" is very comprehensive. It encompasses any operation or set of operations involving personal data, whether or not by automatic means, such as the collection, recording, organization, storage, adaptation, alteration, retrieval, consultation, use, disclosure by transmission, dissemination or otherwise making available, alignment, combination, as well as blocking, erasure, or destruction of personal data. The same regime applies to all these uses of personal data.

b. Is there a public interest or newsworthiness exception?

It is generally accepted that the privacy rights of persons having a public function (e.g., politicians, judges) and persons deliberately looking for or attracting public attention are more limited than those of "regular citizens." According to the ECHR, it is clear that the more public the location in which an activity takes place, the more difficult it is for applicants to establish that their right to respect for their private life is involved, although whether such an activity falls within the concept of private life or not must be judged on the basis of the nature of the activity itself.[161] Whether the privacy rights of private persons who become involved in public events or matters of public concern or facts which are the object of public debate or actual public discussion may be limited is, however, still subject to debate.

The absence of protection against press intrusions or the disclosure in the media of highly intimate, nondefamatory details of private life has not yet been subject to significant challenge before the ECHR. Some complaints, such as the Irish case where the applicant complained that an insurance company took photographs of the applicant outside his house, constituted an infringement of the applicant's private life;[162] and the case introduced by Earl and Countess Spencer concerning press coverage of their private lives,[163] have been declared inadmissible for failing to exhaust domestic remedies. As noted above, the determination of whether issues might arise under private life in relation to press intrusion might be influenced by the extent to which the person concerned courted attention, the nature and degree of the intrusion into the private sphere, and the ability of diverse domestic remedies to provide effective and adequate redress.

Furthermore, as far as the Data Protection Law is concerned, the processing of personal data carried out solely for journalistic purposes or for the purpose of artistic or literary expression is exempted from several important provisions of the Data Protection Law. For example, the prohibition to process personal data revealing racial or ethnic origin, political opinions, religious or philosophical beliefs, and trade-union membership, as well as data concerning sex life, health-related personal data, personal data relating to judicial and administrative proceedings (Articles 6 to 8 of the Data Protection Law) does not apply to journalists. Significantly, this information should relate to data that was made public by the person concerned or is closely related to the public character of the person involved or the fact to which he or she is involved.

c. Is the right to privacy based in common law, statute, or constitution?

The right to privacy is based on Article 8 of the Convention (as interpreted by the ECHR), Article 22 of the Belgian Constitution (as interpreted by the Belgian courts), as well as the Data Protection Law (as interpreted by the Belgian courts).

Article 8 of the Convention provides that "everyone has the right to respect for his private and family life, his home and his correspondence." It is important to note that the right to respect for these aspects of privacy under Article 8 is qualified. This means that interferences by the state are permissible, but only if they satisfy the following conditions: any interference with the right should be (1) in accordance with the law; (2) in pursuit of one of the legitimate objectives spelled out in Article 8(2) of the Convention; and (3) proportionate (i.e., serve a pressing social need).

Similarly, Article 22 of the Belgian Constitution provides that "everyone has the right to the respect of his or her private and family life, except in the cases and conditions determined by law."[164]

15. May reporters tape-record their own telephone conversations for note-taking purposes (not rebroadcast) without the consent of the other party?

Yes. It is accepted that reporters may tape-record their own telephone conversations for note-taking purposes without the consent of the other party.[165] Article 314*bis* of the Belgian Criminal Code imposes important criminal sanctions on any person who (1) either deliberately uses any equipment, monitors, takes cognizance of, records private communication or telecommunication, in which he or she does not participate, during its transmission, without consent of all persons participating in that communication or has this communication monitored, taken cognizance or recorded; (2) or with intent to commit one of the criminal offences mentioned above, installs equipment or has it installed.[166]

Journalists should be advised that if the conversation is confidential in character and the other party has explicitly highlighted the confidential nature of the conversation, the disclosure of certain facts might give rise to tort liability as a breach of confidence.

16. If permissible to record such tapes, may they be broadcast without permission?

Although the case law on this issue is scarce, one court ruled that it is prohibited to broadcast tapes without the consent of the parties involved in the conversation on the tape recording.[167] In addition, broadcasting tapes without the permission of the other party may also constitute a violation of copyright.

17. Is there a recognized evidentiary privilege preventing the disclosure of confidential sources relied upon by reporters?

Until recently, Belgium had no specific law protecting a journalist's sources. However, journalists in Belgium could invoke Article 10 of the Convention in order to protect their journalistic sources. In its landmark judgment *Goodwin v. United Kingdom*,[168] the ECHR ruled that "without such protection, sources may be deterred from assisting the press in informing the public on matters of public interest. As a result, the vital public watchdog role of the press may be undermined and the ability of the press to provide accurate and reliable information may be adversely affected."

The protection of journalistic sources under Article 10 of the Convention is however not absolute. The ECHR has decided that an order of source disclosure is possible in certain circumstances, namely if interests are involved that are more imperative and more important than the freedom of expression. According to the ECHR, it is only when it is "justifiable by an overriding requirement in the public interest" that a disclosure order can be assumed to be in accordance with Article 10 §2 of the Convention. Furthermore, the ECHR underlines the idea that limitations on the confidentiality of journalistic sources "call for the most careful scrutiny by the Court."

In *De Haes and Gijsels v. Belgium*,[169] the ECHR applied the right of journalists to maintain secrecy of a source in a case in which journalists De Haes and Gijsels were held liable for defamation in criticizing some members of the judiciary. In its judgment, the ECHR held that Article 6 of the Convention does not allow national courts to reject an application from an accused journalist to consider alternative evidence besides the disclosure of the source of information by this journalist if such alternative evidence for the proof of the journalist's statements is available to the judiciary. The ECHR ruled that the journalists' concern not to risk compromising their sources of information by lodging the documents at stake themselves was legitimate. The rejection of the Belgian courts to analyze at least the opinion of the three experts, whose reports had prompted De Haes and Gijsels to write their articles, was considered a breach of Articles 6 and 10 of the Convention.[170]

Notwithstanding the protection provided by Article 10 of the Convention, the Belgian legal framework in relation to the confidentiality of journalistic sources was not very well developed and gave rise to legal uncertainty. This was again demonstrated in the case initiated by Bourlard and NMBS/SNCB, the Belgian national railway company, against *De Morgen*, a Flemish newspaper. Upon request of a director of the NMBS/SNCB, two journalists of the newspaper *De Morgen* were ordered to submit a copy of an internal document they had referred to in an article criticizing the financial management of the NMBS/SNCB in a project relating to the construction of a new railway station for the TGV-line in Liège. On May 29, 2002, the president of the Brussels Court of First Instance ordered the journalists of *De Morgen* (De Coninck and Vandermeir) to produce a copy of the document they referred to under forfeiture of a penalty payment of €25 per hour of delay. According to the president, the order could not be considered as a breach of professional secrecy of the journalists. De Coninck and Vandermeir appealed the order of the president of the Brussels Court of First Instance. Referring to the ECHR *Goodwin* judgment, the judge on appeal decided in favor of the journalists, stating that there was a risk that a protected source would be disclosed if the journalists had to submit a copy of the document.[171]

The existing legal uncertainty was taken away by the adoption of the Law on the Protection of Journalistic Sources (the "Law") on April 7, 2005.[172] Pursuant to Article 2, the Law applies to (1) "journalists" (defined as any person "who regularly and directly contributes to the processing, drafting, production or distribution of information to the public through a certain medium"); and (2) "editorial staff" (defined as any person "who in the execution of his or her function is obliged to become acquainted with information that may lead to the disclosure of a source, regardless of whether this happens through the processing, drafting, production or distribution of such information").

Article 3 of the Law provides that journalists and editorial staff have the right to refuse disclosing their information sources. Particularly, they cannot be forced to provide information, recordings, or documents that would, *inter alia,* reveal: (1) the identity of the source; (2) the nature or origin of the information; (3) the identity of the author of the text or audiovisual production; or (4) the content of the information or documentation.

Journalists and editorial staff may only be forced to reveal their sources where obliged to do so by a court order. Such a court order may be issued only if (1) the information is necessary to prevent acts threatening the physical integrity of one or more persons; (2) it is established that the information of the journalist or editorial staff is crucial to prevent these crimes; and (3) the information cannot be obtained in any other way.

Body searches, home searches, seizures, and telephone tapping may not relate to the data relating to the information sources of journalists or editorial staff, unless the aforementioned conditions apply.

18. In the event that legal papers are served upon the newsroom (such as a civil complaint), are there any particular warnings about accepting service of which we should be aware?

Accepting service of legal papers served upon the newsroom is a non-issue in Belgium. Article 43 of the Belgian Judicial Code states that persons to whom copies of legal papers are handed should sign the original to acknowledge receipt. If the addressee refuses to sign, the bailiff enters a note to that effect on the writ. As a result, in all cases, there will be proof in writing that the document has been served.

If a legal paper is served upon the newsroom, it is advisable that the company immediately contacts a local attorney-at-law (*advocaat/avocat*) who will (1) verify whether the legal paper is served in accordance with the law (e.g., service at a registered office of the company; compliance with the requisite minimum period between the service date and the date of the introductory hearing; etc.); and (2) represent the company in court.

19. Has your jurisdiction applied established media law to Internet publishers?

As a general rule, it should be noted that the Belgian legal provisions also apply, subject to the private international law rules on jurisdiction and applicable law, to infringements committed on the Internet. Belgian courts have thus already applied the legal provisions on libel, privacy, disparagement, or racism to Internet publishers.

In a recent case, the Court of First Instance of Brussels held that libelous statements made on the Internet must be deemed to have been made in all places where those statements can be received and read and held that Belgian courts have jurisdiction to rule upon the matter.[173] A similar conclusion was reached by the Commercial Court of Mons, which thus considered, in application of Article 2 of the Convention of 27 September 1968 on jurisdiction and the enforcement of judgments in civil and commercial matters,[174] that it had jurisdiction to hear the case. In the latter case, the Court nonetheless held that Belgian law did not apply, as the act which was at the origin of the damage had been accomplished in the United States.[175]

As mentioned above, in order for the provisions on libel contained in the Belgian Criminal Code to apply, the sued-upon statements must have been made in public (e.g., mailing lists (but not private e-mails), newsgroups, discussion forums, and information on the World Wide Web).

A practical application of the provisions on libel was made in a case where the Bishop of Liège and his diocese sought a cease-and-desist order against the Raelian sect in order to have the contents of an Internet site accusing Catholic priests of being pedophiles removed and to prohibit the creation of any other Internet site having a similar content.[176] The Court of First Instance of Liège thus ordered the defendant as well as the Internet hosting service provider to delete the defamatory content from the Internet site and also ordered penalties in case of noncompliance.[177] This ruling was criticized as it did not distinguish the roles of the protagonists of the case: both the author of the Internet site and the hosting service provider were condemned. It was argued by some legal scholars that the hosting service provider was not actually able to *modify* the content of the Internet site, but could only delete or block access to the litigious Internet page.

Courts and tribunals do not always order the deletion of libelous statements from Internet pages. The Court of First Instance of Brussels considered it was sufficient to insert, next to the electronic version of the complained-upon article, a hyperlink referring the readers to the article mentioning the acquitting of the plaintiff.[178]

Belgian courts have also applied the legal provisions on product disparagement for infringements committed on the Internet. It was thus considered that a trader having, on its Internet site, a discussion forum on which the general public could share its opinion on a competitor, was guilty of disparagement.[179]

In a ruling of December 22, 1999, the Brussels Criminal Court held that racist acts on the Internet amounted to a violation of the laws governing the press. In this case, an officer of the judicial police was prosecuted for having made racist statements in various Internet discussion groups.[180]

20. If established media law has been applied to Internet publishers, are there any ways in which Internet publishers (including chat room operators) have to meet different standards?

As the same legal provisions apply to publishers, whether they operate on the Internet or not, it can be considered that Internet publishers or chat room operators do not have to meet different standards than other publishers.

However, the Belgian Law of 11 March 2003 on Certain Legal Aspects of the Services of the Information Society (the "Law on Electronic Commerce")[181] provides immunity for hosting service providers if certain conditions are fulfilled. Article 20 of the Law on Electronic Commerce provides that a hosting service provider is not liable for information contained on Internet sites which it hosts, subject to the conditions that (1) it does not have knowledge of the illegal activity; (2) it acts promptly to render access to the information impossible or to remove the information, if ordered to do so by the public prosecutor.

It has also been held that a violation of the laws governing the press committed on the Internet should be considered as a "continuing offense" (*voortdurend misdrijf/délit continu*), as long as the statement in contention is easily accessible to any person surfing the Internet to find information on particular topics. Moreover, libelous statements which have been made in Internet discussion forums are archived and can thus easily be accessed with the use of search engines and hyperlinks. Such qualification as a "continuing offense" mainly has a bearing on limitation periods, the expiry of which precludes any criminal prosecution.

21. Are there any cases where the courts enforced a judgment in libel from another jurisdiction against a publisher in your jurisdiction?

We are not aware of any cases where Belgian courts enforced a judgment in libel from another jurisdiction against a publisher in Belgium.

Chapter Notes

1. Belgian Supreme Court, 26 January 1976, Pas., 1976, I, 591.

2. Belgian Supreme Court, 20 May 1992, Pas., I, 895; President of the Court of

First Instance of Brussels, 2 March 2000, not yet reported, RR 2000/77/C.

3. Belgian Supreme Court, 10 July 1916, Pas., 1917, I, 191; Court of First Instance of Marche-en-Famenne, 6 May 1992, *J.L.M.B.*, 1993, 1066.

4. Brussels Court of Appeal, 29 October 1987, Pas., 1988, II, 52.

5. Belgian Supreme Court, 19 June 1991, Pas., 1991, I, 913.

6. Court of First Instance of Liège, 22 October 2004, not reported, available at http://www.barreaudeliege.be.

7. The Assize Court is the highest criminal court in Belgium, where jurors rule upon the guilt of the accused person. The Assize Court sits on an *ad hoc* basis. Its judgments cannot be appealed.

8. *Belgian Official Journal,* 29 May 1999.

9. Belgian Supreme Court, 30 January 1980, *J.T.,* 1981, 290.

10. Belgian Supreme Court, 11 December 1979, *Pas.,* 1980, I, 452; Belgian Supreme Court, 21 October 1981, *Pas.,* 1982, I, 259; Brussels Court of Appeal, 1 April 1982, *J.T.,* 1982, 636; Belgian Supreme Court, 23 January 1984, *Pas.,* 1988, 942; Brussels Court of Appeal, 29 October 1987, *Pas.,* 1988, II, 52.

11. There has only been one case since World War II (Assize Court of Mons, 28 June 1994, *J.L.M.B.,* 1994, 520).

12. Belgian Supreme Court, 9 December 1981, *Pas.,* 1982, I, 482.

13. Belgian Supreme Court, 28 May 1985, *Pas.,* 1985, I, 1219.

14. Brussels Court of Appeal, 5 February 1990, *Pas.,* 1990, II, 154; Court of First Instance of Brussels, 12 January 1990, *J.L.M.B.,* 1990.

15. In this regard, it should be noted that the failure to observe the obligation of prudence of Articles 1382 *et seq.* of the Belgian Civil Code does not constitute the *animus iurandi* of Articles 443 *et seq.* of the Belgian Criminal Code (Belgian Supreme Court, 18 November 1992, *Pas.,* 1992, I, 1269). See also President of the Court of First Instance of Brussels, 2 March 2000, not reported, RR 2000/77/C.

16. The fault standard is further described under Question 6.

17. Court of First Instance of Liège, 22 October 2004, not reported, available at http://www.barreaudeLiège.be.

18. Criminal Court of Brussels, 11 April 1991, *Rev. dr. étr.,* 1991, 214, *J.L.M.B.,* 1991, 804.

19. Liège Court of Appeal, 28 November 2001, *J.T.,* 2002, 308.

20. Brussels Court of Appeal, 20 December 1991, *Rev. dr. pén. crim.,* 1992, 686.

21. Court of First Instance of Brussels, 29 June 1987, *J.T.,* 1987, 685.

22. Court of First Instance of Brussels, 13 September 1994, *A.J.T.,* 1994–95, 128.

23. Court of First Instance of Liège, 7 May 2002, A&M 2002, 370.

24. Court of First Instance of Liège, 22 October 2004, not reported, available at http://www.barreaudeliege.be.

25. Criminal Court of Charleroi, 13 March 1954, *J.T.,* 1954, 334.

26. Criminal Court of Neufchâteau, 13 May 1993, *J.L.M.B.,* 1993, 965.

27. Court of First Instance of Liège, 1 April 1993, *J.L.M.B.,* 1993, 1144.

28. Court of First Instance of Brussels, 2 July 1993, *A&M,* 1996, 161.

29. Court of First Instance of Brussels, 23 June 1998, not reported, R.G. 96/10933/A.

30. Court of First Instance of Brussels, 28 December 1990, *J.L.M.B.,* 1991, 672.

31. Court of First Instance of Brussels, 11 April 1991, *J.L.M.B.,* 1991, I, 804.

32. Court of First Instance of Brussels, 10 March 1998, *A&M,* 1998, 377.

33. Belgian Supreme Court, 5 February 1900, *Pas.,* I, 141; Court of First Instance of Brussels, 28 December 1990, *J.L.M.B.,* 1991, 672.

34. Court of First Instance of Brussels, 10 March 1998, *A&M,* 1998, 377.

35. Brussels Court of Appeal, 28 June 2001, *J.T.,* 2002, 49.

36. President of the Commercial Court of Kortrijk, 27 November 2000, *Annuaire Pratiques du Commerce & Concurrence,* 2000, 217.

37. Brussels Court of Appeal, 19 May 1998, *Annuaire Pratiques du Commerce & Concurrence,* 1998, 118.

38. *Belgian Official Journal,* 29 August 1991.

39. Article 23.6 of the Law on Unfair Trade Practices.

40. Brussels Court of Appeal, 28 June 2001, *J.T.,* 2002, 49; Brussels Court of Appeal, 26 June 1998, *Annuaire Pratiques du Commerce & Concurrence,* 1998, 127.

41. Brussels Court of Appeal, 28 June 2001, *J.T.,* 2002, 49; President of the Commercial Court of Kortrijk, 16 September 2002, *Annuaire Pratiques du Commerce & Concurrence,* 2002, 650.

42. Article 23.7 of the Law on Unfair Trade Practices. Articles 23.6 and 23.7 of the Law on Unfair Trade Practices are mutually exclusive: if the disparagement is made in the framework of a comparison, Article 23.7 applies (President of the Commercial Court of Kortrijk, 11 December 2000, *Annuaire Pratiques du Commerce & Concurrence,* 2000, 238).

43. Article 23*bis*.5 of the Law on Unfair Trade Practices.

44. President of the Commercial Court of Antwerp, 23 October 2003, *Annuaire Pratiques du Commerce & Concurrence,* 2003, 660.

45. President of the Commercial Court of Tongeren, 1 June 1999, *Annuaire Pratiques du Commerce & Concurrence,* 1999, 616.

46. President of the Commercial Court of Kortrijk, 27 November 2000, *Annuaire Pratiques du Commerce & Concurrence,* 2000, 217.

47. Antwerp Court of Appeal, 30 November 1933, *R.W.,* 1934–35, col. 558.

48. Court of First Instance of Brussels, 16 November 1999, not reported, RG 98/7351/A.

49. *Belgian Official Journal,* 8 August 1981.

50. Article 4 of the Preliminary Title of the Belgian Criminal Procedure Code; Belgian Supreme Court, 15 December 1976, *Pas.,* I, 483.

51. Court of First Instance of Brussels, 14 September 1988, *J.T.,* 1989, 8.

52. President of the Court of First Instance of Brussels, 2 March 2000, not yet reported, RR 2000/77/C.

53. Court of First Instance of Brussels, 12 January 1990, *J.L.M.B.,* 1990, 424.

54. Commercial Court of Brussels, 7 February 1984, *J.T.,* 1984, 345.

55. Court of First Instance of Leuven, 15 January 1996, *A&M,* 1996, 460.

56. Court of First Instance of Brussels, 21 September 1999, *A&M,* 2000, 334; Court of First Instance of Brussels, 26 April 1991, *J.T.,* 1992, 315; Court of First Instance of Antwerp, 22 September 1997, *A&M,* 1997, 407.

57. Court of First Instance of Brussels, 26 October 2001, *A&M,* 2002, 88.

58. Ghent Court of Appeal, 11 May 1978, *R.W.,* 1977–78, 46; Court of First Instance of Brussels, 23 June 1998, *A&M,* 2000, 96; Court of First Instance of Brussels, 30 March 1999, *A&M,* 2000, 102; Court of First Instance of Brussels, 23 December 1999, *A&M,* 2000, 138; see also Court of First Instance of Brussels, 9 November 2001, *A&M,* 2002, 288.

59. Brussels Court of Appeal, 5 February 1990, *R.W.,* 1989–90, 1464; Ghent Court of Appeal, 14 March 1995, *A&M,* 1996, 159.

60. Court of First Instance of Brussels, 28 December 1990, *J.L.M.B.,* 1991, 672.

61. Court of First Instance of Brussels, 13 September 1994, *A.J.T.,* 1994–95, 128.

62. Brussels Court of Appeal, 16 February 2001, *A&M,* 2002, 282.

63. Court of First Instance of Brussels, 21 November 1990, *J.L.M.B.,* 1991, 24.

64. Court of First Instance of Brussels, 4 May 1999, *A&M,* 2000, 106; Brussels Court of Appeal, 30 September 1998, *R.W.,* 2000–01, 93.

65. Court of First Instance of Brussels, 29 June 1987, *J.T.,* 1987, 685.

66. President of the Court of First Instance of Antwerp, 8 June 1999, *A&M,* 1999, 388; President of the Court of First Instance of Brussels, 2 March 2000, not reported, RR 2000/77/C.

67. *Lingens v. Austria,* 8 July 1986. The judgments of the ECHR are available on the following Internet site: http://www.echr.coe.int and in this chapter will be referenced only by mention of their name and date on the basis of which they can be retrieved from the aforementioned Internet site.

68. Court of First Instance of Brussels, 29 June 1987, *J.T.,* 1987, 685.

69. Court of First Instance of Neufchâteau, 31 May 1961, *J.L.,* 1961, 293.

70. Court of First Instance of Brussels, 14 October 1988, *J.L.M.B.,* 1988, 1224.

71. Court of First Instance of Brussels, 28 December 1990, *J.L.M.B.,* 1991, 673.

72. Court of First Instance of Brussels, 2 April 1996, *A&M,* 1997, 314.

73. Brussels Court of Appeal, 25 September 1996, *A&M,* 1997, 76.

74. See Question 6b.

75. President of the Court of First Instance of Antwerp, 8 June 1999, *A&M,* 1999, 388; President of the Court of First Instance of Brussels, 2 March 2000, not reported, RR 2000/77/C.

76. Court of First Instance of Brussels, 29 June 1987, *J.T.,* 1987, 685.

77. President of the Court of First Instance of Brussels, 12 October 1990, *Journ. Procès,* 1990, No. 181, 27.

78. Brussels Court of Appeal, 25 June 1969, *J.T.,* 1970, 155.

79. Brussels Court of Appeal, 14 May 1981, *J.T.,* 1981, 415.

80. Brussels Court of Appeal, 25 June 1969, *J.T.,* 1970, 153. See also Antwerp Court of Appeal, 28 March 1977, *R.W.,* 1977–78, 1445.

81. Brussels Court of Appeal, 4 January 1985, *J.T.,* 1985, 237.

82. President of the Court of First Instance of Brussels, 23 April 1999, *J.L.M.B.,* 1999, 1072.

83. OJ 2003 L96/16.

84. *Belgian Official Journal,* 4 September 2002.

85. Article 19 of the Belgian Constitution provides that the freedom to dem-

onstrate one's opinions on all matters is guaranteed, except for the repression of offenses committed when exercising this freedom.

86. Belgian Supreme Court, 6 March 1986, *Arr. Cass.*, 1985–86; Belgian Supreme Court, 10 May 1985, *Arr. Cass.*, 1984–85, 1230.

87. *Sunday Times v. UK*, 26 April 1979.

88. *Lingens v. Austria*, 8 July 1986.

89. *Castells v. Spain*, 23 April 1992.

90. *Thorgeirson v. Iceland*, 25 June 1992.

91. 24 February 1997.

92. 29 March 2001.

93. 25 June 2002.

94. 20 April 2004.

95. 6 March 2003.

96. 7 December 1976. See also *Lopes Gomes da Silva v. Portugal*, 28 September 2000.

97. See also Court of First Instance of Neufchâteau, 31 May 1961, *J.L.*, 1960–61, 292; Liège Court of Appeal, 30 November 1951, *J.T.*, 1952, 400; Court of First Instance of Brussels, 26 April 1991, *J.T.*, 1992, 315.

98. Brussels Court of Appeal, 25 June 1986, *R.W.*, 1986–87, 804.

99. Court of First Instance of Kortrijk, 17 November 1989, *T.G.R.*, 1990, 116.

100. Court of First Instance of Brussels, 21 September 1999, *A&M*, 2000, 334.

101. Court of First Instance of Brussels, 26 April 1991, *J.T.*, 1992, 315.

102. Brussels Court of Appeal, 25 September 1996, *A&M*, 1997, 76.

103. Court of First Instance of Brussels, 4 November 1992, *Journ. Proc.*, 1992/228, 24.

104. Court of First Instance of Brussels, 30 May 2001, *A&M*, 2002, 291.

105. Court of First Instance of Brussels, 26 October 2001, *A&M*, 2002, 88.

106. Brussels Court of Appeal, 5 February 1990, *R.W.*, 1989–90, 1464. See also Brussels Court of Appeal, 5 February 1999, *A&M*, 1999, 274.

107. Court of First Instance of Brussels, 26 October 2001, *A&M*, 2002, 88.

108. Court of First Instance of Brussels, 13 September 1994, *R.W.*, 1994–95, 955; Court of First Instance of Brussels, 30 June 1994, *R.G.A.R.*, 1995, 12473; Brussels Court of Appeal, 5 February 1990, *R.W.*, 1989–90, 1464.

109. Court of First Instance of Brussels, 21 March 2000, *A&M,* 2000, 460.

110. *Belgian Official Journal,* 8 August 1981.

111. *Belgian Official Journal,* 30 March 1995.

112. *Belgian Official Journal,* 15 April 1965.

113. Court of First Instance of Brussels, 26 October 2001, *A&M,* 2002, 88.

114. Court of First Instance of Brussels, 14 December 1993, *A.J.T.,* 1994–95, 70; Brussels Court of Appeal, 25 September 1996, *A&M,* 1997, 76.

115. Court of First Instance of Brussels, 13 September 1994, *A.J.T.,* 1994–95, 128.

116. Court of First Instance of Liège, 7 May 2002, *A&M* 2002, 370.

117. *Belgian Official Journal,* 8 July 1961.

118. On December 17, 2004, the Council of Europe's Committee of Ministers adopted a Recommendation on the right to reply in the new media environment. The Recommendation urges member states to extend the right to reply—which until now applied to the written press, radio, and television—to online communication services providing information edited in a journalistic manner. The right to reply is a particularly appropriate remedy in the online environment, as contested information can be instantly corrected and replies from those concerned can easily be attached.

119. Court of First Instance of Ghent, 25 June 2003, *A&M,* 2004, 79, err., *A&M,* 2004, 367.

120. Ghent Court of Appeal, 25 May 2004, not reported, referred to in: Belgian Supreme Court, 7 December 2004, not reported, available at: http://www.just .fgov.be/index_nl.htm.

121. Belgian Supreme Court, 7 December 2004, not yet reported, available at: http://www.just.fgov.be/index_nl.htm.

122. Ghent Court of Appeal, 3 March 1995, *R.W.,* 1996–97, 540.

123. 29 March 2001.

124. Brussels Court of Appeal, 5 February 1990, *R.W.,* 1990, 1464; Brussels Court of Appeal, 16 February 2001, *A&M,* 2002, 282; Court of First Instance of Brussels, 14 December 1993, *A.J.T.,* 1994–95, 70; Court of First Instance of Brussels, 13 September 1994, *A.J.T.,* 1994–95, 128.

125. Court of First Instance of Kortrijk, 27 November 1989, *T.G.R.,* 1990, 116.

126. See Article 4.3.3 of the circular letter of the Minister of Justice of 30 April 1999 as well as Article 35 of the Police Act as interpreted by a circular letter of 10 October 1995.

127. *Belgian Official Journal,* 15 April 1965.

128. Belgian Supreme Court, 21 May 1987, *Pas.,* 1987, 1160; Belgian Supreme Court, 13 September 1990, *Pas.,* 1991, 41.

129. *Observer en Guardian v. United Kingdom,* 26 November 1991; *Sunday Times v. United Kingdom,* 26 November 1991.

130. President of the Court of First Instance of Brussels, 21 February 1990, *R.W.,* 1990–91, 89.

131. President of the Court of First Instance of Brussels, 9 January 1997, *A&M,* 1997, 197; President of the Court of First Instance of Liège, 12 January 1999, *A&M,* 1999, 287.

132. President of the Court of First Instance of Antwerp, 4 July 1994, *A.J.T.,* 1994–95, 84.

133. President of the Court of First Instance of Antwerp, 19 September 1997, *A&M,* 1997, 408.

134. See, e.g., President of the Court of First Instance of Brussels, 18 October 1996, *A&M,* 1997, 83; President of the Court of First Instance of Brussels, 24 October 2001, *J.T.,* 2001, 780, confirmed on appeal: Brussels Court of Appeal, 21 December 2001, *J.L.M.B.,* 2002, 425–31 and Brussels Court of Appeal, 22 April 2002, *Journ. Procès,* 2002, No. 436, 26.

135. Brussels Court of Appeal, 8 May 1998, *J.L.M.B.,* 1998, 1046; Brussels Court of Appeal, 21 December 2001, *J.L.M.B.,* 2002, 425; Brussels Court of Appeal, 22 April 2002, *Journ. Procès,* 2002, No. 436, 26.

136. President of the Court of First Instance of Brussels, 30 January 1997, *J.L.M.B.,* 1997, 319 (confirmed on appeal). See also Belgian Supreme Court, 29 June 2000, *A&M,* 2000, 443.

137. Brussels Court of Appeal, 22 March 2002, *Journ. Procès,* No. 436, 26.

138. Belgian Supreme Court, 29 June 2000, *Journ. Procès,* 2000, No. 398, 25; *J.L.M.B.,* 2000, 1589.

139. President of the Court of First Instance of Brussels, 24 October 2001, *Journ. Procès,* 2001, No. 423, 20; Court of First Instance of Brussels, 30 June 1997, *A&M,* 1998, 264.

140. Belgian Supreme Court, 13 September 1991, *R.W.,* 1991–92, 464.

141. Brussels Court of Appeal, 25 November 1981, *J.T.,* 1982, 275 (re: privacy of the Royal family).

142. Court of First Instance of Brussels, 26 April 1991, *J.T.,* 1992, 315.

143. Court of First Instance of Ghent, 22 November 1999, *A&M,* 2000, 148, confirmed in Ghent Court of Appeal, 12 June 2001, *A&M,* 2002, 169. See also

Brussels Court of Appeal, 25 November 1981, *J.T.*, 1982, 275; Antwerp Court of Appeal, 18 January 1984, *R.W.*, 1986–87, 2860; Court of First Instance of Ghent, 16 December 1981, *R.W.*, 1983–84, 2968.

144. *Costello-Roberts v. the United Kingdom*, 25 March 1993.

145. This list only includes some examples and is not exhaustive.

146. *Von Hannover v. Germany*, 24 June 2004; *Stjerna v. Finland*, 25 November 1994; *Burghartz v. Switzerland*, 22 February 1994.

147. *Guillot v. France*, 24 October 1996.

148. *Schüssel v. Austria*, 21 February 2002; *Friedl v. Austria*, judgment of 31 January 1995.

149. *X & Y v. the Netherlands*, 26 March 1986. While some interferences with the physical integrity of an individual may impinge on the private life of that person, not all such actions will do so. *Costello-Roberts v. the United Kingdom* (25 March 1993) concerned the compatibility with Article 8 of the corporal punishment of a little boy. The ECHR noted that measures taken in the field of education may, in certain circumstances, affect the right to respect for private life but not every act or measure which may be said to affect adversely the physical or moral integrity of a person necessarily gives rise to such an interference. In the case at hand, the ECHR concluded that having regard to the purpose and aim of the Convention taken as a whole, and bearing in mind that the sending of a child to school necessarily involves some degree of interference with his or her private life, the ECHR considers that the treatment complained of by the applicant did not entail adverse effects for his physical or moral integrity sufficient to bring it within the scope of the prohibition contained in Article 8. Both the slight nature of the punishment and the fact that it had been imposed in the formal school environment were central to the ECHR's decision in this case.

150. *Niemietz v. Germany*, 16 December 1992.

151. *Dudgeon v. the United Kingdom*, 22 October 1981. However, not every sexual activity carried out behind closed doors necessarily falls within the scope of Article 8. In *Laskey, Jaggard & Brown v. the United Kingdom* (19 February 1997), the applicants were involved in consensual sado-masochistic activities for the purposes of sexual gratification. While the ECHR did not formally have to determine the issue of whether the applicants' behavior fell within the scope of private life, it expressed some reservations about allowing the protection of Article 8 to extend to activities which involved a considerable number of people, the provision of specially equipped chambers, the recruitment of new members, and the shooting of videotapes which were distributed among the members.

152. *Kerkhoven v. The Netherlands*, 19 May 1992.

153. *Peters v. The Netherlands*, 6 April 1994.

154. Appl. No. 10435/83, 12 July 1978.

155. *Herczegfalvy v. Austria*, 24 September 1992.

156. See, e.g., *McFeeley v. United Kingdom*, 15 May 1980.

157. *Niemietz v. Germany*, 16 December 1992.

158. *Halford v. the United Kingdom*, 25 June 1997.

159. See, *inter alia*, B. Oversteyns, "Het recht op eerbiediging van het privé-leven," *R.W.*, 1988–89, 490.

160. *Belgian Official Journal*, 18 March 1993.

161. *Tsavachidis v. Greece*, 28 October 1997.

162. *Appl. No. 18760/91 v. Ireland*, 1 December 1993.

163. *Spencers v. United Kingdom*, 16 January 1998.

164. See also Article 15 of the Belgian Constitution ("The domicile is inviolable; no visit to the individual's residence can take place except in the cases provided for by law and in the form prescribed by law") and Article 29 of the Belgian Constitution ("The confidentiality of letters is inviolable").

165. See, e.g., President of the Court of First Instance of Liège, 9 October 1992, *J.L.M.B.*, 1994, 235.

166. See also Article 109*ter* d of the Law of 21 March 1991 according to which it is prohibited to "willfully gaining knowledge of data relating to telecommunications which concerns another person."

167. President of the Brussels Commercial Court, 21 March 2000, *A&M*, 2000, 344.

168. 27 March 1996.

169. 27 February 1997.

170. See also *Ernst and others v. Belgium*, 25 June 2002.

171. President of the Court of First Instance of Brussels, 7 June 2002, *A&M*, 2002, 459.

172. *Belgian Official Journal*, 27 April 2005.

173. Court of First Instance of Brussels, 19 February 2004, not reported, R.G. No 2004/622/A.

174. Convention of 27 September 1968 on jurisdiction and the enforcement of judgments in civil and commercial matters, replaced by the Council Regulation (EC) No. 44/2001 of 22 December 2000 on jurisdiction and the recognition and enforcement of judgments in civil and commercial matters (OJ 2001 L12/1).

175. Mons Commercial Court, 15 June 2001, not reported, R.G. No. A/00/2512.

176. Liège Court of Appeal, 28 November 2001, *J. T.*, 2002, 308.

177. See also President of the Court of First Instance, 2 March 2000, not reported, RR 2000/77/C, where an Internet Service Provider undertook to delete and prevent, by all technical means, the publication of libelous statements on the Internet site of one of its customers.

178. Court of First Instance of Brussels, 25 June 2002, *A&M*, 2004, 367.

179. President of the Commercial Court of Antwerp, 9 August 2001, *Annuaire Pratiques du Commerce & Concurrence*, 2001, 666.

180. Brussels Criminal Court, 22 December 1999, not reported, available at http://www.droit-technologie.org/4_1.asp?jurisprudence_id=33.

181. *Belgian Official Journal*, 17 March 2003.

CHAPTER 12

England and Wales

MARK STEPHENS

Finer Stephens Innocent

Finer Stephens Innocent
179 Great Portland Street
London W1W 5LS
United Kingdom
Phone: +44 (0)20 7323 4000
Fax: +44 (0)20 7580 7069
www.fsilaw.co.uk
mstephens@fsilaw.co.uk

Introduction to the
United Kingdom Legal System

The United Kingdom has three distinct legal jurisdictions: Scotland, Northern Ireland, and England and Wales. Although there are subtle differences among the three independent judicial systems, they share much of the same common law. This introduction will focus on fundamental court structure in England and Wales. The Scottish and Northern Ireland systems are similarly structured with separate branches for criminal and civil actions. Each branch has a trial court, known as county courts or high courts, appellate courts, magistrate courts, and a house of lords.

New laws in the UK common law system originate from either Parliament or common law through judicial decisions. Parliament, composed of the House of Commons and the House of Lords in a bicameral structure, has authority to pass various Acts of Parliament, also called statutes, to create new laws. Case law cannot overrule statutory law; however, case law does serve as a practical tool for determining contemporary application or enforcement of a statute. The hierarchical structure of the British court system demands that all lower courts must abide by any higher court's ruling.

Civil actions, depending on the financial magnitude of the claim and the societal implications of the legal issue at hand, are initially heard in either a County Court or a High Court. County Courts, dispersed in counties throughout the country, are used to hear claims of marginal financial value or type of legal issue. County Court decisions are binding solely to the county of that particular court; however, parties may appeal a County Court decision, on questions of law only, to the Court of Appeal in the civil division. Appeals are then heard in the House of Lords—the highest court of appeal in England and Wales.

Criminal actions are handled in a similar fashion; less serious cases are heard in magistrate courts and are decided by magistrates with limited sentencing powers. More serious cases are sent to a higher crown court and are tried by a more established high court judge with a jury. Appeals from a magistrate court can go to a high court and appeals from the high court must go to the House of Lords.

1. What is the locally accepted definition of libel?

Libel occurs when a defamatory statement is published about someone, in written or some other permanent form, or broadcast. A defamatory statement is simply one that damages a person's reputation or makes others think less of him. It is possible for text, still or moving pictures, headlines, photographs, cartoons, jokes, and illustrations to be defamatory.

2. Is libel-by-implication recognized, or, in the alternative, must the complained-of words alone defame the plaintiff?

English law recognizes that, whereas some statements are not defamatory on their face or in their ordinary meaning, they may still carry discreditable implications to those with special (as opposed to general) knowledge, and thereby convey a defamatory imputation.

To cite a popular illustration, to say that someone was seen entering a particular house may be perfectly innocuous in its ordinary meaning, but would contain a defamatory imputation for anyone who knew that house to be a brothel. This is libel "by innuendo."

3. May corporations sue for libel?

Corporations and companies may sue for defamation but only for statements which damage them in their trade or business reputation. Partnerships and LLPs may also sue. Local authorities cannot. Trade unions and most unincorporated associations cannot sue for libel, but their members can.

It has become increasingly common, e.g., for senior executives responsible for the actions of a corporation to sue as its proxy.

4. Is product disparagement recognized, and if so, how does that differ from libel?

Where statements focus on the product, rather than on the actions of the producer, manufacturer, or supplier, there is less chance of a claim for libel. However, a claim may lie for malicious falsehood for product disparagement or "slander of goods." Such actions are rare and difficult. The producer has to prove a heavy burden: that the statement was false (contrast libel actions where falsity is presumed by law) and the maker of the statement was malicious (in other words, he made the statement knowing it to be false or recklessly published the statement); and the publication must cause financial loss or be likely to cause such loss.

5. Must an individual be clearly identified (by name or photograph) to sue for libel? Can a group of persons sue for libel, even though not named?

A person may bring a libel action if it is possible to identify an individual who is not named in a defamatory statement, but is discernable from the context in which the statement appears. Examples are photographs, clues given about the individual, or other information which tends to lead readers to identify the individual. The legal test is an objective one: whether reasonable readers would understand the statement to refer to the individual concerned (even where there are a number of other persons who might also be identified by the statement).

It is also possible to wrongly or unintentionally identify individuals who reasonable readers could conclude was the subject of the article. In the famous fictional story about Artemus Jones who was said to enjoy gambling, horse racing, and the company of French prostitutes, Jones was misidentified for a real-life Welsh Baptist who was most virtuous.

6. What is the fault standard(s) applied to libel?

a. Does the fault standard depend on the fame or notoriety of the plaintiff?

The law holds that a uniform standard of fault applies to Claimants regardless of their fame or notoriety or whether they are generally perceived as good or bad persons. It is presumed that the Claimant has a good reputation. Practice may present a slightly different picture, however, because most libel actions are before juries who, when faced with someone who is famous, may have a difficult task in divorcing their own preconceptions about the celebrity from the facts at issue. Conversely, in extreme and rare cases, it might be reasonable to adduce evidence that a person has a bad reputation.

In relation to damages, the tendency is toward larger damages awards for celebrities than for ordinary people, and for derisory awards (e.g., £1) for Claimants who win—technically—but whose conduct finds disapproval with the jury.

b. Is there a heightened fault standard or privilege for reporting on matters of public concern or public interest?

Absent the sort of constitutional protection afforded by the First Amendment to the U.S. Constitution, English law has evolved in case law to a point where it can best be summarized as follows: Where matters of public interest are reported and the media has a legitimate duty/interest in doing so and the recipient has a corresponding duty/interest in receiving it, the report may attract the protection of the defense of "qualified privilege" where it satisfies the nonexhaustive criteria which were set out by the House of Lords in 1999 in the leading case of *Reynolds v. Times Newspapers Limited.*[1]

Those criteria are:

1. ***The seriousness of the allegation.*** The more serious the charge, the more the public is misinformed and the individual harassed by the adverse impact on them if the story turns out to be false. Thus, the more serious the allegation, the more weighty the reporter's responsibility to be correct.

2. ***The nature of the information, and the extent to which the subject matter is a public concern.*** The more important the story is to the public's welfare, the more leeway for error will be granted.

3. ***The source of the information.*** Some sources have no direct knowledge of events. Some have their own axes to grind, or are being paid for their stories. The credibility of the source, and the reporter's efforts to ascertain that credibility, will be examined.

4. ***The status of the information.*** The allegation may have already been the subject of an investigation which commands respect.

5. ***The steps taken to verify the information.*** Fact-finding, research, interviews, and investigation all combine to convince a judge that the qualified privilege should be applied.

6. ***The urgency of the matter.*** Whereas news is viewed by some as a perishable commodity, courts are less likely to be swayed by urgency arising from press-competitive pressures and more likely to be convinced by the public's immediate need for the information.

7. ***Whether comment was sought from the claimant.*** He may have information others do not possess or have not disclosed. An approach to the claimant may not always be necessary. As a practical tip, because much litigation now centers on this area, it is often

useful to have proof of contact and the matter put to the target, as well as showing that the target has a reasonable opportunity to inform himself, respond meaningfully, and that response should be fairly included in the article.

8. **Whether the article contained the gist of the claimant's side of the story.** Stories that unfairly edit a denial of wrongdoing may be found libelous.

9. **The tone of the article.** A newspaper can raise queries or call for an investigation. It need not adopt allegations as statements of fact.

10. **The circumstances of the publication including the timing.**

This is sometimes known colloquially as the defense of "responsible journalism." UK media defendants are faced with considerable legal presumptions to overcome at trial: both falsity and damage are presumed by law.

Truth (called "justification") is an absolute defense. In cases where an error has been made, or proving the truth is impossible, once a claimant has proved the words to be defamatory and to refer to him, the onus falls on the media defendant to prove that it acted "responsibly" (by reference to the above *Reynolds* criteria).

Of course, substantial evidential difficulties can be faced. For example, where the media has relied upon confidential sources, it is impossible to prove the reliability of those sources without compromising that confidence in some way. There is a perception that the *Reynolds* Qualified Privilege is aimed at protecting investigative journalism rather than tabloid sensationalism, but very frequently it is investigative journalists who need to rely on confidential sources.

7. Is financial news about publicly traded companies, or companies involved with a government contract, considered a matter of public interest or otherwise privileged?

Owing to the importance of financial news to markets, this information will usually be of public interest, although there is little decided case law on the point. Such publications may fall within the protection afforded by:

1. Statutory qualified privilege which extends to "fair and accurate" reports of: public meetings; proceedings at general meetings of UK public companies; copies of documents circulated to members of public companies in the UK/Channel Islands or Isle of Man and any findings or decisions by certain trade/business/industry/professional associations. Note that for this privilege to attach, the publication must not be prohibited by law or be malicious, and the subject matter must be of public concern.

2. *Reynolds* Qualified Privilege (described in Question 6b. above).

8. Is there a recognized protection for opinion or "fair comment" on matters of public concern?

The defense of fair comment protects statements of opinion or comment on matters of public interest. The defendant must be able to prove, in order to fall within this protection: that the statement was indeed comment (and not a statement of fact); that there is sufficient factual basis for the comment, i.e., the comment must be based on facts which are substantially true; that the comment is one which an honest person could hold (an objective test); and that the subject matter is of public interest. Fair comment will not apply if a claimant can prove the source, author, or publisher was malicious.

9. Are there any requirements upon a plaintiff, such as demand for retraction or right of reply, and if so, what impact do they have?

No such steps are prescribed. It is for the claimant to specify to the defendant what remedies he is seeking, depending on the circumstances. Pursuant to the Pre-Action Protocol for Defamation, he must set out clearly the remedies he seeks when he first complains. Typical remedies sought are for publication of an apology and retraction (form and prominence to be agreed); an undertaking not to repeat the same or similar allegations; removal of an offending publication from a Web site; payment of damages; and payment of the claimant's legal costs.

There are currently legislative moves afoot to introduce a statutory right of reply. The practical difficulties with regard to implementation are presently proving most complex.

10. Is there a privilege for quoting or reporting on:

a. Papers filed in court?

Privilege will apply to documents filed at court which are "publicly available," e.g., the claim form, pleadings (now known as "statements of case"), and witness statements which have been read by the judge in a public hearing, judgments, and court notices.

In the case of any other documents concerned in the litigation (such as papers drafted by litigants but not read by the judge) which do not fall into the above category, anyone who publishes their contents will be taken to have repeated any defamatory statements within them and may be vulnerable to a libel claim.

Absolute privilege attaches to statements made in "fair, accurate and contemporaneous" reports of judicial proceedings in open court in the United Kingdom.

Very limited documents are available directly from the Court Office.

Increasingly, however, Masters (Junior Judges) are permitting journalists access to the Court file if they first explain their reasons for requesting it.

b. Government-issued documents?

Same as above.

c. Quasi-governmental proceedings?

Statements made by one officer of state to another in the course of duty are protected by privilege, as are "fair and accurate" copies/extracts/reports of: any register kept by statute; government publications; matter published by international organizations and conferences; notices from governments; local authority meetings; inquiries, public meetings, parliamentary papers and proceedings; company meetings; and association meetings.

11. Is there a privilege for republishing statements made earlier by other, bona fide, reliable publications or wire services?

No. Anybody republishing or repeating defamatory statements will be treated for the purposes of a libel claim to have made those statements himself. It is no defense to say you were merely repeating what you had been told, however reliable or reputable the source. Similarly, it will not aid a journalist to sprinkle a piece with words such as "allegedly" or "it is claimed"; he will be taken to have said the words himself.

12. Are there any restrictions regarding reporting on:

a. Ongoing criminal investigations?

In terms of libel, in reporting criminal investigations and prosecutions, publishers should at all times have regard to the laws of libel. However, UK law is well-known for restrictions of what reporters may or may not publish from court proceedings. At the heart of these "Contempt of Court" rules is the avoidance of publications that "create a substantial risk that the administration of justice will be seriously impeded or prejudiced." This is usually directed at the press prejudicing a jury by introducing facts or material not yet offered into evidence at trial that if publicized, would prejudice that trial.

This is a strict liability offense. The journalist's intention is irrelevant and is not dependent on there being a specific court order in place.

In relation to criminal *investigations,* potential liability for contempt applies from when the proceedings become "active," meaning when a summons for the defendant's arrest is issued by a Court, or when the defendant is charged.

b. Ongoing criminal prosecutions?

Such risk of liability continues through the criminal *prosecution* and comes to an end when a defendant is acquitted or sentenced, or the action is otherwise discontinued. Serious prejudice is likely to arise from publication of the following matters: a defendant's previous convictions or details of his bad character; suggestions that a witness is unreliable; and details of evidence likely to be contested at trial. Note that revealing similar fact evidence is a particularly fraught area, especially the closer you get to trial.

In addition to the general rule above, under section 4(2) of the Contempt of Court Act 1981 a court may specifically order that publication of any report of the proceedings may be postponed if it appears necessary to avoid substantial risk of prejudice to the administration of justice in those proceedings or any other proceedings pending or imminent. These orders are general in nature, that is, they are directed to the press at large and not to specific publications.

In practice, section 4(2) orders are often made to prevent the media from reporting on a particular piece of evidence which the judge in a libel case does not believe should be put before the jury. Such an order will as a rule be posted on the court door and notice-board for the attention of reporters attending.

Committal proceedings: Under the Magistrates' Courts Act 1980, reports of proceedings in which magistrates' courts commit an accused for trial and remand hearings, may only cover the barest essentials, namely the accused's name, address, the charges, any decision to commit, and arrangements for bail. Background information about the crime alleged should be kept distinct from any report of the proceedings. An accused may request reporting restrictions be lifted, but this is rare in practice. The reporting restrictions applied to the committed proceedings cease if the magistrates decide not to commit, or if they proceed to try the case themselves, or when the Crown Court trial itself is concluded.

Reporting of sexual offenses and young persons: Publishers must comply with statutory provisions, punishable by criminal sanction, prohibiting the identification of victims of certain sexual offenses such as rape, and the identification of young persons (under 18) in proceedings in which they are either a defendant or witness.

Liability for prosecution costs: In a relatively recent development, the Courts Act 2003 empowers courts to impose costs upon third parties such as the media where there has been serious misconduct (whether or not amounting to Contempt of Court) by the media organization and where the court considers it appropriate. This provision was introduced after reporting by the *Sunday Mirror* led to the aborting of a criminal trial involving a number of Leeds footballers (*R v. Woodgate and others*),[2] necessitating a re-trial and where wasted costs were estimated at about £1 million. The media organization would potentially be liable for the wasted costs of the prosecution, defense, and court administration costs.

c. Ongoing regulatory investigations?

No specific restrictions apply but, as above, reporters must keep in mind the law of libel. Objectivity and balance in a story, rather than the taking of sides, are paramount if a publisher is to successfully raise the protection afforded by qualified privilege.

d. Ongoing civil litigation, or other judicial proceedings?

Contempt of Court is a possibility. Civil proceedings become "active" when a matter is set down for trial (usually about halfway through the litigation process) and ends on judgment or discontinuance. However, in reality it is unlikely that in civil cases heard by a judge alone there will be a risk of strict liability contempt; judges are almost invariably presumed to be above influence by the media. However, jury trials are commonplace in libel actions and the media certainly needs to keep an eye on contempt of court in covering these.

Except where judgment or proceedings are held in open court, it is a contempt to reveal reports of proceedings relating to children, family cases, mental health, national security, secret processes, and inventions or where there is a specific court order based on some proper source—note this is not an unencumbered freestanding right.

Civil Procedure Rules: These rules govern the conduct of civil litigation and forbid parties from using for any purpose other than the litigation itself documents and witness statements disclosed by the parties. If the media come into possession of any such documents, great care needs to be exercised. Publication of such documents could amount to *Contempt of Court* where the documents or witness statements have not been read by the judge in a hearing in open court. The same applies to any pleadings which are not on the public court file. Thus, publishers should contact local counsel prior to basing reports on such documents.

13. Are prior restraints or other prepublication injunctions available on the basis of libel or privacy, and if so, what are the standards for obtaining such relief?

Yes, although there is a general rule against "prior restraint." Applications for prepublication injunctions on the basis of libel are very seldom successful because they can be defeated if the media organization asserts that it will defend any libel claim with a defense of truth/justification, or any other substantive defense such as fair comment or privilege. If a publisher has an arguable defense, the publication will not be restrained no matter how damaging the allegations may be: the Claimant may always seek damages after the publication.

As a general rule, the courts will be exceedingly slow to make interim restraint orders where the applicant has not satisfied the court he will probably ("more likely than not") succeed at trial on privacy grounds. A number of considerations apply. Applications for injunctions arising out of privacy issues follow the general rules set out in the *American Cyanamid* case,[3] requiring the following criteria to be satisfied: there must be a serious issue to be tried which has some prospect of success at trial; the balance of convenience must favor the applicant; if at this stage the parties are equally balanced, the court will permit the status quo to prevail; or, should none of these tests succeed, the court will consider the merits of the case. Following the case of *Cream Holdings v. Banerjee*,[4] the court must be satisfied that the claimant has established that it is "likely" that the publication should not be allowed and that this threshold test was "a real prospect of success, convincingly established."

14. Is a right of privacy recognized (either civilly or criminally)?
Following the enactment of the Human Rights Act 1998 which enshrines the "right to respect for private and family life" (Article 8), the established common law cause of action in breach of confidence has developed into a modern concept of "misuse of private information" or "unjustified publication of personal information," now known colloquially as breach of privacy.

a. What is the definition of "private fact"?
No specific definition exists of "private fact" or "private information."

b. Is there a public interest or newsworthiness exception?
In *Naomi Campbell v. Mirror* (2002),[5] a breach of privacy was found after the tabloid published details of the supermodel's attendance at meetings of Narcotics Anonymous, accompanied by a photograph of her leaving a drug rehabilitation clinic. The court held that the photograph disclosed private facts (in this case medical information) about the model. It is suggested that a prudent approach by the media would involve: identifying each element of arguably private information in the proposed publication; deciding whether in relation to each such element the subject of the article would have a reasonable expectation of privacy; considering whether in the case of any such element there is a public interest justification for the proposed publication (such as the correction of a false denial or disclosure of crime or other serious wrongdoing); in relation to any element where there is no public interest justification weigh the value of the free speech

right against value of the privacy right. In the case of photographs, which have a particularly intrusive quality, these should be considered separately from the story by reference to the above criteria.[6]

The European Court of Human Rights decided in the 2004 *Princess Caroline* case[7] that there had been unauthorized publication of photographs of an everyday princess engaging in ordinary activities in public places. The ECHR held that the commercial interest of the press in publishing the photos had to yield to Princess Caroline's right to effective protection of her private life. This decision will have to be taken into account in future English cases in this area.

Examples of cases where "private facts" or "private information" have been at issue:

- *Beckham v. MGN* (2000)[8]—injunction granted: photographs of the interior of a footballer's house.
- *A v. B* (2002)[9]—injunction granted but overturned on appeal: details of a married footballer's affairs with two women.
- *Theakston v. MGN* (2002)[10]—injunction refused: written details of a night spent at a brothel by a television presenter. Injunction granted in relation to photographs of those same activities. Pictures are considered to be more intrusive and more likely to be subject to injunction.

15. May reporters tape-record their own telephone conversations for note-taking purposes (not rebroadcast) without the consent of the other party?

In theory, the United Kingdom is a one-party consent state, but EU legislation (Data Protection Acts and Regulation of Investigating Powers Act) has now effectively made this into a two-party consent state on pain of criminal sanction.

16. If permissible to record such tapes, may they be broadcast without permission?

The use of such one-party tapes may present a possible issue with breach of confidence if:

1. the information broadcast/published "has the necessary quality of confidence" (e.g., is private and secret); and
2. the source imparted the information in circumstances where, or where by making it clear, there would be a duty of confidence (e.g., an employee giving information confidential to his employers; or evidence disclosed in litigation or official secrets); and
3. there has been unauthorized use of that information to the detriment of the person who communicated it.

17. Is there a recognized evidentiary privilege preventing the disclosure of confidential sources relied upon by reporters?

Section 10 of the Contempt of Court Act 1981 provides some limited protection for journalists to protect their confidential sources: "No court may require a person to disclose, nor is any person guilty of contempt of court for refusing to disclose, the source of information contained in a publication for which he is responsible, unless it is established to the satisfaction of the court that disclosure is necessary in the interests of justice or national security, or for the prevention of disorder or crime." In practice, the journalists' statutory protection is rarely challenged as it was reinforced by the European Court of Human Rights decision of *Goodwin v. UK*.[11]

The Police and Criminal Evidence Act (PACE) 1984 sets out the circumstances in which the police may apply to a judge, and a judge may grant disclosure of journalistic material. Before making an order, a judge has to be satisfied that: there are reasonable grounds for believing that a serious arrestable offense has been committed; the evidence would be admissible and of substantial value; other methods to obtain the material have failed or are bound to fail; and that disclosure would be in the public interest.

Because failure to obey a court order is punishable by a contempt charge, reporters facing such demands should contact local counsel immediately.

18. In the event that legal papers are served upon the newsroom (such as a civil complaint), are there any particular warnings about accepting service of which we should be aware?

Strict procedural rules govern the service of papers commencing legal proceedings (e.g., a claim form, previously known as a writ), requiring service on either the registered office within the jurisdiction of the media company or on solicitors who act for the company and who have confirmed expressly that they have instructions to accept service. There may be valid and fundamental legal points to be raised in relation to the validity of service and a newsroom should not carelessly accept service of a claim; there is no obligation to do so.

An injunction is a mandatory court order requiring compliance under pain of fine or imprisonment, and is therefore a very different matter. It would be foolhardy in the extreme for a newsroom to ignore or reject an injunction which it receives as it will be taken to have been served with the injunction, and therefore have knowledge of its contents, from the moment it receives the document, even if it receives the injunction by way of a report from, e.g., a wire service. No longer do claimants have to serve each and every newsroom directly.

19. Has your jurisdiction applied established media law to Internet publishers?

Yes, especially in the areas of libel and confidential information. Recent reported libel cases involving publication on the Internet include the following: *Yousef Jameel v. Dow Jones & Co Inc* (2005 Court of Appeal)[12] (lawsuit brought on only five Internet hits held to be an abuse of process); *Don King v. Lennox Lewis* (2004 Court of Appeal)[13] (whether England was the correct forum in respect of defamation on the Internet); *Richardson v. Schwarzenegger* (2004 Queen's Bench Division)[14] (liability for republication in respect of a publication on the Internet, and forum conveniens); *Hewitt & Others v. Grunwald & Others* (2004 QBD)[15] (application to strike out a defense of qualified privilege failed in circumstances where publication of the press release was complained of on the Internet); *Vassiliev v. Frank Cass & Co Ltd* (2003 QBD)[16] (whether the defendant was protected by common interest privilege where there was publication on the Internet); *Godfrey v. Demon Internet Ltd* (1999 QBD)[17] (defendant was allowed to show other postings in news groups in mitigation of damages).

Confidential Information cases on the Internet in England include: *J K Rowling v. Persons Unknown* (2003 High Court)[18] (injunction granted restraining publication by the world at large of stolen Harry Potter manuscripts); *Covance Laboratories v. J* (2003 Chancery Division)[19] (whether Internet publication defeated a claim in confidence); *Attorney General v. Times Newspapers Ltd* (2001 Court of Appeal)[20] (whether a publisher should be required to obtain prior approval from the Attorney General before publishing material which might be damaging to national security even where the information was already in the public domain as a result of Internet publication).

20. If established media law has been applied to Internet publishers, are there any ways in which Internet publishers (including chat room operators) have to meet different standards?

Generally the same standards apply as apply to publications in other forms, but an Internet service provider (ISP) may be able to avail itself of the safe-harbor defense of "unintentional publication" under Section 1 of the Defamation Act, 1996, where the ISP can show it was not author of the defamatory statement, that it took reasonable care in relation to the publication, and that it did not know, or had no reason to believe, that it had caused publication of a defamatory statement.

Following the *Godfrey v. Demon Internet* case (see Question 19 above), it seems that the prudent course for ISPs is that once they receive a complaint, they should consider temporarily removing the offending material immediately or they risk not being able to avail themselves of the unintentional publication defense. In practice, many ISPs ask for an indemnity from the Claimant to abide the event of wrongful removal.

21. Are there any cases where the courts enforced a judgment in libel from another jurisdiction against a publisher in your jurisdiction?

This issue has arisen only rarely because of the ease with which reciprocal enforcement can be recognized by treaties among Commonwealth States and also among E.U. States.

It is possible to register money judgments from any jurisdiction which meets the UK's basic procedural standards. It is not possible to register foreign injunctive orders without commencing separate proceedings.

In any event, given that London is notoriously the "libel capital of the world" and a claimant-friendly environment in which to sue, most claimants come to the English courts to sue in the first place.

Chapter Notes

1. *Reynolds v. Times Newspapers Ltd* [2001] 2 A.C. 127; [1999] 3 W.L.R. 1010; [1999] 4 All E.R. 609; [2000] E.M.L.R. 1; [2000] H.R.L.R. 134; 7 B.H.R.C. 289; (1999) 96(45) L.S.G. 34; (1999) 149 N.L.J. 1697; (1999) 143 S.J.L.B. 270.

2. *R v. Woodgate, Bowyer, Clifford and Others* (unreported).

3. *American Cyanamid Co v. Ethicon Ltd (No.3)* [1979] R.P.C. 215.

4. *Cream Holdings Ltd v. Banerjee* [2004] UKHL 44; [2004] 3 W.L.R. 918; [2004] 4 All E.R. 617; [2005] E.M.L.R. 1; [2004] H.R.L.R. 39; [2004] U.K.H.R.R. 1071; 17 B.H.R.C. 464; (2004) 101(42) L.S.G. 29; (2004) 154 N.L.J. 1589; (2004) 148 S.J.L.B. 1215.

5. *Campbell v. Mirror Group Newspapers Ltd, 14 October 2002* [2002] EWCA Civ 1373; [2003] Q.B. 633; [2003] 2 W.L.R. 80; [2003] 1 All E.R. 224; [2003] E.M.L.R. 2; [2003] H.R.L.R. 2; (2002) 99(42) L.S.G. 38; (2002) 146 S.J.L.B. 234.

6. *Campbell v. Mirror Group Newspapers Ltd* [2004] UKHL 22; [2004] 2 A.C. 457; [2004] 2 W.L.R. 1232; [2004] 2 All E.R. 995; [2004] E.M.L.R. 15; [2004] H.R.L.R. 24; [2004] U.K.H.R.R. 648; 16 B.H.R.C. 500; (2004) 101(21) L.S.G. 36; (2004) 154 N.L.J. 733; (2004) 148 S.J.L.B. 572.

7. *Von Hannover v. Germany* (59320/00) [2004] E.M.L.R. 21 (ECHR).

8. *Beckham v. MGN Ltd, QBD,* June 28, 2001 (unreported).

9. *A v. B Plc* [2002] EWCA Civ 337; [2003] Q.B. 195; [2002] 3 W.L.R. 542;

[2002] 2 All E.R. 545; [2002] E.M.L.R. 21; [2002] 1 F.L.R. 1021; [2002] 2 F.C.R. 158; [2002] H.R.L.R. 25; [2002] U.K.H.R.R. 457; 12 B.H.R.C. 466; [2002] Fam. Law 415; (2002) 99(17) L.S.G. 36; (2002) 152 N.L.J. 434; (2002) 146 S.J.L.B. 77.

10. *Theakston v. MGN Ltd* [2002] EWHC 137; [2002] E.M.L.R. 22.

11. *Goodwin v. United Kingdom* (28957/95) [2002] I.R.L.R. 664; [2002] 2 F.L.R. 487; [2002] 2 F.C.R. 577; (2002) 35 E.H.R.R. 18; 13 B.H.R.C. 120; (2002) 67 B.M.L.R. 199; [2002] Fam. Law 738; (2002) 152 N.L.J. 1171.

12. *Dow Jones & Co Inc v. Jameel* [2005] EWCA Civ 75; (2005) 149 S.J.L.B. 181 Times, February 14, 2005; Independent, February 10, 2005.

13. *King v. Lewis* [2004] EWCA Civ 1329; [2005] E.M.L.R. 4.

14. *Richardson v. Schwarzenegger* (2004) EWHC 2422 (QBD).

15. *Hewitt v. Grunwald* [2004] EWHC 2959.

16. *Vassiliev v. Frank Cass & Co Ltd* (Defamation: Qualified Privilege) [2003] EWHC 1428; [2003] E.M.L.R. 33.

17. *Godfrey v. Demon Internet Ltd (Application to Strike Out)* [2001] Q.B. 201; [2000] 3 W.L.R. 1020; [1999] 4 All E.R. 342; [1999] E.M.L.R. 542; [1998–99] Info. T.L.R. 252; [1999] I.T.C.L.R. 282; [1999] Masons C.L.R. 267; (1999) 149 N.L.J. 609.

18. *Bloomsbury Publishing Plc (2) J K Rowling v. Newsgroup Newspapers Ltd (2003)* [2003] EWHC 1087 Ch.

19. *Covance Laboratories v. J* (20 and 27 March 2003 Chancery Division), unreported.

20. *Attorney General v. Times Newspapers Ltd* [2001] EWCA Civ 97; [2001] 1 W.L.R. 885; [2001] E.M.L.R. 19; (2001) 98(9) L.S.G. 38; (2001) 145 S.J.L.B. 30 *Times,* January 31, 2001; *Independent,* January 30, 2001.

CHAPTER 13

France

DOMINIQUE MONDOLONI

Willkie Farr & Gallagher LLP

Willkie Farr & Gallagher LLP
21-23, rue de la Ville l'Evêque
75008 Paris, France
Phone: +33.1.53.43.45.00
Fax: +33.1.40.06.96.06
www.willkie.com
dmondoloni@willkie.com

Introduction to the French Legal System

The French legal system, adhering to the principles of civil law, uses courts of first instance, appeals courts, and a court of last resort to resolve both civil and criminal actions. Proceedings are traditionally heard by a panel of magistrates, the parties being generally represented by attorneys that assist the plaintiff and/or defendant. With the notable exception of divorce and juvenile proceedings, all trials are open to the public.

Magistrates govern and enforce the French judicial system. The two kinds of magistrates are sitting magistrates and standing magistrates. Sitting magistrates serve as judges and deliver verdicts; standing magistrates represent state and public interests, prosecute criminal offenses, and ensure equitable and consistent enforcement of state law. Magistrates are assisted by clerks and ushers who record the verdict and ensure the sentence is served.

Civil and criminal actions, although handled in different courts, have similar progressions in the French system. Civil actions are initially tried in a court of first instance (*tribunaux de grande instance*). The proceedings are dominated by written submissions by the attorneys, and a verdict is often announced, in writing, by the panel of magistrates serving as judges many weeks or months after the trial. Verdicts can be re-evaluated by an appeals court (*Cour d'Appel*) and at the highest court, the Court of Cassation (*Cour de Cassation*). Unlike the civil *tribunaux de grande instance,* criminal tribunals, designated to hear criminal offenses, are organized into three groups. Police tribunals hear petty offenses, *tribunaux correctionnels* hear mid-level crimes, and the *cour d'assises* hear the most serious offenses. An appeals court, and possibly the Court of Cassation, can re-evaluate the tribunal court's decision.

1. What is the locally accepted definition of libel?

Libel, and more generally defamation (French law does not distinguish between libel and slander), is statutorily defined as "any allegation or imputation of a fact which is contrary to honor or to the consideration in which is held a person or an institution."[1]

Defamation is an offense and as such is actionable in the criminal courts, but the plaintiff may choose to bring his action exclusively in the civil courts. The essential elements of the offense are:
1. the making of a defamatory statement;
2. the publication of that statement;[2] and
3. the identification of the plaintiff as the person defamed.

1. The Defamatory Statement

The complained-of words must be such that they constitute a factual allegation as against the plaintiff or the imputation of a fact[3] to the plaintiff that is contrary to "honor" or is such that it injures the "consideration" in which that person is held by the community.

"Honor" is a concept common to all men and consists of the notion that one's conduct conforms to moral standards. A man of honor is one who accomplishes his duties and acts according to his conscience. "Consideration" is the respect and esteem in which one is held by the community. To defame is to impute or allege conduct that is contrary to honor or that will damage someone's consideration. In general, defamation tends to involve charges that fall within the following categories: accusation of a crime; sexual impropriety or immoral behavior; disgraceful behavior; bankruptcy, financial irresponsibility, or dishonesty; or professional misconduct in one's business.

2. Publication

"Publication" means that the defamatory statement must have been made public. According to Section 23 of the Law of 29 July 1881, defamation is actionable if the defamatory statement was made orally in a public speech or declaration, or in print through the use of words, engravings, sketches, drawings, and generally any form of image, and was made public through any medium of mass communication including through the sale and distribution of printed material (e.g., books, newspapers, magazines), billboards, or any other support of the voice or images (e.g., radio, cinema, television, Internet).

3. Identification
The complained-of words must identify the plaintiff or be such that the plaintiff is identifiable. For example, if the complained-of words concern a small number of people, none of whom are identified individually in the statement but all of whom are nonetheless identifiable, then all those persons which form the group are entitled to act against the defendant. Such would be the case, say, of a statement to the effect that "the Board of Directors of Company X agreed with the CEO's decision to pay a kick-back to the president of West Africa in order to obtain the contract for the construction of the capital's subway system."

2. Is libel-by-implication recognized, or, in the alternative, must the complained-of words alone defame the plaintiff?
Defamation is actionable even if the words in and of themselves are not libelous but, put in context, become defamatory.

3. May corporations sue for libel?
Yes.

4. Is product disparagement recognized, and if so, how does that differ from libel?
No, unless the denigration of a product is a means of injuring someone's reputation (e.g., "Butcher X's meat is rotten" can be defamatory for the plaintiff because it implies that Butcher X sells rotten meat, which is a statement that can damage his reputation).

However, whereas product disparagement in and of itself is not actionable as defamation, it can give rise to a civil action in tort between competitors on the basis of the theory of unfair competition. A medium that would publish or make public a denigrating statement by an economic operator of his competitor's goods would be actionable on the same grounds.[4]

5. Must an individual be clearly identified (by name or photograph) to sue for libel? Can a group of persons sue for libel, even though not named?
The plaintiff must be identified by name, photograph, or drawing or be identifiable (see discussion in Question 1 above). Group libel is possible

in France. If a statement concerns a group of persons who are identifiable as a result of their membership in the group (e.g., the Town Council of City A, or the Board of Directors of Company X), then all can act against the defendant. The theory of *par ricochet* also allows a cause of action to lie when the unnamed plaintiff is closely associated with the subject of the story in such a manner that the story evokes his image in the mind of the reasonable reader.

6. What is the fault standard(s) applied to libel?

Defamation is an offense so in principle it requires that the plaintiff demonstrate that the defendant acted in bad faith (i.e., with the knowledge that his statement was defamatory). However, Article 35*bis* of the Law of 29 July 1881 has instituted a notable exception to this principle of French Criminal Law by providing that the defendant's bad faith shall be presumed. The plaintiff only has therefore to establish the material elements of defamation.

a. Does the fault standard depend on the fame or notoriety of the plaintiff?

No.

b. Is there a heightened fault standard or privilege for reporting on matters of public concern or public interest?

There is no heightened fault standard from the perspective of the plaintiff (i.e., the fact that the plaintiff is a public figure does not place additional burden on the plaintiff or provide defenses).

However, when reporting on matters of public interest or concern, certain defenses will be more readily available to the defendant. For example, truth of the defamatory statement is a defense that is available in most libel cases except, *inter alia,* when the facts alleged or imputed as against the defendant concern his privacy. Privacy will however be construed more restrictively when the defendant is a public figure. Matters that concern, e.g., a person's finances are generally considered to fall within the scope of privacy. Truth is therefore not an admissible defense in such an instance. But truth will be admitted as a defense if the defendant is a public figure where the aspects of his personal financial situation could have a bearing on the way that person will deal with public funds. Aspects of his intimacy (e.g., the existence of a liaison or the plaintiff's sexual preferences, etc.) will remain outside the scope of the *exceptio veritatis* defense.

Notwithstanding, good faith is a defense upon which the defendant in that situation could rely. Good faith will be more readily admitted by the courts when, for example, the issues at stake concern matters of public interest. The courts will acquit the defendant on that basis provided that the journalist had at least carried out a basic verification of the information from the source (which is a duty of the journalist).

It should also be noted that in French procedure, proving the truth of defamatory allegations, reporters may only rely upon material that they had actually acquired prior to publication. They may not use material learned through investigation after publication to justify the sued-upon article.

7. Is financial news about publicly traded companies, or companies involved with a government contract, considered a matter of public interest or otherwise privileged?

There is no particular privilege in relation thereto, but to the extent the information is of public concern, the defendant will be more readily admitted in his good faith defense.

8. Is there a recognized protection for opinion or "fair comment" on matters of public concern?

To some extent, yes. An opinion is not as such actionable as a defamation. But there is a fine line between an opinion expressed by a journalist as to, say, the way a person manages his business and defamation. Any factual allegation of impropriety in the management of a business, for example, would exceed the limits of fair comment or opinion.

9. Are there any requirements upon a plaintiff, such as demand for retraction or right of reply, and if so, what impact do they have?

The Law of 29 July 1881 provides for a "right of response" which is available to any person whose name was cited in an article or television program.[5] This right of response is open to all persons whose name was cited, irrespective of whether the statements made in relation thereto are defamatory or not.

This right must be exercised within the three months which follow the first publication of the relevant person's name. It takes the form of a letter sent to the "director of publications"[6] requesting an insertion of its content at the same place and in the same font as those of the initial article. The "director of publications" is not entitled to refuse the request except if it exceeds the statutory length, is not in relation to the initial article (i.e., is not truly a response to the article), is defamatory in its content, or is such that it implicates third parties or the journalist. An illegitimate refusal or failure to print the response at the same place and in the same font as the initial article constitutes an offense that is actionable by the plaintiff.

The Law of 29 July 1881 does not provide that the plaintiff address a demand for retraction to the defendant before he files a complaint for defamation. The "right of response" is not a substitute for a complaint in defamation, and if the initial article is defamatory, the plaintiff is entitled to sue for defamation at the same time as he is entitled to exercise a right of response.

Section 65 of the Law of 29 July 1881 provides that criminal and civil actions in defamation are time barred within three months from the initial publication of the defamatory statement. The action must be introduced before the statute of limitation period expires and there is typically no prior notice required before service of the writ.

10. Is there a privilege for quoting or reporting on:

a. Papers filed in court?

Yes. A good faith accounting of the content of papers filed in court is covered by the immunity provided for in Section 41 of the Law of 29 July 1881.

b. Government-issued documents?

Section 41 of the Law of 29 July 1881 provides for immunity from criminal or civil prosecution for defamation in relation to speeches made in parliament or written reports emanating from either chambers of parliament as well as all good faith journalistic accounts of such speeches or reports. The same immunity exists in relation to documents issued by either chamber of parliament.

It would not, however, immunize documents issued by a government administration or agency to the extent such documents would be defamatory. The good faith defense would however be available.

c. Quasi-governmental proceedings?

The immunity from prosecution provided in section 41 of the Law of 29 July 1881 would not apply, but the good faith defense might exonerate the defendant, provided the reporter used due care in reporting. In turn, this would entail examining the reliability, reputation, and methods used by the source paper upon which the defendant is relying.

11. Is there a privilege for republishing statements made earlier by other, bona fide, reliable publications or wire services?

Not *per se*, but this would typically be a situation where the good faith defense would be admitted by the courts.

12. Are there any restrictions regarding reporting on:

a. Ongoing criminal investigations?

As a matter of principle, criminal investigations are conducted under a rule of secrecy (Section 11 of the French Code of Criminal Procedure). All those persons who participate in the conduct of an investigation (Police, Investigating Magistrate, the Clerk) are bound by the rule of secrecy. Violation of the rule by those bound to it is an offense. But this rule is not enforceable as against persons who do not participate in the investigation (such as journalists).

However, a journalist may be held liable as an accomplice if he participated or in some way aided or instigated a person bound by the secrecy rule to violate that rule (e.g., an Investigating Magistrate who gives an "interview" to a journalist. The Investigating Magistrate would be guilty of violating the rule and the journalist could be held liable as an accomplice because he provided the means by which the Magistrate was able to violate the rule). The journalist may also be held liable for aiding and abetting the disclosure of secret documents (i.e., documents which were produced or obtained in the course of an investigation and which are also covered by the rule of secrecy) if he publishes those documents.

A caveat to the above is a consequence of Section 109 of the French Code of Criminal Procedure. A journalist is not obligated to reveal his sources. So, if a journalist obtains information about an ongoing investigation from sources which are not and cannot be identified other than through the testimony of the journalist (which he is at liberty not to give), then prosecution for complicity in the violation of the secrecy rule (assuming the source is bound by the rule) will not be practicable.

b. Ongoing criminal prosecutions?

Criminal prosecutions are reported under the same guidelines as investigations.

Two specific rules deserve attention here: (1) "the presumed innocent" rule and (2) Section 2 of the Law of 2 July 1931, which considers an offense the fact of making public the existence of criminal complaint filed by the victim acting as a party to the procedure.

1. Section 9-1 of the French Civil Code provides that all persons are presumed innocent and institutes a specific action in tort and specific interlocutory relief (i.e., *inter alia,* the publication of a communiqué) in favor of any person who, under criminal prosecution or investigation, is publicly presented as being guilty of the facts for which he has been charged, until a final judgment has been made against that person.

2. Article 2 of the Law of 2 July 1931 considers it an offense for any person to make public the existence of a criminal complaint

filed in the criminal court by the victim acting as a party to the procedure (*plainte avec constitution de partie civile*). The Law of 2 July 1931 was held by the European Court of Human Rights (*Du Roy and Malaurie v. France* application no. 34000/96, 3 October 2000) as contrary to Article 10 of the European Convention on Human Rights because its terms are too broad and provides a disproportionate sanction, incompatible with the ECHR's interpretation of freedom of expression. The French Supreme Court, in a decision dated January 16, 2001, applied the ECHR's ruling and reversed on the same grounds a decision of the Court of Appeals of Aix-en-Provence. A subsequent decision, notably from the Court of Appeals of Paris, has, notwithstanding, continued to apply the Law of 2 July 1931 (Court of Appeals of Paris, 31 October 2001, *Légipresse,* 2002, no. 189, III, p. 31, note E. Durieux).

c. Ongoing regulatory investigations?

There is no general rule, but the statutes which engender regulatory agencies (e.g., AMF, Conseil de la Concurrence) contain provisions similar to the secrecy rule applied to criminal investigations according to which those persons participating in a regulatory investigation are bound to a secrecy rule. Question 12a. above would therefore apply to most regulatory investigations.

d. Ongoing civil litigation, or other judicial proceedings?

There is no specific restriction in respect of civil proceedings.

13. Are prior restraints or other prepublication injunctions available on the basis of libel or privacy, and if so, what are the standards for obtaining such relief?

Yes. Section 809 of the French Code of Civil Procedure allows the President of the Court of first instance to order "any provisional and conservatory measure" to prevent an imminent injury or loss from occurring or to put an end to a clearly illicit behavior. All forms of in limine relief are available, including prepublication injunctions and press releases. The plaintiff has only to provide a *prima facie* case that the publication under criticism is defamatory, injurious, or generally violates an existing rule. Urgency is not a condition.

As a matter of practice, however, obtaining immediate injunctive relief on the basis of libel is complicated by the fact that, pursuant to Section 55 of the Law of 29 July 1881, the defendant must, in all cases of defamation, be granted a period of ten days from the date of service of the complaint in order to administer evidence of the truth of the defamatory statement (an additional five days being granted to the plaintiff to administer counterevidence). This provision of the Law of 29 July 1881 is a matter of public policy and applies even to applications for injunctive relief. So, as a practical matter, no hearing can take place before at least ten days from the complaint, which thus ensures that a publication will remain on the stand for at least that period of time. Likewise, a prepublication injunction, in relation to a television program, for example, will only be efficient if the plaintiff has had at least ten days' prior notice of the fact that the program will be aired. This rule, however, only applies in matters of defamation and does not apply in matters where the plaintiff invokes another rule, say, a violation of the statutes which protect privacy.

14. Is a right of privacy recognized (either civilly or criminally)?

Yes. It is recognized both civilly (Section 9 of the Civil Code) and criminally (Section 226-1 *et seq.* of the French Criminal Code).

a. What is the definition of "private fact"?

There is no academic definition of a "private fact" but it is generally considered that all aspects of a person's intimacy are protected. This includes not only events which concern someone's family life but also more generally all those aspects of a person's life which he can legitimately expect will not be made public. In this respect, reproducing a photograph of someone or a recording of his voice without his authorization is a violation of his privacy. It is for this reason that the French press often blurs or otherwise masks the faces of bystanders in photographs. The protection is far-reaching. For example, if a person agrees to give an interview to a magazine and reveals certain aspects of his intimacy (love life, children, etc.), another magazine would not be entitled to report the same without the person's authorization.

b. Is there a public interest or newsworthiness exception?

The scope of someone's intimacy will shrink if that person is a public figure. Yet, the aspect of his family life will remain private.

c. Is the right of privacy based in common law, statute, or constitution?

The right of privacy is codified both civilly and criminally.

15. May reporters tape-record their own telephone conversations for note-taking purposes (not rebroadcast) without the consent of the other party?

Yes. As a matter of ethics, journalists should refrain from recording interviews without the consent of the interviewee. Furthermore, if the journalist keeps a record of the interview, the tape-recording may be seized in the course of a criminal investigation, which will of course dampen the journalist's ability to protect his source (see Question 17 below).

16. If permissible to record such tapes, may they be broadcast without permission?

No. Broadcasting a tape recording of an interview without the interviewee's consent is a violation of Section 9 of the Civil Code and Section 226-1 *et seq.* of the French Criminal Code (see Question 14 above).

17. Is there a recognized evidentiary privilege preventing the disclosure of confidential sources relied upon by reporters?

Section 109 of the French Code of Criminal Procedure provides that a journalist may refuse to testify and disclose his sources.[7] But the rule only applies to the journalist's testimony. It will not apply to work in progress or other documents or papers he may have gathered and which are susceptible of being seized in the course of a criminal investigation.

18. In the event that legal papers are served upon the newsroom (such as a civil complaint), are there any particular warnings about accepting service of which we should be aware?

Yes, especially with respect to a criminal complaint for defamation. A journalist (e.g., the author of an article considered as libelous) can be prosecuted as an accomplice (the "director of publications" being considered as the statutory principal offender). But service of the writ to appear before the criminal court is not valid unless delivered to the journalist himself or, in his absence, at his place of residence. Service at his professional office is not valid. Because the statute of limitations is extremely short (three months), the invalidity of the service will often bar prosecution if it is not reinstated within the limitation period. So, as a practical matter, journalists and generally all persons other than the "director of publications" (who can validly be served at the registered office of the news medium) should never accept service at their place of work and service should never be accepted on their behalf at their place of work. Civil complaints likewise should not be accepted by the defendants or on behalf of the defendants at their place of business.

19. Has your jurisdiction applied established media law to Internet publishers?

Yes. The Law of 21 June 2004, which amended the Law of 29 July 1982, has subsequently regulated Internet publications.

20. If established media law has been applied to Internet publishers, are there any ways in which Internet publishers (including chat room operators) have to meet different standards?

Although Internet publishing is by and large subject to the same rules as those which apply to television and radio broadcasting (notably, as regards the Law of 29 July 1881 and the obligation, pursuant to the Law of 29 July 1982, as amended by the Law of 21 June 2004), Internet publishers, like television and radio broadcasters, must appoint a "director of publications" (see Note 6 above). In addition, a specific regime applies, according to the Law of 21 June 2004, to the Internet host which is defined as the company that organizes "the storage of either signals, writings; frames, sounds or every kind of messages provided by the recipients of those services."

Hosts have immunity under the Law of 29 July 1881 if they can prove that (1) they had no knowledge of the exact content of the Web site *and* (2) they acted on short notice to withdraw the illegal information or restrain the access to it as soon as they were informed of its content. A host will be deemed to be aware of the circulation of unlawful information on the site, and those liable under the Law of 29 July 1881, as soon as he receives accurate complaints describing the offense. The Constitutional Council has however held, in a decision dated 10 June 2004, that this presumption of liability is deemed to comply with the Constitution provided only that (1) the information described in the complaint is clearly illegal or (2) a prior judgment has ordered its withdrawal.

21. Are there any cases where the courts enforced a judgment in libel from another jurisdiction against a publisher in your jurisdiction?

To our knowledge, there are no such decisions. As a matter of principle, nothing should prevent a foreign decision from being registered in France, provided it complies with the conditions set forth, either in the relevant bilateral treaties on the enforcement of foreign decisions or, in their absence, the general rules of registration of foreign judgments.[8] A criminal judgment rendered abroad will not be enforceable in France although, if the foreign decision contains an order for the payment of damages to the victim of the offense, that portion of the decision will be susceptible to being registered in France like any other civil foreign decision.

A judgment made by a foreign civil jurisdiction will be enforceable in France provided it is registered in France.[9] The application for registration of a foreign judgment will be dismissed if the foreign decision does not comply with due process or if the rule which has been applied by the foreign jurisdiction is considered as contrary to French international public policy. In this respect, it is likely that an application for registration of a foreign judgment will be dismissed if those laws do not afford the defendant the same degree of protection as is available under French law. For example, a foreign judgment under laws that did not provide a defense based on truth would probably be considered as contrary to French international public policy.

Chapter Notes

1. Section 29 of the Law of 29 July 1881.

2. Nonpublic defamation (i.e., the making of a defamatory statement by the defendant in a private setting) is a misdemeanor.

3. The complained-of words must be susceptible to being proven as true. If they cannot be, then the offense is that of injurious language. The distinction is important from a procedural point of view because the plaintiff must choose the grounds upon which he acts and both actions cannot be presented in the alternative.

4. Supreme Court of France, 2nd Ch., 8 April 2004, *Légipresse,* 2004, I, p. 76.

5. There is no right of response in relation to the publication of a photograph. The right of response for communications on television and radio is governed by Section 6 of the Law of 29 July 1982 (as amended by the Law of 21 June 2004). The conditions are slightly different than those that exist in relation to the written medium in the sense that the right of response for television and radio communications may only be exercised if the initial communication on the air is considered as defamatory; this is not the case for both the written medium and Internet, where it suffices that a person be named or cited in the article to claim a right of response.

6. The Law of 29 July 1881 has instituted a list of statutory defendants in all cases which are governed by this law. The "director of publications" is the statutory principal offender. All news media must appoint a "director of publications" who will be held personally liable for the offense (the news medium being vicariously liable for civil damages but not criminally); the "director of publications" is the chief executive officer of the company which exploits the medium. Likewise, the Law of 29 July 1982 (as amended by the Law of 21 June 2004) has instituted a similar list of statutory defendants with respect to television (including cable television), radio, and Internet communications, where each one of these mediums must appoint a "director of publications" who will be held personally liable for the offense.

7. The European Court of Human Rights has also held that an injunction ordering a journalist to disclose his source is contrary to Article 10 of the European Convention on Human Rights which protects the freedom of expression (*Goodwin v. United Kingdom,* application no. 17488/90 dated 22 February 1996).

8. There are no treaties between France and the United States on this point.

9. Registration is obtained through an application in the French Courts either *ex parte* in the context of a treaty or *inter partes* in the absence of a treaty.

CHAPTER 14

Germany

JAN HEGEMANN AND SLADE R. METCALF

Hogan & Hartson LLP

Jan Hegemann
Hogan & Hartson LLP
Potsdamer Platz 1
10785 Berlin, Germany
Phone: +49 (30) 72 61 15-303
Fax: +49 (30) 72 61 15-106
www.hhlaw.com
jhegemann@hhlaw.com

Slade R. Metcalf
Hogan & Hartson LLP
875 Third Avenue
New York, NY 10022 U.S.A.
Phone: 212-918-3000
Fax: 212-918-3100
www.hhlaw.com
srmetcalf@hhlaw.com

Introduction to the German Legal System

Germany has adopted a traditional civil law system. The German Constitution of 1949, called Basic Statute (*Grund-gesetz*), is the central document in the German judicial system. Acts of Parliament are the sole method for statutory reform and codification. Civil, private, and criminal laws are codified in separate government groups; however, all actions regarding the constitution are heard in the German Federal Constitutional Court (*Bundesverfassungsgericht*).

The German legal system does not have separate federal and state branches. There are a series of state courts, organized by subject matter jurisdiction, where actions can be brought. Appeals are heard in federal courts, and the constitutional court is accessible to any citizens claiming their constitutional rights have been impinged.

1. What is the locally accepted definition of libel?

Under German law, libel is a broad term that describes statements in verbal, written, or other form that injure a person's reputation. A false *allega-*

tion of fact, be it defamatory or not, enjoys no protection under German law and will, as a rule, be prohibited by the courts upon application of the person concerned. "False information," as the Federal Constitutional Court has put it, "is not covered by the right to free speech and freedom of expression." A false and, as the case may be, defamatory allegation of fact may be justified only if the person having made the allegation has acted "in the pursuit of legitimate interests."[1]

With regard to press statements, such public interest will be presumed if the journalist has observed the rules of conduct established in the case law for members of the press. However, these rules are strict and compliance with them is often difficult to prove. By contrast, *expressions of opinion* are generally free from liability (see Question 8 below). Despite the protection given to opinion under German law, courts will allow libel claims to stand where the statement is only meant to revile and vilify another person.

The following statements have been found to be defamatory by German courts: The Federal Constitutional Court (*Bundesverfassungsgericht*) held that the description of a politician by a songwriter as "such a heap of federal shit that you would not want to step into it" was defamatory. The Court further held, however, that the newspaper which had published the statement was not liable for its publication since it had sufficiently distanced itself from it.[2] Crude swear words such as "pig," "swine," or "bastard"[3] as well as unfoundedly discrediting expressions like "total loser"[4] are usually deemed defamatory. According to the Köln Court of Appeal (*Oberlandesgericht Köln*), the expression "courtesy journalism" can be defamatory if it creates the impression that the publishers of a magazine have sold their journalistic independence to their major advertising customer.[5] An unproved statement that a person has worked for the ministry of state security (*Ministerium für Staatssicherheit*) of the former German Democratic Republic is commonly found to be defamatory by the courts.[6]

The following statements have been found to be not defamatory by German courts: The statement that a politician running for the mayor's office in a small town was "a scrupulous liar who stuck to nothing and spurned the legal order" was held to be protected under the right to free speech.[7] Likewise, the expression "Stop the child-murder in mother's womb on the premises of the N. clinic. Then: Holocaust, today: Babycaust" made by anti-abortionists with regard to the body responsible for an abortion clinic was not regarded as defamatory.[8] The Karlsruhe Court of Appeal (*Oberlandesgericht Karlsruhe*) held that it was permissible under freedom of speech to call a doctor who had widely criticized the methods of traditional medicine a "pseudo-religious vitamin guru," a "butcher," and a "charlatan."[9] The statement "soldiers are murderers" was held to be protected under the right to free speech by the Federal Constitutional Court.[10]

2. Is libel-by-implication recognized, or, in the alternative, must the complained-of words alone defame the plaintiff?

German law recognizes libel-by-implication. Thus, a statement does not necessarily need to defame a plaintiff expressly to be considered libelous. For a statement to be deemed libelous, it does not necessarily matter what the journalist expressly asserts. It primarily matters what the reader perceives.[11]

However, the German Federal Court of Justice (BGH) demands a high standard for claims of libel-by-implication. For such a claim it does not suffice that a reasonable reader might have concluded that the author intended to imply a libelous allegation. Rather, this conclusion must be compelling in order to be considered libel-by-implication.[12]

3. May corporations sue for libel?

German press law is not restricted to the protection of individuals: corporations may sue for libel. It also protects a corporation's reputation against defamatory criticism that evidently aims at insulting or disparaging the corporation,[13] and grants protection against inaccurate allegations of fact, especially if the statement of such facts has a negative effect on the corporation's credit rating.[14] However, a corporation's reputation enjoys less legal protection against libel than that of an individual, and German courts recognize that reports on corporations and their products are often a matter of great and legitimate public interest.[15] Thus, a corporation must accept critical reports of its performance and business standing, and courts will narrowly read a complaint for defamatory allegations to succeed. Coverage of such issues will not be considered libelous as long as it keeps to the facts and does not aim at disparaging the corporation.[16]

4. Is product disparagement recognized, and if so, how does that differ from libel?

German law recognizes product disparagement. The standards for product disparagement do not differ from libel. Product disparagement may particularly be claimed in two cases: Either (1) a specific product is negatively reviewed in a (comparative or noncomparative) product test; or (2) a report may criticize a whole line of business and name a certain product as an example. In both cases, the report has to comply with the standards of libel law. Thus, critical commentary of a product is allowed as long as the allegations are true and do not primarily aim at disparaging the product, its manufacturer, or distributor.

A journalist who alleges, for example, that an entire line of products contains toxic substances must make sure that these allegations are true with regard to each particular product that is being singled out for the purpose of illustrating the allegations. Product tests must at least comply with a minimum of neutrality, expertise, and impartiality.[17] Higher standards regarding the objectiveness of a report apply to comparative product tests.[18]

5. Must an individual be clearly identified (by name or photograph) to sue for libel? Can a group of persons sue for libel, even though not named?

Under German law, an individual does not need to be clearly identified by name or photograph to sue for libel. The individual must only be identifiable. Similarly, a group of persons may sue for libel, even though not named, provided that the members of the group are identifiable. In many cases a statement refers to an individual without clearly identifying him by name or photograph. This does not mean, however, that the individual may not sue for libel.

German courts consider it to be sufficient if the statement refers to a certain person covertly. Identification can be constituted by reference to the name, by pictures, initials, nicknames, or by a description of the plaintiff's life story, profession, or any other identifying circumstance.[19] The courts do not make high demands on showing that the plaintiff is identifiable. The test is whether the statement could reasonably lead persons acquainted with the plaintiff or any other readers to believe that he was the person referred to.

Similarly, a member of a group can sue for libel, even though not named, provided that he is able to show that the statement referred to him. In that case the identification often depends on the size of the group of persons referred to. If the group is so small that a person would reasonably believe that each member of the group was pointed out, then each member may sue.[20]

6. What is the fault standard(s) applied to libel?

a. Does the fault standard depend on the fame or notoriety of the plaintiff?

The fault standard does not depend on the fame or notoriety of the plaintiff. However, press coverage of famous or well-known figures will often be of public interest. Matters of public interest are subject to the heightened fault standard applied under the "public interest" defense. In that defense, even if a statement is false and defamatory, liability will not attach provided the journalist can show that: (1) the subject is indeed in the public interest; and (2) the story was crafted with a requisite degree of journalistic care.

b. Is there a heightened fault standard or privilege for reporting on matters of public concern or public interest?

The fault standard applied to libel also depends on the relief sought by the plaintiff. In cases where a plaintiff seeks injunctions or the right to retraction, libel is essentially a strict liability tort. By contrast, claims for damages require proof of at least negligence, which may be defeated by the defense of proper journalistic caution. This defense usually requires proof of careful, methodical research of the issue.[21]

7. Is financial news about publicly traded companies, or companies involved with a government contract, considered a matter of public interest or otherwise privileged?

Financial news about publicly traded companies or companies involved with government contracts is not automatically privileged. With regard to companies in general, however, German courts recognize that coverage of corporations is often a matter of great public interest, given the fact that they may be heavily unionized, publicly held, or enjoy contracts with the government.[22]

8. Is there a recognized protection for opinion or "fair comment" on matters of public concern?

German press law recognizes the defense of fair comment on a matter of public interest. Recognizing that there is no such thing as a false or untrue opinion, persons must tolerate sharp, unfair, or even insulting criticism as long as it is somehow issue-related. An expression of opinion will only be deemed libelous if it deliberately and primarily aims to injure a person's reputation.

The intentional attack on a person's reputation must clearly be in the foreground of the comment. According to the case law, this can be assumed if the statement in question, even from the critic's point of view, has no factual basis and is only meant to revile and vilify another person. Unlike U.S. law, where the more heated and hyperbolic the words, the more protection the statement may enjoy, German law does not abide by gratuitous or overly vitriolic language, and such writing may be *prima facie* evidence of an intentional attack.

Gratuitous attacks excepted, under German law, the expression of opinion is widely protected. There is a legal presumption that the expression of one's opinion is permissible.[23] Since this presumption does not apply to statements of fact, the distinction between allegation of fact and expression of opinion becomes crucial in determining the outcome of many lawsuits.[24]

The expression of opinion that is defamatory, however, is actionable. The degree of public interest, again, determines the standard for defamation. Thus, statements that concern a matter of public interest are more likely to be considered permissible by German courts. They even may be exaggerated and polemic as long as they still refer to the matter of public interest.[25]

9. Are there any requirements upon a plaintiff, such as demand for retraction or right of reply, and if so, what impact do they have?
Under German law, an action for damages or injunctive relief does not require that the plaintiff has demanded a retraction or right of reply. However, the plaintiff's damage claim may be reduced if the defendant has published a retraction without delay. In this respect it is irrelevant if the plaintiff has demanded a retraction or if the defendant has independently retracted the statement.

10. Is there a privilege for quoting or reporting on:

a. Papers filed in court?
Coverage of public proceedings of a court is conditionally privileged. In general, the media is entitled to report on all judicial proceedings. Therefore, German press law excludes any claims arising from the coverage of judicial proceedings, as long as the coverage truthfully reports on the trial.

However, there are some restrictions of importance. First, the privilege normally extends only to the publicly available documents of the court. Accordingly, Section 353d No. 3 of the German Criminal Code prohibits literal quotations from indictments or other parts of an investigation *before* the case is brought before a public hearing. The provision does not, however, prohibit publishing of a rough summary of an indictment. In the event that a pretrial summary or contemporaneous report is published, the media must not infringe on the privacy of the persons involved in criminal cases. Thus, the accused or the witnesses may not be mentioned by name or identified by other details unless the case concerns serious crimes or other offenses that are of public interest.[26]

b. Government-issued documents?
Coverage of legislative or parliamentary debates is similarly privileged.[27] By contrast, republication of government-issued documents or proceedings and statements from government bodies are not privileged.

c. Quasi-governmental proceedings?

Basic reports on quasi-governmental proceedings are not privileged, but may satisfy the "public interest" privilege, but failure to verify facts contained therein that may be "obviously" incorrect, inaccurate description of legal terms, failure to provide for comment, and failure of other journalistic fundamentals may result in liability.

11. Is there a privilege for republishing statements made earlier by other, bone fide, reliable publications or wire services?

Yes. German law recognizes a privilege for republishing statements made earlier by other, bona fide, reliable publications or wire services, unless there is reasonable doubt about the reliability of the statement. In general, courts consider the press not to be obliged to conduct further research on a statement if the report comes from one of the established wire services.[28] However, further research is required if there is reasonable doubt that the statement is reliable. Other bona fide, reliable publications include information from public authorities like the public prosecutor or the police.[29] Such information can be relied upon unless there is reasonable doubt about the reliability.

12. Are there any restrictions regarding reporting on:

a. Ongoing criminal investigations?

Coverage of investigations and prosecutions may be permissible provided that there is a public interest, but German law places some restrictions on reporting ongoing criminal investigations and prosecutions. Section 353d No. 3 of the Criminal Code expressly prohibits literal quotations from indictments or other parts of an investigation *before* the case is brought before a public hearing.

b. Ongoing criminal prosecutions?

The law does not prohibit the publication of a rough summary of the trial. The media does not have to wait for the completion of investigations before coverage is allowed. In all cases, however, reports on ongoing investigations or prosecutions must respect the presumption of innocence and may not suggest that the alleged offender has already been found guilty.[30] Names of the parties, witnesses, or other involved persons may only be mentioned in the case of serious crimes or other offenses that are of particular public interest.[31]

c. Ongoing regulatory investigations?

None.

d. Ongoing civil litigation, or other judicial proceedings?

Reports on ongoing regulatory investigations, civil litigation, and other judicial proceedings are not subject to any particular restrictions but must still comply with the standards of general libel law.

13. Are prior restraints or other prepublication injunctions available on the basis of libel or privacy, and if so, what are the standards for obtaining such relief?

Prior restraints and other prepublication restraints on the basis of libel or privacy are available under German law. However, the standards for obtaining this sort of relief are high.

German law requires a plaintiff seeking a prepublication injunction to present substantial evidence that the defendant is likely to commit the alleged libel ("likelihood of commission").[32] Thus, the plaintiff must precisely describe the alleged libel to the court, demonstrating both its falsity and defamatory quality. In most cases, the plaintiff will not be able to adduce proof of the likelihood of commission, unless he somehow came into possession of the rough draft of the statement. The mere fact that a journalist has been doing research on an issue does not suffice to adduce such evidence.[33] If a journalist, however, expressly announces that he is going to publish the alleged libel, the required proof may be accepted by the court, and an injunction issued, provided the complaint meets the test laid out above.

14. Is a right of privacy recognized (either civilly or criminally)?

a. What is the definition of "private fact"?

German civil and criminal law recognize a right of privacy. It is part of the so-called general right of personality (*allgemeines Persoenlichkeitsrecht*). This all-embracing right of the individual to protection of one's personality was first recognized by the Federal Supreme Court in 1954[34] and has since been further elaborated by the courts.[35] It is based not in statute but directly in Articles 1 and 2 of the Basic Statute which warrant the inviolability of the human dignity and the individual's right to free development of one's personality. Article 13 of the Basic Statute guarantees the inviolability of the home as one specific aspect of the right of privacy. In addition, the right of privacy is protected by a wide range of statutory provisions, in civil as well as in criminal law, such as Sec. 22 of the *Kunsturheberrechtsgesetz* (KUG), which protects against the unauthorized publication of a person's image, or Sec. 201a of the StGB (German Criminal Code), which prohibits the infringements of a person's right to privacy by taking pictures of that person in his or her home or any other secluded space.

The Federal Supreme Court held that the publication of photographs showing Princess Caroline of Monaco at a candlelight dinner in a secluded part of a restaurant infringed on her right of privacy. Even though a person did, in general, not have a reasonable expectation of privacy in a public place, the remoteness and familiarity of the place in question made it obvious to everyone that the princess wished to be left alone. The Court placed special emphasis on the fact that the pictures had been taken surreptitiously and by telephoto lens.[36] In contrast, the Courts deemed the publication of pictures showing the princess in a Monaco beach club,[37] in a marketplace, or while riding a horse or a bike, lawful.[38] This finding, however, was recently challenged by the European Court of Human Rights.[39]

b. Is there a public interest or newsworthiness exception?

In general, German privacy law acknowledges three "spheres of privacy," each of which is protected to a different extent.

The *core private sphere* (*Intimsphaere*) enjoys the broadest legal protection. It must absolutely not be intruded into.[40] In particular, the core private sphere includes any information relating to the sexuality of a person.[41] Coverage of those issues is not permitted without the consent of the person concerned.[42] There is no public interest exception.

Issues that concern the *private sphere* (*Privatsphaere*) particularly include the domestic area[43] and family affairs[44] as well as a person's physical condition[45] or religious views.[46] Coverage intruding into a person's private sphere is prohibited,[47] but there is a public interest exception, which is strictly limited to those issues that are most essential to the public.[48]

The *public sphere* comprises those areas of life that by definition are open to everybody. A person enjoys least protection when acting in the public sphere.[49] Thus, a movie actor or a lawyer involved in a public trial cannot refer to privacy law in order to prevent coverage of their public behavior.

Newsworthiness, defined here as news that serves the public interest, may justify disclosure. Press reports about a person's marital life, including marital conflicts, adulterousness, and divorce, are usually deemed unlawful if not directly related to preeminent public interests that would justify a publication.[50] With regard to a case where Prince Ernst August of Hannover had sued a German tabloid for reports about his (then) adulterous relationship with Princess Caroline of Monaco, the Federal Supreme Court held that because the prince was an eminent representative of high nobility, the reported facts were true, and since the foreign press had already reported about the incident, the publication was permissible.[51]

Finally, information about the relationship between parents and their underage children enjoys particular protection under German law and must, therefore, not be published except in cases where outstanding public interests exceptionally outweigh the children's interest in an undisturbed development of the child's personality.[52]

c. Is the right of privacy based in common law, statute, or constitution?

The right is both statutory and constitutional.

15. May reporters tape-record their own telephone conversations for note-taking purposes (not rebroadcast) without the consent of the other party?

No. Under German law, tape-recording of a telephone conversation without the consent of the other party is generally prohibited. German privacy law grants every person the right to decide on his own whether his words may be tape-recorded and by whom the tape may be played. Moreover, according to Sec. 201, subsec. 1 No. 1 of the German Criminal Code, tape-recording a telephone conversation without the consent of the other party is considered a criminal offense. The section applies regardless of the purpose of the tape-recording. Thus, it does not matter if it is for note-taking or other purposes.

16. If permissible to record such tapes, may they be broadcast without permission?

Section 201 of the German Criminal Code not only prohibits the tape-recording of a conversation but also the broadcasting or other uses of a tape that has been recorded without the consent of the other party.

17. Is there a recognized evidentiary privilege preventing the disclosure of confidential sources relied upon by reporters?

Under German law, a plaintiff cannot force the disclosure of any sources relied upon by reporters, nor can a journalist be ordered by the court to disclose a confidential source. However, the defendant, by refusing the disclosure of his source, may run the risk of losing his civil case if that confidential source is the basis by which a defamatory statement would otherwise be relied upon.

18. In the event that legal papers are served upon the newsroom (such as a civil complaint), are there any particular warnings about accepting service of which we should be aware?

There are no particular warnings about accepting service of legal papers. In general, a defendant is obliged to accept the service of a civil complaint. However, you should be aware that the acceptance of service of a legal paper often triggers a statutory period within which a reply should be filed.

19. Has your jurisdiction applied established media law to Internet publishers?

The principles of German media law described above apply equally to Internet publications. Section 186 of the German Criminal Code declares punishable, in general terms, the publication of untrue facts, which are defamatory, about others. Likewise, the publication of private facts, if not justified by overweighing public interests, is deemed unlawful by Sec. 823 (1) of the German Civil Code in conjunction with Articles 1 and 2 of the Basic Statute. Publication means *any form* of passing on the information in question[53] by any means, including the Internet.[54] Thus, Internet publishers are, in general, equally as liable as press publishers or broadcasters for the publication of untrue, defamatory, or private facts.

20. If established media law has been applied to Internet publishers, are there any ways in which Internet publishers (including chat room operators) have to meet different standards?

According to German statutory law, different standards of liability apply for Internet service providers which offer their own content or adopt third parties' content as their own ("content providers") on the one hand, and Internet service providers which merely give access to third parties' content ("access providers") on the other hand.[55] Whereas content providers are fully responsible for the information published according to the general rules set out above, access providers are, in principle, only obliged to remove or disable access to the unlawful information in question.

The responsibility of ISPs in German law is governed by two statutes, the *Mediendienstestaatsvertrag* (Media Services Treaty—MDStV) and the *Teledienstegesetz* (Telecommunication Services Act—TDG). Media services are defined as information and communication services for the general public, in text, sound, or image, which are transmitted by electromagnetic waves (Sec. 2 MDStV). This includes online services such as online newspapers or magazines, and similar mass media services, which put an emphasis on the editorial layout and aim to add to the general public debate. In contrast, telecommunication services are electronic information and communication services which are intended for individual use and transmitted by telecommunications (Sec. 2 (1) TDG) such as, for example, telebanking, electronic market places (e.g., eBay), or online data services such as weather services and traffic services as well as Internet access service providers.

It is often difficult to differentiate between media services and telecommunication services. For example, it is disputed whether chat room operators provide services for the general public or for individual use.[56] However, since the provisions of the Media Services Treaty and the Telecommunication Services Act are largely identical, a distinction between media services and telecommunication services is in many cases not necessary. Thus, under both the Media Services Treaty and the Telecommunication Services Act, ISPs that offer their own content or adopt third parties' content as their own ("content providers") are responsible for the information published according to the general rules of civil and criminal law (Sec. 6 (1) MDStV, Sec. 8 (1) TDG).

In contrast, ISPs that *merely give access* to third parties' content ("access providers") are liable only if they have positive knowledge of the unlawful information or the circumstances establishing the unlawfulness of the information in question (Sec. 7 sqq. MDStV, Sec. 9 sqq. TDG). The liability of access providers is further restricted by the statutory rule that providers are not obligated to control the information to which they give access or to trace evidence of possibly unlawful information (Sec. 6 (2) MDStV, Sec. 8 (2) TDG).

Access providers made aware of unlawful content are obligated to remove or disable access to such content according to the general rules of civil and criminal law (Sec. 6 (2) MDStV, Sec. 8 (2) TDG).

21. Are there any cases where the courts enforced a judgment in libel from another jurisdiction against a publisher in your jurisdiction?

Although there are no reported cases, under German law, foreign judgments are generally enforceable if the decision has become final and binding and is recognizable according to the rules of German civil procedure.[57] Provided that these requirements are met, foreign judgments in libel cases can, in principle, be enforced on German territory.

Chapter Notes

1. Sec. 193 German Criminal Code.

2. *Bundesverfassungsgericht,* (2004) Archiv für Presserecht (AfP) 49.

3. Cf. *Oberlandesgericht Hamburg,* (1990) AfP 135.

4. Cf. *Landgericht Oldenburg,* (1995) AfP 679.

5. *Oberlandesgericht Köln,* (2001) AfP 332.

6. Cf. *Oberlandesgericht Hamburg,* Judgment of May 28, 2004 (unpublished).

7. *Bundesverfassungsgericht,* (2003) Neue Juristische Wochenschrift (NJW) 3760.

8. *Bundesgerichtshof,* (2000) NJW 3421.

9. *Oberlandesgericht Karlsruhe,* (2002) Neue Juristische Wochenschrift—Rechtsprechungs-Report (NJW-RR) 695.

10. *Bundesverfassungsgericht,* (1994) NJW 2943; (1995) NJW 3303.

11. *Bundesgerichtshof,* (1980) NJW 2801, 2803; *Oberlandesgericht Köln,* (2000) NJW-RR 470.

12. *Bundesgerichtshof,* (1980) NJW 2801, 2803; (1994) AfP 295.

13. *Bundesgerichtshof,* (1975) NJW 1882, 1883; *Oberlandesgericht Stuttgart,* (1976) NJW 628.

14. Sec. 824 BGB (German Civil Code).

15. *Bundesgerichtshof,* (1966) NJW 1617.

16. *Bundesgerichtshof,* (1976) NJW 620.

17. *Bundesgerichtshof,* (1987) NJW 2222; (1976) NJW 620.

18. *Bundesgerichtshof,* (1965) NJW 484.

19. *Bundesverfassungsgericht,* (2000) NJW 1859; (1971) NJW 1645; *Landgericht Berlin,* (1992) NJW-RR 1379.

20. *Bundesgerichtshof,* Decisions of the Federal Supreme Court in Criminal Matters (BGHSt), vol. 19, p. 235.

21. *Bundesgerichtshof,* (1987) NJW 2225.

22. *Bundesgerichtshof,* (1966) NJW 1617.

23. *Bundesverfassungsgericht,* (1958) NJW 257.

24. *Bundesverfassungsgericht,* (2003) NJW 277, 278; (1983) AfP 215.

25. *Bundesgerichtshof,* (2002) NJW 1192.

26. *Oberlandesgericht Nürnberg,* (1996) NJW 530; *Oberlandesgericht Frankfurt,* (1980) 597.

27. See Sec. 5 (5) of the Berlin Press Act.

28. *Landgericht München,* (1975) AfP 758; *Landgericht Hamburg,* (1990) AfP 332.

29. *Bundesgerichtshof,* (1971) NJW 698, 700; *Oberlandesgericht Hamburg,* (1977) AfP 35; *OLG Karlsruhe,* (1993) AfP 586.

30. *Bundesgerichtshof,* (2000) NJW 1036, 1037.

31. *Oberlandesgericht Frankfurt,* (1980) NJW 597; *Oberlandesgericht München,* (2003) NJW-RR 111.

32. *Oberlandesgericht Nürnberg,* (2002) NJW-RR 1471.

33. *Oberlandesgericht Hamburg,* (1992) AfP 279; (2000) AfP 188; *Landgericht Frankfurt* (1991) AfP 545.

34. *Bundesgerichtshof,* (1954) NJW 1404.

35. See *Bundesverfassungsgericht,* (1973) NJW 1221, 1223; (1984) NJW 419, 421.

36. *Bundesgerichtshof,* (1996) NJW 1128, 1130; confirmed by *Bundesverfassungsgericht,* (2000) NJW 1021 sqq.

37. *Oberlandesgericht Hamburg,* (1999) AfP 175, 176; confirmed by *Bundesverfassungsgericht,* (2000) NJW 2192.

38. *Bundesgerichtshof,* (1996) NJW 1128, 1130; confirmed by *Bundesverfassungsgericht,* (2000) NJW 1021 sqq.

39. *European Court of Human Rights,* (2004) NJW 2647.

40. *Bundesgerichtshof,* (1981) NJW 1366; *Oberlandesgericht Hamburg* (1967) NJW 2314, 2316.

41. *Bundesgerichtshof,* BGHSt vol. 11, p. 67, 71.

42. Cf. *Oberlandesgericht Hamburg,* (1991) AfP 533.

43. *Bundesgerichtshof,* (2004) AfP 116.

44. *Oberlandesgericht Köln,* (1973) 479; *Landgericht Bielefeld,* (1975) NJW 54.

45. *Bundesgerichtshof,* (1996) NJW 984, 985.

46. *Oberlandesgericht München,* (1986) NJW 1260.

47. Cf. *Bundesverfassungsgericht,* (1997) NJW 2669, 2670; *Oberlandesgericht München,* (1993) AfP 762; *Oberlandesgericht Celle,* (1999) NJW-RR 1477.

48. *Bundesverfassungsgericht,* (2000) NJW 2189, *Bundesgerichtshof* (1979) AfP 647.

49. *Bundesgerichtshof,* (1995) AfP 404, 407.

50. Cf. *Bundesgerichtshof,* (1974) Gewerblicher Rechtsschutz und Urheberrecht (GRUR) 794; *Oberlandesgericht Hamburg,* (2000) Zeitschrift für Urheber- und Medienrecht—Rechtsprechungsdienst (ZUM-RD) 142.

51. *Bundesgerichtshof,* (1999) NJW 2893, 2894 sq.; confirmed by *Bundesverfassungsgericht,* (2000) NJW 2189.

52. Cf. *Bundesverfassungsgericht,* (2000) NJW 1021 sqq.

53. Cf. *Bundesgerichtshof,* (1996) NJW 1131, 1132.

54. Cf. *Landgericht Hamburg,* (1998) ZUM-RD 389, 390; but see *Landgericht Berlin,* (1998) NJW-RR 1634.

55. Cf. *Oberlandesgericht Köln,* (2002) NJW-RR 1700, 1701; *Oberlandesgericht München,* (2002) AfP 522, 523.

56. See Hoeren/Sieber (eds.), *Handbuch Multimediarecht* (2003), para 29.54 sqq.

57. See Sec. 328, 722 sq. of the Code of Civil Procedure (ZPO). In 1992, the Federal Supreme Court held that U.S. judgments awarding a significant sum in punitive damages can, in general, not be recognized and enforced under German law (*Bundesgerichtshof,* (1992) NJW 3096).

CHAPTER 15

Italy

MARIO GALLAVOTTI

Gallavotti Honorati & Pascotto

Mario Gallavotti
Gallavotti Honorati & Pascotto
Via Po, 9
00198—Roma, Italy
Phone: +39 06 85823 1
Fax: +39 06 85823 200
www.ghplex.it
mgallavotti@ghplex.it

Alvaro Pascotto, Esq.
Of Counsel, Morrison & Foerster
1800 Century Park East, Suite 1111
Los Angeles, CA 90067-1600 U.S.A.
Phone: (310) 203-4035
Fax: (310) 203-4040
apascotto@mofo.com

Introduction to the Italian Legal System

When publishing material that may be accessed in Italy, journalists and publishers are well advised to consider two important points. First, Italy is a Civil Code system, meaning that precedent in case law is limited in application, and courts evaluating speech-related issues will first and foremost weigh the relevant facts against a strict interpretation of statutes, rather than case law. Only decisions of the *Suprema Corte di Cassazione* (hereafter "Cassation") are binding precedent on trial courts.

Introduction to Italian Media Law

Media-related statutes must be understood as reflecting a balance of constitutionally derived rights. In the Italian legal system, persons have a constitutional right to reputation and privacy. These rights (called "publicity" rights) are intertwined and treated interchangeably. Although Section 21 of the Italian Constitution recognizes liberty of the press, peoples' rights of reputation, image, and honor have been deemed to have superior constitutional value.

1. What is the locally accepted definition of libel?

Libel is actionable under both civil and criminal law in Italy. Pursuant to Section 595 of the Italian Criminal Code (hereinafter referred to as Codice Penale or c.p.), libel is an offense committed in the form of communication with several individuals that is "injurious to the reputation of another person," and is punishable by imprisonment for up to one year or a fine of up to €1032. If the article in question falsely attributes a specific act of wrongdoing (as opposed to an unjustified attack on one's character), fines may be doubled. Italian law, recognizing the power of mass media, actually applies a higher duty of care to publishers than to nonmedia defendants.

Damage to reputation or honor is given broad interpretation in Italian law: reputation may be injured simply by allegations that "damage the esteem" in which the offended person is held by his or her community or that engender contempt for that person.

Under Italian law, the line of what is and is not considered defamatory is flexible. The very elastic concept of libel is molded according to the person offended, to his or her social condition and professional activity, and to his or her family and marital status; to the peculiarities of the addressees of the communication; and to the person, role, and activity of the libeler. Not least, the context in which the libel takes place is also considered. In general, Italian law will broadly attribute defamatory meaning to almost any statement that impugns "honor," "dignity," or "reputation." Following are examples of speech found to be defamatory in nature.

The Supreme Court of Cassation found it defamatory to refer to a business person as "insolvent" or "unreliable." This statement was made by employees of a bank with whom the plaintiff did business. The Court said that to refer to someone in print as "insolvent" and "unreliable" means to negatively label the person in relation to his or her economic activity.[1] The Cassation found defamatory the title of a magazine article about the president of the Italian Chamber of Deputies, which read "Young Ignorant." Finding the word "ignorant" offensive in itself, the Court stated that such definition could not even be justified by the right to inform or by the right of political criticism (discussed in Question 8 below). The Cassation found that the publication was an offense repugnant to the politician's personal identity.[2] A radio broadcaster was also found liable for announcing the imminent cessation of business due to economic problems of the subject company. This news, which subsequently proved to be untrue, caused considerable harm to the company's goodwill due to deterioration in its credit and loss of customers.[3] The Cassation also deemed libelous the sentence in a story about a famous journalist: "Be prepared to see anything. That man has the glance of an hired killer, and [...] with some flashes of sadism that promise disaster."[4] A story suggesting that a female television journalist on the Italian public television channel "advanced her career because of political connections and a close friendship with the President of the Republic" was deemed prejudicial to her honor and reputation.[5]

The criminal offense of libel is often flanked by tort suits for damages (envisaged in general terms by Section 2043 of the Italian Civil Code [hereinafter referred to as "Codice Civile" or c.c.]). In practice, preference is normally given to civil lawsuits for damages over private prosecutions and consequent criminal action against the offender. Civil court judges may order compensation for noneconomic (that is "reputational and emotional") damages (see Section 2059 c.c. and Section 185, paragraph 2 c.p.).[6]

2. Is libel-by-implication recognized, or, in the alternative, must the complained-of words alone defame the plaintiff?

In the Italian legal system, libel may take the form of both explicit defamation and implicit or "allusive" defamation. In particular, the defamatory intention may be realized indirectly, by means of "underhanded" allusions. Defamation of this sort is likewise punishable under the criminal and civil laws. Indeed, even equivocal, insinuating, allusive, unsaid, ambiguous, and suggestive expressions may constitute libel if they can engender in the reader "a willingness to accept the actual correspondence of the narrated facts with the truth. This possibility must be investigated on a case-by-case basis."[7]

The Cassation will censure and condemn a journalist's "lack of clarity," and in several decisions[8] has mentioned a number of "deceptive techniques" as examples of this defect:

1. *The clever implication,* consisting in the use of expressions with the awareness that the reading public will understand them either in a different way or even contrary to their literal meaning;
2. *Suggestive combinations* of facts that refer to the person to be cast in a bad light with other facts (that somehow negatively affect one's reputation) regarding other, unrelated individuals;
3. *A disproportionately scandalized and indignant tone;*
4. *Out and out insinuations,* which are made when, even without openly stating facts or judgments, matters are related in such a way that the reader interprets them to the detriment of a specific individual's reputation.

Sloppy or careless editing of stories is a particular danger. Even though there may have been no intentional defamatory meaning on the reporter's part, if the statement at issue is capable of defamatory construction, claims may proceed. Because defenses to libel claims are adjudicated on an objective basis (a measure of reasonable care) rather than a subjective basis (the reporter's state of mind), an innocent and unintended meaning does not raise a significant defense.

3. May corporations sue for libel?

Yes. In the Italian legal system, it is commonly accepted that legal entities—"*persone giuridiche*" (that is, corporations, foundations, partnerships, and nonprofit organizations)—may take action to defend their honor and reputation.[9] In general terms, harm to the honor and reputation are encompassed by the broader concept of harm to the rights of personality, which also include protection of the personal identity and all other aspects evoking the personality of the organization.[10]

In general terms, in order for injury to honor and reputation to justify compensation of damages to corporate entities, it must cause economic harm, which may be proved by lower company sales.[11] Once the threshold of economic damages is met, additional noneconomic damages are available.[12]

4. Is product disparagement recognized, and if so, how does that differ from libel?

Yes. In the event that a company's goods or services are defamed, companies can bring libel claims based on impact on the company's reputation.[13] Product disparagement is envisaged in Section 2598 c.c., n. 2, in the context of unfair competitive practices, where "news and appraisals of the products and activities of a competitor, capable to cause its or their disrepute" are spread out, or the case where the competitor "appropriates the merits of a competitor's products or enterprise." Claims sounding in unfair competition are limited to competitors.

Italian law respects the right to publish consumer protection news and product reviews, but it is subject to a high duty of care. Italian courts have held that whereas publication of consumer-related testing reviews (*Warentest*) represents a manifestation of the right of criticism envisaged and protected by Section 21 of the Italian Constitution (in regard to the right of criticism, see Question 8 hereunder), on the other hand, there is a limit beyond which the right of criticism interferes with the right to exercise economic activities, a right protected by Section 41 of the Italian Constitution. The publication of inaccurate product reviews falls outside the Section 21 protection because the inaccurate article is not helpful to consumers.[14] Reporting of or publishing comparison test results is considered legitimate only if and when it satisfies the demands for objectivity and accuracy.

The Court of Rome has outlined clear limits to the reporting of consumer reporting:

> [F]or publication of defamatory results of the Warentest in the press and on television to be considered a legitimate manifestation of the freedom of opinion and not involve civil liability, the following conditions must be satisfied: 1) the news must be socially useful; 2) the presentation must be formally correct; 3) the presented facts must be true (this requirement is considered satisfied when the journalist, after carefully verifying the competence of the experts and scientific seriousness of the analysis, presents the investigative methods and results in the body of the article).[15]

5. Must an individual be clearly identified (by name or photograph) to sue for libel? Can a group of persons sue for libel, even though not named?

In general terms, it is held that the individual subject to libel must be identified or identifiable with certainty. The leading case in Italian court decisions is the case where the image of a famous singer was improperly used in an advertisement. In that case, the ad only reproduced the hat and round spectacles normally worn by the musician.[16] This referential imagery reasonably conjured up the singer, and satisfied the identification requirement. The rule laid down by Italian law is that textual, visual, and phonetic components must be analyzed with a view to the evocative effect of the whole, and whether that effectively conjures the person alluded to.[17]

Italian law allows *indirect* causes of action in libel.[18] For example, even though a statement might be directed at the directors and management of a specific corporation, the organization for which they work might be implicated. In one case, the inaccurately reproduced quotations of a famous political leader gave his party standing to bring an action in libel, complaining of a damaging distortion of its ideological position.[19]

In another case of indirect libel, a tobacco company published editorial advertising that contained excerpts of an interview released by the president of a well-established cancer institute. The statements were edited to state that the cancer institute's president believed that light cigarettes were less dangerous than regular cigarettes. Because such a statement would imply that the president was hypocritical, and the notion of such a man "endorsing" tobacco would offend his honor, the tobacco company was found liable to *both* the president and the cancer institute.[20]

Group libel is also possible in Italy, where libelous remarks are generically addressed to an undifferentiated group of individuals associated by their belonging to the same ethnic group or faith, or engaging in the same professional activity, or sharing the same political beliefs. Older court decisions have denied group claims, as in the case of libel generically addressed to Jews.[21] Nonetheless, more recent court rulings have rejected a flat ban on group libel, particularly in those cases where it is possible to identify a single entity representing the injured interests, which thus becomes an ideological plaintiff. The right to damages has been recognized in a group libel form:

1. to religious congregations or the union of them, in those cases where all members of a particular faith are libeled, even though not all of the members feel that they have been offended;[22]
2. to religious sects, when accused of fraudulent intents because of actions committed by some of their members, if the whole sect is targeted by libelous expressions;[23]
3. to professional associations, when a person sentenced for bribery was wrongly described as belonging to such professional category because such incorrect reporting is deemed harmful to the association's identity.[24]

6. What is the fault standard(s) applied to libel?

a. Does the fault standard depend on the fame or notoriety of the plaintiff?

The plaintiff's societal role has some bearing on the fault standard. Although free press interests are weighed against a constitutionally derived personality interest, Italian law does recognize a common law privilege for statements of defamatory facts, provided three strict criteria are met. In a leading case,[25] the Supreme Court of Cassation identified these criteria in order for a publication to be considered lawful, despite carrying a defamatory sting:

1. the social utility of the information;
2. its objective (or at least presumed) truth;
3. a sober form in reporting the story.

b. Is there a heightened fault standard or privilege for reporting on matters of public concern or public interest?

If all three of the above-referenced requirements are satisfied, a consolidated line of decisions[26] grant a privilege for publication and will not allow liability to attach, despite the fact that the article in question injures another person's reputation.

1. *The social utility of the information.* Although it is certainly difficult to define, the general rule of social utility forces the judge to determine in any given case whether there is a genuine social interest in the people to be informed about the news item(s) under review. The plaintiffs' status, their role in society, and their position of authority will inform the court as to the social utility. This should not be read as a "public figure" defense: courts recognize that even the famous and infamous have a personality right that should be protected. Courts instead ask whether journalists are fulfilling their mission to inform the public about news it needs to protect itself, rather than mere gossip or prurient interest. For example, in a case adjudicating an article about a famous television broadcaster and her allegedly improper relationship with a politician, the Court held that "no social utility could be realized from informing the readers [...] and the public in general" of this "alleged intimate personal relationship."[27]

2. *The objective truthfulness of the information.* Truth is not an absolute defense in Italy: if a statement is true yet defamatory but not in the public interest, the publisher will be held liable without regard to truth or falsity. The social utility element must be satisfied.

Moreover, there is no "substantial truth" defense in Italy: the article must be correct in all statements of fact. The line of decisions equates false news to "half truths" or incomplete truths. The publication of a story that is objectively true in itself but accompanied by silence regarding other facts that are so closely related to the reported news as to distort its content, "is [ruled] more dangerous than the exposition of individual falsehoods [...] on account of the greater ease with which reporting or hearing a report of a patently false fact, rather than a true but incomplete fact, may be defended."[28]

3. *The "sober form" in reporting the story.* This last requirement, which is also referred to as the criteria of moderation, is specified in a series of hypothetical cases considered by the court decisions in question. In particular, the press is expected to use moderate and cautious language not considered rude or discourteous or disrespectful. Articles may be considered libelous when the language:

   i)   exceeds the proposed aim of providing information,
   ii)   is not calm and objective,
   iii) tramples that minimum amount of dignity to which all individuals have a right,
   iv)   is not characterized by sincere clarity.[29]

Italian law also recognizes a *de facto* "good faith" defense, provided that an article (even if inaccurate) serves the social utility and is soberly expressed. The essential rules of conduct in the reporting of news are the subjective standards of prudence and skill. A journalist publishing an error will be released from liability *only* if he proves that he acted with a high degree of diligence, described by one court as the "fruit of serious and documented research."[30]

The reliability of the news source is not a dispositive factor, although it is one of the parameters used by judges in determining the standard of diligence applied. Thus, for example, a line of decisions has held liable the director of a newspaper that mistakenly identified, as the perpetrator of a grave offense, a person whose surname coincided with that of the actual culprit. The editor defended himself by affirming that he had questioned the reporter about the story, but the court found that this did not satisfy the high degree of care required to assert the defense. The failure to question all sources thoroughly or to exhibit skepticism of defamatory allegations will result in a rejection of the defense.[31] Sections 342 and 595, last paragraph of the Codice Penale envisage the aggravating circumstance of libel targeting a political, administrative, or judicial institution.

7. Is financial news about publicly traded companies, or companies involved with a government contract, considered a matter of public interest or otherwise privileged?

Although it has not been litigated in Italy, the prevalent view is that at least with regard to publicly traded companies, news about their behavior and actions is in the public interest, because Italy's market regulator, CONSOB, oversees almost all aspects of corporate governance in the name of public interest. Thus, news that relates to corporate governance is most likely to be recognized as serving the same public interest.[32]

There is controversy over whether public institutions can be recognized as having a right to privacy and, in particular, whether it is possible to extend the law protecting the privacy of personal data to them. No guidance on this point has yet been provided by court decisions. Press law proponents have argued that public institutions should not be accorded privacy rights, because laws allow the press and public access to their documents.[33]

8. Is there a recognized protection for opinion or "fair comment" on matters of public concern?

Yes. Subject to the restrictions of libel law described above, Section 21 of the Constitution treats criticism in the fields of politics, science, literature, etc. as having equal status with news reporting. Therefore, defamatory references are allowed, provided that the social utility and diligence to finding the truth of any asserted facts is satisfied,[34] and the language is guided by moderation and restraint.[35]

Courts have provided more leeway to publishers in the area of political discourse, where harsh, polemical, and aggressive expressions are considered legitimate.[36] The more socially relevant the reported or criticized activity is, the more severe the language can be.[37] Moreover, relevant to the right of political criticism, weighing the offensive nature of a statement, the judge is supposed to consider the general historical and political situation and especially the fact that political disputes are usually characterized by aggressive language.[38] However, criticism of a public person must address a subject's public, not private life.[39]

9. Are there any requirements upon a plaintiff, such as demand for retraction or right of reply, and if so, what impact do they have?

Italian law recognizes a right of reply. The Italian legal system holds that individuals whose image has been published or who have been subjected to statements they consider harmful to their dignity or contrary to the truth have the right to ask the directors of newspapers, periodicals, or press agencies to publish their replies free of charge. It has been held that the function of the correction is not to re-establish the objective truth of the published news report but rather to ensure publication of the subject's point of view and publicize a possible different interpretation of the facts in the interest of pluralism in the news media.[40] Italian law allows parties who have made a written demand for a right of reply to seek judicial intervention and an order requiring the publication to publish the reply.[41]

The right-of-reply laws are complicated and detailed, and include rapidity of response, selection of particular typeface, periodic frequency, and position requirements. One court noted that "The right to correction of the published news represents the fundamental right of the person to protect his or her image and dignity. Therefore, the correction must be published in conformity with the request, without the newspaper director or judge having any right to modify its text, or control the truthfulness of its content."[42] The right-of-reply statutes do not apply to radio and television.[43]

10. Is there a privilege for quoting or reporting on:

a. Papers filed in court?

Italian law does not recognize "privileged" documents, meaning documents deemed by themselves as stating the truth. The Supreme Court of Cassation was forced to wrestle with this issue, and said that no documents, by themselves could "release the journalist from his duty of: (a) examining, controlling, and verifying the facts he relates [...];(b) proving the care that he exercised in verifying the facts to remove all doubts [...]

as to the truth."[44] However, accurate and fair reports of judicial proceedings may satisfy the prudence and skill elements required in a good faith defense.

b. Government-issued documents?

There is no specific privilege for government-issued documents; however, such documents may be relied upon in the exercise of prudence and skill as described above.

c. Quasi-governmental proceedings?

There is no specific privilege for documents or statements made in such proceedings; however, such sources may be relied upon in the exercise of prudence and skill as described above.

11. Is there a privilege for republishing statements made earlier by other, bona fide, reliable publications or wire services?

No. Journalists cannot in any case invoke the appearance of the reported news or story in another newspaper or agency press release as an extenuating circumstance. Court decisions denied the existence of extenuating circumstances in the case of news by wire services such as ANSA or AGI republished without further checking.[45]

It should be noted that the following have not been recognized as reliable sources sufficient to release the journalist from his obligation of checking the facts: sources of information such as newspapers, press agencies, RAI—Radiotelevisone Italiana;[46] rumors heard in legal circles;[47] and unofficial news issued by police agencies. This latter case is addressed in a decision by the Court of Cassation, which ruled that: "pursuant to law, Government agencies are governed by specific rules for reporting their activities, outside of which information shall not be considered official."[48]

12. Are there any restrictions regarding reporting on:

a. Ongoing criminal investigations?

Italian law restricts the right of the press to report on ongoing criminal investigations and trials. This is in order to protect the efficacy of investigative activities. Reporting on prosecutions and investigations certainly represents a public interest, and thus the right to news reports prevails over the right to protection of privacy. Nevertheless, news coverage of prosecutions and investigations suffers from a series of restrictions that serve to protect investigative activities and thus are not dictated by the need to guarantee and protect the person involved in the prosecution.

b. Ongoing criminal prosecutions?

Italian law places a series of restrictions on the ability of the press to reproduce documents from criminal proceedings. Sections 114 and 329 of the Italian Code of Criminal Procedure (hereinafter referred to as Codice di Procedura Penale or c.p.p.); Section 684 c.p.p., and Section 114, c.p.p., paragraph 1, outlaws any sort of publication of court documents (*atti coperti da segreto*), including summaries, until the investigatory phase is completed.[49] Italian law gives special treatment to the naming and depiction of minors involved in the justice process. The Constitutional Court first gave concrete form to the concept of "the minor's interest not to be publicized" as a strong value in contrast with legitimate publication: "the reporter's activity must respect personality and, therefore, there can be no dispute that the protection of minors assumes a special set of norms regarding formation of the personality."[50]

c. Ongoing regulatory investigations?

Section 114, paragraph 3 c.p.p., states that publication of the documents contained in the court trial record is prohibited until the decision of the court of first instance is issued, and documents in the public prosecutor's file are secret until the decision is under appeal. There are some exceptions to the rule of secrecy, including: documents used to cross-examine witnesses; documents produced by parties in the preliminary investigation phase[51] and knowable by the indicted, such as preliminary testimonies.[52] Secrecy rules do not apply to documents introduced in court but knowable from different sources.[53]

The Cassation has given a strict interpretation of the matter, discerning between secrecy of the document, operating within the proceeding (internal secrecy), and total publishing bans (external secrecy).[54] Under Section 684 c.p., violation of secrecy and improper reporting of court documents may be punished with imprisonment up to thirty days or a monetary fine from €51 to €258.

Section 114, paragraph *6bis,* c.p.p., forbids the unconsented publication of the image of a defendant deprived of his or her personal freedom, if handcuffed or subject to other means of restraint.

d. Ongoing civil litigation, or other judicial proceedings?

Civil cases are not subject to the same restrictions. However, it must be remembered that pursuant to Section 76 of the Implementation and Transitional Provisions of the Codice di Procedura Civile, only the parties and the defense counsel with power of attorney may have presumed access to the acts and documents in the court record.

13. Are prior restraints or other prepublication injunctions available on the basis of libel or privacy, and if so, what are the standards for obtaining such relief?

Yes. The Italian legal system expressly provides for urgent, preventive protection in the case of traditional personal rights, such as the right to one's name (Sec. 7 c.c.), the right to a pseudonym (Sec. 9 c.c.), and the right to privacy (Sec. 10 c.c.), for which preventive actions are standardized. Section 700 c.p.c. also provides a cause of action for the seizure of defamatory material on an expedited basis.

14. Is a right of privacy recognized (either civilly or criminally)?

a. What is the definition of "private fact"?

Pursuant to Section 4, letter B, Law 30 June 2003 (hereinafter "Privacy Code"), "personal fact" has been interpreted as "any information regarding a physical person, a legal entity, an institution, or an organization that are directly or indirectly identified or identifiable by referring to any other information, including a personal identification number."

Therefore, the definition of "private fact" in Italian law is very broad.

b. Is there a public interest or newsworthiness exception?

There is a codified newsworthiness exception. Pursuant to Sections 136 and 137 of the Privacy Code, it is not necessary to obtain the express consent of the interested party for the treatment of personal data "when it is performed in the course of exercising the journalistic profession and exclusively for the purpose of pursuing relative aims."

c. Is the right of privacy based in common law, statute, or constitution?

The right of privacy is codified in Section 2 of the Italian Constitution, which acknowledges to all citizens equal social dignity and a right to protect privacy, right to honor, reputation, personality, personal image.

15. May reporters tape-record their own telephone conversations for note-taking purposes (not rebroadcast) without the consent of the other party?

Italy allows telephone recording with the consent of only one party. Such recording is deemed to have a documentary nature and the fact that it occurs with only one of the party's consent does not represent an offense to the other party's freedom of self-determination.[55] Any subject, if directly involved in a conversation he is a party to, is free to record the content of the conversation, by telephone as well as by voice, in order to acquire the most proper documentation of it.[56]

16. If permissible to record such tapes, may they be broadcast without permission?

No. The prejudice to the right to the voice (a form of the right to personal image) may be damaged by unconsented broadcast, even if no offense to the individual's honor or reputation took place. Someone's voice is deemed an expression of personal identity. Also, the Copyright Act (Law April 22, 1941, No. 633) devotes three sections to the right to portrayal; two of which, Section 96 and Section 97, may be applied to the right to the voice.

17. Is there a recognized evidentiary privilege preventing the disclosure of confidential sources relied upon by reporters?

Yes, although this right is not absolute. Section 2, Law February 3, 1963, No. 69 (Ruling about Journalism Profession) provides that "journalists and publishers are required to respect the professional secrecy relevant to the source of information when this is required by its confidential nature."

However, the Codice di Procedura Penale, while recognizing journalistic confidentiality, still may require a journalist to provide the investigating magistrate with the information in circumstances of demonstrated need: "journalists entered in the professional register, regarding the names of the persons that provided them with confidential information in the course of their professional work. Although, if the information represents evidence necessary to prove the offense being prosecuted, and its truthfulness can be ascertained only by identifying the source of the news, the judge shall order the journalist to name the source of information" (Sec. 200, paragraph 3, c.p.p.).

This shield law only applies with the following restrictions:

1. secrecy is extended only to the sources of the information but not its content;
2. the information must be of a confidential nature;
3. the person asserting the shield must be a professional journalist.

The European Court of Human Rights has frequently ruled that the protection of journalistic sources is one of the fundamental aspects of liberty of the press, considering that "the lack of such protection could dissuade journalistic sources from aiding the press in informing the public about matters of general interest."[57] No Italian shield law cases have yet been brought to the ECHR.

18. In the event that legal papers are served upon the newsroom (such as a civil complaint), are there any particular warnings about accepting service of which we should be aware?

In Italy, only bailiffs or other public officers may provide service of process, by delivering to the served person a true copy of the document to be served or sending it through the regular postal service. Legal papers are served to the legal domicile of the person to be served. However, servicing by personal delivery may also occur wherever the served person is met by the bailiff. Newspapers and publishers named in complaints can be served at the publicly listed office.

In the case of individual defendants, servicing through the regular postal service must be made only to the legal residence/domicile of the served person. A civil complaint must be served to a defendant at his or her home, not workplace. If an individual is sued but served at work, it is advisable not to accept the service on behalf of the defendant.

19. Has your jurisdiction applied established media law to Internet publishers?

In relation to libel perpetrated by the Internet, the Cassation stated that, notwithstanding the lack of specific legislation expressly related to telecom libel, online libel may be punished according to the Italian criminal system.[58] The sole communication between the actor and third parties fulfills the conduct requested for the perpetration of the crimes envisaged by Section 595 c.p. The crime is perpetrated when the readers perceive the libelous expressions. Therefore, such action may as well offend someone's reputation when the libelous news is introduced on the Internet. Publication or accessibility in Italy most likely satisfies jurisdictional requirements.

Furthermore, the Supreme Court added that such Internet publications be considered as potentially more offensive than the traditional case, being able to spread the libelous message *erga omnes* (meaning to the address of everybody—even if, in this case, only among people with the technical means to receive it) and perpetrating, therefore, an aggravated case of libel.

20. If established media law has been applied to Internet publishers, are there any ways in which Internet publishers (including chat room operators) have to meet different standards?

Italian law does not envisage a higher fault standard for Internet publishers regarding the event of online libel, and Italian Press Law does not address Internet publication. Thus, webmasters are not expected to meet the same standards as traditional news publishers.

However, the European e-commerce directive may be applied to provide hosts with a degree of immunity (2001/31/EC).

21. Are there any cases where the courts enforced a judgment in libel from another jurisdiction against a publisher in your jurisdiction?

To be enforced in the Italian legal system, a foreign judgment needs to be previously recognized through a short proceeding to verify that it meets all the requirements that an Italian decision must have, which briefly are:

- the sentence must not violate constitutional principles of the Italian legal system;
- the parties' right to defense has been respected: all of them had the chance to join the proceeding and to defend their arguments;
- the sentence is finally binding;
- there is no conflict with any Italian sentence nor with pending proceedings before Italian courts.

Therefore, it is possible to enforce in Italy a foreign conviction decision for libel, in consideration of both its criminal and civil effects. However, we are not aware of any case of foreign conviction of publishers being enforced in Italy.

Chapter Notes

1. Cassation, Criminal Section, December 21, 2000, n. 6920.

2. Cassation, Criminal Section, November 15, 2000, n. 598.

3. Cassation, Criminal Section, June 1, 1976, in *Rep. Foro it.*, 1976.

4. Cassation, Criminal Section, November 7, 2000, n. 14485, in Dannone Resp., 2001, N. 29, with note by CARBONE.

5. Tribunale Roma [Court of Rome], November 24, 1992, in *Dir. inf.*, 1993, 403.

6. Cassation, Criminal Section, May 31, 2003, n. 8827.

7. Cassation, Criminal Section, June 8, 1992, in *Cassazione Pen.*, 1994, p. 592, 1, and in *Giur. It.*, 1993, II, p. 518; on the same point, see also Tribunale Roma, November 24, 1992, in *Dir. inf.*, 1993, p. 403.

8. The leading case is Cassation, October 18, 1984, n. 5259, in *NGCC*, pp. 84 and 214, with note by ALPA and ROPPO.

9. The Restatement of law adopted by Law 30 June 2003, n. 196, entitled "Code relevant to the protection of personal data" (hereinafter, Privacy Code), under Section 4 includes legal entities among the "holders" of personal data (letter f)

and among the "interested parties" (letter i) beneficiaries of certain rights. They are covered by the same norms that apply to persons, with the specification, under Section 9, Paragraph 4, that "If the interested party is a legal person, an entity or an association, the request [to know and access its personal data stored by any subject and to effect assured rights] shall be proposed by the physical person appointed to act as by internal statutes."

10. Tribunale Roma, June 7, 1991, in *Dir. inf.*, 1992, 72, with note by ZENO-ZENCOVICH.

11. Tribunale Milano, September 18, 1989, in *Dir. inf.*, 1990, 144; Cassation, May 10, 2001, n. 6507, in *Guida al diritto*, n. 21, June 2, 2001, 32.

12. The leading case is Cassation, June 22, 1985, n. 3769. More recently, Cassation, July 10, 1991, n. 7642, in *Giur. it.*, 1991, I, 1, 96; Cassation, March 3, 2000, n. 2367, in *Danno e resp.*, 2000, p. 490, with note by CARBONE.

13. A specific case relevant to services provided to a hospital, Cassation, March 3, 2000, n. 2367, in *Danno e resp.*, 2000, p. 490, with note by CARBONE, *Il pregiudizio all'immagine e alla credibilità di una S.P.A. costituisce danno non patrimoniale e non danno morale.*

14. Tribunale Milano, September 28, 1972, in *Giur. it.*, 1973, I, 2, 1; Tribunale Roma, July 23, 1984, in *Foro it.*, 1984, I, 1963; Cassation, United Sections, May 22, 1991, n. 5787, in *Foro it.*, 1992, I, 2204, with note by DI VIA.

15. Tribunale Roma, June 18, 1997, in *Dir. inf.*, 1998, 282, with note by RESTA.

16. Tribunale Roma, April 18, 1984, in *Foro it.*, 1984, I, 2030.

17. Cassation, March 12, 1997, n. 2223, in *Dir. inf.*, 1997, p. 542.

18. Pretura Roma [Rome Magistrate's Court], May 7, 1974, in *Giur. it.*, 1974, I, 3227; Cassation, Criminal Section, April 27, 1998, in *NGCC*, 1999, I, 793, with note by FUSARO, *Diffamazione dell'ente mediante offesa rivolta ad un suo componente. La lesione dell'onore della Corte dei Conti.*

19. Pretura Roma, May 11, 1981, in *Giust. civ.*, 1982, I, 817.

20. Cassation, June 22, 1985, n. 3769, in *Foro it.*, 1985, I, 2211, and in *Dir. inf.*, 1985, 965, with note by FIGONE, and in *NGCC*, 1985, I, 647, with note by ZENO-ZENCOVICH, and in *Resp. civ.*, 1985, 578, with note by PONZANELLI.

21. Appello Genova [Court of Appeals in Genoa], January 28, 1963, in *Giur. it.*, 1964, II, 47, with note by LARICCIA, *Tutela dei culti e libertà di offendere. Considerazioni intorno al reato di offese a culto ammesso nello Stato mediante vilipendio a chi lo professa*; Cassation, Criminal Section, February 24, 1964, in *Giur. it.*, 1964, II, 241, with note by LARICCIA, *Sulla tutela penale delle confessioni religiose acattoliche.*

22. Cassation, Criminal Section, January 16, 1986, in *Dir. inf.*, 1986, 458, with note by LARICCIA and ZENO-ZENCOVICH, *Il diritto all'onore delle confessioni religiose e dei loro fedeli.*

23. Cassation, Criminal Section, October 7, 1998, in *Dir. eccles.*, 1999, II, 96, with note by PIGNEDOLI.

24. Tribunale Roma, February 28, 2001, in *Dir. inf.*, 2001, 464, with note by PINO.

25. Cassation, October 18, 1984, No. 5259, abovementioned.

26. Among the most significant ones, Cassation, Criminal Section, October 15, 1987, in *Riv. pen.*, 1989, 428; Cassation, Criminal Section, April 27, 1992, in *Giur. it.*, 1993, II, 688; Cassation, July 25, 2000, n. 9746, in *Danno e resp.*, 2001, 146, with note by MACCABONI.

27. Tribunale Roma, November 24, 1992, in *Dir. inf.*, 1993, 403.

28. Cassation, October 18, 1984, n. 5259, abovementioned.

29. Cassation, October 18, 1984, n. 5259, abovementioned.

30. Cassation, February 14, 1984, n. 1138, in *Mass.*, 1984.

31. Tribunale Roma, July 18, 1991, in *Dir. Inf.*, 1992, 83.

32. It is worth noting that Italian law prohibits the publication of confidential company information. See Sections 2622 and 2628 c.c.

33. Law 7 August 1990, No. 241.

34. Cassation, February 14, 1984, n. 1138, in *Mass.*, 1984.

35. Cassation, Criminal Section, November 24, 1993, in *Giust. pen.*, 1994, II, 496; Cassation, Criminal Section, February 12, 1987, *Riv. pen.*, 1988, 79.

36. Cassation, Criminal Section, May 22, 1984, in *Cassazione pen.*, 1985, 617.

37. Cassation, Criminal Section, February 7, 2001, in *Guida al dir.*, 2001, XXX-IV, 97, with note by AMATO.

38. Cassation, Criminal Section, April 18, 2001, in *Foro it.*, 2002, II, 2; Cassation, Criminal Section, March 15, 2001, in *Foro it.*, 2002, II, 4; Cassation, November 7, 2000, n. 14485, in *Danno e resp.*, 2001, 29, with note by CARBONE, and in *Giur. it.*, 2001, 1360, with note by BAROLI.

39. Cassation, Criminal Section, February 2, 2000, in *Cassazione. pen.*, 2000, 698; Tribunale Milano, April 7, 1997, in *Giur. it.*, 1997, I, 2, 409; Pretura Roma, July 15, 1986, in *Dir. inf.*, 1986, 926, with note by ZENO ZENCOVICH; Tribunale Napoli, October 5, 1977, in *Giur. it.*, 1978, II, 172.

40. Pretura Roma, April 29, 1991, in *Dir. inf.*, 1991, 889.

41. Section 700, Code of Civil Procedure. See also Section 8 of the Press Act, as amended by Section 42 of Law No. 416 of 1981.

42. Tribunale S. Maria Capua V., January 22, 1999, in *Foro napoletano*, 1999, 37.

43. Tribunale Roma, February 27, 1982, in *Giur. costit.,* 1982, II, 1802; Constitutional Court, November 11 1985, N. 259, in *guir. costit.,* 1985, N. 2124.

44. Cassation, Criminal United Sections, June 30, 1984, in *Foro it.,* 1984, II, 531. Following such decisions are the subsequent Cassation, Criminal Section, April 17, 1985, in *Cassazione pen.,* 1985, 1078; Cassation, Criminal Section, February 13, 1992, in *Cassation pen.,* 1993, 2266.

45. Tribunale Napoli, October 11, 1989, in *Dir. Inf.,* 1990, 987.

46. Cassation, Criminal Section, May 9, 1980, in *Riv. Pen.,* 1980, 11; Cassation, Criminal Section, March 21, 1991, in *Riv. Pen.,* 1991, 912.

47. Tribunale Roma, February 5, 1991, in *Dir. inf.,* 1992, 459.

48. Cassation, Criminal Section, June 14, 1996, in *Cassation pen.,* 1998, 448.

49. Tribunale Milano, April 8, 1991, in *Dir. inf.,* 1992, 56; Cassation, December 18, 1980, in *Giust. Pen.,* 1982, II, 139.

50. Constitutional Court, February 10, 1981, n. 16, in *Foro it.,* 1981, I, 601.

51. Cassation, October 10, 1995, in *Cass. pen.,* 1996, 1183.

52. Tribunale Bologna, March 17, 1994, in *Critica del diritto,* 1994, IV, 74, with note by Rossi; Gip (Judge for preliminary investigation) Tribunale L'Aquila, June 30, 1993, in *Dir. inf.,* 1994, 530, with note by Lodato.

53. Cassation, July 11, 1994, in *Arch. nuova proc. pen.,* 1994, 821.

54. Cassation, October 3, 2002, in *Ced Cass.,* rv 222662.

55. Cassation, April 8, 1994, in *Riv. pen.,* 1994, 856.

56. Cassation, January 9, 1987, in *Riv. Pen.,* 1987, 1124.

57. Quotation from the ruling by the European Court of Human Rights in the case *Goodwin v. United Kingdom,* issued on March 27, 1996.

58. Cassation, Criminal Section, November 17, 2000, in *Dir. inf.,* 2001, 21.

CHAPTER 16

Netherlands

JENS P. VAN DEN BRINK

Kennedy Van der Laan

Kennedy Van der Laan
Haarlemmerweg 333
1051 LH Amsterdam, Netherlands
Phone: 00-31-20-550 68 43
Fax: 00-31-20-550 69 43
www.kvdl.nl
jens.van.den.brink@kvdl.nl

Introduction to the Dutch Legal System

The Dutch legal system has evolved from being almost identical to the French civil law system to one that incorporates several aspects of a number of different legal systems in Europe. Guided by traditional civil law principles, the Dutch system is divided into three main branches, the civil branch, the administrative branch, and the criminal branch. The court of first instance in all three branches is called the *rechtbank* (the district court). The administrative system has a number of sector-specific supreme courts, organized by subject, that hear appeals and select cases.

The civil system has a sub-district court, the so-called *sector kanton*, which has recently been made a separate department of the *rechtbank*. The *sector kanton* hears cases of lesser importance as well as real estate and labor cases. The civil and criminal branches have a court of appeals and the *Hoge Raad* (or Supreme Council), which is the Supreme Court. Appeals from both the sub-district courts and the district court are heard in the appeals court. The Supreme Court, comprised of a president, seven vice presidents, and thirty-one justices, ensures that law is being properly applied. Dutch courts do not have the authority to test an Act of Parliament or an international treaty against the Dutch Constitution. Dutch courts do test Acts of Parliament against international treaties.

Introduction to Netherlands Media Law

The Netherlands is a member of the European Convention on Human Rights (the Convention); thus, this section contains regular citations of case law of the European Court of Human Rights (ECHR). Article 94 of the Dutch Constitution contains the general principle that clauses with direct effect in international treaties override national law. Whereas the freedom of speech as laid down in section 10 of the Convention has direct effect on press rights, Dutch courts directly apply the relevant ECHR case law in their judgments.

Conflicts relating to press publications may also be brought before the Council for Journalism, which is a self-regulatory entity. Its decisions are not binding and it cannot apply any sanctions. The Council will give its opinion on whether a journalist has operated carefully and whether a publication has exceeded the boundaries of what is acceptable in society, taking into account journalistic responsibility.

1. What is the locally accepted definition of libel?

As a criminal matter, article 261 of the Dutch penal code defines common libel as the "intentional damaging of a person's honour or good name by accusing that person of something, while aiming to make this fact public."

Slander is defined as a libel committed with the knowledge that the accusations are untrue (article 262 Criminal Code). Offending a person by exposing him to rash accusations and thereby harming that person's reputation may also constitute a tort under article 6:162 of the Dutch Civil Code.

Any limitation of freedom of speech should meet the test of article 10 of the Convention. In short, the limitation should be (a) prescribed by law, (b) serve one or more defined legitimate aims,[1] and (c) be necessary in a democratic society. The role of the press as public watchdog will be taken into account: the press fulfills an essential function in a democratic society. The freedom of speech also entails the right to use speech which offends, shocks, or disturbs,[2] and journalistic freedom also covers possible recourse to a degree of exaggeration, or even provocation.[3]

If statements are unlawful or punishable by criminal law (and therefore prescribed by law), it should still be determined under article 10 of the Convention whether the limitation of the freedom of speech serves one of the defined aims and is necessary in a democratic society. The latter will be determined by weighing the freedom of speech against the personal (or dignitary) rights of the person implicated (often the right of privacy).

This is a case-by-case analysis; there is no order of priority between these rights.

The following statements have been found to be defamatory under Dutch criminal law: The accusation "that G.R. mistreats and/or threatens women on the streets" was found to be libelous (Supreme Court, November 6, 2001). By contrast, the implicit allegation that "H. may be seduced by a bag of candy" was not found to be libelous (Supreme Court, October 24, 1989).

The following statements have been found to convey defamatory meaning under Dutch civil law: a medical watchdog group calling a physician a "quack doctor";[4] accusing the president of a Dutch football club of being a "dictator who lies and cheats";[5] accusing a Dutch TV presenter of being a "programme thief."[6] The following statements have been held lawful under Dutch civil law: "malafide trade-practices mislead agrarian entrepreneurs";[7] "reprobate swindler" and "professional liar."[8]

2. Is libel-by-implication recognized, or, in the alternative, must the complained-of words alone defame the plaintiff?

Yes, libel may occur by implication only.

3. May corporations sue for libel?

Yes, a legal entity can sue for libel. This has recently been confirmed by the ECHR.[9] Libel toward a company may also create criminal liability.[10]

4. Is product disparagement recognized, and if so, how does that differ from libel?

Yes, product disparagement may constitute a tort, e.g., if the reputation of the producer of that product is harmed. For example, a product may be libeled in a publication through the use of demeaning language that implies wrongdoing on the part of the producer. The abovementioned guidelines on libel apply.

If it concerns advertising which directly or indirectly mentions the product or name of a competitor, the rules on comparative advertising apply (section 6:194a of the Dutch Civil Code). Comparative advertising is allowed if the statutory conditions are met (article 194a Civil Code, which is an implementation of European Directive 97/55/EC). This also comprises the rule that the reputation of the competitor may not be harmed and no denigrating language may be used.

5. Must an individual be clearly identified (by name or photograph) to sue for libel? Can a group of persons sue for libel, even though not named?

Even if a publication does not clearly identify an individual by name or photograph, that individual may sue for libel if that person can be identified by other means.[11] A group of persons which is not named may also sue for libel. For example, the Anne Frank Foundation has successfully acted against Holocaust revisionist publications.[12]

6. What is the fault standard(s) applied to libel?

a. Does the fault standard depend on the fame or notoriety of the plaintiff?

Yes, Dutch law holds that a public figure should in general tolerate more harsh speech than a nonpublic figure, especially if that person actively seeks out publicity for his private life himself. The limits of acceptable criticism are especially broader when it concerns politicians and when the debate is in the general interest.[13] With respect to public figures who do not exercise public functions, the "public figure" defense has recently been curtailed by the ECHR.[14]

b. Is there a heightened fault standard or privilege for reporting on matters of public concern or public interest?

Yes, the more an issue reflects on the public interest, the more freedom the press has to examine and disclose such problems.

Dutch law uses a balancing test to determine liability for potentially defamatory speech. Under tort law, it should always be assessed which interest prevails: the interest of an individual not to be confronted with rash accusations in the press weighed against the public interest involved in the exposure of wrongs in society to the general public. This balancing of interests has been given shape in Supreme Court case law,[15] which determines that journalists should take the following elements into account:

1. The nature of the accusations and the seriousness of the expected consequences for the person to whom the accusations relate;
2. The seriousness—as seen from the general interest—of the abuse which the publication tries to expose;
3. The extent to which the accusations were supported by factual material available at the time of the publication;
4. The way the accusations have been formulated;
5. The probability that the general interest which the publication strived for could have been achieved in a different, less damaging, manner;
6. Would the statements or accusations have been published anyway?

Similar considerations regarding the general interest will play a role under criminal law. Article 261(3) of the Criminal Code provides a ground of justification for libelous statements if the perpetrator assumed in good faith that the charged fact was true, while the accusation was in the general interest.

7. Is financial news about publicly traded companies, or companies involved with a government contract, considered a matter of public interest or otherwise privileged?

Yes, financial news about publicly traded companies, or companies involved with government contracts, may be considered a matter of public interest. Nevertheless, the press must not overstep certain bounds, in particular with respect to the reputation and rights of others and the need to prevent the disclosure of confidential information.[16] In each case, the balancing of interests should take place. The making public of confidential corporate documents which have been obtained through a criminal act is criminally punishable (article 273 Criminal Code).

8. Is there a recognized protection for opinion or "fair comment" on matters of public concern?

There is no distinction between political discussion and matters of public concern, because both fall under the role of the press as "public watchdog."[17] ECHR case law even provides that it is the duty of the press to impart information and ideas on all matters of public interest.[18]

According to established case law, a distinction should be made between opinions or value judgments on the one hand and statements of fact on the other. The former provide much more leniency to journalists than the latter. Whereas the existence of facts can be demonstrated, the truth of value judgments is not susceptible to proof.

9. Are there any requirements upon a plaintiff, such as demand for retraction or right of reply, and if so, what impact do they have?

Dutch law does not provide for a right of reply following a publication. There is no pre-litigation requirement for the plaintiff to demand some form of retraction before starting defamation proceedings. However, in some cases damages are limited by a fair and timely correction. If the plaintiff refuses a right of reply which is offered, this might be used against him by the court.

Dutch law does not contain a general obligation to provide the person involved with a right of reply or a right of inspection prior to publication.[19] However, serious allegations may not be expressed rashly and must be founded on the then-available facts. The more serious the allegation, the more stringently the publication should be researched. In some cases, this may lead to an obligation for a journalist to provide the person involved with a right to reply (otherwise the publication would be unlawful).[20] If it can be shown that obtaining a reply or comment has been attempted, but failed, this may suffice.[21] If the plaintiff was contacted, but refused to provide commentary, this may lead the court to conclude that the press has fulfilled its duty to investigate. Please note that if a reply is published, this does not necessarily make the publication lawful.

10. Is there a privilege for quoting or reporting on:

a. Papers filed in court?

There is no statutory privilege for papers filed in court; however, there is a common law privilege as courts have held that if it encompasses statements regarding matters of public concern from a bona fide third party source (and that would include government sources), no further research is required.[22]

Statements which are included in procedural documents of a criminal case may relieve the journalist of his duty to investigate the factual basis of those statements, even if the person who made the statements withdrew them at a later stage.[23]

b. Government-issued documents?

There is no specific privilege for government-issued documents. As a general rule, under Dutch law, information concerning administrative matters originating from the government should in principle be available to the public. Any citizen (including journalists) may request copies of such documents on the basis of the Code Publicity Public Administration (*Wet Openbaarheid Bestuur* or "WOB").

c. Quasi-governmental proceedings?

There is no specific privilege.

11. Is there a privilege for republishing statements made earlier by other, bona fide, reliable publications or wire services?

Although there is no codified republication privilege, under Dutch law statements pertaining to matters of public concern derived from bona fide third parties do not require further investigation on the reporter's part.[24] However, in some cases, particularly harsh or accusatory statements may require establishing distance with the third-party source, e.g., by explicitly stating that it concerns statements from a third-party source.

12. Are there any restrictions regarding reporting on:

a. Ongoing criminal investigations?

Generally, no. However, publishing (or even obtaining) government documents which should be kept classified in the interest of the State constitutes a criminal offense (Dutch Penal Code articles 98–98c). Please note that in exceptional circumstances, those asserting the freedom of speech might prevail.

b. Ongoing criminal prosecutions?

No.

c. Ongoing regulatory investigations?

Articles 10 and 11 of the WOB define circumstances which provide for an exception to the duty of the public administration to supply information as laid down in the WOB. These exceptions include information the disclosure of which would endanger the safety of the State or criminal investigation and/or prosecution and/or the privacy of persons.

In the *"King Kong"* case,[25] a journalist requested a copy of government information, which the Dutch State regarded as classified. The court decided that, although the files concerned the Dutch secret service, and thus the safety of the State, this information did not contain information which would *per se* endanger the State when made public. Therefore, the documents had to be provided to the requesting journalist.

There are no special restrictions regarding reporting on ongoing regulatory investigations.

d. Ongoing civil litigation, or other judicial proceedings?

There are no special restrictions regarding reporting on ongoing civil litigation or other judicial proceedings and/or criminal prosecutions.

However, such reporting often implicates the privacy of persons involved in a criminal case. For that reason, in most cases, the names of the defendant and convicted in a criminal case are only mentioned by using initials (this is customary, and not laid down in a statute). Please note that the full name may be provided under certain circumstances, e.g., to warn the public, if the person involved cooperated with the publication or if the full name is already published by other media.[26]

13. Are prior restraints or other prepublication injunctions available on the basis of libel or privacy, and if so, what are the standards for obtaining such relief?

Article 7(2) of the Constitution provides that prior restraint is not allowed. However, if it concerns repeated broadcasts or publication, or if the content is known to a sufficient extent prior to the broadcast or publication, it may be forbidden on the basis of libel or tort law.[27]

14. Is a right of privacy recognized (either civilly or criminally)?

Yes, the right of privacy has been recognized both in civil (article 8 of the Convention, article 10 of the Constitution, and the Act on the Protection of Personal Data) and in criminal law (articles 138–139g of the Criminal Code). Further, the right of privacy has been laid down in the so-called portrait right clauses of the Dutch Copyright Act 1912 (articles 19–21). If the portrait has not been made at the request of the person portrayed, that person may prevent the publication of the portrait if he has a reasonable interest (usually privacy related) which opposes such publication.

a. What is the definition of "private fact"?

"Private fact" as such is not defined. However, the Convention defines the right of privacy as follows: "Everyone has the right to respect for his private and family life, his home and his correspondence."

b. Is there a public interest or newsworthiness exception?

There is no absolute general public interest exception. In the case of a publication which might infringe on the right of privacy, a balancing of interests will have to take place. If the infringement of privacy is necessary in the public interest, it might be a lawful infringement. Circumstances mentioned in case law which specifically relate to the balancing of interests in case of a privacy infringement comprise the following:

- the seriousness of the privacy infringement;
- the nature and extent of intimacy;
- the length of the period within which the infringement took place;
- the nature and importance of the published facts;
- the extent to which the published facts shed new light to what is already known;
- the persons involved;
- did the person involved actively pursue public interest for his private life?;
- the position of the person involved;
- the aim and the nature of the publicizing medium.

The following cases have been found to be unjustified intrusions upon privacy: the use by a welfare institution of a report on a woman who was on social security, which was the result of information provided by her neighbor (also director of a social security institution) who regularly "spied" on her;[28] publication of stories and photos by a gossip magazine about the children of a Dutch princess who the magazine had also followed around;[29] publication of a photograph of a woman engaged in a sexual act in public.[30]

The following have been found to be justified publications of private facts: the publication of a photographic portrait of the killer of Gerrit-Jan Heijn (brother of the founder of the famous Dutch supermarkets Albert Heijn), due to the high newsworthiness of the portrait and the special quality of the picture (which won a prestigious photographic prize);[31] publication of a summary of gossip concerning the editor of a famous gossip magazine (allowed in part because of the manner in which the person exposed worked as a journalist himself);[32] the publication of tax forms of the director of Peugeot (allowed because of the public interest and because the facts substantiated the accusations made against the executive).[33]

c. Is the right of privacy based in common law, statute, or constitution?

The right of privacy has been statutorily recognized both in civil law (article 8 of the Convention, article 10 of the Constitution, and the Act on the Protection of Personal Data) and in criminal law (articles 138–139g of the Criminal Code).

15. May reporters tape-record their own telephone conversations for note-taking purposes (not rebroadcast) without the consent of the other party?

Yes, provided the reporter is a party to the conversation.[34] However, a reporter relying on such documents to defend her case may face evidentiary challenges in court. Under Dutch law a party in a legal dispute may ask for submission of exhibits by the other party under article 843a of the Dutch Code of Legal Procedure. The foregoing means that in case an interview has been recorded, the one being interviewed may request a copy of the recording in order to assess whether the interview has been correctly reproduced. Depending on the circumstances, such an application may be granted.[35]

16. If permissible to record such tapes, may they be broadcast without permission?

This will depend on a balancing of the interest of: (a) the individual involved not to be confronted with rash accusations in the press; and (b) the public interest in exposing wrongs in society to the general public. Broadcasting such a conversation may, depending on the circumstances and content of the tape, be a wrongful act due to an infringement of the right of privacy.

In one case,[36] a journalist published the contents of an illegally recorded telephone conversation (to which he was not a party). The court found that the freedom of speech overruled the criminal provisions on illegal taping. Therefore, even the broadcasting of illegally recorded phone conversations might be allowed.

17. Is there a recognized evidentiary privilege preventing the disclosure of confidential sources relied upon by reporters?

Yes. Although Dutch law does not provide for a statutory right of nondisclosure for journalists, case law does. According to the Supreme Court, the protection of journalistic sources is one of the basic conditions for press freedom, to prevent sources from being deterred from assisting the press in informing the public on matters of public interest. A journalist may only be forced to reveal his confidential source if this would be justified by an overriding requirement in the public interest.[37]

18. In the event that legal papers are served upon the newsroom (such as a civil complaint), are there any particular warnings about accepting service of which we should be aware?

No.

19. Has your jurisdiction applied established media law to Internet publishers?

The European E-Commerce Directive (2000/31/EC) contains limitations of liability for intermediaries providing mere conduit, caching, or hosting services. For example, an Internet service provider which merely hosts information is not liable for the information transmitted. However, liability does arise if the ISP, as soon as he obtains knowledge of apparent illegal activity or information, fails to act expeditiously to remove or disable access to that information.

This exception has been implemented in article 6:196 (c) of the Dutch Civil Code and article 54a of the Dutch Criminal Code. This rule is based in part on a landmark Dutch case (*Scientology v. XS4all*, http://www.spaink .net/cos/verd2eng.html), in which the same rule was found to apply in general to service providers which merely pass on information, without making a selection or adapting the information.[38] Please note that for a publisher who acts in the more traditional sense and selects or adapts the content of its publications, the normal rules on the freedom of speech apply.

There appears to be no specific Dutch case law with respect to Internet publishers (case law with respect to Internet publications does exist; in general this case law does not differ from case law with respect to offline publications). Related case law does exist. In the "*Deutsche Bahn*" cases, a Web site of a left-wing group contained a manual for sabotaging the German railways. The Amsterdam court of appeal found that this publication constituted a tort and ordered the Dutch ISP of the Web site to shut it down.[39] However, mirror sites with the same content had already appeared. On its Web site, Indymedia provided a hyperlink to one of those mirror sites, which contained the same manual. Indymedia was summoned by the German Railways to remove the hyperlink. The court found that, by knowingly linking to material which a court had already deemed tortious, Indymedia committed a tort itself.[40] In arriving at this conclusion, the court also noted that the text which accompanied the hyperlink stimulated the visitors to use the link and visit the connected Web site (with wrongful content).

20. If established media law has been applied to Internet publishers, are there any ways in which Internet publishers (including chat room operators) have to meet different standards?

As soon as an Internet publisher obtains knowledge of an apparent illegal activity or information, it must act expeditiously to remove or disable access to that information.

21. Are there any cases where the courts enforced a judgment in libel from another jurisdiction against a publisher in your jurisdiction?

Such case law has not yet been decided. Foreign judgments in libel cases have the same status as "normal" judgments. This means that a judgment given in a foreign jurisdiction is not enforceable in the Netherlands, unless such foreign country has entered into an agreement thereto with the Netherlands. Within Europe, the EEX Regulation[41] provides that judgments given in EU member states may relatively easily be executed in the Netherlands. Please note that no bilateral agreement exists between the United States and the Netherlands concerning the execution of U.S. judgments in the Netherlands.

In case of libel through a publication in several EU member states, the offended person may take the publisher to court in the jurisdiction where the publisher is incorporated, or in the jurisdictions where the publication was disseminated and where damage was done to that person's reputation.[42]

Chapter Notes

1. Article 10 (2) of the Convention defines the following interests: territorial integrity or public safety, for the prevention of disorder or crime, for the protection of health or morals, for the protection of the reputation or rights of others, for

preventing the disclosure of information received in confidence, or for maintaining the authority and impartiality of the judiciary.

2. ECHR 26 April 1979, NJ 1980/146 (*Sunday Times*).

3. ECHR 26 April 1995, Series A no. 313 (*Oberschlick v. Austria*).

4. Court of Appeal Amsterdam, 19 October 2000, Elro no. AA 7654.

5. President Court of Utrecht 20 September 2001, Elro no. AD 3844.

6. President Court of Amsterdam 5 April 2005, LJN no. AT 3177.

7. President Court of Breda, 15 July 1991, KG 1991/260.

8. President Court of Assen 1994, Mediaforum 1994, p. B68.

9. ECHR 15 February 2005 (*Steel and Morris v. the U.K.*).

10. Supreme Court 22 April 1986, NJ 1986/827.

11. Cf. Court of Arnhem 1 April 1999, Mediaforum 1999-5, nr. 27.

12. Court of Appeal Amsterdam 27 April 2000, Mediaforum 2000-7/8, nr. 45.

13. ECHR 8 July 1986, NJ 1987, 901.

14. ECHR 24 June 2004, Mediaforum 7/8, nr. 27 (*Caroline of Monaco*).

15. Supreme Court 24 June 1983, NJ 1984, 801 (*Council Member X*).

16. ECHR 20 May 1999, no. 21980/03 (*Bladet Tromso*).

17. ECHR 25 June 1992, Ars Aequi, 1993-9, 687–93.

18. ECHR 23 September 1994, Series A no. 298, p. 23 (*Jersild v. Denmark*).

19. Cf. Court of Appeal The Hague 25 May 1993, Mediaforum 1993, p. B62 and Court of Appeal Den Bosch 18 February 1999, Mediaforum 1999-3, nr. 17.

20. Supreme Court 6 January 1995, NJ 1995/422 (*Parool – Van Gasteren*).

21. ECHR 2 May 2000, NJ 2001/65 (*Bergens Tidende*).

22. ECHR Bladet Tromso, see note 11 above, and Supreme Court 15 June 1990, NJ 1990/432 (*McDonalds*).

23. President Court of Maastricht, 28 January 1998, KG 1998, 81.

24. ECHR Bladet Tromso, see note 11 above, and Supreme Court 15 June 1990, NJ 1990/432 (*McDonalds*).

25. Council of State (judiciary department) 2 January 1986, AB 1986, 216.

26. Cf. ECHR 11 January 2000, NJ 2001/74 (*News Verlag*); Court of Appeal Amsterdam 25 February 1960, NJ 1960/502; Court of Amsterdam 14 August 1996, Mediaforum 1997-5, B78-82; President Court of Amsterdam 1 December 1988, KG 1989, 15.

27. Supreme Court 2 May 2003, Mediaforum 2003/6, nr. 30 (*Storms/Niessen*).

28. Supreme Court 9 January 1987, Computerrecht 187-2, 110–15.

29. Supreme Court 4 March 1988, NJ 1989/367 (*Children De Bourbon Parma*).

30. Court of Amsterdam 10 July 1996, Mediaforum 1996-10, pp. B136–B138 (*Wasteland*).

31. Supreme Court 21 January 1994, NJ 1994/473 (*Ferdi E.*).

32. Court of Haarlem 19 August 1997, Mediaforum 1997-9, pp. B130–B132 (*Van der Meyden*).

33. ECHR 21 January 1999, NJ 1999, 713 (*Fressoz and Roire*).

34. Court of Amsterdam 28 October 1998, NJ 1990/440 (*Huibregtsen v. De Volkskrant*).

35. Court of Appeal Amsterdam 22 June 1989, KG 1989/344 (*Nieuwe Revu v. Stuart*).

36. Court of Amsterdam 2 January 1996, Mediaforum 1996-2, pp. B30–B35.

37. ECHR 27 March 1996, NJ 1996/577 (*Goodwin*) and Supreme Court 10 May 1996, NJ 1996/578 (*V.d. Biggelaar/Dohmen en Langenberg*).

38. Court of The Hague 9 June 1999, Computerrecht 1999, pp. 200–205. Confirmed on appeal Court of Appeal The Hague 4 September 2003, Mediaforum 2003-10, nr. 45.

39. Court of Appeal Amsterdam 7 November 2002 (*Deutsche Bahn v. XS4ALL*).

40. Court of First Instance Amsterdam 20 June 2002 (*Deutsche Bahn v. Indymedia*).

41. Council Regulation (EC) No 44/2001 of 22 December 2000 on jurisdiction and the recognition and enforcement of judgments in civil and commercial matters.

42. European Court of Justice 7 March 1995, NJ 1996/269 (*Shevill v. Presse Alliance*).

CHAPTER 17

Russian Federation

ANNA OTKINA, NELLIE ALEXANDROVA,
AND ELENA KIRILLOVA

Denton Wilde Sapte

Denton Wilde Sapte—Moscow Office
Bolshaya Dmitrovka 7/5
Building 2
Moscow
Russia
125009
Phone: +7 095 255 7900
Fax: +7 095 255 7901
www.dentonwildesapte.com
moscow@dentonwildesapte.com
anna.otkina@dentonwildesapte.com
nellie.alexandrova@dentonwildesapte.com

Denton Wilde Sapte—London Office
One Fleet Place
London EC4M 7WS
United Kingdom
Phone: +44 (0) 20 7242 1212
Fax: +44 (0) 20 7246 7777
www.dentonwildesapte.com
elena.kirillova@dentonwildesapte.com

Introduction to the Russian Legal System

The Constitution of the Russian Federation of 1993 spurred a significant reform of the Russian legal system. The Russian system, based on the tenets of civil law, has a three-branch court system. The three branches include a four-level "regular" court system with a court of last resort (Supreme Court) for civil and criminal actions, a three-level arbitration court system for business-related actions, and a constitutional court system composed of one Supreme Court for constitutional actions.

The "regular" court system is similar to the traditional hierarchical structure in many other countries. There are four levels of courts: the Supreme Court of the Russian Federation, supreme courts of the republics, *krai* and *oblast* courts, and courts of cities of federal importance.

Almost every civil or criminal action is initially heard in the People's

Court. Each city, or area, has a People's Court that, unlike many other civil law systems, does not organize courts by the subject matter of the case being tried. The appeals process is in a hierarchical structure, from an intermediate court to the Supreme Court.

There are several methods of determining a verdict in a case. The most common structure of adjudicating bodies consists of either a panel of three judges or a single judge. The reform of the mid-1990s led to experimentation with twelve-member juries. Juries are currently reserved for serious crimes that are designated to *oblast* courts.

1. What is the locally accepted definition of libel?

Libel is a criminal offense, and defamation is a civil offense.

Criminal Law

The Criminal Code of the Russian Federation No. 63-FZ dated 13 June 1996 (the "Criminal Code") defines libel in section 17 as "Crimes against the freedom, honour and dignity of a person" by "spreading (circulation) of deliberately false information denigrating the honour and dignity of a person or undermining his reputation."[1] "Spreading or circulation" is understood by the Criminal Code as communication of information to one or more persons other than the claimant in written, oral, or video form.[2]

The Criminal Code has been read to mean that "disseminating deliberately false information" means that the speaker knows the information is false or that it could be false.[3]

Under the Criminal Code, the statement itself must be capable of defamatory meaning, and has been read to require a statement of a fact evidencing that the subject of the publication is in breach of the law or of any moral values. This requires that the sued-upon statement must be specific and contain factual statements capable of being verified. By contrast, a statement that someone is "bad" is a matter of personal opinion and is not sufficiently specific to constitute criminal libel.

Like other criminal laws, libel is also capable of being an aggravated offense, and two specific instances are most likely to occur: (1) "libel contained in a public speech or in a work performed in the public or in mass media," and (2) "a defamatory statement alleging that a person has committed a grave crime." An aggravated libel is punishable by either four or six months' detention, or by up to three years' imprisonment. (An ordinary libel is punishable by a fine,[4] in the amount of the defendant's monthly income, or up to one year of penitentiary works.)

Accusing a person or entity of committing a serious crime is the basis of most criminal libel claims. *A and B v. D* (1999) is such a case, wherein the Lomonosov Regional court of the city of Arhangelsk found that in an interview to a newspaper and his letter to the president of the Russian Federation, Mr. D "circulated deliberately false and denigrating information regarding Mr. A and Mr. B, stating that they had committed a serious crime."[5] According to Mr. D, in 1989 Mr. A and Mr. B, being employed by the state legal entity "Arkhangelskribprom," sold to another legal entity in Germany a batch of crayfish for the value of US$740,000. Mr. D alleged that this money was subsequently stolen by Mr. A and Mr. B and used to establish their own business. Mr. D was convicted of aggravated libel. On appeal, the guilty verdict was reversed. Mr. D was found innocent and the decisions of the lower courts were reversed. In its decision the Supreme Court looked at the factual as well as formal requirements of part 3 Article 129 of the Criminal Code. Criminal libel requires that the circulated information must be distributed with knowing falsity: a difficult standard to meet. According to the facts of the case, Mr. D had been in charge of an investigation related to embezzlement at "Arkhangelskribprom" and had documents indicating that Mr. A and Mr. B were directly involved in receipt of the money in the transaction in question. However, the criminal investigation of the matter by the local prosecution office was not completed. Recognizing the difference between an error and an intentional falsity, the Supreme Court concluded that under the circumstances Mr. D could have been genuinely confused as to the real circumstances of the case and therefore found him not guilty of libel.

By contrast, in *Antoshin v. Rzhevsky* (2003) the trial court of the city of Kalitva found Mr. Rzhevsky guilty of aggravated libel. The court found that in July 2002, during a meeting of the city council in the presence of 147 people, Mr. Rzhevsky publicly claimed that Mr. Antoshin, the deputy mayor of the city, was guilty of embezzlement of RUR 10 million granted as part of federal support of the coal mining industry of the city of Kalitva. The court found that the allegation of embezzlement had been the subject of a previous investigation by the local prosecutor's office and was found to be untrue. Before making his defamatory statement, Mr. Rzhevsky had already obtained written conclusions from the office of the prosecutor to this effect. Therefore, at the time of making the statement, Mr. Rzhevsky knew that he was circulating deliberately false and denigrating information and was therefore guilty of criminal libel.[6]

In practice, few courts in the Russian Federation actually apply the criminal sanctions to libel, because of the difficulty of proving the knowing falsity that law requires. It should be noted, though, as a civil law jurisdiction, Russian courts do not recognize court precedent as a formal source of the law, and although the lower courts generally take account of and follow the recommendations and legal practice of the Supreme Court of the Russian Federation (the "Supreme Court"), each case is reviewed independently on its merits and with reference to the statutory provisions of the law.[7]

Civil Law

Unlike the criminal context, the defamatory meaning required in civil law to trigger liability is considerably broader: a statement simply "discrediting the honour, dignity or business reputation" made in the mass media.

The civil law is designed to protect persons against defamation under the heading of "protection of freedom, dignity and business reputation" (Article 152 of the Civil Code of the Russian Federation No. 51-FZ dated 30 November 1994 [the "Civil Code"]). The Article provides as follows: "any person has the right to demand in court the refutation of communications defaming his honour, dignity, or business reputation, unless the person who disseminated of such communications shows that they correspond to reality."

By contrast to the criminal courts, the commercial courts of the Russian Federation[8] hear annually a substantial number of cases on protection of freedom, dignity, and business reputation. The courts are mindful of the right of the mass media to fair comment, as provided by the Mass Media Law, and thus, many claims are unsuccessful, on the basis that the statements in question are either true or within the protection for fair comment.[9]

In *"Alliance Group" v. "Publishing House of Rossiskaya Gazeta"* (2004), the publicly traded "Alliance Group" filed a claim against "Publishing House of Rossiskaya Gazeta." The claimant asked the court to rule the publication of an article to be false and discrediting its honor, dignity, and business reputation. The article in the newspaper *Rossiskaya Gazeta,* said that Alliance Group, using "dodgy methods of business," corrupted officials and participated with criminals to the detriment of the Russian economy. The Commercial Court of the city of Moscow found the newspaper liable for defamation and ordered them to publish a retraction of the allegations made in the article. The appellate court reserved its decision and reviewed the case de novo. In its decision, the appellate Federal Commercial Court of the Moscow Region stated that the lower court failed to give sufficient weight to the following points: (1) whether the claimant had proved the allegations made in the article were false; and (2) whether the statements made in the article in fact could be considered "an opinion" of the journalist and thus fall within the definition of fair comment.[10]

2. Is libel-by-implication recognized, or, in the alternative, must the complained-of words alone defame the plaintiff?

The Criminal Code and the Civil Code each take the position that in order to constitute a libel, the defamatory statement has to be clear and precise and must make factual allegations, the truth of which is capable of verification.

3. May corporations sue for libel?

Yes. Any legal entity can sue for libel. Criminal proceedings for libel are brought by a public prosecutor following a complaint of a person or a legal entity. A civil lawsuit is initiated by a claimant for protection of honor, dignity, or reputation.

4. Is product disparagement recognized, and if so, how does that differ from libel?

Product disparagement is prohibited by Article 6 of the Federal Law No. 108-FZ dated 18 July 1995, "On Advertising" (the "Advertising Law"), where it is regarded to be a part of unfair advertising practice. Unfair advertising practice is understood to be any advertising which:

- discredits legal or natural persons who do not use the advertised product;
- contains tactless comparisons of the advertised product with other product(s) of other legal or natural persons, as well as containing statements or images denigrating the honour, dignity or business reputation of competitor(s);
- "misleads consumers as to the advertised product by way of imitation (copying, resembling) images, texts, advertising logos, pictures, musical or sound effects which have been used in the advertisement of other products, or by way of abuse of the trust of natural persons or misuse of their lack of experience or lack of knowledge, including by omitting of a part of significant information from the advertisement."[11]

There are two ways of bringing actions against unfair advertising: either to file a complaint with the State Antimonopoly Committee (an administrative process), or to initiate litigation in a court of general jurisdiction or a state commercial (commercial) court (a civil law process). The remedies in each case can include a refutation,[12] fine(s), and/or damages.[13]

In addition, the Advertising Law distinguishes similar offenses such as "inaccurate advertising" (Article 7), "unethical advertising" (Article 8), and "intentionally false advertising" (Article 9), all of which are prohibited.

5. Must an individual be clearly identified (by name or photograph) to sue for libel? Can a group of persons sue for libel, even though not named?

The claimant must be ascertainable by name or by photograph to be able to sue for libel. The right to bring an action is of a personal nature and is vested only with a natural person (who can appear in a court in person or via his representative), or a legal entity (which can be represented in a court).

A group of individuals, which might be identified by certain criteria (e.g., religion, profession, employment by the same company, etc.) cannot bring an action for libel. Such action must be brought by each individual who will have to prove that the defamatory statement concerns him personally (and not him as a member of the group). However, where all suits are brought against the same defendant, they can all be brought at the same time and a judge can decide to hear all the cases together.

6. What is the fault standard(s) applied to libel?

In order to be liable for libel, the person has to have acted in bad faith, although there is not much direction as to what constitutes "bad faith." It has been suggested that in the civil context, reporters will be held liable for careless, sloppy, or reckless reporting techniques that result in a false and defamatory publication. In criminal libel, the statutes require that the publisher act with knowing falsity.

a. Does the fault standard depend on the fame or notoriety of the plaintiff?

No, the fault standard has no relevance whatsoever to the social standing of the claimant.

b. Is there a heightened fault standard or privilege for reporting on matters of public concern or public interest?

There is no diversity of fault standard depending on whether the matter is of public concern or public interest.

7. Is financial news about publicly traded companies, or companies involved with a government contract, considered a matter of public interest or otherwise privileged?

Not generally. Furthermore, all Russian open joint stock companies (publicly traded companies) are bound by various reporting and disclosure requirements, particularly in relation to their major financial results and corporate governance events.[14] The standards for such disclosure are much higher in situations of public offering and placement by stocks and bonds,[15] or when securities are listed and traded at stock exchanges,[16] or reporting of banking institutions.[17] Information on corporate mergers and acquisitions in excess of 20 percent of stock is also subject to reporting and disclosure requirements.[18]

Finance, banking, and insurance businesses and those dealing with investments are restricted in the types of information they can include in their advertisements by the Advertising Law. For example, it will be contrary to the Advertising Law, if such a company makes representations or promises on its profitability in the future, or guarantees dividends on its ordinary stocks, or makes any statements as to the future growth of the market value of its securities.[19] A similar requirement is contained in the Federal Law No. 39-FZ dated 22 April 1996, "On Securities Market," specifically in relation to the public offering of stocks, bonds, and derivatives.

8. Is there a recognized protection for opinion or "fair comment" on matters of public concern?

Yes. The right of fair comment as well as the prohibition on any kind of censorship are provided for in the Mass Media Law.[20] However, this right is balanced against the limitations set out by the Criminal and Civil Codes on libel. The rights guaranteed to publishers are not absolute and must also be balanced against the prohibitions of disclosure of state secrets and any other statutorily protected information.

In *LLC "AN Rosbuilding" v. closed joint stock company Publishing House "Ekonomicheskaya Gazeta"* (2004), the defendants published an article stating that "sooner or later it is possible to become a victim of skillful speculators like Rosbuilding." The claimaint sued, alleging that the statement discredited its honor, dignity, and business reputation. The claim was denied, and the court referred to Article 47 of the Mass Media Law and the right of the journalist to fair comment. The court did not find that the statement was defamatory, because the statement did not allege provably false facts, and was found to be the personal view of the author of the article. The court offered its linguistic analysis of the statement and found that the words "skillful speculators" can be viewed only as the author's personal opinion and are allowed under the Mass Media Law as a matter of personal comment, whether positive or negative.[21] The appellate court upheld the decision.

9. Are there any requirements upon a plaintiff, such as demand for retraction or right of reply, and if so, what impact do they have?

Article 43 of the Mass Media Law provides that claimants have a right to demand retraction of any audio, video, or printed publication. The retraction should be made in the same form as the defamatory statement. If the statement was made in a printed form, the retraction should be published on the same page as the original statement, and if broadcast, it should be broadcast at the same time.

The right of retraction does not exclude the rights of the claimant to bring an action in court. Retraction is regarded as a remedy of supplementary nature and does not prevent the claimant from claiming full damages or loss, including moral damage, that have resulted from the defamatory publication.

10. Is there a privilege for quoting or reporting on:

a. Papers filed in court?

Provided that the republication is accurate, Russian law provides immunity for statements made in these contexts. According to Article 57 of the Mass Media Law, liability for dissemination of false or dishonoring information shall not attach if the mass media organization proves that it has merely reproduced a press release issued by a state body, an organization, an institution, or a social association, or alternatively, that the information has been reproduced from an official response to a request sent by such mass media organization.

b. Government-issued documents?

Yes, as above.

c. Quasi-governmental proceedings?

There are no particular privileges on such materials. As a matter of practice, mass media often follow the exact wording of press releases in relation to quasi-governmental proceedings, because this most likely relieves them from any liability under Article 57.

11. Is there a privilege for republishing statements made earlier by other, bona fide, reliable publications or wire services?

Yes. Under the Mass Media Law, the mass media organization is exempted from liability for republication where: (1) the statement republished is a word-for-word copy of the information or the statement previously made by another public source; and (2) this source can be located and if false and defamatory, held liable under Russian law.[22]

In *LLC "Pentakom" v. LLC "NPF Softvideo"* (2002), LLC "Pentakom" filed the claim against LLC "NPF Softvideo" in the Commercial Court of the Moscow Region, claiming that the defendant broadcast false and denigrating information on the claimant's business activities. In the television program in question a reference was made to different newspaper articles as the source of information. The claim was denied. In its decision the court referred to the Mass Media Law and stated that the publishing house or the news agency is not liable for any defamatory information where the latter was reproduced from another media publication, and the latter could be located as the source of information.[23]

12. Are there any restrictions regarding reporting on:

a. Ongoing criminal investigations?

Yes. Reporting on ongoing criminal investigations is not allowed unless consented to by a public prosecutor or by an investigator in charge. Dissemination of such information may lead to criminal liability under Article 310 of the Criminal Code. Presidential Decree No. 188 dated 6 March 1997 (the "1997 Presidential Decree") introduced a "List of Types of Information Regarded Confidential" which covers information obtained during a criminal investigation.

In the event that an investigatory search of a home brings to light certain circumstances of a person's intimate life, the investigator is obliged by law to take steps necessary to prevent further disclosure of such circumstances to the public.[24] If a criminal investigation requires any intrusion into a person's private life (for example, by conducting a personal search or a search of a person's home; removing personal belongings, seizing correspondence, recording conversations, etc.), such actions currently require a prior approval of a public prosecutor, or, alternatively, a court decision. The option for a public prosecutor's approval is abolished as of January 1, 2004.[25]

No information obtained during a criminal investigation may be disclosed unless such disclosure has been specifically approved by a public prosecutor or an investigator in charge and only to the extent it is justified by good reason. No disclosure of information relating to the private life of parties to a criminal investigation or criminal prosecution can be made without their consent.[26]

b. Ongoing criminal prosecutions?

If a criminal case is heard in open court, there are no specific restrictions on covering it in the press. A journalist attending the hearing may take notes (including shorthand notes), or make sketches, or even make audio recordings, unless it interferes with the proceedings.

However, specific permission of a judge is required for filming, taking photographs in a courtroom, or broadcasting proceedings on radio and television.[27] Similar rules apply in relation to commercial litigation in a commercial court[28] and to proceedings on civil law matters in a court of general jurisdiction.[29] A judge can make a decision to permit or not to permit these actions, either on his own initiative or in response to a request of any party to the proceedings.

When a criminal case is heard in a court, judges traditionally deal with protection of privacy, for example, by ruling on holding closed hearings, particularly where facts of intimate personal life will be discussed.[30] Similarly, the identity of crime victims may not be disclosed without consent prior to publication.[31]

c. Ongoing regulatory investigations?

There is no specific regulation of this issue, but it is customary to hold regulatory investigations in closed proceedings.

d. Ongoing civil litigation, or other judicial proceedings?

Although civil litigation is traditionally open to the public, the law requires that civil or administrative hearings must be held closed if the discussions may lead to the exposure of facts of the person's private life (e.g., adoption of a child), or any other secrets protected by law.[32]

Most proceedings in a civil law court are of open character; however, where the case involves a state secret or a secret of adoption, a judge will rule on keeping the proceedings closed (which means that no information leaves the courtroom). Judges have discretion to keep the proceedings closed in other circumstances too, for example, responding to a request filed by one of the parties, if it is motivated by prevention of disclosure of a commercial secret, protection of private life, or any other right or interest the court deems legitimate.[33] Similar rules are provided by the Commercial Procedure Code in relation to litigation in a state commercial court.[34]

Covering cases involving juveniles requires special care. The Mass Media Law provides for additional protection for young persons (those under 18 years old) who are involved in criminal or administrative proceedings. Their identities are treated as confidential information in itself. Editors may not bring to the public any information which leads explicitly or implicitly to the identification of a young person who has committed a crime, or is suspected in the commission of a crime, or has committed an administrative offense or any other action of antisocial character, without the consent of the person in question or his legitimate representative.

13. Are prior restraints or other prepublication injunctions available on the basis of libel or privacy, and if so, what are the standards for obtaining such relief?

Generally, interference or restraints prior to the publishing of any materials or information is not allowed.[35] However, secrecy is required by legislation in certain situations. For example, the Mass Media Law provides that mass media sources may be restrained in relation to "disclosure of any information constituting a state secret or other secret information specifically protected by law."[36] If a mass media source discloses information regarded as a state secret, this will qualify as "a misuse of freedom of information" under Article 59 of the Mass Media Law and could lead to a range of criminal and administrative penalties and liabilities.

The same approach is taken by Federal Law No. 5485-1 dated 21 July 1993, "On State Secrets," which limits access to and reporting on any information related to state secrets to persons with due authorization.

In case of pending litigation, injunctive relief (i.e., restraining a defamatory publication) may be sought under Article 91 of the Commercial Procedure Code, or Article 140 of the Civil Procedure Code, which contain identical rules on this issue. Both laws allow the judge to "prohibit a defendant from taking certain actions before hearing the case if this is necessary in order to prevent further violation of somebody's rights."

14. Is a right of privacy recognized (either civilly or criminally)?

It is recognized in a number of legal sources. Primarily, the Constitution of the Russian Federation (the "Constitution") recognizes a right for privacy as a principal right of an individual: "Everyone shall have the right to the inviolability of private life, personal and family secrets, the protection of honour and good name."[37] The Constitution also states that: "The collection, keeping, use and dissemination of information about the private life of a person shall not be allowed without his or her consent."[38]

Violation of privacy may be actionable on different grounds, including criminal prosecution, depending on the nature of information disclosed. For example, it is a criminal offense to illegally collect or disseminate information on the private life of a person which is his/her personal or family secret.[39] Alternatively, a civil action may be brought in order to protect inviolability of private life, personal and family secrets, and such claims are often coupled with claims for moral damage. In case of a positive outcome, compensation at the discretion of the court and retraction may be awarded (although sometimes courts also award apologies which are, strictly speaking, not on the legislative list of potential remedies).

If privacy has been violated by a state body, an official, or a nongovernmental organization, the action may be brought on the basis of Article 2 of the Law "On Challenging to Courts any Actions and Decisions that Violate Rights and Freedoms of Citizens," No. 4866-1 dated 27 April 1993.

Truth is not a defense to privacy claims, and the law seeks to redress the intrusive nature of the crime or tort. One recent example was a claim based on the filming of a couple during their wedding. The seven-second fragment of the film was featured in a television program devoted to marriages, and also appeared in promotional spots for the program, which turned on the theory that "all marriages via advertisements are 'calculated marriages'." Broadcasting of the film in such a program suggested that these newlyweds met each other through a marriage advertisement, which was actually true, but nevertheless was considered an unwanted intrusion into their private life, heightened by the negative comment on such marriages made in the program.

The court ruled in favor of the couple, taking into account that they were recognizable in the video recording included in the program, although no names or other personal data were broadcast in the program.

a. What is the definition of "private fact"?

There is no commonly recognized legislative definition of a "private fact," and its interpretations vary widely.

The 1997 Presidential Decree does not contain the term "private fact," but effectively outlines this concept by qualifying as confidential "any information on facts, events or circumstances of a private life of an individual, which allows his/her personality (personal data) to be identified, except for any information that is subject to dissemination in mass media in the circumstances set up by Federal laws." A nonexhaustive list includes: information with limited accessibility derived from professional activity (such as a medical secret,[40] an attorney-at-law's secret); correspondence; telephone, postal, or telegraph communications; a secret of adoption;[41] a secret of confession;[42] a secret of will and other actions of a notary;[43] a secret of monetary deposits;[44] and a secret of personal data. This also extends to impermissibility to have a person shadowed and to have private conversations overheard.[45]

A similar approach is taken by the Federal Law "On Information, Informatization and Protection of Information" No. 24-FZ dated 20 February 1995 ("Law on Information"), which states the following: "Collecting, storing, using or disseminating any information on private life as well as any information violating a personal secret, a family secret, a secret of correspondence, a secret of telephone communications, postal, telegraph or other communications of an individual without his consent is not allowed, unless it is based on a court decision."[46]

b. Is there a public interest or newsworthiness exception?

Not in the legislation, but there is a common understanding of the situations which would justify intrusion into someone's private life for the sake of the public interest. The examples are as follows: (1) investigation of a crime or other serious offense; (2) protection of health or public security; (3) protection of the public from a fraud attempted by a person or by an organization through any word of mouth or any actions; (4) bringing to the public's attention the significant incompetence of an official. In each case, proportionality between any action and the public interest served is required.

c. Is the right of privacy based in common law, statute, or constitution?

The right of privacy is based on the Constitution.

15. May reporters tape-record their own telephone conversations for note-taking purposes (not rebroadcast) without the consent of the other party?

No. Article 49 of the Mass Media Law requires that journalists must let sources know that they are being recorded.

16. If permissible to record such tapes, may they be broadcast without permission?

The broadcasting of tape-recordings made without the consent of the source of information (as set out in Question 15 above) is admissible in the following situations:

1. if such broadcasting does not violate the constitutional rights of an individual, for example, by identifying them; or
2. if it is necessary for protection of a public interest and all measures have been taken not to identify a third party without a good reason; or
3. if such broadcasting is based on a court decision.[47]

17. Is there a recognized evidentiary privilege preventing the disclosure of confidential sources relied upon by reporters?

There is a limited shield law, but prosecutors would most likely succeed in overcoming it.

18. In the event that legal papers are served upon the newsroom (such as a civil complaint), are there any particular warnings about accepting service of which we should be aware?

No, except those that relate to general civil procedure. Under the Civil Procedure Code of the Russian Federation No. 138-FZ dated 14 November 2002 (the "Civil Procedure Code"), the service of summons is effected either via registered mail or by personal delivery. The time of delivery is reflected in the receipt which is returned to the court. The summonses are served either on a particular journalist, or if the claim is against a company, on its authorized representative (e.g., an editor in chief). One can refuse to accept the summons, in which case the person effecting delivery makes a note on the receipt, and for the purpose of litigation this is regarded as effective service.

19. Has your jurisdiction applied established media law to Internet publishers?

Currently in the Russian Federation there is no specific legislation regulating the rights and obligations of Internet publishers. Nevertheless, the courts of the Russian Federation have developed a practice of applying the Mass Media Law to Internet publishers. However, as the Russian Federation does not have a system of precedent, such court practice will vary depending on the case and application of the law by the particular court.

Currently in Russia there could be three different parties involved in administering an Internet site: (1) the domain owner, which is the person in whose name the domain is in fact registered; (2) the person who is providing the technical support or content of the Internet site; and (3) the person on whose behalf the Internet site provides the information. In practice often all of the above-mentioned parties are different legal entities. The legal issue arises as to who should be responsible for any defamatory publications on the site. The courts are of the opinion that the responsibility should rest with those entities for whose benefit such site is in fact administered. Although the actual registration of the domain name may lie with another party, such "beneficiaries" are considered to be the owners of the sites.[48]

Another legal issue arises out of the question of which law should apply to the Internet publishers. Formally, an Internet publisher does not fall within the definition of a mass media source. As a consequence of the latter, publishers are currently trying to avoid the liability attached to the registered media by the use of disclaimers, stating that: (1) they are not required under the law to register; and (2) the Internet web pages are merely their "hobby."[49] The courts, however, are increasingly taking the approach that (1) the legislation on libel as well as on protection of freedom, dignity, and business reputation should be applicable to Internet publishers independently of their legal "status"; and (2) Internet publishers should be regarded as an electronic mass media source.

In at least one case, it appears that there is no immunity for Web site operators who host chat rooms, despite not knowing about the content of postings in those rooms. In *"Troyka steel" v. LLC "Megasoft"* (2004), "Troyka steel" filed a claim against "Megasoft," claiming that the information posted in a chat room hosted on its Internet site www.metaltorg.ru, denigrated its honor and dignity and undermined its reputation. Subtance of the postings aside, Megasoft argued that: (1) it cannot be considered an entity circulating the information on Internet site www.metaltorg.ru as neither the site nor the respondent can be considered a mass media source; and (2) the fact that the site belongs to the respondent does not mean that it should be responsible for the denigrating information published in the chat room of the site. The Federal Commercial Court of the Moscow Region ruled in favor of the claimant, applying the provisions of the Civil Code and stating that: (1) the liability for publishing information denigrating honor and dignity of a person or undermining his reputation is not directly linked with the status of the legal entity as a mass media source; and (2) the fact of creating and supporting the site by the defendant made it possible for such denigrating publications to take place.[50]

20. If established media law has been applied to Internet publishers, are there any ways in which Internet publishers (including chat room operators) have to meet different standards?

No. The analysis in Question 19 above applies.

21. Are there any cases where the courts enforced a judgment in libel from another jurisdiction against a publisher in your jurisdiction?

We are not aware of any such cases. Any foreign judgment in the Russian Federation is enforced on the basis of a convention for the mutual recognition of judgments. Currently Russia has entered few such conventions, except with the countries of the former USSR.

Chapter Notes

1. Article 129, the Criminal Code.

2. Article 129, the Criminal Code.

3. Article 129, the Criminal Code.

4. A statutory minimum wage currently amounts to Rubles 100 (approximately US$3.40).

5. The Decision of the Supreme Court of the Russian Federation dated 29 June 1999 (abstract from the ruling).

6. "The court found Rzhevsky guilty of libel," article from the newspaper *Perekrestok,* dated 20 November 2003.

7. The review of the cases by the Supreme Court or any other high court of the Russian Federation is intended only for the purpose of observing diligent and accurate interpretation of the law by the relevant courts. Constitution of the Russian Federation 1993, Chapter 7.

8. The word "commercial" in this context is used only for the purpose of defining

the type of courts, which review the cases between the legal entities in the Russian Federation.

9. For more detailed analysis of the matters related to fair comment, see the discussion in Question 8 of this chapter.

10. The Decision of the Federal Commercial Court of the Moscow Region dated 14 October 2004 No. кг-А40/8331-04.

11. Article 6, the Advertising Law.

12. Article 29, the Advertising Law.

13. Article 31, the Advertising Law.

14. Article 92 of the Federal Law No. 208-FZ dated 26 December 1995 "On Joint Stock Companies" specifies the major types of information subject to disclosure and reporting requirements; the detailed procedure is governed by "Procedure for Publication of Annual Book Accounts by Open Joint Stock Companies" approved by Ministry of Finance on 28 November 1996 No. 101.

15. "Statute on Procedure and Volume of Disclosure of Information by Open Joint Stock Companies in Relation to Placement of Stocks and Securities Convertible to Stocks through Subscription," approved by the Federal Commission for Securities Market ("FCSM") No. 9 dated 20 April 1998; Resolution of the FCSM No. 8 dated 7 May 1996.

16. Resolution of the FCSM No. 1-PS dated 4 January 2002.

17. Statute of the Central Bank of Russia No. 227-P dated 14 May 2003 "On Order for Keeping Records and Submission of Information on Affiliated Persons of Credit Organisations."

18. "Statute on Procedure for Publication of Information on Acquisition by a Joint Stock Company of more than 20% of Voting Shares in another Joint Stock Company," approved by FCSM on 14 May 1996 No. 10.

19. Article 17, the Advertising Law.

20. Article 3, the Mass Media Law.

21. Decision of the Federal Commercial Court of the Moscow Region dated 5 October 2004 No. кг-А40/8753-04.

22. Article 57, the Mass Media Law.

23. Decision of the Federal Commercial Court of the Moscow Region dated 21 February 2002 No. кг-А41/609-02.

24. Article 182, the Criminal Procedure Code.

25. Articles 29 and 182–186, the Criminal Procedure Code.

26. Article 161, the Criminal Procedure Code.

27. Article 241, the Criminal Procedure Code.

28. Article 11, the Commercial Procedure Code.

29. Article 10, the Civil Procedure Code.

30. Article 241, the Criminal Procedure Code.

31. Article 41, the Mass Media Law.

32. Article 10, the Civil Procedure Code; Article 24.3, the Code of Administrative Offenses; Article 241, the Criminal Procedure Code.

33. Article 10, the Civil Procedure Code.

34. Article 11, the Commercial Procedure Code.

35. Article 3 and 57, the Mass Media Law.

36. Article 4, the Mass Media Law.

37. Article 23, the Constitution of the Russian Federation.

38. Article 24, the Constitution of the Russian Federation.

39. Article 137, the Criminal Code.

40. Protection of medical secrets has been consistently dealt with in a few other sources, such as Articles 30 and 61 of the Basics of Health Protection of Citizens; Article 9 of the Law "On Mental Help and Guarantees to Individuals Taking It"; Article 52 of the Federal Law "On Sanitary-Epidemiological Well Being of Population"; and Article 12 of the Law "On Avoidance of Spreading out of Tuberculosis in Russian Federation."

41. Article 139, the Family Code; Article 155, the Criminal Code.

42. Article 3 of the Federal Law "On Freedom of Conscience and Religious Associations."

43. Article 1123, the Civil Code.

44. Article 857, the Civil Code; Article 26 of the Federal Law "On Banks and Banking Activities."

45. Article 11, the Law on Information.

46. Article 11, the Law on Information.

47. Article 50, the Mass Media Law.

48. "Retraction of the information on the Internet: legal peculiarities," V.V. Bulichev, *Zakonodatelstvo,* N9, October 2004.

49. "Internet will be viewed as Mass Media," dated 8 July 2004, http://www.media-online.ru.

50. Decision of Federal Commercial Court of Moscow Region dated 9 March 2004 No. кт-А41/390-04.

CHAPTER **18**

Spain

ALMUDENA ARPÓN DE MENDÍVIL AND
SANTIAGO LARDIÉS

Gómez-Acebo & Pombo

Gómez-Acebo & Pombo
Paseo de la Castellana, 216
28046 Madrid, Spain
Phone: (34) 91 582 91 00
Fax: (34) 91 582 91 20
www.gomezacebo-pombo.com
aam@gomezacebo-pombo.com
slardies@gomezacebo-pombo.com

Introduction to the Spanish Legal System

The Spanish Constitution of 1978 provides the framework for the Spanish legal system, and the Organic Law of the Judicial Power contains that country's fundamental laws. As described in the Constitution, the General Council of the Judiciary (*Consejo General del Poder Judicial*) is the sole group controlling the Judicial System. The Council is composed of twelve judges and eight lawyers and other established legal professionals. Council members serve a five-year term and may not serve beyond one term.

Spain is divided into several levels of geographical judicial areas. These areas, from smallest to largest, are municipalities, judicial districts, provinces, and autonomous communities. Municipalities only have courts of the peace, judicial districts have courts of first instance, provinces have provincial courts, and autonomous communities have a high court of justice. The Supreme Court and the National Court are the only courts with complete jurisdiction.

Spanish courts are also organized by subject matter. Civil and commercial issues are addressed in civil courts, criminal offenses are heard in criminal courts, social security and employment issues are heard in social courts, and the administrative court is used for public administrative issues. The courts are in a hierarchical structure where lower court decisions can be appealed to higher courts and higher court opinions override those of the lower courts.

1. What is the locally accepted definition of libel?

The Dictionary of the Royal Academy of the Spanish Language defines libel as "the act of discrediting someone by publishing something against his/her good opinion or fame."

Under Spanish law, defamatory meaning is broad, and libel is most often defined as "an illegitimate intrusion in someone's right of honor" under the Organic Law 1/1982, of 5 May, on Right of Honor and Privacy (hereinafter, Law 1/1982). If serious enough, and if the communication in question is made in a public forum, it may also constitute a criminal offense sanctioned by the Spanish Criminal Code, which defines libel as "the action or statement that injures someone's dignity, discrediting his/her fame or as an attack on his/her own esteem."

The Constitutional Court, in Judgment 223/1992, defines libel as "harming the reputation of someone within the public consideration, as a consequence of statements expressed with discredit or disrespect or that were considered as an offence within the public context."

Slander is a higher or aggravated degree of libel, essentially the publication of a statement that similarly injures reputation, but is also made with the knowledge that the statement is false. Slander is also an offense under the Criminal Code.

Spanish law is also unforgiving with regard to hyperbolic language that might be seen as "insulting." For example, in Judgment 1882/2002, the Supreme Court found the following statement defamatory, in this case, made by Ramón Mendoza, a former president of Real Madrid Football Club: "There are people who manipulate the public opinion, and the biggest bastard of them is José María García, who, by means of lies and defamations, creates suspicion and doubts among Real Madrid supporters (...) Maybe when Mr. García speaks about some people's private life and their economic reputation he is trying to protect his friends, who are seated on the bench."

By contrast, in Judgment 3927/2000, the Supreme Court did not find defamatory an economic magazine calling a group of financial companies a "gang of swines" under the title "How to Hide Money." The Court held that these words could be defamatory, but not within a context referring to a well-reported financial scandal, which was of public significance and related to persons who held professions with a public scope. The Court also stated that the journalists carried out the required diligence in order to verify what they published. (See the discussion in Question 6 below.)

2. Is libel-by-implication recognized, or, in the alternative, must the complained-of words alone defame the plaintiff?

Libel-by-implication is recognized under Spanish law even though no reference is made in this regard in Law 1/1982. In order for the plaintiff to sue for libel, the individual needs to prove that the statements expressed in relation to him- or herself are defamatory within the context in which they were stated.

For example, the Supreme Court found a newspaper liable for publishing a letter that criticized, without evidence, how the principal of a school was appointed, and accusing the principal of getting his job through means that did not comply with all legal requirements. Although the words used were not libelous by themselves, these words, when taken as a whole, were found defamatory and the newspaper that published the letter was held liable for defaming the teacher (Judgment 679/2004).

3. May corporations sue for libel?

The Constitutional Court has established in various judgments that corporations may sue for libel.[1]

4. Is product disparagement recognized, and if so, how does that differ from libel?

Disparagement of products is generally limited to statements made by or between competitors in the marketplace, under Article 9 of the Law on Unfair Competition. Unfair competition may be found simply when the statement is capable of damaging the product's reputation within the relevant market. Likewise, publicity disparaging a competitor's product may also be considered as "unfair publicity" under Article 6 of the Law on General Publicity.

Product disparagement itself cannot be considered an illegitimate intrusion in the right of honor since only persons (either natural or corporate), and not products, are holders of dignitary rights. However, in very extraordinary cases, denigration of a product could be considered a libel upon the manufacturer's reputation.

5. Must an individual be clearly identified (by name or photograph) to sue for libel? Can a group of persons sue for libel, even though not named?

An individual does not need to be clearly identified to sue for libel as long as that person's honor, privacy, or image is damaged. A group of persons can also sue for libel, even though not named.[2] Group libel was recognized in 1991 when Spanish Jews brought a successful libel claim upon a statement made by a German World War II veteran: "If there are so many Jewish people, it is difficult to believe that they left crematoriums so alive; the problem with Jewish people is that they always want to be the victims, if they do not have enemies, they invent them (…) We need a leader (…) but nowadays there is not a person like the Fürher" (Constitutional Court Judgment 214/1991).

6. What is the fault standard(s) applied to libel?

It is worth noting that Spanish law conflates to a degree the right of privacy and the right to be free of defamatory falsehoods. In order for liability to attach, the defendant must have published either:

1. The disclosure of facts relating to someone's private life, which affects his/her reputation and good name; or
2. The attribution of facts or the expression of statements that injures someone's dignity, discrediting his/her fame; and
3. Either of the above publications must be unprivileged, that is, "an illegitimate intrusion" into the dignitary rights of the subject.

In civil libel, the fault standard is objective, not subjective, thus the author's state of mind is not relevant to a defense. The Constitutional Court defines "illegitimate intrusion" in the following manner:

- The facts or expressions do not serve the public interest.
- The information lacks the requirement of veracity (i.e., genuine efforts to verify the truth of the report, and generally accepted reportorial technique).
- Clearly humiliating, insulting, or opprobrious language with no relationship to the factual matter of general interest is used.

As regards the press and the freedom of speech, Spanish case law is still debating whether or not to apply a subjective standard in favor of the press, i.e., to exonerate the publication of untrue news when the media has used reasonably required efforts in order to find out the truth.

a. Does the fault standard depend on the fame or notoriety of the plaintiff?

In principle, no. However, the fault standard depends on the notoriety of the plaintiff in the sense that the greater the popularity of the affected person, the less right the person has to privacy.

b. Is there a heightened fault standard or privilege for reporting on matters of public concern or public interest?

Yes. Spanish law recognizes a public interest exception to defamation. This is narrowed by an examination into the truth-finding efforts of the reporter. News stories, even if defamatory, may not be the subject of liability when a historic, scientific, cultural, or public interest exists.[3] Public figures have also been deemed to have a limited right of privacy compared with ordinary individuals.[4]

In the civil context, truth is not an absolute defense to libel. If the public interest is not served by the publication, then liability may still attach. Truth is a defense to criminal libel in the narrow instance that the subject of the story is about government employees and relates to facts regarding the exercise of their public function or the commission of either criminal or administrative offenses.

7. Is financial news about publicly traded companies, or companies involved with a government contract, considered a matter of public interest or otherwise privileged?

Financial information regarding important known corporations and publicly traded companies is generally considered to be of public interest. The criteria applied to news about corporate activity do not differ from the general criteria applied to individuals. If the information published is in the public interest and the veracity of what is published was duly checked, the right of the press would prevail over the right of honor.

8. Is there a recognized protection for opinion or "fair comment" on matters of public concern?

Freedom of speech and the right to express opinions are fundamental rights recognized by the Spanish Constitution. Truthfulness of the opinion or the implications that an opinion might engender are not subject to the ordinary degree of diligence, as might be the case with a traditional news story.

However, the freedom of speech and opinion is not absolute. Therefore, if the opinion expressed by a reporter includes humiliating expressions directed at a person (natural or corporate), then an illegitimate intrusion in the right of honor may have occurred.

Protection of the freedom of speech and right to opinion is greater when opinions refer to matters of public concern or toward persons who hold a public service or profession. For example, the Supreme Court did not find defamatory the following statements included in a Spanish Socialist Party's press release: "The company La Palma TV is acting in a sectarian and partial way (…) The news broadcasted does not comply with the necessary pluralism and impartiality (…) they do what Coalición Canaria (the party in the government) orders them to do." The Court explained that damage to La Palma TV's honor did not occur since what the Socialist Party disseminated was criticism protected by the freedom of speech and right to opinion (Judgment 4937/2004. See also Judgments 336/1993 and 79/1995).

9. Are there any requirements upon a plaintiff, such as demand for retraction or right of reply, and if so, what impact do they have?

Yes. Aggrieved parties may make application to the Court for a right of reply. There is no requirement upon the plaintiff to demand a retraction before he or she files a complaint for libel. Section 2 of Article 9 of Law 1/1982 enumerates the remedies available to prevailing plaintiffs to put an end to the illegitimate intrusion against the right of honor and to be compensated for damages. The subject of a news story can choose one or more of the remedies granted by Law 1/1982:

• ***Right of reply:*** The right of reply is established by a judgment on the facts. The purpose of this remedy is to rectify and clarify the untrue facts and statements disseminated by the defendant. The right of reply is usually carried out in the terms specified by the Court in its judgment against the publisher.

• ***Money damages in tort:*** Both Law 1/1982 and the Constitutional Court recognize the right of the plaintiff to receive pecuniary compensation for the moral and material damages suffered. Presumed (or "Moral") damages are allowed (*iuris tantum presumption*); however, claims for actual damages (called "material damages") must be supported by proof.

• ***Retraction right:*** Law 2/1984 on Right of Retraction establishes that anyone has a right to demand a retraction of the information published in relation to facts about the subject that the individual considers false and the disclosure of which can injure that person's right of honor.

• ***The dissemination of the judgment:*** This remedy is aimed at compensating the plaintiff for the moral damages suffered. The judge shall decide whether the defendant has to publish the whole judgment or only some part of it and the specific media where the judgment has to be published.

Notwithstanding the above remedies, other measures can be requested by the plaintiff and granted by the judge.

10. Is there a privilege for quoting or reporting on:

In general terms, in reporting on matters of a governmental nature, as long as public persons are involved, and provided the journalist is diligent with regard to the veracity of the information reported, the right of information shall prevail over the right of honor. Thus, statements that within a different context might be considered libelous will not be seen as an illegitimate intrusion.

a. Papers filed in court?

Under Spanish law, governmental and judicial documents are not the proper object of copyright. Therefore, unless a secrecy obligation exists with regard to judicial proceedings or judgments (see answer to Question 12 below), there are no particular restrictions on the reporters to be able to quote or report on documents issued by the courts. By the same token, the general contours of media law still apply to reports from judicial proceedings; thus, insulting or offensive language may not be tolerated.

Documents filed by lawyers are the subject of copyright and, consequently, they cannot be freely disclosed or broadcasted absent the lawyer's consent.

b. Government-issued documents?

Article 71 of the Spanish Constitution establishes that members of Parliament and senators shall enjoy immunity for the statements declared during the course of their public functions. Similarly, under Article 8 of Law 1/1982, statements made by competent government authorities according to law shall not be considered an illegitimate intrusion in someone's right of honor. Thus, official statements from government agencies acting within their lawful capacity may not be the basis of a defamation claim.

Except in the case of insulting or opprobrious language, the public interest privilege would almost always be satisfied by basing reporting on documents issued by the government. As stated above, legal documents generated by the Court or government agencies are not the object of copyright.

c. Quasi-governmental proceedings?

No statutes or cases have treated statements made by these kinds of bodies as on equal footing with government statements; therefore, reporters are urged to act with due diligence in reporting any such statements.

11. Is there a privilege for republishing statements made earlier by other, bona fide, reliable publications or wire services?

Yes. This principle is known in Spain as the "neutral report doctrine." This doctrine allows reporters to accurately quote other, earlier publications, as long as the report is a matter of public concern or public interest (see, e.g., Judgments 232/93, 136/99, and 134/99).

12. Are there any restrictions regarding reporting on:

a. Ongoing criminal investigations?

Yes. In accordance with Article 301 of Law on Criminal Procedure, criminal investigations conducted by the investigating judge (called a "magistrate") shall be carried out in secret until the opening of the oral proceedings.

b. Ongoing criminal prosecutions?

There are no restrictions for reporting on the existence, development, and outcomes of ongoing criminal prosecutions.

Article 680 of Law on Criminal Procedure states that criminal litigation shall be public during the oral proceedings. However, the president of the Court can require secrecy when so required because of morality or public order reasons, or out of respect for the victim or the victim's family.

c. Ongoing regulatory investigations?

There are no restrictions regarding regulatory investigations.

d. Ongoing civil litigation, or other judicial proceedings?

Except for reporting on matters referring to minors, marital status, or other very personal rights, such as adoptive parents' names, there are no restrictions regarding civil proceedings.

13. Are prior restraints or other prepublication injunctions available on the basis of libel or privacy, and if so, what are the standards for obtaining such relief?

Precautionary measures are expressly allowed in Article 9 of Law 1/1982. These interim measures are aimed at preventing an alleged illegitimate intrusion into someone's right of honor. However, granting interim relief only occurs in very extraordinary cases.

In order for a precautionary measure to be granted by the courts, applicants must provide preliminary proof of the violation of their right of honor and must also post a bond to make good the damages that the precautionary measure might cause to the defendant if the libel claim is unsuccessful.

14. Is a right of privacy recognized (either civilly or criminally)?

Yes. This right is recognized and protected both by Law 1/1982 and by the Spanish Criminal Code. The Constitutional Court considers that the information disclosed represents an illegitimate intrusion into someone's right of privacy when the disclosure is not consented to, and lacks public interest, regardless of the veracity of the information.

The Constitutional Court has held that the following facts represented an illegitimate intrusion into the right of privacy: broadcast of a videotape from an ambulance depicting the agonizing death of a famous bullfighter who was mortally injured in the ring (Constitutional Court Judgment 231/1988); disclosure of the identity and activities of the natural mother of a child adopted by a well-known artist (Constitutional Court Judgment 134/1999); disclosure of the fact that an architect suffered from AIDS (Constitutional Court Judgment 20/1992); publishing unauthorized photographs of the interior of a famous person's home and detailing that person's personal likes and dislikes in their home life (Constitutional Court Judgment 115/2000).

a. What is the definition of "private fact"?

It is a constitutional doctrine under Article 20 of the Spanish Constitution that a "private fact" is that kind of fact found within someone's personal and reserved sphere, kept private by the right's holder and "necessary to keep a minimum quality of human life." Usual examples are intimate family or medical information, details about children, and financial information.

b. Is there a public interest or newsworthiness exception?

Yes. The public interest is the dispositive criterion to assess whether certain information deserves protection under the right of privacy or, on the contrary, constitutes a legitimate exercise of the right of freedom of information.

Thus, when certain information refers to a public matter, that is, to facts or an event that affects the whole of the citizens, then the information does not represent an illegitimate intrusion in someone's right of privacy.

c. Is the right of privacy based in common law, statute, or constitution?

The right of privacy (as well as the right of honor) is based on the Spanish Constitution, which considers this right fundamental and, therefore, subject to the highest legal and judicial protection.

15. May reporters tape-record their own telephone conversations for note-taking purposes (not rebroadcast) without the consent of the other party?

Yes. Although Article 7 of Law 1/1982 prohibits secret placement of tape-recording devices with the aim of recording someone's private life, the

Constitutional Court has also held that anyone may tape-record their own conversations without the consent of the other party.

By contrast, a third party may not record a conversation to which he is not a party without consent.

16. If permissible to record such tapes, may they be broadcast without permission?

In principle this would represent an illegitimate intrusion in the right of privacy. However, in the right context, the public interest exception may apply. If the person involved in the conversation was a public figure and the recording related to a matter of public interest, it may be justified.

17. Is there a recognized evidentiary privilege preventing the disclosure of confidential sources relied upon by reporters?

Yes. Pursuant to the Reporters' Statute, reporters are obliged to keep secret the identity of their confidential sources. Reporters may not be compelled to disclose their sources to their employers, the public authorities, or judicial authorities except in extraordinary cases, when, as a consequence of the disclosure, the commission of an offense against someone's life, integrity, health, freedom, or sexual freedom can be prevented.

In most circumstances, a reporter summoned to reveal a source's identity in a judicial proceeding must invoke the right to confidentiality. Breach of the promise to a confidential source can be considered an offense under the Criminal Code.

18. In the event that legal papers are served upon the newsroom (such as a civil complaint), are there any particular warnings about accepting service of which we should be aware?

No. Article 155 of the Law on Civil Procedure establishes that the defendant's residence for the purposes of the first summons can be that person's place of work. Thus, it is common in Spain that legal papers are served upon the newsroom and no consequences will arise by accepting service.

19. Has your jurisdiction applied established media law to Internet publishers?

Law 1/1982 protects the right of honor and privacy and constitutes a limit to the right of information regardless of the nature of the media (radio, television, press, Internet, etc.). For example, the Court of First Instance number 43 of Barcelona found "Leading Activities at Canadian Abroad Network Online Associates, S.A." liable for publishing false information on its Web site regarding the alleged sexual affairs of some members of a football team in a Madrid hotel. The company was ordered to pay damages to the football players and to publish the judgment on its Web site (Judgment 23/2003).

20. If established media law has been applied to Internet publishers, are there any ways in which Internet publishers (including chat room operators) have to meet different standards?

The standards that Internet publishers have to meet are the same as those explained above. No distinctions are made regarding the media used to diffuse the information.

21. Are there any cases where the courts enforced a judgment in libel from another jurisdiction against a publisher in your jurisdiction?

As far as we know, there are no cases where Spanish Courts enforced a judgment in libel against a publisher from another jurisdiction. However, this does not mean that it is not possible.

Chapter Notes

1. See, e.g., the Constitutional Court Judgment 139/1995 or the Supreme Court Judgment 751/2004, which found the Socialist Party liable for some statements in which it accused the plaintiff, *"Radio Television La Palma, S.L."* (limited corporation), of being partial on political matters.

2. The Jewish associations B'Nai B'Rith de España and Amical de Mauthassen had standing to bring an action against the author of a comic book considered xenophobic (Constitutional Court Judgment 1761/1995).

3. As the Constitutional Court Judgment, 22/1995, of 30 January 1995 states: "it is reiterated constitutional doctrine that only the information referred to facts of public concern and obtained and contrasted with a minimum of diligence, that is, truthful information, can be protected by Article 20.1.(d) of the Spanish Constitution (which guarantees the freedom of information right) and prevail over the right of honor guaranteed by Article 18.1. of the Spanish Constitution."

4. Thus, the Constitutional Court has held that the right of honor is weakened when the holder of the right is a public person, a person who holds public functions, or a person who takes part in matters of public concern, since they are obliged to bear the risk of their right of honor being discredited as a consequence of expressions or statements of public interest (Constitutional Court Judgments 165/87, 107/88, 20/92, and 320/94).

CHAPTER 19

Switzerland

ROLF AUF DER MAUR

VISCHER

VISCHER
Schützengasse 1
P.O. Box 6139
CH-8023 Zurich
Switzerland
Phone: +41 (44) 254 34 00
Fax: +41 (44) 254 34 10
www.vischer.com
ram@vischer.com

Introduction to the Swiss Legal System

Switzerland is divided into twenty-six states, called cantons. Each canton has significant law-making powers which are evident in the mixture of cantonal law and federal law in each individual canton. The Swiss Federal Supreme Court is the only federal court in the Swiss system and is used as the court of last resort. The cantonal courts are divided into civil, criminal, and administrative courts. Procedural law is generally canton-specific, while more substantive laws tend to be federal laws. All cases are dealt with in the court system of the canton with jurisdiction and can be appealed up to the Supreme Court.

1. What is the locally accepted definition of libel?

Various federal statutes provide civil and criminal sanctions against libel, slander, defamation and, in more general terms, disparaging statements. Whereas the freedom of speech and the freedom of the media are guaranteed by the Constitution (Articles 16 and 17 of the Swiss Federal Constitution, herein referred to as "SFC"), these civil and criminal sanctions constitute limits to the media which are clearly distinctive from those applicable in other European countries or in the United States.

Three statutes are of particular relevance: (1) the Civil Code of December 10, 1907 (herein referred to as "CC") for the protection of personality rights; (2) the Penal Code of December 21, 1937 (herein referred to as "PC") for the protection of the right of honor; and (3) the Unfair Competition Act of December 19, 1986 (herein referred to as "UCA") for the protection of fair competition. Additionally, the Data Protection Act of June 19, 1992 (herein referred to as "DPA") may also have to be considered.

As a consequence, there is not a single definition of "libel," "slander," or "defamation" but rather a framework of legal provisions, which must be examined on a case-by-case basis. Ultimately, these provisions incorporate (and are construed by the courts in accordance with) the constitutional rights to human dignity (Art. 7 SFC), privacy (Art. 13 SFC), and the right to enjoy free access to and free exercise of private economic activities (Art. 27 SFC).

Infringement of the Personality Right (Civil Law)

Article 28 CC protects the rights connected with the personality of an individual or legal entity, i.e., all aspects that make a person or entity unique. The personality right includes the right to live, the right to physical integrity, the right to personal freedom, the right to bear a name, the right to one's own image and voice, the right to privacy, and the right to be recognized as a person of dignity. More specific rules relating to the protection of personal data are set out in the DPA. It is noteworthy that the DPA does not only relate to personal data of individuals but also to those of legal entities.

Anyone whose personality is injured by a wrongful act can seek judicial measures against any person who takes an active part in the injury. An injury is illegal when it is not justified (1) by the injured person's consent, (2) by a prevailing private or public interest, or (3) by the law.

Article 28a CC provides for (1) injunctive relief, (2) removal of an existing infringement, (3) a declaratory judgment (if the effect of the infringement is continuing), and (4) a claim for rectification or publication of the judgment. Furthermore, the injured party may ask for compensatory damages or an account of profits and for moral compensation. Damages are only due when the offender was acting with fault, i.e., with intent or with negligence.

Infringement of the Right to Dignity (Penal Law)

The object of legal protection in criminal law is the right to dignity (i.e., the moral reputation of a person as opposed to the social or professional reputation). Social and professional reputations are protected only by Art. 28 CC (and to some degree through the UCA, as outlined below).

The two most important provisions of criminal law are defamation, in accordance with Art. 173 PC (*Üble Nachrede*), and Art. 174 PC (*Verleumdung*). Both provisions apply to the dissemination of false and dishonorable information vis-à-vis a third party or the public. Article 174 (*Verleumdung*) applies only if the false statement is made knowingly (i.e., the infringer knows that the statement is not true), whereas Art. 173 (*Üble Nachrede*) applies if the defendant was not aware of the statement's inaccuracy.

The dissemination of a defamatory value judgment (e.g., the allegation that someone acts like a "clown") as opposed to a statement of fact, or the dissemination of a factual statement only to the subject of the statement (i.e., not to third parties or to the public) will be qualified as an insult, in accordance with Art. 177 PC (*Beschimpfung*).

Under Articles 173 and 177, the publisher is allowed a so-called proof of exoneration, which consists of a "proof of truth" and a "proof of good faith": to avoid criminal sanctions, the offender must show either that the defamatory statement was true (proof of truth) or that he or she had good reasons to believe, in good faith, in the truth of the defamatory statement (proof of good faith).

The following represent some examples of defamation made by media:

A weekly business magazine accused a manager of dubious business practices. The manager resigned from his professional position before the defamatory article was published. As a result of the defamatory article, he was not able to find new employment. The Federal Supreme Court held that the article in question infringed the manager's personality rights and granted compensation for damages of SFr 1.7 million.[1] A daily newspaper published an article about criminal proceedings that took place twenty years ago and published the name of the then-juvenile delinquent who had been successfully reintegrated into society by the time of the publication. The Federal Supreme Court held that the media company infringed the personality rights of the former delinquent and argued that there exists a "right to forget." The Court awarded the plaintiff moral compensation of SFr 40,000 for suffering a severe depression after the publication of the defamatory article.[2]

2. Is libel-by-implication recognized, or, in the alternative, must the complained-of words alone defame the plaintiff?

Defamation-by-implication is recognized, i.e., even if a statement is not by itself defamatory, it can become actionable if it is put in a libelous context.

3. May corporations sue for libel?

Corporations may sue for defamation under both civil and criminal law. There is a dispute, however, as to the extent a corporation's "honor" can be infringed under Articles 173, 174, and 177 PC.

4. Is product disparagement recognized, and if so, how does that differ from libel?

Under Art. 3a UCA, it is considered unfair (and therefore illegal) to disparage another person or entity, its products, works, services, prices, or other business affairs by making false, misleading, or unnecessarily infringing statements. The disparaging statement must be of some gravity and it must influence the competition between the person or entity and its competitors.

Contrary to laws against unfair competition in most other countries, the UCA also applies to parties who are *not competitors* (e.g., to media reporting on businesses, thereby impairing their competitive status). An aggrieved party may initiate civil (Art. 9 UCA) and criminal (Art. 22 UCA) actions against the infringing party.

Thus, the dissemination of false, misleading, or unnecessarily infringing statements about products, and which affect the competitive status of the products, may be subject to civil and criminal sanctions. In a newspaper interview, the manager of a sewing machine company was quoted as saying that a competitor's technical standards were outdated and that his own products were "always technically ahead." The Federal Supreme Court held that the journalist who published the interview infringed Art. 3a UCA.[3] The European Court of Human Rights (ECHR) has in the past reversed similar judgments under Swiss law. A scientist wrote in an academic journal that food prepared in microwaves is a health hazard. The Federal Supreme Court held that the statement infringes Art. 3a UCA.[4] The ECHR reversed the judgment of the Federal Supreme Court, arguing that the statement of the scientist was protected by Art. 10 European Convention on Human Rights.[5]

5. Must an individual be clearly identified (by name or photograph) to sue for libel? Can a group of persons sue for libel, even though not named?

It is sufficient if the aggrieved party is *identifiable* by the public concerned in the context of a defamatory statement. An explicit identification (i.e., by name, photograph, voice, etc.) is not required.

A group of persons can sue in civil and criminal actions if organized as a legal person (e.g., as a corporation). Unincorporated groups without legal capacity do not have standing to bring actions in Swiss law for defamation (e.g., boards of directors, governmental administrations, ethical or social groups) and each person must file a lawsuit individually.

6. What is the fault standard(s) applied to libel?

The verification of the source of potentially defamatory information is a significant part of the journalist's professional duties of care. If severe allegations are to be published, the journalist is required to submit the allegation for comments to the person concerned prior to publication and to publish such comments along with the allegation, unless there is not sufficient time for obtaining the comment of the person concerned (principle of "*audiatur et altera pars*," stipulated as principle nr. 3.8 of the guidelines relating to the Swiss charter of journalists, published by the self-regulatory body "Presserat").

Swiss law recognizes a "good faith" defense. The headline in a tabloid: "Rightist Extremist Works for the Protection of the State" was not found to be infringing the right of honor because the defendant could show that he believed with good faith in the truth of the statement.[6]

Each case requires an assessment of the public interest versus the interest of the person concerned. The decision rendered by the European Court of Human Rights in the matter of *Princess Caroline of Hannover vs. Germany* will surely further tighten the practice of the Swiss courts, thereby limiting the media's freedom to report on matters not directly related to the public function of a person.

a. Does the fault standard depend on the fame or notoriety of the plaintiff?

The fault standard does not depend on the fame or notoriety of the plaintiff.

b. Is there a heightened fault standard or privilege for reporting on matters of public concern or public interest?

Yes. Reporting on matters of public concern or public interest is privileged under both civil and criminal law, and such publications may be defended from monetary damages by "good faith," a showing that the article was published without malicious intent or negligence, and was subjected to a degree of fact-finding and scrutiny or truth-seeking by the reporter. When the issues at stake concern matters of public interest or public concern, the courts will more readily admit good faith. Further, the courts will acquit the defendant on that basis, provided that the journalist has carried out "professional duties of care."

Under civil law, the Swiss jurisprudence follows the so-called theory of spheres that distinguishes between the person's (1) intimate sphere, (2) private sphere, and (3) public sphere. A further distinction is made between persons of public interest, where the doctrine further distinguishes between "absolute and relative persons of contemporary history" ("absolute und relative Personen der Zeitgeschichte") and private persons in whom the public has no interest.

Absolute persons of contemporary history (such as the president of a State, a minister of national importance, a CEO of a [multi]national corporation, a leading celebrity or artist) cannot prevent the media from reporting on matters related to their public function (whether or not such matters are in the public, private, or even intimate sphere of these persons).

Relative persons of contemporary history (i.e., persons who are temporarily in the public eye or only in relation to a limited subject matter, such as a scientist) can prevent the publication of any facts that are not related to their public function.

Private persons can challenge the publication of any facts about them unless such facts are part of public life (e.g., a picture taken of a person who is part of a crowd in a sports stadium).

In criminal actions against the infringement of the right to dignity and against insult (Art. 173 and 177 PC), the public interest is taken into account as part of the "proof of exoneration."

In either a civil or criminal action, based on Art. 3c UCA, public interest is taken into account when assessing whether a statement is "unnecessarily infringing."

7. Is financial news about publicly traded companies, or companies involved with a government contract, considered a matter of public interest or otherwise privileged?

There is no particular privilege, as such, protecting the publication of financial news, neither with respect to publicly traded companies nor with respect to companies involved with a government contract. A public interest, however, in information related to publicly traded companies and companies involved with government contracts is likely to be inferred.

8. Is there a recognized protection for opinion or "fair comment" on matters of public concern?

An opinion is not as such actionable as a defamation under criminal law (Art. 173 and 174 PC) but it can be actionable under civil law (Art. 28 CC and Art. 3a UCA). The line between an opinion expressed by a journalist and a defamatory statement of fact can be a fine one. Good faith is a defense upon which the defendant could rely under criminal law ("proof of exoneration" under Art. 173 PC).

9. Are there any requirements upon a plaintiff such as demand for retraction or right of reply, and if so, what impact do they have?

A person who is affected (but not necessarily infringed) in his personality rights by the publication of facts (as opposed to value judgments) in periodically published media, in particular, the press, radio, or television, is entitled to publish a counter-statement (right of reply, "*Gegendarstellung,*" Art. 28g CC). The text of the counter-statement must be brief and restricted to the subject matter of the publication to which the right to reply applies. The person concerned must send the text of the counter-statement to the media company within twenty days from having taken notice of the published facts, but in no case later than three months after the publication. The media company must immediately inform the person concerned, stating when the counter-statement will be published or stating the reasons why it is rejected. When the purpose of the right to reply can only be achieved through the publication of a picture instead of a text, the applicant can request that the media company publish the picture.[7]

The counter-statement shall be published as soon as possible and in such a manner that it reaches the same audience as the facts to which it relates. The counter-statement must be marked explicitly so that it can be recognized as such. The media company is entitled to add a declaration, regarding whether it maintains the previously published position, and it may also add the sources of its findings. The counter-statement must be published free of charge. If a media company refuses to publish a counter-statement or if it is published incorrectly, the person concerned may file a request with the court.

The law does recognize a mandatory right of reply; however, neither civil law nor criminal law requires a plaintiff to demand retraction of an infringing statement or to exercise a right of reply prior to taking legal action.

A request for criminal prosecution due to defamation needs to be filed within three months from the day when the injured party becomes aware of the identity of the infringer (Art. 29 PC).

The right to publish a counter-statement can be abused ("*rechtsmissbräuchlich*") if the person affected was offered the opportunity to provide his comments on the facts before their publication.[8]

10. Is there a privilege for quoting or reporting on:

a. Papers filed in court?
There is no privilege for quoting or reporting on papers filed in court. Such reports are still subject to due diligence of responsible reporting.

b. Government-issued documents?
There is no privilege for quoting or reporting on government-issued documents.

Journalists who quote from official governmental documents, legally declared secret by the appropriate authorities, may be subject to criminal prosecution for indiscretion.[9] This penal code provision has been criticized because it criminalizes the media for disseminating information whether or not the public is interested in this information, while the public official is not.

c. Quasi-governmental proceedings?

There is no privilege for quoting or reporting on quasi-governmental proceedings, such as those issued by professional associations.

11. Is there a privilege for republishing statements made earlier by other, bona fide, reliable publications or wire services?

There is no privilege for republishing statements made earlier by other, bona fide, reliable publications or wire services. The "proof of exoneration," according to Articles 173 and 177 PC, however, may be successful in certain contexts.

12. Are there any restrictions regarding reporting on:

a. Ongoing criminal investigations?

Criminal investigations and prosecutions are governed by cantonal laws (but a nationwide federal law is currently in preparation). All cantons stipulate that criminal investigations shall be conducted secretly. A public official who infringes the secrecy obligation is committing a criminal offense.[10] A journalist who publishes secret information obtained from an official who broke the secrecy obligation will not be sentenced as an accomplice but may be charged with indiscretion.[11]

b. Ongoing criminal prosecutions?

Criminal prosecutions are open to the public: "The court hearing shall be public, and the judgment shall be publicly proclaimed."[12] The public has the right to attend criminal prosecutions. This right does not include the media's right to broadcast the criminal prosecution to the public.

The public and the media may, however, be excluded from all or part of the prosecution in the interest of morals, public order, or national security; where the interests of juveniles or the protection of the parties' private life prevail; or under special circumstances when publicity would prejudice the interests of justice.[13] All cantonal statutes enumerate exceptions to the rule of publicity, within the scope given by the Convention.

c. Ongoing regulatory investigations?

Regulatory investigations are conducted secretly, but the authorities may make public any investigation of public concern. Some laws, including Art. 25 of the Federal Antitrust Act of October 6, 1995, provide explicitly that the authorities must respect secrecy of investigations under Art. 320 PC (see 12a. above). A journalist who publishes information obtained from an official who breaks the secrecy rule may be sentenced for indiscretion.[14]

d. Ongoing civil litigation, or other judicial proceedings?

As a general rule, civil litigation or other judicial proceedings are open to both the public and the media.[15] Most procedural rules provide that secret proceedings are to be conducted if legitimate reasons are at stake, such as morality or family interests.

13. Are prior restraints or other prepublication injunctions available on the basis of libel or privacy, and if so, what are the standards for obtaining such relief?

Prior restraints and other prepublication injunctions are available on the basis of defamation and privacy. Article 28c CC states that a person may apply for precautionary measures, when that person can substantiate that he or she has been infringed in his or her personality rights by an illegal act; that he or she must fear that an act will infringe his or her personality rights; and that from this infringement, a disadvantage will arise, which cannot be easily compensated.

Where an infringement is caused (or threatens to be caused) by periodically published media (i.e., by press, radio, or TV), the court can only take steps to restrain or to remove the infringement when: (1) the personality rights infringement involves a particularly serious disadvantage to the aggrieved party; (2) there exists obviously no justification for the infringement; and (3) the prepublication injunction does not appear to be disproportionate.

Yeslam Binladin (the half-brother of Osama Bin-Ladin) and his company, Saudi Investment Company, SICO Corporation, applied successfully for precautionary measures (ban of publication) before the distribution of a book in Switzerland, published by French authors and entitled *The Forbidden Truth. The Involvement of the USA with Osama Bin-Ladin.* The Federal Supreme Court repealed the decision on a review of the defamatory meaning complained-of, holding that neither Yeslam Binladin nor his company are put in the perspective of terrorism; the publication was therefore neither capable of harming their reputation nor violating their personality rights.[16]

14. Is a right of privacy recognized (either civilly or criminally)?

Yes. Swiss law recognizes a right of privacy, which is stipulated in Art. 13 SFC. As mentioned above, under civil law, the Swiss jurisprudence follows the so-called theory of spheres that distinguishes between the person's (1) intimate sphere, (2) private sphere, and (3) public sphere. A further distinction is made between persons of public interest, where the doctrine further distinguishes between "absolute and relative persons of contemporary history" ("absolute und relative Personen der Zeitgeschichte") and private persons in whom the public has no interest.

a. What is the definition of "private fact"?

No definition of "private fact" is found in any legal statute. All aspects of a person's intimate and private life are protected as "private fact." This concerns all those aspects of a person's life, which he or she can legitimately expect will not be made public. Private facts include photographs and/or recordings of private or intimate situations, information on health, on social security measures, or on sexual preferences. Information has, perhaps, held the public's interest at the time it initially occurred, but this interest may dissipate over time.

b. Is there a public interest or newsworthiness exception?

The protected scope of a person's privacy is reduced if that person is active in matters of public concern (see Question 6 above). Private aspects may only be published if a public interest is given (e.g., it is of public interest when a person with a pedophile past is applying for a position for the protection of children's rights within the local government; on the other hand, purported romantic involvements of celebrities are generally not a matter of public interest).

c. Is the right of privacy based in common law, statute, or constitution?

The right of privacy is based in the Constitution (Art. 13 SFC) as well as in statutes (Art. 28 CC, Art. 173 ss. PC, and Art. 1 DPA).

In one case, a journalist took a photo of a man involved in a criminal proceeding and who had just been released from a pretrial confinement. The subject was standing in the doorway of his house and explicitly told the journalist that he did not want to be photographed. The Federal Supreme Court held that taking a picture of someone, against his will, in the doorway of his house, is a violation of this person's privacy right. Note: the plaintiff sued the journalist for infringing his intimate and private sphere through use of a tape recorder.[17]

15. May reporters tape-record their own telephone conversations for note-taking purposes (not rebroadcast) without the consent of the other party?

According to Art. 179ter PC, without the consent of the other party, reporters may not tape-record telephone conversations for note-taking purposes. This law also applies even if the conversation or extracts of the conversation is not intended for rebroadcasting.

16. If permissible to record such tapes, may they be broadcast without permission?

No.

17. Is there a recognized evidentiary privilege preventing the disclosure of confidential sources relied upon by reporters?

Art. 27bis PC recognizes the evidentiary privilege of confidential journalistic sources ("*Quellenschutz*"). The privilege includes the right to refuse to testify in a court, to disclose research material, and to reveal journalistic sources. The privilege may be suspended, however, if specific, legally protected interests of importance are at stake.

The law contains a comprehensive list of offenses that suspend the evidentiary privilege, in particular, offences such as murder;[18] armed robbery;[19] sex crimes;[20] hardcore pornography;[21] membership in a criminal organization, financing of terrorist organizations;[22] money laundering and related crimes;[23] corruption;[24] and serious drug trafficking.[25]

The legal doctrine also requests that a test of proportionality be conducted in each case before a journalist is requested to disclose research material and sources.

18. In the event that legal papers are served upon the newsroom (such as a civil complaint), are there any particular warnings about accepting service of which we should be aware?

In Switzerland, the delivery of legal documents is carried out by the courts and not by the parties themselves. In general, the courts deliver legal papers to the defendant at the address provided by the plaintiff.

Should delivery fail because the defendant rejects receipt of the legal documents, effective delivery may be presumed under the applicable cantonal or federal procedural law. If delivery fails because the defendant has no domicile or habitual residence at the address the plaintiff provided, the court may ask the plaintiff to provide an accurate address.

If legal documents in criminal or civil matters against a media company are delivered to the premises of the media company, receipt should not be rejected (because it may otherwise be deemed to have taken place).

The documents should be forwarded directly to the person who can make the appropriate decisions on the proper course of action, such as local counsel.

If legal papers in criminal or civil matters against a journalist, whether employee or regular contributor, are delivered to the media company's premises, these documents should be received and forwarded to the proper person. If the journalist is not a regular contributor, receipt should be rejected by explicitly stating that the defendant is not related to the media company. It should be taken into account, however, that legal documents may be published (and thereafter deemed delivered) if these documents cannot be delivered to the defendant.

Receipt of legal papers at the media company premises does not prevent the journalist from appealing the validity of the service at a later stage. Further procedural rules should be considered in accordance with the cantonal laws applicable at the media company's domicile.

19. Has your jurisdiction applied established media law to Internet publishers?

The above law applies to Internet publishers, but there has been no specific precedent to this effect.

20. If established media law has been applied to Internet publishers, are there any ways in which Internet publishers (including chat room operators) have to meet different standards?

Internet publishers do not, as such, have to meet different standards, but they may be held liable for content contributed by users and published in discussion forums or chat rooms. Therefore, Internet publishers need to establish clear rules as to the nature of the content that may be published by users. They should also establish appropriate monitoring procedures to ensure that no illegal content can be published by users and that noncomplying content is removed immediately upon the publisher being made aware of it.

Legislation that stipulates a primary responsibility of the publisher and grants relief from criminal prosecution to access providers and (to a lesser extent) to hosting providers is currently in preparation.

21. Are there any cases where the courts enforced a judgment in libel from another jurisdiction against a publisher in your jurisdiction?

There are no cases in Switzerland where the courts enforced a judgment in libel from another jurisdiction against a Swiss publisher.

Chapter Notes

1. Art. 28 CC, Art. 41 Code of Obligations, Federal Supreme Court, BGE 123 III 385 and case 5C.57/2004, September 2, 2004.

2. Art. 28 CC, Art. 49 of the Swiss Code of Obligations, Federal Supreme Court, case 5C.156/2003, October 23, 2003.

3. Federal Supreme Court, BGE 117 IV 193.

4. Federal Supreme Court, BGE 120 II 76.

5. *Hertel v. Switzerland,* 59/1997/843/1049.

6. Articles 173 and 174 PC, successful "proof of good faith," Supreme Court of the Canton of Zurich, case DF30002/U, March 1, 2004.

7. Federal Supreme Court, BGE 130 III 1.

8. Federal Supreme Court, BGE 120 II 273.

9. Art. 293 I PC, "*Verbot der Veröffentlichung amtlicher geheimer Verhandlungen.*"

10. Violation of the official secret, Art. 320 PC, "*Verletzung des Amtsgeheimnisses.*"

11. Art. 293 I PC, "*Veröffentlichung amtlicher geheimer Verhandlungen.*"

12. Art. 30 III SFC and Art. 6 I European Convention for the Protection of Human Rights and Fundamental Freedoms of November 4, 1950.

13. Art. 6 I European Convention on Human Rights.

14. Art. 293 I PC, "*Veröffentlichung amtlicher geheimer Verhandlungen.*"

15. Art. 30 III SFC and Art. 6 I European Convention on Human Rights.

16. Federal Supreme Court, case 5P.362/2002, December 17, 2002.

17. Art. 179 PC, "*Verletzung des Geheim- oder Privatbereichs durch Aufnahmegeräte,*" [Federal Supreme Court, BGE 118 IV 41].

18. Art. 111–113 PC ["*Tötungsdelikte*"].

19. Art. 140 IV PC ["*qualifizierter Raub*"].

20. Art. 187, 189–191 PC ["*strafbare Handlungen gegen die sexuelle Integrität*"].

21. Art. 197 III PC ["*harte Pornografie*"].

22. Art. 260ter and 260^{quinquies} PC ["*kriminelle Organisation*" and "*Finanzierung des Terrorismus*"].

23. Art. 305bis PC ["*Geldwäscherei*"] such as 305ter PC [lack of care within financial transactions, "*mangelnde Sorgfalt bei Finanzgeschäften und Melderecht*"].

24. Art. 322ter - 322^{septies} PC ["*Bestechung*"].

25. ["*schwerer Drogenhandel*"] Art. 19 I of the Narcotics Act ["*Betäubungsmittelgesetz*"].

PART FOUR

ISSUES OF GLOBAL INTEREST

International Media Law and the Internet

Special Issues for Book Publishers

Enforcing Foreign Judgments in the
United States and Europe

Fair Use

The Emergence of Privacy as a Claim
in the UK

CHAPTER 20

International Media Law and the Internet[†]

CHARLES J. GLASSER JR., *Bloomberg News* AND
JONATHAN D. HART, *Dow, Lohnes & Albertson, PLLC*

Dow, Lohnes & Albertson, PLLC
200 New Hampshire Avenue, N.W., Suite 800
Washington, D.C. 20036 U.S.A.
Phone: 202-776-2000
Fax: 202-776-2222
www.dowlohnes.com
jhart@dowlohnes.com

Introduction

Much of the law as it applies to the Internet might be described as "old wine in a new bottle." The fact that news and commentary may now be disseminated globally, seamlessly, virtually, and instantaneously doesn't often change the standards by which courts around the world hold publishers accountable for alleged wrongs related to news and commentary.

What *has* changed is that now almost anyone, anywhere can be a publisher. Although we are now all potential Gutenbergs, the "anyone" component is problematic because libel, privacy, and intellectual property cases arising from Internet speech are not infrequently brought against people who had no idea that their statements might be subject to restrictive media laws.

Moreover, the "anywhere" component has raised problems, because Internet publishers have been sued by people thousands of miles from their computers, sometimes in places the publisher has never even visited.

[†] This article is based upon excerpts from *Web Law 2005: A Field Guide to Internet Publishing,* by Jonathan D. Hart; published by Bradford Publishing Company, Denver, Colorado.

The conflict is clear: states have a duty to protect the interests of citizens alleging harm, and at the same time there seems something fundamentally unfair about a publisher being hauled into the court of a far-flung place that the publisher never thought about.

These questions of Internet jurisdiction—who can sue whom, in what nation, and under what law—are complex. Each case requires factual analysis that can't be accomplished in the abstract. The best this guidebook can do is to provide the substantive libel law of various jurisdictions, and to highlight details of any treatment of Internet cases in each of those jurisdictions.

The reader is encouraged to question whether the subject of publication may have a connection to any particular jurisdiction, and then to review the substantive law of that nation and publish accordingly. For the purpose of providing more material upon which better risk analysis may be made, this guidebook also contains a section on the enforcement of judgments across borders (see Chapter 22, "Enforcing Foreign Judgments in the United States and Europe: When Publishers Should Defend"), and readers are encouraged to review it. As always, no guidebook can substitute for the advice of experienced local counsel, and readers are implored to seek that guidance.

The Internet is a rich medium, laced with sound, music, artwork, motion pictures, and other "multimedia" functionality. Here, where intellectual property and data privacy rights may clash with a Web publisher's interests, the "old wine in a new bottle" cliché falls apart. This chapter raises these issues and outlines some of the questions that Web publishers should ask themselves. Web publishers are also encouraged to periodically review them and make an informed decision as to what extent—if at all—the publisher determines compliance is called for.

Trademarks on the Web

Generally speaking, a trademark is a designation that is used to identify the source of goods and to distinguish that source from other sources. A service mark is a designation that is used to identify the source of services and to distinguish that source from other sources. A mark (whether a trademark or service mark) can consist of a word or words, a stylized rendition of a word or words, a number or numbers, a design, a color, a sound, or any combination of these elements.[1] The term "trademark" is frequently used to encompass both trademarks and service marks, and the law applicable to each is essentially the same. Most Internet-related trademark disputes reflect a trademark owner's desire to establish or maintain online brand recognition and loyalty. A Web site operator may be liable for trademark infringement, depending on the applicable national law, for displaying another's trademark on a Web site without permission, in a way that implies an association between the Web site and the trademark owner; that "tarnishes" the mark's reputation, or somehow "dilutes" the strength of the association between the mark and the public's association of a specific source with that mark.[2]

Liability for Third-Party Provided Content: Internet service providers (ISPs), as well as persons who create Web sites that allow third-party contribution (such as blogs, bulletin boards, chat rooms, and other forums to which users post content), may be liable for contributory trademark infringement under U.S. and other law. Publishers allowing third-party contribution should consider whether it makes sense to acquire indemnities from suppliers of such content, whether to periodically review such forums and remove potentially actionable material, or in the alternative to take a "hands-off" approach.

Is Linking or Framing Trademark Infringement? One of the defining features of Internet publishing is the ability to provide readers with direct links to other Web sites. Generally speaking, linking from one Web site to another Web site, by itself, does not amount to trademark infringement.

However, linking *may* present trademark infringement questions if the link implies an endorsement by or association with the linked-to site. "Deep-linking" (linking directly to particular pages within a Web site rather than the Web site's home page) may also raise trademark infringement issues if the deep link leads consumers to believe there is an association between the sites. Most questions will be judged against whether the challenged use creates a "reasonable likelihood of confusion" in the mind of the viewer. Publishers are cautioned that their good-faith intent is rarely dispositive on this question, though their innocent intent might mitigate the amount of damages available to the plaintiff.

Framing a Web site (displaying another's Web site within the pages of one's own Web site) can potentially constitute trademark infringement, if the frame confuses Web site visitors into believing there is an affiliation or association between the Web sites. Webmasters should be very careful here to weigh the use of their own company's logos or trademarks when "wrapped around" the content of another party, because presenting both logos at the same time might be construed as an implied association or endorsement, and is more likely to be viewed as causing a likelihood of confusion.

Metatags and Infringement: A metatag is a word or code embedded in a data field on a Web site that is not normally part of any publicly viewable web page. Search engines read a Web site's metatags to determine the subject(s) addressed on the site so that the search engine can determine whether the site is responsive to a search query input by a user. Some Web site operators include metatags on their sites that incorporate the trademarks of their competitors. In this way, when a user searches for a competitor, the search results include the Web site operator's site as well. Courts have found that using a competitor's trademark in metatags may constitute trademark infringement when such use causes users confusion about the origin or affiliation of the Web site. In some instances, use of metatags will not amount to trademark infringement if the use is not intended to deceive or confuse consumers.

Copyright on the Web

Most fundamentally, copyright law does not protect pure ideas or facts, which are, by definition, in the public domain. Instead, copyright attaches to the unique manner in which ideas and facts are expressed. By way of example, the fact that "Christopher Columbus discovered the New World in 1492" is not subject to ownership: it is a fact for the world to own. On the other hand, to say "Bravely, Columbus stood on the weather-beaten oak deck of his ship, looked over the azure waters of the Caribbean and prayed that God would deliver his three ships safely to his dream of a New World" is protected expression. The facts are in the public domain, but the prose is an author's property.

Unlike libel law, which varies dramatically from country to country, much international conflict has been avoided due to a series of treaties and conventions that bind most of the world to some degree of harmony in copyright. The primary issues of how to avoid infringing others' work and how to protect your own work on a global basis are treated in a separate chapter (see Chapter 23, "Fair Use: It Stops at the Border"). This chapter addresses some of the issues that are unique to the Internet because of its technical qualities.

Liability for Third-Party Provided Content: Internet service providers (ISPs) as well as persons who create Web sites that allow third-party contribution (such as bulletin boards, chat rooms, and other forums to which users post content) are generally exempt from liability for copyright infringement based on infringing content posted by such third parties.[3] However, this exemption does not apply when the host is put on notice that material over which they have control is alleged to be infringing,[4] under U.S., EU, and other law.

Is Linking or Framing Copyright Infringement? Linking from one Web site to another generally does not constitute copyright infringement. Providing a "deep link" to a page that is not the home page of the linked site may have copyright implications, although a number of courts have held that such practice does not infringe copyrights.

Several courts have found that framing another's site without permission may be a copyright infringement, because it makes the framed content appear to be incorporated within the framing site.

Data Collection and Privacy on the Web

Although businesses have long collected data about consumers, the rapid growth of the Internet has sparked a new debate about the collection of personal information and the consumer's right to privacy. In the online world, information often can be gathered and processed more quickly than in the offline world. As in the offline world, the mechanisms by which this is accomplished may not be immediately apparent to consumers.

On the one hand, Web publishers—like other businesses online and off—want to gather information about their customers that will allow them to better serve those customers (and their advertisers). On the other hand, some consumers care passionately about restricting the information businesses gather, and controlling how it is used. Many jurisdictions have begun to legislate controls over the use of that data.[5]

Privacy and Data Collection under European Law

The EU Directive: The European Union (and by extension, its Member States) has taken perhaps the most restrictive approach to the restriction of data collection on the Internet. The EU's Directive on Data Protection (95/46BC) became effective on October 24, 1998. Article 25 of the Directive prohibits the transfer of personally identifying data to countries that do not provide what the EU considers an "adequate" level of privacy protection.

The EU takes a broad definitional approach to the meaning of "personally identifying." This definition includes: full names; addresses; financial data; dates of birth; passport, national identity or social security numbers; or information concerning "racial or ethnic origin, political opinions, religious or philosophical beliefs ... [or] concerning health or sex life." Web masters are strongly encouraged to review this list prior to configuring web pages and processes that collect such information.[6]

Among other requirements are that data can be collected only for "legitimate purposes"; there are severe restrictions on the ability of data collectors to transfer data to a third party, and individuals about whom data is collected have considerable notice rights and a right to correct incorrect data.

"Safe Harbor" for U.S.-based Web sites: Because of the Directive's potential to lead to disputes that could seriously hamper U.S.–EU trade, the United States and the EU worked for years to devise a way for U.S. companies to comply with the EU Directive without unnecessarily harming online commerce. The United States and European Union reached agreement on May 31, 2000 (the "Safe Harbor Agreement"), with the EU Member States unanimously approving the U.S. "safe harbor" proposal. The European Commission approved the Safe Harbor Agreement on July 26, 2000. The agreement took effect on November 1, 2000. The agreement is a compromise between the two culturally divergent approaches to privacy, and is an attempt to accommodate both the U.S. self-regulatory framework and the EU's strict standards. As of December 31, 2004, more than 700 companies had taken advantage of the safe harbor by registering with the Department of Commerce.

The decision to enter into the safe harbor is voluntary; companies may qualify for the safe harbor in different ways. For example, a company can join a self-regulatory privacy program that adheres to the safe harbor principles, or it can develop its own self-regulatory privacy policies that conform to the principles. U.S. companies adhering to the agreement's principles will be viewed as providing adequate privacy protection, and would gain "safe harbor" from prosecution or lawsuits by EU governments. Although European citizens do not lose their rights to sue U.S. companies directly, they are encouraged to follow a process under which they first raise any complaints with the potential defendant and go through out-of-court dispute resolution before proceeding with any suit.

To take advantage of the safe harbor, companies self-certify by providing an annual letter to the Department of Commerce or its designee, signed by a corporate officer, containing the information required by the Safe Harbor Agreement. The Department of Commerce or its designee maintains a list of all organizations that file such letters. Both the list and the self-certification letters submitted by the organizations are publicly available. All companies that self-certify for the safe harbor must also state in their relevant published privacy policy statements that they adhere to the safe harbor principles. Companies do not need to subject all personal information that they retain to the safe harbor principles; rather, they need to make sure that personal information received from the EU after they have joined the safe harbor is handled according to the principles. The Safe Harbor Agreement does not cover the financial services sector. Webmasters are encouraged to consult counsel about how to comply with the safe harbor provisions.

Other Data Privacy Laws

Canada. Canada has taken a comprehensive approach to online privacy similar to that of the EU, passing the Personal Information Protection and Electronic Documents Act (PIPEDA), which took effect January 1, 2004. The law requires organizations to obtain an individual's consent before collecting, using, or disclosing his or her personal information, and such personal information may only be used for the purpose for which it was collected. The law also requires that businesses appoint the equivalent of an internal privacy compliance officer. The law does not specify the type of consent that must be obtained—i.e., opt-in or opt-out—but leaves to the organization soliciting the information the discretion to decide on a mechanism, based on the "sensitivity of the information" and the "reasonable expectations of the individual." Canadian law also requires that companies that have collected personal information prior to the law's enactment notify the individuals from whom the information was collected about the new law and their privacy policies.[7]

Japan. On May 23, 2003, Japan enacted the Personal Information Protection Law, which applies to the national government, independent public corporations, municipal governments, and other related bodies. Effective 2005, it also applies to private companies that use personal information. Under the law, entities that collect and use personal information must notify the owner of the information, refrain from providing such information to third parties without owner consent, correct errors promptly, and provide the owner of information, upon request, with the name of the collecting entity and the purposes for which it will use the information.[8]

South Africa. In December 2002, South Africa passed the Regulation of Interception of Communications Act, which subjects private companies to fines for monitoring employees' e-mail, mail, and telephone calls without the employees' consent. Individuals who violate the Act may also be subject to jail sentences.[9]

Electronic Contracts

The term "electronic contracts" refers to agreements that are similar to traditional contracts, except that they are made online or using electronic media rather than on paper. An electronic contract involves the formation of an agreement between two or more people or entities, just like a traditional contract, written on paper and signed in ink. Not surprisingly, courts have applied familiar principles of traditional contract law when deciding disputes involving electronic contracts.

Web site Disclaimers and User Agreements: Web publishers often seek to reduce exposure to liability and to protect the integrity and proprietary value of their content by posting "visitor agreements" on their Web sites. Such agreements contain various disclaimers of liability and notices concerning rights to content, restrictions on site use, and the like. Similarly, computer manufacturers and software publishers often include license agreements that are either printed on or included within a product's packaging materials. Case law indicates that these disclaimers and user agreements, which are often referred to as "click-wrap" or "browse-wrap" agreements, may constitute enforceable contracts. Generally, disclaimers and agreements that require readers to actively click on "I Agree" buttons before any other screen can be accessed are more likely to be held enforceable. Depending on context, pages that merely contain a link at the bottom to terms that a reader can ignore may be judged as less binding; the question is whether reasonable users would have understood that they were entering into an agreement.

Electronic Signatures (E-Signatures): An electronic signature has the same function as a traditional signature: to affirm the signer's intent to abide by the terms of the contract to which he or she affixes the signature. In the case of e-signatures, this affirmation takes place digitally instead of by the use of ink on paper. The U.S. government has passed legislation mandating that electronic signatures be given the same validity as ink signatures (15 U.S.C. § 7001). All state-level governments in the United States have passed legislation to the same effect.

Visitor Agreements: Web publishers often use visitor agreements (also referred to as "user agreements," "terms of use," "terms of service," and the like) to establish the ground rules for access to their Web sites and use of the contents provided within. Users who violate the visitor agreement may be denied access to the site in the future. They may also be liable for breach of contract. Visitor agreements also often include language intended to limit the publisher's liability and reduce the publisher's exposure to lawsuits.

Visitor agreements typically notify users that the publisher and those who license content to the publisher hold copyright in the content that appears on the site. The publisher often includes language alerting users that, though they are free to use material on the Web site for personal, noncommercial purposes, they may not reproduce or distribute content found on the Web site without permission from the copyright holder. Such a provision may put users on notice of the terms on which they are being granted access to the content on the site. The visitor agreement may also advise users how they can contact the site if they want permission to publish content appearing on the site.

Chapter Notes

1. See 15 U.S.C. § 1127 (The "Lanham Act").

2. Corporations that believe their products are unfairly maligned may bring libel cases against critics in jurisdictions that do not have the same extent of speech protection as is enjoyed in the United States. See "McDonald's Wins Record-setting Libel Case," *USA Today,* June 20, 1997, at http://www.mcspotlight.org/media/press/usatoday_19jun97.html.

3. See Digital Millennium Copyright Act of 1998 ("DMCA"), Pub. L. No. 105-304, available at http://www.copyright.gov/legislation/dmca.pdf.

4. See http://www.copyright.gov/titlel7/92chap5.htmM512.

5. See, e.g., list of Internet activities under jurisdiction of U.S. Federal Trade Commission at http://www.ftc.gov/bcp/conline/pubs/buspubs/dotcom/index.html.

6. *Id.*

7. A copy of the law is available at http://www.parl.gc.ca.

8. Personal Information Protection Law, Law No. 57.

9. See Penny Sukhraj, "New Law Stops Bosses Spying on E-Mail," *Sunday Times* (Johannesburg) (Feb. 2, 2003), available at http://allafrica.com/stories/printable/200302010167.html.

CHAPTER 21

Special Issues for Book Publishers

SLADE R. METCALF

Hogan & Hartson LLP

Hogan & Hartson LLP
875 Third Avenue
New York, NY 10022 U.S.A.
Phone: 212-918-3000
Fax: 212-918-3100
www.hhlaw.com
srmetcalf@hhlaw.com

Libel rules affecting book publishers under U.S. law are signifi-cantly different than the rules applicable to newspaper publishers, primarily due to the fact that almost all authors of books are in-dependent contractors and accordingly there are separate bases of liabil-ity for the authors and book publishers. Unlike the employer/employee relationship for most newspaper publishers and the rather simple writ-ten agreements between magazine publishers and writers, book publish-ers generally enter into detailed written agreements with their authors, who are considered independent contractors. These detailed contractual relationships influence (and often are determinative of) the rights and liabilities of book publishers and authors. This is not always the case in non-U.S. jurisdictions, especially those where a strict liability standard may apply. Book publishers should carefully consider the libel laws of the various nations presented elsewhere in this book, and consult with counsel prior to publication. As a starting point, publishers should ask themselves where the book will be published, and whether or not the subject of the statement at issue has a significant relationship to that nation.

Book publishers face more than libel claims in terms of the legal issues they confront. Although most book publishers use, at least as a starting point, a standard-form written agreement, most authors—particularly the more celebrated ones—can negotiate certain clauses and adjust certain provisions to suit their needs. The following discussion will treat various aspects of the book publishing agreements as well as other issues arising outside of the publishing agreement.

Author Agreements and Electronic Publishing

A book publisher should be sensitive and aware of the separate rights that it can acquire from an author in a written agreement. Generally, a trade book publisher will acquire at least exclusive first rights to publish the author's manuscript (the "Work") in the hardcover edition for a specific geographic area, whether the United States, North America, or worldwide. Some of those rights that a book publisher can acquire are as follows:

- Softcover or paperback rights
- Syndication rights for newspapers or magazines
- Anthology rights
- Abridgement or condensation rights
- Foreign language rights
- Rights to subcontract publication in other countries
- Motion picture rights
- Derivative rights
- Theatrical rights
- Book club rights
- Rights for publication in Braille or large-size type
- Audio rights
- Electronic rights

It is important for book publishers to consider the scope of the electronic rights that it may be acquiring. If there is a negotiation as to particular electronic rights, some of the rights to be considered should include:

- Electronic retrieval rights such as Nexis or other subscription data services
- Rights for the publishers' Web sites
- Electronic commerce (or e-book rights)

Although the commercial viability of e-books seems to be softening, every book publisher, to the extent that they obtain electronic rights, should clarify that they are receiving rights to publish the Work in e-book format.

Noncompetition Clauses

Book publishers may from time to time preclude certain authors from having manuscripts published that are competitive to a book already under contract to the publisher. These prohibitions on competitive works are subject, of course, to reasonable time restrictions. Such a competitive restriction would not be upheld, for example, for the life of the copyright of the published Work. These competitive restrictions are more likely to be upheld as reasonable if they preclude books by other publishers on the same or similar topics as the initial book published. With respect to "similar" topics, it is helpful to describe and delineate the scope of the subject matter that is restricted. Frequently, a book publisher will obtain from the author an option to publish the next book or books by the author, or secure the right of first refusal or a right to match a competing offer made to the author.

Publishers' Obligations and Warranties

The publisher generally accepts the responsibility to edit, print, bind, and distribute the Work as submitted by the author. The publisher rarely, if ever, takes on the obligation to ensure that the facts contained in the manuscript are accurate. Occasionally, the publisher will take on the obligation to "use its best efforts" to market the Work. However, the publisher, except in those cases when a contract is with a very well-known author, will assume the exclusive rights to determine such aspects as the distribution of the book, layout of the book, quality of the paper, price of the book, nature of binding, advertising efforts, markets for distribution, and publicity relating to the ultimate publication.

Authors' Obligations and Warranties

First and foremost, the author agrees to provide a publishable manuscript within a certain deadline and of a certain length, both of which are set by the publisher. The author generally agrees to obtain appropriate releases and permission forms for photographs and illustrations or reprinted material which will be included in the published book. The author also warrants and represents that the manuscript as submitted is original to her or him and will be free from any claims of libel, invasion of privacy, and copyright infringement, and that it will not be harmful to the reader. Frequently, a book publisher will require an author to certify that the manuscript is accurate to the best of the author's knowledge. The author also generally agrees to indemnify the book publisher for any costs, including reasonable attorney's fees, which arise as a result of any claims made against the published work. Some book publishing agreements limit the indemnification only to those occasions where a claimant *successfully* pursues a claim against the publisher or the costs arise from a breach or alleged breach of the author's warranties.

The issue of warranties and indemnification should be addressed at the commencement of any libel, invasion of privacy, or copyright suit. To the extent that the publisher agrees that it is appropriate to have the same outside counsel represent both the book publisher and the author, it is important to discuss and specify with the author the nature of the relationship with the joint outside counsel and how the indemnification might work. Sometimes a book publisher will "freeze" the royalty account of the author so that there will be a fund to pay the legal expenses at the end of the case. Both the book publisher and the author should resolve the questions of what might happen if their interests diverge as the suit proceeds. For example, it may turn out that the author was aware of certain information that he or she did not share with the publisher. That might well impose increased liability on the author, and the publisher might prefer to make a significant issue of the failure of the author to disclose that relevant information.

Insurance Coverage for Authors and Publishers

Book publishers commonly have insurance policies for the books that they publish. Those policies may also provide coverage for the authors who are independent contractors. The policy may spell out the deductible (or retention) under the policy, which is the maximum amount of money for defense costs and settlement that will be owed by the publisher. The book publisher, in turn, may have an arrangement with the author in the written agreement, whereby the publisher and the author pay the retention amount on a certain percentage basis. For example, if there is a $200,000 deductible and the publishing agreement provides that the author and the publisher would share the retention on a 50/50 basis, then the author would be obliged to reimburse the publisher in an amount of up to $100,000. That amount might well be deducted from the author's royalty account, if there are any monies owed or to be owed to the author. The insurance policy may provide that the publisher (or insured) can select counsel to represent it with respect to claims filed against it, but that right is often subject to the approval of the insurance company. The policy may or may not specify whether the insurance company will pay for separate representation of the author in the event that the interests of the publisher and the author diverge during the course of the lawsuit. The author will always have the option of retaining his or her own counsel, but such representation would be at the expense of the author. In order for the insurance company to cover the cost of separate representation, the conflict between publisher and author generally needs to be apparent.

Differences in Liability Between Author and Publisher

Unlike the newspaper business, because the author is not generally an employee of the book publisher, there is no *respondeat superior* manner of responsibility or liability. As an independent contractor (which the publishing agreement usually specifies), the author has her or his own basis for liability. The separate basis often translates into a heightened level of protection for the book publisher. Libel in the United States differentiates between public persons and private figures. Individuals (and corporations) who are deemed to be public figures or public officials must satisfy the onerous burden to show by clear and convincing evidence that the publisher and/or author either knew that the offending language was false or had serious doubts about the truth of that language. This so-called "constitutional malice" standard for public persons frequently means that the book publisher will avoid liability because the publisher generally relies on the *bona fides* of the author and the representations and warranties of the author in the publishing agreement that he or she has taken appropriate steps to ensure the accuracy of the manuscript. The publisher may incur liability if it is put on notice prior to publication that certain facts in the manuscript are false and defamatory, and the publisher takes no steps whatsoever to obtain assurances that the material is in fact accurate. For example, if a book publisher were provided with a tape recording of a meeting that directly contradicts the author's portrayal of that meeting in the manuscript, and the publisher takes no steps to obtain independent corroboration or modify the wording of the manuscript, then the book publisher may be held liable under the constitutional malice standard. On the other hand, the author may be subject to liability even in a libel suit brought by a public person if that author was a part of a particular event and it was shown that the author's rendition of that particular event was false. The plaintiff will argue that the author knew that the portrayal in the manuscript was false because he or she participated in the event and therefore must have known that the wording was contrary to the actual facts.

When a libel suit is brought by a private person, the standard to be imposed in a particular case is dependent on the law of the appropriate state that governs the proceedings. That standard of liability may range from a simple negligence standard (as in most states) to a gross negligence standard (as in New York State) to a constitutional malice standard (as in Colorado, Indiana, and New Jersey). Where a negligence standard applies, it is extremely difficult for a libel case to be dismissed prior to trial. Courts will generally allow a jury to make a determination whether the publisher and/or the author used reasonable care in researching, writing, and publishing the offending language. Such evidence would thus be evaluated under the negligence standard. Frequently, book publishers will submit testimony from professional editors or journalists to show what the book publisher and author did with respect to the book at issue in the lawsuit was reasonable under the circumstances and that the efforts of the defendants evidenced reasonable and due care.

Product Liability

From time to time, purchasers and readers of books claim that they have been physically injured or have suffered some kind of economic damage from material contained in a book. Although infrequent, those claims can have a severe adverse impact on a book publisher and its authors. For example a cookbook might contain a recipe that inadvertently contained the wrong ingredient or incorrect amount of the ingredient. If the misnamed ingredient was in fact dangerous, it could certainly cause health hazards to the reader.

Indeed, in one unfortunate case, a book contained the wrong name of a mushroom to be picked and eaten and a reader died from ingesting poisonous mushrooms. In another case, a medical textbook contained the wrong name of a chemical substance to be injected for an enema. A nurse who purchased the book used that incorrect chemical when she self-administered an enema and the chemical burned her insides. United States courts have generally found in those circumstances that the book publisher does not have a duty to the reader to ensure the accuracy of the information contained in the books. In other nations, particularly those without a constitutional right to press freedom, publishers of instructional, how-to, and other informational books may be held liable for incorrect information that results in monetary loss or physical harm. Again, it is strongly suggested that publishers consult with local attorneys prior to distributing books in multiple jurisdictions.

It is also worth noting that even in the United States, courts have not been so clear that the individual author does not owe a corresponding duty of care to the readers. In the case involving the self-administered enema, the court dismissed the book publisher from the case but did not dismiss the author from the case.

Courts have also rejected claims when certain financial information turns out to be untrue. For example, incorrect listings of prices of securities have not provided a basis for a claim based on negligent publication. As another example, a book publisher came out with a book about battered women. The book contained a listing of attorneys who were familiar with the area of the law. One of the attorneys listed turned out to have been sanctioned by a state disciplinary organization. A reader who relied on the book in selecting the attorney learned, unfortunately, that the attorney had ignored her case and that the statute of limitations had expired on her claim. The court found that the book publisher again did not have a duty of care to the reader and, although the information about the attorney was not current, the plaintiff could not pursue any claim. For whatever reason, the plaintiff in that case chose not to sue the two authors of the book and therefore the court did not have occasion to decide whether both of the authors had a duty to take reasonable steps to make sure the information in the book was accurate.

A separate category of cases in this area arises when a publisher endorses or guarantees the quality of a product or a service. For example, a court declined to dismiss a case against *Good Housekeeping* magazine when it placed its "Good Housekeeping Consumers Guaranty Seal" on a product that allegedly was defective. Courts on rare occasions have found that certain advertising that contains harmful information can be grounds for a lawsuit. However, those cases are generally restricted to the commercial speech or advertising context. A rare exception concerned the manual called *Hit Man: A Technical Manual for Independent Contractors*. There, the author gave precise instructions on what to do in the event you wanted to kill someone. A man looking to obtain his son's $2 million trust fund, derived from the settlement of a personal injury suit, hired an assassin to murder his ex-wife, his son, and the son's nurse. The assassin succeeded. Certain relatives of the decedent wife and son sued the book publisher on the theory that the publisher aided and abetted the assassin. A federal appellate court found that the publisher could be held responsible for information that was so clearly offensive and dangerous on its face.

CHAPTER 22

Enforcing Foreign Judgments in the United States and Europe

When Publishers Should Defend

KURT WIMMER

Covington & Burling

Covington & Burling
1201 Pennsylvania Avenue, N.W.
Washington, DC 20004-2401 U.S.A.
Phone: 202-662-5278
Fax: 202-778-5278
www.cov.com
kwimmer@cov.com

For decades, international treaties have promised freedom of expression "regardless of frontiers."[1] The Internet finally has provided a means by which this promise may be achieved. National borders, however, remain crucial to risk management even on a borderless medium such as the Internet. This is particularly true for publishers that now find themselves being sued or prosecuted in foreign courts for libel, invasion of privacy, or other causes of action based on content, usually accessed through the Internet outside the United States.

The prospect of foreign litigation is a constant challenge for publishers because of the complexity, inconvenience, and expense involved in defending an action outside the United States. But these traditional concerns pale compared to the increased risk profile of publishing on the Internet because of the growing potential for a foreign court to apply a body of law that does not protect speech as robustly as does U.S. law. Multinational plaintiffs, governments, and courts have begun using the Internet to manipulate jurisdictional principles to avoid application of the U.S. law—and its First Amendment—to claims against U.S.-based publication of content through the Internet.

The extent of the real danger to U.S. publishers depends on whether a judgment rendered by a foreign court can be enforced in countries where the publisher has assets. If a publisher has no assets in the jurisdiction issuing the adverse decision, then the risk level is diminished. Although a foreign libel judgment might be outstanding, U.S. courts have steadfastly refused to enforce these defamation judgments arising from legal systems that do not provide protections similar to those provided by American constitutional law. If American courts continue to refuse to enforce foreign libel judgments that are not consistent with the First Amendment, there is less chance that American media companies, authors, and webmasters without substantial assets and reporting staffs abroad will be significantly affected by the potential for foreign liability. Media companies with significant assets abroad, however, may need to make different decisions.

This chapter considers the likely success of actions by foreign claimants to enforce content-liability judgments rendered by distant courts in the United States. First, for publishers with assets based entirely or largely with the United States, it reviews the consistent refusal by U.S. courts to enforce foreign libel judgments. Second, it provides practical advice for publishers with assets or reporting staffs outside the United States.

The United States and the First Amendment

Courts' Refusal to Enforce Foreign Content Judgments

Rachel Ehrenfeld, a respected U.S. scholar and the director of the American Center for Democracy, wrote a book entitled *Funding Evil: How Terrorism Is Financed and How to Stop It*. Dr. Ehrenfeld's book was published in the United States, and fewer than thirty copies entered the United Kingdom. Yet, a Saudi national, Sheik Khalid Salim a bin Mahfouz, filed suit against her in London, alleging that Ehrenfeld defamed him by writing that he arranged financing for Islamic charities that supported terrorism. Ehrenfeld decided not to show up in England to defend against the Sheik's suit. On December 7, 2004, English Judge Eady entered a default judgment against her for defamation. Ehrenfeld has no assets in England, and will defend herself against enforcement of the Sheik's judgment by arguing that it would violate the First Amendment for a U.S. court to enforce that judgment against her. (In fact, she has asked a U.S. court to declare the judgment unenforceable even if Bin Mahfouz does not seek to enforce it.)

The *Ehrenfeld* case illustrates the "guts play" of international libel disputes. If a U.S. publisher is sued in a court outside of the United States, the first question to consider is whether the publisher has assets outside the

United States. If the answer to that question is "no," then the publisher has the option of simply not defending against the suit, which will result in a default judgment being rendered against it. The publisher then can fight the enforcement of that judgment—that is, the efforts by the plaintiff to try to collect the judgment against U.S.-based bank accounts and assets. (The publisher also can defend against the suit in the foreign country, and *also* attack any attempt to enforce a judgment against it if it loses.) Under the First Amendment, there is a line of precedent under which U.S. courts refuse to enforce foreign libel judgments.

The risk involved in this gambit is, however, significant. If a court does decide to enforce the judgment, there will be no opportunity for the publisher to argue against the specific facts or law underlying it. Once a default judgment is issued, any defenses the publisher might have had to the underlying cause of action are waived. The foreign court, moreover, has the discretion to award the foreign plaintiff any amount of damages it wishes to award.

An alternative is the "two bites at the apple" strategy, in which a publisher defends in the foreign court but later argues against the enforcement of any judgment entered against it. This approach has the significant advantage of permitting the publisher to make all the substantive arguments it can to prevent a judgment from being entered against it in the first event (although victories in foreign jurisdictions are rare because the state of the law is typically stacked in favor of the claimant). If the publisher wins, the game is over (except perhaps for appeals). But if it loses, it still has the constitutional defense that U.S. courts should not enforce any foreign judgment rendered against it. The disadvantage, of course, is cost—defending in a foreign jurisdiction can be very expensive and time-consuming.

The Constitutional Defense. As a practical matter, the assertion of jurisdiction over U.S. media companies who do not maintain substantial assets abroad will be limited by the fact that the jurisdictional requirements of U.S. law must be satisfied in order for these judgments to be enforced, at least insofar as such requirements are grounded in the constitutional guarantee of due process. The Restatement (Third) of the Foreign Relations Law of the United States § 482 explains that, "[a] court in the United States may not recognize a judgment of the court of a foreign state if the judgment was rendered under a judicial system that does not provide … procedures compatible with due process of Law." The Supreme Court has repeatedly made clear that jurisdictional standards of minimum contacts and purposeful availment are rooted in the Due Process clause of the Constitution.[2] Accordingly, U.S. courts cannot enforce a foreign judgment rendered without sufficient contacts or purposeful availment to justify jurisdiction.[3]

U.S. courts generally enforce foreign-money judgments under principles of comity—the respect of one country's courts for the courts of another country.[4] However, U.S. courts are not required to enforce foreign judgments where such judgments conflict with U.S. public policy.[5] Cases in which U.S. courts have refused to enforce foreign judgments on policy grounds have been relatively rare outside the First Amendment context.[6] Within the First Amendment context, however, courts have consistently refused to enforce foreign libel judgments on policy grounds.

In *Matusevich v. Telnikoff,*[7] the leading case in the area, the plaintiff brought an action to preclude enforcement of a British libel judgment. The U.S. District Court for the District of Columbia granted the defendant's motion for summary judgment, holding that recognition of the British judgment would violate both Maryland's Uniform Foreign-Money Judgments Act (which tracks almost exactly the U.S. act) and the First and Fourteenth Amendments to the U.S. Constitution. In so holding, the court compared the differing libel standards of the English and U.S. jurisdictions. For example, the English libel scheme starts out assuming the falsity of the statements at issue, while under U.S. law, plaintiffs are required to prove that the article in question is false. The U.S. court determined that the speech found libelous under English law would have been protected by the First Amendment in a U.S. action. Emphasizing the drastic distinction between the two standards,[8] the U.S. court ruled that it would not enforce the UK libel judgment.[9]

In the most recent and high-profile application of the *Matusevich* principle, Yahoo! Inc. succeeded briefly in its efforts to avoid French jurisdiction over the dispute concerning Nazi speech on its global Internet site. In France, it is illegal to publish material that supports or encourages Nazism. In *Yahoo! Inc. v. La Ligue Contre Le Racisme et L'Antisemitisme,*[10] Yahoo! convinced a district court in California that the French court's orders "are not recognizable or enforceable because they violate the U.S. and California public policy of protecting free speech" and because they "constitute an unconstitutional prior restraint on speech that is protected by the First Amendment to the U.S. Constitution and by Article I of the Constitution of California."[11] The district court first held, importantly, that it did have jurisdiction over the French defendants against whom Yahoo! initiated its U.S. action (the plaintiffs in the French action) by virtue of the fact that they sought to avail themselves of the benefits of U.S. law by, among other things, serving Yahoo! with their French complaint with the assistance of U.S. marshals.[12] It then granted summary judgment to Yahoo! Inc., preventing enforcement of the French judgment against it. (On appeal, the U.S. Court of Appeals for the Ninth Circuit found that the district court did not have jurisdiction over the French defendants and reversed this decision; the full panel of Ninth Circuit judges currently is reviewing that decision.)

This decision illustrates a new strategic avenue for the defense of foreign actions by U.S. Internet publishers. Although publishers with assets and subsidiaries in foreign countries always will be vulnerable to off-shore litigation and the enforcement of foreign judgments against those assets and subsidiaries, the *Yahoo!* decision suggests that the *Matusevitch* doctrine applies with full force and effect to Internet publishing in contexts additional to defamation judgments. In *Yahoo!,* the matter at stake was not defamation, as has been the case in most cases where U.S. courts have refused to enforce foreign judgments, but other speech that was protected by the First Amendment. If it is affirmed on appeal, this case may make it more feasible for U.S. Internet publishers to extend the *Matusevich* doctrine to cases involving invasion of privacy, the increasingly controversial area of hate speech that is criminalized under the laws of many European countries, prosecutions for newsgathering offenses, and the like.

The *Matusevitch* principle has been applied straightforwardly in a variety of different factual contexts outside of the Internet. In *Abdullah v. Sheridan Square Press,*[13] for example, the U.S. District Court for the Southern District of New York, applying New York choice of law doctrine, refused to apply British libel law against a New York publisher in an action by a former Jordanian army officer living in Britain because "establishment of a claim for libel under the British law of defamation would be antithetical to the First Amendment protection accorded the defendants."[14] In *Bachchan v. India Abroad Publications Inc.,*[15] an Indian national sought to enforce a British libel judgment granted by the High Court of Justice in London against the New York operator of a news service; the court held that the values underlying the First Amendment "would be seriously jeopardized by the entry of foreign libel judgments granted pursuant to standards deemed antithetical to the protections afforded the press by the Constitution."[16]

The principle has been applied in suits initiated in U.S. courts as well. In *Desai v. Hersh,*[17] for example, the former prime minister of India asked a U.S. court to apply Indian defamation law in a suit against the U.S. author of an allegedly defamatory book published in both the United States and India. Indian law, unlike U.S. law, does not require a public figure to prove actual malice on the part of a libel defendant, and the court thus refused to apply Indian law. Notably, however, the *Desai* court refused to adopt the defendant's broad argument that the First Amendment applies to all American-written documents published abroad. The court used the public figure/actual malice requirement as a constitutional dividing line—it held that where a libel action is brought by a foreign public figure in U.S. court, the public figure must show actual malice on the part of the U.S. defendant.

Finally, some cases have applied foreign law but added First Amendment protections to that law. In *DeRoburt v. Gannett Co.,*[18] for example, the president of Nauru brought a federal action for defamation against a U.S. newspaper publisher under the law of Nauru. Nauru law contains no analog to the First Amendment. The court adopted a choice of law analysis, rather than categorically refusing to apply foreign libel law, and viewed the First Amendment as one of the policies that should be considered in the choice of law calculus.[19] The court ultimately held that Nauru law could be applied, but only as modified by the imposition of First Amendment safeguards.[20]

In sum, these cases illustrate the reluctance, if not absolute refusal, of U.S. courts to apply foreign libel law in American courts, or to enforce foreign libel judgments based on laws inconsistent with the First Amendment. This is perhaps the single most important protection against the increasing trend toward aggressive assertion of jurisdiction over Internet content claims by courts outside the United States.

International Law

Judgments Typically Are Enforced

The First Amendment, and the way in which it has been applied, is unique in the world. The refusal of U.S. courts to enforce judgments rendered under foreign libel law, in turn, also is unique. Other countries are not as hesitant to enforce judgments rendered outside their borders.

The European Union is a high-profile case in point. Under the Brussels Convention on Jurisdiction and Enforcement of Judgments in Civil and Commercial Matters, and under legislation that has followed on from that agreement, a judgment entered against a person or entity in any of the twenty-five Member States of the European Union generally may be enforced against that person or entity in any Member State.[21] A similar treaty exists among the member states of the Organization of American States (excluding the United States).[22] Other treaties exist as a bilateral matter between particular countries.

There may be opportunities to raise objections to the enforcement of such judgments based on the public policy of the country in which the judgment is sought to be enforced, similar to the procedure in the United States under which a publisher can object under the First Amendment to the enforcement of a judgment rendered under a law with insufficient protections. The difficulty, however, is that European law is largely uniform on defamation, privacy, and other content-liability issues. A judgment rendered in the United Kingdom, therefore, is unlikely to offend public policy in France, and vice versa.

Because of this important distinction, publishers with either assets or reporters in an EU country may not be able to employ the "guts play" of simply ignoring a foreign suit and challenging enforcement of a default judgment. For a publisher with significant assets outside of the United States, the first step in determining whether to defend against a suit is to determine whether any resulting judgment can be enforced against it. For example, if the publisher has assets in France and the suit has been filed in Portugal, the judgment would be enforceable, even without assets in Portugal, and the publisher should be advised to defend the suit aggressively. If the publisher has assets in the United Kingdom and has been sued in Australia, again the answer should be "yes"—Australia and the United Kingdom have a bilateral treaty permitting judgments rendered in Australian courts to be recognized and enforced in English courts. The question, and the answer, depend on the countries involved.

Of course, this raises the strategic question of whether a publisher ought to consider structuring its assets so that it can avoid enforcement of any judgments entered by foreign courts. To the extent that it is practical as a commercial matter for assets to be located in the United States, following such a strategy may be workable.

Conclusion

U.S. publishers can, and should, consider the location of their assets as an important strategic matter. Those who can, consistent with commercial realities, limit their holding of assets to the United States have an important benefit—they can argue that a U.S. court cannot constitutionally enforce a defamation judgment against them because that judgment was rendered by a foreign court applying law that was not consistent with the demands of the First Amendment. The strategic decision then is whether to defend the case, and later argue against its enforcement against the publisher, or to permit the suit to result in a default judgment.

If a publisher cannot structure its assets in this manner, it should nonetheless determine its strategy for defending against international suits based on the treaties that are binding in any country in which it does own assets. If that country is in the European Union, for example, the publisher should anticipate being required to defend any suit filed against it in an EU Member State. In all cases, however, it is wise for publishers to think through their options carefully *before* being forced to consider them under the pressure of the initiation of litigation. In a world in which foreign courts routinely exercise jurisdiction over publishers based solely on Internet publication, the most likely question is not *whether* a publisher ever will be sued in another country, but *when.*

Chapter Notes

1. See, e.g., United Nations, Universal Declaration of Human Rights, Article 19; European Convention for the Protection of Human Rights and Fundamental Freedoms, Article 10.

2. See, e.g., *International Shoe Co. v. Washington,* 326 U.S. 310 (1945); *World-Wide Volkswagen Corporation v. Woodson,* 444 U.S. 286 (1980).

3. The same section of the Restatement provides that a U.S. court may not enforce a foreign judgment where the foreign court was without jurisdiction to adjudicate under the principles of § 421. However, jurisdiction in this analysis means jurisdiction in accordance with the law of the foreign country. See § 421(b) and Comment c. The argument outlined in the text does not assert that the foreign court was without jurisdiction but that the jurisdiction it in fact exercised failed to comport with Due Process of law.

4. Note that the enforceability of foreign judgments is determined on the basis of state law. See 13 A.L.R. Fed. 208 (1972). States provide for such enforcement under the Uniform Foreign Money-Judgments Act. Federal cases have often relied on principles of comity as the rationale for enforcement. See, e.g., *Hilton v. Guyot,* 159 U.S. 113 (1895).

5. See, e.g., Maryland's Uniform Foreign-Money Judgments Recognition Act of 1962 and the Uniform Enforcement of Foreign Judgments Act of 1964, at Md. Code Ann., Cts. & Jud. Proc. § 10-703.

6. See, e.g., *Tahan v. Hodgson,* 662 F.2d 862 (D.C. Cir. 1981)(enforcing Israeli default judgment though process served upon defendant while in Jerusalem was in Hebrew).

7. 877 F. Supp. 1 (D.D.C. 1995) (answering question certified from the D.C. Circuit Court of Appeals), 1998 U.S. App. LEXIS 556 (D.C. Cir. May 5, 1998), *conforming to judgment of Maryland Court of Appeals,* 702 A.2d 230 (Md. 1997).

8. The court noted that the judgment did not require the plaintiff to prove falsehood; that the judge had instructed the jury to disregard context in contravention of *Moldea v. New York Times Co.,* 22 F.3d 310 (D.C. Cir. 1994); and that the judgment did not rest upon a finding of actual malice, in contravention of *New York Times v. Sullivan.* See *id.*

9. See *id.* at 4.

10. 169 F. Supp. 2d 1181 (N.D. Cal. 2001).

11. Complaint at 10 (http://www.cdt.org/speech/international/001221yahoo complaint.pdf).

12. *Yahoo! Inc. v. La Ligue Contre Le Racisme et L'Antisemitisme,* Case No. 00-21275 JF (N.D. Cal June 7, 2001) (available at http://www.cdt.org/jurisdiction/010607yahoo.pdf).

13. 1994 WL 419847 (S.D.N.Y. May 4, 1994).

14. *Id.*

15. 154 Misc. 2d 228 (N.Y. Sup. Ct. 1992).

16. *Id.* at 235; see also *Ellis v. Time, Inc.,* 1997 WL 863267 (D.D.C. Nov. 18, 1997).

17. 719 F. Supp. 670 (N.D. Ill. 1989).

18. 83 F.R.D. 574 (D. Haw. 1979).

19. See *id.*

20. See *id.* at 580.

21. See Council Regulation (EC) 44/2001 of 22 December 2000 on jurisdiction and the recognition and enforcement of judgment.

22. See Inter-American Convention on the Extra-Territorial Validity of Foreign Judgments and Arbitral Awards.

CHAPTER 23

Fair Use

It Stops at the Border

NANCY E. WOLFF

Wolff & Godin, LLP

Nancy E. Wolff, Esq.

Wolff & Godin, LLP

118 West 79th Street

New York, NY 10024, U.S.A.

Phone: 212-787-1640

Fax: 212-787-8355

http://www.wolffgodin.com/

NEWOLFF@aol.com

The ease with which people can select, cut, and paste photos and text in our globally wired, Internet-accessible world has made the infringement of copyrighted material a more pervasive problem than ever. What makes this problem particularly reoccurring is not only that copying other's work is just so simple—a few mouse clicks—but that the idea of *fair use* is widely misunderstood.

This doctrine is unique to U.S. copyright law, although the principles have been recognized to a lesser degree in part by the Berne Convention, which is a global treaty on copyright.[1]

Fair use is a defense to infringement of copyrighted material. The defense is codified in the Copyright Act embodied in 17 U.S.C. §107. In sum, the defense of fair use allows for the reproduction of copyrighted material in certain instances, including criticism, comment, news reporting, teaching, scholarship, or research without obtaining consent from the copyright owner. The reproduction of copyrighted material in these instances is not an infringement of copyright, whether the copyright owner agrees with the new use or not. The purpose of this chapter is to explain in better detail what those instances are, and what limitations apply to fair use.

Four Factors, But No Bright Line Test

There are no bright lines in determining whether an unauthorized use would be considered "fair" and non-infringing or simply infringing. The Copyright Act offers guidelines as to what factors the court should use in determining fair use, and does not list any rules. Accordingly, there is no generally applicable definition of fair use, and each case raising the question must be decided on its own facts.[2] In determining whether the use made of a copyrighted work in any particular instance is "fair," the factors include:

1. the purpose and character of the use, including whether such use is of a commercial nature or is for nonprofit educational purposes;
2. the nature of the copyrighted work;
3. the amount and substantiality of the portion used in relation to the copyrighted work as a whole; and
4. the effect of the use upon the potential market for or value of the copyrighted work.[3]

When fair use is raised as a defense to a copyright infringement action, the court uses these four factors to analyze the case. Although no single element is most important, the fourth factor, the effect of the use upon the potential market or the value of the copyrighted work, is often given more weight than the others by the courts.

Is It "Transformative"?

The issue turns on the persuasiveness of the justification. In writing for the *Harvard Law Review* in 1990, Judge Pierre N. Leval noted that the issue of justification for the fair use defense turns on whether, and to what extent, the challenged use is transformative.[4] To be transformative, the use must be productive and employ the quoted material in a different manner or for a different purpose than the original. If a quotation of copyrighted material merely repackages the original work, it is unlikely to pass the test. However, if the secondary use adds value to the original—if the quoted matter is used as raw material, transformed in the creation of new information—the fair use doctrine is intended to protect such a use.[5] A transformative use does not guarantee success of a fair use defense: the transformative justification must still overcome factors favoring the copyright owner.[6]

Checklist for Fair Use

Each of the four factors to be considered in fair use determinations has a number of conditions which will support or hinder a fair use defense.[7]

1. ***Purpose and character:*** In analyzing the first factor, courts will generally ask whether such use is of a commercial nature or if is for non-profit educational purposes. Similar conditions favoring a finding of fair use include: teaching, research, scholarship, criticism, comment, news reporting, parody, transformative or productive use that changes the work for new utility, restricted access (such as to students or other similar groups), and use by a nonprofit educational institution. By contrast, conditions that will hinder a fair use defense include: use for commercial activity, profiting from the use, use for entertainment, bad-faith behavior, and denying credit to the original author.

2. ***The nature of the copyrighted work:*** In analyzing the second factor, conditions that support a fair use defense include: use of published works, factual or nonfiction-based works, and use important to favored educational objectives. Conditions which may defeat a fair use defense under this factor include: use of unpublished works, use of highly creative works, such as art, music, novels, films, and plays, and use of fictional works.

3. ***The amount and substantiality of the portion used:*** In analyzing the third factor, conditions which support a claim of fair use include: use of a small quantity, use of a portion that is not central or significant to the entire work, and use of an amount that is appropriate for the educational purpose. Conditions that hinder a fair use defense under this factor include use of a large portion or the whole work and use of a portion which is central to the work or the "heart of the work."

4. ***Effect upon market potential:*** In analyzing the fourth factor, conditions which support a fair use defense include: whether the user owns a lawfully acquired or purchased copy of the work, the number of copies made, the lack of a significant effect on the market or potential market for the copyrighted work, and whether there is a licensing mechanism. Conditions which will overcome a fair use defense under this factor include: a use that could replace the sale of the copyrighted work, uses that significantly impair the market or potential market for the copyrighted work or a derivative, the reasonable availability of a licensing mechanism for use of the copyrighted work, the availability of affordable permission for using the work.

Examples of Fair Use

A useful example of a successful fair use claim is seen in *Mattel Inc. v. Walking Mountain Products.*[8] Thomas Forsythe, of Walking Mountain Products, took a series of seventy-eight pictures of Mattel's Barbie doll being attacked by vintage household products. Here, the strongest fact in favor of fair use was the ability to use copyrighted work for the express purpose of criticizing or commenting upon the original work. Here, because the Barbie doll is a cultural icon, and the use of the copyrighted features was central to any critique, the Court found Forsythe's reproduction of Barbie fair. The Court reasoned that Forsythe's use was a parody meant to criticize Barbie, Forsythe only copied what was necessary for his purpose, and Forsythe's photographs could not affect the market demand for Mattel's products. One good indicator of fair use is whether it is impossible to avoid using some of the copyrighted work in order to write a review or critique of the copyrighted work.

By contrast, the fair use defense failed in *Elvis Presley Enterprises Inc. v. Passport Video.*[9] The owners of various copyrights involving Elvis Presley, such as Elvis's appearance on *The Ed Sullivan Show,* his songs, and still photographs of him, brought suit against Passport Video, which made a 16-hour documentary of Elvis using the copyrighted material. Approximately 5–10 percent of the documentary was made up of the copyrighted material owned by the Presley estate. The Court found that Passport's use was commercial in nature, and sought to profit directly from the copyrights it used without license. Whereas television footage may be properly characterized as newsworthy, the Court stated that still photographs and songs are not as newsworthy and comprised the photographer's and composer's artistic product. The nature of the use—here, the repetition of the same clip several times—swayed the Court to rule that the use was not "fair." The Court also noted that though the clips were short in length, they tended to comprise the heart of the work. "What makes these copyrighted works valuable is Elvis's appearance on the shows, in many cases singing the most familiar passages of his most popular songs. Plaintiffs are in the business of licensing these copyrights. Taking key portions extracts the most valuable part of Plaintiffs' copyrighted works." In analyzing the fourth factor, the Court stated that Passport's use is commercial in nature, and thus can assume market harm. Passport expressly advertised that its documentary contained the television appearances for which Plaintiffs normally charge a licensing fee. "If this type of use became wide-spread, it would likely undermine the market for selling Plaintiffs' copyrighted material." The Court stated that this conclusion does not apply to the music and still photographs, as it seems unlikely that someone in the market for these materials would purchase the documentary instead.

Foreign Limitations on Fair Use

As described earlier, the United States is the only country that has a well-defined fair use doctrine. Other countries, including almost all of Europe, have specific statutory exemptions to copyright infringement. In order for a use of a copyrighted work to be found non-infringing, the use of the work must fall under one or more of these statutory exemptions. Instead of "guidelines," these countries have rules.

Illustrative are the statutory exemptions of the United Kingdom under the idea of "fair dealing," which tends to be narrower in scope than fair use in the United States. Specific exemptions include use for research and private study, library and archival uses, educational uses, charitable and related uses, criticism and reviews or news, recitation and incidental uses, government uses, and public interest uses.

One infringement exception is when the copyrighted work is used for research or private study. This exception requires that the use be noncommercial, and applies to literary, dramatic, musical, or artistic works, and has limited application to computer programs. Three factors are looked at to determine if the use is reasonable: the quantity appropriated, the financial effect on the copyright owner, and whether the owner makes the material available.

A second exception to infringement for the use of copyrighted works applies to library and archival uses. Libraries may make copies for individuals for their noncommercial research or private study use at cost and in accordance with clear regulations. The library may copy up to one article per issue and a reasonable extract from any other publication. Libraries may also make one or more copies under specific statutory circumstances.

A third category of exceptions is use of copyrighted works in an educational setting. Specific exceptions in this category include copying literary, dramatic, musical, or artistic work in giving or preparing instruction, provided the copying is not done by a reprographic process; use of copyrighted work in preparing and giving examinations; performing, playing, or showing works before teachers and pupils at an educational establishment; lending of copies of work by an educational establishment; and copying abstracts of scientific or technical articles.

A fourth category of copyright exceptions is use for charitable and related uses. This category has a few, very specific, exceptions. By example, copyrighted sound recordings may be played, provided that (1) the organization is not established or conducted for profit, (2) the main objects of the organization are charitable, (3) any proceeds for admission are solely for purposes of the organization, (4) any proceeds from goods sold are solely for the purposes of the organization, and (5) the work is played by a person acting to benefit the organization.

A fifth category of copyright infringement exceptions is use for criticism, reviews, and news. Generally, any work available to the public may be copied to some extent for the purpose of criticism or review of the work itself or of another work, provided there is adequate acknowledgment of the author.

Recitation and incidental uses provide a sixth category of exceptions to copyright infringement. One exception in this category provides that a solo reading or recitation or a reasonable extract may be made in public with sufficient acknowledgment. Another exception provides that a copyrighted work is not infringed by incidental inclusion in an artistic work, sound recording, film, or broadcast, such as the use of a copyrighted picture in the background of a film.

A seventh category of copyright infringement exceptions is government use. Generally, the government is allowed to use artistic works, broadcast programs or works, and computer programs and databases without infringing the copyright.

An eighth category of exceptions to copyright infringement is if the use is in the public interest. There is no statutory provision for this exception, which was first recognized in the 1970s by the High Court. The exception is very narrow, however. In rare circumstances, it may justify infringement; however, those circumstances can't be described in advance.

Copyright law in most of Europe falls under the Berne Convention.[10] The Right of Reproduction language provides a three-step test to determine whether use of a copyrighted work is infringement of that work. The test provides three separate but cumulative conditions that must be satisfied before the national law of a county may rely upon an exception to copyright infringement. First, the reproduction must only be allowed "in certain special cases." Second, the reproduction should "not conflict with a normal exploitation of the work." Third, the reproduction should "not unreasonably prejudice the legitimate interests of the authors."

The Centre for Copyright Studies Ltd.[11] has provided some guidelines in interpreting the three-step test. In interpreting the first condition, the exception should be clearly defined and narrow in scope and reach. There is no public policy or exception circumstance that must justify this exception.

In determining what the "normal exploitations" are under the second condition, regard must be given to the existing, as well as potential, uses of a work from which the copyright owner can extract an economic benefit. Neither existing nor future exceptions will be in conflict with a normal exploitation of a work just because they involve uses that would be of economic benefit to the author. The test is whether they enter into or will enter into economic competition with the author.

In interpreting the third condition, "legitimate interests of the author" include both economic and personal, or moral rights, interests. The prejudice to the author's interests by the proposed usage may be substantial or material, but must not be "unreasonable" in the sense of being disproportionate. "Unreasonable prejudice," therefore, may be avoided by conditions on the usage, including a payment requirement.

Chapter Notes

1. The Berne Convention contains a number of provisions directed at the same issues that make up the foundation of fair use, specifically, "freedom of information" in the cases of teaching, reporting current news, and making public speeches. See *Berne Convention of Paris,* July 24, 1971, articles 10(2) and 11, available online at http://www.law.cornell.edu/treaties/berne/overview.html.

2. House Report 94-1476.

3. 17 U.S.C. §107.

4. Pierre N. Leval, *Toward a Fair Use Standard,* 103 Harv. L. Rev. 1105, 1111 (1990).

5. *Id.* at 1111.

6. *Id.*

7. Copyright Management Center, IUPUI, *Checklist for Fair Use,* available at http://www.copyright.iupui.edu/checklist.htm, last visited February 28, 2005.

8. 353 F.3d 792 (9th Cir. 2003).

9. 357 F.3d 896 (9th Cir. 2003).

10. Article 9(2) states: "It shall be a matter for legislation in the countries of the Union to permit the reproduction of such works in certain special cases, provided that such reproduction does not conflict with a normal exploitation of work and does not unreasonably prejudice the legitimate interest of the author."

11. The Centre for Copyright Studies Ltd. was established in 1993. The primary purpose of the Centre is to undertake and promote research into copyright. The Centre is funded by Copyright Agency, Ltd., a copyright collecting society representing authors and publishers.

CHAPTER 24

The Emergence of Privacy as a Claim in the UK
Theory and Guidelines

AMBER MELVILLE-BROWN

David Price Solicitors & Advocates

David Price Solicitors & Advocates

21 Fleet Street, London, EC4Y 1AA, United Kingdom

Phone: +44 (0) 7793 001 023 / +44 20 7353 9999

Fax: +44 20 7353 9990

www.lawyers-media.com

amelville-brown@lawyers-media.com

Introduction

Despite its shy and retiring nature, privacy never ceases to muscle its way into the limelight—concerning photographs of a footballer in his underwear on a private Portuguese balcony;[1] a secret drug addict on a public road and a private doorstep in London;[2] a naked radio presenter in a private villa in the Seychelles;[3] a Monaco princess skiing and horseback riding;[4] and Hollywood royalty caught out at their own wedding.[5]

But although privacy protection and exposure are two great national pastimes in the UK, with celebrities and public figures fighting for the one and the press and the media seeking to secure the other, the fact of privacy's high-profile place in the UK is all the more surprising given that historically English law has not recognized a right to privacy. Although a variety of causes of action and legislation have provided some protection, there is no Privacy Act in the UK; there is no English constitution enshrining a right to privacy; historically there has been no free-standing tort of privacy.

But things began to change with the implementation of the Human Rights Act 1998 (the HRA)[6] incorporating into UK law the European Convention of Human Rights (the Convention), and the article 8 right protecting privacy. With the global spread of information, it is also impossible to ignore the rulings of the European Court of Human Rights (ECHR), whose long fingers probe the domestic laws of every member country. As Lord Nicholls said in his judgment in the House of Lords in *Campbell v. MGN* (*Campbell*), "the protection of various aspects of privacy is a fast developing area of the law, here and in some other common law jurisdictions." Indeed, significantly the UK Court of Appeal has recognized "for the first time" in *Douglas v. Hello* that post the ECHR case of *Caroline von Hannover v. Germany* (*von Hannover*), "the courts have a duty to recognise and protect privacy rights."[7]

As referred to in *Campbell*, a picture is worth a thousand words, conveying important information readily to the reader, so it is often cases involving the publication of photographs, perhaps more so than in any other medium, that give rise to complaint. This may be especially so in the UK, where celebrity magazines and tabloid newspapers abound; photographs of those in the public eye are as popular as they are potentially invasive of those parties' privacy.

So, how did we get to the stage in the United Kingdom where the right to freedom of expression weighs heavily in the balance, where the public is ceaselessly transfixed with the minutiae of other people's lives while fiercely protective of their own, and where there is no law *per se* protecting privacy, but privacy is nevertheless protected? The courts have now confirmed that "the ECHR has recognized an obligation on member states to protect one individual from an unjustified invasion of private life by another individual and an obligation on the courts of a member state to interpret legislation in a way which will achieve that result."[8]

The author does not attempt here to provide an exhaustive legal treatise on the development of privacy law in the UK, and there are respected professionals in the field who have discussed the subject further. The aim of this chapter is to seek to give a brief background and some practical advice with particular regard to the important subject of the use of private information contained in photographs. This may assist those at the front lines of the media industry, faced with making daily decisions as to the content of their publications to protect their freedom of expression while not unnecessarily infringing the rights of others.

To do that, it is worthwhile considering the history of privacy law as meted out by the courts of England and Wales. This is not just an interesting academic exercise, but it is important to know how the law has developed to see how the courts may react in any given set of circumstances, and how the law is likely to develop further.

Historical Perspective: England and Wales

There was perhaps no more vivid example evidencing the lack of an English privacy law than the case of *Kaye v. Robertson*,[9] concerning the publication of unauthorized photographs of a well-known British actor recuperating in the hospital from a very serious accident. Given that the purported interview and photographs which formed the subject of the claim concerned his medical treatment, it is almost certain that it would constitute an infringement of his right to privacy in the post–*Campbell* regime. The House of Lords in *Campbell* was prepared to protect Campbell's right to keep confidential the details of the treatment that she was undertaking. In *Kaye,* Lord Bingham expressed the unsatisfactory nature of the law as it stood then as follows:

> The defendants' conduct towards the plaintiff here was a monstrous invasion of privacy. If ever a person has a right to be let alone by strangers with no public interest to pursue, it must surely be when he lies in hospital recovering from brain surgery. It is this invasion of privacy which underlies the plaintiff's case. Yet it alone, however gross, does not entitle him to relief in English law.

The push for better ways to protect privacy has included the creative use of various causes of action. Among others, malicious falsehood, trespass, harassment, copyright, and data protection sometimes fit the facts and can be used to achieve justice, but the most frequently used cause of action has been the common law tort of breach of confidence.

Breach of Confidence: Privacy's Germinal Start

This longstanding tort—in evidence as a mechanism for privacy actions since as long ago as 1848 when it was used by Queen Victoria's husband to protect private etchings from further dissemination[10]—prevents, at the instigation of the person to whom the confidence is owed, the publication of private information given to or obtained by a person in confidence. The original test propounded in *Coco v. Clarke*[11] was as follows:
- the evidence has to have the "necessary quality of confidence about it,"
- the information must have been "imparted in circumstances importing an obligation of confidence," and
- there must have been an "unauthorised use of the information to the detriment of the party communicating it."

What will be considered to be confidential or private information and have the necessary quality about it will be decided on the facts of the case in question. It may cover various classes of information, including secrets between partners in life, in employment, and in business.

The definition of the second requirement has been radically widened so that there is now no longer the need for a close relationship between the imparter and the discloser of the information, such as, for example, a contractual relationship or the relationship between doctor and patient. The circumstances in which a duty of confidence could now be held to exist was accepted in Earl Spencer's ECHR case in 1998[12] as being as follows:

> A duty of confidence arises when confidential information comes to the knowledge of a person … in circumstances where he has notice, or is held to have agreed, that the information is confidential, with the effect that it would be just in all the circumstances that he should be precluded from disclosing the information to others.

So a publisher who does not obtain private information himself but does so, for example, from a freelance photographer in circumstances which put him on notice of the confidential nature of the material, would be equally liable if he publishes it as if he had obtained it in breach of confidence himself.

Misuse of Private Information: Privacy Takes Root

The evolution of this tort into the privacy arena has led to it being referred to by the House of Lords in *Campbell* as "better encapsulated now as misuse of private information." This might suggest at a cursory glance, erroneously in the author's view, that the traditional breach of confidence has been replaced. Rather, the two now co-exist, the original based on the nature of the relationship between the parties and/or an obligation, and the new based on the nature of the information and a reasonable expectation of privacy. If both exist, then one has to consider at the outset what type one is dealing with and adopt the correct tests. In respect of the new, the test to be applied is:

- is the information private, and
- did the subject have a reasonable expectation of privacy with regard to the information in question, and
- did the subject suffer harm or a risk of harm as a result of the wrongful disclosure of the information in question?

The Human Rights Act: Synching Up With Europe

The implementation of the HRA significantly impacted our privacy laws. It incorporated into UK law the European Convention's twin rights of freedom of expression[13] and the right to respect for private and family life, *aka* privacy.[14] As was quite clearly set out by Nicholls LJ in *Campbell*, "the time has come to recognise that the values enshrined in articles 8 and 10 are now part of the cause of action for breach of confidence." And like two naughty siblings they are constantly fighting for attention and arguing over who is the stronger. Neither has automatic precedence. The UK courts must act consistently with the ECHR rulings and must balance the two rights in any given set of circumstances.

Before von Hannover*: Practice*

Although there are a number of cases evidencing the courts' approach to the publication of potentially private photographs (see cases below), those taking or publishing photos in the UK had not previously had much of a firm hand exercised over them for a number of reasons.

First, the Press Complaints Commission (PCC), which is charged with enforcing the Editors' Code of Practice with which publishers voluntarily comply, has been criticized by some to be a dog with a bark but no bite. It provides guidelines as to what is considered good practice, but it cannot impose a fine or demand compensation be paid to a successful complainant, only that the offending publication publish its adjudication. However, its current chairman, Sir Christopher Meyer, is keen to ensure that this image is dispelled and is proud of its policy of being "fast, free and fair." Additionally, compliance with the Code will also be taken into consideration by the courts in any relevant litigation by virtue of section 12 of the HRA.[15] Ofcom, the regulatory body for the broadcasting industry since the beginning of 2005, has a new Broadcasting Code in force from July 25, 2005. Both Codes are available on the relevant Web sites.[16]

Second, and of greater practical importance, is that whereas the PCC does receive complaints from private individuals and celebrities/public figures alike, many in the public eye or aspiring to be there may have been more likely to think twice before making any complaint given that they need the media to survive. There is a highly competitive and thriving celebrity market in the UK, with numerous magazines dedicated solely to picturing celebrities in authorized—and very popular unauthorized—photo spreads, not to mention the many pages devoted to celebrities in our tabloid newspapers and numerous celebrity television shows. "Live by the camera, die by the camera" is not only on the lips of those seeking to exploit the celebrities for commercial gain, but will almost certainly be in the minds of those seeking similarly to exploit the media on their way up the celebrity ladder.

So, whereas the Code and the law may set out guidelines and requirements, in practice a failure to comply may not historically have led to a complaint. A blatant disregard for the Code or the Court can *never* be condoned, and indeed if there is evidence of this it will certainly sound in damages in any subsequent legal action. It should not be forgotten that the PCC Code is said to be HRA/ECHR compliant and, also by virtue of section 12 of the HRA, is to be taken into account when the court is considering granting an interim injunction.[17] Therefore, its clauses and its rulings merit consideration.

Although this is not an exhaustive list, the following examples of English cases in which the question of private information regarding photographs has been addressed show how, over recent years but pre–*von Hannover,* our courts have considered the issues.

Attard v. Greater Manchester Newspapers Ltd *[2001]* This Family Division case effectively allowed an outing of the principle later expounded by the Court of Appeal in *Douglas v. Hello!* that a "hybrid" privacy right of private and commercial information can be a commodity that can be sold, without "the owner" losing the right to protect their privacy. The case dealt with the publication of photographs of conjoined twins, one of whom died. The court was prepared to grant an injunction preventing publication of photographs of the surviving twin, taken on the steps of the hospital where the operation to separate her from her sister had taken place, and then to vary that order to allow publication of photographs in the one newspaper with whom the parents then entered into an exclusive deal for publication. Interestingly, this approach was considerably frowned upon by the PCC, which said that privacy was not a commodity that could be sold on one person's terms.[18] The right to commercial confidence has now been approved by the Court of Appeal in *Douglas.*

Venables and Thompson v. News Group Newspapers Ltd *[2001]*[19] In what was then an unprecedented move, lifelong anonymity—effectively guaranteeing privacy—was granted in 2001 to two child killers, Thompson and Venables, on reaching maturity. The murder they committed was considered to be particularly abhorrent because perhaps of the age of the toddler victim, the young age of the killers, and the fact that there had been CCTV footage at the shopping center, shown nationwide on mainstream television, of the killers leading the little boy away to his ultimate torture and death. Accordingly, the public outcry over the murder was huge and the danger to the boys' lives on release from the youth offenders institution was evident. Dame Butler Sloss granted lifelong anonymity to the boys, naturally including a prohibition against the publication of photographs of them, in order not to protect their *private* lives but under section 2 of the Convention to protect their very lives. The Court found that the law of confidence could be used in this way to injunct the media where there was a real possibility of serious injury or death and this was the only way to guard against it.

A similar injunction was granted to protect Maxine Carr,[20] the former girlfriend of child murderer Ian Huntley, given the public outcry over her involvement in the matter. Her crime was not murder but only providing a false alibi for her then partner, but again the public outcry was such that her life was threatened and in danger. As a by-product, her right to respect for her private and family life under article 8—accordingly preventing the publication of photographs of her—was also protected.

Douglas v. Hello *[2002]* (First instance) The well-publicized breach of confidence case of Hollywood couple Catherine Zeta Jones and Michael Douglas, who sought protection over invasion into their private lives as a result of *Hello!* magazine's publication of surreptitiously taken photographs of their wedding,[21] specifically identified a "hybrid" right foreshadowed in *Attard* of commercial confidentiality. In this case, the first instance judge, Mr. Justice Lindsay, agreed that the couple's wedding was a private affair the privacy of which they had worked hard to try to protect. It mattered not that they had entered into an exclusive deal with *OK!* magazine for the publication of some photographs of their wedding, under controlled circumstances, and that photographs of the wedding would therefore have been published and available to the public anyway. This did not deprive them of their right to protect their "hybrid" right, partly private/personal and partly commercial in nature. Despite this additional twist, in fact the judgment found in the claimants' favor on longstanding breach of confidence grounds. Further clarity was given to the right to privacy concerning photographs in the Court of Appeal decision handed down in May 2005. This is discussed below.

Theakston v. MGN Ltd *[2002]* This case related to an injunction application to prevent the publication of an article about a children's television presenter's visit to a brothel, and salacious photographs taken by one of the women working there. Ousley J was not prepared to grant an injunction preventing publication of the article but did prohibit the publication of the photographs:

> I concluded that this part of the injunction involved no particular extension of the law of confidentiality and that the publication of such photographs would be particularly intrusive into the Claimant's own personality ... Publication of photographs taken there without his consent could still constitute an intrusion into his private and personal life and would do so in a peculiarly humiliating and damaging way.[22]

Note the use of the word "humiliating" which was also addressed in *Campbell* and *von Hannover* and shows that the nature of the activity photographed will bear upon the court's decision.

Peck v. United Kingdom *[2003]* UK courts do not always get it right as far as the ECHR is concerned. This is illustrated in *Peck,* featuring a disturbed individual caught on CCTV camera trying to take his life. As a result of the numerous times unauthorized photographs of the claimant at this distressing time were published and subsequently broadcast, it was held that our law did not properly protect the rights of this individual.[23]

Naomi Campbell v. MGN Ltd *[2004]* The extent to which the publication of photographs impacted on the right to respect for one's private life was dealt with substantially by our House of Lords in the case of *Campbell.*[24] The well-known and frequently photographed supermodel, Naomi Campbell, did not complain about being outed as a drug addict by the *Mirror* newspaper; she had lied about her addiction publicly so had to accept that there was a legitimate public interest in exposing her as a hypocrite. Neither did she specifically complain over the taking of the photographs themselves. Instead, her complaint was that the combination of the photographs, taken on the steps of where she was undergoing her therapy, and the unnecessary private and confidential detail about her treatment in the article infringed her privacy.

Taken all the way to the UK House of Lords, the eventual outcome of the case was success for the claimant. Some disagreement on the application of the law to the specific facts can be found in the judgments of the Law Lords, with the senior judges Lords Nicholls and Hoffman in favor of dismissing the claim, while the other three, Lords Hope and Carswell and Baroness Hale, upheld it. This disparity turned on the margin of appreciation to be allowed to the editor in adding color to the story that it legitimately proposed to publish.[25] But some useful general principles can be seen, including that:

- everyone, even those in the public eye, can retain some vestige of privacy worthy of protection;[26]
- whether one has a privacy to protect will turn on the "touchstone" of whether the subject had a reasonable expectation of privacy with regard to the disclosed fact;
- the nature of the activity photographed will be key to a privacy claim;
- the circumstances in which the photograph was taken will be relevant;
- the likely damage that may be done by the publication will be taken into account;

- information of a medical nature is almost always likely to be protected, save for a public interest defense.[27]

Echoing what was said by the judge in *Theakston,* Lord Justice Hoffman's dissenting judgment in *Campbell* considered that photographs of incidents which might be in the public interest could themselves be a step too far; for example, he said that there might be a public interest in the disclosure of a sexual relationship between a politician and someone whom he or she has appointed to public office, where "the addition of salacious details or intimate photographs is disproportionate and unacceptable. The latter, even if accompanying a legitimate disclosure of the sexual relationship, would be too intrusive and demeaning." So disclosure of the fact of the relationship would be acceptable, but private photographs evidencing it would, in his view, not be.

But he also considered that a photograph might be actionable where it disclosed nothing embarrassing, but where it was taken "by intrusion into a private place (for example, by a long-distance lens)."

Although neither of the rights guaranteed by article 8 or 10 took priority, in a foreshadowing of the "debate of general interest" test later set out in *von Hannover* in the ECHR (see below), Baroness Hale said that in a case where they vied for superiority the test to be applied was "whether publication of the material pursues a legitimate aim and whether the benefits that will be achieved by its publication are proportionate to the harm that may be done by the interference with the right to privacy." In other words, a proportionate balancing exercise had to be undertaken. In this case, it was very much the public policy issues of a recovering drug addict seeking to get over her addiction, and the harm that publication of photographs and information about her recovery would do to that process and to people in general in her situation, which swayed the House of Lords. Medical treatment, be it conventional or alternative, and details of such treatment, whether in narrative or photographic form, are now almost certainly protected except where disclosure is in the public interest, given the great harm that would likely be done both to the individual and in general public policy terms, should it be disclosed.

Privacy After Campbell

These cases, coupled with the principles that come out of *von Hannover,* of which more is given below, show that:

- A person in the public eye is still able to maintain some degree of privacy, despite the fact that they may be seeking to exploit it themselves and despite their public position. It is impossible for a publisher simply to argue that a public figure is in all circumstances "fair game" or that they "can't have their cake and eat it."

- There are considerations for an editor to take into account in relation to each aspect of the story he intends to publish. Perhaps most importantly, given their intrusive nature, photographs are to be given separate consideration.

- There is a margin of appreciation for editors as to the language and "furniture" which they use in their articles in order to convey the information to the public, including the use of photographs.[28]

- Where a publisher is faced with a threat of and/or an application for a pretrial injunction to prevent publication of private information/photographs, he should refer to the higher test, recently clarified (*Cream Holdings*[29] in the House of Lords) which sets out that the applicant must in most cases show that he is "more likely than not" to succeed at trial in establishing that the information should not be published and that he "probably" will succeed at trial in obtaining a permanent injunction.

Although the checking process post–*Campbell* is fairly extensive, it cannot stand alone as by virtue of section 2 of the HRA, judgments of the ECHR must also be taken into account by our domestic courts.[30] The decision of *von Hannover* in the ECHR took the matter one step further. And the case of *Douglas* confirmed the applicability in the UK of its finding of an obligation on the court to protect the privacy of individuals from infringement.

Von Hannover *and the ECHR Ruling*

Princess Caroline von Hannover, the eldest daughter of Prince Rainier III of Monaco, had during the 1990s and beyond, brought a number of actions over the publication in Germany of photographs which she said both invaded her privacy and, contrary to the German Basic Law, infringed her right to the protection of her personality rights. These pictures featured her going about her normal daily business. Some included shots of her with her children, or at the end of a secluded courtyard, and these were found in one landmark decision in the German Constitutional Court in 1999 to have breached her rights under German law. But whereas the pictures taken in France, as many of them were, of her horseback riding, skiing, shopping and so on would have breached stricter French privacy laws, published in *Bunte, Freiseit,* and *Neue Post* in Germany they did not. The German courts found that as a public figure "par excellence" she had to tolerate photographs of her in public places, be they of her at public functions or of her private life. If she could not show that she was in a secluded place out of the public eye, she would have to put up with what she maintained was constant harassment from photographers cataloguing virtually her every movement.

The ECHR did not find it acceptable that she should have to tolerate this and indeed, the way in which the photographs were taken and "the harassment endured by many public figures in their daily lives" was referred to and taken into account by the ECHR, who heard the case after numerous hearings and applications throughout the various German courts. The ECHR judgment made on June 24, 2004 found that Princess Caroline's rights guaranteed by Article 8 of the Convention had been infringed and that the laws of Germany had not sufficiently protected her.

According to the ECHR, the deciding factor in balancing the protection of private life against the right to freedom of expression was the contribution that the publication of the photographs made to "a debate of general interest." As those photographs published did not refer to any public function but merely to Princess Caroline's private life, and had been taken in public but without her consent, they did not contribute to any such debate. There were no special circumstances to justify the publication and even as a public figure—in an echo of *Campbell*—she had a legitimate expectation that her private life would be protected. The ECHR held:

> A fundamental distinction needs to be made between reporting facts—even controversial ones—capable of contributing to a debate in a democratic society relating to politicians in the exercise of their functions, for example, and reporting details of the private life of an individual who, moreover, as in this case, does not exercise official functions. While in the former case the press exercises its vital role of "watchdog" in a democracy by contributing to impart[ing] information and ideas on matters of public interest … it does not do so in the latter case.

Albeit that Princess Caroline was not a private individual and that the public might be interested in seeing the photographs, the court found that they did not concern her taking part in any official functions and did not contribute to a debate of general interest:

> The publication of the photos and articles in question, of which the sole purpose was to satisfy the curiosity of a particular readership regarding details of the applicant's private life, cannot be deemed to contribute to any debate of general interest to society despite the applicant being known to the public.

Gasps of horror could be expected around the picture desks up and down Fleet Street. Was this the death knell of the tabloid newspaper and celebrity magazine market? Well, it appears not.

Privacy After von Hannover

Adopting what we might call "the Milk Bottle Test," Baroness Hale in *Campbell* considered that a celebrity out and about buying a pint of milk in public at her local shop would be fair game; "If this had been ... a picture of Naomi Campbell going about her business in a public street, there could have been no complaint ... Readers will obviously be interested to see how she looks if and when she pops out to the shops for a bottle of milk." But this would be unacceptable according to the principles of the ECHR decision in *von Hannover*. Although the press might consider itself after *Campbell* to be free to publish photographs of Naomi Campbell buying a pint of milk, after *von Hannover* they would not be free to do the same regarding the princess. This disparity makes the position slightly unclear, but one must remember the specific facts of alleged press hounding in the *von Hannover* case. Accordingly, an editor and his lawyer considering and advising on a proposed publication must consider the principles both in *Campbell* and *von Hannover* and attempt to draw some general conclusions from them, regardless of any disparities.

It is also important to consider when the invasion of privacy occurs. If the harassment of the photographer is to be taken into account when deciding on the facts if an invasion of privacy has taken place, it would suggest that the invasion takes place at the time that the photograph is taken. Or is it the case that it takes place when the photograph is published? The view favored by the author is that the latter is the case and this was said in *Campbell*.[31] However, the circumstances in which the photograph was taken may have a bearing on whether the subject had a legitimate expectation of privacy and may impact on the publisher accordingly.

The UK press industry appears to be taking *von Hannover* in its stride and not to be overly phased by any fears that this judgment has disastrously far-reaching implications. Their pages still abound with unauthorized shots of celebrities going about their daily lives. They are not, it seems, subjugating their freedom of expression in deference to the privacy of those who pack their pages. We have started to see more pixellating of the faces of children, but it is not necessarily directly as a result of this case that they do so; the PCC Code lays down guidelines with respect to children. The extent to which the principles in *von Hannover* will be applied by our national courts remains to be seen; it would be difficult to imagine our domestic courts flagrantly ignoring the ruling and/or acting inconsistently with it, even if the celebrity magazine market appears comfortable to continue as before. But taking a conservative approach, there are some questions that an editor should ask himself which will assist in highlighting areas of potential concern and accordingly, which might assist in minimizing the risk to those publishing in the UK.

In the author's view, the two most important principles to come out of the *von Hannover* judgment are: (1) that the courts have an obligation to protect individuals from invasion of privacy by others, as confirmed in *Douglas;* and (2) that although the press will be praised for its role as Watchdog of Society, it will be reprimanded where it extends that role and acts to the detriment of others as lap dog to the public's prurient interest for pure entertainment and titillation. Given that magazines and newspapers flirt with doing just that—while the tabloids may have a better argument that they are publishing stories in the public interest or which contribute to a debate of general interest—it is not easy to see how this will be dealt with by the courts in the future. Certainly the courts will consider the circumstances in which the photograph was taken, what it portrays, and the identity of the subject. It would appear from *von Hannover* that the publication of photographs taken with a long lens camera, even if of celebrities in public places, will be unacceptable if the subject is engaging in a private rather than a public function. Although public figures will not have a "reasonable expectation of privacy" with regard to their public functions, they will have with regard to their private life and unless there is a "debate of general interest" to which the private information and/or the photograph contribute, it will be actionable.

One matter of interest for the press and the media is how heavily in the balance will weigh the commercial nature of the press in a democratic society if the wider policy issues are taken into account in the decisions of any court. Our courts have discussed the issue, for example in *A v. B*[32] and by some of our Law Lords in *Campbell.*[33] Indeed, in *A v. B* Lord Woolf effectively suggested that what the public was interested in was in the public interest[34] and it certainly seems, even though such a bold statement may not have been made subsequently, that the UK courts are prepared to consider the readers' interest in what they read and the commercial nature of the newspapers themselves, to be matters which may merit protection in the pubic interest. This is a vital issue that our press and media will undoubtedly raise at every opportunity, and how our judges deal with it post–*von Hannover* will have a significant impact on what approach is expected of the media in future.

Douglas v. Hello!

The UK's common law approach, now with the added burden of ECHR case law, means that we are all assessing matters on shifting sand. No sooner does one set of rules appear to apply than the court makes a decision which moves the goalposts. The Court of Appeal decision in *Douglas* has upheld the Douglases' claim for privacy, confirming that they have a right to protect a commercial confidence, but it has overturned the huge award of damages previously made to *OK!* magazine, finding that the Douglases' right to commercial confidence is not one that can be transferred to any third party.

Hello! had appealed against *OK!*'s judgment, arguing that it had no cause of action over the publication of unauthorized photographs simply because it had entered into an agreement to publish authorized shots. It also appealed the damages awards made to the Douglases. *OK!* counter-appealed on the dismissal of its economic tort claims. Significantly, the Court of Appeal followed *von Hannover* regarding the obligations of member states to protect their citizens from invasions of privacy as referred to above. This earns the case its place as a landmark decision in the development of the law of privacy in the UK.

Having accepted its obligations and the claimants' right to protection, it upheld the Douglases' claim, finding that photographs of a private wedding had been taken surreptitiously in circumstances where the photographer knew that his presence at the wedding was forbidden; and that those who bought them must have been aware that there had been some trespass or deceit in obtaining them. Moreover, they must have known that the Douglases would fairly and reasonably consider the material in the photographs to be confidential or private and that they had a reasonable expectation that it would remain so. That would comply with the definition of the obligation of confidence as set out in *Earl Spencer* referred to above. Accordingly, it found that: "photographs of the wedding plainly portrayed aspects of the Douglases' private life and fell within the protection of the law of confidentiality, as extended to cover private or personal information."

Importantly, it did not accept the defendants' argument that, by entering into an agreement to publish authorized photographs elsewhere, the couple forfeited their rights to protect the *un*authorized photographs: "Once intimate personal information about a celebrity's private life has been widely published it may serve no useful purpose to prohibit further publication," the court said, but it went on, "the same will not necessarily be true of photographs." There is a fresh invasion of privacy every time the photograph is viewed and this can potentially cause more distress each time. The Court found that "the offence is caused because what the claimant could reasonably expect would remain private has been made public." So, a right to privacy can be a right to commercial confidence and this can be exploited for financial gain at the "owner's" choice:

> Where an individual ("the owner") has at his disposal information which he has created or which is private personal and to which he can properly deny access to third parties, and he reasonably intends to profit commercially by using or publishing that information, then a third party who is, or ought to be aware of these matters and who has knowingly obtained the information without authority, will be in breach of duty if he uses or published the information to the detriment of the owner.

Importantly, however, this right is not transferable and it is this finding that robbed *OK!* of its million-pound damages. *OK!* had no claim to damages for the publication of photographs which, while their publication spoiled their scoop, belonged to the Douglases and not to them. They had an exclusive and very valuable right with regard to the authorized photographs that the Douglases chose to give them; they had nothing with regard to those photographs which remained private.

The judgment is also significant in that it concluded with an obiter comment from the judges that they did not consider that the injunction granted at the outset should have been overturned. Damages were not, in this case where an individual's right to privacy was at stake, a sufficient remedy. This is likely to be seized upon by those seeking to injunct the publication of photographs, with claimants seeking to persuade the lower courts that it was the Court of Appeal's intention to make the ordering of injunctions for privacy invasions more readily available. How this will work out in practice remains to be seen and indeed may be confirmed further in the appeal to the House of Lords.

Conclusion

Privacy in the UK has come a long way since its tentative beginnings over 150 years ago. The courts have finally accepted that they have an obligation to protect an individual's right to privacy from interference by others and, on the other hand, that that individual has a right to exploit that privacy right for commercial purposes. The courts are laying down, case by case, a series of guidelines as to what may be considered to be private material as well as how and in what circumstances privacy may be invaded.

Being able to see in the historical context why the courts are concerned with the privacy of individuals and how they seek to protect those rights will allow the journalist or lawyer to become better at making judgment calls when needed. But all cases are different and general guidelines need to be carefully applied to the specific facts. In summary, they boil down to this:

- Is the information to be published in the photographs of a *private* rather than a public nature?
- Is there a *debate of general interest* to which the photograph contributes (at least this is what *von Hannover* suggests) or alternatively is it in the public interest?
- Does the subject have a *reasonable expectation of privacy* with regard to the photograph, which may be assessed by considering the circumstances in which it was taken—the where, when, and how—the nature of the photograph in terms of offensiveness and/or embarrassment to the subject, and the subject's current/past relationship with the press.

The courts are attempting to create a fair balance between the rights guaranteed by Articles 8 and 10, privacy and freedom of expression, not seeking to stifle legitimate reporting and/or allow stories in the public interest to be covered up. They are seeking to steer a middle ground between protecting the rights of the press to inform the public (and, at least as far as some decisions of the English courts suggest, to run a successful commercial business) and the rights of individuals which might be affected by the exercise of the rights of the press. If an editor also tries honestly and fairly to do the same, he or she should be able to minimize the risk to the publication.

"Publish and be damned" has been a philosophy and right treasured by our press for centuries. By carefully navigating the choppy waters between free speech and privacy, with practical guidance as a life-line, publishers may still be able to publish, but with less risk of ultimate damnation.

Anyone in any doubt should take legal advice where they have concerns, and although it is hoped that this chapter will raise awareness of the issues to be considered, it does not pretend to be exhaustive or a specific advice. In these interesting yet dangerous and fast-moving times, this safety line should not be relied upon as the only means of protection and cannot be a substitute for specific legal advice. Whether damnation will ensue will be decided on the particular facts, and editors will have to use their judgment as relying on past experience may not now be sufficient in this new era.

Chapter Notes

1. The Football Association sought in June 2004 to protect the privacy of England's football captain David Beckham when photographs of him in his underwear on the balcony of his hotel room, during the European cup in Portugal, were

circulated to newspapers. It was reported that they complained to the Newspapers Publishers Association, warning that any publication would be an invasion of Beckham's privacy and arguing that the use of such photographs in Portugal would be illegal and any use of them in the United Kingdom would result in a complaint to the Press Complaints Commission. Having closed the door to his hotel room, the FA is reported to have argued, and given the exclusion zone around the hotel complex, Beckham had a reasonable expectation of privacy. The London-based picture agency involved agreed to pay damages to a charity of Beckham's choice for having taken the photographs and agreed to destroy its copies. Nevertheless, they were still published on the print pages of two UK tabloids, *The Sun* and *The Star*. The FA has reportedly also sought an apology and damages from these newspapers and it is not known at the time of writing if this matter has been resolved.

2. *Campbell v. MGN Limited* [2004] UKHL 22 on appeal from [2002] ECWA Civ 1373. The model Naomi Campbell had sued the UK tabloid *The Mirror* over the speculation of an article which outed her as a drug addict and which was illustrated by photographs of her leaving a Narcotics Anonymous (NA) meeting and included some details of the therapy that she had been receiving. Her cause of action was in breach of confidence and under the Data Protection Act 1998, but only the former was addressed in the House of Lords, with the DPA claim standing or falling with the confidence claim. Campbell had conceded that she could not complain about being outed as a drug user, as it was in the public interest for the newspaper to correct the false impression that she had given that, unlike other models, she did not use drugs. Bur her complaint was that the meat put on the bones of the story invaded her privacy. On a three-to-two majority, their Lordships found that the detail in the article had invaded her privacy.

3. *Sara Cox v. MGN Limited*. The British radio presenter Sara Cox brought an action for breach of confidence against *The People* newspaper over the publication of photographs of her on her honeymoon in the Seychelles, naked in a Jacuzzi with her husband. She was honeymooning in a private villa and the photographs had been taken with a long lens camera in breach of the PCC guidelines. She complained to the PCC, who ruled in her favor that the Code had been breached. The Code provides that: "(i) Everyone is entitled to respect for his or her private and family life, home, health and correspondence. A publication will be expected to justify intrusions into any individual's private life without consent. (ii) The use of long lens photography to take pictures of people in private places without their consent is unacceptable. Note—private places are public or private property where there is a reasonable expectation of privacy." She followed her successful complaint with proceedings which were settled with a payment of £50,000 damages.

4. *Von Hannover v. Germany* (application number 59320/00); www.echr.coe.int/ Eng/Press/2004/June/ChamberjudgmentVonHannover240604.htm.

5. *Douglas v. Hello Ltd,* [2005] EWCA Civ 595 (neutral citation number). The Hollywood actors Michael Douglas and Catherine Zeta Jones sued for breach of confidence and breach of the Data Protection Act 1998 over the publication of unauthorized photographs of their private wedding at the Four Seasons Hotel in

New York, taken surreptitiously by an infiltrator to the wedding notwithstanding the security measures taken. The couple had entered into an exclusive deal with *OK!* magazine to license exclusively for nine months, photographs taken by the couple's chosen photographer that they authorized for release. *OK!*'s rival *Hello!* proposed to publish the surreptitious shots taken by the infiltrator. In the first instance the couple were successful in having the magazine injuncted from publishing. However, on appeal this injunction was lifted and the photographs were published in *Hello!* The magazine *OK!*, which had intended to run the authorized shots over two weeks, attempted to mitigate the damage by the loss of the scoop, getting their issue out on the same day as *Hello!*'s including the authorized photographs. At first instance on the question of damages, Mr. Justice Lindsay awarded the couple damages for distress, under the DPA and for wasted costs in relation to the work that had to be undertaken to get authorized photographs approved for the earlier deadline, of £14,600 each. He awarded *OK!* just over £1 million for the loss of the scoop out of which they would have generated that sum. The matter went on appeal to the Court of Appeal, where the court upheld the damages award to the Douglases to compensate them for the invasion of privacy, but overturned the award to *OK!* on the grounds that it had no claim to compensation over the publication of the Douglases' private photographs to which it was not entitled under its agreement with them. The matter has subsequently been appealed to the House of Lords.

6. http://www.hmso.gov.uk/acts/acts1998/19980042.htm.

7. 5RB. www.5rb.co.uk. 5RB is the set of barristers' chambers that is home to three of the four counsel in the case, Desmond Browne QC and David Sherborne for Douglas, Zeta Jones and Northern & Shell for *OK!*, and James Price QC for *Hello!* James Price's junior is Giles Fernando of 11 South Square.

8. *Douglas v. Hello!* [2005] EWCA Civ. 595.

9. *Kaye v. Robertson* [1991] F.S.R. 62, CA. The British actor Gordon Kaye suffered serious head injuries in an accident, and required extensive surgery. While in the hospital, he was visited by a photographer and journalist from the tabloid *Sunday Sport* who ignored hospital signs asking visitors to see a member of staff before visiting patients. They proceeded to interview and take photographs of him in his hospital bed. It was accepted by the Court of Appeal that Kaye had been in no fit state to give any informed consent to the interview, but there had been no unlawful entry into the hospital and no physical damage done to Kaye. The family was unable to stop the publication in its entirety, but the Court of Appeal took a creative approach and granted an injunction in malicious falsehood—a cause of action that had not been raised by the claimants and which requires proof of falsity, malice, and financial loss—to prevent the paper from alleging in its article that he had consented to the interview. The claim was founded on the court accepting that the newspaper intended to publish a false suggestion that Kaye had consented to the interview, maliciously given they knew that to be untrue, and calculated/likely to cause financial loss given the article would deprive him of the opportunity of later selling his exclusive story to another newspaper. Although the Court of Appeal judges lamented their in-

ability to protect Kaye altogether, the newspaper simply went on to publish the story, making it clear that Kaye had not consented to the interview.

10. Prince Albert successfully used the tort to prevent the publication of a catalogue containing etchings of himself and Queen Victoria, made for their own private amusement, copies of which had been made by a commercial opportunist.

11. *Coco v. AN Clarke (Engineers) ltd* [1969] RPC 41; [1968] FSR 415.

12. *Earl Spencer v. United Kingdom* [1998] 25 EHRR CD 105.

13. Article 10 ECHR. Article 10—Freedom of expression. 1. Everyone has the right to freedom of expression. This right shall include freedom to hold opinions and to receive and impart information and ideas without interference by public authority and regardless of frontiers. This article shall not prevent States from requiring the licensing of broadcasting, television or cinema enterprises. 2. The exercise of these freedoms, since it carries with it duties and responsibilities, may be subject to such formalities, conditions, restrictions or penalties as are prescribed by law and are necessary in a democratic society, in the interests of national security, territorial integrity or public safety, for the prevention of disorder or crime, for the protection of health or morals, for the protection of the reputation or rights of others, for preventing the disclosure of information received in confidence, or for maintaining the authority and impartiality of the judiciary.

14. Article 8 ECHR. Article 8—Right to respect for private and family life 1. Everyone has the right to respect for his private and family life, his home and his correspondence. 2. There shall be no interference by a public authority with the exercise of this right except such as is in accordance with the law and is necessary in a democratic society in the interests of national security, public safety or the economic well-being of the country, for the prevention of disorder or crime, for the protection of health or morals, or for the protection of the rights and freedoms of others.

15. Section 12 Human Rights Act 1998. Freedom of expression.

(1) This section applies if a court is considering whether to grant any relief which, if granted, might affect the exercise of the Convention right to freedom of expression.

(2) If the person against whom the application for relief is made ('the respondent') is neither present nor represented, no such relief is to be granted unless the court is satisfied-

> (a) that the applicant has taken all practicable steps to notify the respondent; or
>
> (b) that there are compelling reasons why the respondent should not be notified.

(3) No such relief is to be granted so as to restrain publication before trial unless the court is satisfied that the applicant is likely to establish that publication should not be allowed.

(4) The court must have particular regard to the importance of the Convention right to freedom of expression and, where the proceedings relate to material which the respondent claims, or which appears to the court, to be journalistic, literary or

artistic material (or to conduct connected with such material), to-
> (a) the extent to which-
>> (i) the material has, or is about to, become available to the public; or
>> (ii) it is, or would be, in the public interest for the material to be published;
> (b) any relevant privacy code.

(5) In this section- 'court' includes a tribunal; and 'relief' includes any remedy or order (other than in criminal proceedings).

16. PCC @ www.pcc.org.uk; Ofcom@ www.ofcom.org.uk.

17. HRA section 12 - (1) This section applies if a court is considering whether to grant any relief which, if granted, might affect the exercise of the Convention right to freedom of expression.
(4) The court must have particular regard to the importance of the Convention right to freedom of expression and, where the proceedings relate to material which the respondent claims, or which appears to the court, to be journalistic, literary or artistic material (or to conduct connected with such material), to- (b) any relevant privacy code.

18. *Attard v. Greater Manchester Newspapers Ltd,* Fam 14/15 June 2001, Bennet J. During an application in the Family Division regarding the operation to separate the twin babies, the parents successfully applied for an injunction to prevent publication of photographs of their children. The operation went ahead, but unfortunately only one of the children survived. The parents entered into an exclusive deal with the *News of the World* and the *Mail on Sunday* to publish photographs of the surviving twin and successfully applied to the court to vary the order to allow publication. Meanwhile, the *The Manchester Evening News (MEN)* had obtained long lens photographs of the baby on the steps of the hospital which it published. The parents applied to the court, again successfully, for an injunction to prevent further publication. The judge held, in a foreshadowing of Douglas and Zeta Jones to come, that the baby and/or her parents on her behalf, had a right to privacy which could be sold (Attard and *The Manchester Evening News,* PCC Adjudication 15 June 2001, (Report 55)).

Contrast this to the view of the PCC to whom a complaint was made by the parents over the publication of the photograph that had been published by the *MEN.* Their complaint was not in respect of the main privacy clause of the Code, but in respect of that which relates to children under 16 being photographed on matters concerning their welfare without their parents' consent. The claim was not upheld, with the PCC finding that the photograph did not concern the child's welfare, but more importantly it stated as follows:

> It is not the function of the Commission to seek to protect the financial position of complainants through the use of privacy sections of this Code. Indeed the Commission has always taken the common sense view that where a complainant releases or sells information or photographs, then they become disentitled to the protection of the Code in certain circumstances. Privacy is—in the Commission's Opinion—not a commodity which can be sold on one person's terms.

19. *Venables and Thompson v. News Group Newspapers Ltd* [2001] (2001) Fam 430 (2001) 2 WLR 1038 (2001) 1 All ER 908 (2001) HRLR 19 (2001) UKHRR 628 TLR 16/01/2001 2001 WL 14890.

20. *Maxine Carr v. News Group Newspapers Ltd* (24/2/2005).

21. *Douglas & Ors v. Hello! Ltd & Ors*, [2003] EWHC 786 (Ch). The Hollywood actors Catherine Zeta Jones and Michael Douglas were married on November 18, 2000, at the Plaza Hotel in New York. They wanted to keep the affair private and guests were admitted by invitation only, and guests and all those at the ceremony and after-ceremony celebrations, including staff, were made to sign agreements to keep the wedding confidential. There had been negotiations between *Hello!* magazine and the couple, and *OK!* magazine and the couple, for an exclusive deal with them for photographs of the ceremony. *OK!* had been the successful party in securing the deal. Unbeknown to them at the time, a paparazzi photographer infiltrated the wedding and took photographs, transmitting them to the offices of *Hola* from where they were included in copies of *Hello!* magazine on November 19 and distributed to England the next day, thus frustrating the exclusive deal signed by the couple with *OK!* They obtained an injunction on November 20th to prevent further publication in *Hello!,* which was discharged by the Court of Appeal on November 23, and commenced proceedings for breach of confidence and/or invasion of privacy, breaches of the Data Protection Act, and unlawful interference/conspiracy. The judge found that the claimants' rights in confidence and under the DPA had been breached; that the wedding was a private event; that it was reasonable that they should seek to make it so given the extent to which, in the public eye, their private lives were curtailed; that they had a hybrid right of confidentiality which was partly private and partly commercial in nature; and that the fact that they had done a deal for some of the photographs of the wedding, in a controlled environment, to be published, did not rob them of that right.

22. *Theakston v. MGN Limited,* [2002] EMLR 398.

23. *Peck v. The United Kingdom.* The applicant, a UK national, at a time when he was suffering from depression, walked alone down Brentwood High Street with a kitchen knife in his hand, and attempted suicide by cutting his wrists, unaware that he had been filmed by a closed-circuit television (CCTV) camera installed by the Borough Council. The CCTV footage did not show the applicant cutting his wrists; the operator was solely alerted to an individual in possession of a knife. The police were notified and arrived at the scene, where they took the knife, gave the applicant medical assistance, and brought him to the police station, where he was detained under the Mental Health Act 1983. He was examined and treated by a doctor, after which he was released without charge and taken home by police officers. On October 9, 1995, the Council issued two photographs taken from the CCTV footage with an article entitled "Defused—the partnership between CCTV and the police prevents a potentially dangerous situation." The applicant's face was not specifically masked. Various local newspaper and television articles followed. After being told by friends that they had seen him, unmasked, on trailers for a forthcoming television program, he complained to the Council, who contacted the producers who confirmed that his image would be masked in the program.

Although he was masked in the main program, he was recognized by friends and family. He made a number of media appearances thereafter to speak out against the publication of the footage and photographs. He complained to the Broadcasting Standards Commission (BSC) alleging an unwarranted infringement of his privacy, and the BSC upheld his complaint. He then complained to the ITC concerning another broadcast on Anglia Television and they found that his identity was not adequately obscured and that the ITC code had been breached. Given an admission and apology by Anglia Television, no further action was taken. He then complained unsuccessfully to the Press Complaints Commission concerning press articles. He applied to the High Court for leave to apply for judicial review concerning the Council's disclosure of the CCTV material. His request and a further request for leave to appeal to the Court of Appeal were both rejected.

24. *Campbell v. MGN Limited.* See note 2.

25. *Campbell v. MGN Limited* [2004] UKHL 22. The minority judges found that the material was within the legitimate margin of appreciation:
  • Lord Nicolls found the material "added colour and conviction" to the "legitimate and sympathetic newspaper story"; "We value freedom of the press but the press is a commercial enterprise and can flourish only by selling newspapers. From a journalistic point of view, photographs are an essential part of the story."
  • Lord Hoffman found that "photographs are an essential part of the story. The picture carried the message, more strongly than anything in the text alone, that the *Mirror*'s story was true. So the decision to publish the picture was in my opinion within the margin of editorial judgment and something for which appropriate latitude should be allowed."

But the majority judges found otherwise:
  • Lord Hope found that, "had it not been for the publication of the photographs, and looking to the text only, I would have been inclined to regard the balance between these rights [privacy and freedom of expression] as about even. Such is the effect of the margin of appreciation that must, in a doubtful case, be given to the journalist… but the text cannot be separated from the photographs."
  • Baroness Hale considered that "the photographs would have been useful in proving the truth of the story had this been challenged, but there was no need to publish them for this purpose. The credibility of the story with the public would stand or fall with the credibility of *Daily Mail* stories generally."
  • Lord Carswell held that "publication of the details about the appellant's attendance at therapy carried out by Narcotics Anonymous, highlighted by the photographs printed, constituted in my judgment a considerable intrusion into her private affairs which was capable of causing substantial distress, and on her evidence did cause it to her."

26. *Campbell v. MGN Limited* [2004] UKHL 22. Para 57: "A person may attract or even seek publicity about some aspects of his or her life without creating any public interest in the publication of personal information about other matters." Para 120: "it is not enough to deprive Miss Campbell of her right to privacy that she is a celebrity and that her private life is newsworthy."

27. *Campbell v. MGN Limited* [2004] UKHL 22. General helpful comments from the judges include the following:

- everyone is entitled to their privacy, even those who had courted the press to some extent;

- "the fact that the photographs in question had been taken without the subject's consent was not enough to amount to a wrongful invasion of privacy. We have not so far held that the mere fact of covert photography is sufficient to make the information contained in the photograph confidential. The activity photographed must be private."

- "the famous and even the not so famous who go out in public must accept that they may be photographed without their consent, just as they may be observed by others without their consent ... But the fact that we cannot avoid being photographed does not mean that anyone who takes or obtains such a photograph can publish them to the world at large."

- "the widespread publication of a photograph of someone which reveals him to be in a situation of humiliation or severe embarrassment, even if taken in a public place, may be an infringement of the privacy of his personal information."

- "Likewise, the publication of a photograph taken by intrusion into a private place (for example, by a long distance lens) may in itself be such an infringement, even if there is nothing embarrassing about the picture itself."

- "the taking of photographs in a public street must, as Randerson J said in *Hosking v. Runtin* [2003] 3 NZLR 385, 415, para 138, be taken to be one of the ordinary incidents of living in a free community. The real issue is whether publicizing the content of the photographs would be offensive ... A person who just happens to be in the street when the photograph was taken and appears in it only incidentally cannot as a general rule object to the publication of the photograph ... But the situation is different if the public nature of the place where a photograph is taken was simply used as a background for one or more persons who constitute the true subject of the photograph."

28. *Campbell v. MGN Limited* [2004] UKHL 22. Para 112: "The respondents are also entitled to claim that they should be accorded a reasonable margin of appreciation in taking decisions as to what details needed to be included in the article to give it credibility."

29. *Cream Holdings Ltd and Others v. Banerjee and Another.* The test to be applied for the grant of an interim injunction before trial, to prevent the publication of confidential information where a party's article 8 rights are engaged, is now whether applicants can show that they are "more likely than not to succeed at trial," that is, they have a greater than 50 percent chance of success in establishing that they will be granted a permanent injunction. This is higher than the previous test accepted by the majority of the court of Appeal, that the claimant only had "convincingly to establish a real prospect at trial."

30. Section 2 (1) of the Act provides that: "A court or tribunal determining a question which has arisen in connection with a Convention right must take into account any ... a) judgment, decision, declaration or advisory opinion of the European Court of Human Rights."

31. *Campbell v. MGN Limited* [2004] UKHL 22: Photographs in public "must be taken to be one of the ordinary incidents of living in a free community. The real issue is whether *publicising* the content of the photographs would be *offensive.*"

32. *A v. B Plc* [2003] *QB 195:* "the Courts must not ignore the fact that if newspapers do not publish information which the public are interested in, there will be fewer newspapers published, which will not be in the public interest."

33. *Campbell v. MGN Limited* [2004] UKHL 22: Lord Hope, para 77: "we value the freedom of the Press but the press is a commercial enterprise and can flourish only by selling newspapers"; Baroness Hale, para 143: "one reason why Press freedom is so important is that we need newspapers to sell in order to ensure that we still have newspapers at all."

34. *A v. B & C* [2002] ECWA, Civ, 337, para 11, xii. Where an individual is a public figure, he is entitled to have his privacy respected in the appropriate circumstances. A public figure is entitled to a private life. The individual, however, should recognize that because of his public position he must expect and accept that his actions will be more closely scrutinized by the media. Even trivial facts relating to a public figure can be of great interest to readers and other observers of the media. Conduct which in the case of a private individual would not be the appropriate subject of comment can be the proper subject of comment in the case of a public figure. The public figure may hold a position where higher standards of conduct can be rightly expected by the public. The public figure may be a role model whose conduct could well be emulated by others. He may set the fashion. The higher the profile of the individual concerned, the more likely that this will be the position. Whether you have courted publicity or not, you may be a legitimate subject of public attention. If you have courted public attention then you have less ground to object to the intrusion which follows. In many of these situations it would be overstating the position to say that there is a public interest in the information being published. It would be more accurate to say that the public has an understandable and so a legitimate interest in being told the information. If this is the situation, then it can be appropriately taken into account by a court when deciding on which side of the line a case falls. The courts must not ignore the fact that if newspapers do not publish information in which the public is interested, there will be fewer newspapers published, which will not be in the public interest. The same is true in relation to other parts of the media.

CROSS-REFERENCE CHART

ISSUE	AUSTRALIA	BELGIUM	BRAZIL	CANADA	CHINA	ENGLAND & WALES	FRANCE
Truth as Absolute Defense?	Y	Q, St.	Y, Q	Y	N	Y	Y
Libel by Implication?	Y	Y	Y	Y	U	Y	Y
May Corporations Sue for Libel?	Y	Y, St.	U	Y	Y	Y, Q	Y
Product Disparagement?	Y	Y, St.	Y, St.	Y	Y	Y	N
Group Libel?	N	Y, St.	Y	Y, Q	U	N	Y
Higher Public Figure Fault Standard?	N	Y, C.L.	N	N	N	N	N
Public Interest Defense?	Y, Q	Y, C.L., Q	Q	Q	N	Y, Q, C.L.	Y
Company Reporting as Public Concern?	Y, Q	N	Y	N	Q	Y, Q	U
Fair Comment or Opinion?	Y	Y, St., Q	Y, St.	Y, C.L.	N	Y, Q	Y, Q
Right of Reply?	N	Y, St.	Y, St.	U (VARIES BY PROVINCE)	N	N	Y, St.
Privilege for Government Documents?	Q	N	Y, St.	Y, Q	Q	Y	Y, St.
Wire Service Defense?	N	Y, C.L., Q	Y, Q	N	N	N	N
Contempt of Court?	Y	N	N	Y, CL., Q	N	Y	Q
Prior Restraints?	Y, Q	Y, St., Q	N	Y, Q	Y, C.L.	Y, Q	Y, St.
Privacy Recognized?	N	Y, St.	Y, St.	Y, Q	Y	N	Y, St.
Shield Law?	N	Y, C.L., Q	Y, St.	Q	N	Q	Y, Q, St.
Law Applied to Internet?	Y	Y	U	Y	Y	Y	Y, St.

KEY: **Y** = Yes, **N** = No, **U** = Unclear, **St.** = Statutory, **C.L.** = Common Law, **Q** = Qualified or Limited

GERMANY	HONG KONG	INDIA	ITALY	JAPAN	KOREA	NETHERLANDS	RUSSIA	SINGAPORE	SPAIN	SWITZERLAND	USA
N	Y	Y	N	Y, Q	Y, Q	Q	Y	Q	N	Q	Y
Y	Y	Y	Y	Y	Y, C.L.	Y	N	Y	Y	Y	Y
Y	Y	Y	Y	Y	Y, C.L.	Y	Y	Y, St.	Y	Y, St.	Y
Y	Y, St	Q	Y, St., Q	N	Y	Y, St.	Y, St.	Y, Q	N	Y, St.	Y, Q
N	N	N	Y	N	Y	Y	N	N	Y	Y, Q	N, C.L.
N	N	Y, Q	N	N	N	Y	N	N	N	N	Y, C.L.
Y, Q	Y, Q	Y	Y, Q	Y, C.L.	Y, C.L.	Y	N	Y	Y	Y, St.	Y
U	Y	Q	U	N	N	Y, Q	N	N	Y	N	Q
Y, Q	Y, Q	Y	Y, Q, St.	Y	Y	N	Y, St.	Y, Q	Y	Y, St., Q	Y
N	N	N	Y	N	Y	N	Y, St.	N	Y, St., Q	Y, St.	N
Q	Y, Q	Y	N	N	N	Q, C.L.	Y	Q	Y, Q	N	Y, Q
Y, Q	N	N	N	N	N	Y, Q	Y, St.	N	Y	N	Y, Q
Q	Y, St.	Q	Y	N	N	N	N	N	N	N	N
Y	Y	Y	Y, St., Q	Y	Y, St.	N	N, Q	Y	Y, St.	Y, St.	N
Y	N	Y	Y, St.	Y, St.	Y, St.	Y, St.	Y, St.	N	Y, St.	Y, St.	Y
Y	Y, C.L.	Y, C.L.	Y, St., Q	N	Q	Y, C.L., Q	Y, St.	N	Y, St.,Q	Y, St., Q	Y, Q
Y, St.	Y	Y	Y, C.L.	Y	Y	Y	Y	N	Y	N	Y, St.

INDEX

ABOUT BLOOMBERG

Bloomberg L.P., founded in 1981, is a global information services, news, and media company. Headquartered in New York, the company has sales and news operations worldwide.

Bloomberg, serving customers on six continents, holds a unique position within the financial services industry by providing an unparalleled range of features in a single package known as the BLOOMBERG PROFESSIONAL® service. By addressing the demand for investment performance and efficiency through an exceptional combination of information, analytic, electronic trading, and Straight Through Processing tools, Bloomberg has built a worldwide customer base of corporations, issuers, financial intermediaries, and institutional investors.

BLOOMBERG NEWS®, founded in 1990, provides stories and columns on business, general news, politics, and sports to leading newspapers and magazines throughout the world. BLOOMBERG TELEVISION®, a 24-hour business and financial news network, is produced and distributed globally in seven languages. BLOOMBERG RADIO℠ is an international radio network anchored by flagship station BLOOMBERG® 1130 (WBBR-AM) in New York.

In addition to the BLOOMBERG PRESS® line of books, Bloomberg publishes *BLOOMBERG MARKETS®* magazine. To learn more about Bloomberg, call a sales representative at:

London:	+44-20-7330-7500
New York:	+1-212-318-2000
Tokyo:	+81-3-3201-8900

FOR IN-DEPTH MARKET INFORMATION and news, visit the Bloomberg website at **www.bloomberg.com**, which draws from the news and power of the BLOOMBERG PROFESSIONAL® service and Bloomberg's host of media products to provide high-quality news and information in multiple languages on stocks, bonds, currencies, and commodities.

Also by Susan Isaacs

Novels
Past Perfect
Any Place I Hang My Hat
Long Time No See
Red, White and Blue
Lily White
After All These Years
Magic Hour
Shining Through
Almost Paradise
Close Relations
Compromising Positions

Screenplays
Hello Again
Compromising Positions

Nonficton
*Brave Dames and Wimpettes: What Women Are Really Doing
on Page and Screen*

As Husbands Go

A Novel

SUSAN ISAACS

Scribner
New York London Toronto Sydney

Scribner
A Division of Simon & Schuster, Inc.
1230 Avenue of the Americas
New York, NY 10020

First Scribner hardcover edition July 2010

SCRIBNER and design are registered trademarks of The Gale Group, Inc., used
under license by Simon & Schuster, Inc., the publisher of this work.

For information about special discounts for bulk purchases,
please contact Simon & Schuster Special Sales at 1-866-506-1949
or business@simonandschuster.com.

The Simon & Schuster Speakers Bureau can bring authors to your live event.
For more information or to book an event contact the Simon & Schuster Speakers
Bureau at 1-866-248-3049 or visit our website at www.simonspeakers.com.

Designed by Carla Jayne Jones

Manufactured in the United States of America

10 9 8 7 6 5 4 3 2 1

Library of Congress Control Number: 2009052241

ISBN 978-1-4165-7301-2
ISBN 978-1-4165-7984-7 (ebook)

To St. Catherine and Bob Morvillo with love

Here, take this gift,
I was reserving it for some hero, speaker, or general,
One who should serve the good old cause, the great idea, the
progress and freedom of the race,
Some brave confronter of despots, some daring rebel;
But I see that what I was reserving belongs to you just as
much as to any.

—Walt Whitman, "To a Certain Cantatrice," *Leaves of Grass*

Chapter One

✄ ─────────────────────────────────────

Who knew? It seemed a perfectly nice night. True, outside the house, the wind was whoo-whooing like sound effects from a low-budget horror movie. The cold was so vicious that a little past seven, a branch of the great white spruce on the front lawn that had been creaking all afternoon suddenly screamed in pain. Then a brutal *CRAAACK,* and it crashed to the frozen ground.

But inside our red brick Georgian in the picturesque Long Island town of Shorehaven, all was warmth. I went from one bedroom to another to kiss the boys good night. Despite the sickly yellow gleam of the SpongeBob Squarepants night-light in his bedroom, Mason, the third-born of our triplets, glowed pure gold. I stroked his forehead. "Happy dreams, my sweetie." He was already half asleep, thumb in mouth, but his four other fingers flapped me a good night.

A flush of mother love reddened my cheeks. Its heat spread. For a moment, it even eased the permanent muscle spasm that had seized the left side of my neck seconds after Jonah and I gazed up at the sonogram and saw three little paisley curls in utero. My utero. Still, a perpetual neck spasm was a small price to pay for such a wonderful life, one I had hardly dared dream about as a little girl in Brooklyn.

Okay, that "wonderful life" and "hardly dared dream" business does cross the line into the shameless mush of Mommyland, where "fulfillment" is all about children, not sex, and where mothers are jealous of each new baby-shoe charm on their friends' bracelets. Feh.

Sure, sure: Sentiment proves you're human. Feelings are good, blah, blah, blah. But sentimentality, anything that could go on a minivan bumper sticker, makes me cringe. Take this as a given: Susan B Anthony Rabinowitz Gersten (i.e., me) was never a Long Island madonna, one of those moms who carries on about baby Jonathan as if he were Baby Jesus.

What kind of mother was I on that particular night? A happy one. Still, it wouldn't have taken a psychologist to read my emotional pie chart and determine that the sum of my parts equaled one shallow (though contented) human being. One third of that happiness was attributable to the afterglow of the birthday present my husband had given me two weeks earlier, a Cartier Santos watch. Another third was courtesy of Lexapro (twenty milligrams). A little over a sixth came from the pure sensual gratification of being wrapped in a tea-green Loro Piana cashmere bathrobe. The remaining sliver was bona fide maternal bliss.

Maybe I'm still shallow, just deluding myself that after all that's occurred, I've become a better person. On the other hand, even at my superficial worst, I wasn't terrible. Truly, I did have a heart.

Especially when it came to my immediate family. I loved them. So I gloried in that moment of mommy bliss. I remember thinking, *Jonah and I have some lucky star shining down on us.* Along with our three boys, my husband, Jonah Paul Gersten, MD, FACS (picture a slightly older—and significantly shorter—Orlando Bloom, with a teeny touch of male pattern baldness), was the light of my life. Naturally, I had no clue about what was happening with Jonah twenty-six miles west, in Manhattan.

How could I possibly know that right at that very instant, he was stepping into the Upper East Side apartment of a call girl who had decided a month earlier that the name Cristal Rousseau wasn't projecting the class-up-the-ass image she had been aiming for. Lately, there hadn't been much of a market for the refined-type fuck, so she'd changed her image and her name to something still classy yet more girl-next-door—Dorinda Dillon.

Why would a man of Jonah's caliber bother with someone like Dorinda? Before you go "heh-heh," think about it. It's a reasonable question. First of all, Jonah never gave me any reason to believe he wasn't devoted to me. Just a couple of months earlier, at the annual holiday party of his Park Avenue surgical practice, I had overheard the scheduling coordinator confide to one of the medical assistants, "Dr. Gersten always has that look of love, even when Mrs. Gersten is standing right beside him in those four-inch heels that—I hate to say it—make her *shockingly* taller."

Also, being a plastic surgeon with a craniofacial subspecialty, Jonah was a man with a sophisticated sense of beauty. He had the ultimate discerning eye. No way would Dorinda Dillon's looks have pleased him. Objectively speaking, I swear to God, she looked like a ewe in a blond wig. You'd expect her to go *baa*. Genuinely sheepy-looking, whatever the word for that is. All my life I've read much more than people ever gave me credit for, and I have a surprisingly decent vocabulary—though obviously not decent enough.

Anyway, Dorinda had a long, wide sheep nose that sloped down straight from her forehead. It took up so much room in the middle of her face that it kept her eyes farther apart than human eyes ought to be. Despite her loyalty to some hideous blackish-red lipstick, her mouth came across more as dark two-dimensional lines than actual lips.

Not that I was gorgeous. Far from it. All right, not that far. Still, most people saw me as . . . well, fabulous-looking. I guess

I should apologize because that sounds arrogant. Okay, obnoxious. A woman who comes right out and says, "Hey, I'm stunning!" (even when she is) is violating what is probably the real First Commandment, the one that somehow got replaced by the "I am the Lord thy God" business, which never really made a lot of sense to me because how is that a commandment? Anyway, the true numero uno of human conduct is "Thou shalt not speak well of thyself."

Because of that, every great-looking woman has to apologize not only by acting nicer than she really is but by showing she's paid her dues, à la "I had major zits when I was fourteen and was totally flat-chested and, like, so self-conscious nobody even knew I was alive. I'm still, like, really, really shy deep down."

So let me get with the program. For most of my life, whenever I looked in the mirror, I honestly did feel insecure. In fact, throughout my childhood in Brooklyn, I kept waiting for someone to shout "Hey, Bucktooth!" which would inevitably become my nickname until I graduated high school. Weird: No one ever did. Years passed without any cruel mockery. My confidence grew—a little. And after Jonah came into my life, it flourished. Someone like him genuinely wanted someone like me! Yet I always knew my overbite stood between me and actual beauty.

Braces would have fixed me up, but I didn't get them. With perfect clarity, I still see myself at age ten, gazing up at Erwin Monkarsh, DDS, a blobby man who looked like he'd been put together by a balloon-twisting clown at a birthday party. Even though he didn't seem like a guy who could answer a maiden's prayer, my young heart fluttered with hope. I put all my energy into willing him not to do . . . precisely what he now was doing: shaking his head. "No, her bite's actually okay," he was telling my mother.

In that instant I understood I was doomed. No orthodontia. "However, I'm not saying she couldn't use braces for cosmetic reasons," he added. "She definitely could."

At that time my mother was in her Sherry the Fearless Feminist and Scourge of the Frivolous stage, and she responded with a single humorless chuckle. "'Cosmetic reasons'!" Then she snorted at the notion that she would spend money on a treatment that would aid in transforming her daughter into a sex object.

For the next ten years of my life, I spent thousands of girl-hours on self-criticism—gazing into mirrors, squinting at photos, having heart-to-hearts with my girlfriends and department store makeup artists. What I finally concluded was that my overbite was clearly not a plus. The good news was that it made me look a little dumb but not unappealing. Sometimes after I changed my hairstyle or got a new coat, I'd catch myself in a mirror. In that fraction of a second before I realized it was me, I'd think, *Great look, but double-digit IQ.*

Still, as I explained to Andrea Brinckerhoff, my business partner as well as my official best friend (you're not a true woman unless you have one), men liked what they saw when they looked at me. I still got frequent second and, once in a while, third looks. Naturally, no guy ever went—I demonstrated by pressing both hands over my heart and gasping—"Omigod!" the way a guy might if he bumped into an indisputable, acknowledged beauty, a Halle Berry or Scarlett Johansson. On the other hand, Halle and Scarlett weren't rolling carts down the household-detergents aisle of a Long Island Stop & Shop.

"Why do you even waste two seconds worrying about your appearance?" Andrea demanded. "Look who you're married to. A plastic surgeon. Not just any plastic surgeon. A plastic surgeon who made *New York* magazine's top doctors. You know and I know, way before Jonah even went into medicine, he had a gut understanding about what 'stunning' meant. He couldn't marry a d-o-g any more than he could drive an ugly car. With all he has going for him, he could have had almost anyone. He has a good family background. Well, not Social Register, since

they're . . . you know. But still, he is Ivy League. Then he stayed
at Yale for medical school. And he's hot in that Jewish-short-guy
way. He could have picked a classic beauty. But he chose you."

Andrea may have been irritating and snobbish, but she was
right: I was close enough to beauty. Take my eyes. People called
them "intriguing," "compelling," "gorgeous." Whatever. They
were very pale green. At Madison High School in Brooklyn,
Matthew Bortz, a boy so pasty and scrawny that the only type
he could be was Sensitive Artiste, wrote me a love poem. It went
on about how my eyes were the color of "liquid jade mix'd with
cream." Accurate. Sweet, too, though he got really pissed when
I said, "Matty, you could've lost the apostrophe in 'mix'd.'"

It wasn't only great eyes, the kind that make people say a
real woof is beautiful just because she has blue eyes and three
coats of mascara. I also had world-class cheekbones. They were
prominent and slanted up. Where did I get them? My mother's
face was round, my father's was closer to an oval, but both their
faces were basically formless, colorless, and without a single feature that was either awful or redeeming. My parents could have
pulled off a bank heist without wearing masks and never have
been identified.

I was around thirteen and reading some book about the Silk
Road when I began to imagine that my facial structure came
from an exotic ancestor. I settled on a fantasy about a wealthy
handsome merchant from Mongolia passing through Vitebsk.
He wound up having a two-night stand with one of my great-
great-grandmothers. She'd have been the kind of girl the neighbors whispered about: "Oy, Breindel Kirpichnik! Calling that
green-eyed minx a slut is too good for her. They say she's got
Gypsy blood!"

It's a long story I won't go into here, but I was twenty when
I sought out and actually found where my looks came from:
my no-good grandmother who'd taken a hike, abandoning not
only her boring husband but her eight-year-old daughter—my

mother. Grandma Ethel was tall, willowy, with liquid-jade-mixed-with-cream eyes. She was me minus the overbite. She told me I could thank her for my hair, too, light brown with gold highlights. She was pretty sure hers had been my color, but she'd become a blonde in 1949 so couldn't swear to it.

But back to me. My mouth was better than Grandma Ethel's, but "better" is mostly luck, since I'd been born into Generation X, a global slice of humanity that tolerates fat only in lips. Other women were forever asking me, "Did your husband inject collagen or some new filler into your lips?"

My body was good, which made me one of maybe five females within a fifty-mile radius of Manhattan who did not have a negative body image. I was blessed with an actual waist, which came back (though not 100 percent) after the triplets. Long legs and arms. Enough in the boob department to please men without having them so cantaloupish as to make buying French designer clothes an act of willful idiocy.

My mind? No one would ever call me brilliant, unless those MacArthur people gave grants for genius in accessorizing. Still, I was smart enough not only to make a beautiful life for myself but to be grateful for my incredible blessings. Plus, to get people to ignore any "she's dumb" thoughts courtesy of my overbite (also so they wouldn't think I was all style, no substance), I listened to *The NewsHour* on PBS five nights a week. Jonah helped, because having gone to Yale, he went for subtitled movies about doomed people, so I saw more of them than any regular person should have to. I read a lot, too, though it was mostly magazines because I never got more than fifteen minutes of leisure at a shot after Dashiell and Evan and Mason were born. Still, there was enough stuff about books in *Vogue* that when all the women at a luncheon talked about, say, *Interpreter of Maladies,* I'd read enough about it to say "exquisitely written" and not "hilarious." I did like historical fiction, but more the kind that got into eighteenth-century oral sex, or the marchioness's brown wool riding jacket with silver braid, and didn't linger on pus-filled sores on the peasants' bare feet.

So, okay, not a great mind. But I definitely had enough brains not to let my deficiencies ruin my happiness. Unlike many wives of successful, smart, good-looking doctors, I didn't make myself crazy with the usual anxieties: *Ooh, is Jonah cheating on me? Planning on cheating on me? Wishing he could cheat on me but not having the guts or time?*

To be totally truthful? Of course I had an anxiety or two. Like knowing how fourteen years of marriage can take the edge off passion. We still enjoyed gasping, sweaty intimacy now and then. Like one starry Long Island evening that past August. We did it in a chaise by the pool after three quarters of a bottle of sauvignon blanc. Also in a bathtub in the Caesar Park Ipanema Hotel during an International Society for Aesthetic Plastic Surgery convention.

But with three four-year-olds plus two nineteen-year-old live-in Norwegian au pairs (twins) and a five-day-a-week, eight-hours-a-day housekeeper, our chances for hot sex were close to zero—even when Bernadine wasn't there and Ida and Ingvild had a weekend off. After "Sleep tight, sweetie" times three, Jonah and I were rarely finished being parents. We still had to deal with Evan's nightmares about boy-swallowing snakes, Dashiell's nighttime forays downstairs to play with remote controls, and Mason's frequent wakenings. So even ho-hum marital hookups weren't as common as they had been. On those exceptional nights when I still had enough energy to feel a tingle of desire, Jonah was usually too wiped from his ten-hour day of rhinoplasties, rhytidectomies, mentoplasties, genioplasties, office hours, and worrying about what the economy was doing to elective surgery to want to leap into bed for anything more than sleep.

Even though I was clueless about what my husband was doing when he was actually doing it (though now I can picture

Jonah stepping onto the leopard-print carpet of Dorinda's front hall, his milk-chocolate-brown eyes widening at the awesome display of lightly freckled breasts—which of course he would know weren't implants—that rose from the scoop neck of her clingy red tank dress), I do remember sighing once or twice over how Jonah's and my private time lacked . . . something.

Fire. That's what was lacking. I knew I—we—had to figure out some way to cut down the noise in our lives so we could once again feel desire. Otherwise? There could be trouble down the road.

Not that I didn't trust him. Jonah was a one-woman man. A lot of it was that he had an actual moral code. Not just the predictable DON'T SHOPLIFT AT BERGDORF'S MEN'S STORE. Seriously, how many super-busy, successful guys in their thirties were there who (like Jonah) absolutely refused to weasel out of jury duty because they believed it was a citizen's obligation to serve?

Also, Jonah was monogamous by nature, even though I hate the word "monogamous." It always brings to mind a nature movie from eighth grade about a mongoose that had dried-out red fur and brown eyes. Just as I was thinking, *Oh my God, it looks like the Disney version of my mother!* the mongoose gave a gut-grinding shriek and *whomp!* It jumped on a snake and ripped it apart in the most brutal, revolting way.

Okay, forget mongoose and monogamous. Jonah always had one girlfriend at a time. We met standing on line in a drugstore when he was a senior at Yale. I was a freshman in the landscape architecture program at the University of Connecticut at Storrs but was in New Haven for a party and had forgotten lip gloss. The weekend before, he'd broken up with a music major named Leigh who played the harp. That we actually met, going to schools sixty-five miles apart, was a miracle. Right from the get-go, I became the sole woman in his life. I knew that not only in my head but in my heart.

And in the years that followed? At medical school, lots of the women students were drawn to him. At five feet eight, Jonah couldn't qualify as a big hunk, but he was a fabulous package. He looked strong with that squared jaw you see on cowboy-booted politicians from the West who make shitty remarks about immigrants, which of course he never would. Plus, he was physically strong, with a muscled triangle of a body. And the amazing thing was, even though Jonah was truly hot in his non-tall way and had that grown-up-rich-in-Manhattan air of self-possession, he gave off waves of decency. So his female classmates, the nurses, they were into him. But he had me. He never even noticed them. Okay, he knew he was way up there on lots of women's Ten Most Wanted, which couldn't have hurt his ego. But my husband was true by nature.

However, a girl can't be too careful. Since I wanted Jonah more than I wanted to be a landscape architect (which was a good thing, because with the department's math and science requirements, my first semester wasn't a winner), I quit UConn five minutes after he proposed. There I was, eighteen, but I knew it was the real thing. So I moved in with him in New Haven. At the time I was so in love—and so overjoyed at never again having to deal with Intro to Botany or Problem Solving—that dropping landscape architecture seemed all pros and no cons.

I transferred to Southern Connecticut State in New Haven as an art major and wound up with a concentration in jewelry design, an academic area that evoked double blinks from Jonah's friends at Yale (as in *Could I have heard her right?*) followed by overenthusiastic comments of the "That sounds sooo interesting!" variety.

Much later, it hit me how sad it was, my tossing off my life's dream with so little thought. From the time of my third-grade class trip to the Brooklyn Botanic Garden, when I gaped at the thousands of roses covering arches and climbing lattices, the bushes laid out in a plan that had to one-up the Garden of Eden, and inhaled the mingling of roses and sweet June air, I understood flowers were somehow my ticket to a world of beauty. Those scents transformed me from a shy kid into an eight-year-old live wire: "Hey, lady!" I hollered to the guide. "What do you call someone who thinks all this up?"

"A landscape architect."

Strange, but until I talked to my guidance counselor in my senior year at Madison, I never told anybody this was what I wanted. No big secret; I just never mentioned it. The librarians knew, because two or three days a week, I walked straight from school to sit at a long table and look at giant landscape books. When I got a little older, I took the subway to the garden itself or to the main branch of the Brooklyn Public Library. The librarian in the Arts and Music section there, a guy with a face like a Cabbage Patch doll's, would always ask, "What do you want to look at today, garden girl?"

Though I did turn out to be a quitter, landscape architecture-wise, I wasn't a loser. First of all, I snagged Jonah. I got my BA in art from Southern. Also, from the get-go in New Haven, I proved I wasn't going to become one of those burdensome, useless doctors' wives. I moved my things into Jonah's apartment on a Saturday while he fielded hysterical calls from his parents. By late Monday afternoon I had landed a late-afternoon/weekend design job at the crème de la crème of central Connecticut florists by whipping up a showstopping arrangement of white flowers in milk, cream, and yogurt containers.

Why am I babbling on like this? Obviously, I don't want to deal with the story I need to tell. But also because I never bought that business about the shortest distance between two points is a straight line. What's so great about short? Too often it's the easy way out. Plus, a straight line is minimalist, and my work is all about embellishment. Any jerk can stick a bunch of thistle into an old mayonnaise jar, but what will people's reaction be? *Why couldn't that thistle-pulling bitch leave the environment alone?*

But I take the identical thistle and jar, grab a few leaves or blades of grass, and voilà! create an arrangement that makes those same people sigh and say, *Exquisite. Makes you really appreciate nature. And so simple.* It really wasn't simple, but if your design shouts, *Hey, look how brilliant I am,* it's not much of a design.

Anyway, after Jonah graduated from college and then finished Yale med school, we moved on from New Haven. With time ticking away like that, a lot of men who marry young start thinking, *Do-over!* Not Jonah. Even after ten years of marriage (along with two failed attempts at in vitro), when some other deeply attractive senior resident in plastic surgery at Mount Sinai might have dropped a starter wife for a more fertile number two (maybe one from a Manhattan family even richer and more connected than the Gerstens, one who could push his practice), Jonah stayed in love with me. Never once, in word or deed, did he communicate, *It's not my fault you can't conceive.*

Once we were settled back in New York, I began realizing my chosen career shouldn't have been chosen by me. I did not love jewelry design: Finding brilliant new ways to display pyrope and tsavorite garnets in Christmas earrings wasn't a thrill. Living in Manhattan made me want to work with something real, and I yearned for the smell and feel of flowers.

So I wound up with a design job at Bouquet, which billed itself as "Manhattan's finest fleuriste." While I was still finding myself, Jonah was already a success, and not just in the OR. He was surrounded by enamored patients. Housewives and advertising executives, beauties and battle-axes. So many had crushes on him. They would have given anything for a taste of his toned pecs, his status, his obvious decency. Except those women only got what they paid for—a first-rate surgeon and a caring doctor. Not that I was complacent. Throughout our marriage, I saw what happened to other doctors' wives as well as to some of our neighbors when we moved to the North Shore of Long Island. I understood: Marriage is always a work in progress.

On that particular night, I was too wiped to be inventive about how to turn up the romantic heat. In fact, I was too wiped to do anything. So instead of calling Andrea to discuss what seasonal berries would be right for Polly Kimmel, who wanted ikebana arrangements for her daughter's bat mitzvah, or exfoliating my heels, or reading *The Idiot* for my book club because Marcia Riklis had said, "Enough with the chick lit," I flopped onto our Louis XV–style marriage bed without my usual satisfied glance at its noble mahogany headboard and footboard with their carvings of baskets of flowers and garlands of leaves. Almost instantly, I fell into an all-too-rare deep, healing sleep. Sure, some internal ear listened for any sound from the boys' rooms, but one thing I'm certain of: I would have been deaf to the soft tread of Jonah's footsteps as he climbed the stairs.

If he had.

Chapter Two

✄——————————————————————————————

"What?" I mumbled about ten hours later. I didn't want to exchange the pleasure of French lavender sprayed on my pillowcase for the daily blast of triplet morning breath, which for some reason reminded me of the cheap bottled salad dressing my mother bought, the kind with brown globules and red pepper flecks suspended in a mucous-like vinaigrette. The boys were fraternal, not identical, triplets. Yet not only did they smell alike, they also had that multiple-birth juju, sharing some magical connection, like their triplet alarm clock that rang only for the three of them at the same instant each day, right before five-thirty.

Jonah always said if he'd known about the five-thirty business, he wouldn't have agreed to get them big-boy beds for their third birthdays. But he knew we really didn't have any choice. Dash and Evan had inherited my height and all three of them had variations on Jonah's solid musculature. If we hadn't gotten the beds, we'd have had to deal with three little King Kongs breaking through the bars of their cribs or climbing over the rails.

That morning, like every other, the boys raced toward our

bedroom. Outside our open door, as usual, they merged into a single wild-haired, twelve-limbed creature that climbed up Jonah's side of the bed. The game never changed: He would grab them one by one and bench-press them up from his chest to arm's length. Then there would be the usual breathless laughter and shrieks of "Daddy, Daddy, I'm flying!" As he finished with each one, he'd set him down between us.

So I knew that within a minute, Evan, Dash, and Mason would be climbing all over me, wild from their high flying, to yell into my ear: "Cocoa Krispies!" "My Band-Aid came off! I need a new one!" "Put on *Rescue Heroes* now!" When I wouldn't respond, one of them, usually Mason, would remember there was a concept called politeness and scream, "Please!" which would bring forth an earsplitting chorus.

Except that morning they woke me with something completely different: a quiet question. "Where's Daddy?" My mind started to reply, *Probably downstairs getting a cup of coffee,* but before the words made it to my mouth, I turned my head.

The white duvet over Jonah's side of the bed was like a predawn snowfall, immaculate. The sham on his pillow with its subtle off-white monogram, sGJ, was pristine. The hideous plastic digital clock with its cracked red and gray Camp Chipinaw medallion that he insisted on keeping on the hand-tooled leather top of his English Centennial nightstand read 5:28.

"Where's Daddy?"

"Where's Daddy?"

My gut must have understood something was terribly wrong before I did, because I reacted so primitively. My eyes darted across the white linen field, and an instant later, I took the same path. Like a snake with prey in sight, I slithered over the undisturbed duvet at amazing speed and grabbed the phone on Jonah's side of the bed. The optimist in me took over. I pressed it to my ear, ready for the beep of a voice-mail signal. I even shushed the children so I could key in our password and hear Jonah's message. Yet when all I heard was the standard steady dial tone, some small, shadowed thing inside me was not surprised.

"Where's Daddy?"

Say anything, I commanded myself. Don't let them see you panic. Because there's no reason for panic yet. Cause for discomfort? Yes. Fear? Of course. But say something Mommyish. Lighthearted or at least reassuring, like "Daddy had to—" The sentence would not finish itself in my head, much less emerge. I vaulted out of bed and ran toward the bathroom. The boys followed, calling out, "Mommy?" With each step, each second without a response, their voices rose.

As I ran, I tried to think what could have happened to Jonah. A freak accident? Maybe last night, when I'd poured my Dramatic Radiance TRF cream into my hand, a tiny blob had dropped on the floor. When he'd gone in there as I slept, he'd slipped on the blob and cracked his head against the white onyx counter! The image was so vivid: him on his back on the Carrara marble floor, eyes closed. No, wait. Eyes open, blinking, because even though he had been unconscious the whole night, he was now coming to. Aside from a slight headache and an ugly red bump on his left temple, he was all right! In my mind I was kneeling beside him, crying out, "Oh Jonah, oh God, oh my God," then calming myself so I could turn to the boys and say, "See? Daddy's fine."

Except Jonah wasn't there. My mind went blank because fright took over and pushed everything else out. It got hold of my body, too. All I felt was that scary internal vibration from nonstop adrenaline, like a running engine that couldn't be turned off.

I braced my hands on the strip of countertop in front of the sink. My back was turned to the boys. All of a sudden, some basic animal instinct for keeping the nest intact momentarily overcame my fright. It seized control, forcing me into action, if not rationality. I grabbed the Bio-Molecular firming eye serum I'd left by the faucet the night before and put it back in the medi-

cine cabinet. Then I yanked a hand towel off the rack and polished the fingerprint I'd just made on the mirror. I folded and
refolded the towel lengthwise into thirds and hung it up again.

Since Evan, Dash, and Mason rarely asked a question without each of them repeating it at least three times, I was still getting pounded with "Where's Daddy?" There was no fright in
their voices, maybe discomfort over my leap from the bed, some
concern, but mostly bright curiosity over this intriguing change
in the morning's routine.

I was about to charge over to the linen closet and get a
fresh bottle of L'Essence de Soleil liquid hand soap when
the endangered-animal-trying-to-get-control nesting instinct
exhausted itself and the terror returned. I whimpered, a high
sound in my throat. In the movies it would have built into a
shriek of pure terror, but since it was me in my bathroom, I
made myself turn and face the boys. "I'm not sure where Daddy
is." Evan, more fearful than his brothers, always on guard
against any monster beyond a closed door or inside a toy chest,
cocked his head and watched me through narrowed eyes. "Probably . . ." I threw out the word, stalling until I could come up
with something that would pacify not just Evan but me. "There
was an emergency at the hospital and he had to go there. Maybe
he was in the operating room all night. He could still be there."
The marble floor was ice that rose through my feet. I knew I
hadn't been standing there that long, but the bones of my feet
felt frozen; my ankles ached from the cold. At the same time, my
hands perspired. I wiped them on my nightgown, but the apricot
silk charmeuse wouldn't accept anything as déclassé as sweat.
"Breakfast time!" I announced in an upbeat tone. I guess I was
trying to come off confident, like one of those TV-commercial
microwaving moms whose brains lack despair neurons.

Instead of following the boys downstairs to pour out Evan's
and Mason's usual additive-rich, dye-laden cereal (for which,
truly, I did feel guilty) and hand Dash his unvarying choice, a

container of vanilla yogurt, I rushed past them, through the bedroom, down the long hall to the other side of the house, and
banged on the door of our au pairs. "Ida! Ingvild!" My voice
ascended to whatever pitch was one notch below hysteria. I
tried to pull it down an octave. "I need both of you right away!"

I commanded myself, *Stop overreacting.* A normal woman
discovering her husband had not spent the night at home
wouldn't be on the brink of psychosis. She wouldn't be so sick
with dread that she wanted to puke up last night's fusilli prima-
vera: *wanted* to, as a purge from the horror poisoning her. At
most, a normal wife would be frantic—*Oh my God, maybe he
was in a terrible car crash!* Or super pissed off—*How stupid is he
that he thinks I'll believe some stupid excuse: He got so sick from
E. coli nachos at a sports bar that he passed out for eight hours?*
Already I was miles beyond that. I pounded on the girls' door as
if my clenched fists were racing each other. "Ida! Ingvild!"

Every other second it hit me how important it was that I
didn't lose control. The boys, right behind me, would absorb
my fright. I couldn't hold back: Terror was appropriate. Jonah
was unfailingly dependable: the ever-responsible Dr. Gersten. A
man of routine. A man of decency, too. Would he ever willingly
leave me open to this kind of fright? Not in a billion years.

If there had been some horrific urban emergency that had
pulled Jonah into Mount Sinai for unscheduled surgery, he'd
have had someone call me. Later, right from the OR—surgical
mask in place, skin hook in hand—he'd have demanded someone double-check that the call to his wife had been made. If he'd
been in an accident, it would have occurred hours before, on his
way home, and someone would have phoned.

Ingvild, who had plucked away her nearly invisible blond
eyebrows and who, by day, replaced them with penciled circum-
flex accents, opened the door so fast she nearly got punched by
my pounding fists. Fresh from sleep, her round, browless face
showed about as much emotion as a picture drawn by one of the

boys in the first year of preschool: a big circle with minuscule circle eyes and nose plus a crooked line for a mouth.

I could definitely read the alarm on her sister's face. Ida was standing a little farther back, and I felt her apprehension: *Has something awful happened? Did we do anything wrong? Is this some bizarre American holiday nobody told us about that begins with waking people before sunrise on a Tuesday in February?* The two of them wore pajama bottoms and T-shirts with the names of bands I'd never heard of.

"Maybe it's nothing," I began slowly. But then I couldn't stop my words from rushing out. "My husband didn't come home last night! It's definitely not like him to do something like that. You know him well enough to know that." The girls seemed to be getting the gist of what I was saying. They weren't sophisticated Scandinavian types, students whose English was so flawless that they comprehended every nuance, who spoke with such slight accents that they might have come from some far corner of Minnesota. Ida and Ingvild were from a small farming community near the Arctic Circle. As they stared at me—watching my eyes dart insanely from one of them to the other, at my hair, which I suppose was sticking out scarecrow-fashion—they were probably pining for the security of the old chicken coop back home. I tried to slow myself down. "I'm worried about my husband. I need to make a few calls."

Though no doubt longing to shoot *What the fuck?* glances at each other, they both managed to keep their eyes on me. I forced my shoulders into a more relaxed position, since I realized I must look like I was expecting blows from a blunt instrument. I didn't want them to think I was out of control. The two of them, at least, should stay calm so as not to communicate any more fear to the boys. "It's probably nothing," I said. "Please take the boys and give them breakfast. And then—whatever. Keep them busy downstairs."

"Okay," Ingvild said.

"Mrs. Gersten," Ida finished. They divided a lot of what they said into halves. I once told Jonah I worried the boys would assume this was some practice of multiples, and they'd wind up splitting whatever they had to say into thirds. If they went off to separate colleges, they wouldn't be able to complete a sentence until Thanksgiving vacation.

The triplets were eyeing me, probably hoping what they feared—Mommy thought something *bad* was happening—wasn't true. They wanted Mommy to be okay and everything to be wonderful. I flashed them my razzle-dazzle smile, the one I employed at medical conventions. It always worked.

Except Evan saw through it. His Mommy radar was picking up bleeps of phoniness. Now he would be agitated all day. When the girls took them all down to the kitchen, he'd still be so rattled by the mere fact of my falseness that he'd puke up his breakfast. That would set off a chain reaction: Mason would gag at the pink and yellow blobs of Froot Loops on the polyure-thaned bamboo kitchen floor, then Dash would have to display how tough he was by mimicking Mason's retching sounds. Evan would vomit again, this time from overstimulation.

The five of them headed to the stairs. Ida, who had the crowd-control instincts of a collie herding sheep, rushed ahead so she could set the pace of the boys. Ingvild descended slowly, not holding the banister, like a bride making her entrance. Racing back toward the bedroom, I fell down flat as my nightgown slid around my legs and hobbled me. I managed to push myself up to my knees but couldn't catch my breath to take in enough air and propel myself to a standing position. Alone, I was hit again with panic. Where could Jonah possibly be? I was no longer befuddled from sleep, but my fear so overwhelmed me that I could barely manage to get up off the floor. Thinking things through was beyond me.

When my feet left the sturdy hallway carpeting and felt the soft rug in our bedroom, I relaxed enough to let my mind escape into fantasy: *Oh! Wait! I know: Maybe our phone's ringer is off. Yes! That could definitely be it.* Maybe Jonah had an accident, and someone in an emergency room had called to tell me. Not wanting to leave a frightening message, that nurse had left a note for the chief resident on the next shift: *Please notify wife of traumatic brain injury, bed 7. Collapsing scaffolding in front of building on Madison Avenue. (FYI his ID from Sinai/he's MD!!). Tell her he's here.* I hiked up my nightgown and hurried around the bed to the phone.

The ringer was on. To double-check, I raced back to my side of the bed and grabbed my BlackBerry from my nightstand. My hands were trembling so uncontrollably, it took me a couple of tries to press the speed dial, H for home. As our phone shrilled its first ring, I jumped, then ran back around the bed, fleetingly forgetting I had just dialed myself. *It's Jonah, and he feels absolutely terrible because he forgot*—then I glanced down and saw my cell number on the regular phone's caller ID readout.

I wanted to heave my BlackBerry across the room, hard, and create a vicious bruise on the Venetian-plaster finish on the wall opposite the bed. But my shaking hands decided to obey some barely conscious command from my brain: I brought up Recent Calls on the little screen of the phone. Hope lived under a second. My last incoming call had come at 6:47 P.M. the night before: Aurora Hartman saying, "It would be a major blessing for the community if you'd co-chair the Trike-a-thon event for Tuttle Farm nursery school, because this could be a huge, huge fund-raiser for Tuttle, and you do *everything* with such style, and oh my God, your energy—I'm always in awe—and, Susie, this is our chance to make a major difference in our kids' lives."

What had sounded so comfortably familiar the night before—Aurora failing to be charming yet again—now, because of its ordinariness, felt like a smack in the face. My heart couldn't keep up with its own pounding; it slammed against my chest wall so hard . . . how could it not explode? I pictured pieces of cardiac muscle pierced on the shards of my shattered ribs.

Jonah hadn't come home the night before. He hadn't reached out to me. Therefore, something unthinkable had happened. Absolutely. Sure, I could imagine him walking in the door and running upstairs shouting, "Susie, Susie, you're not going to believe what happened to me!" But it was getting harder each minute to take off on any flight into fantasy.

My husband was missing. Then I thought, *Missing? If I'm lucky.*

Chapter Three

I sat on the edge of the mattress. Instead of doing what I meant to—covering my face and sobbing—I started sliding and almost landed on my ass. My nightgown again, and the perils of the good life: Everything was so smooth, there was hardly any friction between the gown and the Egyptian cotton sheet. My bare feet saved me with an up-down, up-down step, like in one of those folk dances performed by people trailing ribbons. When at last I got steady, I was panting, almost gasping, from the effort. This was crazy. I was strong, fit, well coordinated if not brilliantly athletic.

Except the bottom had dropped out of my life. Ninety-nine percent of me believed that. But that other one percent was almost afraid to call Jonah's cell: He would answer with his cold, busy voice: "For God's sake, Susie, there's an emergency here! Dammit, don't you think if I had a free second—if anyone here had a free second—you'd have gotten a call?"

I called anyway. Three rings and then "This is Dr. Gersten. I can't answer the phone right now. To leave a message, please wait for the tone. If this is an emergency, please press the number five and the pound key."

"Jonah, sweetheart, I know something's happened—your not coming home at all last night—and I'm terribly worried. Please call me as soon as you can, or have someone call me to let me know how you are. I love you." Right then it hit me. Maybe something had happened in the city during the night and I didn't know about it yet. I rushed for the remote. But my hands started shaking again, so it took four tries to turn on the TV. I didn't care whether it would bring terror or relief. I just needed to know what was out there. That was what I'd done for months after 9/11, turning on the TV every few hours, ready for the worst but hoping for the sight of Nothing Catastrophic. I'd longed for boring weather forecasters standing before maps, McDonald's commercials. And that was exactly what I got now: normality as presented by News Channel 4. Darlene Rodriguez was asking Michael Gargiulo if he knew why people used to eat oysters only in months that had an R in them. The sports guy glanced up at Darlene and Michael from his papers. From his grin, it looked like he'd been born with double the normal number of teeth; all of them gleamed with pleasure at his knowing the oyster answer.

I switched off the TV and paced back and forth on the carpet, trying for grace under pressure—or at least enough self-control so I wouldn't howl like a dying animal. I leaned against the footboard. Considering all the crap I'd read in my life, how come I'd never come across a magazine article entitled "What to Do When You Wake Up and Your Husband Isn't There"? It would have had a bullet-pointed sidebar of suggestions that could flash into my head.

The only information I could imagine in such a sidebar was "Phone police." No, that probably wasn't right. I remembered a TV show on which the wife called the cops and the guy on the phone asked, "How long has he been missing?" When she said, "Well, he didn't come home last night," the cop told her, "Sorry. We can't take any action until he's gone for three days. Try not to worry. Nine times out of ten, they just show up." The cop had an edge to his voice—world-weary, snide—as if he were picturing a staggering-drunk husband, or one with the lousy luck to fall asleep after having sex with his bimbo girlfriend.

I walked across the bedroom toward the window that faced the front and sat in Jonah's favorite chair in the world, a Regency bergère with gilded wood arms and legs. It was upholstered in creamy silk with a ribbon motif. When I'd spotted the bergère at an auction house, an embarrassingly loud "Ooh!" had escaped me. It was a beauty, fit for British royalty—and okay, suburban Jewish doctors, too.

Because I wasn't the only one blown away by its beauty; Jonah had wanted the chair way more than I did. He'd sat on it and noted in his objective clinician's tone that it wasn't comfortable. You didn't see it, but you could feel its back angled in a bizarre way. Instead of sitting straight, you felt pitched slightly forward, as if you were examining your knees. But he added in his deeper-than-usual, I've-got-a-refined-aesthetic-sensibility voice, "It's a splendid piece." Also a decent investment. But there was more: I could feel the chair's power over him. It made him feel not just well-off—*Hey, I can afford this exquisite objet*—but incredibly refined. If George the Whatever had needed a court plastic surgeon, Jonah knew he would have been tapped. In a flash of marital ESP, I caught all this in under a second. We bid. We bought. For both of us, sitting in that chair always made us feel elegant and rich. Protected, too: *We've made it. We're upper-class, and therefore things go the way we wish them to go.*

Even in that instant, petrified that life was about to give me the cosmic smack in the face that would make every woman on Long Island tell her best friend, "Thank God I'm not Susie Gersten," I knew if I were sitting in a repro Regency covered in polyester damask, I would feel worse.

A second later, as I glanced back at my cell phone, the chair vanished from my head. I got up and called information. When the computer said, "City and state, please," I told it, "New York, New York," then enunciated "Donald Finsterwald" even while knowing the computer wouldn't get it, having obviously been programmed not to comprehend New York accents by some hostile Southern Baptist; except for twice in my entire life, I'd always had to wait for an operator.

Even though it was not yet six in the morning, Donald Finsterwald, the administrator of Jonah's plastic surgery practice, sounded not just alert but primed, up on the toes of his orthopedic loafers, ready and eager to handle the day's first crisis. "Hello!" His extreme loyalty to Manhattan Aesthetics always creeped me out because it resembled patriotism more than simple dedication to work. Jonah said I didn't have an organization mind-set, that every decent-sized office needed a Donald.

"Hi, Donald. Susie Gersten. Sorry to call so early." My voice came out squeaky; plus, I was still breathless. I tried calming myself by taking a Lamaze breath through my nose and exhaling it through pursed lips as silently as I could so he wouldn't think, *Partner's wife breathing hysterically. Watch what you say!* "I'm concerned . . . I am worried about . . . Jonah didn't come home last night. I didn't get any messages from him."

"Oh, I'm sure—" He always strung out his vowels—"Ooooh, Iiii'm suuure"—so even in the best of times, it took practically a week till he got out a sentence. Also, he had one of those unisex voices, so nearly every time he called, if he asked for Dr. Gersten and didn't say, "Hi, Mrs. Gersten, it's Donald," I'd wonder if it was a patient with a question about her new chin implant who'd managed to get Jonah's home number, or the Irish dermatologist who always sat at the Manhattan Aesthetics table at any Mount Sinai fund-raising gala.

I said, "Listen, Donald, something is really wrong. Jonah doesn't not come home. And before you think—"

"Mrs. Gersten, I would never think—"

"I know. Of course you wouldn't." Truthfully, I had no idea

what he would think. Despite his almost pathetic eagerness to please, Donald Finsterwald had always repulsed me. I know I was being unfair, but I couldn't help it. I saw him as (like antimatter and the Antichrist) the Anti-style, a man who always picked the most heinous clothes and accessories and wore them with total seriousness. What would make someone have his thick prescription lenses stuck into narrow black frames that made him look like he was Peeping Tom checking out the world? Why would he wear strangulating turtlenecks that pushed up his double chin until it hung like a feed bag? Donald's inner life—he must have one, since everyone was supposed to—was a mystery. "Sorry. Forgive my manners," I apologized. "I'm so beside myself, Donald. In all the years we've been married, Jonah's never not come home. I mean, if he's going to be over a half hour or forty-five minutes late, he calls. Or has someone call."

"Don't I know it," he said. "There have been a fair number of times I got word from Dr. Gersten, 'Have someone call my wife.' The very moment I get an order like that, it's carried out."

"Jonah tells me about the great job you're doing," I said. "And I know if you'd heard from him, you'd call me immediately. What I'm wondering, though, is if you heard . . ." The phone was in my right hand; I used my left to massage my temples with my thumb and middle finger. "Have there been any calls from the police? Or from the office's alarm company? Maybe a hospital? I mean, not about one of his patients but about something happening to Jonah?"

"No. Of course not. I would have called you immediately, Mrs. Gersten."

"I know, but I just wanted to be sure you weren't, whatever, protecting me or waiting until, like, around seven o'clock, before calling me or Dr. Noakes or Dr. Jiménez." Jonah's partners, Gilbert John Noakes and Layne Jiménez, would have called me right away if they'd heard anything.

"Oh no, no. I wouldn't have waited to get in touch."

"Okay, fine. I just wanted to be sure before I started making any other calls."

"Oh. Who were you thinking of calling? I mean, could it be better to wait, it being so early? Dr. Gersten, maybe if he had some sort of emergency at Sinai, he might have gone to one of those rooms where residents can rest, because he wouldn't want to disturb you at this hour."

I was on the verge of saying, "Oh no, he knows I'd be up because the boys always wake us at five-thirty." Then I realized Donald was buying time so he could figure out if Jonah's not coming home could be a potential catastrophe for the practice. Was Jonah sick or dead or God knows what? Or was his absence the result of some marital misunderstanding that could end in either tears and kisses ("Oh, sweetie, I was so worried!") or else in a gargantuan retainer to a matrimonial lawyer? Maybe Donald was stalling so he could call Gilbert John Noakes, the practice's senior partner, and get some guidance on dealing with a hysterical wife.

Except I wasn't hysterical. In talking with Donald Finsterwald, I had concentrated on sounding calm. Calm was good, wasn't it? Under normal circumstances, I came across like a calm person. Pleasant, friendly. An excellent doctor's wife, with just enough sex and sparkle to keep me out of the ranks of Xanaxed zombie ladies or sugarplum spouses who smiled in lieu of talking. I had my own career, but I didn't bore the crap out of people by carrying on as if floral design were the answer to the world's prayers.

And just now with Donald, I'd been courteous, balanced. Totally nonhysterical. Good, I'd paid my dues to Manhattan Aesthetics. So instead of agreeing to wait before making any calls, or telling Donald that I appreciated his input and would give it the serious consideration it deserved, I dropped the nice and snapped, "I've got to go."

Then I hung up and called the police.

Chapter Four

It wasn't only that I had what in the flower business is called "a great nose," a highly sensitive sense of smell: Anyone with two nostrils would instantly know that Detective Sergeant Timothy Coleman's body odor was over-the-top. And his generous application of synthetic lime cologne did nothing to camouflage it.

"Please excuse me, Mrs. Gersten," Nassau County's finest said after he cleared his throat. His manners were exquisite, as if to apologize for his pungency. Maybe as a child he'd been beaten and forced to memorize *Emily Post's Etiquette;* his politeness was as aggressive as his BO. "Are you sure it's all right if I sit down?"

"Of course," I said, fast as I could. "Please." I couldn't wait to get to the couch. The chemical reaction of his smell added to my ever escalating fear was so explosive that—*ka-boom!*—I got dizzy two seconds after I'd opened the door for him. Now I almost dove onto the couch so I wouldn't risk swooning into it.

"Thank you *so* much," he said.

We had already spent twenty minutes talking at the kitchen table, but then my housekeeper had arrived, toting a bag of her own microfiber cloths. Driven as Bernadine was by her obsessive-compulsive need to empty the dishwasher before she took off her coat, the detective and I couldn't stay in the kitchen. However, bringing Coleman into the living room hadn't changed the environment. He stank. And his excessive courtesy was simultaneously exhausting me and making me a nervous wreck. *What's his game? What does he want from me?*

"The reason I'm asking for all this information now, ma'am, is so I don't need to keep having to come back to you for more. I hope you understand and can bear with me."

"Of course. I appreciate . . ." Besides the dizziness, my mind kept veering off in a hundred directions. It didn't seem like I'd offered any helpful information about Jonah that Detective Sergeant Coleman could use. Not one single "Good, I see, right" had escaped his lips. So I felt doubly pressured to make a positive impression. I wanted him to think I was a fine, deserving person so he'd work day and night to find my husband. But he wouldn't think I was so fine if I went berserk, which I felt I could do at any second. If I started screeching hysterically—"I want my husband! I want my husband!"—while grabbing the detective's lapels and shaking him, he would get sidetracked. Maybe he'd decide I was one of those "She seemed so nice" wives who, three days before her period, axes her husband and shoves him into a calico-covered Container Store box with the croquet set and pool toys—then saunters back to the kitchen to make zucchini bread.

The tension was too much. Also, from the minute I opened the door, I was afraid he'd be hostile because of my height. Tall women get to some short guys, and not in a good way. And Coleman was short, like he'd been zoomed down to 75 percent. With me at five feet nine inches, I didn't want him to feel I was the type who didn't take mini-men seriously, even though he'd never see the five-five he probably lied about on his driver's license. I wasn't hung up on height. Jonah was shorter, but not dollhousey like Coleman. Jonah was solid and strong.

Then I got upset with myself: *It's not about you or Detective Sergeant Smell-o-rama. It's about Jonah.* I hung my head with shame—not a good idea, because the sudden shift of position made me want to throw up.

Coleman, perched on the edge of the seat of a carved Sri Lankan chair, kept the questions coming. I suppose I answered. Images kept flashing inside my head and overpowered any thought: Jonah writhing on the floor in some obscure men's room at Mount Sinai, delirious with fever from a superbug he'd caught in the hospital. Jonah carjacked, bound and gagged in the black, near airless trunk of his BMW.

"I hope you don't mind my asking," Detective Sergeant Coleman said, "but has Dr. Gersten ever, uh, not shown up before? Not come home?"

"Never. Jonah is completely reliable. I can always count on . . ." The tears I'd held back in the kitchen started to spill. I wasn't actually crying; my eyes just became full and overflowed, like a stopped-up sink. "He's so responsible." It came out as a froggy sound because I was choked up. "That's why I think it must be something bad, because . . ." The tears cascaded down my cheeks. Coleman sat there. Instead of averting his eyes, he watched. A tiny spiral-bound notepad rested on his knee. Its size seemed grossly inadequate for recording the huge facts of Jonah's vanishing.

Finally, I found the energy to propel myself up. "Excuse me," I said. I rushed into the guest bathroom, blew my nose, wiped my eyes.

When I returned to the living room, Coleman was still at the edge of his chair. "I didn't know whether to call the police this soon," I told him. "I remember from movies when detectives say they have to wait forty-eight hours or three days until they can look into a matter."

"Oh no, ma'am. If someone who keeps a regular pattern suddenly doesn't show up, we should know about it. A lot of times the local precinct only sends in regular officers to take the initial report, like if it's a teenager who's probably with a friend, or if it's someone with a history of instability. The next day, if that sort of person is still unaccounted for, the department follows up with a detective. But with someone like Dr. Gersten, what with his position in the community, well, you know."

"Right."

"Now, when we were in the kitchen, you mentioned your last conversation with your husband was yesterday afternoon."

"Yes."

"Can you recall what each of you said in that conversation, ma'am?" I was examining a medallion of roses and laurel leaves on the needlepoint rug. He repeated "Ma'am?" louder, which made me jump.

"I don't know. Let me think. It was a regular late-afternoon phone call. Jonah still had a couple of post-op patients to see. Then he had some odds and ends to do in the city before he came home."

"Did he happen to say what they were, ma'am?"

"The only thing he mentioned was maybe going to Tod's. It's about twenty blocks downtown from his office. A shoe store."

"To . . . ?"

To have a martini, shmuck. "To try on a pair of shoes," I said. "Brown suede lace-up shoes. He'd seen them in the window. But he was pretty tired, so chances were he wouldn't bother."

"He said he probably wouldn't bother, or was that your sense of things?"

"He said it."

"Had he been under any special pressure lately?" I must have given him a *Duh* look because he added, "That he was tired from a more-than-usual workload? Or maybe family pressure?"

"No. I mean, he's in a great surgical practice. Well, it's been less than stellar lately, the economy being what it is, but they're doing better than most of their colleagues. So far, so good." Coleman blinked. I noticed he had no sign of beard, as if he used Nair instead of a razor. Imagining stroking a hairless, almost poreless man's cheek was so repulsive that I forgot I was in the middle of answering his question. When Coleman uncocked his head and looked into my eyes straight-on, I quickly said, "Sorry, I lost my train of thought."

"You were saying your husband wanted to build up his practice," he said.

"Right," I said. Coleman wiped the tip of his pen on the pad. He seemed ready to jot down some significant detail. "A lot of his business comes from referrals from other doctors, so he needs to stay active in the medical community. Like if a woman asks a doctor she knows, 'Can you recommend someone for . . . ?'" I patted the underside of my chin with the back of my hand to demonstrate. "Jonah says if that doctor has run into him in the last week or two, he's likely to say, 'Jonah Gersten. Definitely. He's first-rate.' Which he truly is. If you're not well trained and gifted, no one's going to risk recommending you. But Jonah knows being out and about is important, too. And he's big on PR. If he's quoted somewhere, like in O or *Allure,* he'll get calls for the next few months. All that takes time and planning. Plus being a surgeon, he has to keep up professionally. So his hours are incredible. And since the triplets were born—"

"They're how old again?"

"Four. They're usually asleep when he gets home. They go to bed at seven. We decided that instead of family dinner, we'd have family breakfast. But I know Jonah wishes he could have more time with them, not just mornings and weekends. I guess you could call that pressure, too."

"What about financial pressure, ma'am?"

"We're okay." Early on in my marriage, I'd overheard my mother-in-law telling one of her friends that it was très LMC— lower-middle-class, a heinous crime—to say "X is rich." "God in heaven," she said, "'rich' is so crass." She meant saying it, not being it. Anyway, within a month after moving from New Haven to New York, I'd come to understand that "rich" was fine to describe Rembrandt's colors or a veal stock. But when it came to even really big bucks, I knew to say "X does nicely." Detective Sergeant Coleman was fingering his hairless cheek, trying to figure out what my "we're okay" meant. So I added, "Jonah's making a very good living."

Coleman's fast 180 scope of the living room apparently gave him confirmation because he started nodding like a bobblehead. "You mentioned earlier he has partners in his plastic surgery practice," he said.

"Yes."

He didn't hear me because he was busy flipping through his little pad, stopping every couple of pages. Maybe he was fascinated by notes he'd made. Or he couldn't read his own writing. "I hope you don't mind my asking, but do Dr. Gersten and his partners get along?"

"Yes."

"No financial disagreements? Egos? That sort of thing?"

"They're fine," I said.

"If I might ask, how are things within your family?"

"Fine. Great. He loves the children, loves me. And vice versa."

"The two girls you say are living here?"

"Our au pairs," I said. His lids fluttered. "Mother's helpers. They're here from Norway." More flutters. "They're all legal and everything. They have valid work permits and—"

"Dr. Gersten has no issues with them, ma'am?" He wrote something on his pad.

The dizziness that had eased sneaked back, maybe because I could almost hear Coleman thinking, *Two Scandinavian girls. Blondes, I bet.* True, they were blondes. But Ida and Ingvild bore such a resemblance to Miss Piggy that I was waiting for their visas to expire before buying the DVD of *The Muppets Take*

Manhattan for the boys. "No issues at all. Jonah thinks they're great with the boys. Listen, my husband is, you know, easygoing. Friendly but polite. Respectful." He underlined whatever he had just written.

"Ma'am?" he asked.

"Yes?" I had to raise my head slightly to look at him. Dizzy again, like the floor had switched places with the ceiling.

"When we're called in on a case, we're put in the position of having to ask questions that may seem, you know, not polite. But we have to ask them anyway."

"I understand." He was going to ask me if Jonah screwed around.

"So I hope you don't mind if I ask you . . . You said your husband loves you, and I'm sure he does. But some men do have a midlife-crisis thing."

"Jonah's thirty-nine. I don't know if that qualifies, but—"

"Is it possible that there is someone else—"

"I'm absolutely sure there isn't."

"Maybe a patient—"

"Jonah says any surgeon who takes up with a patient has a fifty-fifty shot at a malpractice suit, and no sex in the world is worth that."

He smiled and nodded at Jonah's remark. But what doctor wouldn't say that to reassure a suspicious wife? "What I meant to ask was if there has been any patient calling or stalking him in any way. Sometimes with doctors—"

"No. Our home number is unlisted. And he knows how to deal with patients who get emotionally dependent or pushy or a little crazy."

Coleman flipped to a clean page in his pad. He held the pen against his upper lip, just south of his nostrils, and took a deep breath, like he was working on an ink-fume high. "Are Dr. Gersten's parents still alive?" he asked.

"Yes. Clive and Babs—Barbara—Gersten. They're still very

active, professionally, socially. They live in the city." I saw he wanted more. But I was so wiped from all the frantic hours I'd spent since I'd woken to "Where's Daddy?" that it was getting too much to think up more words and then push them into speech. Coleman rotated his pen near his nose a few times. Even though I was looking at my wedding ring, I could feel him gazing into my eyes. Finally, I got it together enough to answer.

"His father's a radiation oncologist in Manhattan. Clive Gersten." To look at my father-in-law, you wouldn't think he was in that field. He smiled all the time. Or at least the corners of his mouth turned up. I sometimes wondered if he'd had a stroke early in life because his personality was un-smiley. Not morose. Just bland. If he were ice cream, he wouldn't even be vanilla. But his patients adored him, clearly taking the rising corners of his mouth as either an optimistic smile or a compassionate one, depending on their diagnosis.

"Oncologist is cancer, right?"

"Right. Jonah's mother is marketing director of Gigi de Lavallade Cosmetics." Babs Gersten was the person who, back in the eighties, had convinced millions of white women all over the world that they should wear brown lipstick and bronze blush. In the nineties she got millions of black women converted to maroon cheeks, not red. Currently, she was working on a major campaign to get Asian women out of rose-tinged foundation, to open themselves up to the untapped potential—the actual brilliance!—of much maligned yellow.

"Does your husband get along with his folks?"

"Yes."

"Does he see a lot of them?"

"We usually see them every couple of weeks. They have a place in Water Mill, in the Hamptons. They sometimes stop here on their way out or back. It's easier that way. Having the triplets running around their apartment is a little much for my in-laws. They collect pre-Columbian art. Lots of clay figurines. We do visit them at the beach, but even that's pretty chaotic if the weather's not good."

Coleman wrote what appeared to be a long sentence in his pad, then turned back a page and made what looked like three dots. "Any other children? Your husband, I mean. Does he have any brothers or sisters?"

"He has a younger brother. He's a casting director."

"Do they get along?"

"Jonah and Theo?" His brow furrowed, which was what usually happened when people first heard it, because it sounds more like a lisp and diphthong than an actual name. Whenever I had to introduce him, I fought the urge to say "Thith ith Theo." "T-h-e-o," I spelled. "They talk on the phone . . . I guess about once a week. Whenever they see each other, they have a good time. It's a solid relationship."

He closed his pad and stuck it in the outside pocket of his jacket. "Would you mind taking me for a look around?" he asked as he stood.

"Of course. I mean, I'll be glad to show you." Coleman didn't seem the house-and-garden type. I assumed he had some sort of checklist he needed to go through in a missing-person case. Suddenly, those words, "missing person," hit home. They ricocheted around my brain and grew more powerful with each repetition as they brought home the reality: I not only didn't know where Jonah was, I couldn't even guess.

Now that Coleman was no longer seated, some hostess gene made me pop up from the couch. Not the best idea. I swayed sideways and made a stupid grabbing gesture with each hand as I tried to get hold of something to steady me. There was only air. It was scary, not being able to distinguish between up and down.

He rushed over and braced my elbows until he was sure I could stand perpendicular to the floor. We spoke at the same time: "Are you okay?" "Sorry, I got dizzy."

That was followed by a couple of eternal seconds of silence.

Coleman moved himself out of the narrow space between couch and coffee table with the klutzy sidestep slide of someone who should not bother trying tennis. "Are you okay to take me around the house?" he asked.

"Yes. It'll be fine."

I'd sent the boys off to preschool to get them out of the way. Ida and Ingvild would hang out there in the mommies' room in case of—whatever.

So it was just the two of us, me and Detective Sergeant Coleman. The dizziness was gone, but I definitely didn't feel normal. Every few minutes my heart banged with an almost audible boom. *But listen,* I told myself, *considering everything, I'm functioning.* Leading him to the basement, then through all the rooms on the first floor, I was at least reassured I could control myself sufficiently to go through the motions.

Only after we climbed the stairs and he opened the linen closet outside our bedroom did I comprehend that he wasn't just hunting for some subtle clue to Jonah's whereabouts. When Coleman had peered in cabinets and armoires and opened the tops of the benches that ran across one wall in the basement playroom, he'd been searching for Jonah's dead body.

"Do you ever find the person somebody says is missing right there, in the house?" I asked. "Or do you just find clues?"

"Sometimes an individual writes a note," Coleman said carefully. "He's in a rush and winds up leaving it in the weirdest place." He must have decided I was thinking, *Note? Does he mean suicide note?* Not wanting me to tilt and maybe pass out, he said real fast, "'Dear So-and-so, I have to go to . . . whatever, someplace . . . for a few days' and so forth." I noticed he wasn't answering my question about discovering the missing person right there at home.

We went through Jonah's closet and then the bedroom. Other than gaping at the lineup of Jonah's tassel loafers—which admittedly was a little excessive, the same shoe over and over,

as if some weird form of asexual reproduction were going on—
Coleman didn't seem to find anything worth noting. In the bedroom, he didn't cringe at the plastic Camp Chipinaw clock on
Jonah's nightstand the way I did, and completely ignored the
book lying beside it, *Einstein: His Life and Universe,* not even
saying something like "Hey, Dr. Gersten really must be a genius
to be reading about a genius." He didn't pick it up and shake it
the way detectives do on TV—where paper falls out that's inevitably a clue. So I picked up the book and pretended to be pag-
ing through it. Nothing fell out because Jonah didn't even use a
bookmark, just bent down pages. He was up to page 104. I held
it against my chest, closed my eyes, and told myself, *He's going
to get to finish this book,* even though I dreaded he wouldn't. But
I didn't say that out loud because I wasn't the plucky-heroine
type. As I was laying it down again, I quickly leafed through it.
Nothing: just his name, written in his graceful, non-doctorish
script, and his usual underlinings and margin notes, as if he'd
never gotten out of Yale. Inside the back cover, he'd even written a shopping list: *Mach3,* his razor blades, *black shoe polish,*
and *check red cap,* probably something to do with capsules.

Then the phone rang. I knew it was Jonah's office because all
the calls from there and his answering service rang with a special
bing-bing-bing tone. A little Tinker Bell–ish, I'd told him. Now
it sounded beautiful. A burst of hope propelled me to the phone.
It wasn't until I was almost bellowing "Hello" with desperate
eagerness that it hit me it might be someone else and not Jonah
finally, finally calling to explain why—

"Susie?" Not Jonah. It was Layne. "I'm here with Gilbert
John on speakerphone."

Layne Jiménez was from New Mexico, so she had that no-
accent all-American accent television journalists have. Her tone,
though, was doctor-gentle rather than reporter-crisp. "We hate
to bother you, Susie. Donald told us about Jonah," she said.
"We kept going back and forth: Should we call, shouldn't we

call? You've got to be waiting for the phone to ring. But we're so concerned. Have you heard anything?"

I shook my head for a few seconds until the shuffle of shoes coming through their speakerphone made me realize they were nervously waiting for my response. "No. No calls." I put my hand over the mouthpiece and murmured to Detective Sergeant Coleman, "Jonah's partners."

"Susie?" Gilbert John Noakes this time. He had that gorgeous bass voice you'd expect to be singing "Ol' Man River," in his case, without the customary African-American inflection. Gilbert John had a grand accent, slightly more British than Boston. He sounded like he'd been born on some elitist island in the mid-Atlantic. His pronunciation of my name was "Syu-see?" His appearance matched his voice. Handsome, like one of those manly actors with thick white hair who played rich, potent older men on daytime soaps.

"Yes. I'm here."

"How are you holding up, dear?" he asked.

"All right."

Over the years, I'd come to believe that Gilbert John's supercilious delivery was a minor case of snobbishness made much worse by shyness—and dullness. He never had much to say about anything except the most tedious surgical matters—or in migraine-inducing detail, his latest mosaic. He made his compositions from found objects. That had the potential to be interesting, but Gilbert John didn't understand how not to be boring. Listening to him, you wanted to gasp for air. He'd go on (and on) about smashing up a souvenir plate from the 1989 Philadelphia flower show, and about how half of creating mosaics was getting the right-sized shards. Even if you were backing out of the room, he'd stay with you step for step to give you his secret for getting the proper consistency of grout. The weird thing was, in spite of his aggressive tediousness, his mosaics were fresh, even lively.

"Has either of you heard anything?" I asked. "Anything at all?"

"Not a thing," Layne managed to say. She had a catch in her gentle voice. I tried to think of something to comfort her so she wouldn't burst into tears and then feel terrible because, by crying, she'd made it harder on me. But she was able to go on. "We have the whole staff calling hospitals, but no one like Jonah has come in," she said. "You know, Susie, I've been thinking. Maybe you should call the police. Or Gilbert John says you might want to think about a private investigator. You know, if you don't want word getting around."

"Up to you entirely," Gilbert John said. "We simply want you to know we'll do anything we can if you need us."

"Absolutely," Layne said. "Whatever you want done—or not done—you only have to ask."

That instant I started second-guessing myself. Had I been stupid to call the Nassau County police when Jonah very well could be in the city? Should I have called the NYPD instead? He could be anywhere.

Maybe he would wind up being one of those vanishing husbands who turned up decades later, living a different life in some other country. Years from now, when the triplets were in high school, or later, when I was on my deathbed, we'd learn Jonah had been living as Dottore Giovanni Giordano, treating the poorest of the poor in the slums of Naples, not taking even a *lira* for his work.

Except that wasn't what happened.

Chapter Five

"I know you came here to keep yourself from staring at the phone, trying to will it into ringing," Andrea Brinckerhoff said brightly. She picked up a speck of floral foam from our worktable and flicked it into the green plastic trash can. Andrea rarely said anything non-brightly. She seemed to have modeled her personality on one of those debutantes in 1930s movies: a martini in one hand, a cigarette holder in the other, laughing in the face of doom. "Though I'm assuming you call-forwarded so it would ring here."

"So it would ring on my cell. Car, bathroom: I could be anyplace and I'd be able to hear it."

"Excellent!"

I understood Andrea's over-the-top brightness on this morning was an effort aimed at keeping up my spirits—though her detractors might claim she simply wasn't touched by other people's sorrow.

She headed for the coffeepot, her head swiveling slowly back and forth as she walked, searching for stray bits of stem or leaf on the concrete floor. Not that I watched her every step. I was flipping through the pocket-sized brown leather phone book I'd brought with me, the one Jonah had used until two years earlier, when he finally surrendered to a BlackBerry. I finished his A's and B's and began the C's, copying down names and numbers of anyone who might be in his life currently, people he could have seen or spoken to in the last couple of weeks.

Andrea handed me coffee in one of her L'Objet porcelain mugs. She'd chosen the Aegean-green style; its handle was twenty-four-karat gold. "If I might suggest . . ."

I listened. Andrea was thorough. While we both did the same jobs—floral design, client development, running the business—we both accepted reality and roles. She was the efficient, let's-create-a-system one. I was the more imaginative and (despite Andrea's copy of the Social Register that leaned against *Contemporary Approaches to Floral Art* on the shelf above her desk) had the more upmarket aesthetic. Not that Andrea was Miss Azalea Plant in a Green Plastic Cachepot, but she had too many musts and no-nos to be an exciting designer. She stuck to the old tired-out rules, like no bear grass or carnations ever or that heritage roses and English ivy in Grandmère's 1780 silver teapot were the ultimate word in elegance.

"Instead of writing a list," she said, "put a mark next to each name. That way you can tell at a glance who you need to call."

"Good idea," I murmured. Was it? I hadn't a clue, but she sounded authoritative. My thoughts were dark and swirling, like a tornado. The mere idea of a system was soothing.

"See? Make a dot on the left side of the entry. After you speak to that person, put a check mark on the right."

I either knew or had heard Jonah mention about half the names I'd gotten to in his phone book. That I didn't know the others wasn't particularly meaningful. Like many surgeons, my husband was meticulous to the point of being a pain, or worse. When he hung a tie on his pull-out rack, the pointy bottom of all the ties had to be at the same level. If he was in the kitchen when I was cooking and overheard me mumble to myself, "Where the hell is the dill?" he'd stare at me not just in disbelief but with displeasure, as in *How can you go through life and not have a precise place for everything?* I'd told him the need for a precise place for things was a definite plus for a guy who reconfigured faces. He had to be finicky about detail: like *Where are the sutures?* or *How many millimeters to the right do I move this nose?* And the proof was right there in his phone book. Nearly all the entries I didn't recognize had a teeny P above the name. Patient. Well, I assumed P meant patient, as Jonah's universe wasn't peopled with peony growers or philosophers.

"One more suggestion?" Andrea said. I nodded. "Drink your coffee. You need some . . . you don't want to sound so" — she combed her straight blond hair off her forehead with her fingers — "so down."

"I am down. I'm terrified."

"Susie, I know that. You know that. But if your cell rang and it was Jonah saying, 'My car went over a cliff — '"

"Where are there cliffs between Manhattan and Long Island?" I snapped.

"I'm talking in, you know, whatever that stupid fucky word people always use — something terms."

"Metaphorical terms?"

Andrea was hostile to words over three syllables. "Right," she said. "So let's assume he'll be fine. And if he is fine, you don't want him saying, 'I hear you called Dr. Schwartz' — I'm sure there's always a Dr. Schwartz — 'asking about me. Schwartz said you sounded totally down, like you'd lost all hope.' I mean, if I know Jonah, he wouldn't be thrilled."

"No. He'd be humiliated." I came close to smiling at the thought of Jonah clapping his hand to his forehead, jaw dropping, when he heard I'd called the names in his phone book. Then it hit me that he might be not embarrassed but proud I'd taken such initiative. On the other hand . . . Angry, definitely angry. *I know you must have been frightened, Susie. But call-*

ing everyone . . . God! Can I ask you one simple question? Why couldn't you have waited twenty-four hours? What the hell am I going to say to all these people?

"Humiliated?" Andrea said. She had seen Jonah's flash of temper—rage, almost—when I'd said or done something to hint that maybe he had a flaw or two. "No. He'd be pissed beyond belief. But it's not just about Jonah getting mad that you called his entire phone book sounding like the 'Before' in an antidepressant commercial. You need to get some caffeine into you so you don't sound like you mainlined Ambien."

I picked up the mug. Andrea had paid for them herself because she believed clients should know that Florabella had a profound understanding of what beautiful was. L'Objet mugs were, in her view, irrefutable proof. I'd vetoed them, telling her yes, they were gorgeous, but Bergdorf's could get four hundred thirty-two bucks for six coffee mugs from someone else, not us. But they did get it: from Andrea herself. Self-indulgence came easy for my partner, because she'd married a hedge fund. Well, technically, she'd married Hugh Morrison, whom most people called Hughie. She called him Fat Boy. I'd pointed out to her that "Fat Boy" was cruel as well as pointless; anyone seeing a three-hundred-pound guy whose ankle flab hung over his Italian driving moccasins could figure out his nickname wasn't Slim.

"You might want to start phoning the people you've marked off already, because some of them will have to call you back. Especially the doctors."

"Do you think I should leave my home phone number when I call? If I'm on my cell getting an important lead, I don't want to be interrupted by call waiting. But if the police want to reach me, or if Gilbert John or Layne hear something, I need to know right away." I set the mug on the worktable as a wave of the morning's dizziness came back. Not a tidal wave, but I pictured myself saying, "I was wondering if you'd spoken to Jonah recently . . ." to some snooty ENT guy while my cell vibrated with another incoming call and I wound up cutting off the ENT and missing the other call, which would turn out to be Jonah, and in the end all I'd have were his final inexplicable words on my voice mail: "I love you, Su—" Then silence. "And there's another problem. When I'm talking and a call comes in, I know I'm supposed to push the Send button, but half the time that doesn't work."

"Calm down," Andrea said. She jerked her head back. Apparently, I'd gone from being emphatic to yelling.

"*Why?*"

"Because you need to stop fixating on phones and think clearly." I found myself nodding slowly, like what she said was wisdom so dazzling it couldn't be absorbed all at once. "This is what you should do: Give them my cell number, okay? You'll take my phone. Don't even think of arguing with me. I want to get a new one anyway. That Vertu Rococo." I struggled. "I can't believe you haven't heard of it. It would be the Rolls-Royce of cells if the Rolls didn't suck. Listen, this makes sense for both of us. You take my cell because then I can get a new number and not tell my mother-in-law. She has me on her speed dial as A. Every time she shoves her phone into her handbag—it's as full of shit as she is—it dials me. Just don't answer any call that comes from Palm Beach."

Andrea lifted her hair with both hands and let it fall back. It covered her shoulders like a short cape made from the fur of a gleaming blond animal. An unkempt animal. Though she'd never admit it, she thought having scraggly ends was cool. She saw herself as an aristocrat and looked down on the nouveau riche as trying too hard with their pricey blunt cuts or exquisitely scissored layers.

In an era where there were (maybe) a hundred people left in New York to whom pedigree mattered, hardly anyone gave a rat's ass that one of Andrea's Brinckerhoff ancestors had come to New York (Nieuw Amsterdam then) in 1559. From the way she sneered at most of humanity, it was clear her lineage was the central fact of her existence. It offered her a reason to feel superior. It gave her (she'd decided) license to transgress any social or moral law—like a lady should have a good haircut. Like it's tasteless not to mock one's obese husband in public. Like it's seemly to refrain from committing adultery with members of your husband's family, country club, and church.

"Okay, I'll take your cell." Then I remembered to add, "Thank you."

"You're welcome." She paused. "Are you going to make those calls?"

"Now?"

"Why not now? Do you need six more months of therapy to work through your Brooklyn accent anxiety?"

I rubbed my forehead as if that would encourage an idea or two. It didn't. "It's not about that. It's that I won't know what to say if someone takes the call. I'll end up going, 'Uuuh, uuuh, I'm Jonah Gersten's wife. I don't know if you remember me, but now uuuh, uuuh.' And if I get their voice mail, do I say, 'Hate to bother you on a workday, but I'm Susie and my husband, Jonah Gersten, vanished from the face of the earth, and did you . . .'"

"Go on," Andrea said. "Did you what?"

"I don't know. Speak to him recently? Have any idea where he might be? Listen, calling people is stupid. God knows why I even thought of it. Everything was fine with Jonah. No one out there knows anything about him I don't know. He's not a secret-life kind of guy."

"You believe that."

"Yes!"

"I do, too, actually," Andrea said. She spoke so slowly that for two seconds she forgot her brightness. "But some men with a secret life really want to keep it that way—not like the assholes who leave Amex receipts on top of their dresser. Fat Boy used to do that, before he got too fat to fuck anybody but me, probably because he's afraid he'll drop dead from excitement and crush the girl and it'll make *The Financial Times*. Anyway, if Jonah wanted to keep a secret, you wouldn't know, and neither would I. And no, I don't think he has any secrets worthy of the name."

"He paid a scalper a fortune for Giants play-off tickets. But then he told me about it."

"But someone in here"—Andrea tapped his phone book with her index finger—"might know something you don't. Or it doesn't even have to be a secret. Maybe someone heard him say, 'There's a store up in Litchfield that has fabulous antique chronographs—'"

"What?"

"Those watches with all the little dials on the faces. Classics. Très popular right now. And maybe that means you should be calling hospitals in Connecticut because—"

"Do you honestly think that after a hideously long day, he'd drive up to Connecticut?"

"No. I was just making up an example."

"Jonah would never collect—"

"Susie, listen to me." She set her elbow on the table. Instead of resting her chin on her hand, like most people do, she stuck out her thumb and put the deep cleft of her chin on it: Andrea's "I'm deep in thought" pose. Finally, she said, "If you keep saying Jonah wouldn't do this or that, you're closing your mind. Am I right?" I didn't answer. "Am I being logical?"

"Yes."

"So you shouldn't decide not to listen to something that could be useful simply because it doesn't jive with your version of your husband."

"But my version is the right one." I said it in almost a whisper.

I shuffled into the small office that took up part of the space between our reception area and the workroom. Then I returned with a pen and a piece of our billing stationery. *Make it first-rate with Florabella,* it said along the bottom. When I got back, I jotted down a few talking points along with Andrea's cell number. I knew I'd be needing a script.

After a half hour, I got good at leaving voice mails and getting past secretaries and nurses by saying, "This is an urgent call about Jonah Gersten, and I need to speak with whoever now." Then I'd immediately add, softening my voice from powerful to genteel, "if that's possible." I got through right away to a fair number of the names, but by the time I began the D's, I'd learned only two things I hadn't known before. Jonah wished he'd taken clarinet instead of piano lessons as a kid. And about a month earlier, when he'd run into a friend from Yale, he'd said the biggest change with having triplets was that there never was a time he wasn't exhausted. I chewed on my knuckles for half a second as I listened to this, then got up the courage to ask, "Did he sound depressed?" Not at all. In good humor, actually, accepting perpetual fatigue as a fact of life.

Between each call, I'd close my eyes to blank out reality, but it was there anyway: I kept picturing the boys. Today would be all right, not counting the trauma I could be inflicting on them by playing down the terror I'd felt about Jonah not being in bed and them seeing through my act. Everyone said kids were so smart that even toddlers knew when their parents were faking emotion. They'd grow up not trusting me.

I worried about them in triplicate: as a threesome, as individual boys, and how each would affect the others. Closing my eyes, I got an image of Jonah and me making triplet sandwiches, snuggling the boys between us. If he didn't come back, would I have to explain those open-faced sandwiches with teeny fronds of dill they always serve at Wasp weddings, and wouldn't a Mommy canapé be fun? Would they think I was pathetic? I pictured furrowed-brow Evan growing closer with Mason, who would resume his thumb-sucking but still have enough security to give Evan a little boost, and Dashiell, who'd try to swagger through it all, being ostracized by the other two because they'd think he didn't care.

What could I do for my kids that I wasn't doing? That second, I wanted to embrace them, soothe them, though truthfully, part of me wished they could go visit Norway with Ida and Ingvild and milk reindeer until this nightmare blew over.

Except if Jonah didn't come back, it would never blow over. At that moment, I had a selfish or even depraved thought, which was: Did Jonah have enough insurance? I might even have worried that I'd have to sell the house, move to a garden apartment, and buy store-label toilet paper instead of Charmin Ultra, but then I thought, *No, my in-laws would help us out,* if only for the boys' sakes, because without them, Babs probably wouldn't care if I had to cut up *The New York Times* into four-by-four squares to keep beside the toilet, though without insurance, I wouldn't be able to afford home delivery anymore.

"Oh my God!" The words burst out of me.

"What? What is it?"

"My in-laws don't know!" I must have looked both pleading and stricken. I guessed I hoped that Andrea would respond: "Listen, your mother-in-law is not a piece of cake, and I know you work yourself up into a froth over dealing with her. So let me call her and explain what's going on."

She exclaimed, "'Oh my God' is right! Here you are, calling up everybody who knows Jonah! One of them—shit, so many doctors!—one of them could call Clive. You better call this *instant.* Which one? Him or her?"

Him, my father-in-law, was infinitely preferable. Clive wasn't nice, but on the other hand, he wasn't not nice. I'd never gotten beyond his blah-ness, but maybe that was because there was no beyond. So while no one, including his children and his wife, ever went to Clive looking for love, you could take being with him. You'd never have to fear getting worn down by high-pressure charm. Nor would you have to worry about getting hit with a Babs zinger. With my father-in-law, you never had to be on the lookout for hostility so gracefully disguised it sounded amazingly like flattery.

But with Babs, I never once said goodbye to her without feeling that some small but significant number had been deducted from the sum of my soul during the encounter. "Her," I said to Andrea. "If I don't call her, she'll think I was afraid."

Which of course I was.

Chapter Six

B abs sat on the dark red leather couch in our den, her elbows resting just above her knees, her hands veiling her eyes and cheeks. Her nails, coated with Gigi de Lavallade's Crème Caramel, precisely matched the hue of some new liver spots her dermatologist hadn't gotten to. She uncovered her face and said, "Of course you're doing everything that can be done, Susie . . ." I nodded, except she wasn't finished with the sentence. "But we're always here for you if you have any doubts. Never, ever hesitate to call on us."

Clive sat beside her looking at me, though I wasn't sure he was seeing me. He was swaying slowly from side to side, like Ray Charles keeping time to a ballad. I waited for him to add something, but he was silent. Then Babs took a deep breath that looked like preparation for a long sentence. But she didn't speak.

So I did. "Right before you got here, I called back Detective Sergeant Coleman, the Nassau County cop who came this morning. I hadn't heard from him again, not even to say they hadn't gotten any leads. Maybe they don't do that—call to say they don't have anything to tell you. But since he'd said he—a detective—had been sent here instead of a regular cop because of Jonah's 'position in the community,' I figured I could push it a little." Clive stopped his swaying when he was at a 100-degree angle away from Babs. I waited for him to right himself. He didn't, so I continued. "I told Coleman that since Jonah spent so much time in Manhattan, there was a good chance that if, God forbid, something bad happened to him, it could have happened there. I asked if he'd been in touch with the New York police. He said yes. So then I asked him for a name."

"Good," Babs said. I couldn't tell if she was approving or thinking, *How come you didn't think of this five hours ago, asshole?* Not that she would use a word like "asshole." In a confrontation, I imagined that, since she'd graduated from Vassar, she would more likely say "unmitigated fool." She cocked her head at the same weird angle as Clive's upper body, as if they shared a choreographer. "And he gave you the name?"

"He said it might be in the notes he'd typed up, but he wasn't near a computer." My in-laws kept their gaze on me, though I sensed they were controlling themselves, aching to exchange a glance, maybe hoping I'd look away. Was I reading something into the situation? I didn't know. Yet their silence also told me they'd vowed to each other to be gentle: Families could split apart under this kind of pressure, and the Gerstens weren't that sort. I could hear Babs telling Clive on their drive out from the city, "I want this to be civilized. No recriminations. Even if we have to bite our tongues." And Clive, hands gripping and pushing against the wheel as if to fuse it to the steering column, murmuring in a choked monotone, "Unless she's making a complete hash of it and putting Jonah in peril. Then we cannot remain silent. Am I correct?" Clive came from a middle-class New York background, but when he did speak, his vocabulary was kind of grand, as if he had a screenwriter specializing in biblical epics writing his dialogue. He was so worshipful about his wife's privileged background, I guess he kept wanting to sound like the man he thought she deserved. Now, though, he had nothing to say.

Possibly what I was reading from their silence was my own tale, composed totally in my head, and they were simply waiting for me to talk again. "I got the feeling Coleman's 'not near a computer' might be some kind of delaying tactic. So I asked him, 'Could you do me a favor and just check that notepad you carry? Maybe you jotted it down.' And he waited, like, a few seconds too long. It could have been that he was hoping I'd tell him not to bother if it was an inconvenience. But I kept quiet. So he gave me the name."

"Which was?" Clive asked. He loosened the knot on his tie, an orange Hermès with teeny giraffes all over. Its cheeriness was making me uncomfortable, and I wished he'd worn something in a gray basket weave.

"Lieutenant Paston," I told him. "Gary McCorkle Paston. From the Nineteenth Precinct detective squad."

Babs leaned forward. "Did you get a chance to call Lieutenant Paston?" she asked with the sweet neutrality of a social worker, which made it sound like she'd sprouted a second personality.

"Yes, I did call him. He'd already gotten some details and the picture of Jonah I'd given to Detective Sergeant Coleman— I'm not sure whether he's called Detective or Sergeant or both because he only gave me his card. I don't think he said, 'I'm so-and-so.' Maybe he did. I guess I just wasn't paying attention." I was starting to sound ditsy, and probably not only to myself. I inhaled one of those conscious diaphragmatic breaths they teach you in yoga to relax. I could have used a few more, but then my in-laws might think I was acting weird or even on drugs. "Anyway, Lieutenant Paston asked if I had any more pictures, so I scanned a couple and e-mailed them to him. He said he'd call Gilbert John and Layne, and whoever else police call. A few of Jonah's other contacts. But he said the good news was that he'd checked: There weren't any reports of people resembling Jonah who were, you know. Unidentified."

Even though the den was the warmest room in the house, all

three of us seemed to feel the ice of my unsaid words: "morgue," "dead body." In the same instant, we each tried to get warm. Babs pulled the shawl collar of her taupe sweater tighter against her neck. Clive clenched his hands, brought them to his mouth, and breathed hot air on them. I lifted up my cup of tea, but its warmth was gone, and the aroma of the cold, smoky Earl Grey made me shudder.

We were quiet too long. Maybe because they were in my house, I felt obliged to say something, but I'd already gone the "coffee? tea?" route twice since they'd arrived. So I picked up the pad and paper I had ready to make a note or take down an address if I got a call. I wrote down Detective Sergeant Coleman's and Lieutenant Paston's names and numbers. "These are the Nassau County and NYPD detectives I've been dealing with. If something pops into your head that could be useful, feel free to call them."

I hoped they understood I was giving them permission to tell the cops anything they might know that they wouldn't want me to hear: that Jonah had experienced some bizarre mental disorder in childhood involving running away from home. Or that he had a girlfriend—who didn't have embarrassing parents—he was planning on leaving me for.

My father-in-law appeared grateful as he took the paper, though given those upturned corners of his mouth, he could be thinking the most horrible thoughts and still appear smiley. My mother-in-law pursed her Bronze Méditerranéen–glossed lips but overdid it. Instead of appearing reflective, she looked like she was about to give me a great big air kiss.

I wish I could say that one of us let our humanity shine through long enough to reach over and squeeze a hand, or stand and offer a long, comforting hug. But providing comfort didn't seem to pop up on any of our to-do lists.

Babs, who had been staring at the bare, dead-looking aerial roots of an Evening Star orchid I had on the end table beside her, turned back to me. Managing to keep any hint of dread out of her voice, she asked, "Are your parents coming over?"

Oh, shit! I thought. The idea of my mother and father—the very fact of their existence—simply hadn't occurred to me. "I haven't called them yet." I was sure Babs was relieved. "I didn't want to scare them and then have Jonah walk in."

She nodded and refolded the left cuff of her sweater as if it hadn't already been precisely folded back the same number of centimeters as the right. Like many Manhattan women, Babs was meticulous in her casualness. Her black hair with silver at the temples and subtle gold and platinum streaks shot through was blown dry, then artfully disarranged by Sabine, her hairdresser, every other day. God could have created my mother-in-law to counterbalance my mother's denial of adornments. Not that Babs was fussy. Her clothes were Armani and Jil Sander in black, white, and a narrow spectrum of pale browns. Jewelry wasn't a problem for her, either, as Upper East Side good taste discouraged all gems except diamonds and all metals but gold and platinum. Still, beside the pale green petals and violet red lips of the fully bloomed orchid she'd been staring at, my mother-in-law looked less chic than sick. Just the couple of hours of knowing Jonah was a missing person had been enough to bring out deep beige shadows beneath her eyes. Even her knuckles and wrist bones seemed mysteriously altered in the fading afternoon light in the den, so her hands looked like a crone's.

We hung out for another fifteen minutes, forcing conversation. At one point, I almost asked if they thought I should hire a detective agency, the way Gilbert John and Layne had suggested. Some mental censor clapped a hand over my mouth just in time. If they said no and I decided I needed one, they'd find out. No detective could call half of Manhattan (the upper half, where Jonah came from and worked) and hide it from my in-laws. And if they did think hiring an investigator was a dandy idea, they'd take over—Clive saying that John Doe of the Doe Agency, you know, international reputation, had a mother who'd been a patient. Then Babs would chime in that she'd gone to Fieldston with Jane Roe, whose husband had formed the Strategic Inquiries Group, or some Washington-esque name, after he left the Department of Justice, where he'd been Janet Reno's right arm.

Periodically, one of us would glance at the silent phone, which would give the others a millisecond of hope that there had been some kind of pre-ring in a decibel range just below their hearing. But then nothing would happen, so one of us would mutter a sentence or two to cover the embarrassment of our naive optimism.

My ears did pick up what theirs didn't: the crunch of one of the minivan's tires as Ida veered slightly off the driveway, which she did about 50 percent of the time, riding the pebbles that protected the bases of the boxwood and lavender shrubs that ran along the driveway from the street all the way up and around to the garage. The triplets coming in—the sudden clomp of Ugg boots, the thud of backpacks on the floor, accompanied by "I gotta pee," "No, me first! I gotta pee worse!" and "Apple slices with peanut butter!"—startled my in-laws, as if all the time they'd been in the house, they hadn't remembered they had grandchildren.

I got up to go into the kitchen. Clive and Babs stood also but stayed where they were, in front of the couch. "Do the boys know?" Babs asked.

"They know he wasn't here this morning. They get up at five-thirty. Jonah's always there, but they didn't seem to attach any real importance to it. If any of them had a clue at all, it would be Evan."

"He is very sensitive," Babs said, the strain already in her face growing more intense, as if her inner colorist had brushed on another coat of ashen concern. This time, however, she didn't get a chance for her usual "I do worry about Evan, though I know his sensitivity will be an asset in the long run" or "He's like my brother Bill, with his nerve endings so close to the surface," because Clive cleared his throat. He did it so loud that it made her flinch and cry, "Ooh!"

"Susie," he said, "we are not in any way criticizing you. But we should be working together on this." Standing, I was taller than either of them. My height never bothered Jonah: One of his nicknames for me was Stretch. But I could tell Clive wasn't so crazy about it.

What did he mean, "working together"? Sometimes I didn't understand the dialect the Gerstens spoke. I got all the words, but it was like one of those communiqués you hear on the news about the State Department, where they say, "We had a full and frank exchange of views, and warm wishes were exchanged over cups of tea and the traditional almond cakes." The only way you could comprehend what was going on was if you were an insider and knew the lingo. We shared the last name, but I often found myself longing for subtitles. "Working together?" The way he used that phrase made me feel like something had grabbed the intestines behind my belly button and twisted. But I knew I had to be cool. I couldn't get elbowed out of the way in the search for Jonah, yet I needed his parents to stay on my side.

"Of course we'll work together on this," I told him. "That's why I telephoned you as soon as I saw . . . the lay of the land. I mean, I didn't call my parents. I only checked with Jonah's office manager to make sure he hadn't been called in for some emergency. Then I notified the police." I didn't mention I'd been at Florabella making calls and talking through everything with Andrea. "Then I immediately called you."

"What we are trying to say," Babs said carefully, "is that perhaps going to the police so very soon might not have been— how can I express it?—the quickest way to get an answer. It's not that I'm questioning your judgment, Susie. It's that they are a bureaucracy. And bureaucracies are notoriously inefficient." Standing straighter, she kicked out one leg, then the other, to align the pleats in her black pants. For an instant, she teetered on one of her black alligator boots with its four-inch heel, but she quickly righted herself.

"In this case, they seem to be responding pretty well," I said. "Nassau County sent a detective, and he got the NYPD on to it right away. I called the police in because"—I wanted to sound authoritative, or at least like I wasn't a total screw-up—"the cops have the power to get information from hospitals and police departments, their own and in other places." The boys would be racing around the house any second, searching for me, calling out, "Mommy." I talked faster: "Were you thinking along the lines of the investigative agency?" They nodded. "I agree with you completely. It's something we should consider. As far as I'm concerned, we should look into it today."

"One of my patients—" Clive began.

But he was cut off as Dashiell careened around the doorway of the den. Dash's hazel eyes with their awning of thick brown lashes opened wide: *Wow! So great that you're here!* their sparkle seemed to say. I'd trained the boys not to demand "Got a present?" each time Babs and Clive arrived, even though my in-laws came bearing gifts on every visit. Naturally, I'd asked them not to. "Just little tokens," Babs had explained the next time as she handed out packages artfully wrapped in high-end silver foil to look like a giant Hershey's kiss. But the last time they were over, Dash had hinted not at all subtly for a Webkinz bulldog. This time he knew not to ask. He blinked once, then twice, trying to come up with something interesting to say, a simple "Hi" obviously not occurring to him. I shook my head at him: *No. No presents today. Don't expect* . . . But he cut off my silent protest with a grin toward his grandparents. "I got a riddle!" he told them.

"You've got a riddle?" Babs said. "Tell me, Dash."

"Guess who didn't go to bed last night?" he asked. He gave her no time to answer. "My daddy!"

Chapter Seven

Other than sighing "Heaven!" over a hot fudge sundae or a great orgasm, ordinary people don't talk about paradise much. But everyone's heard a million definitions of hell. I remembered one of Jonah's fraternity brothers at Yale, drunk out of his mind, sweat streaming through his sideburns, across his jaw, and down his neck, yelling, "You know what the existentialists say hell is, cocksuckers? Other people! That means you!" And someone famous enough that I vaguely recognized the name wrote about hell being the torture of a bad conscience. Et cetera. But every hour or so over the next couple of days, I wanted to cry out, "Those definitions are crap. Hell is what I am living."

Not knowing if my husband was alive or dead. If he was pinned inside the smashed metal skeleton of his car after an accident, screaming in pain from crushed bones. If he was held in a stinking basement, tortured by some psychopath like a victim on *Dexter*.

Once or twice I felt temporarily normal, like when I helped the boys make zebra cookies with chocolate and vanilla stripes for the Tuttle Farm school's zoo carnival. Then I'd be back to hell, picking up (or making up) Jonah's screams of unspeakable pain. I'd calm down, though only slightly, picturing him in an East Sixty-fifth Street town house sipping martinis with the shockingly rich, once-homely, now-stunning former patient he'd decided to leave me for.

After my in-laws went back to the city and I whispered, "Thank God," I had a long phone conversation with Gilbert John and Layne: What to say to Jonah's patients, especially the ones scheduled for surgery? Layne was totally against trying to take over the surgery themselves because it was too much pressure and they wouldn't have time to get to know the cases. Gilbert John was most concerned about managing what he called "the situation" in a way that wouldn't provoke gossip. He kept interrupting himself with a single cough either from something in his throat—peanut speck, post-nasal drip—or overtaxed nerves. Between coughs, his main point was Protect Jonah's Good Name. That might have been Gilbert John Noakes–ese for Protect the Practice, but it did make sense. So did his suggestion, which we all agreed on, to say simply that Jonah had had an emergency and they had to cancel his appointments for the time being.

The days began to take on a rhythm. Once I caught the beat, I began living a regular life. True, it was in an irregular regular life, like living in some war-ravaged country. You knew a bomb could blow you away a minute from now, but meanwhile, you were out of dishwasher detergent. I did only what needed doing, the basics.

I was responsible for the boys. Funny: One of Jonah's tender, ironic names for Evan was Killer, because he was such a high-strung kid. I worried he'd be the one most disturbed by his father's absence, but he didn't even get teary. On the other hand, Dash, who generally possessed the sensitivity of a dump truck, couldn't seem to stop talking about how Daddy wasn't there. Mason, as usual, was Mr. Moderate, neither unglued nor unruffled; a couple of times each day, he asked if Daddy would be home on Saturday to make waffles. I managed a bright "I hope so."

After the triplets' day at preschool was finished, I had the twins keep them out of my way. I needed a break from their usual "You're a poopy head!" shouts at one another. Even the thought of having to holler "No!" when they tried yet again to climb the bookshelves was too much for me. I was so exhausted and overstimulated. I felt one more decibel would kill me.

February was a lousy month for a husband to disappear, with its snowless days of cold wind and rain. The house seemed airless yet bursting, as if it wanted to break open and expel the boys into the fresh air. Me? I still had to deal with my parents. But when I tried to call them, fortified by many deep, relaxing breaths, I couldn't. The effort of picking up the phone and lifting it to my ear pushed me over the edge—a place I was getting used to.

I ordered myself, *Get it over with,* but I wound up half sliding onto the kitchen floor and sat there sobbing. My back pressed against the pantry door, my legs splayed out, and I, the Pilates queen, couldn't summon the strength to haul myself up. I stayed there on that wood floor for nearly thirty minutes, long after the dial tone had changed into the loud, high-pitched cry that signals the receiver is off the hook, my mind whirling in a vicious circle of crazy thoughts all those self-help books urge you to avoid.

First I kept imagining that when I'd been at Florabella the previous morning and sent the boys to preschool—with the twins in the Mommies' Room—Jonah might have come back briefly. Finding no one home, he'd decided to leave forever. The whys—where had he been? why would he do such a thing?—came fast. Madness, I decided. Madness induced by a hit on the head by a gun butt during a mugging. No, from eating a salad with "wild mushrooms" that were actually never-before-seen hallucinogens. All right, maybe not actual madness. Just a nervous breakdown from four years of mornings with triplets, afternoons operating on patients who were still whining that the cost of genioplasty should include a freebie chin cleft even as they were going under anesthesia. And, of course, evenings with too much of my "I think we should repaint the boiler room floor" and too little sex.

Then I thought that maybe Jonah hadn't come back when I'd been out. No, it was his kidnappers who'd dropped by to leave a ransom note. Finding no one around, they'd decided not to bother—just to kill him and snatch a richer doctor whose wife didn't go gallivanting on a day when she should have been home. On and on, sitting motionless on the kitchen floor on the balls of my ass, while my head swirled with frightening what-ifs.

The few seconds of silence between horrific scenarios offered enough clarity for me to glimpse not only the hugeness of Jonah's absence but its profound and awful mystery. That profundity business lasted only about thirty seconds; I'd never been the plumbing-the-depths type who knew from cosmic despair.

I finally got up and took a giant bottle of San Pellegrino and a water goblet from our Baccarat crystal that we'd registered for but never gotten a full set of, and I went into Jonah's study. Bernadine and her vacuum cleaner were approaching, and I didn't want to be sitting at the kitchen table when she turned on FOX News and then have to watch her clean between the two wall ovens with a Q-tip dampened with her own saliva even though I'd gently pointed out three times that it wouldn't be much harder to wet it at the sink. Anyway, Jonah's study was the most businesslike room in the house. It contained only a desk, computer, phone, and shelves of books on plastic surgery I never looked at because not only were they technical and boring, they were also filled with hideous illustrations of surgical procedures and, even worse, photographs printed on thick, glossy paper.

It was a calm place. I'd made it that way. The walls were covered in a watered silk the same color as the lightest amber in his bird's-eye-maple desk. The room emitted a golden warmth that avoided the decorator-trying-for-scholarly-humanist ambiance.

I called Manhattan Aesthetics and punched in Gilbert John's extension, grateful that despite my protests of "tacky" and "user-unfriendly," the practice had switched to a voice-mail system and I no longer had to speak to Karen, the receptionist who looked as if she'd been manufactured by the same company that had done Schwarzenegger as the Terminator.

Gilbert John took my call within seconds. Even though my first words were "Sorry. No news," he didn't sigh or tsk or indicate any disappointment. In fact, he was pretty compassionate, for Gilbert John. So while he wasn't oozing empathy, he sounded genuinely concerned, not just about Jonah but about how I was doing.

"Holding together," I told him. "I'd love to fall apart and have to be heavily sedated, but I can't."

"The boys," he observed.

"Yes, and also . . . I don't know. Maybe I can think of something, or at least have a working mind, if someone says something that has any potential."

"I understand. The toughest part for me is the worry," he said. "No, let me be more precise. The fear. And for you? I cannot begin to imagine." I could hear him take a deep breath to settle himself. "A nightmare. A heartache."

"Yeah," I agreed, then wanted to bite my tongue because I hadn't said "Yes." Jonah once told me that when I got emotional, I got Brooklyn, and he hadn't meant it as a compliment on being myself and not putting on airs. He could take only so much of my authenticity. "You're right," I said. "This whole thing is every word for awfulness you can think of. But I'll tell you what I would like. One or both of you mentioned something about hiring an investigator, detective, whatever. Can you get me a name or two? Obviously, the sooner the better."

"I'll get right on it," Gilbert John said, pronouncing each word as if the survival of properly spoken English rested solely on him. "Is there anything else, Susie?" I told him no and thanked him, probably a little too profusely.

Before I even hung up, I was pulling open the top right-hand drawer of Jonah's desk. True, I had watched Detective Sergeant Coleman search the desk. And I had seen for myself that he hadn't found anything. Then we'd moved upstairs.

During our entire search, neither Coleman nor I had found anything in the room to make me think Jonah was anything other than what I believed him to be. No pieces of paper with mysterious, scribbled phone numbers, no hate mail, no blackmail demands, no charge slips at La Perla for a G-string in size P. But I was hoping to find a clue that might prove at least a beginning. Maybe Coleman and I had overlooked something, the way you finally discover the Advil in your handbag that you'd failed to find after two thorough searches.

But with Jonah being as orderly as he was, there were no surprises. Even his paper clips in the top drawer's tray all lay on the horizontal, though I doubted he'd consciously arranged them that way. Maybe in the back of my mind was the belief that objects, like people, bent to Jonah's will. Not that he was a bully: It was just that his way always wound up seeming so reasonable.

I was about to get up and start leafing through his books, shaking them, too. Maybe something would fall to the floor that would make me go "Aha!" But the phone rang. It was Gilbert John with the names of two investigative agencies.

"I'm told these are the crème de la crème," he said, "although technically, I suppose only one can be the cream of the cream." I couldn't tell if he was correcting himself or if he thought I needed a translation. "In any case, I have contact names: David Friedman at InterProbe, though he might be in Dubai this week." I pictured a Jewish guy with a hundred-dollar haircut at a conference table with a bunch of Arabs in keffiyehs on the eightieth floor of a building overlooking a futuristic city like you see on the covers of science fiction paperbacks. I decided David Friedman might be a little too high-powered. "The other one is Liz-beth—*Lizzzbeth*, with a Z, no E, no A—Holbreich at Kroll."

Lizbeth, it turned out when I called her, sounded pretty high-powered herself, with a low-pitched, southern-accented voice that conveyed the confidence born of an earlier life as Miss Tuscaloosa or, more likely, a brigadier general in the army. She had no trace of the flirty, rising inflection that turns southern women's sentences into questions. In fact, her actual questions sounded more like commands.

I spent nearly an hour on the phone with her, going over a lot of the same ground I had covered with the police. Was Jonah under stress? Going through a difficult time? She came right out and asked if I thought he could have committed sui-cide. I told her, "Jonah is the last person in the world who would take his own life." She wanted even more details than the cops, data on everyone in Manhattan Aesthetics and infor-mation on Ida and Ingvild, our housekeeper, Bernadine Pietro-wicz, plus people she called vendors, everybody from the guys who picked up the garbage to the plumber. I swallowed hard and agreed to a twenty-thousand-dollar retainer and faxed permission for her to speak with our accountant, lawyer, and stockbroker, and to examine the hard drive on Jonah's comput-ers at work and at home. She said she would talk to Gilbert John Noakes about getting the names of Jonah's patients to see whether any of them were suing him (no) or were wack jobs (yes). As we talked, I e-mailed her Jonah's cell phone number, e-mail address, head shot, and the URL for his biography on the practice's website.

"I don't want to frighten you," she said. "Well, any more than you already are, which is more than enough. So let me be clear that kidnapping is very, very rare in the U.S. Most of the cases we deal with happen abroad. Even so, it's a good idea that if the police haven't done it already, we get the FBI on this and also put recording devices on your phone."

"In case of—" I stopped cold. This conversation was so far away from anything I ever thought I'd be talking about that it felt like I was being forced to read from a script meant for somebody else. "Are you talking about a ransom demand?"

"Yes. But as I said, that scenario is highly unlikely."

I didn't have the courage to ask what scenario she'd put her money on. But by the time we were finished, Lizbeth didn't scare me anymore. While not exactly in the ninety-ninth percentile for effusiveness, she sounded decent: Two or three times she'd said some version of "You must be going through absolute hell." And when she opened Jonah's picture, she'd remarked, "He looks like an absolutely lovely man."

Fifteen minutes later, I felt the urge to get out and go to Florabella. Andrea told me not to come in, saying that she would call in Marjorie, a retired florist who helped us out during busy times, squeezing us in between her daily Alcoholics and Overeaters Anonymous meetings. Still, I yearned for an hour or two of the mindless comfort that always came to me when I was using my hands, like greening out hunks of floral foam, covering them with leaves or moss as the basis for table arrangements. But now I was too scared to trust call forwarding; I worried that some vital message from the cops would not only go unanswered but not make it to voice mail. And I wanted to be home in case . . . I caught myself in what Jonah would have called "doing a Sherry," sighing my mother's *It's hopeless* sigh. He could do a hilarious imitation of my mother that included shaking his head in despair, followed by an "oy" and a few tsk-tsks, even though she never actually said "oy" and at most gave a single tsk. But how could I not sigh? With each hour he was gone, it got tougher to come up with a Jonah-coming-home fantasy powerful enough to divert me for longer than ten seconds.

Bleak. Every few years, Jonah would tell me I really should read his favorite novel, *Bleak House*. Except it was incredibly long and the title wasn't exactly a grabber. Also, it was by Dickens, and okay, maybe something was deeply wrong with me, because whenever someone brought up Charles Dickens, everybody else nodded with reverence and got that funny little smile that's supposed to signal "Literature has added so much meaning to my life." Except the only thing in high school I hated more than *A Tale of Two Cities* was *David Copperfield*. So I kept telling Jonah, "You're right and I'd love to. As soon as I finish whatever for my book club, I'm going to read it. Then we can go out to dinner, just the two of us, and really discuss it. Plus, I'll finally get to see what makes you so passionate about it."

The house was silent except for the occasional gust of wind that rattled the shutters. I walked purposefully from Jonah's study to the den, thinking that I would find his leather-bound copy. Maybe in the back of my mind I was picturing him coming home so quietly I didn't even hear his key in the lock. He'd find me reading *Bleak House* and be incredibly moved.

Except I passed the den, went into the kitchen, and made myself a sugar-free hot chocolate. I drank it standing up, leaning against the island where the stovetop was, thinking, *Bleak House? You want fucking* Bleak House? *I'm in it.* But I was barely halfway through the thought when I realized there was a house even bleaker, the one I'd grown up in. Not bleak from tragedy. Bleak from perpetual simmering, silent resentment. I decided I really had to call my parents.

Chapter Eight

My mother answered the phone. She always did. Her "hello," as usual, came across as a challenge, as if she expected every call to be a fund-raiser from some organization whose position she'd once been passionate about and then lost interest in: NOW, NARAL, Emily's List, Americans United Against Gun Violence, Greenpeace. She'd bought a T-shirt from No God 4 Me at an atheist street fair on Amsterdam Avenue, but she'd never gotten on any sucker list because she'd switched to her most recent cause, libertarianism, which she seemed to define as being at liberty not to do anything for anybody and listening to deeply unattractive people on C-SPAN talk about abolishing the Federal Reserve.

"Mom, it's me."

"Susan?" I was an only child. Her voice was frosty; I hadn't called her in over a week. Not that she ever called me, apparently being under the impression that the telephone was a one-way instrument.

"Yes. Listen, I have some . . . not-good news." Why did I expect a nervous intake of breath or a terrified "Are the boys all right?" Beats the hell out of me. I definitely shouldn't have, because after a lifetime of phone calls, I knew it was my job to set the tone of our conversations. I usually tried to be affectionate (extending an invitation to a Mother's Day barbecue) unless the occasion called for a little dab of melancholy (inquiring where Cousin Ira's funeral services would be held).

I'd always low-keyed it around my parents, even during my years of the usual teenage derangement, because their emotional gamut ranged from a high of not unhappy to a low of vaguely depressed. On the rare occasion when they were directly confronted with someone else's hilarity or heartache, they'd practically stagger, as if they'd been hit with a Category 4 hurricane. So I kept my hysterics to myself. Still, when I blurted, "Jonah's been missing for two days," I couldn't subdue my agitation vibes.

"Two days?"

"Yes."

She burped, and I let myself think the news was a shock to her system. "You don't have any idea where he is?" she asked.

"No. Nobody has any idea."

"Are you going to call the police?"

"I already did. So far I haven't heard anything."

"That's not like him," she observed. "Two days?"

"Yes."

The ball was in my mother's court, but she couldn't do any more than stand there and watch it bounce. "Effectual" wasn't a definition for either of my parents. Even when they sensed something was expected, they rarely managed to figure out what it was. If there had been a Rabinowitz family crest, *Think on your feet* would not have been its motto.

Now, however, my mother's silence lasted longer than usual. Another time (more in the interest of "Let's move it along" than out of kindness) I would have offered a hand to pull her out of her emotional hole. Why not? I'd been doing it most of my life, once I decided that, through either the grace of God or recessive genes, I had what they lacked: sense.

I'd grown up being their guide around Normalville. This time, though, all I could do was get angry and think, *Can't you even ask me, "Is there anything I can do?" Aren't there any limits to your insecurity? You're my mother, for crissakes!* Just then she asked, "Would you like us to come over?" I decided she was hoping I'd say, "No, don't bother." Before I could stop myself, I told her it would be great if they could. Maybe I was thinking that someday in the future, I'd be saying, "Listen, my parents are far from perfect, but when the chips were down, they were really there for me!"

There for me? Maybe I was fantasizing my mother calling my father at work and saying "Susie needs us!" then grabbing a cab out to Long Island and him driving eighty-five miles an hour from Queens to comfort me. Maybe—though I knew that despite her fifteen-year flirtation with feminism, she never went anywhere without my father. She'd flunked her driving test forty years earlier and found taxis too filthy and obscenely expensive. Public transportation was, in her view, too public: crowded with male riders who saw buses and subways as prime turf for humiliating women via the rush-hour penis prod.

Anyway, by the time my father left work, drove back to Brooklyn to pick her up, and crept out in rush-hour traffic to the house via the expressway, since side roads could still have ice from January, they arrived after six.

"Maybe he's at a medical conference," my father, Stanley Rabinowitz, suggested, "and just forgot to mention it to you." He was sitting at the kitchen table wearing one of his Mr. Rogers cardigans, this one a weary green covered with decades of pilling. Very little actual sweater remained, yet the tiny pill balls somehow hung together and seemed to have acquired balls of their own. I set a large plate of grilled cheese sandwiches on the kitchen table because naturally, they had shown up at dinner-time expecting to be fed. When I sat, they seemed taken aback that there was no soup or salad. My mother, glancing around at the place mats and finding neither forks nor spoons, reluctantly took a half sandwich.

The boys and Ida and Ingvild were in the den with their cheese sandwiches, apparently charmed by the sophisticated wit of Lenny the Wonder Dog, giving me time to bask in the warmth of my parents' company. My father always ate sandwiches from the outside in: His grilled cheese sat on his plate with even denture marks all around the perimeter, like a decorative scalloped edge. He picked it up and took another bite.

"He's not at a medical conference," I replied calmly. "First of all, Jonah wouldn't forget to tell me he was going someplace. Even if he did, he would have had to plan for going out of town. There isn't any sign of planning. He had operations scheduled, appointments at the office. He just disappeared. Didn't come home, didn't show up at his office or the hospital. His partners are as mystified as I am."

My father shrugged to show he was stumped, too. When no one else spoke up, he added, "Maybe foul play?"

"Maybe." Just those two syllables used up all the energy I had left.

My mother shook her head, a movement that communicated *Gee, too bad* rather than *Catastrophic.* When she'd come in, she'd given me her usual awkward hug, where her upper arms performed the actual hugging and everything else, from elbows to fingertips, hung awkwardly in the air behind me. Now, though, she seemed to realize some comforting maternal gesture was in order, so she reached across the big round table to squeeze my hand. However, her arms were short. In order to do my part and get my hand squeezed for comforting, I wound up stretching forward until, from the waist up, I was almost flat on the table.

"Thanks, Mom," I said.

She muttered something into her sandwich. It could have been "No problem."

My mother was short and chunky. Not a stylish combo, but short, chunky women can be tough/adorable or else little dynamos throwing off sparks of energy. Sherry was neither. She was belligerently unattractive, almost as if she'd been created in the late sixties by a male-chauvinist cartoonist as a malicious caricature of a feminist.

Periodically, one of my friends would tell me I was too harsh about her; that, okay, she would never win any awards in the mother-love department, but wasn't that because she thought herself less than lovable? Probably. Her own mother, Ethel, had walked out when she was eight. Little Sherry had been raised by her father, my grandfather, Lenny "the Loser" Blechner. After failing early on to be a nightclub singer, probably because he had a mediocre voice and kept forgetting to smile between songs, he'd become a bookkeeper for Calabro Brothers Flounder in the Fulton Fish Market.

"So," my father said, "where do you go from here?" An outsider would think he was wracked with emotion because his voice quavered so much, but I knew better. For as long as anyone who knew him could recall, he'd always talked as if the section of floor he was standing on were vibrating. Now and then some less than diplomatic soul would ask, "Hey, uh, what's with your voice? You got Parkinson's or something?" He'd reply, "Huh?" He never got it.

"I honestly don't know where I go next," I told him. "I want so much to do something. But the police are on it, and a private investigative agency. I wish I could think of something else to do."

"Terrible, terrible," he said. His eyes fell to his plate, and I sensed he was trying to come up with a suggestion, but nothing came to mind, so he picked up his sandwich.

Some people would call my father a nebbish. I certainly did.

Other than despising my mother, an emotion he projected mostly by flaring his nostrils whenever she spoke, he had few strong opinions. He was bald and colorless. Even if he'd committed some terrible crime, he would never be picked out from a lineup because it was impossible to remember his face. He worked as a salesman in a store called My Aching Back, although he wasn't particularly successful at it. As a kid, I had sensed his boss kept him on because even though he was only borderline competent, he was very reliable. Stanley was without ambition to be any better off than he was, so he was truly reliable. His commissions were enough for us to live on. Also, his shaky voice made some customers believe he was becoming emotional about their back pain, so he was never fired. I guess he liked his job; the only time I saw my father anywhere close to animated was when he was holding forth on sciatica.

"Maybe you should go on TV," my mother said. "All those missing women? You always see their parents on the *Today* show with their home movies of the one who's missing. The husbands sometimes do it, although ninety-nine times out of a hundred, you know what?"

"What?" I knew what.

"What?" my father asked.

"The husbands turn out to be batterers who finally went over the line and did what all the friends and relatives always knew they would." In case we weren't clear on what this was, she added: "Kill the wife. And then the relatives all have the chutzpah to say, right on camera, 'Oh, I *begged* her to get out while she still could, but she just wouldn't listen.'"

"I did give some thought about publicity," I told her. Her mock turtleneck was covered by some weird little capelet, squares of black and forest green that looked like an afghan someone had abandoned when they realized they hated crocheting. The capelet had captured a lot of sandwich crumbs and three orange teardrops of melted cheese. I went on, "I may have to resort to going public. There are even organizations that help you with PR. But right now it's only been two days. If something's happened to Jonah that he or I or his partners wouldn't want public, going on TV or whatever would put it all out there. Something embarrassing could mean the end of his career."

"Like what?" my mother asked. "What could he be doing that couldn't be public? He's not a drinker, as far as I know." I shook my head: No, Jonah wasn't a drinker. "So he wouldn't be lying in the gutter on the Bowery. Is there something you haven't told us?" She shrugged. "Drugs? You hear about doctors getting hooked because they have easy access. Homosexuality? Some other . . . whatever."

"No. To the best of my knowledge, which I truly believe is excellent, Jonah is what he seems to be: honorable and sober. And heterosexual." Since she looked as if she still didn't get it, I explained, "It doesn't have to be a major issue. Sometimes even the best people get into trouble."

Silence. Maybe someone else's mother would have clearly disagreed about not seeking publicity and told her daughter that finding Jonah was of paramount importance. "You have to risk bad publicity in order to find him. The more time elapses, the colder the trail gets."

But my mother had strong opinions only on matters with no direct effect on our lives, like what had been printed on her T-shirt the previous summer: SOCIAL WELFARE REVERSES EVOLUTION, which I'd spent half a barbecue thinking was an anagram I couldn't figure out.

"Well," she said, "I guess you know what's best."

The few good-hearted thoughts I had about my mother were like: *Okay, she's embarrassing, grabbing on to causes, letting the slogans on her T-shirts substitute for snappy conversation and a philosophy of life. Amazing. There is absolutely nothing she can do well or even competently—cook, clean, talk about a TV show, buy shoes, show affection (much less love). To be fair, she's like someone who had a terrible accident as a kid and can't walk. Her own mother abandoning her when she was eight was exactly like that—a terrible accident. It left my mother permanently crippled. She can't do all the simple, normal things in life that other people take for granted.*

That abandonment was obviously the central fact in my mother's life, and maybe in mine. If Ethel had left Lenny the Loser but kept little Sherry with her, my mother might have been different. Okay, maybe she wouldn't have been fun or kind or had a sense of style. But she could have been emotionally savvy enough not to need MapQuest to find her way across a room to hug her grandsons.

My mother had very little to say on the subject of her own mother other than "I hardly remember her." The times I pushed for more information, all I got was "I have almost no memory of her." No memory? The only memory she ever dug up for me was: "One time we heard her screaming at the top of her lungs. My father and I went running into the bedroom. She was holding a stocking in her hand, and she screamed at us, 'My last pair of stockings, and I got this huge run!' Then she went right back to screaming."

Eventually, I stopped asking my mother, but that was when I was ten or eleven, old enough to take aside some cousins nearer to my mother's age and ask them about the woman I thought of (with bizarre familiarity) as Grandma Ethel. Cousin Marcia told me she'd heard that someone had seen Ethel in a nightclub in Miami Beach wearing serious jewelry in the company of an Italian-looking guy. However, further inquiry by Cousin Danny led to finding out the man was Ethel's husband, Sidney Nachman, of Nachman & Company, distributors of wine and spirits. Cousin Naomi made a few calls to Florida and learned the Nachmans had no children. About ten years later, Cousin Marcia told me that her best friend from high school, who'd moved to Coral Gables, had sent her a clipping of Sidney Nachman's obituary from the *Miami Herald*: *Nachman is survived by his wife, Ethel, and a sister, Rita Umelitz of Creve Coeur, Missouri.*

And that was—almost—that. Although my mother never told me, I heard from assorted cousins that she knew Ethel was alive and well and wearing serious jewelry. However, she made no attempt to contact her mother. Maybe she was waiting for Ethel to make the first move. That never happened.

Just before my twentieth birthday, a half year after Jonah and I were married, we were on a flight to Miami for the wedding of one of his camp friends. I'd had a couple of vodka tonics to dull the sound of the engine (it was only the third or fourth plane ride of my life, and I was still terrified). In a what-the-hell mood, I said, "Hey, we'll be in Miami. Maybe I'll try to find my grandmother." I waited for Jonah to say, "Are you crazy?" When he didn't, I asked, "Do you think I'm crazy?" He said no, not at all, but I should be prepared for someone who was a total bitch and who would refuse to see me—and don't forget I'd made a hairdresser appointment at the hotel at four-thirty on Saturday.

Finding her wasn't as easy as it would be today; we were in the pre-Google era. But after an hour at the Miami Beach public library that Saturday morning, Jonah and I discovered Ethel Nachman had married Roy O'Shea, a man who owned several Honda dealerships in South Florida. The O'Sheas definitely had an active social life. As we sat looking into the microfilm viewer at newspaper photos of parties and benefits, Jonah kept saying, "I can't believe how much she looks like you!" I kept saying, "Oh my God!" I also said, "Do you think my mother remembered what she looked like and saw the resemblance and that's why she always held back with me emotionally?" Jonah said, "Everything doesn't need a psychological explanation." We went back to the microfilm and discovered that in the mid-eighties, "gregarious and charming socialite Ethel O'Shea" was high on a list to take over as the new host of a local late-morning TV show, *Talk of Miami*. Ethel got the job. Ethel was a hit. Within a year, Roy O'Shea was history.

I didn't get up the courage to call her—not that I had her unlisted number. But while I was at the hairdresser, Jonah called the TV station, said he was Jonah Gersten from the Yale School of Medicine and that Ethel O'Shea had asked him to mail something to her at her home address. Sadly, he'd lost it. Who would have believed a story like that? Anybody. I'd always told him I trusted everything he told me. Whenever I said that, he'd smile and say, "Why wouldn't you?" But most other people had that reaction to him, too. So at nine the next morning, four hours before we had to leave Miami to get back to New Haven, the two of us rang Grandma Ethel's bell.

"I'm . . ." I began to say to the woman at the door. She was me plus forty-something years—assuming a good dermatologist and a great colorist and plastic surgeon. Her jaw dropped. She barely looked at Jonah before turning back to me. Even without makeup, her eyes were her most beautiful feature: pale green jade. Her smooth skin was an almost completely unwrinkled pearly pink, and her hair an incredibly believable blond. She was built like me, too, tall and long-legged. Even though we didn't have any money yet, I already knew enough about fashion to realize the satin robe she had on was a Donna Karan.

"You're mine?" Grandma Ethel asked at last. She knew the answer. Before I could say a single word, she took my arm and brought me inside.

But my blocking out the reality of my parents' alternating grilled cheese and diet-ginger-ale burps with the memory of my grandparent ceased when my father boomed, "Excuse me!" It so startled me that I twitched, dropping my last bite of sandwich, a near-perfect circle, onto the floor. "I know this is a bad time for you," he said.

He does have empathy, I thought. "Thank—" I started, but

never got out the "you" because he cut me off: "Maybe you haven't gone shopping, but do you happen to have a piece of fruit?"

One navel orange and two decafs later, they left. Four hours after that, the police rang my doorbell.

Chapter Nine

On either side of the front door, there were tall, slender panes of glass, so even before I opened it, I could see Detective Sergeant Timothy Coleman looking down at the doormat. He stared with an intensity born of a desire to face anything but the person who would open the door. Beside him stood an African-American guy in his forties—the ex-jock type who looked like he'd discovered doughnuts, though only recently. He had on a gray overcoat and a long black knit scarf, the kind male models wrap around their necks a hundred times. It ended at his knees in a hysterical eruption of fringe. He studied me through the narrow window. It was nearly midnight, but he appeared more weary than physically tired, probably because he knew too well what the next hour would bring.

As if to live up to his expectations, I began to cry as I tried to turn the stiff, heavy lock. I clutched the brass knob, and it felt like forever before I was able to turn it.

"Mrs. Gersten," Coleman said, "this is Lieutenant Gary McCorkle Paston from the NYPD."

"Corky Paston," the other cop said.

It wasn't until the gusting icy wind made me shiver that I

realized my hand was still gripping the knob and the two men were outside. "Sorry. Please come in." I led them into the living room, though all I wanted was to stand right there in my bare feet on the cold marble floor of the hall and shout at them, "For God's sake, just say it! Get it over with!" I was still crying as we passed through the hall, yet when we got to the living room and I turned, a small part of me expected to see Paston smiling and giving the thumbs-up to signal, *Hey, no reason to cry. I'm here with good news. Your husband's fine: just a little worse for wear.*

"I'm sorry, but I have bad news," he said.

"Is Jonah dead?"

"Yes."

I didn't move. I didn't wail. I stared at his scarf and thought it looked hand-knit.

"We found him just a few hours ago."

"What happened?" My voice emerged as an awful croak. I got so busy clearing my throat again and again that I didn't notice Paston had guided me over to a chair until I felt the frame and seat cushion against my leg. But it was the wing chair, Jonah's chair, and sitting in it would have been indecent, like flag-burning or even idol worship. I stepped away quickly and moved to the deep corner formed by the arm of the couch. I motioned for them to sit. Neither went near the wing chair. Coleman took the chair he'd had the last time, and Paston sat on the middle cushion of the couch.

"I'm sorry to have to tell you: Your husband was murdered," Lieutenant Paston said.

"Oh my God!" I said, covering my face with my hands. "Oh my God!" I may have groaned. Shock: That was what was so weird. I'd spent so much time in the past two days picturing not just something terrible happening to Jonah but murder, specifically murder, in ten or twenty or maybe a hundred different ways. I made an awful grunting sound, but that was because the words "How?" and "Who?" crashed into each other as they came out.

The detectives' silence lasted way too long, and I realized they were waiting for me to say something. I uncovered my face and put my hands in my lap. A second later, I was crossing my arms and clutching them tight against my ribs: holding myself together. "What happened?" I asked Paston. His first few words didn't register because I got lost staring at the red blood vessels in the whites of his eyes. They were thin and twisty, like the lines indicating bad country roads on a map.

". . . in the chest."

"What? Sorry, I didn't hear what you said."

"Dr. Gersten appears to have been stabbed in the chest with a long, pointed pair of scissors."

I heard the words, but all I could say was "I'm sorry. I forgot to take your coats." Lieutenant Paston took off his scarf and stuck it in the sleeve of his coat, but it must have been Trauma Time, like during a car crash, when everything slows. I saw his hand grasp the scarf near his collarbone and imperceptibly make an arc behind his neck until three feet of black wool hung from either side of his hand. He slipped out of one coat sleeve, then another, in what seemed to be a series of jerky pictures—more like primitive animation than fluid motion. *Funny,* I thought, because he looked graceful, like one of those extra-large men who surprise you by moving like Fred Astaire on a dance floor. It was only as I got mesmerized watching him snake the scarf into a sleeve that Coleman's sheepskin jacket suddenly appeared in my hands. With that, time returned to its normal speed.

"Surgical scissors?" I asked Paston.

"No. More like the ones barbers use," he said. "Your husband seems to have been stabbed twice." Paston had even more of a New York accent than I did—his "more" came out like "maw." "It'll be clearer once an autopsy is performed." He lowered his voice to a funeral-parlor hush. "We'll let you know when that will be." I watched as he took a deep breath. I knew something I didn't want to hear was coming. "Then you can make your arrangements for . . . whenever you want to. I know at this point nothing can comfort you, but you ought to know—the doctor from the medical examiner's office at the scene indicated that after the second wound, it couldn't have been long at all."

I'll treasure that thought, shmuck, I thought. "I don't understand," I said. "A barber's scissors? Did it happen—"

"No, no." Coleman cut in so fast, it was clear that Paston running things wasn't sitting well with him. "That's just a description of the kind of scissors."

"Well," I snapped at him, "where did it happen, then?"

"Let me start at the beginning," Paston said, flashing Coleman a *This happened on my turf, so shut up* look. The little cop's lips pressed together to show a slash of resentment. "Naturally, we'd been working on your husband's being missing. But a call came in to the NYPD around six tonight," Paston continued. "Someone living in an apartment on East Eighty-seventh Street got home from work and called the building's superintendent. Said there might be a problem in the apartment next door."

One half of me wanted to stick my fingers in my ears and go *la-la-la* real loud so I wouldn't have to hear any of what he was going to say. The other half urgently needed to know every detail. "What kind of a problem did the neighbor report?" I asked.

"I haven't had a chance to speak to the individual, so I can't say for sure. In any case, the superintendent tried to contact the tenant but wasn't successful. He didn't want to enter the premises without permission, so he called the police. Two patrolmen came from the Nineteenth Precinct. He let them in. They found Dr. Gersten just past the front hallway."

"Was anyone else there?" I asked.

"No." Maybe he sensed Coleman was about to say something, because he turned, flashed him a beady-eyed glance, then continued, "The apartment is sublet to someone named Dorinda Dillon. Do you know her?" I shook my head. "Ever heard the name mentioned?"

"No. Who is she?"

"Actually, that's only one of her names. She changed it a few months ago. Before that, she was known as Cristal Rousseau."

"What?"

"Cristal Rousseau." He spelled it out. "That probably isn't her real name."

"What kind of a person would call herself Cristal Rousseau?" My voice was so loud it made me sit up straight. I tried to think of something more to say to show I was in control, but nothing came to mind.

"Ma'am," Coleman cut in, "would you like me to call somebody for you? A friend or family member? You know, just to have someone with you."

It sounded like the right thing to do. Except I couldn't think of anyone I wanted to be with me. No one in either of our families. Not any of my you-know-I-am-always-there-for-you Shorehaven friends who would try to hold my hand or hug me. If I'd said anything, they'd murmur "I hear you." Of course, the whole time they'd be making mental notes so their "I was with Susie Gersten the night she found out" story would be filled with rich insights and examples of their sensitivity.

"No one," I said.

"Are you a hundred percent sure, ma'am?"

No, not Andrea. She'd offend Coleman with a single blink of contempt at his low-end shoes; Paston by eyeing his slightly over-the-belt gut. The cops might forgive her bad manners if they got distracted by her body—basketball-sized boobs stuck on a lean, boyish frame. Once that happened, they'd quickly turn into admirers, especially once they realized her excessive blondness was natural. Andrea was okay for sexy comedy, but she wouldn't fit into a horrible dark story.

I shook my head. No one. But I realized they hadn't seen my dismissal because they were eyeing each other. Maybe glaring. Any second it could escalate into NYPD/Nassau County, black/white, big guy/mini-man hostility. I cleared my throat. "There's no one I want here now." Except Jonah. An insane thought flew through my head: Once he came home, I'd feel so much better. "Please, for God's sake, just tell me everything. Who is this Dorinda Dillon?"

Coleman opened his mouth to speak but then realized he didn't have anything to say. Lieutenant Paston leaned forward in his chair. "She's an escort," he said. I didn't react. Maybe I was trying to think of a way to ask him what he meant by "escort." Could it be a new term for someone who took around Europeans looking for plastic surgery bargains? But he dissolved any potential for sugarcoating: "By 'escort,' I mean a call girl. A prostitute."

I shook my head hard—no, no way!—even as I understood he was telling the truth. Jonah had been murdered in a call girl's apartment. "She did her work . . . ? Was that apartment her place of business?"

"Yes."

"East Eighty-whatever," I said. "That's a good neighborhood." Paston didn't say anything, and Coleman flexed his ankles to study the Velcro closings on his little brown shoes. "I don't mean that it's better to get killed on the Upper East Side than, say, someplace else." I realized I was babbling, but I didn't want Lieutenant Paston to get the idea that I was thinking, *Oh, God forbid! To be stabbed to death in Harlem.* "What I meant was that Jonah's office is in that area, so maybe he dropped in to see her on his way home. Maybe she was post-op. If there was some minor problem, he could check up on her without her having to go to the office."

"It's only been a few hours since we found him," Lieutenant Paston answered. Either he hadn't heard or didn't care about my "good neighborhood" comment. I decided that mentioning that Jonah had switched from Hilary to Obama early on would be tacky. "First thing tomorrow," he went on, "I'll ask someone at Dr. Gersten's medical office to check if she ever was a patient."

My mind kept going to stupid things. Should I offer them coffee? Could I ask Paston to tell my in-laws about Jonah so I didn't have to call them? Even if he did, I realized, I'd still have to let Gilbert John and Layne know.

Soon everyone would know. Soon everyone would be shaking their heads and saying, "Susie Gersten won't believe Jonah went to a hooker for sex. Is that willful ignorance or what? So sad."

Part of my mind must still have been functioning because I surprised myself by suggesting: "You might want to check at Mount Sinai, too. Jonah and his partners were sometimes on call for victims of domestic violence—" But then I cried some more. One of the cops must have gotten up; a moment later, the tissue box from the downstairs guest bathroom was set on the coffee table. I felt a couple of tissues being tucked between my thumb and index finger. I blew my nose and went on, "They do pro bono work for victims of domestic violence, women and children whose faces . . . Prostitutes, you know, they get abused. So if Jonah had any dealings with someone like that, I'm sure it was to help her."

"It's definitely a possibility," Lieutenant Paston said. His eyes moved from me to the table beside him, to an old green Derby tureen I'd filled with preserved yellow Dendrobium orchids and pale orange roses. I could tell he wanted to touch the flowers to feel if they were fake. "We'll look into it."

"Lieutenant Paston, if I could only listen to myself, I'd probably be saying, 'Poor thing. She is *so* trying to deny reality, swearing her husband wouldn't go to a prostitute for sex.'"

"Not at all," Detective Sergeant Coleman said.

"Except this is the thing," I explained to Paston, "I know my husband. You don't." He nodded. "But maybe, in a way, you know more than I do." Believing Jonah wouldn't cheat on me, especially with a call girl capable of calling herself Cristal Rousseau, was one thing. But now, to ask a specific question . . . I saw it as a test. Was my faith in Jonah the real thing? Or was it self-deception to keep the horror to a manageable size, as in "Sure, my husband may have been stabbed to death in a whore's apartment, but he was there for severe facial trauma, not a blow job"?

"Jonah had his clothes on, didn't he?"

"Yes."

I don't think I said "Thank God" out loud. "It wasn't like he was killed without clothes and someone dressed him."

"No," Paston agreed, "the wounds were made through his shirt. Mrs. Gersten, I'll be glad to talk to you about the crime anytime. But maybe this isn't the moment. Let me explain. Dr. Gersten's been missing for several days, so there must have been moments when you expected the worst. But no wife is prepared for the cops to knock on the door late at night and tell her that her husband has been the victim of a homicide. You're in a state of shock. It may be better to skip the details now. You don't need images of graphic violence in your head. Tomorrow, next week, next month: All you have to do is call and you have my word, I'll describe—"

"No. I'd like to know now." I crossed my arms again, tight. I needed my own embrace because the mere thought of not being held together, of resting my elbow on the arm of the couch or setting my hands in my lap, made me feel sick. "Let me try to explain," I said. "I'm a floral designer. My work is getting images in my head." Paston glanced at the orchids and roses in the tureen and turned back to me. I went on, "If I know what happened to Jonah, I can deal with it. I have to. But if there's a blank, I'll need to fill it in. I'll create a thousand images in my mind, and a lot of them will be more horrible than anything you can tell me. I don't want to go through that again, because I've been there since he's been gone. That's all it's been. I can't live through hundreds of wide-awake nightmares anymore. Let me deal with just one."

Coleman had been eyeing me, expressionless. Now the side of his mouth formed a curlicue of doubt. Not a good idea, he was guessing, giving details to the victim's wife. But he couldn't signal to Paston because the Manhattan detective was too busy thinking and nibbling tiny bits of skin off his chapped lips. Finally, Lieutenant Paston sat back in the chair. "Dr. Gersten was stabbed through his shirt. He was fully dressed in a tie and suit jacket, though the jacket was open. He may have been holding his overcoat because it was found near him on the floor."

"Doesn't that back up what I was saying?" I asked him. "About Jonah not being there as a customer?"

"You say you want to deal with reality now, so I'm going to take you at your word," Paston said. "If you're looking for the truth, you have to keep an open mind at this stage. We're just hours into the investigation. We know only a small percentage of what we need to know. It's too early for conclusions. For us, that's a definite. Naturally, how open-minded you want to be is up to you. Being fully dressed may be evidence that your husband wasn't using Dorinda Dillon's professional services. But the homicide might have occurred as he was entering the premises. Or as he was leaving."

I began nodding to show I was comprehending, though I was so tired I was still processing what he said. At last I asked, "When you say 'leaving,' you mean he might have been leaving after having sex with her and getting dressed again?"

"Yes. We'll know more once we get the medical examiner's report."

"You mean if he . . ."

"Yes." I was grateful to Paston for not saying "ejaculated" in front of Coleman. I wouldn't have minded if Paston had said it five hundred times—if Coleman hadn't been there. But there was something about the Nassau County cop's prissy politeness, and his looking at me like I was a piece of sculpture with jade eyes, that made me uncomfortable in my own living room. "I'll keep an open mind," I told Paston.

"Good," he said. I doubted he believed me.

"So you haven't found Dorinda Dillon?"

"No. It looks like she left the building the night Dr. Gersten was killed. We haven't found anyone who has seen her since. Her normal pattern is either working—men coming and going days, nights—or being up there by herself. The only time she seems to go out is in the afternoon, to have her nails done or to pick up a few groceries. Maybe get drugs, too. She's had two arrests for possession. Cocaine. Charges dropped the first time. The second time she pleaded guilty to a Class C nonviolent felony and got a suspended sentence."

"Do you think she was the one who killed him?"

"We don't know at this point."

"You're keeping an open mind," I said. Coleman's brow furrowed, but Paston didn't take it as a sarcastic remark, which was good, because I hadn't meant it to be.

"Yes. We need to be able to weigh whatever evidence comes in, so it doesn't make sense to close off our options." He stood and walked around the coffee table and over to the fireplace mantel. He was tall enough to lounge against it and rest his elbow on its ledge, but after a couple of seconds, he came back and sat beside me. "Had to stretch my legs," he said. "Sorry."

"It's fine." I shifted slightly to face him. When he spoke again, his voice was so soft I had to strain to hear it. Just the two of us: He wanted Coleman out. "Once we leave, a person going through what you have to deal with should have a friend in the house. A person to rely on. Sergeant Coleman says you have two Norwegian girls who work here. They'll probably be busy keeping those triplets of yours under control, right?"

"Yes. And they're teenagers. I wouldn't . . ." I wanted to ask him what I should tell the boys. He would know the right thing.

"So what Sergeant Coleman suggested, you calling a friend or a family member, you need to do that. At some point you're going to have to sleep. You'll need somebody with a good head on their shoulders to answer the phone, do what needs doing." I didn't say anything. "Your parents are alive?"

"Yes. But not them."

"Dr. Gersten's—"

I shook my head. "I'll call my business partner. She's my best friend, too. I didn't want to before because she can be . . . She's a little much on the cool, calm, and collected side."

"Got it. But some cool can come in handy at a time like this." He took a card case from his inside jacket pocket and handed me two of his business cards. Lieutenant Gary McCorkle Paston, Manhattan North Homicide Squad. The NYPD shield was flat. I imagined some New York City budget gap that had needed closing decades before had meant the end of embossment. "You can reach me day or night. If for any reason I can't come to the phone, there will be other detectives assigned to the case who can help you or get a message to me. If you think of anything that might help, or anyone it might be good for us to speak to, let me know right away. Don't worry about bothering me or calling with some small detail. We need whatever you can come up with." I nodded, although I didn't realize I'd closed my eyes again until I got startled when he spoke. "This is a shock and a terrible loss. Nothing I do can make it better for you. But I'll do everything I can to find out who did this to your husband."

"Thank you." Before he could say "You're welcome" or anything else, I added, "I feel confident having you on this case." Before he could thank me and we'd wind up in some embarrassing gratitude match, I said, "One more thing: Jonah's parents."

"Right. I heard about them. He's a big deal at Sloan-Kettering. She's a big deal at some makeup company."

He seemed to have gotten the picture before he even drove up to the house. Just to be clear, I said, "This is going to be devastating for them, too. They're very fine people, wonderful grandparents to our kids. But they're the types who are used to being in charge of stuff, respected. Also, they are very well connected. I'm sorry if this sounds obnoxious, but you should know: They probably know the chief of police and the DA and half the judges in the city. My father-in-law is involved with some charity with Mayor Bloomberg."

"I understand."

"Over the years they've come to like me, or at least have learned to live with me. Our relationship is . . . how would my mother-in-law describe it? Perfectly pleasant. But bottom line, they think Jonah could have done better, that I don't have enough class for him and that I'm not smart enough—except for me having the brains to reel him into marriage while he was still too young to know better." I was glad Paston didn't go into the "Oh, I'm sure that can't be true" business. "They may call you. No, they will call you. I'm telling you all this because although I'd appreciate it if you could talk to them, I don't want them pushing me out of the picture. I want to feel free to speak to you and find out—"

"I understand. I'll tell your husband's parents the truth, that you're the legal next of kin, and that means, while I'll speak with them, I deal only with you."

"Thank you." I didn't cry again. I just started to shake, pretty violently.

Coleman decided his help was needed, so he practically flew over and stood between the couch and the coffee table, so he was right beside me. "If you give me your doctor's name, ma'am," he said, "I'll be glad to call him or her. A sedative might—" He had sweat on his upper lip.

"Thank you, but no sedatives. I can't take drugs with three little boys in the house." He fell silent, though he didn't move. He just stood next to me, his shins an inch from my knees, as if he had a front-row seat to some all-star nervous breakdown. I wanted Paston to tell him to get the hell away, but he didn't.

After a few minutes, my shaking eased to mere trembling. My head cleared so I could remember Andrea's number. I gave it to Coleman so he could call her and tell her to come over. Only then did he go back to his chair to get busy on his cell.

"I didn't tell him the truth," I murmured to Paston. "About drugs. I actually have enough Xanax to calm a herd of crazed elephants."

"Good," he said. "You're going to need it."

Chapter Ten

✂—————————————————————————————————

Andrea must have arrived soon after Detective Sergeant Coleman called her. I heard her voice at the front door, followed by the purr of small wheels. She'd brought the small Vuitton suitcase she always kept packed in case Fat Boy finished some hedging deal early and called her to join him in Shanghai or Dublin. I saw her as she stepped into the room, and I watched as she came over to pat the back of my hand—the Andrea equivalent of a regular person's loving embrace. She said, "Oh, Susie, this is dreadful. I'm so sorry." Maybe I nodded, and I think I retreated farther into the softness of the couch's corner, where the overstuffed back met the fat arm. At some point the detectives left. For all I knew, they simply evaporated. I heard no goodbyes, no footsteps, no closing doors. "Tell me what you need me to do, Susie," Andrea said.

"Calls." I exhaled it more than I actually said it. "I need you to call . . . everybody. Not tonight. I think it's too late."

"Yes. It's almost one in the morning."

"Maybe you should go home, come back later. I don't know. They told me I needed someone to be here. I can't think clearly." My arms were still crossed so tight over my chest that my shoulders ached, but I couldn't seem to release them. "Do I have to call his parents now?"

"Yes, you do. Soon, I would think."

"What?"

"They can't hear this on the news."

"They're asleep at this hour."

"But someone they know might hear of it and call them."

"Oh God, I can't believe I didn't think about that."

One of Andrea's usual snotty retorts got to the tip of her tongue, but this time she stopped it before it came out. She didn't even look like herself. She was wearing just lipstick. Without other makeup, her eyes were almost lost under puffy pink lids and uncurled blond lashes. Her face seemed magnified, a white oval with a glossy brick-red mouth that appeared glued on, as if she'd cut it out from a Chanel ad. "And you'll have to call your parents. Unless you want me to do it."

I shook my head. The movement loosened up some words. "No friendship could survive that kind of strain."

"I can do it."

"No, I'll call them. Don't worry. They won't be able to cope with coming back out here. Most likely, they'll wait till nine-thirty or ten in the morning. That way, they can get the car washed before they stop at GNC because they're low on acidophilus. But then they'll be on their way."

"To offer their usual nonstop comfort," Andrea added. We'd been partners and friends long enough that I knew, even before she did it, that she'd start to look up to heaven but quickly avert her gaze, knowing that when it came to my parents, even God couldn't help.

"Well, when they do show up," I said, "they're bound to be wonderful with the boys." I knew I sounded bitter.

That was when it hit me: *I have children.* It must have been too awful to think about the boys immediately after I heard the news. I just blocked them out. I wished I could do that again.

The thought of Evan, Dash, and Mason missing Jonah while not truly comprehending what had happened was too sad to dwell on. And what about their growing up without a father? My head flopped down. I was defeated. "I can't take this, Andrea."

"You have to."

"Take your stiff-upper-lip Wasp bullshit and shove it."

"I'm not Anglo-Saxon, as you well know. I'm Dutch. And I don't expect you to stiff-upper-lip it, Susie. You should know that. This is beyond horrible. I'm only saying that you're eventually going to have to find a way to take it because . . ." She swallowed. "You're all the boys have now." Her eyes closed for what was either a very long blink or a prayer: *Thank you, God, that it isn't me.* "The good news is, they won't be up until their ungodly wake-up time. You don't have to think about them this second. You have other fish to fry now: your in-laws, your parents. And what about Gilbert John? Layne? You do have to call them tonight, don't you? Or can I call them and you call the others?"

I made all the calls. It was worse than I'd imagined because I had to live through everybody else's shock. I don't recall having even a milligram of compassion. I wished I could get away with "Listen, I hate to tell you this, but Jonah's been murdered. I'll know more tomorrow. Speak to you then," and hang up. Take three Ambien. No, two, because of the boys. Three wouldn't kill me, probably, but I couldn't risk even a little soothing brain damage.

If I could have made the calls and heard "You poor thing!" over and over again, I might have dealt with giving them the news. But I had to listen to my father-in-law's terrible groan, like that of a lion gone mad with pain, and Babs screeching in the background, "What? What? Tell me! For God's sake, tell me!" So I had to go into the whole thing, repeating large parts of it because they put me on speaker and then couldn't understand half of what I was saying.

And of course it wasn't "Your son was stabbed to death in the midst of performing some noble act." The answer to their wheres and hows was "In the apartment of a call girl named Dorinda Dillon, aka Cristal Rousseau, who'd had a couple of arrests for cocaine." With a pair of those long-bladed scissors you see in barbershops. All this interrupted by moans and cries and me saying, "I'm sorry, I'm so sorry," too many times to count.

Gilbert John Noakes, MD, FACS, didn't scream or groan. In fact, he was almost speechless except alternating in a shaky voice between "Good God!" and "I'm sorry, Susie" a few times. He didn't ask questions, and after I'd told him Jonah had been stabbed, I heard what sounded like a sigh filled with pain. "I don't know what to say. It's brutal." He sounded so wiped out that I couldn't bring myself to tell him about the call girl. At the end of the conversation, he said he'd call Layne, but I told him I'd do it, since I figured they had to hear the Dorinda details that, barring some international tragedy or celebrity overdose, would be on the news.

I hadn't realized Andrea had left the living room until I saw her coming back in. She handed me a mug and said, "You had some actual cocoa. This is true hot chocolate, not your diet shit. Drink it."

"Thank you." Andrea had to be thanked constantly, even at work, like when she was just handing you pieces of sphagnum moss every two seconds.

She said, "You're welcome. I brought Xanax. Do you want any?"

I shook my head, then said, "No, thank you." She gave me the raised-eyebrows, flared-nostrils look she gave to clients who were making a foolish decision, like wanting lollipops on ribbons in table arrangements for a First Communion luncheon. It worked 99 percent of the time. I added, "I don't need anything. I'm numb." I couldn't say "What I'd like is an overdose of something so I can die and not have to face the rest of my life." Not that I'd have done that: I knew I had to be there, as whole as possible, for the boys. But it would have been nice to say it and hear a passionate "I know it's terrible for you, but you can't even think that way!" Except Andrea would have added, or at least thought, *Don't be a self-indulgent ass*.

When I called Layne, she was on the other phone with Gilbert John, but she was back to me within seconds. She talked for too long, but it was bearable because she spoke the way decent people are supposed to, the way you see in the older movies when you're surfing channels. "What a horror for something like this to happen to such a fine, honorable man. A good man! My heart . . . my heart goes out to you." She either swallowed a lot or cried for a few seconds. "And your wonderful boys. Susie, I don't have to tell you how much he loved all of you. You know those office watercooler chats? Every single time Jonah and I would talk, a light would come into his eyes. I always knew the next sentence out of his mouth would be about one of the triplets. Or all of the triplets. He'd get this gleam—"

"Layne, thank you so much, but I have to tell you—"

"Jonah wasn't just a partner and mentor to me. He was a great friend. When he was senior resident—"

"Layne." Not that I would actually tell her to save it for the funeral home and the shiva, but one of the reasons everyone said "Oh, Dr. Jiménez is such a fine, fine person" was that Layne didn't stint on kindness. She was never too busy for a good word—or, more to the point, words linked into paragraphs. "Gilbert John sounded so shaken up that I didn't want to go into detail," I began.

"And if you can't handle it, you don't have to with me, Susie. Whenever you're ready . . ."

"You both need to know something now, before you hear it on the news or anywhere else."

"What is it?" she asked cautiously.

"Jonah was killed in a call girl's apartment."

"No!" Her "no" came out so spontaneously that a huge sigh of relief escaped me. Thank God for that reaction. Clearly, I'd been dreading the overlong silence I'd be forced to translate into "Oh, you found out about his whore habit." Maybe I was misinterpreting. The "no" could have been pure reflex on Layne's part. But I grabbed on to it as if she were saying "He was too much in love with you to even consider any other woman, much less a call girl."

That was all the reassurance I was going to get, although I didn't realize it for another twelve hours. Andrea got a little pushy—in a good way, I guess, urging me to go up and get a couple of hours' sleep, or at least rest, before the boys woke up. If she hadn't been there, I probably would have spent the night on the couch.

I didn't want to go upstairs. I was afraid. Climbing the steps (right foot, left, right, as if I were on a Level 4 hike instead of walking up to the next floor) was too much effort. I was terrified. Spooked. I stood before the black rectangle of the door frame, staring into the unlit bedroom. I was sure I'd take one step onto the carpet, reach for the light switch, and suddenly— a gut-ripping noise, half howl, half shriek—and the enraged ghost of Jonah would boil the air an inch from my face. I didn't know why I was so crazy, or why, even if I didn't believe in ghosts, which I didn't, except maybe the week after I saw *The Sixth Sense*, Jonah's spirit would be anything but benevolent toward me.

Yet I had to force myself to lie down in our bed. My heart fluttered, then slammed against my chest in panic at the sudden, jarring silence when the heating system turned off. A second later, a current of warm air puffed across my ear and blew a strand of my hair onto my cheek. I suppressed a scream. Maybe that strand had been there all along. Yet the air above the bed felt agitated by invisible goings-on in some parallel sphere.

At times during the night, the fear vanished. I was in the bedroom I had once shared with my husband, although now I was a widow. I censored that line of thought not because of what it represented but because I'd always hated the word. It conjured up old ladies in shapeless black dresses gray with lint. Or those black spiders with gross hairy legs.

But I forced myself to stay where I was. I mumbled aloud what I knew of the Twenty-third Psalm—not much—again and again. If I couldn't whip it up for the Lord being my shepherd in the Valley of Death and getting me through this night of grief and hysteria, it would be the start of big-time bedroom phobia, a truly embarrassing fear. Because truthfully, how could I tell my therapist, Francine Twersky, that my dead husband's vengeful soul was whirling around the Regency bergère chair and that the very air of the bedroom stank of sulfurous fury? I could tell her—and doom myself to session after boring session of her getting me to understand that what was haunting the bedroom was coming from my head.

Speaking of heads, I covered mine with the duvet, then started worrying that if I suffocated, the boys would go to Theo, Jonah's brother. Jonah once said, "Even though my folks are hip enough to appreciate one sciencey kid and one arty one, they know I'm the winner and Theo is . . . They always try to act like he's my equal or a close second with the silver medal. But deep down? All four of us know he's the loser."

If something happened to me and Theo got the boys? Within weeks, one of his friends would convince him to coproduce a reality show—giving him the excuse it would be a public service. *TV Guide* would write, *Sparks fly in SINGLE WITH TRIPLETS when a young Maserati-driving Manhattan casting director gets surprise custody of his four-year-old nephews.* I rearranged the duvet so my nose and mouth were out in the air.

At five-thirty, the boys startled me awake, so I must have gotten a little sleep. "Come up on the bed," I said, patting the mattress. My chest ached from holding back sobs, though I didn't completely rule out a heart attack. "I want to talk with you." I had to wait while Dashiell used the bathroom. I made the mistake of telling him to use ours. Within a second, the other two were demanding the privilege. I got all choked up, so I nodded. They ran in, and even before the giggling became wild laughter, I could visualize the puddles of pee I'd have to wipe up. Jonah wouldn't be calling on his cell, bored in bridge traffic, and my "They're the Jackson Pollocks of urine" would forever stay unsaid.

When they returned, they were so high from the excitement of a triple toilet experience that I had to get up and grab them as they raced around the room. I plopped them hard onto the bed. By the time I finally caught Mason, I was screeching like the Wicked Witch of the West, "Shut up! For God's sake, shut up and listen to me!" over and over again. Naturally, I spent the next few minutes weeping and apologizing—"I'm so, so sorry, sweeties. Oh God, I'm so sorry"—and calming them down, especially Evan. His bony shoulders jerked with each of his sobs. Mason's eyes were still wide with fright at my rage while Dash stared at me with concern mixed with contempt.

I pulled them close, for the thousandth time envying mothers of twins, who had an arm for each kid. It was only then, as I was kissing one of their heads and trying to banish non-mournful thoughts like *He needs a shampoo* that I realized I had no idea what to tell them. During the days of waiting, imagining every terrible outcome except the one that had happened, why hadn't I turned on the computer and Googled "explain child death parent"? My eyes grew heavy. I so longed to go back to sleep with them, bony shoulders and smelly heads snuggling against me, even though their wakefulness and squiggliness were proof of what an idiot fantasy that was.

"I have something very sad to tell you," I said. All three of them looked downcast, but it struck me that they didn't understand that "very sad" had to do with Jonah's not being around. Their "sad" was more "Carvel has run out of rainbow sprinkles." "You know Daddy hasn't been home for a couple of days." I guess I expected children-as-seen-on-TV behavior: nodding, gazing up at me curiously. But all three of them talked at once.

"Where is he?"

"When's he coming home?"

"Where's Daddy?"

"Is he bringing us presents?"

"Can I—"

I said, "Shhh!" loud enough to drown them out. "Evan, Dash, Mason! Let Mommy finish. Okay? This is very important." I took a deep breath. I knew I had to say something fast, before they started babbling again. "Daddy . . . Something very sad happened to Daddy. He got hurt, really hurt. He died. You know what that means, don't you? It means—"

"He's dead!" Mason said, triumphant at having beaten out his brothers. "When somebody dies, he gets dead!"

"Yes. Very good. That's right. But it's also very sad because it means he's not coming back anymore."

"Jake's grandpa isn't coming back," Evan said. "He died. He got too old." Then he added hopefully, "Daddy's not too old."

"Daddy can go to the hospital," Dash said. "They'll get him all fixed. Then he can come home."

"I wish more than anything that could happen. But Daddy didn't die because he was old or sick. He got hurt so bad that . . ." I started to cry, which maybe wasn't so terrible; all the articles say that kids feel the passions that are swirling around them, even if they don't comprehend. So if they remembered this, at least they'd know I was talking from my heart. I did try to calm down a little, so I could keep talking. "When someone dies, it means their body got hurt—or sick—so bad that nobody could fix it. Not even the best doctors."

"Daddy's the best doctor," one of them said.

"I know that. He was the best doctor in the world. Except even Daddy couldn't get someone who is dead to come back . . . to be not dead."

I had to stop not because I was still crying, though I was, but because I couldn't think of what to say next. They hadn't asked me how he'd gotten hurt, and I didn't want to tell them it was an accident, because they might soon be hearing words like "killed" or— I prayed not, but I had no reason to believe that at some point they wouldn't run into a neighbor or relative who would be stupid or cruel enough to say something like "stabbed with scissors."

It definitely wasn't the time to explain that a very bad person had killed Daddy. Or a sick person, a crazy person. Instinct, along with four years as their mother, told me that right then the boys could deal with only one basic fact: Their father was dead. That was all the horror they could take.

Usually, they had the normal fears that came, went, and sometimes traveled from triplet to triplet: alligators under the bed; automatic flush toilets in restrooms; being the first belted into his car seat, at which point the minivan would slide shut its doors and, driverless, zoom off; Goofy Goober from *Sponge-Bob Squarepants* hiding in our basement. They didn't have to deal with the concept of bad/sick/crazy people who kill daddies.

"But we have to remember one thing," I said. "Daddy loved all of us more than anything. Do you know what he called you? 'Our miracle boys.' We wanted so much to have a baby, and Daddy said, 'God gave us a very special present. Not one baby—'"

"Three babies!" they sang out. We'd been through this story too many times to count, but they loved it.

"Three wonderful, gorgeous baby boys. And when Daddy looked at all three of you right after you were born, he said, 'I am the happiest, luckiest man in the world, because I am the daddy of these perfect babies!'" Actually, right after they were born, I'd been fixating on my episiotomy incision and whether the OB had been as careful as she'd sworn she would, so I hadn't been paying attention to whatever Jonah had been going on about. But this sounded good enough, although way too flowery for Jonah. "So even though Daddy won't be here to tell you how much he loves you, you know he did. Right? He always said 'I love you' when he kissed you good night."

"He said 'Go to sleep,'" Mason piped up.

"He said—" Dash began.

I cut him off. "But mostly, he said 'I love you.' So even though we won't see him again, we know how much he loved us. And every night before each of us goes to sleep, we'll think about Daddy, about saying 'I love you.'" If I'd expected tears from them, I would have been let down. But Dashiell said he was hungry as a bear, and Evan wanted to know if Jonah would come back when they were five.

Let me go back to sleep, I thought, wishing there was some way the boys could knock on Ida and Ingvild's door and say, "Mommy asked us to tell you that Daddy's dead and not coming back, and could you give us breakfast and take the phone, and she'll definitely be up by ten-thirty or eleven."

As I followed them downstairs, I felt overwhelmed by two warring emotions, grief and anger. Grief that Jonah would not see the boys grow up. Anger at Dorinda Dillon. What had happened in that apartment? It made no sense. What could have made anyone, even a crazy whore, want to kill a wonderful man like Jonah Gersten?

Chapter Eleven

Jonah had been wowed by our house before he saw it. Just as the real estate agent announced, "Here it is!" he realized he couldn't see anything except an old-fashioned green mailbox on a white post, two weeping cherries, and a row of rounded boxwoods, beautifully pruned, standing guard on either side of the driveway. Imposing yet inviting. Tasteful, too. Proof to his Manhattan parents that moving to Long Island didn't mean he'd chosen a life of LICENSED TO GRILL barbecue aprons.

When we curved around to the front of the house, Jonah, who'd been sitting in front next to the broker, leaped out to open the car door for me, mainly so he could whisper, "You can't see the house from the street!" I'd nodded but didn't really get into picturing his parents' dropped jaws. I was too hard at work being what I'd set out (and failed) to be, a landscape architect. Already my mind was sketching in . . . what? Oh, perfect! Lavender shrubs. That would soften the tight-ass formality of all that boxwood. It registered, though barely, that Jonah was being cool for the broker—giving the slate roof a critical eye, dilating his nostrils with displeasure at the perfectly fine lunette window over the door, even though his knowledge of construction was limited to the difference between a shingle and a brick.

Still, both of us must have been throwing off rays of excitement. From that second on, even before we walked between the white columns and stood on the grand front portico, the broker went from nervously chirping, "You okay?" every three seconds to acting so relaxed it looked like she'd been popping Valium instead of Velamints. She knew she'd made the sale.

So given that long, curving, upwardly mobile driveway, it took me a while to find out what was going on beyond our house. All had seemed quiet enough when I went to the kitchen with the boys shortly after five-thirty, gave them breakfast, and parked them in the den with a *Let's Learn Spanish with Frank & Paco* video. I didn't hear anything unusual when I went back upstairs just after six. I had to tell Ida and Ingvild about Jonah. Tears plus a lot of what must have been "Oh my God!" in Norwegian, and they kept taking turns hugging me, which did nothing except make me realize that Ida, who always looked like she'd just jumped out of a shower, wasn't very good at washing her neck. I finally slipped away so they could get dressed.

As I closed their door, I bumped into Andrea in the hall. "When did you get here?" I managed to gasp. "Who let you in?" I was so shocked that there was someone in the house I hadn't known about that I could hardly catch my breath.

"What are you talking about? I was here the whole night." She was already dressed—in pale pink cashmere pants and a matching sweater that had a cowl neck the approximate size of Cape Cod, the sort of getup you'd expect in a Neiman Marcus catalog, not in life. "Remember? I came over with my carry-on."

"Sorry. Obviously, I'm not thinking clearly. I guess I assumed you left after I went upstairs."

"Why would I do that? You needed someone here with you, right? That's what the detective told me when he said to come over. What if I'd gone home and at three o'clock in the morning you wanted to talk? Anyway, I went to the guest room and looked through your eight hundred thousand *World of Interiors* magazines and was fine."

"Was everything okay?" I asked. I seemed to be flying on some sort of automatic pilot, making conversation that meant nothing to me. I'd found myself comforting Ida and Ingvild, telling them that Jonah had been so grateful to them for being with us and how he'd thought the world of them, when in fact he'd been pushing to get "a proper nanny," which showed he'd been having too many hands-free chats with his mother during his drive home from the city.

"The guest room is fine," Andrea said, "but you really need to tell Bernadine to put fresh soap in the shower right after a guest leaves. So she doesn't forget."

"I did tell her. She's like you, always making lists. I can't believe she forgot. Her urge not to waste is probably stronger than her obsessive—" Automatic pilot must have stopped working, because all my thought processes crashed. So I said, "My husband's dead."

"I know," she said as gently as she could, which would be a sensitive person's callous. "I didn't want to say, 'Oh, your husband's dead and we ought to sit down and make a list of what needs to be done,' because . . . I don't know. It might sound coarse. Speaking of coarse, Fat Boy is coming over with a few things I need. But you don't have to look at him this early in the morning. I'll get rid of him—"

"No, it's fine if he comes in."

The bell rang, but it was someone from Kroll, the investigative agency, coming for Jonah's hard drive. Since I didn't think of saying it was too late because he was dead, I let Andrea take him to the study.

When she came back, she was still on Fat Boy. "Don't say it will be fine if he comes in. It will be awkward and horrible. I know that, you know that."

While a nail-gnawing, socially buffoonish, three-hundred-pound, waxy-skinned man wasn't most women's idea of a dreamboat, Hugh Morrison wasn't that bad. All he ever wore, four seasons a year, were short-sleeved Ralph Lauren Polo shirts, but when he came in I noticed he'd put on a black one to show respect in a house of mourning, and the shirt was so spotless that I couldn't even guess what he'd had for breakfast.

"Hey, Susie."

"Hey, Hugh."

He squeezed my shoulder, and I could feel the wetness of his palm through my sweater. Andrea said he didn't hug or kiss other women because he was shy. I'd always thought the reason was he feared they might misinterpret a friendly gesture, assume he was coming on to them, and not be able to hide their distaste. "Sorry about Jonah," he said. He spoke so fast that it came out "SarboutJo."

"Thank you."

He held out a stuffed Vuitton duffel for Andrea. She walked to him with the dread and dignity of an aristocrat going to the guillotine, and they exchanged their usual greeting—puckering lips and kissing on the points of pucker. Then she grabbed the bag out of his blubbery hand. "Did you remember to ask Cora to pack the Louboutin Mary Janes?" He nodded. Side by side, the Morrison-Brinckerhoffs were a perfect ten, she a willowy numeral one, he a jiggly zero. Andrea seemed surprised and perhaps disappointed that he'd remembered the shoes, but she offered him a dour "Good work, Fat Boy."

For once I was able to resist watching the awful spectacle of their marriage, and I headed off to the kitchen. It occurred to me that I hadn't excused myself, but it didn't matter: Fat Boy shuffled up beside me. (Long ago, I realized I should think of him as Hugh, but my mind had accepted the name his wife had assigned him.)

"You got a problem out there," he said.

Comprehending any sentence of his usually took double time: First I had to break down the whiz of sound that came out into words. Plus, I was now so numb—or maybe paralyzed with grief—that there were whole minutes I really didn't comprehend Jonah was dead. I was down deep, drowning in pain, and I could make it to the surface, to reality, only when grabbed by someone and pulled up. "What?" I asked. "A problem out where?"

"End of the driveway." I panicked for a second: One of the weeping cherries had been uprooted by a blast of winter wind. Jonah would be beside himself because he loved those trees. Also, it would cost thousands to replace it with one of the same size, and we'd have a fight about whether that was necessary.

Then I realized Jonah was somewhere in Manhattan, ice cold, on his back in one of those stacked stainless-steel refrigerators like on *Crossing Jordan*. My breath blasted from me like a tire blowout, with such force that I would have careened into the wall of the hallway and crashed to the floor if Fat Boy hadn't grabbed me from behind. He held me under my armpits. When I glanced down, I could see his huge fingers sticking out, pale and porky like bratwurst waiting to be grilled. He propelled me into the dining room, pulled out a chair with his foot, and plopped me into it.

"Sorry," I mumbled.

"Forget about it. Y'okay?"

"I know you just told me something, Hugh, but I forget what it was."

"The end of the driveway. TV trucks and cameras and a bunch of reporters." My brain took far too long to get from *Why are reporters in Shorehaven?* to *Oh shit!* My face must have finally registered something close to comprehension because he started talking again: "Before I got out of my car, I called the cops. They can't keep the press off the streets. But they'll send a couple of guys over to keep them from putting a foot on your property." I nodded a thank-you. "Your tax dollars at work," he added.

Real crime, like big-time burglary or homicide, was handled by the Nassau County PD. But Shorehaven Estates was one of those privileged little incorporated villages that had a police force all its own for lesser offenses. It appeared to be made up entirely of white guys so shiny-faced and clean-shaven they looked like Mormons parachuted in from Utah. My only contact with them had taken place a year before, when I'd called asking what to do about a demented raccoon staggering alongside our house. They arrived three minutes later, shot it with a tranquilizer dart, and carted it away.

"What do reporters want here at the house?" I asked. "It didn't happen here." Had I been thinking straight, I wouldn't have had to ask, but I wasn't.

"They want whatever piece of Jonah they can get," he said. "Like you. You go to your mailbox, and you'll see yourself ten times an hour on CNN. And if they get a shot of the boys in the backseat of your minivan? Listen, Susie, they're pros for a reason. They're going to swear they'll go away if someone comes out and talks to them."

"A 'family spokesman,'" I said.

"Yeah. But they won't go." Fat Boy knew about media coverage. His hedge fund was in an overly glassed and marbled office building in Great Neck, fifteen minutes west, but he hardly went there. Not that it was such a depressing place: Unlike so many formerly smart financial types, Fat Boy had not been lured by skyrocketing real estate profits or exotic offshoots like mortgage derivatives. Instead of assuming all those investments were too sophisticated for him to understand, he'd told Andrea that the speculators and bankers "couldn't tell a pile of shit from a hot rock" and bet big against the boom. And of course he'd won.

Most of the time, his global dealings took place in the vibrating Barcalounger in his home office. With a headset blinking blue just over his right ear, he was commander of the six-line phone on a table beside him and the notebook computer on his lap. Four feet opposite him was a wall of TV monitors tuned to business and news channels, none of which were muted.

Fat Boy had the multitasker's dream brain, seemingly capable of absorbing every stream of data coming at it. Thus, he had the same total recall of Scott Peterson's murder trial as he did of Goldman Sachs's estimates for European metals and mining in 2005, and how many million hectares India was devoting to the production of soybeans. He said now, "They'll send in helicopters. Your house will come off so magnificent in an aerial shot it will make *The Great Gatsby* look like crap. You know what the crawl will say? 'Lush Long Island estate of Park Avenue plastic surgeon Jonah Gersten found stabbed to death in NY call girl's apartment.'" Had Andrea been around, this would have been when she snarled, "Shut your fat mouth, Huge." But she'd gone someplace—probably up to the guest room to put on her Mary Janes.

The thing was, Fat Boy hadn't meant to be cruel. He wasn't one of those financial freaks who specialized in tactless remarks and had zero knowledge of other people. Not that he'd ever win the Tobey Maguire Male Sensitivity Medal, but at his worst, he was simply a gauche guy who wasn't helped by being wrapped in layers of fat and decorated with swirls of sweat and splotches of snack food.

But, God, was he sharp. Fat Boy lived for data and assumed that the more anyone knew, the better. So right there in the dining room, two hours before I heard an awful *whomp-whomp*, ran outside, and saw the local stations' news helicopters circling over the house like mechanical vultures, I understood he was right: Jonah's murder was a nightmare for his family, colleagues, and friends, but it was a media dream. I had better be prepared that, besides being a personal and police matter, the story was public property. Anyone with a TV or computer could savor our tragedy.

"What am I going to do?" My hands were covering my face,

so my voice was probably muffled. Anyway, it was no big deal if I couldn't be understood. My question was one of those biggies to God, not an inquiry I expected to get answered.

"You need somebody to go out and talk to the press. A family spokesman."

"But you said that won't satisfy them that—"

"It won't." Fat Boy pulled out the dining room chair next to me. It was a nineteenth-century reproduction of an eighteenth-century Hepplewhite: in other words, a piece of furniture designed for slender aristocrats. I immediately put all my energy into not stiffening as he sat down. "Look," he explained, "nothing will satisfy them until a new scandal comes along. Meantime, you've got to deal."

"Okay, but can you do me a favor, Hugh? Talk a little slower."

"Sure, sure, sure. What I'm saying is, you need to deal—now. But hey, there's no law saying you can't do it from the bottom of the deck." He started cleaning under the nails of his left hand with his overlong right pinkie nail. "Here's the thing: You can have someone you trust strolling up your driveway to a bank of microphones three times a day. Except what will that get you? A guarantee to keep them here in Shorehaven throwing Starbucks cups into your storm sewer. No, you've got to give them a spokesman who'll say . . ." He put on what I took as his idea of a sensitive voice, high-pitched, all R's and T's articulated clearly. "She's devastated. Right now all she can think of is how to protect her kids. No, make that 'protect her three little boys.'"

"But isn't that giving them—"

"You don't do it, for Christ's sake," he said, cutting me off. "Oh, I forgot. I need to be really nice to you. Sorry."

"Don't worry about nice. Just tell me what you think I should do."

"Strategize. Give them their family spokesman. But . . . I'll tell you what. Give it to them in the city. That way most of them will be out of here in a day or two. The news outlets won't want to spend the money on two teams of reporters. You'll get the freelancers, the paparazzi, but between the local cops and a couple of weeks of hired security—I'll pay for it—you can probably deal."

"Thank you, but I can pay—"

"Hey, Sus, don't look a fuckin' gift horse. You know the exact balance of your checking accounts, what your credit card bills are? You know your net worth like you know your phone number?"

"No, but I do have some sense of what we have. And Jonah was great at details and on top of everything. So I'm sure—"

"Look, ninety-nine percent of women avoid reality because it isn't pretty." I would have said "That's such a dumb, narrow-minded remark from such a smart person," but Fat Boy talked too fast, and I barely had enough energy to think it, much less say it. "But your reality is that less than a week ago, you thought Jonah was Dr. Nice Guy and in a million years he wouldn't go to a hooker—"

"Listen to me. I am positive—"

"—and that he'd live to be a hundred-year-old stud without eye bags. So be positive, if that's how you want to play it. Believe what you need to believe. But just understand there's a lot about your life you may not know shit about. I'm telling you that as a friend."

He wandered into the kitchen. By the time he came back fifteen minutes later, covered with streaks of confectioners' sugar, I'd forgotten he was in the house. I'd been concentrating on who could be a family spokesman and was getting nowhere.

"You had some good cookies in the freezer," he said.

I looked at the powdery streaks on his mouth and fingers and said, "Lemon curd cookies."

"Hey, I thought they tasted lemony."

"They're better at room temperature," I murmured. "I was thinking about a spokesperson. I considered calling Jonah's brother, Theo, asking him to find an appealing older actress, you know, someone with a big, comforting bosom and a lot of authority to play the role. Do you think that's a possibility?"

"S-U-X," Fat Boy said. "Sucks. Let me draw you a picture, Susie. You get an actress who depends on Theo for jobs, and you'll get someone willing to spout whatever lines he and his parents want to put out there, which could turn out to mean making them look good and you look bad. And don't ask me"—he raised his voice into a falsetto—"'why would they want to make me look bad if we're all family?'"

"Every time you imitate a woman," I said, "it comes out sounding like the same profoundly irritating person."

"I'm sure that's a comment fraught with psychoanalytic insight or some shit, but you're changing the subject. Still, the actress thing isn't a totally stupid idea."

"Thank you."

"Sure. You do need a pro. Don't even think of your cousin Schnooky or someone who's going to become an egomaniac after two minutes standing in front of a microphone bank. You need a PR type who's not in PR, because that went over like a fucking lead balloon with the JonBenét Ramsey parents." Fat Boy closed his eyes in thought and twisted his watch, which had gotten caught on one of the fat folds on his wrist. Then he looked at me. "Listen, I'll find someone. If you do it, you'll make the wrong calls, or start crying and sound like a potential pain in the ass, or try to get them to work for twenty bucks an hour."

"I wouldn't do that."

"It doesn't matter what you do. I'll do it better and faster," Fat Boy said. "You'll have someone in time for the six o'clock news."

Fat Boy was true to his word. Late that afternoon, he actually walked the quarter of a mile to the house. He was exhausted and triumphant, as if he'd just completed the Ironman. His shirt was soaked, like laundry when the spin cycle doesn't work. I handed him a giant glass of water and even managed my hydration speech, which he seemed to enjoy; I thought it made him feel like a jock. He told me he'd gotten a family spokesperson for me, someone named Kimberly Dijkstra, who had done some freelance writing for his hedge fund. "She was a reporter for *BusinessWeek* a hundred years ago. Steel-trap mind but comes off as warm and fuzzy—with big, maternal boobs, which is what you said you wanted. I kind of always liked those kind. Anyway, Andrea said you met her at one of our tree-trimming parties, so Kimberly can legitimately say she's known you for years. Trust me: She's good. She lives on East Seventy-fifth, in a town house, serious family money—and her parents were nice enough to die young, so it's all hers. She'll meet the press, so to speak. Do it in front of her house, which makes a good visual. A tree, window boxes, wealth . . . you will like it." I told him fine, although right now I couldn't think of anything I wanted. to say privately, much less publicly. "You don't have to think," Fat Boy said. "Kimberly will. And if she's stumped, she knows I'll have the answer."

Chapter Twelve

By the time of the funeral, I'd broken apart. Now I was two people. Naturally, there was Susie the Wreck, the new widow who slept two or three hours a night, who had to fight herself not to break into hiccupping sobs when she was with her boys. That wound up being twenty hours a day, since besides my not being able to sleep, Evan, Dashiell, and Mason each developed his own brand of insomnia.

In Evan's case, insomnia was plain not sleeping. I could see his exhaustion getting worse day by day. His endearing little-boy skinniness—ribs and vertebrae on display—went from healthy to skeletal. His fair, lightly freckled skin grew pale, then took on a greenish undertone. Red smudges appeared under his eyes, then darkened until he looked like a creepy character in a Tim Burton movie. In those rare hours I managed to fall asleep, I'd wake myself. *Evan? Is everything okay with Evan?* I pictured him lying on his side, eyes wide open, though not really seeing the stuffed animal sharing his pillow. My in-laws had brought one for each boy from their trip to Machu Picchu. I'd done the aren't-you-marvelous daughter-in-law bit: "What absolutely gorgeous llamas!" Even before the "ma" in "llama" was out of my mouth, Babs was shaking her head. "Actually," she said, "they're vicuñas."

Dashiell would wake up screaming. No words, just an endless shriek that slashed through the suburban night. One of Jonah's and my private names for him had been Blabbo the Talking Boy—Dash had been born with no internal shutoff device. But now, at night anyway, he'd become mute. "Dash, sweetie, tell Mommy what the bad dream was about." He'd suck in his lips and shake his head violently, *No! No!* as if he were certain an evil Someone was listening in to make sure he didn't break the code of silence.

Mason had never completely given up his infant sleep habits. It hadn't been that terrible; Jonah and I had taken turns getting up whenever he woke, going to his room to kiss his forehead. At worst, we'd have to sit on the edge of his bed for a couple of minutes, saying, "Shhh, go to sleep, Mase." After that, he'd be fine for another three hours. Maybe we should have Ferberized him early on, but he'd been the easiest of the triplets, so without even discussing it, we'd just allowed him the right to be a little annoying. Besides, our sleep deprivation had been so off the charts that our visits to his room barely registered.

Now, though, Mason was wide awake for at least a half hour each time he got up. I'd hold him and whisper "Easy, sweetie" or "Shhh." But no comfort could get him to stop pleading with me to come downstairs with him and wait for Daddy. I knew I had to be patient. I would explain exactly what I'd explained a few hours earlier: Daddy wasn't coming back. "Remember, honey? We talked about it, that Daddy died. And what did we say?" His head swiveled frighteningly fast. No, no, no. He wanted no part of reality. "When someone dies," I went on, "they *can't* come back. No matter how much we wish they could." No, no, no.

So there was that half of me, Susie the Wreck. But beside this exhausted, shaken, grieving mess, another me took form. Enraged Susie. "Enraged Susie" did sound ridiculous, even to me—Premenstrual Barbie meets Bride of Chucky. Except my rage had such power I was frightened by its destructiveness. What I couldn't deal with was the fury; I was consumed with flaming anger even when I had zero energy to drag myself from room to room. The tabloid headlines could barely get through the wall of my grief, yet at the same time, they sent me into a frenzy. I wanted to scream louder than any human being ever had. Neighbors, acres away, would call 911 in horror. The cops would hear my shrieks over their sirens as they sped from headquarters.

Left to myself, shielded by Kimberly the Spokesperson and Fat Boy's gift of two weeks of security goons watching the house, I wouldn't have seen those headlines. From the morning I woke up and Jonah wasn't there, I let the *Times* and *The Wall Street Journal* rot in their plastic bags in the driveway. And was I going to drive to the newsstand at the LIRR station to get a look at *The New York Post* and *The Daily News*? I saw the headlines because relatives and friends had decided the widow of a murdered thirty-nine-year-old man needed to know what the world had to say about her husband.

DOC SHOCK PARK AVENUE PLASTIC SURGEON FOUND SLAIN

UNKINDEST CUT COPS SAY PARK AVENUE "FACE ACE" STABBED.

NO TRACE OF "FACE ACE" HOOKER COPS STEP UP HUNT FOR MISSING CALL GIRL.

If I'd had a minute to reflect, I wouldn't have found the crassness of those front pages such a shock. A young, successful doctor, married, three kids, is stabbed to death in a whore's apartment. Was that a tabloid story or what? Sure, I would hate it. But no rational person would believe *The New York Post* would rethink its mission and decide, *Oh no, hawking this story would be cruel, to say nothing of tasteless!* But I hadn't had that minute to reflect.

I could have borne Susie the Wreck better if not for Enraged Susie. Sure, I knew about the connection between depression and anger; I'd had enough therapy to understand that just by pressing Play in my mind, I could hear the placid but breathy voice of my shrink, Dr. Twersky, saying: "Depression is anger turned inward."

"For God's sake," I told Dr. Twersky five hours before Jonah's funeral. "I am not turning my anger inward. I'm angry! I know I'm angry." There she was, in my kitchen, a shrink making a house call and at seven-thirty in the morning, so I could get to Manhattan in time. I'd been to the funeral home before: It was every Jewish doctor's last stop between New York and eternity, upscale, dowdy, but reassuring. The chapel didn't have crosses, though the vaulted ceiling had fluffy clouds painted on it. *Hey, don't worry,* the azure sky seemed to be reassuring, *there actually is a heaven, and you'll get in.*

"Inward anger is one thing," I went on. "Mine is outward!" Actually, I shouted it. But it was the sort of whispered shouting you do when you don't want to be overheard—like by your children. I'd made the mistake of telling Ida and Ingvild it would be okay if the boys raced their Hot Wheels trucks along the upstairs hallway. "What I'm feeling is actual rage!" Except by whispering it, I was coming off more like an angry Muppet than the near-psychotic I was. "Even if I wanted to keep it inward, goddammit, I couldn't."

"You just told me—" She always spoke slowly. Either she weighed her every word or feared making some hideous and eternally mockable Freudian slip. "—that you—" I watched and waited. She was wearing a pantsuit and hadn't wanted to take off the jacket. Now, as she sat in the straight-backed kitchen chair, the shoulders were riding way up. She looked like one of those overpadded, neckless football linemen, except in heavy navy tweed.

I didn't let her finish. "I just told you . . . what? That I'm depressed? Of course I am." I was on the verge of saying I felt like a dead person, but I stopped myself. She'd say, "Let's talk about what you mean by 'dead person.'" Instead, I said, "I feel like shit. Except shit would be an improvement."

Dr. Twersky nodded. Some weak sun made it through the window and shone on her reddish-blond hair. It lit up her frizzy corkscrew curls into something painterly. Usually, she looked like Little Orphan Annie's grandmother. "Feeling like shit . . ." she said carefully. "That sounds like an appropriate response to me."

"But if I'm feeling so dead and empty, plus on the verge of hysterical weeping, how can I also have all this rage? It's almost impossible to control. I'm so exhausted. I need it to stop. I'm afraid I'll lose it and start screaming. Or hurt everybody."

"Everybody?"

"Well, not the boys. But with everyone else, I get wild with fury at even the dumbest remark. You know, something just thoughtless, not even cruel. Or at least not intentionally cruel. I got crazed by people who were calling here to talk to me. Why the hell can't they wait for the funeral? Then I get angry at all the others, the ones who don't call: Do they have to stand on fucking ceremony?"

"And you say you have none of this anger toward the boys?"

"No, not toward them." I smoothed the ribbed cuffs of my sweater. I don't know how long I'd stood in my dressing room, debating what to wear for a shrink home visit on the day of my husband's funeral. Wool pants? No, too afternoony for such an early hour. I finally threw on jeans and a black sweater. But when the doorbell rang and I was running down the stairs, I thought, *Oh God, what if she thinks I'm going to wear this to the service?*

I hadn't wanted Dr. Twersky at the house. She'd called a couple of hours after the news of Jonah's murder got on TV, and started going on and on about how sorry she was. I wanted to pretend the connection was bad; if she thought I couldn't hear her, I could say "What? What? I can't hear you" and hang up. I did try to lose her with "I really, really appreciate your calling" and babbling about how I wished I could get over to see her but I really didn't have time because as soon as the medical examiner released the body—Jonah—we'd have the funeral the next day.

That was when she offered to come over, which naturally made me wonder, *Is she doing this because she just wants to get a look at the house?* Because when I'd gone on and on in one session about picking yellow alabaster for the countertop in the downstairs guest bathroom—even though I wasn't supposed to be, because talking about objects was masking a psychological issue I obviously wanted to avoid—I realized she was leaning forward. Yellow alabaster! Obviously high on Dr. Twersky's emotional resonance chart.

Then I kept worrying if this session was going to be a freebie because I definitely didn't ask her to come. She volunteered. Or would she send me a bill? Fine, it was a professional relationship, but what if she billed me for, like, time and a half because it was so early in the morning, or because it was a house call? Now, sitting with her at the kitchen table, that all-American place for honesty, I realized I couldn't get away with saying I hadn't gotten angry at all with the boys. Fine: I admitted to her that I was so wiped that I didn't have my usual resistance to their noise, and that Mason's inability to comprehend that dead meant dead after I'd explained it a hundred times was getting to me. It made me want to break down and cry. In fact, one time I did. But I left out how a couple of times I wanted to grab him by the shoulders and shake him until his head rocked and he cried "What? What do you want, Mommy?" and I'd scream, with spit flying out of my mouth, "Never, ever talk about Daddy coming back again!"

Then I changed the subject to how, within a few hours of the newspapers coming out, before they even got to the autopsy, I'd picked up the remote in our closet–dressing room area, just out of habit. FOX News came on because Bernadine, our housekeeper, was not only a right-wing nut but had a fixation on Bill Hemmer that went way beyond a crush. Just as I was about to turn off the TV, I glanced up. They were cutting from a reporter in front of the UN back to the news desk.

Behind the anchor—a woman who'd had serial face-lifts that made her mouth look like it was experiencing major g-forces on blastoff—was a giant screen. On it was Jonah's photo from Manhattan Aesthetics' website. And Awful Face-lifts on FOX was telling her male co-anchor, Obvious But Not Terrible Eye Job, that Jonah had been "stabbed to death in the apartment of a notorious Upper East Side prostitute." She went on about Jonah being known as "king of the tummy tuckers," which wasn't true; he did much more face and some breast work. Then she said he was "a well-known Democrat activist," which was true if that meant someone who'd gone to one cocktail party for Obama.

Then she got to the family: first, Kimberly the Spokesperson, saying, "Mrs. Gersten has no reason to doubt her husband's love for her and their little boys." Then they played a video of me and Jonah. It must have come from somebody's black-tie wedding, or maybe a Mount Sinai benefit, because I was in an Armani, a strapless cobalt taffeta, from about five years before, that had never fit in the bust after my pregnancy. Jonah's arm was around me, and we were standing in a group, but they'd put our heads in a highlighted oval. It made us not just more visible to TV viewers but look like some golden couple among grayed-out dullards. I couldn't follow much of what the anchor was saying beyond "wife and triplets, four years old!" as if the boys being four made Jonah's murder or his being at a prostitute's— whichever—infinitely worse than if they'd been three or five.

"And," I added, "they had a close-up of our 2008 holiday card, with the boys sitting on a beautiful horse. Light chestnut or something. From when we were up in Aspen, in a glen with Ponderosa pines and aspens all around. Well, of course aspens. There's a . . . I guess it's a lake in the background. I don't remember it, but it's there on the card."

Dr. Twersky gave a nod and said something. Maybe "Uh-huh."

"It was really strange," I went on. "I was so shocked at seeing all of us up there that it felt like my heart stopped beating. But I was too stunned to worry *Am I getting a heart attack?* And I didn't get at all angry then."

"Do you remember anything else you might have felt?" For the second time, I saw her glancing over to the cooking island. I'd hollowed out a giant Savoy cabbage and filled it with white roses and Genista. She was probably thinking how superficial I was, bothering about arranging flowers when I had a dead husband to worry about. To be fair, maybe she was thinking that it was healing that I could lose myself in flowers, even for a couple of minutes.

Once Dr. Twersky left (after an inordinate amount of time in the yellow alabaster guest bathroom), I spent the next hour making brown sugar cookies with the boys, for whoever came back to the house after the cemetery. I figured it would be a good way to get the three of them to calm down after their truck races and also let them feel they were participating in the day. Also, I wanted to give Ida and Ingvild a break; based on their kindness over the last few days, they could qualify for sainthood.

I cried so much that day. Not just from grief, because I'd been grieving since they found Jonah, and even before, in anticipation. This time my tears were from being in this packed chapel with almost three hundred people demanding face time to tell me "What a terrible, terrible loss." Many of them meant it. "Susie, I'm so sorry." It was like someone else's car radio you couldn't turn off; I was stuck with listening to their every word. Yet all I heard of the rabbi's eulogy was "We have a right to ask, 'Where is God in all this?'" The rabbi probably offered an answer, though I didn't catch it.

Apparently, he went on for a while. One of Florabella's best customers, Caddy Demas, came running over—or whatever it's called in stiletto heels with anorexic ankles—just as I was getting into the limo to go to the cemetery. Her gloved hand tugged at my coat sleeve. "Susie, I just have to tell you. That rabbi may have gone on for what? twenty minutes? but it was so incredibly moving that nobody cared." Her gloves were persimmon suede with black satin skirtlike things flaring out at the wrists, a look for the woman whose devotion to fashion was so maniacal she was proud to look like the fourth musketeer.

By that time, I was little more than a robot programmed to respond "Thank you" when spoken to. But Caddy had a standing five-hundred-dollar-a-week order with us, and so was capable of overriding my circuitry. I wound up saying, "Oh, Caddy, thank you *so* much for sharing that with me," a sentence I normally would not only refuse to utter but would make me gag. Maybe it wasn't that she was a valuable customer; maybe it was dawning on me that I needed to be nicer to people.

With three little kids, I was facing the world as a different person. Whatever points a widow inherited from her husband's status weren't going to guarantee me a spot on the A-team anymore. "Stabbed to death" might make for interesting conversation, but Jonah's demise at a call girl's apartment would be taken to mean that Susie hadn't been able to satisfy him. Or that someone like me had managed to score a privileged-attractive-charming-gifted-successful Yale doctor only because he was one deeply twisted dude.

Chapter Thirteen

"How has it been, dealing with her?" my brother-in-law asked. Our heads turned toward the living room and his mother.

"Fine," I said. Theo gave me a look, so I said, "Doable. But she seems to be avoiding eye contact with me. Normally, that would throw me. But I'm too far gone to be thrown."

"Let me tell you: When a person comes to the end of her rope and she's sure there are no more terrors life can hold, that's only because she hasn't met my mother yet. You're never too far gone."

"Your mother can be a challenge, to put it mildly," I agreed. "But she loved Jonah so much. She and I are going through the same hell now. The last thing I want is for her to withdraw from me. Trust me, Theo: I understand what your parents—and you—are living through now, what you went through from the minute Jonah was missing. This is just as terrible for you as it is for me."

Theo flipped his stylishly messy hair off his forehead. "No. Look, they lost a child, but he'd had a life: He accomplished, he gave them grandchildren. I lost a brother who was always great

to me, even way back, when I was *the* primo pain in the ass."
Jonah would not have put that completely in the past tense, but
I nodded. "For me, a brother like him was a perpetual reminder
that you don't have to be a shit or a bore to get where you want
to go. He was such a good man, but he didn't wear his goodness
like, you know, Thomas More in *The Tudors*. He was fun. But
for you: We're not just talking close relative here. We're talking father of your children, triplets, for God's sake. And your
lover."

"My dearest friend, too." My voice might have trembled a
little, but by late afternoon, I was cried out, at least until after
everybody left. "He understood me so totally, right from the
start. And he loved me a hundred percent. He wasn't looking to
make changes."

"Sucks," he murmured.

"And then some."

It was the third night of shiva, the weeklong period of mourning. Theo and I had successfully hidden ourselves in plain sight
in the hallway between the guest bathroom and living room.
Momentarily, we were safe from the damp kisses and messy
condolences from the almost two hundred visitors coming each
day.

The seven-day grieving period probably had been a brilliant custom for a sixteenth-century Polish village, where you
could spend a whole lifetime meeting fewer than two hundred
people. But in the twenty-first century, Babs, Clive, Theo, and
I were overwhelmed with visitors from the different universes
we inhabited. We had doctors, of course, smooth-browed plastic surgeons and rumpled oncologists. Babs's crew of cosmetic-
industry executives was discernible because they looked like
they'd inherited their eyelashes from a mink. The theater and
New York movie types from Theo's casting life reminded me of
academics—the only other group I knew who wore their scarves
indoors.

From my life, floral types set down flowers that could have been plucked from the Garden of Eden when God's back was turned. Event planners came bearing excessively inventive sympathy baskets. Someone brought French preserves, a wheel of Reblochon, and baguettes tied around and around with tricouleur ribbon probably left over from a Bastille Day party. Another came with a Limoges plate on which she'd arranged gargantuan dried apricots and pears into a giant rose.

Neighbors came, too, from all the Gersten territories, suburban Long Island, Manhattan, the Hamptons. So did our best friends from high school, college, and the present. Obscure third cousins appeared, insisting on drawing family trees on the backs of business cards. It was all too much.

Every few sentences, Theo or I would glance over at Babs. She sat so far back in the wing chair—Jonah's chair—that her black lizard Manolo flats weren't touching the floor. I kept waiting for her to inch forward, as she was in deep dialogue with her blue-eyed rabbi. It seemed like a one-way conversation—she talked, he leaned in to listen. But she sat straight, speaking slowly but intensely, her head pressing against the chair's high back.

"I'm glad I'm not a fly on that wall," Theo remarked. "I'm sure she's saying something that would infuriate me." He shuddered in a way that made his glossy, longish hair flop charmingly. "Or humiliate me beyond belief."

"Maybe just embarrass you," I countered.

"Not that 'embarrass' is a natural segue, but are your parents coming tonight?" Even when trying to hide distaste, a lot of people broadcast it through small gestures—nose wrinkling or corner-of-mouth twisting. Theo's giveaway was always over the top in its lack of subtlety. He would jerk back his head in distaste as if he'd just spotted a conga line of cockroaches. I thought it was hilarious, though Jonah had a theory that Theo's hostility level was so off the charts that while politeness required everyone else to hide their "What a loser" or "Outrageously cheap wine" comments, Theo had to let it out. His "your parents" and head jerk occurred in the same instant.

"No, they're not coming," I told him. "My mother had a sinus attack. From my flowers, she said. She disapproves of flowers inside houses. Right after I dropped out of school and moved to New Haven, she went through an environmental-activist phase. It lasted about three weeks. But that was just when I moved in with Jonah and landed a designer job with *the* best florist in New Haven. When I told her about it, she did her quiet 'oh' first. She just says 'oh,' then stops. Gives you enough time for your heart to sink. Then she said, 'There are some of us who believe nature is a not-for-profit corporation.' I had some brilliant response, like 'Huh?' She got this really huffy tone: 'Some of us might ask if the florist business is ethical. You have to admit it does rip off nature.' So I asked her, 'What about farmers?' She couldn't think of an answer, so she backed down.

"But a couple of months later, she was sitting next to a basket of dahlias and bittersweet I'd done. All of a sudden she started clearing her throat about a million times. Then she said, 'The doctor thinks I may have developed an allergy to flowers indoors, when there's no ventilation.' She still does her allergy act whenever she remembers. Sometimes she rubs where her sinuses hurt. Except Jonah said where she's rubbing would be for TMJ pain, not sinusitis. Anyway, my father offered to come by himself tonight, but I could hear the relief in his voice when I told him he should stay home, rest up."

A minute later, we glanced back into the living room. Babs had fallen silent. The rabbi looked like he was trying to recall Pastoral Relations 101, the lecture called "When Communication Is Awkward." Suddenly, Babs burst into tears. She patted her lap, blindly searching for her handkerchief, unfolded it, and pressed it against her eyes with both palms.

"You can't see from here," Theo said. "But I bet you anything her Gigi de Lavallade waterproof mascara is still working."

I stopped the smile before it got to my face and said, "Theo, stop!" My brother-in-law had the bad-boy appeal of a precocious kid. People were forever shaking their heads at his scandalous remarks while being charmed at his wicked assessments. With him around, I was the nice one, but we'd always enjoyed verbal tennis, volleying remarks back and forth. So in this brief, bright time-out from the darkness of Jonah's murder, I was on the verge of responding that Babs could use the mascara's reliability for a first-person "My Tragedy, My Mascara" ad campaign. Theo would like that one, but I couldn't take the risk. He could easily become a loose cannon, and my remark was great ammunition the next time he decided to zing Babs: "I know your mother is in terrible pain."

Theo leaned back, tilting one of the antique prints of ferns hanging in the hallway. Though he obviously heard the scrape of frame against wall, he didn't say anything like "Oh, sorry," the way most people would have. He just shifted and spoke, his voice relaxed yet somehow flat, as if he were chatting about an actress not quite talented enough to play the mother in a movie he was casting. "She's probably in pain because my father wants to go straight back to work and not take a post-shiva week in Saint Barth to console her, which means she's feeling pressure to go back to work before she's ready."

"So you're telling me not to go gently with her?" I asked. "I mean, if she's feeling pressured."

"No. Be however you want to be. Say whatever needs saying. Well, easy for me to say. I am her son, which I guess entitles me to special treatment from her. The Best of Babs: Good, Bad, Ugly. You know, I had an internship at a rep company out in L.A. the summer between my junior and senior years at Wesleyan. Okay, I'd been to camp and on teen tours, but that was the first time I was really away from my parents' world. Not that summer theater is the place to go if you're big on genuineness, but I felt so *right* there. What's really strange, though, is even driving out there, I went through Terre Haute, Indiana, and I thought how much easier my life would have been if I'd grown up there. I'd never realized before how—I don't know—complex, difficult, it had been living in my parents' world."

I could almost feel Jonah beside me, whispering in my ear, "See? You asked a question about you, and what did it become? All about Theo." He'd be smiling, less with pleasure than with satisfaction that he had his brother's MO down pat.

I had to get back into the living room. Heads were starting to swivel. Visitors were searching for me so they could say, "This must be such a nightmare for you!" and still have enough time to get home for *American Idol*. But my bro-in-law didn't want to let me go.

"I call it my parents' world," Theo continued, "but my mother rules."

I'd told Jonah once that Theo reminded me of those sprites or whatever in a Shakespearean comedy. Not gay, I'd added. He was definitely a hetero sprite, but he was unusually graceful and was always making delightfully wicked comments. Jonah replied that the problem was his brother often didn't see the difference between being wickedly witty and being a mean little shit.

I waved to Andrea at the far end of the living room, but she missed the urgency of my *Come get me!* signal and just waved back. I hoped a few seconds of silence would discourage him, but Theo wasn't going anywhere. I finally said, "You'd think with your father being an oncologist, he'd be more . . . not aggressive. Assertive. He'd know what's important in life."

Theo took over. "He knows cancer is important. But cancer isn't all there is in the world. The only other thing he ever knew was that being the son of a podiatrist with a plantar's-wart specialty wasn't a ticket to the A-list. More than anything, my father wanted to be a someone. He was like the Little Match Boy, staring in on people living—whatever—elegantly. He so wanted in, but he didn't have a key to the door. That's where my mother came in. 'This is the biography to read, the film to see, the primary candidate we should support. Wear a white dinner jacket for formal occasions between Memorial Day and Labor Day. Stop ordering risotto because risotto is so 2001.' It's all about surfaces with her. Look what she does for a living: marketing director for a cosmetics company. Can you get more superficial than that?"

Naturally, I didn't say "How about the last movie you cast?" *Call 666-SATAN* was not only superficial but supremely lousy. Also, as Jonah pointed out, totally miscast. Then again, Theo wasn't exactly coming home to voice mail from Martin Scorsese. He worked for deeply minor theater companies and film directors whose common goal seemed to be making bad imitations of successful horror, soft-core porn, and hacked-up teenager movies. So I said, "I don't know about superficial, but your mother is capable of love. You—" Theo shook his head: *No. She doesn't love me.* Arguing with him would have taken too much time, so I kept going. "She loved Jonah."

"Absolutely."

"She loves the boys. I know she sees them as individuals, not just the triplets."

"That's true. She—the two of them—are the quintessential doting grandparents. Granted, it's baby-boomer chic, being crazy about your grandchildren. But they are completely besotted. Well, she told my father he was completely besotted, so that's what he is. And that will be great for you."

I didn't get what he meant. Normally, to avoid the Gersten I-Must-Be-Patient-with-Your-Stupidity deep breath, I would have said sure, but I'd waited too long. As Theo inhaled, I was forced to ask, "What do you mean, great for me?"

"I mean she's not going to do anything to alienate you. Don't you see why? She's smart enough to know that, ultimately, alienating you would also mean alienating the grandchildren. You are the doorkeeper."

"What?"

"You control access to the boys. Also, if my parents didn't do right by you and word got out, they'd look bad. It's not comme il faut to fuck over your late son's widow."

Just as I was wondering if he meant his parents could deal with their son's murder but not with looking bad, Fat Boy came into the hall, double-timing it from the living room on his way to the bathroom. I noticed a macadamia nut drop from the huge fistful he was trying to hide by stuffing his hand into a too-tight side pocket. Since I didn't want to make him uncomfortable about having to squeeze by the two of us, I parted from Theo with "Later."

"Later" took quite a while, because I made the mistake of saying "Why don't we sit down?" to Gilbert John Noakes and his wife, Coral. She was a long-limbed Englishwoman. Though her looks made you think, *Oh, more graceful than a gazelle,* Coral lurched through life like a bad actor imitating a drunk, which I guessed she was. It was hard to tell, because all she ever drank in public was sparkling water, yet she showed the signs: Most of her sentences made you wonder whether you'd mis-heard—they were Britishly enunciated and probably grammatical, but they didn't make sense. Also, she was dangerous in any space containing antique vases and other people's feet—such as my living room.

Once we were seated, though, I was hardly able to speak to the Noakeses. People kept crowding around me like I was a Nancy Gonzalez sale table at Bergdorf's. I got that phobic feeling of *Oh my God, not enough air,* so I stood. That left the two of them gazing up at me, but at least I didn't feel like the oxygen was being sucked out of my lungs.

I sensed Coral and Gilbert John would understand my getting up, or pretend to, or not notice, and they wouldn't disappear from my life. I could look forward, unfortunately, to still being asked to their dinner parties. Gilbert John would invite a mix of doctors, potential patients, and what he called "interesting young people," which meant anyone under thirty who wore retro eyeglasses. Coral used a caterer who always served what Jonah had called "elderly chicken" with halves of grapes and a curdled white sauce. But maybe I'd be too tainted by the scandal of Jonah's murder to be asked to dine chez Noakes. They might take me to a restaurant every six months. Without the comfort of knowing I could at least laugh about them on the ride home, how could I bear it? Gilbert John would rake a fork tine on a tablecloth to show me the pattern of his newest mosaic, thereby competing with Coral's convoluted conversation about English gardens of her youth, though she could never remember the names of flowers: "The purplish ones with . . ." She'd fluff a couple of fingers outward, waiting expectantly, so I'd wind up guessing iris, anemone, cosmos. No to each. "Passionflower, echinacea?" Again a no.

At very long last, they stood to say goodbye. Gilbert John's chapped lips felt like an emery board against my cheek. "We'll speak soon," he said. Coral put her cheek to mine. As I kissed the air, she said, "If there's anything . . ." She must have thought she'd completed a sentence, because she turned and walked away. Gilbert John hurried to catch up and grab her elbow. He steered her across the rest of the living room so if she did trip over any feet, they would be her own.

I realized that by standing up, I'd become a one-woman receiving line for friends, relatives, and everyone else, from the long-retired coach of Jonah's high school tennis team to a Baptist minister who'd sat with me on the board of the Nassau County Coalition Against Domestic Violence. All the heartfelt words that came my way—"So very, very sorry" and "I know nothing I say can ease your pain, but . . ."—were offset by Buddy Gratz, a local pharmacist who elbowed his way into a knot of neighbors and in history's loudest recorded whisper confided to them, "Hey, can you *believe* the cops haven't found that hooker yet?"

Shudders passed through the room. But before the whispered "Oh my God's" that would mortify me even more got started, there was a Distraction with a capital D—as well as Drama. As "that hooker" still echoed, every head turned to a spot ten feet behind me. Right on the borderline between the entry hall and living room stood a tall, slim exclamation mark of a woman. Something about her drew attention, like the giant horseshoe magnets in science class that pulled in all those iron filings.

And there she was, Ethel O'Shea, my mother's mother, a woman I'd seen only twice in my life. Grandly, she swooped into the living room on the arm of her lover, Felicia Burns, whom everyone called Sparky. Halfway over to me, Ethel came to a halt. As we all waited for her to speak, she lifted her liposuctioned chin. In a voice that made Buddy Gratz's remark sound like silence, she declared, "Susie, dear girl! Grandma is here!"

Chapter Fourteen

For Babs, the blue-eyed rabbi became history. Like everyone else's in the living room, her gaze kept racing from Grandma Ethel to me and back again. For those who knew my family history, here, in pants and a black Malo turtleneck, was the anti-mom, the dreadful woman who'd walked out on her eight-year-old child. Heartless. But hey, did she look fabulous.

For the rest—showtime! There was the new widow greeting a woman who was practically her clone. Except the clone had called herself Grandma, so she must be, what? In her late seventies? Amazing, because the clone was simply not an old lady. She had fabulous hair, astoundingly lush for someone her age, deep gold and platinum—colors from a treasure chest. She wore it twisted into a soft knot pinned with careful casualness on top of her head.

Their thoughts were so loud I could hear them. *Look at her and Susie!* The same long arms and legs. Necks that came close to qualifying for swan status. Straight noses that Jonah once swore no plastic surgeon could replicate. Cheekbones like that of Mrs. Genghis Khan. And those mesmerizing eyes, so pale they were barely on the green side of white.

Seeing Ethel O'Shea was seeing the future me. Thankfully, since I was a superficial person, it was not a nightmare vision, though it didn't make me think, *Hey, I can't wait till I'm seventy-eight!*

I kissed my grandmother on the cheek, inhaling the Gardenia Passion I'd smelled the other two times we'd been together. I kissed Sparky, who was scentless. I'd met her about five years earlier, when she and Ethel had come to New York and Jonah and I had taken them out for dinner. My grandmother had introduced us by putting her arm around Sparky's shoulders and saying, "This is the love of my life." Sparky had grinned and said, "Ethel's got that line down pat."

"Susie, I am so, so sorry," Sparky began. She was a civil liberties lawyer. Every word she spoke, probably even "with milk and Splenda," came out loaded with passion and conviction. "Jonah was a wonderful guy. I only wish we'd had the chance to spend more time with him."

"He was beyond wonderful," Grandma Ethel corrected. "A total doll." Those in the audience close enough to hear her lines nodded in agreement. "You couldn't help loving him. He didn't hold back, you know what I mean?" Sparky nodded. Since she was the expert on how to handle my grandmother, I decided nodding was the way to go. "You know what was remarkable about Jonah? None of that 'Let me see if you're worth my while before I'm nice to you' crap. He was so decent. To everyone, even the waiter. Remember? Also, there wasn't an ounce of that bullshit gemütlichkeit successful men use to show they're not the arrogant putzes they actually are."

Compared to Grandma Ethel's greeting and what I'd come to recognize as her brassy talk-show-hostess style, her remarks were soft-spoken. Still, that didn't stop her magnetism. She didn't have to shout to draw all the attention in the room, even from those out of hearing distance. Babs, along with everyone else, was probably reflecting on the triumph of nature over nurture, as in: *The two of them have the same taste in clothes! Look at them. Black slacks, black turtlenecks, diamond stud earrings. True, the grandmother has about ten gold bangles on her right wrist, while Susie's wearing a wide gold mesh cuff. But that's more a generational thing than a different fashion sensibility.*

Finally, I sensed the *Oy!* and *Good grief!* reactions to the resemblance had gotten played out. Almost everyone in the room, Babs included, lost interest in me and got busy assessing the dynamics between Grandma Ethel and the woman whose arm she was holding. *That is definitely not the way an old-fashioned lady would take the arm of a hired companion or a good friend—not with her boob brushing the other one's upper arm.*

As for that other woman, mid- to late fifties. She's wearing a pantsuit. Wait, call it what it is: a suit that probably had GEN-TLEMEN'S CUSTOM CLOTHIER *on the label. Tropical wool, winter white. Worn with an open-necked white shirt. She looks like a sugar magnate in pre-Castro Cuba, minus the mustache, of course. She is definitely not masculine.*

Not that she's feminine, either. Though she, too, is wearing diamond stud earrings, hers are major, close to three carats each. By the time she gets to be the grandmother's age, her earlobes could resemble a beagle's. She isn't wearing a stitch of makeup, but she's good-looking in that "dark brown hair, sparkly brown eyes, tanned skin, pug nose" way. She could belong to any group that fell under the heading Caucasian, from English in a sunny climate to Sicilian with a nose job.

I glanced through the knots of visitors and watched my mother-in-law rising from her chair. Though only five feet three, Babs had that head-held-high posture that demanded deference: *I get introduced first.* She saw me looking at her and smiled a little—sadly, of course. Still, it was enough to tell me my social quotient had risen with the arrival of a stylish lesbian grandmother (carrying a Prada clutch under her arm). If, in the past, Babs had formed any mental picture of Ethel the Abandoner, it probably had been a crone version of my mother, Sherry Rabinowitz: Mrs. Potato Head but much more wrinkled, wearing a T-shirt that said DON'T CALL ME SWEETIE . . . IT'S BAD FOR YOUR TEETH.

"My grandmother Ethel O'Shea and Felicia Burns," I began, using the Spanish/Miami pronunciation Felicia preferred— *Fee-lee-see-a.* "This is my mother-in-law, Barbara Gersten."

Since shiva was not just a sad occasion but a religious tradition with its built-in formality, there was no follow-up of "Please call me Sparky/Babs." Grandma Ethel took Babs's hands in hers, closed her eyes for a moment as if searching, searching, for the perfect words. "Oh, Barbara. I am so sorry we have to meet on such a terrible occasion. But what a first-rate man Jonah was! Trust me. I've been around the block many, many times in my life, and I never met a better man than Jonah."

She was right. Throughout our entire marriage, I did believe there was no better man than Jonah. Still, I knew there was a 97 percent chance my grandmother's tribute was full of shit. Not that she didn't think positively about him—doctor/charming/ Gen X non-homophobe/nice pecs, not flabby tits—but that was probably as far as her enthusiasm went. Nevertheless, my mother-in-law, so wise in the ways of social fakery (having the ultimate insider's view), appeared genuinely moved by Grandma Ethel's words.

"He was wonderful," Babs agreed. "The best." She could barely get the words out because she was so choked up. "Thank you for saying so."

"I just met him once," Sparky spoke up. "But I knew right away, this guy is the real deal. I'm sorry that you, your husband, Susie, your whole family have to suffer a loss like this."

"I can't tell you how much I appreciate your kindness," Babs said. "Coming up here from Miami in the middle of winter."

"How could we not?" Grandma Ethel demanded. "We're family."

As Babs and my grandmother went back and forth, I watched

them with something between disbelief and awe. Grandma Ethel had spent twenty-five years hosting *Talk of Miami*. Even in the bit of it I'd gotten to see, in a single week, she could run the gamut of emotions from A to Z, then back from Z to A— depending on if she was interviewing a celebrity chef, a victim of ethnic cleansing in Rwanda, or a sixty-something actress who had written a memoir claiming simultaneous affairs with Adlai Stevenson and Grace Kelly. I couldn't decide if my grandmother felt all those emotions, or any of them. But she'd definitely acted as if she did.

And then there was my mother-in-law. Babs's life was dedicated to convincing women around the world that by laying out seventy-two dollars for a jar containing a buck's worth of petroleum jelly and chemicals, they would soon look like a million. She and Grandma Ethel shared two dualities: an ability to manipulate other people and a powerful ambition to be a somebody. Most likely, they also shared a common ruthlessness. What felt weird was watching my self-centered grandmother trying so hard to make my mother-in-law feel better—and my snooty mother-in-law reaching out to someone from my family, of all people, for the comfort and healing no one else seemed able to provide.

Just as I started to worry about what to do after their conversation ran its course, Sparky put her hand on my grandmother's shoulder. "Eth, honey, let's see if we can find a quiet spot so we can spend some time with Susie." She offered a brief, regretful smile to Babs, who offered her an *Of course I understand* nod. As Babs retreated, Andrea teleported over, and Grandma Ethel managed to simultaneously charm her and brush her off with a "Heard so much about you/loved meeting you" goodbye.

Sparky, definitely a take-charge type, herded my grandmother and me toward the piano bench and commanded, "Sit there." The living room was packed with people, and there was no seat for her. Glancing around, she decided Cousin Scott the tax examiner didn't need the chair he'd carried in from the dining room for himself. She had him bring it over and place it beside us, then gave him a thank-you that conveyed, without words, *Get out of here*—which he did.

"Is that nerdy man a relative of mine?" Grandma Ethel asked.

"No," I said. "He's a Rabinowitz. He's a semi-decent guy, actually."

"'Semi-decent' is not a ringing endorsement. Does your father wear hideous ties like that? What made someone think green and black ought to be combined into a houndstooth pattern?"

"My father's ties are hideous in a different way. He's into random splotches." I took a deep breath. "In case you're worried about my parents being here tonight, you can relax. They're not coming."

"I know," Grandma Ethel said.

"You know?—"

Sparky cut in, "We came up the second we heard about Jonah. But then Ethel thought our coming here might set off your mother, which would be rough for you, and—"

"We didn't want to give you any more grief," my grandmother said. "You have enough. So I looked up their number and called it the next couple of nights. No one answered. What's with them that they don't have voice mail? In any case, I called tonight, and she answered." I couldn't find the words to form a "And what did you say?" question, but she answered it anyway. "Naturally, I wasn't going to talk to her. I hung up. But at least I knew the coast would be clear for us to come here." She pulled back her head and gave me a haughty look. "What was there for me to say to her? 'Hello, little Sherry, this is your mother' would be awkward. And am I supposed to say 'I'm sorry I walked out and left you with that loser Lenny'?"

"What would be wrong with that?" I asked, amazing myself.

"Ethel's too ashamed," Sparky said, aligning the cuffs of her jacket. "And probably scared shitless."

"I am not!" Grandma Ethel snapped at her.

"Of course you are. The only thing in the world you're afraid of is your own child."

"I am not afraid! Except of being bored. When we had dinner with you and Jonah, Susie sweets, and you brought those pictures from your wedding, I took one look at Sherry and said—I think I said it to myself—that kid grew up to be one heavy piece of furniture. You know? Something in the middle of the room everyone wishes wasn't there but can't move."

"You just said you don't want to give Susie any more grief, Eth," Sparky snapped, "so why don't you zip it up about her mother?"

"Fine," my grandmother snapped back. She slid back on the piano bench to see me better, but we were still pretty close. Looking into her eyes was like seeing my own eyes in a magnifying mirror, except all the skin around them was covered with fine wrinkles, like a veil on an old-fashioned ladies' hat. "I wish there was something I could do for you, Susie," she said to me. "I mean it."

"Thank you," I said.

"Is there something?" I shook my head. She went on, "I wasn't kidding about what I said about Jonah, you know. Not my customary crapola. Good guy. Emotionally developed. Not your typical surgeon. And he was crazy for you. You know that."

"I thought so."

"Listen, sweet one, I'm an expert. I can smell a lousy marriage a mile away. Anyone's, not just the three stinkos I wound up with. But yours, it smelled like a rose. An antique rose, like you said the first time we met, when I wanted to know why roses didn't smell anymore and you told me about . . . antique and something else."

"Rosa rugosa, probably."

"Right. Anyway, the two of you were the real thing. You had a *marriage* there. Not just a husband."

Finally, I said, "Then why did it have to end like this?"

"You mean in his being killed?"

"Not just that. I could have dealt with Jonah dying, even with him being murdered. Painful beyond belief, a wound that would never heal completely, but still, I'd keep going. But to have him stabbed to death *there,* in an apartment of someone like her. It's too much." Somehow I was able to speak those last three words quietly, even though they wanted to be shrieked.

"It is too much," Sparky responded. She said it like an established fact, which for some reason made me feel better. "Are you getting a lot of 'You have to go on for the sake of the children'?"

"That's all I hear. 'Terrible, terrible, but you have to go on for the boys.' Like I don't know that. I want to tell them, 'You know, I was thinking of giving up and letting them raise themselves, but thanks to you, I'll keep going.'"

"People are shmucks," Grandma Ethel said.

"Some of them," Sparky agreed. "But others understand the awfulness of the circumstances. I'm not trying to make chicken salad out of chicken shit. Say, three quarters of the people in this room are loving the schadenfreude thrill, wallowing in the pleasure of someone else's misery; most of them also feel grief for you. Compassion, too." Sitting on the piano bench in the corner, I kept glancing one way to my grandmother, then the other to Sparky, whose vivid personality and wide shoulders blocked off the rest of the room. I'd temporarily forgotten the house was filled with people I should be paying attention to, though I couldn't think of a way to get up and say "Excuse me." Also, I didn't want to be with anyone else, just the two of them. "Listen," Sparky went on, "I'm a civil liberties lawyer. By nature and profession, I'm cynical. I fight for causes most people don't even want defended. But I've learned that too much cynicism can hurt you. If you let yourself be overly skeptical of other people's motives, all you'll do is isolate yourself."

"What Sparks is really saying," Grandma Ethel broke in, "is

that you might be . . . what's the psychological term for what you're doing? I forget. Transposing? Displacing? Anyway, you're putting what you're thinking on to them. Like you've got it in your head, *They're laughing about Jonah — happy husband, ha ha — getting killed by a hooker.* But you tell yourself it's what they're thinking because you can't deal with the anger, embarrassment, whatever. That he was with someone like her."

"Fuck off, Eth," Sparky said quietly. "That's not what I was saying. And not at all what I was thinking."

"Whatever you say, Sparky."

"And you shouldn't be talking that way in front of Susie." As there seemed to be zero comprehension on my grandmother's part, Sparky added, "She's your granddaughter, for God's sake. Act protective. No, excuse me. *Be* protective." Her eyes got an angry crinkle on the sides as she spoke. When her gaze returned to me, her eyes didn't exactly mist up, though they did soften into a sad benevolence. "She didn't mean to hurt you," Sparky said.

"What? Did I leave the room so you can explain me to my granddaughter?" Grandma Ethel demanded. She patted the top of my hand twice. Then, sensing something more in the way of maternal warmth might be called for, she offered a third pat. "Susie, I didn't mean to hurt you."

"I know." I took Sparky's word for it more than hers.

"The minute we heard about Jonah on CNN? I mean, it's good I've got a heart of stone. But right then and there, I knew I had to be with you. Not that there's anything I can do, but . . . I don't know."

"I'm glad you both came," I said. "I'm sorry I didn't think to call you, so it's extra meaningful that you just picked up and came on your own." Sparky nodded. My grandmother did an *aw-shucks* shrug/head tilt — as if auditioning for a cowgirl role — and gazed down at her suede ankle-high boots. I continued, "You're right about me being angry. Humiliated, too. I mean, God, Jonah being killed at a hooker's. But, Grandma Ethel,

I'm not taking my thoughts and sticking them in other people's heads. I read expressions. I overhear remarks." She looked up at me. I wondered whether her lashes had always been sparse or if she'd lost them with age. "Trust me: There are plenty of 'What do you think was missing in their relationship that made Jonah need a whore?' conversations going on. And comments like 'Susie is all about appearances, and with a crappy economy affecting Jonah's practice, he probably just wanted a nice, simple fuck without any pressure or demands.'"

"I'll take your word for it," Grandma Ethel said.

My back was hurting from sitting on the piano bench without any support. My neck ached from the weight of my head. Grandma Ethel, on the other hand, sat straight and looked supremely comfortable. I said, "My mind understands what Jonah probably went to Dorinda Dillon's apartment for. It has to, because it can't find any other explanation that it can believe. But you want to know something? My heart will never accept it. It's contrary to everything I ever knew or felt about him and our relationship." She nodded. I turned to Sparky. She wasn't nodding, so I added, "Maybe because not accepting it is the only way I can keep going."

"Then let me give you some advice," Grandma Ethel said. "Fuck logic. Why torment yourself? If your heart says, 'He was a good and faithful husband,' go with it. You have every right to tell yourself, 'Maybe he was in a whore's apartment, but not for sex.' Period. End of sentence."

Chapter Fifteen

Closer to eleven o'clock than ten, after all the goodbyes, I didn't feel just exhausted. I felt physically weak. When I got to the staircase, I had to clutch the railing with two hands, lean forward, and pull with all my strength to get up the first step. What kept me from sitting right there, resting my head on the third step, and sleeping like that the whole night was fear that Mason would wake up. Not finding me in bed, he would come rushing downstairs thinking Daddy had come back. Then I heard a scraping sound: footsteps coming out of the kitchen. I'd been sure everyone was gone. A surge of adrenaline I didn't know was in me rocketed me up. I was ready to grab the boys, lock us all in my bedroom, and call the cops.

Then I heard "Susie?" Theo's voice, but he said my name in an odd way. Had he heard me practically crawling up the stairs? I turned. He was holding what was left of my last organic Pink Lady apple; his mouth was full. "Anything wrong?" he asked, the words muffled by apple.

"No, nothing. I was going to check on the boys."

"I was waiting for you in the kitchen."

"Sorry, I thought you went back to the city with your parents."

"I told them . . ." He flipped back his hand in a *get out of here* gesture. A piece of apple pulp slipped from his mouth and onto his black silk shirt, but he didn't notice. "You said we'd talk later. I assumed you still needed to unload after everyone left and that you wanted me to stay late or stay over."

"I did!" I lied. I flashed what I hoped was more grateful smile than mere display of teeth. "Let me run up and check on the boys."

When I forced myself to come back down, Theo was stretched out on the living room couch. My hope that he'd fallen asleep was dashed when he popped up into a sitting position.

"Were you in the living room when my neighbor asked if the cops had any lead on the call girl?" I asked. "Lovely moment."

"No," Theo said. "I was hanging in Jonah's study with my father. But my mother caught it, so naturally, I'll be hearing 'Can you believe the unmitigated gall of that tacky, tacky man' for the next two or three years. What a dumb pièce de shit. Your neighbor—not my mother, who, as you know, is not dumb."

"I do know." Every part of me was so heavy with exhaustion I dreaded moving. If anyone else in the world had been stretched out on my couch, eating my last Pink Lady, I would have been honest and said I was vanquished, beyond fatigue, and—though I was deeply and profoundly sorry—if I didn't sleep immediately, I would drop dead. We'd have to talk tomorrow.

The price of Theo's charm was saying yes to whatever he wanted. He hardly ever got anything but yeses, since nobody could deal with what came after the no. If I gave the slightest indication that I wouldn't go along with what he wanted, I'd be in for any of fifty different responses, all of them unpleasant. He'd rage out of the room in angry silence, shout "You think you're the only one who's exhausted?" Pull a passive-aggressive "I just want to help, but if it's more than you can handle . . ." hurl the apple across the room, and then stomp out.

But I hadn't said "No, I can't talk," so he leaned back his

head against a pillow and gave one of those half-smiles that people get when recalling a nice moment. "You know," he said, "when your grandmother walked into the room . . . Amazing! I knew instantly who she was. I mean, God, the resemblance!" His eyes opened wide, and he mouthed a silent "wow." "And her lover. You've got to give both of them credit. It can't be easy coming into a living room full of suburban types. But your grandmother has, shall we say, a certain chutzpah. Maybe even a kind of courage."

"I guess so. But 'courage' is such a positive word. Is it courageous to turn your back on an eight-year-old kid, your own flesh and blood?"

"I don't know," Theo said. "How can we judge what the mind-set was pre-feminism? It was a different world. Anyway, what is the deep dish?" He gave me what I guess was meant as an expectant raised-eyebrow look, except, as with most people, both brows lifted. "Come on," he said. "You and Granny were next to each other on the piano bench with the girlfriend right beside you. Into heavy-duty conversation." I waited for him to say more, but he sighed, like he was giving up on me.

"There wasn't anything special we were talking about," I said quickly. "Just about Jonah. They really thought he was a wonderful guy. And my grandmother obviously wanted to see me, to say how sorry she was. I'm surprised by how moved I was when I looked up and . . . Grandma Ethel. And I like Sparky a lot. She works very hard—long hours—so it meant a lot that she came, too."

"She's a civil rights lawyer?"

"Civil liberties. First Amendment stuff, keeping government out of people's personal lives."

"Does it pay?" Theo asked. "Not keeping government out of people's lives. I mean does it pay financially?"

"Probably not a bundle. But if you remember, no one has to hold a fund-raiser for Grandma Ethel." Theo nodded. I continued, "Two really profitable divorces. Highest-paid TV personality in Miami for years."

"I remember you guys talking about it."

Jonah and I had described going up to my grandmother's endless white fifties-style ranch house on some elegant little island off Miami Beach. It had high double front doors with double knobs right in the middle. The brass back plates formed a two-foot sunburst. "When Grandma Ethel and Sparky walked in tonight, it was such perfect timing," I said. Theo nodded again. I could tell I had become boring with a couple of sentences. But he wasn't getting up to go, so I added, "Actually, I was talking to them about Dorinda Dillon." Theo exhaled a long "oh." I had stopped being boring. "This may sound hopelessly naive, but do you know what I was telling them?"

"What?"

"That I still can't get my mind around the fact that Jonah went to someone like her." Maybe Theo murmured a response. It was difficult to tell, because he sat up, taking so long to change positions that it became the Theo Slo-Mo Demo and I was momentarily distracted.

Finally, he turned his head toward me and said, "I hear you, Susie." Too many seconds—maybe three—went by before he found something better to say: "He really, really loved you."

"The thing of it is," I told him, "he never turned off me the way some husbands do over time. We couldn't have kids right away because he was in med school and I had to work. Then I had all those fertility problems. So we had more years to be honeymoonish than most couples. There aren't lots of opportunities for intimacy when you have triplets, active boys, but I never doubted that Jonah was, you know, drawn to me. Even when he looked at other women, he was appreciating them, like *Hey, she is really spectacular,* but it was more as a connoisseur than a guy actively lusting. Or sometimes he'd look at them clinically, like someone would think he was gazing into their eyes while he was saying to himself, *I could make her look so much better with a brow lift.*"

"I hear you," Theo said again. "Let's put it this way: If you had exactly your personality and looked like a dog, I don't know if Jonah . . . you know how he was. About clothes, decoration, art. He had a strong aesthetic opinion about, really, everything. And for him, you were the best. My parents finally accepted they could never change his mind about you because his attraction was so strong."

"Were they hoping he'd get bored with me and see me as I really was—not an aristocrat?" *You Gerstens aren't exactly bluebloods,* I so wanted to say. *What do you have that I don't? A two-generation head start on my family in upward mobility and maybe an extra twenty-five IQ points?*

"I don't know what they thought," Theo said. "I didn't ask. The way I saw it was I loved my brother and you made him happy."

"I did. Listen, I admit I want to believe that he wasn't at Dorinda Dillon's for sex. And I do believe it. But what I'm after is the truth, even if it's an ugly truth that forces me to face something about Jonah or our relationship that I don't want to look at. Theo, the times you talked to him, did you get the impression that anything was wrong?"

"I don't know." He caressed the gold band of his thirtieth-birthday Rolex, but he couldn't check the time because the watch face was hanging down now that it was hip to wear watches loose. "I don't think anything was wrong with him, but I think he felt pressured."

"Pressure from me? Supporting me, the whole house and everything, in the style—"

"No. Possibly that's my mother's theory, but not mine."

"I wasn't that terrible a drain. I mean, for all that I'm high-maintenance, I'm doing part of the maintaining. I work. Florabella isn't making a fortune, but it's doing all right. So even with the economy and people cutting back on elective surgery, I didn't feel like I had to put the thermostat down to sixty-five degrees or buy Vanity Fair panties."

"He never complained to me about you. Period."

"The kids?"

"Well, they are a handful. As far as they went, all he ever complained about—and it wasn't in any really bad way—was their noise level. He said there were never five consecutive seconds of silence from the minute they got up to when they fell asleep. But he said it in kind of an amused way or a fond way, like 'They are so fucking noisy, but they're mine, and aren't they adorable?'"

"Then what do you think caused the pressure?"

Theo turned up his hands in an *I don't know* gesture. "I'm trying to think. Maybe he felt pressure about work. He never came right out and said it, but I sensed he didn't feel he was getting enough support from his partners. He had all the responsibility, making all the business decisions, following up on everything. Does that sound right to you?"

"It does. I mean, I don't know how much pressure he was feeling, because Jonah never was one of those husbands who took up the whole night telling you about his day. But he did feel he had too much on his plate. Gilbert John was doing his Grand Old Man thing on the international conference circuit, plus his pro bono work and philanthropy stuff. And when he wasn't busy with his usual grandness, he was getting ready for a gallery show of his mosaics. Jonah said Gilbert John was taking out the most money but working as though someone had named him surgeon emeritus. And Layne? She's the ultimate sweetie. Great with patients, but she can't or won't exert any authority over the staff."

I had to get upstairs. I suppressed a yawn so enormous, my eyes began to water.

"I think there might have been something else getting to

Jonah," Theo said. "I'm not saying it was a conscious thing. I don't know."

"What?"

"At some level, he may have been angry at not being able to live life as graciously as he wanted to."

"What do you mean?" I asked, sensing that I was going to hear something I wouldn't like.

"You know, he loved beautiful things. He wanted beautiful things. And with him being the first child, *and* the most gifted, the fact of all the pressures in his practice and of earning enough to sustain the lifestyle he wanted . . . It pissed him off, having to work so hard and still not be able to get what he dreamed of."

Everything seemed to go silent except the ticking of the wall clock in the kitchen, which I could suddenly hear. "What did he want that he didn't have?" My fatigue gave my question a flatness I wasn't feeling, but I was grateful for being able to sound as cool as Theo.

"He said it would be great to be able to afford a driver so he could have some downtime between home and work. And he really wanted to get rid of those au pair twins who had to be treated like family and were always around—going out to dinner with all of you, even—and get a top-drawer nanny."

"He was angry over that?" I asked. The flatness was gone. If any word could describe my tone, it was disbelief. Yes, Jonah could get angry, but he wasn't the type to seethe over the injustice of our not having upscale servants. Theo's shrug meant either *I'm not sure* or *I won't push it because you're in total denial.*

He left a minute later. It was nearly midnight. I had to sleep fast. Given the boys' recent insomnia, along with their usual five-thirty rise-and-shine, I'd be lucky to get four hours. I would have been asleep before my head hit the pillow, but as I was pulling down the duvet, I noticed Lieutenant Paston's card. I'd stuck it among the pinkish-white Rosalind roses I'd arranged in Jonah's Yale tenth-reunion mug on my nightstand. Paston had said to call him any time if I thought of something. Midnight was definitely any time, but the number wasn't his cell, so it wouldn't be like I was waking him. And if he wasn't working the late shift, he'd told me someone familiar with the case would be on duty.

After a couple of minutes on hold, a woman's voice came on. "Mrs. Gersten, Sergeant Maureen Ferrari. I'm sorry about your loss."

"Thank you. I know it's late, but I haven't heard anything in a couple of days. Maybe I should have waited until the morning to speak to Lieutenant Paston, but—"

"No problem." Her voice was smoky, like one of those babes in old detective movies whose hair dips over an eye. But she spoke in a fast staccato, so she didn't come across as babelike. "I wish I had something solid to report. So far, none of our leads to Dorinda Dillon has panned out."

"She's the only one you're looking for?" I asked. "I mean, was there any evidence that somebody else was involved? Her just disappearing: You don't think she had an accomplice to help her get away? Or else—this may sound far-fetched—maybe somebody did her in because"—even to myself, I was coming across like an overambitious rookie detective on *Touching Evil*—"if she was caught, she could be persuaded to talk?"

"There's really nothing to make us think anyone else was involved," Sergeant Ferrari said. "But I promise you, Mrs. Gersten, this case is our top priority. We'll find her. She left in a hurry."

"How do you know?"

"Because we found a salable amount of drugs, cocaine. In a plastic bag in a frozen pizza box. She glued the box shut, so it looked unopened." She took a deep breath. I sensed an announcement. "If Dorinda had a personal phone book or a PDA, she took it. But she did have a pad in the kitchen with a list of her . . . appointments for that day. It said six-forty-five

Jonah. I'm sorry to say this, but it's written in the same way as with all her clients—first names and the time they were coming."

I closed my eyes. "How many names were on the list for that day?"

"Dr. Gersten was her third," she said. "Third and last."

Chapter Sixteen

The end of the week of mourning coincided with the travel agent calling to remind me that Presidents' Week was two days away and, "Heavens," she said, "this is sooo awkward to have to say, but did you happen to remember that Dr. Gersten got plane tickets and put down a deposit for a ski vacation in Utah?"

"Oh my God, I forgot! And he kept reminding me about some new ski wax with Teflon . . ."

Every time I was doing something ordinary and mindless—like at that moment, making tea and answering the phone—and Jonah's name came up, my heart stopped. It beat *lub,* but then I kept waiting for the *dub,* except it felt like it was never going to happen and my life wouldn't go on. My final act on earth—in this case, bobbing a Dragon Pearl jasmine tea bag in and out of hot water—seemed both commonplace and so magical that Vermeer should have captured it: *Woman Dunking Tea Bag.* I held the phone between my ear and shoulder and wrapped my hands around the hot mug. As I lifted it, the jasmine went straight up from my nostrils and saturated my brain with sweetness.

Utah? It wouldn't be the worst thing in the world to get away for a few days, give the boys a change of scene. Maybe I'd be smart to take some of the unasked-for advice people kept giving me: Do a Variety of Activities with the Kids to Create a More Meaningful Bond; No Major Challenges the First Year, but Do Take on Small Ones; Time Heals; Don't Let Your Exercise Routine Go Because You Need Those Endorphins.

In the time it took to tear open a packet of Splenda, I decided the combination of a twelve-hour-long altitude headache, seven days of anxiety over Evan feeling abandoned in ski school, and me schussing down a mountain, sobbing so hard I wouldn't see the ponderosa pine four feet ahead and—whoops!—leaving three orphans, did not sound enticing. Even Jonah had been having second thoughts about the boys being too young and also (being a surgeon) about his hands after a day skiing in fifteen-degree temperatures. I suggested to the travel agent that considering the circumstances, a refund seemed the way to go.

Her call back showed that all the revolting publicity did have one upside: The reservations departments of both the Deer Valley Resort and Delta Airlines had heard about Jonah's murder and, as my travel agent put it, "How could they not understand?" It also helped that the boys had only a vague concept of time— Mason and Dash still believed that "tomorrow" meant any time in the future—and wouldn't understand that the ski vacation Jonah had been going into raptures about was supposed to be happening now. So we spent Presidents' Week at home.

I had tiny flashes of fun, although in terms of elapsed time, they lasted as long as the flare when a match is struck. I discovered an ice rink nearly an hour farther east on the Island and signed up the triplets for Tots on Ice lessons. Ida and Ingvild came along. Considering they were Norwegian, it wasn't a shock that they skated. But as I watched them swirl around the ice, I was amazed: With their round faces and red down-filled jackets, they were roly-poly Frosty the Snowgirls. Who knew they had been on a synchronized-skating team in high school?

They wowed everyone at the rink with their athleticism, including a routine that involved skating backward, then somehow, spinning faster and faster with the tops of their heads touching—while doing arabesques.

They even talked me onto the ice, not easy after I'd spent twenty-five perfectly happy years off. Within a half hour, I recovered whatever ability I'd had when I was ten. Rhythmic movement—running on a treadmill, sex, gliding around the rink—almost always suckered me in. For moments at a time, I forgot I had on rented skates that had been worn by strangers whose unwashed socks reeked from toe cheese and sweat. Once, the movement of my freezing cheeks even let me know I was smiling. (Of course I immediately felt ashamed and punished myself with a flash memory of Jonah's grave just before they lowered the coffin; I'd been transfixed by the horrid nakedness of a tree root sticking out from the cold, packed dirt.)

We went back to the rink twice that week. On another day, I let each of the boys invite a friend over, gave them charcoal and paper, and had them draw portraits of one another. One morning we took graph paper and diagrammed a vegetable and herb garden for the spring and taped it to a window that overlooked the garden.

Grief is supposed to take you over. A bright memory may break through, but mostly, it's full-time misery. One thing's for sure: The pain doesn't kill boredom. I was so bored. Other than the months I took off just before and after the boys were born, I'd been working since I was eighteen. Floral design was never nine-to-five, but there was always something to keep me engaged.

But after what was no doubt the hysteria of Valentine's Day, which obviously I missed, Florabella was completely quiet. In a good year, Presidents' Week meant seven bud vases of red, white, and blue flowers at six bucks a pop for the Lions Club luncheon. So when Andrea said, "Don't you dare show your face at the shop," I'd felt grateful and nearly guilt-free. Except that being bored at work would have been better than having nothing to do in a house where Jonah's anorak was on a peg by the back door and his J was monogrammed on every towel.

I wound up watching a couple of runway shows from Milan on Fashion TV. Just as I was thinking I could probably give Dolce & Gabbana a pass forever, it dawned on me that the accountants still hadn't given me the word on my financial future. Even if I was as economically secure as they were "quite confident" I would be, Italian couture—or any couture—was unlikely to find its way into my closet or my life.

At the thought of money, a memory of the retainer I had sent to the investigator at Kroll popped up. *Twenty thousand dollars shot to hell*, I thought. Grabbing a Diet Coke—decaf, since any financial uncertainty fried my nerves—I headed for the golden calm of Jonah's study to call the investigator, Lizbeth Holbreich.

"I am so terribly sorry it turned out this way," she said southernly. While her style was too formidable for honeyed charm, there was something in the way she was speaking that kept me from my post-Jonah robotic response: Wait for the person to finish their condolence spiel, then offer a "Thank you, I really appreciate, blah, blah, blah," as if their expression of sympathy was not just profoundly moving but also amazingly original.

Not knowing what to say when I actually was touched, I went with "Thank you."

"Is there anything at all we can do for you?" she asked. "I was going to call, but I didn't want to intrude quite yet." Her "quite" came out "quaaat."

"I appreciate that." I was thinking she and I were both business types. In my work, if the bride or groom didn't show at the wedding, I'd feel terrible, but I couldn't give a refund. Florabella had paid for the flowers and done the labor. In Lizbeth's case, I had hired her company to find out whether there was some secret part of Jonah's life that had led to his disappearance — and where he could have gone. Since only a couple of days had passed before he was found, murdered, I couldn't imagine they could have had time to do much investigating. "At the risk of sounding cheap," I began.

"Your twenty-thousand-dollar retainer."

"I was wondering . . . can I get any of it back, Ms. Holbreich?"

"Call me Liz, please. Some of it, I'm fairly sure. I'll need to check. But we did do some work on your behalf. I took it upon myself to go ahead and write a preliminary report. I'd be happy to sit down with you and review everything. I'll gladly drive out so we can talk. Of course, if you'd rather, I could messenger it to you with a detailed letter. Once you read it—"

Considering this was my second phone conversation ever with Lizbeth Holbreich and that I'd never been comfortable with letting anything, from bra straps to emotion, hang out, I surprised myself by blurting, "Listen, I've *got* to get out of this house. It's like there are bars instead of walls here." My volume went too high. In a quieter voice, I added, "Sorry. I'm usually not like this. Would it be all right if we met in your office?"

"Of course."

"I promise, no big emotional displays."

Lizbeth Holbreich's office was austere yet comforting. The walls were covered in a pale gray sueded paper, a hue to soothe. If its texture was as luxurious as it looked, it was thick enough to absorb all clients' shrieks of outrage and crying jags. Liz's lacquered black desk was one of those midcentury designs, asymmetrical, somewhere between an artist's palette and a boomerang. The only part of her computer that was visible was the monitor, a black rectangle jutting from the wall on a jointed steel arm; it could be angled up, down, or side to side if you pressed the edges of a quarter-sized control to the right of the mouse. It was so high-tech, I would have believed it could access the Internet via mind control from a teeny Bluetooth device embedded in the frontal lobe. But Liz pulled out a hidden drawer in front of her desk that held a keyboard.

Liz Holbreich was younger than her voice, which sounded at least fifty. She was probably my age, mid-thirties, slightly imposing but not scary. She wore what I was 98 percent sure was an Escada, a peacock-blue suit, with pointy-toed pumps that had princess heels. Her shiny dark hair was cut chin-length. She had the powerful-woman-politician look. However, being small-boned in the extreme, she looked less Nancy Pelosi and more a modern-dressed version of the elf Viggo Mortensen married in *Lord of the Rings*.

"This way we can literally be on the same page," Liz said as she pressed a control and the screen angled more toward me. "Naturally, before you leave, I can give you a printout. And a CD if you'd like."

I nodded, but then I realized she was typing. "That would be fine," I said.

"Let me explain. What I'm showing you represents the work we did so far." I raised my head slightly to read what was up there: a table of contents with listings for items like addresses, names of relatives, education, employment history, professional associates, personal associates, credit report. "What isn't up there," she continued, "though the fact is noted in the intro, is that there is absolutely no evidence that Dr. Gersten had hidden any sort of criminal record or used any Social Security number other than his own legitimate one."

It bordered on hilarious, the thought of Jonah hiding a criminal record. But how could I laugh when, if anyone had told me my husband was going to stop at a call girl's place before he drove home to Long Island, I would have . . . well, laughed.

Liz Holbreich continued her rundown. "No record of litigation, either—no pending lawsuits, including malpractice, which, considering his specialty, is amazing."

"One of his patients did threaten to sue about a year ago," I said. "I mean, it happened just three weeks after surgery. She claimed one of her eyes was higher than the other. She even got a lawyer. Jonah told her it would be fine once the swelling went down. It was, and the lawyer called him to say they weren't going to pursue the matter. Like two months later, that same lawyer wanted to hire Jonah as an expert witness in one of his cases."

Liz didn't show any signs of being impatient, but I began to feel I was wasting her time with unnecessary talk. This business was all business. Floral design was so much about major events in people's lives that, along with showing pictures of centerpieces and pulling together a fast nosegay to demonstrate an idea for the cocktail tables, you heard the saga of the bar mitzvah boy's triumph over developmental arithmetic disorder. You and the client chatted about wonderful weddings and tacky ones; confirmation parties that should have worked but fell flatter than the crabmeat crepes; the issue of themed bat mitzvahs; the etiquette of floral displays at funerals. A bride, noting your style, sought your advice about what shoes to wear with a tea-length dress, while her mother asked how to get rid of slugs in her hostas. You, in turn, admired the groom-to-be's riding boots but knew not to ask where he stabled his horse. In my world, business rarely felt like business. In Liz's, it definitely did.

She swiveled her chair to face me and leaned back. Not the usual leather office throne but a fifties-style chair that resembled one of those nut scoopers at Whole Foods. She rested her elbow on her desk, which I took to mean the meeting wasn't over.

"You gave us authorization, so we were able to get a preliminary look at Dr. Gersten's office and home hard drives, along with his e-mails and Internet use," she said. "Our findings and conclusions are in the report. There's also a good deal of backup data on the CD that I'll give you before you leave. Now, do you want the bottom line?"

Whatever "a state of suspended animation" actually meant, I was suddenly in it—a cone of silence that wouldn't lift until she spoke. Would I hear "He had no secret life"? Or would it be something that would change everything, like "Dr. Gersten secretly operated on bin Laden and made him look like Calvin Klein"? "Yes," I managed to say. "Bottom line."

"Nothing major," she said. I realized how tight I'd been clasping my hands only when I eased up; my knuckles ached from where my fingers had been pressing on them. "No evidence of an affair or sexual liaisons."

I couldn't feel relieved. "Anything with prostitutes?" I asked.

"Nothing we were able to find."

"Isn't that kind of a lawyerly answer?" I asked.

"I'm not a lawyer," Liz said. "But if you mean it sounds qualified, I'd go with that. Look, the conclusions in the report don't exist in a vacuum. We have to take into account real-life circumstances. Dr. Gersten was killed in a prostitute's apartment. It's entirely possible he was there for a purpose that had nothing to do with sex."

"But you don't think so."

Liz was wearing a large aquamarine ring on her right ring finger. She twisted it around a few times, more thoughtful than nervous. "Let's put it this way: Is it more likely for a man to be visiting a prostitute for sex or for an undetermined reason—perhaps a benevolent reason? And if the reason was to help her rather than to use her services, why would this particular prostitute, a woman with a criminal record, go into her own medicine cabinet, take out long-bladed scissors, and stab him?"

"But that's what I don't get. Isn't her criminal record for drugs? I mean, she wasn't in trouble for anything violent. I didn't hear she was ever involved in something where anyone got hurt."

"True," Liz said. "In any case, there is one more point I should make. An entry was added to Jonah's office computer calendar around eleven-thirty the morning of the day he was killed. According to the police, his calendar hadn't yet been synced when he died, because the event wasn't on his Black-Berry. But 'D.D.' was put in the office calendar for six-forty-five that evening."

"Was she on his calendar at any other time?"

"No. Unless it was under an alias both we and the NYPD didn't come up with in our database searches. We contacted the authorities once we heard about Dr. Gersten's death. They understand that in a case like this, private investigative agencies are there to support them, not work against them. The cops passed along the information they and the FBI had because we did the same for them."

"Do you know anything about Dorinda Dillon? Her background, where she comes from?"

"No. Not because we wouldn't be able to get that information. But because you hired us to try to find Dr. Gersten. Not to investigate his murder . . ." She stopped.

A second later, I realized she was waiting because my eyes had filled up. "It's okay," I assured her. "I get teary at least ten times a day. I'm so used to it that half the time I'm oblivious. Well, almost oblivious. Anyway, sorry for the interruption."

"On my own, no charge to you, I ran a quick search on Dorinda Dillon. It's on the CD. But since this case went from being a missing-person case to a homicide, we wouldn't go much further—and keep drawing down against your retainer—without your go-ahead. Actually, I did call you once or twice."

I swallowed and recrossed my legs, all the minor movements to cover social embarrassment. Beneath Liz Holbreich's businesslike courtesy, I sensed sweetness. I said, "I vaguely remember you leaving a message or two. But once I knew Jonah was dead, murdered, plus with dealing with the boys and his family, and then all the publicity. I wasn't . . . I couldn't return phone calls. I started making a list and then stopped. I even stopped checking voice mail."

"Please. No explanation necessary." A small sigh escaped from deep in Liz's chest.

I realized I could be wrong about her. Maybe Liz Holbreich wasn't a sweetie pie, just a cool and extremely mannerly investigator. With all that southern stuff, I could be misreading courtesy as compassion. How could I tell? In the past, I'd trusted my gut because, as guts go, mine was excellent. Now I was too messed up to rely on myself.

"She had just changed her name to Dorinda Dillon a few months before. From Cristal Rousseau. But Cristal's name had come up in a drug case. When the cops got to her apartment to question her—ultimately, it turned out that time she wasn't involved—the super told them Cristal hadn't moved away, just changed her name."

"I'm assuming what you told me is all there is," I said hopefully. "Right? There wasn't anything else?"

"If our investigation had run its course," Liz replied, "there were a few avenues we might have explored."

Now I didn't have any choice except to ask, "Like what?"

"Nothing to be concerned about."

Had I looked concerned? Even after all her reassurance, was I still fearful that she'd spring Percocet addiction, spying for Russia? From the moment of Jonah's disappearance, I'd left no nightmare unimagined—except for some horror I lacked the capacity to conceive of, the one that could kill my love for him. If he was capable of going to a prostitute, was he capable of something much worse? If a husband is alive and a wife learns something awful, she can confront him with "I'll never be able to trust you again." What about a great guy who was maybe not so great and who was dead?

"We found a few e-mails indicating . . ." Liz tilted her head to the side. Shrugged. *Get it over with!* I wanted to scream. "I wouldn't even call them fights," she said at last. "Squabbles. The routine disagreements anybody could have in business or family life. They might be overlooked in the normal due-diligence investigation. But if an individual inexplicably disappears, we need to go the extra mile."

"Can you give me an example of a squabble?"

"Everything's on that CD," she said. She touched the edge of the desk with the heel of her hand, and the bright computer monitor faded to black.

Being an executive at an international investigation agency, Liz Holbreich clearly understood the world in a way I never would. So although I was a reasonably chic, très-upscale sophisticate in my black Proenza Schouler skirt and jacket, I was feeling more like a hick in a purple velour warm-up suit.

"I get the impression there's a lot of stuff on the CD," I managed to say. "So I'd appreciate some guidance. Maybe you can tell me 'I would have looked into this' or 'I wouldn't have wasted my time on that.'"

"Sure. I wasn't trying to blow you off. I'm genuinely sorry if I seemed abrupt. If I was holding back, it's because I was hesitant about giving too much detail," Liz said. "You've been through such hell. It would have been one thing to look over your husband's shoulder in the normal course of events, watch him typing an e-mail, and say to yourself, *Wow, is he pissed.* It's quite another to read or hear about that same e-mail if it was written in the last couple of days of his life. It has a great deal more weight."

"If Jonah had dropped dead of a heart attack, it would be one thing," I said. "But because he was murdered, murdered in a place where I would never in all my life have believed he would go, I need to understand what was going on in his head—and in his life."

"Fair enough. As I said, no matters of great consequence.

There were a number of e-mails between Dr. Gersten and . . . I believe it's the manager of the medical practice. A Donald Finsterwald."

"Yes. Were there problems?"

"Basically that when the going got tough with the economic downturn, Dr. Gersten thought Finsterwald was turning to mush. Doing less marketing, less PR rather than more. Your husband discovered Finsterwald had turned down an offer for one of the three partners to go on *Today in New York* because it was a local show, not national. Finsterwald e-mailed back to Dr. Gersten apologizing profusely. Had there been a history of friction between them?"

"No. Jonah thought Donald was the ultimate suck-up with physicians but too uncaring with staff. Jonah didn't like him personally, but I didn't realize he was so annoyed."

"More than annoyed, I think. Sometimes it's hard to get a reading just from e-mail, because in any office setting, there are always conversations taking place between correspondence. But the last few days, it looked as though your husband was downright angry."

"Anything else with Donald?"

"Yes. Apparently, part of his job was tracking financial performance. Finsterwald sent several e-mails apologizing for not having weekly reports done, saying it was difficult getting numbers, what with Dr. Noakes doing so much pro bono work and traveling. The records were incomplete."

"Gilbert John was good with his medical notations," I said. "But he practiced by himself for so many years before taking on Jonah and then Layne that he couldn't deal with being accountable to partners. And with the practice's businessy computerized systems, he was technologically lame."

The light coming through Liz's window was beginning to soften. Instead of looking overbright, like an HDTV test pattern, her black hair, blue suit, and aquamarine ring were starting to appear washed out, almost fuzzy, more like one of those fifties movies you rent that was done by some cheaper process than Technicolor. "Does everybody call Dr. Noakes 'Gilbert John'?" Liz Holbreich asked.

"Yes. At least, I've never heard him called anything else. It's weird, because he's probably the most boring guy at Mount Sinai, which takes doing, but everyone plays up to him. Part of it is that he's a really good-looking man. But there's something truly formidable about his manner. Jonah always said Gilbert John had a brilliant reputation as a surgeon, and the grand style to go with it."

"Is he a nasty kind of guy?"

"Not at all," I said. "He just has—pardon me—a permanent stick up his ass. And Layne is just the opposite: 'I'm just a down-to-earth gal from Albuquerque, and don't bother calling me Doctor because, gosh, all that formality just isn't me, and now, is there anything I can do to make you feel better about yourself because you're a wonderful person?' My guess is that's why Jonah was so upset with Donald Finsterwald, because he'd been hired to ease the pressure and make it easy for the three partners not to have any issues." My left foot started falling asleep. I wriggled my toes, but as I was wearing pointy stilettos, all I could do was rotate my ankle slowly so Liz wouldn't notice. "You mentioned avenues you might have gone down if you had more time to investigate. Besides Donald and the practice, does anything else come to mind?"

"Let's see." Liz shut her eyes, doing a major *I'm thinking*.

"Please don't be concerned about hurting me. I do flowers. I don't have the background, the way you do, to evaluate what's potentially investigatable."

She nodded and did the pushing-back-cuticle-but-really-looking-at-watch business. Maybe she was thinking her shot at leaving early to check out the shoe sales at Saks would be lost if I dissolved into tears.

"You're absolutely right to ask for a professional's opinion, though in this case, I don't know what it's worth. I was only hesitating because it involves family," she said. I almost laughed because my first thought of family was my parents and assorted cousins, whose existence seemed way too mind-numbing to merit investigation, except by researchers into the nature of boringness. "Dr. Gersten's brother, Theo."

"Theo?" Definitely an interesting life. And a self-centered one. Aside from their being siblings, I couldn't imagine his life and Jonah's crossing in any significant way. Years earlier, when Theo was still trying to be an actor, he kept sending his friends to his brother for consultations, though they seemed to believe Jonah would not only work on them for free but take care of the anesthesiologist and OR costs. After Jonah told them — and Theo — all he could give was a discount, Theo stopped the referrals, but only after telling Jonah that he was appalled at the cheap fuck he had become.

"He recently asked your husband for ten thousand dollars," Liz said.

"He did? Like 'Hey, can you give me ten thou?'"

"He needed it to pay for some fire damage to his apartment building from a sauna he'd had installed. Illegally, it turned out."

All I could do was shake my head. It was so Theo. "Jonah didn't tell me about that one."

"I must say, you don't seem surprised," Liz said.

"I'm not. Unless Jonah gave him the money."

"No. He sent him . . . I wouldn't call it angry, but it was a strongly worded e-mail. Essentially, it said, 'You've got to be kidding, asking me.' Theo came back with 'If you can't see your way to helping me out, could you loan me the money?'" I felt that tennis-volley anticipation, waiting for Jonah's response. "He refused," Liz said.

"How did he put it?"

"Something about Theo already owing him the equivalent

of the national debt. Obviously, I don't know if he was being ironic or if Theo did owe him a large amount." Natural curiosity made her pause, hoping for an answer, but I didn't have one. I hadn't a clue that Theo owed him—us—money. "Us" because everything we had was joint. Still, I couldn't think up a way to make it sound like "Oh, Jonah told me everything." For whatever reason, that was what I wanted Liz to believe. "Dr. Gersten suggested if Theo couldn't get a loan from a bank, he should ask their parents. Then it was a great deal of back-and-forth: Theo writing that Jonah should go F himself and Jonah asking him why, since they're both in their thirties, he should have any responsibility for Theo."

What I couldn't get over was Jonah not saying a word about this to me, not even "Theo's being a pain in the ass again" or "Can you believe my brother put in an illegal sauna and it burned a ten-thousand-dollar hole in his apartment?" Maybe he'd gotten so angry at Theo's immaturity that he couldn't even talk about it—plus, he knew I'd get furious and then he'd have to listen to me, like an echo of his anger.

I took a deep breath. "When did all this e-mailing happen?" I asked.

Liz's voice was soft. "A couple of weeks before Jonah was killed."

Chapter Seventeen

Forget about *Get a life*. It had been almost a month, and even though I'd OD'd on reality, part of me still held on to the primitive, pathetic belief that Jonah would be found alive. "That wasn't your husband in the Gersten plot, three feet away from Grandpa Ben, after all!" I'd be told. There'd be some jaw-dropping explanation involving amnesia, but seeing me would cure it. All the papers and magazines would write editorials apologizing for their gross misreporting, and Rupert Murdoch would send a handwritten letter saying how sorry he was about FOX News and *The New York Post* being *the* most disgusting media about Jonah, and he'd offer his private jet to take me and the boys anywhere in the world for a healing vacation; we'd know he wasn't truly sorry, just afraid of a libel suit because Jonah hadn't been a public figure till his tabloid notoriety had made him one.

If I couldn't get a life, I at least had to muddle on. Those he's-not-dead fantasies were scaring me with their seductiveness. I had to deal. So, having done the only decent thing, giving Ida and Ingvild three days off after their above-and-beyond, day-and-night selfless devotion, I was dealing—and proceeding to go insane.

Worse, it was Saturday morning. I'd been all alone with the boys only eighteen hours. "Evan, get back here! Don't you dare open that door!" I screeched from the kitchen. I heard the *shoosh, shoosh* of his Power Ranger slippers skimming along the marble checkerboard floor of the front hall as he raced to answer the bell. Mason and Dash, lacking their brother's gregarious nature, were still parked on the rug in the den, yukking it up as they watched *Kung Fu Panda* for the fiftieth time.

So much TV. I was afraid of a call from the accountants saying, "We've been going over your expenses, and sad to say, we were overly optimistic. You can no longer afford video on demand. In fact, you can no longer afford any luxury in your life." Whenever I called Wollman & Rubin, LLP, Certified Public Accountants and Profitability Consultants, they tried to soothe me with voices practically dripping in anesthesia: "Not to worry, Susie," "Jonah seems to have been on top of things," "We're almost ready to sign off." But until they did —

"Evan, dammit, if you open that door, you can forget your playdate with Josh! Cross it off your to-do list because there's no way in hell —" Still screaming that last sentence, I careened around the corner and skidded into the front hall.

Lieutenant Gary Paston stood framed by the open door. He was telling Evan, "You shouldn't open the door unless a grown-up tells you it's okay."

"Into the den!" I ordered Evan, who ignored me. He was riveted as Paston flipped shut his gold shield with one hand. Paston obliged him by flipping it open and shut a few more times. "Evan." I forced myself to use my reasonable voice. "You know your brothers won't rewind. You'll miss the best part." He took off.

"Please come in, Lieutenant Paston," I said. It came out too ladylike, the tone you resort to when trying to make someone forget how you'd been shrieking like a shrew. A second later, any notion of graciousness vanished. Normality, as in "Can I take your coat?" was out of the question. Instead, I stood mute, staring at his black fringed wool scarf. It was the same one he'd worn on his other visit. An ordinary knit scarf, but seeing it brought back the moment I'd found out. It was like that guy in Proust who dunked a cookie in tea and got not just a memory but a total five-senses replay. All that hand-tied fringe bursting from Paston's scarf, and I was back in that awful night, when my hope had turned to dread and dread to despair.

A six-feet-something, football-player-sized African-American guy in a gray overcoat was standing framed by my front door, but I couldn't see him. All I could take in was the fringe on his scarf, the fringe of his eyelashes, and the knowledge that in a couple of seconds, he was going to tell me Jonah had been murdered. Post-traumatic stress? Maybe. Probably.

It wasn't until he said, "Mrs. Gersten? Are you okay?" that I realized I was rigid—like in the game the boys played, where one kid yelled "Red light!" and everybody froze. Despite my asking him in, I was blocking his way. "I owe you an apology," he said. "I should have called to see if it would be okay if I drove out. I just thought, *Well, it's a Saturday morning and—*"

"No, it's fine. Really. Please come in." We had an awkward couple of seconds of me wanting to hang up his coat, him saying not to bother, he could put it down somewhere. Then he noticed there was nothing in the front hall except a bombé chest, a mirror, and two antique Chinese chairs that looked like they'd break into smithereens with one good sneeze.

We wound up in the kitchen, where he put his coat on a chair and I got to make a fresh pot of coffee so he would think I was a decent person and not an alternatingly shrewish, catatonic homicide victim's widow. I pushed the button on the coffee machine, and as I turned back to him, he said, "We found Dorinda Dillon."

"Oh." That was all I could think to say.

"That's why I drove out. I wanted to tell you personally and also answer any questions you might have before . . ."

He stopped. Suddenly, I realized that was because I'd turned my back on him again. "Sorry. I just wanted to get down a couple of mugs. What do you take in your coffee?"

"Milk."

I set up the mugs and Splenda, and poured milk into a small pitcher. Then I took a mason jar of gerbera daisies from the windowsill over the sink and set it on the table. "I'll sit down now," I announced. "Sorry I cut you off."

"No problem," Lieutenant Paston said. I sat across the table from him. For an instant we looked at each other. The only sound was the dribbling of the coffeemaker. We had an ESP moment, or at least I think we did: Each of us found the other a decent, likable person, so we took time off—maybe five seconds—not to speak. We wished we could avoid the single awful subject we had in common. Then he said, "She was arrested around three this morning. Midnight in Las Vegas. I'll give you the whole story in a minute, but the department wanted you to be the first to hear it. There's supposed to be a joint announcement of the arrest, us and the Las Vegas police, but these things can leak. I wanted you to be prepared in case there were phone calls or reporters showing up wanting you to comment."

"Thank you." The coffee was still dripping. I was eager for the big hiss that came at the end of brewing so I could jump up to get the pot, not to get away from the table but to have something to contribute. "How did you find her?" I asked.

"We got cooperation from all three of the escort services she occasionally worked with."

"Occasionally?"

"They'd call her if their regulars were booked, away, whatever. If she had free time, she'd take the job, or if things were slow with her, she'd call asking for work. Anyway, none of the services had heard from her. But yesterday afternoon she called

College Girl Companions—the one she did the most business with. She told them she needed the name of a criminal lawyer in New York and tried to get them to advance her some money. She was broke."

"Advance her some money?" I asked. "They do that kind of thing?"

Paston shook his head. "I doubt it, especially when they know she's a person of interest in a murder investigation and isn't likely to be getting anything in the way of income for the next twenty-five years plus. We had advised the owners of all three escort services to stall her, talk, get whatever information they could. Luckily, the girl who spoke to Dorinda was smart, told her to wait a couple of hours, that she'd come up with the names of some lawyers and try to convince the owner to wire some money. We had a recording device on the phone. I heard the conversation. The girl did a great job: very sympathetic, finally got Dorinda to a comfort point where she gave the number of the motel she was at."

"You couldn't trace the call?"

"We did, to a pay phone in a Laundromat. I had one of the guys in my squad fly out to Las Vegas right away. By the time the local cops got to the pay phone, she was gone. No big surprise. But they staked out the motel and arrested her two hours later."

"Did she say anything? About what happened?"

"Initially, she claimed not to know about the killing." He shifted the knot of his tie about a millimeter to the left, then shifted it back. I didn't know why, but I trusted Paston more because he dressed nicely: no shirt gaping between the buttons; no strangely stiff tie that looked lined with cardboard; no fluffed-out mustache like those of detectives on TV shows—and in real life, on the news. A subdued rep tie, white shirt, and a dark gray suit. Not badly cut or old guy, but not trendy either. "She claimed she was in Vegas for a vacation, hadn't been watching TV, and was shocked to hear someone had been murdered in her apartment."

"And then?"

"They didn't question her formally until my guy got there. It went back and forth for a while: she saying she didn't know a thing, my guy telling her, 'Do yourself a favor by cooperating.'"

"Did she have a lawyer by that time?"

"No. Listen, most jurisdictions videotape any questioning of someone involved in a homicide case. So don't worry. Whatever we have is solid. It's on tape, her being read her rights. She did ask for a lawyer—Legal Aid, public defender, whatever they call it out there. One of the Las Vegas cops made the call, and meanwhile, my guy and one of their detectives kept talking to her."

More than anything, I wanted to ask if Dorinda admitted knowing Jonah, but I didn't want Paston to think my only concern was that my husband had gone to a whore and I didn't give a shit about justice. So I didn't interrupt.

"What got her talking a little was my guy. Irish, blue eyes, thinks he looks like Brad Pitt when he smiles, which he doesn't, but women are crazy about him. I'm sure it's on the tape, him smiling and saying 'Give me a break' to everything she said."

"Did she confess?"

"No. She claims she doesn't know anything about what happened. It was when she went to the closet near the door of her apartment to get your husband's coat." He said it matter-of-factly, as if there had never been any doubt in the world that Jonah was her customer. If Paston hadn't been with the NYPD, but a private detective paid by me, he might have told me a little more gently, allowing me a couple of seconds more to hold on to an illusion, but this was the no-frills, publicly funded truth. "She said when she opened the closet door, someone who had been hiding there smashed her in the head with an electric broom she kept in a corner behind the coats. She claimed she was knocked unconscious. She didn't see her assailant. When she came to, Dr. Gersten was on her living room floor. He was dead."

"Do you believe any of what she says?"

"Absolutely not. But let me give it to you straight. If we're going to believe or disbelieve based on someone's status, we're not going to solve many cases. Prejudice gets in the way. So it doesn't matter if Dorinda Dillon is . . . what she is or if she's ambassador to the UN. And it doesn't matter if the victim is a homeless psycho or a high-class plastic surgeon. Those of us who investigate homicides really believe the old 'Thou shalt not kill.' We see our job as putting the scales of justice back in balance." Corky Paston rested his hands on the edge of the table. "But you know and I know we live in the real world. Right?"

"Right."

"So we wind up responding to its pressures. Do you know what I'm talking about?"

"I'm guessing here: a case that's gotten a lot of publicity, or where the victim has . . . Detective Sergeant Coleman mentioned something about Jonah's position in the community."

"Right. So this case, your husband's murder, qualifies on both counts. The words 'thorough investigation' really mean something here. We interviewed the doorman, but he didn't see anyone else come in. These doormen who work in rental buildings are pretty savvy. One look at a tenant like Dorinda Dillon—maybe the rental agent can't figure it out or doesn't want to, but the guys at the door know what she is before she even signs the lease. Same thing when they're standing out front. They can see a man walking down the street and know 'This one is going to the big dinner party in 6A,' and that other man a couple of feet behind him, dressed pretty much the same way, has a date with the hooker."

The coffeemaker gave its last steamy hiss. I brought the carafe over to the table and started to pour, then worried that Paston could be saying to himself, *I cannot believe she's going to serve me from Pyrex!*

"So what you were asking about, whether we believe what she says: The answer is no. There's nothing to back up her claim. No one else got past the doorman after Dr. Gersten asking to go to Dorinda Dillon's apartment. No one who even looked like a client type came around. Also, the doorman was sure everybody who got into the building that afternoon and evening was either a tenant or had some legitimate business in one of the other apartments."

"I see," I said. "Okay."

"The other thing is the closet." I wanted to tell him fine, enough was enough. I believed him. I believed the police did their job. For someone who'd had such a need to know, I was rapidly becoming the don't-tell-me type. Still, there wasn't any way I could make Paston stop. "We didn't find evidence that anyone had been inside the closet other than Dillon herself. There were some prints, a few hairs—long, dyed blond—that matched up with what was all over the apartment. The prints were hers, too. We have them on file because of her previous arrests."

It was weird, but I didn't remember, in all the media coverage, seeing any photo or mug shot of Dorinda, though I must have. For whatever reason, I hadn't imagined her as a blonde, not that I'd really had an image. That in itself was strange for me, because nearly all the time when people described something that had happened to them, or when I was reading, I got vivid mental pictures of what was going on. Jonah once told me, "You have an amazing visual intelligence," which was such an ego-boosting compliment, even if I wasn't totally sure what it meant: maybe my ability to visualize a design or room layout, or what wasn't right about someone's outfit, or why a piece of art didn't work. He'd said it when we were at a Calder exhibit at the Whitney after I'd told him why I didn't love Calder's work, even though I respected it.

"Now that she's in custody, we'll know for sure about the

hair when the DNA tests come back," Lieutenant Paston said, "but there doesn't seem to be any reason right now to think it was someone else's."

"I understand." He took a sip of coffee and seemed to be waiting for something more, so I added, "Sounds right to me."

"Now, as far as the electric-broom thing is concerned." At that point, I was hoping one of the boys—no, all of them—would come in and behave so obnoxiously that Paston would make his excuses and leave. He'd say, "I'll e-mail you the details." But obviously *Kung Fu Panda* was still entrancing. "The only prints on the broom were hers. There was no hair, no blood on it that would be consistent with someone using it to hit her over the head. Just the usual household dirt. Also, electric brooms are mechanical."

"Uh-huh." I wasn't sure what this had to do with anything.

"They weigh something. But most of the weight—this one was eight pounds—is toward the base, where the mechanism is. Eight pounds doesn't sound like much, but because it's bottom-heavy, it would be hard to grab and raise up as a weapon when somebody opened the closet door. Possible but unlikely."

"Thank you. Thank you for all you've done."

"Please," he said. "It's what we do. Before I forget. Speaking of her hair, or what we assume is her hair. There was one of them on Dr. Gersten's jacket, just to the left of the second stab wound." I couldn't really say thank you for that information, so I just nodded. "Oh, and there wasn't any cash in his wallet." I shrugged. All I remembered was someone saying the police had to hold on to his wallet, keys, and BlackBerry—"all Dr. Gersten's effects"—as evidence when I'd asked if I could get back Jonah's photos of me and the boys. "Not even one dollar," Paston added.

"I'm not sure how much he had. Most of the time, he never carries more than a hundred, a hundred fifty." Then I said, "I mean 'carried.'"

"He did make a withdrawal from an ATM near his office late that morning," Paston said.

"How much?"

His slight hesitation made me listen more closely than I might have. "Six hundred dollars."

"I see." How could I not?

"He had lunch brought into his office. Fourteen dollars and change. He doesn't appear to have left there before . . . before he finally left for the day. Of course, he might have paid cash for something, but we didn't find any receipts." I didn't ask what Jonah had ordered for lunch, even though I figured Paston probably knew. A couple of times over the years, Jonah and I had had that dumb conversation about if you knew something was your last meal, what would it be? Even though both of us hardly ever ate beef, I'd said a pastrami sandwich and a real Coke, not diet; he'd said a steak and hash browns from Peter Luger with their best bottle of cabernet.

As Paston headed to his car, I glanced out the window and noticed he had the slightly bowlegged walk of an ex-jock. He'd said, "Call me if there's anything more you want to know." How about why? Maybe Jonah's murder would always seem senseless to me, but right now I felt there were too damn many unanswered questions. I didn't expect Lieutenant Corky Paston and the entire NYPD to share my passionate need to know, but didn't the why of it make them at least a little curious?

Chapter Eighteen

I blessed the Tuttle Farm nursery school's four-hour day, its "yummy, nutritious, all-organic lunch," and its "wide range of exciting, individualized, optional after-school activities." The wide range was two: Yay for Yoga or Creative Clay. My three boys went for clay. Each indulged his unique artistic vision by making humongous plates with SpongeBob and/ or Squidward painted on them. So I was free, and with Ida and Ingvild off with another au pair to explore still more wonders of Long Island mall-dom, I had my Monday in front of the TV in the den watching Dorinda Dillon.

Not that there was much to watch except the perp walk. There she was at JFK, handcuffed, with a quilted jacket too big to be hers draped around her shoulders. Two female detectives for whom the word "strapping" must have been invented led her past a lineup of photographers and reporters who shouted to get Dorinda's attention: "Hey, look over here!" "Did you know him before that night, Dorinda?" "Over here, beautiful!" "Did you ever have plastic surgery?" "Yo! Dor! Why'd you kill the doc?"

CNN and MSNBC had slightly different angles. I went with

CNN's because Strapping Detective #1's shoulder wasn't blocking the camera at the moment Dorinda turned her head to the shoving pack of journalists and rolled her eyes in *Give me a break* boredom. Her expression was more what you'd expect from a celebrity-hounded eighteen-year-old hip-hop star than a handcuffed hooker with no makeup except atrocious blackish-red lipstick, whose shoulder-length hair (not the roots but the part that was still blond) looked like the hay they fed hansom cab horses around Central Park. Too bad for her that her chances of getting near a stylist, or even a box of Clairol Champagne Blond, were iffy—at least for the next twenty-five years.

I couldn't get enough Dorinda. I had recorded a bunch of evening and late-night local news shows so I could watch them first thing the next morning, the instant the boys left for school. After I'd seen them, there was nothing to do except wait for the perp-walk clip on CNN Headline News every half hour. Right after it ran, I'd race upstairs to my computer to check out online videos on a couple of Las Vegas TV websites.

Since I'd spent extra on a high-quality color monitor for viewing flowers, I was able to check out the style and eye-burning purpleness of Dorinda's halter sundress, which had been hidden under the borrowed jacket at the airport in New York. The purple had a sheen not just of the sleaziest polyester ever manufactured but also of newness.

I played those Las Vegas news segments over and over. As I watched them, parallel videos ran in my head. I pictured Dorinda getting to Nevada in New York winter clothes and spending twenty dollars of Jonah's fast-disappearing cash in a dreadful store with filthy linoleum on the dressing room floor. Maybe she thought she looked luscious in the dress. On the other hand, she could have felt miserable knowing such a trashy dress (all she could afford) would discourage the class of customer she wanted. Once or twice I imagined her shoplifting, stuffing the dress into her handbag, thinking she was smart: *This'll never wrinkle.* When she pulled it out, though, it had creases even the hottest iron could never flatten.

To add a little shame and disgust to my Dorinda imaginings—what fun was a fantasy without them?—I envisioned her running out of money and having to work: turning a quick trick, a hand job in an alleyway (assuming there were alleyways on the Strip), or a standup fuck in a place known to locals as the worst hotel in Vegas, beyond some slot-machine room in a corridor that still reeked from cigars smoked in the seventies.

The quality of the Las Vegas TV footage wasn't great. I tried to zoom in on her, see her expression, but even my high-res monitor couldn't get me a decent picture. Still, I saw enough to decide Dorinda Dillon was definitely not pretty. And not just by my standards; she knew it. Even under arrest, a woman who was aware that she was appealing could get paraded and handcuffed and yet hold her head at least a quarter inch higher than someone who felt unattractive. A pretty woman would hope her good bones or shining eyes would please the cameras, tame the ferocious media.

It didn't help that Dorinda was also a mess. Besides the wreckage that was her hair, her crappy bright purple dress sucked the color from everything around it, including her face. Her posture was awful, shoulders slumped, back hunched, which I assumed was what happened when you were in heavy handcuffs attached by chains to your ankles—though I couldn't see below her calves.

It struck me that even if there were a charity benefiting homicidal whores that gave Dorinda the full Day of Beauty package at the best spa in town, she would still be wrong-looking. Her nose was both long and unusually broad, so it pushed her eyes far apart and took up so much space that the sides of her face, reserved for cheeks on other people, were flat. Forget being able to tell the color of her eyes; I could barely see eyes at all, because they were little more than slits. Dorinda reminded me of Dolly, that sheep who was cloned, except without the sheepy dread-locks, which might have been an improvement.

It took me a weirdly long time running between the TV and computer to stop trying to read her face, maybe even her thoughts, and start thinking, *Oh, right, she's a prostitute. Her body is what's for sale. Let me see what that body looks like.*

It looked good. In the Las Vegas footage, I saw the sundress was short enough to show that unless something repulsive was going on around her ankles, she had great legs. The dress was tight enough to reveal a notably small waist. And not an ounce of fat stuck out over the top in back, unusual because the sad fact of life for most women, even thin ones with fantastic arms (which is maybe 3 percent of the world's population), was that the tight-bodiced halter dress was meant more for a fashion spread than a body. In front, the dress was cut low enough to display Dorinda's major boobs—maybe real, or at least well-done fakes, since Jonah had always said the soccer-ball look (those high, round mounds on either side of a canyon of cleav-age) were the sign of a second-rate surgeon.

A little before one o'clock, I decided I needed a break and sat down for my favorite lunch, cut-up apple and cheddar. I started leafing through the latest issue of *Fleur Créatif*, but I'd been on overload with "Idées pour Noël" since early December and hated trying to figure out half of the French words, which were probably on a second-grade reading level. I decided to get lunch over with, so I stuffed a whole bunch of apple slices and cheddar into my mouth.

But I didn't get up, and I didn't chew. Instead, I slid my chair over to a small patch of sunshine. I sat in the warmth with a full mouth and tried to be objective about how people would react to Dorinda. Most of them, I decided, wouldn't look at her and think, *Two-bit whore.* On the other hand, she wasn't exactly exuding gentility. Most neutral observers would take a look and think, *Cheap.*

I spat the apple and cheese into my hand and ate the pieces slowly. They were ooky, saliva-coated, and I wondered if I was already losing whatever polish I'd gotten by marrying up. But being a slob was better than having Ida and Ingvild get back from the Walt Whitman shopping center and find me choked to death on the floor. I ate the lunch in my hand tiny piece by tiny piece. As I did, I told myself, *Trust your gut. Does Dorinda Dillon look like a killer?* The answer seemed obvious at first. No. She did not look murderous. Just stupid.

Then it hit me: The impression she made didn't matter. Stupid or smart didn't matter. Neither did whether she was groomed or disheveled and dirty. All I needed to figure out was this: Could this slitty-eyed, big-boobed, horrid-haired, badly dressed, handcuffed hooker be capable of murdering my husband? This time around, I decided, *Of course. Now get on with your life.*

The next few days, I did get busy at work. Though our business was always slow from Valentine's Day until the week before Passover and Easter, I wound up doing everything from super-scrubbing every flower bucket to scanning all the photographers' proofs of Florabella decorations and arrangements that our clients had given us over the years. We'd tossed them into acid-free boxes and forgotten their existence.

At home, I kept occupied, working with the boys to prepare a Saturday-night dinner party for the four of us. We made pasta by hand, did menus on the computer. I had them create table arrangements from leaves, three dollars' worth of carnations, and things that should be thrown away from each of their rooms. Evan's showed actual talent: He entwined leaves and a blue ribbon all around a sneaker he'd outgrown; stuck more leaves, carnations, and two curled-up baseball cards into the shoe; and hung his Johan Santana Mets key chain from one of the Velcro closings. I was amazed: four years old, and somehow he understood you had to have a theme.

Even keeping busy on those Dorinda days, right after she

was arrested and brought to New York, were rough. War, famine, economic convulsions: None of them made headlines like Dorinda Dillon. First her perp walk. Then TV and the Web got busy with clips from a couple of soft-core movies she'd been in during the late nineties. Networks and cable stuck shaded ovals or rectangles over tops, tushes, penises, and pudenda. I realized how often I'd watched the clips when I began seeing an abstract dance of geometric shapes.

Maybe Dorinda had once dreamed of a film career. Forget about it. All she got to do was be naked, or almost; not a single line of dialogue. She was one of four pole dancers in a bar, an extra girl at what was supposed to be a Hollywood orgy, the second of two blondes climbing all over a guy in high pimp gear who went for the other girl while shaking off Dorinda as if she were a pesky, leg-humping golden retriever. Dorinda Dillon had played the porn equivalent of a wallflower. But a famous wallflower, at least for those few days.

The scenes took on an almost comforting familiarity. They felt like old family movies you've had to watch too often. No more shock, any more than watching (for the fiftieth time) Cousin Mindy curl her lip in disgust as Aunt Edith demonstrates the twist, or watching baby Hannah do absolutely nothing at her first birthday party, an unsmiling Buddha in a frilly pink dress.

The weird thing is, these home movies always take over and become the truest Truth. There may be a million memories in your head, but your mind's basic definition of Mindy is COUSIN WHOSE LIP NEVER STOPS CURLING. For the rest of her life, Hannah will be BLAH PUDGY GIRL. And Dorinda Dillon—Dorinda Before, with long, silky, teased porn hair, and the hay-headed Dorinda After—would, first and forever, come to mind not as prostitute/accused murderer/coke-dealing robber of cash from a dead body who happened to be my husband, but as FORMERLY BARELY-ATTRACTIVE SLUT WHO FORGOT IMPORTANCE OF GOOD GROOMING WHEN ON THE LAM. Even weirder, the image with a lifetime lease that now resided somewhere near Mindy and Hannah would make it feel like Dorinda was somehow part of the family.

Weirdest: A week to the day after Lieutenant Corky Paston dropped by to tell me Dorinda had been apprehended, my obsessive curiosity about her simply stopped. When I got back from Florabella after doing a few centerpieces for local dinner parties and sharpening all our knives, pruners, and deleafers, I switched the cable DVR list to find a *Cook's Country* show I'd recorded. When I saw my endless lineup of local news shows starring Dorinda Dillon, I had one of those *What was I thinking?* flashes. Then I erased them all.

Late that afternoon, my cousin Scott Rabinowitz came over, more to play with the boys than to keep me company. He was a couple of years younger than I was, but he had the social sophistication of a six-year-old. Naturally, that made him a favorite of the boys. The pleasure was mutual. Being an IRS tax examiner, Scott was accustomed to being detested by people. Also, being a pudgy accountant with a juicy lisp, he wasn't a guy's guy. As an extra attraction, he had a unibrow, so he was achingly familiar with the disdain of the glam women he was, unfortunately, attracted to. For a guy like Scott, being considered cool by Evan, Mason, and Dash was an ego-booster. I assumed that for him, a Saturday night building SpongeBob, Patrick, and a bunch of jellyfish from LEGOs was a small triumph and not a defeat.

Since I couldn't completely abandon my cousin, I put him and the boys at the kitchen table. I kept busy making whole-wheat dough and cutting out five-inch circles to freeze for future pizza nights. Now and then Scott and I would exchange a few sentences on how Cousin Kay, researching the Rabinowitz family tree, had discovered a branch of rogue Rabins in Indianapolis, or how it would take years for the IRS to remake the enforcement division after what the Bushies had done to it. Most of the time, though, the boys kept him too busy to make conversation. A good thing.

Suddenly, Dashiell began yelling at Mason for hiding some green LEGOs in his room. As the two of them stomped off to search, Evan sat quietly, ignoring us, balancing LEGO pieces on the backs of his outstretched fingers. Scott got up, looked in my refrigerator, and asked, "Don't you ever eat unhealthy food?"

"Of course. If I kept it in the house, I could eat pounds of it."

"But you don't really *desire* salty pretzel rods, do you? I mean, like, you want one so bad you would go out at three in the morning to a 7-Eleven . . . except they'd probably only have those twisty ones that don't crunch."

"Listen, you pick your poison. If someone said, 'They're selling English florists' bulbs from the Wakefield and North of England Tulip Society on a street corner in the Bronx at three A.M., but you'll have to fight off a gang of crackheads — trust me, I'd be there."

"Bulbs for planting, not eating, right?" Scott asked.

"Right. People don't generally . . . Well, onions are bulbs."

Times like this, I missed Jonah even more than I did at night when I was alone. I could cry then over my loneliness, though I'd be so exhausted from the day that no matter how bad the desolation was, sleep knocked me out. Talking about pretzels with someone who was nice enough but could disappear off the face of the earth and I might not remember he'd existed or been nice to the boys was a worse kind of loneliness.

Right after dinner, I sent Scott *time-to-go* thought waves, but he didn't receive them. Instead, he came upstairs while I bathed the boys — the fast bath, which meant they all stood in the tub while I soaped them, sprayed off the soap, dried them, and gave them each a star stamp on their separate Clean Guy charts, then did the hurry-up toothbrushing with all three around the sink at the same time, which got them another star stamp because they kept to the no-spitting-toothpaste-or-water-at-your-brothers rule.

"How do you do it night after night?" Scott asked after we put them all to bed. "Aren't you completely wiped?"

I took his question as a positive sign, that the boys had worn him out. So I censored "Not completely wiped, just your basic wiped," and offered him what I hoped was a weary smile as I led him downstairs. I made the mistake of turning on a lamp in the living room. He took that as an invitation to stay, plopping down in a club chair, leaning his head back, closing his eyes, and letting his arms dangle over the sides.

In defeat, I grabbed a fringed throw from the arm of the couch, wrapped myself in it, and sat in the corner of the couch. The throw had a pleasing verbena smell from a delicate-fabric wash I'd forgotten I'd bought.

Scott lifted his head and opened his eyes. Then he realized he had nothing to say but couldn't very well close his eyes again. So I told him, "You put on your sincerest voice and say, 'Tell me, Susie. Really. How are you doing?' Put a lot of concern into the 'how.'"

"Okay," he said. "I'll know for next time. So?"

"So, I don't know. Up, down, up, down. Never really up, actually. There's just low-key down and deep down." He nodded, which was fine because there was really nothing to say. "Sometimes I think it can't get any worse, but then I realize it can and probably will."

"Scary." He rubbed his nose with the back of his index finger. I pictured his knuckle hair rubbing against his nose hair.

"Scary on its own," I said. "But with the boys . . . and don't tell me I'm stronger than I think I am. I'm afraid I'll be in the middle of a normal moment a few months or a year from now, doing whatever but thinking about Jonah, and I'll break from the cumulative effect of all the memories."

"When people break down—"

"I'm not talking about breaking down. Breaking, period. As in shattering. Like a champagne flute."

Scott laughed. "A champagne flute?"

I got up, pissed at how he'd pronounced "champagne" with a French accent, as if my mere use of the word was pretentious. But I tripped on the long fringe of the throw, and I wound up right back on the couch. "Dammit! I was talking to you, one human being to another, opening up."

"Susie, listen, I know. I'm sorry. Honestly, I was listening, one human being to another. But we're Brooklyn human beings, and 'champagne flute' was never a word combination in Flatbush."

"Your part of Flatbush."

"Like your parents knew from champagne flutes. Anyway, it just struck me. Believe me, I wasn't—you know—making light of your troubles. Your pain."

"It's okay, Scott. Forget it."

"When I said 'breaking down,' I wasn't talking about you having a nervous breakdown and going to a psych ward or anything. For all I know, that could happen. Except you really are so strong. I was thinking that you got to be what you are not from marrying Jonah, who was a wonderful, wonderful guy. You know I always thought that. He was so nice to me. But you didn't become what you are now just through your looks or your talent or marrying a doctor. Look, I'm a tax examiner. I deal with some rich people. You know what I see? Some of them got where they are through inheritance or brains. Or dumb luck. Or embezzlement, tax evasion. There are loads of ways to make it. But you: You got what you wanted because you had a powerful vision of how you wanted to live. And you got there because of whatever gifts you have—and your strength. You didn't sit around eating bonbons and fantasizing. You worked your ass off. You built a business. You kept up with that fertility business for years, and everyone is in awe of how you deal with the little guys. You were a huge asset to Jonah in his practice."

"Then why would he . . ." I didn't even bother to finish.

"I don't know," Scott said. "But if you're clueless, maybe there's a reason. Maybe it had nothing to do with you." I shrugged. He went on, "What? It sucks if you can't blame yourself? Listen, you've always been the creative type. If you're looking to blame yourself, you'll invent a way. But come on. Was Jonah a shit who always screwed around?"

"No. Of course not. Well, it's possible, but it's so totally against everything I knew about him. He was so dependable. And moral. Also, I can't see where he could have found the time."

"Maybe he had some secret kink he managed to hide from the whole world, including you, that he could satisfy in five minutes."

I had to laugh. Maybe I even did. "Scott, give me a break."

He scratched his jaw. Even though he was in his early thirties, a pear-shaped man in unfashionably baggy jeans and loafers with black tire-tread soles, I still saw him as my kid cousin, so the rasping sound of his fingernails on his five o'clock shadow surprised me. "I don't know if I should be saying this," he began. "Probably not. But anyway, about being duped: People meet some slicko with a ton of hair gel and a bullshit story, and they say, 'That guy is a con man.' But that's not a con man, that's a loser with too much crap on his hair. The successful con man, white-collar criminal, guy who leads a secret life—someone with a big sex secret, or a spy—gives off waves of normalcy. They're nice guys, but not so nice that it calls attention to their niceness. I've been with the IRS for ten years, and you know when my antenna goes up? When someone comes in, tells his story, and my reaction is 'Whoever looked at your returns made a big mistake. I apologize that we wasted so much of your time and energy.'"

I leaned back to mull over what Scott had said. I tried putting my feet up on the coffee table, but Bernadine had moved it farther from the couch, where she believed it belonged, and my heels slipped off the edge. I sat straighter and said, "You're right, and it's the perfect viewpoint for someone working for the government looking for really clever tax cheaters. But it's different living with somebody. I know there are lots of wives who go into shock when they find out their husbands have been fooling around with another woman, or with a guy, for that matter, or that they're involved in some giant fraud. They're always saying, 'I can't believe it!' But almost all the time, if they've missed the signals, it's because they didn't want to pick them up."

"So you're saying you're not that way," Scott said. He sounded more matter-of-fact, as if making an observation, than doubting.

"Scott, I've thought this through again and again, and I can't remember any signals or signs of distress that made me draw back and tell myself, *Uh-oh, I don't want to deal with that because it would jeopardize the marriage or my lifestyle.* And okay, maybe I wasn't well-bred enough for him, or interesting on intellectual subjects, but I don't think it was anywhere near a deal-breaker. Even if it was, does a guy who wants to talk about history cycles go to a prostitute for conversation?"

"No. If Jonah was hostile that you weren't into history cycles, I can't see him taking that route."

"You know what I wish?" I said.

"What?"

"I wish there was someone who'd been Jonah's best friend, someone he really confided in, and that guy could say to me, 'Susie, I swear to God, that one night was the only time Jonah ever cheated on you. We told each other everything, and trust me, I would have known. It was just one stupid moment of weakness in a whole lifetime of love.'"

I could see Scott felt sad for me. Usually, that would have pissed me off, being the object of pity, but I didn't feel any condescension of the "naive little fool" variety that had been coming my way since the cops found Jonah. "Maybe there's something to say that would make you feel better," Scott finally said, "but I don't know what it is."

"Thank you. Listen, your coming over, hanging with the boys because you have fun with them, not because it's the decent thing to do—it means a lot to me. And so does your telling me how strong I am, even though I'm not so sure about that." We sat in what I suppose was called companionable silence. I broke it by saying, "When I tell myself, *All right, Jonah went to a call girl for sex,* and no matter what my gut says, it's a fact, I still hit a wall. I try and try, but I can't imagine a scenario where his being murdered there could happen. How could Jonah set someone off to the point where she'd want to kill him?"

"Maybe . . ." He decided to let it drop.

"You mean maybe he did something awful to her, or asked her for something that was totally disgusting?" Scott nodded. I continued, "But prostitutes get asked to do disgusting stuff all the time. See, that's what I don't understand. Men beat them up or ask them to do dominatrix stuff. All sorts of things that you think, *God, how could anyone be so bent?*"

At that moment, it occurred to me that I had no idea what my cousin did for sex, that maybe he shared a bed with a blowup doll named Titty Rabinowitz and I'd offended him.

"Maybe it wasn't anything Jonah did," Scott said. "Maybe Dorinda was crazy."

"She had arrests for cocaine. But nothing I heard from the detective or the DA's office made me think of her as a violent person."

"Did Jonah have a bad temper? Ever lose control?"

"No. He never screamed like a crazy person or anything. Once in a while we'd have a fight and he was really loud, but so was I. At his worst, he was overbearing, I guess that's the word. A control freak: my way or the highway."

"If she was really deranged," Scott said, "that's the kind of behavior that might have set her off."

"Could be." I guessed that made sense. At least it was an explanation, where none had existed before. I started with the *Time for you to go* thought waves again, but they were as unsuccessful as they'd been earlier.

"No," Scott said. "I don't think I'm right. Because if Dorinda was a total nut job, she would have—sorry to say this—killed him in a crazy way. He was stabbed, what? Twice?"

"Yes."

"It seems to me a crazy person would have stabbed him a freakish number of times. That's what happens if someone is wild with anger, out of control. Right? Doesn't that make more sense to you than just twice?"

"Yes," I said, "it does."

Chapter Nineteen

My conversation with Scott was keeping me up. For the first time since I lost Jonah, I wanted to talk more. Not with my cousin, though.

I could call Andrea, who would welcome any excuse—"Susie needs to vent"—to escape the California king she shared with Fat Boy. But we'd talked so long and so often that before our first word, I knew where we'd end up.

I adjusted my pillows against the headboard and considered my best friend from high school, Jessie Heller. I called her my human resource; she'd been in HR at Goldman Sachs before she had kids. But even though she was smart and practical and had been at the funeral and the shiva, it would take a half hour to bring her up-to-date.

Seconds later, Grandma Ethel's phone was on its third ring. That was when it hit me that she might not be thrilled with such a late call. What saved me from hanging up was remembering that old people are supposed to need less sleep. And I'd always felt that gay people led more exciting lives and so went to bed later than straights.

"I was just thinking about you a few minutes ago," she told me. "I saw the hooker on the TV."

"So how come you didn't call?" I said it in a teasing way, but when it came out, it sounded whiny.

At least I thought so, but my grandmother acted like she'd heard a regular question. "I didn't want to wake up your children."

"The children are boys," I said. "Three of them. Triplets."

"Did you call because you missed me or to give me a hard time? Because to tell you the truth, if you want to give someone a hard time, don't bother me. Call your mother."

I was about to make a snide comment, but then I thought that would be like telling Grandma Ethel, "Boy, were you lucky to get away from her." "Is this too late for you?" I asked.

"Are you kidding? I live in Miami. For half my friends, this is dinner hour. Now, as I used to say to the guests on my show, 'Talk to me, sweetheart.' You wouldn't believe the people I called 'sweetheart.' Cher. Archbishop Desmond Tutu."

"It's not so much about me talking," I said untruthfully. "I could use some wisdom."

"For that you need Sparky." My grandmother's voice sounded cheery and charming, the upbeat voice people use at dinner parties they're delighted to be at but surprised to be invited to.

"Actually, what I want now is grandmotherly wisdom," I said. No one could possibly call my voice upbeat.

She was obviously someone who knew when to leave the party, because when she spoke again, it was clear that she'd let go of the cheery business. "Sure, grandmotherly wisdom . . . if I have any. Tell me. Whatever I can do for you, I'll do it. And don't think that's just Ethel O'Shea's patented bullshit, because I almost never make offers like that." I was about to thank her when she added, "Maybe three times in my life. You don't make commitments, you don't have to back out of them. Know what I mean?"

This wasn't exactly reassuring, but after eleven at night, I couldn't be picky. "Sure."

"Good. Now talk to me."

"Okay. You know how when something bad happens, there's the story of what happened that makes sense to most people. And then there's all sorts of conspiracy theories?"

"Right," Grandma Ethel said. "You should've been around after the Kennedy assassination."

"From what I've seen, a lot of the conspiracy theories are crazy stuff—from paranoids and idiots. Then there are a few that come across as reasonable." I had been lying back in bed. Now I sat up and crossed my legs under me, which had the double advantage of being the posture of a heart-to-heart discussion and also keeping my feet warm. I was so chilled. I prayed the boiler wasn't having its biweekly collapse and I'd have to wait up half the night for the oil burner guy.

"You heard some conspiracy theory about Jonah that you're tempted to believe?" my grandmother asked.

"No. Not really. It's just that the murder case against this Dorinda Dillon is so open-and-shut, which is fine with me. Well, it should be fine. But every time I accept what happened, what all the experienced people like the cops and the head of Homicide at the DA's office say happened, I think, *All right. They're pros. Not emotionally involved. Now it's time to get on with my life.* And just when I do, something starts troubling me."

"What's the something?" Grandma Ethel asked.

"That's just it: nothing specific. It's always one bit of information or another that seems wrong. I keep wishing somebody— me, even—would come up with a conspiracy theory that would take care of all the little doubts I have."

"Tell me the little doubts."

I went through my talk with Scott, saying that if Dorinda had been crazed with anger at Jonah or plain crazy, how come she hadn't stabbed him over and over?

"You don't know for sure that's how a nutsy person would go about it," Grandma Ethel said. "I'm sure some of them would stab him a lot more than twice, but there's no book called *There Is Only One Type of Homicidal Stabbing Behavior for the Criminally Insane*. Right?"

"Right. But stabbing multiple times seems more likely. And even if she was a stab-twice-only kind of person, it doesn't explain why she went and got the scissors and killed him."

"Listen, I interviewed a madam and also a couple of call girls over the years. The madam, I forget her name—that's okay, there's not a chance in hell it was her actual name—she was smart. Well spoken, well put together, reminded me of Rita Hayworth, except not sexy. That was strange, because before her Call Me Madam days, she was a hooker. The madam, not Rita Hayworth, who I think started out as a dancer. Anyway, when I say her 'Call Me Madam' days, that was a Broadway musical. Ethel Merman. But not about a madam. The madam on my show was smart, made a good appearance. You could bring her to a luncheon at your club and not be at all embarrassed. But below the surface, I could feel there was something a little nuts. A cold beyond cold. It's one thing to sleep with a creep because he's rich or famous or you need a guy and he's the only one with a regular paycheck who'll have you. It's a completely different mentality to sleep with twenty, thirty, forty guys a week. What I'm saying is, don't go giving Dorinda Dillon a clean bill of mental health."

"I'm not," I said. I wished now that I could ask her to bring Sparky into the room and put me on speaker. That way there would be someone in on the conversation capable of saying, "Eth, you seem to have used up your daily quota of logic."

"Good, because from what I've seen of darling Dorinda on the television, she looks like she's got a few screws loose."

"Even if she's not a picture of mental health, it still doesn't explain her being a killer. Thousands of prostitutes go through their entire careers without murdering a customer."

I got into explaining what I believed in my heart, that while there were no guarantees in life, I was willing to bet Jonah hadn't had some kind of messy sexual secret, no fetish that could send a pro like Dorinda into a killing frenzy or frighten her into self-defense with a pair of scissors.

"Did he ever hit you?" my grandmother asked a little too casually.

"No! Of course not!"

"Okay, I was just asking. Don't bite my head off. Did he ever call you names or humiliate—"

"Absolutely not! Jonah didn't have an abusive bone in his body."

"Just to make sure I have the picture . . . He wasn't violent, no vicious tirades. Any throwing things, kicking over tables?"

I shook my head but then realized we were on the phone. "No."

"Was he controlling with money?"

"No, only with tight lips. As far as money went, he wasn't at all cheap. Maybe one of the reasons he was so uncritical of me was that he was really good at spending, too. And I was never out of control." I paused. "Well, once."

"What?"

"A red gown. From Valentino's last collection."

"No! Not the strapless with the double flounce on the bottom?" It was a question, but somehow she knew.

"Yes!"

"My God! They had a Valentino spread in . . . I think *The Miami Herald,* and my jaw dropped when I saw that gown! Good for you!"

"But usually, both of us were under control, for two acquisitive personalities. Jonah was never one of those show-offy guys, handing hundred-dollar bills to maître d's. It's weird, I was thinking about this last night, about Jonah and money. Whatever happened at Dorinda Dillon's, I can't imagine him being cheap or not fair. And he would never hold back on paying her, if that's a thing that could set her off. He told me a story over and over again about going out with his parents when they had a lousy waiter. His father left a dollar bill as a tip."

"It upset Jonah?"

"Incredibly. He kept bringing it up."

"He was right. It was petty and vindictive. Probably made him realize his old man was a shtunk." On the phone, I kept forgetting my grandmother was a woman of a certain age—old. Not only was her voice free from shakiness, but even though she was pretty good at digression, she didn't lose her focus. This was especially true when she wasn't being Unforgettable Character and concentrating on her own delightfulness but was focusing on a thought or another person.

"Jonah always said, 'Give someone the benefit of the doubt.'"

"So give Jonah the benefit of the doubt by asking the questions."

"Who can I ask questions? They closed the case. It's over."

"It's not over. Dorinda's in jail, she hasn't been on trial yet, so how can it be over? Go back to the cop or the district attorney and tell them you still have some questions."

"They'll think I'm a real pain in the ass."

"So? Big damn deal if they do. Listen, law enforcement has to cooperate with a victim's widow—unless she's an out-and-out lunatic, which you obviously aren't. They don't want to risk alienating you. You could go to the media and shed a few tears and tell them, 'I'm disappointed in how the police and the DA are handling my husband's murder case.' It would be a nightmare for them: a beautiful widow with three little boys who are also victims of this crime."

"I don't like the role of victim."

"But you've got it," my grandmother said. "This isn't 'victim' as in 'My parents wouldn't pay for a nose job, and when my first husband left me, he called me Pinocchio.' This is genuine victimhood, so you might as well use it. The world loves victims."

"I don't."

"Then be a pain in the ass, a thorn in their side. Be whatever the hell you want to be. But give your husband the benefit of your doubt. And while you're at it, toots, give that to yourself, too."

Chapter Twenty

"You know the chief of the DA's Homicide Bureau's a woman?" my in-laws' lawyer, Christopher Petrakis, asked me.

"Yes," I said. My father-in-law also nodded. My mother-in-law acted as if all she'd heard was silence.

"Just so you know, because her name is Eddie Huber. It's a nickname, but I forget what her real name is." Christopher Petrakis adjusted his French cuffs by holding them at the very edge. This gave us a view of one of his gold scales-of-justice cuff links; a single diamond chip rested on only one pan of the scales, yet the two were in balance. "I call her Eddie Hubris. Obviously, not to her face." He seemed a little surprised that none of us chuckled. You'd have thought that, having once worked in the DA's office himself, he'd figure the parents and widow of a murder victim, who were about to go in to discuss the case against the accused, would not be given to chuckling.

The four of us stood outside the door to the chief's office. A secretary had met us as we got off the elevator, walked us through the hall, then told Petrakis, "She'll send somebody when she's ready to see you." The whole building was so run-down, I felt like I was breathing in not just dust but decades of suspended dirt that normal air currents could not pass through—mildew, tracked-in shoe crud, sneeze droplets from a 1967 flu outbreak.

When I'd called Babs and Clive to tell them I wanted to talk with someone in the DA's office, I didn't mention any of my assorted qualms about Dorinda Dillon. Still, from the moment Babs had asked, "Would you mind terribly if one or both of us come?" I'd said, "Of course not. I was hoping you would." That was immediately followed by Clive on speakerphone responding, "Excellent," but in a tone he might use to offer a dismal prognosis. So I knew meeting with the chief of the Homicide Bureau would be a snap compared to dealing with Babs and Clive.

Babs had called me from her office three days in a row with variations on "Don't you think you should wait until someone from the DA's office calls *you*?" I mumbled some bullshit that included "proactive" and "engaged in the process." She told me she was concerned that if we pushed too hard, the prosecutors might get the impression that we weren't satisfied with their handling of the case. "As you know, Susie my dear," she said, "they've been wonderfully cooperative about keeping us informed. But consider this: If we were seen in the building, word could leak out that the family was putting pressure on the district attorney's office!"

Pressure for what? I wanted to ask. To get them to railroad a poor, innocent hooker? Unlikely, since they were absolutely certain Dorinda Dillon killed Jonah.

My mother-in-law's calls were followed up by one from Clive, wanting to know if I'd have any objections if they brought along a lawyer. "We've got a first-rate man. Fine, fine reputation. He himself used to be with the DA's office. With a midtown firm now. Comes highly, highly recommended."

Their concerns about not wanting me to start trouble seemed over-the-top, especially because they had no clue about my agenda, to the extent that I had one. I wasn't about to confide in them how plagued I was by the small doubts that kept popping up, only to disappear into *How could I have been thinking that?* — moments when my own craziness made me cringe. But later, in those dull-witted hours between the kids' bedtime and mine, the doubts would pop up again, more powerful than ever.

Dr. Twersky, defying my principle (which, thankfully, I'd never mentioned to her in therapy) that women over fifty should never wear leather pants, had uncrossed her legs with a squeak and suggested my in-laws might be overcome with grief and anger at Jonah's death, made worse by the horrible publicity, even the social humiliation. Babs and Clive saw any questions about the case against Dorinda Dillon as . . . overstimulating, overwhelming, oversomething. The Gerstens wanted to let it be. They were older and more fragile than I was and therefore were at their breaking point.

It wasn't until I was driving home from Dr. Twersky's office that I'd considered she might be telling me I was being cruel to subject them to this; I was young enough to be resilient. I could eventually get over Jonah. The Gerstens didn't have that going for them. I'd asked Dr. Twersky if, when someone was feeling fragile, was the remedy to call a criminal lawyer? She'd gone on about them viewing a lawyer as a wise guide or perhaps a protector. Now I thought, *Protection against what? Me?*

I'd pulled over to the curb and parked in front of a tiny house dwarfed by a giant copper beech. I cried for a few minutes until I saw someone coming out of a house two doors down, walking one of the fifty thousand Labrador retrievers in Shorehaven, a community of thirty thousand people. Reasonably sure all my windows were closed, I'd yelled, "Go fuck yourself!" to either Dr. Twerksy or my in-laws, pulled out, and driven home.

Petrakis centered the gold Rolex on his wrist. Other than the watch and the scales-of-justice cuff links, he wasn't a flashy guy. His suit was a gray box, his tie black with unassertive white dots, his shoes black lace-ups that were neither scuffed nor shined. It looked like one person took charge of his jewelry, while another did clothes. "Any minute now," he told us.

"Thank you," Clive said. He turned to inspect the wall next to him. It was peeling, and long pieces of paint hung down like the drooping leaves of a spiderwort. But he was staring, intent, examining the strips of paint as if they were hung in an up-and-coming gallery.

My father-in-law's attire was a lot more elegant than the lawyer's, but then only one person—Babs—was in charge of dressing him. Jonah once complained his father looked like an assistant fashion editor's idea of a successful Manhattan doctor rather than an actual doctor. He'd laughed when I told him it was hostile to make it an "assistant editor."

Petrakis's arm made a sweep of the hall. "You can see for yourself. All the doors are open, so Hubris must be up to her eyeballs in work, or in deep conference with her door closed."

Clive and I nodded. Listening, I could hear the drone of conversation from the other offices, the clicks of keyboarding, phones that honked like geese. Babs didn't seem to have heard Petrakis and also seemed unaware of the noise of business. She stood pale and motionless, swathed in black. It was probably less for mourning than for the simple reason that black was the official color in her set, the Upper East Side's red, white, and blue. The outfit was by a designer whose work I didn't know: black pants that were almost leggings and a great deal of black jersey, somewhere between a dress and tunic, which fell several inches below the knee. All she needed was the face-veil thing to look like Mrs. ibn Saud, but I decided to compliment her on it to get some conversation going.

I was about to go over to her, but her posture stopped me cold. Her arms were rigid, as if she didn't have elbows, and tight against her sides. Maybe she sensed I was going to take a step toward her because her eyes, which had been staring ahead at nothing, now shut tight. Someone facing a firing squad, hearing "Ready, aim . . ." would stand like that.

I felt awful, sick to my stomach that I was making her go through this, because she really did look fragile. Both she and Clive seemed to have lost weight since Jonah died; in fact, they appeared diminished in every way. Then it hit me that coming to the DA's office wasn't a command performance. Babs had asked if one or both of them could come, and there was only one answer I could have given.

The door opened, and three lawyers—well, two women and a man, all wearing glasses and carrying binders—whooshed out of the office and flew down the hall.

"Come in, come in," a voice called. Petrakis tried ushering us all, but Clive held back to put an arm around Babs's rigidity and lead her slowly. He motioned to me to go ahead.

Eddie Huber was already up and circling her desk to greet us. "I apologize for keeping you waiting," she said. By this time, Clive had steered Babs into the room. Eddie approached her first, extending a hand.

I was nervous that Babs would continue with the catatonia business, but my mother-in-law shook Eddie's hand and said, "That's quite all right. It's kind of you to see us." She said it so graciously that I took a closer look at Eddie to see what could bring out that response from Babs. I didn't get it. Not that I had a mental image of the chief of a homicide bureau, but what I saw looked more like a woman in her mid-forties who taught Latin in high school in suburban Boston. She wore a plain sweater in a washed-out green that was probably called sage in the catalog she bought it from. The sweater was tucked into a wool A-line skirt in a wishy-washy color that didn't deserve a name.

After shaking hands with Babs and telling her how sorry she was about Jonah, Eddie did the same with Clive, then me. Her handshake was strong, but if I'd been wearing a ring on my right hand, it wouldn't have gotten squished. As she and Petrakis did the "How are you, Chris?" "Keeping out of trouble, Eddie" ritual, I noticed that her ballet flats looked like the ones from the fifties you see in vintage clothing stores—great leather but a little clunky in the sole-and-heel department. I wondered if she had some preppy/schoolmarm-style thing going. I might even have thought nun who works in the world except she didn't have a cross, and she wore minimal makeup: a touch of mascara and a hint of beigey-pink lipstick. Why she would go that far and not spend fifteen more seconds putting on a little foundation was a mystery.

My in-laws were seated, but Petrakis had to move a pile of file folders from a chair to the floor so I could sit. Eddie, meanwhile, went back to her desk, sat, picked up the phone, and said, "Now. One more chair." The words were snippy, but her tone was neutral, like that of an NPR voice announcing the time.

"Ms. Gersten," she said, looking at me and not Babs, "asked for this meeting so she could have a sense of how we're proceeding on the case."

Even though she wasn't short, it was hard to see more than her head when she was sitting behind her desk. Besides an old, bloated computer monitor, it was covered with piles of files, notebooks, legal documents with metal clasps, newspapers, and panda tchotchkes—wood, ceramic, metal, plastic—not one with any artistic merit as far as I could see. There were yellow legal pads and loose papers, some stained with circles of coffee. A few cardboard cups were balanced atop the piles. One lay on its side; the remains of the coffee left in it made a little pond on one of the few areas of actual bare desk.

"As you know, Dorinda Dillon is in custody. Everything points to her as the perpetrator. We expect her to be indicted soon, and she'll probably be brought to trial within sixty days." Before I could ask "Are you sure?" she continued, "Her prints are on the scissors that were used as the weapon."

"The scissors definitely were hers?" I asked. The door opened. Someone rolled in a secretary's chair for Petrakis, then left.

"At the time she was interviewed in Las Vegas, she wasn't asked. However, forensics has established that the scissors came from the medicine cabinet in her bathroom. The shelves there were full of dust from the compressed powder used in makeup, as well as regular dust and so forth. We found significant traces of that mix on the shank and around the finger rings of the scissors."

Eddie Huber glanced across her desk wreckage at my in-laws, who were seated directly opposite her. Then she looked at me to see if any of us had questions. We didn't. I was slightly off to the side and had to look past Clive to see Babs. What I saw was not encouraging. She was staring right at me, as if she'd been doing it for a while. Somehow she'd decided I merited more attention than the business at hand. Her hands, scarily white as they emerged from her long black sleeves, were gripping the sides of her chair as if she had to restrain herself from grabbing me.

I looked back at Eddie Huber and prayed for her to start talking again. She obliged. "We found what we posited was a strand of Dorinda Dillon's hair near the second wound, as if she bent over Dr. Gersten's body to examine it closely."

I expected a gasp from my mother-in-law just because she was a basket case. The phrase "Dr. Gersten's body" was pretty ugly, especially under the fluorescent lights in that pigsty of an office. But Babs was silent, and I was afraid to check again in case she was still staring at me.

"Are the DNA results in?" Christopher Petrakis asked. I got the impression that he wasn't as much genuinely curious as feeling the need to speak up and justify his five-hundred- or one-thousand-dollar-an-hour fee.

"Yes, we have the results," Eddie Huber said. "And the hair found was Dorinda Dillon's. All right, as I was saying . . ." While the two lawyers didn't seem to dislike each other, they didn't look to have great chemistry. She peered at a piece of yellow legal paper off to her right. "The doorman who was on duty that evening is willing to swear that no one came into the building whom he cannot account for. Ms. Dillon's last, uh, visitor left the building a few hours before Dr. Gersten's arrival."

"Did the doorman describe what that guy, the previous visitor, looked like?" I asked.

While she seemed surprised at the question, she answered in a polite way, which made me feel, despite my pounding heart, that it wasn't an unreasonable query. "An older man. Longish gray hair. The doorman thought he looked either theatrical or Eastern European, though he didn't notice any accent. He believes he's seen the man a fair number of times over the last year or two. Goes up, stays for a half hour or forty-five minutes, then out. Also, he saw no one else during his shift, four in the afternoon until midnight; no one else had any business in Ms. Dillon's apartment. She went for her usual late-afternoon walk and came back under an hour later—alone."

Petrakis spoke up quickly, as if afraid I'd beat him to asking something else. "Was the doorman who was on duty earlier that day also questioned?"

"Yes. He says she had no deliveries, no repair people of any kind. The only client was a regular—a man in his mid- to late seventies—who got there around ten o'clock and was out before eleven. That early-shift doorman saw Dorinda a little later, when she came down to check the mail, but she didn't go out." Eddie Huber had either a trace of a New England accent or that studied way of saying some words—"re-pay-ah" for "repair"—that I'd noticed with a couple of Jonah's friends at Yale. Jonah said it was the last gasp of what used to be the New England boarding school accent, the way Franklin Roosevelt and upper-class people used to talk.

I leaned forward to run my finger inside the back of my shoe, as if it were digging in near my Achilles tendon, but really to look at my mother-in-law. Thank God, her eyes were now on Eddie Huber, and though she was still holding the sides of her chair, her grip didn't seem as desperate. My guess was she had somehow determined the chief of homicide was an aristocrat, not someone working-class from New Hampshire. That was keeping Babs on her best behavior.

"Who's representing Dorinda?" Petrakis asked. "Legal Aid?"

"No. A lawyer named Joel Winters."

"Never heard of him." Petrakis rubbed his forehead. He would have been a nice-enough-looking guy except for his forehead and scalp, a few inches north. Earlier in his life, he must have had a low hairline, but what was left were tufts of fuzz, like bits of brown cotton balls, randomly growing between his forehead and the top of his skull. "Is he any good?"

Eddie Huber shrugged, which I thought was a pretty classy way of saying someone sucked. Maybe she actually was one of those blue-blood types, the kind who behaved as if they'd signed some code of behavior in Ms. Pomfret's penmanship class as soon as they learned script. I'd found that most people who considered themselves American aristocrats were no more honorable than anybody else. Some, in fact, flying first-class through life on family and school connections (not in a middle seat in row 37, where their own abilities would get them), had the moral code of hyenas. Even Andrea Brinckerhoff acted as if eight of the Ten Commandments were too annoying to be taken seriously.

"What's Dorinda's defense?" Petrakis asked, making me glad for the first time that he was there. Lieutenant Paston had given me some details, but I'd been so rattled when he dropped by that I wasn't sure I'd even heard everything he said, much less remembered it.

"She was unconscious. She opened the closet door to get Dr. Gersten's coat; someone was in there with Dorinda's electric broom and hit her over the head with it."

"When she says she opened the closet door," Petrakis said,

"did she mention whether whoever was supposedly in there had the broom raised in readiness? Or did the person pick it up when the door opened?"

"I don't think . . ." Eddie Huber raised herself a few inches out of her chair and leaned forward to one of the higher piles on her desk. She found what she was looking for a few inches from the top, papers held together with a large butterfly clip. Wetting her middle finger, she leafed through them, then put them down. "That was never asked," she said. "And now her lawyer won't let us near her. All right, so she claims she was unconscious. When she came to and discovered Jonah's body, she called a lawyer she had used on the drug charges: Faith Williams."

"Never heard of her, either," Petrakis said.

"Doesn't matter. Williams wasn't in, Dorinda left a message. While she waited for Williams to phone back, she threw a few things into a bag—just in case—though it's on the police video that when she was asked 'In case of what?' she was unable to say. She waited an hour. When Williams hadn't gotten back to her, she put on a pair of gloves, took whatever cash there was in Jonah's wallet, then left. She withdrew an additional four hundred dollars from her account at an ATM and took the subway to Forty-second Street, then the shuttle to Times Square. She stopped in a store, bought a curly red wig. Then she walked over to Port Authority and took the next bus to Las Vegas."

"Did the doorman see Dorinda leave?" I asked.

"No," Eddie Huber said. "Sorry I didn't mention it: Dorinda said she left the building via the service entrance that's off to the side."

I tried to picture it. "Is it, like, around the corner from the entrance to the building?"

"Sort of." I thought I heard the ultra-bland tone in her "sort of" that people put on when they're pissed, but maybe it was two-thirty in the afternoon and she needed another cup of coffee. "The front door of the building is mid-block, so the service entrance is technically on the same street as the front entrance. But it's a fairly large building, and the service door is set in a gap between that building and the one next to it. You go about six feet down an alleyway between the buildings to access the service door."

"So the doorman can't see it from where he stands," I said.

"It's monitored." Eddie Huber barely moved her lips as she said it, so much like a ventriloquist that I wouldn't have been surprised to see an assistant DA dummy perched on her lap. "The doorman has a console at his front desk with closed-circuit TV screens for the elevator, the lobby-level staircase behind the fire door, the service elevator, and the service entrance and alleyway. So he would see whatever is going on."

"Unless he's helping someone with packages or hailing a cab," I said.

"According to the building's management and all the doormen, the service entrance is always locked to the outside by a deadbolt. Of course, it can always be opened from the inside. When someone needs to get in that way, the doorman buzzes the porter. If he has any question about whether to let someone in, he calls the building superintendent."

"But Dorinda got out without anyone seeing her," I said.

Eddie Huber nodded. "Yes, she must have gone down the service elevator." Her thin, straight hair bobbed along with the motion of her head.

"So if the door is unlocked from the inside, it's possible that she or anybody else in the building could have let somebody else in earlier," I said.

"Technically, yes. Technically, anything could have happened. But we have overwhelming evidence, physical and circumstantial, that Dorinda committed the crime. We believe we have proof beyond a reasonable doubt. We wouldn't bring the case if we didn't think so. We also believe she was alone at the time of the murder, had no accomplices, and that's what we're going with."

Didn't you ever hear of anybody taping a lock? Or breaking it so they could get in from the outside? I was taking a deep breath to ask some modified version of that question when I heard the softest "Shh," like an exhalation through clenched teeth. And that's what it was, air through teeth. Not Petrakis, who I figured was annoyed that I was mixing in when he was there; it was my father-in-law, looking straight at me and shaking his head, warning me again to keep quiet.

"We wouldn't be proceeding with our case unless we thought it was not only strong but just," Eddie Huber said, making me realize I hadn't been quite as subtle as I'd thought.

"I think I can speak for all the Gerstens when I say we appreciate and value that," Petrakis said. "All we ask is that you keep us informed, either directly or through me. As I'm sure you understand, Eddie, the family has had more than its share of shocks and surprises."

"Absolutely," Eddie Huber said.

"Mrs. Gersten," he went on, "Mrs. Jonah Gersten, has been through an unimaginable nightmare . . ."

He babbled on, and at first I got steamed by the "Mrs. Jonah" thing. Every time we got an invitation saying "Dr. and Mrs. Jonah Gersten," I'd say something to Jonah, like, "This is enough to get me to put on one of my mother's T-shirts!" He'd start to laugh, and I'd go on, "Give me a break! Aren't I entitled to a name of my own? Is this 1907 or something? How much extra would they have to pay a calligrapher for a Susan?"

". . . a highly developed ethical sense."

I assumed Petrakis was talking about me. He was, because Eddie Huber gave me a nod of recognition, like *Good ethics. Mazel tov.* I nodded back, even though I'd never been totally sure what ethics meant (not counting medical ethics, which had been a huge deal at Yale) and whether they were different from morals.

Practically like the Rockettes, Petrakis and Clive made the same move simultaneously, inching to the front of their chairs, putting their right foot forward and leaning on it as they began to get up. So I said, "One quick question, Ms. Huber. Why would one of Dorinda Dillon's hairs near the second stab wound be proof of her, you know, examining Jonah to see if he was dead? Wouldn't it be even more likely to have gotten there in the course of . . . a prostitute cozying up to her client? I'm not saying you don't have a really good case against her, but—"

Maybe Babs would have yelled or cursed or even smacked me if she didn't believe Eddie Huber was the second coming of Katharine Hepburn, which struck me as showing she really was a total wreck and possibly delusional. Instead, she stood so fast Clive didn't even have a chance to get out of his chair before she was in the hall. My father-in-law hurried after her. I left more slowly because I sensed what fun awaited me. I knew I had gone too far for my in-laws. But not for me.

"How dare you!" Babs shouted at me as I came through the door. "What kind of sick, attention-getting game is this you're playing?"

"What . . . ?" It was such a blast that I staggered backward. It wasn't just her shouting in a public place, it was her shouting, period. The loudest she'd ever been was saying "Damn!" when she couldn't open the clasp of a bracelet. And while I was as familiar with her hostility as with her Gigi de Lavallade Ingénieux scent, it was always in the background, barely noticeable or low-level annoying, like elevator music.

"What are you talking about?" I asked. It sounded like a lame question, because most of the time when you ask it, you know very well what the person is talking about. But I hadn't a clue. A sick, attention-getting game?

"'What are you talking about?'" she mimicked, and the "talking" came out not only loud enough to bounce off the walls but as the meanest imitation of a New York accent I'd ever heard.

"Come on, Babs," Clive urged. He held her arm with one hand and placed his other on her back to maneuver her toward the elevator. "It'll be okay."

"How will it be okay?" she shouted. "Tell me—"

"Mrs. Gersten," Christopher Petrakis said quietly, "why don't we all go downstairs? We can talk outside."

"Why don't you go?" she snapped back. "This doesn't concern you." I was hoping she'd keep at him for a minute or two so I could get out of there, but at that moment she turned back to me. "You realize, I suppose, that your idiot questions could make them rethink the case against that disgusting whore. 'Oh, the poor little widow wants to be sure all the i's are dotted.' And for what? To keep the scandal in the news!"

"You really have to get her out of here," Petrakis told Clive.

"Don't you think I know that?" Clive snapped back. My father-in-law put his arm around Babs and drew her close. "Come, my dear. Let's go home. There are offices all around here, and they might think this is a security situation. We don't want them picking up the phone, calling the police, and saying—"

"You're raising questions about any stupid detail you can think of," Babs kept going at me. "You are in such denial. You really think you had the fairy-tale marriage, princess. You'll do anything to convince yourself that 'Ooh, Jonah loved me sooo much he wouldn't put his life in jeopardy without realizing it by going to a vile, druggy whore. It must be some CIA plot. Or he wandered into that apartment by mistake, and she just happened to be holding scissors and stabbed him.'" The door to Eddie Huber's office slammed shut, but my mother-in-law didn't take the hint. "You turned his life into a hell."

"If you can't deal with this," Petrakis said to Clive, "I'm going to have to escort Mrs. Gersten, the younger Mrs. Gersten, out of—"

But the older Mrs. Gersten wouldn't be stopped. "It was *you* who insisted on going through with having triplets. The doctor made it very clear to you that the pregnancy could be reduced to one or two. I saw the exhaustion in Jonah's eyes every single time we were together. There was *nothing* but tumult in his life. Demands and more demands. What I don't understand is how you can delude yourself that he wouldn't go elsewhere, just for a quick release, just to get away from the constant turmoil. And now you're rewriting history. You're asking questions to—"

I cut her off. "I have a question for you. Mason, Dash, Evan: Which one or two would Jonah have wanted to get rid of? And while we're at it, I've got another question. Did he ever once complain about our marriage? Or me? Or are you the one believing your own fucking fairy tale?"

I left as fast as I could. Only when I was outside did I realize that I had failed to ask Eddie Huber why Dorinda Dillon would have stabbed Jonah only twice.

Chapter Twenty-One

"Babs." Andrea made a noise halfway between a snort and a laugh. "What I don't understand is why her outburst surprised you. You can't expect good breeding from someone who contours their eyes with three browns for daytime."

"She went to Vassar."

"That's education, not class. By the time you're eighteen, you can't even learn how to imitate being polished much less be polished."

"Speaking of classy behavior," I said, "guess who said 'fucking'? I said it right to her face."

"If I stopped saying it, my mother-in-law would think I got run over by a truck and Fat Boy married someone else. Hand me the roll of cloth-covered wire, please."

We were in one of those huge echoing lofts in a nowhere section of downtown Manhattan, doing a wedding both of us hated to the same degree, a rarity. The bride's inspiration was "Make it look like a box from Tiffany!" Andrea's broad hint that this was not an original concept—some might call it trite—hadn't made a dent. Neither had my suggestion that the tiniest touch of red could take it to a whole new level. So, along with our part-timer,

Marjorie, and Tyrell and Nick, two tall Shorehaven High School seniors who helped us with installations, we were stuck decorating sixteen-feet-high structural columns with leaves, white flowers and tulle, aqua ribbon, and bushels of ivory hydrangea that had touches of greenish-blue. Andrea told the bride it was the *Hydrangea Tiffania*. A lie, of course.

I was making bows from six-inch satin ribbon. "When Theo was at the shiva," I said, "he told me I had nothing to worry about from his parents. They'd be good to me if only because I was the gatekeeper to the boys."

"Did I ever tell you he looks like a metrosexual Munchkin?"

"Many times."

"'We represent the Lollipop Guild,'" Andrea sang out in her highest voice. Tyrell and Nick, up on ladders, exchanged looks that said *I'm embarrassed for her.* "Theo was probably right," she went on. "I think Babs has broken under the strain. Nothing really bad ever happened to her. If you're sixty-something and have led a charmed life, you assume you have immunity. So Jonah's death has destroyed her whole view of reality." Andrea clipped a few lengths of wire, then glanced at me. "Don't look so stunned that I said something thoughtful."

"Sorry. I assumed I was hiding it. So, do you think now that my mother-in-law's hostility is out in the open, things can never be fine again?"

"They were never fine. You know that. But will they be okay? Probably, eventually."

"Do you think I should call—"

"Absolutely not! First of all, she owes you an apology. At some point she'll realize it. She'll go, 'Horribly, horribly sorry, Susie sweetness, but shock, breakdown, not myself, blah, blah, blah.' Meanwhile, she's too angry. And too threatened, probably at the thought of even more publicity. But who knows? Anyway, you'll have to accept her apology and move on. Even if you remarry, she'll always be in your life because of the boys."

I spoke quietly so if the high school boys wanted to eaves-drop—which was dubious, because they assumed Andrea and I had nothing interesting to say—they couldn't hear me. "Forget the 'remarry' business."

"I'm not suggesting this June," Andrea said.

"Listen to me: I know what my life is going to be. The accountants called me. It looks like I'll be okay financially. Jonah had enough insurance and pension stuff that it definitely won't be the way it was, but it'll be like ninety-eight percent of the world would like to live." I knew she was thinking what I was: *That's not good enough*. But at least we didn't say it. "You tell me, Andrea: What reasonably nice, semi-cute, single guy—who's going to have hundreds of women after him—"

"Unless he's really poor."

"—would get involved with a mother of three four-year-old boys? You've seen them do it time and again. Evan, Dash, and Mason come in, and they turn a room into a three-ring circus, except ten times noisier. A guy might want me. He might even want them—if he doesn't have kids and has a zero sperm count. But forget even a long weekend: Three hours with them and he'd run out screaming. And don't say 'not necessarily.'" Andrea might have been about to say it, but for once she thought before speaking. "I've thought about it," I went on. "You want to know what the word is for what my life will be? Lonely. My life will be so lonely."

She didn't say I was wrong.

True to what Andrea had predicted, my mother-in-law called to apologize four days after she exploded. She said it had hap-pened because she was a wreck, "an utter wreck," and also had an adverse drug reaction from a new antidepressant that didn't get along with her medication for arrhythmia. There was no way, she told me, to tell me how sorry she was; she only hoped that I would be generous enough to understand and, hopefully, forgive. I did the expected "I understand totally and there's no need to ask for forgiveness." Then I gave what I thought was a pretty moving speech on how I not only treasured my relationship with her and Clive but had always looked up to her as the model of what a wife, mother, and working woman should be. Of course I kept "except that you're a snob and a cold bitch" to myself.

I was trying to move back into the world. At home, whenever someone called, I tried not to think that he or she had put me on their Outlook calendar right after the funeral and forgotten me until — *Oh, dammit!* — the day popped up with *Call Susie Gersten*. When people left messages, I made myself call back, even a woman in my cousin Marcia's mah-jongg group with a terrible stammer who called everyone because in 1962 a speech therapist had told her that was the way to get over it.

I was so busy. I had tried to put Dorinda Dillon out of my head. Maybe the cops and the DA and Babs were all right about her. *The NewsHour,* which I still watched so I wouldn't get caught saying "Huh? Wha?" the next time a teeny country suddenly became important, didn't carry reports on killer whores. The *Times* might have had something on the case, but since the only section I read regularly was Style, I might have missed it. Since those first few days after Dorinda's capture, when I'd watched her perp walk about a thousand times, I hadn't Googled her or looked on YouTube: too addictive, too tempting to stay in that world and forget my own. Also, there was no one shoving a tabloid into my hands while telling me, "You need to see this." For all I knew, maybe some fact or new piece of evidence had come out that really sealed the deal on Dorinda's guilt. But I didn't read about it or see it. And there were definitely no calls from the DA's office or Gersten super-lawyer Christopher Petrakis.

One day, studying the olive oils at Whole Foods, I heard a woman in the next aisle tell someone, "I saw her! Dr. Gersten's wife! The plastic surgeon who got killed. No, *here,* in the store, a minute ago." I thought I'd gotten good at stuff like that, but I left my cart—with all its plastic bags of fruit and vegetables, Greek yogurt, and yet another box of organic cereal to challenge Froot Loops—and walked out.

Once I got the kids to bed that night, I filled my tub with the hottest water I could stand, determined to unwind until the water got cold or my finger pads turned to corduroy. I even dimmed the bathroom lights and lit a jasmine candle. I did succeed in forgetting "Dr. Gersten's wife!" Unfortunately, that left enough room in my mind to think about the photo of Dorinda that I'd seen in a magazine at the pediatrician's office.

It was a head shot with her looking into the camera, unsmiling. She was wearing heavy eyeliner and chandelier earrings, so it wasn't a mug shot. What struck me again was how dumb she looked, like someone who'd gotten lower than 400 on her combined SATs because she'd made too many wrong guesses. I opened my eyes and stared at the candle flame to hypnotize myself and clear my brain. But I couldn't not think. She might be dumb, but was she someone who could as easily stab her way out of a situation than think her way out? After all, she did have enough smarts to slip out the side door of her building and pass on taking a taxi to Port Authority because taxis keep records. She'd stopped in Times Square to buy a wig. True, maybe she'd stabbed Jonah in one insane moment and then was able to think clearly again. But was the DA's case really so solid, so beyond a reasonable doubt, the way Eddie Huber seemed so sure it was?

But where was Dorinda Dillon's lawyer? I wanted to know. If people can't afford a lawyer, they can only get Legal Aid. Dorinda, though, had hired her own lawyer, a guy named Joel Winters. Even if he wasn't any great shakes, and even without me sitting at the computer ten times a day to Google Dorinda Dillon, I should have heard something about Dorinda's side of the story. Okay, she was going to plead not guilty. The case would be going to trial. So why wasn't the lawyer out there defending her? All he had to do was go to the media, talk up some of the issues I'd been wondering about, like her not having a history of violence, like Jonah's personality: nonconfrontational, generous rather than cheap, a man used to putting women at ease and dealing with them directly.

And a couple of new thoughts. A prostitute and convicted drug offender probably wouldn't call 911. But if Dorinda really had killed Jonah, why did she bother calling that first lawyer, the woman who had once represented her for drugs? Why bother waiting around for a callback before getting out of her apartment? Why not just run? She'd waited an hour. Was she so stupid that it would take her that long to figure out to put on gloves, take the cash in Jonah's wallet, and decide it wasn't a cool idea to hang around with a dead body?

And what about the scissors? If you're crazy or threatened or in the mood to commit murder, wouldn't you go to the kitchen and grab a knife? Okay, maybe she didn't have a big set of Wüsthof, but she must have had at least one killer knife. Why would she instead think to go into the bathroom, open the medicine cabinet, and take out haircutting scissors she may have used—how often?—only every two, three, four weeks?

Dorinda probably wasn't paying Joel Winters enough to put a lot of time in. But this had been a high-profile case, all over the news. Wouldn't even a third-rate criminal lawyer recognize that it was a chance to get himself out there? Even if he didn't believe he could get his client off, why wouldn't he grab all that free airtime?

The water was still pretty hot, but I got out of the tub. When I blew out the candle, I was so upset that it was half air, half spit. I'd forgotten to take out a bath sheet, so, shivering, I wrapped myself in a regular towel and thought, *Why is Dorinda my problem?*

Chapter Twenty-Two

"I knew you'd be happy to see me!" Grandma Ethel announced, a display of either her self-confidence or her self-delusion, since all I was doing was standing in my doorway, my mouth hanging open in surprise. I hadn't asked to be made happy by my grandmother flying up to New York.

Just like before, she again showed up at my house without calling. Granted, we'd been speaking pretty often. I'd filled her in on both the briefing inside the DA's office and the drama outside. Sure, I'd wanted her take on it, but more than that, I simply couldn't stop talking about the People of the State of New York against Dorinda Dillon, aka Cristal Rousseau. Too often I found myself alternately fixated on the Meeting with Eddie Huber and the Big Babs Explosion.

Frizzy Francine Twersky definitely thought they were topics worth discussing—and better at two sessions a week. Now that I'd heard from the accountants that my budget could handle psychotherapy, I had no good reason to put Dr. Twersky off. Andrea was glad to talk about my obsessions, in part to satisfy me, but mostly because they appealed to her need for excitement. Entertainment, too. She gave it all her own spin, so instead of it being an episode of *Law & Order* with a gut-wrenching family subplot, she made it into a British drawing-room comedy, the kind on PBS. This one was complete with a social-climbing, overdressed mother-in-law, a charming and virtuous young widow, and a she-devil who happened to be the chief of the DA's Homicide Bureau. Clive and Christopher Petrakis weren't in Andrea's version. In fact, the only man in her cast was the one actor who couldn't make an appearance: Jonah.

Unloading to both your shrink and your best friend generally makes a good one-two combo, but I needed to explain things to someone more objective or maybe more distant. I wasn't looking for insights into my behavior or "You were right but much too nice to Babs." I hoped to analyze what I'd gotten, and not gotten, from my meeting at the DA's.

Maybe my phone calls made it sound like I wasn't so good at analyzing. All I knew was in the early evening of the day following my fourth or fifth phone call with Grandma Ethel, there she was, standing in my doorway—surprise!—telling me not to worry, she was staying in the city at the Regency because she genuinely enjoyed room service. Sometimes she loved going downstairs to the restaurant and seeing who was having a power breakfast. To be totally honest, she didn't particularly care for being a houseguest unless it was in a house with other house-guests and many servants. But I shouldn't take that personally, because when she'd gone to the bathroom during the shiva, she'd been struck with how perfect everything was and how clean—even with all that company!

We talked for almost three hours once the boys went to bed. The good news was that both they and she seemed to find meeting each other interesting. They vaguely understood that someone called Great-grandma Ethel was a member of their family. I was pretty sure they realized I looked like her because their eyes did the "Mommy Great-grandma Mommy" trip at least a dozen times. She gazed at them with some admiration, not hard, since they went from cute (Evan) to beautiful (Mason and Dashiell). She probably credited her genes for their good looks. I was amazed how unrattled she was by their noise and perpetual motion, though from time to time she looked apprehensive, as if she expected them to turn into vicious little monsters, like the Mogwais in *Gremlins*.

That night's talk comforted me. It felt relaxed, warm, fun at times, like a pajama party with your best friends in middle school. Mostly, we discussed what I should do about Dorinda Dillon.

"Do you know anything about ethics?" I asked her.

"Ethics?" Grandma Ethel repeated it like a new vocabulary word. "What about it? Yeah, I guess so. Someone on my show, a rabbi I guess, told a story about some medieval scholar. Jewish. Anyway, some evil king or an anti-Semite hooligan said to the scholar, 'Tell me about the Torah'—or maybe he said the Talmud—'while standing on one foot.' I guess what that meant was he'd have to stand for a long time, so it would be torture. But listen, it's not getting burned at the stake. So okay, the scholar stands on one foot. And you know what he says? 'What is hateful to you, don't do to others. The rest is commentary.' I forgot what happened to the scholar, but it probably wasn't good. It never was. So, Susie, there you have it: everything I know about ethics. It's the 'Do unto others' thing."

"Well," I said, "even though I talked to the prosecutor, I still don't feel comfortable about the case against Dorinda. I'm not saying she didn't do it. I'm sure it will come down to finding out that she definitely did. But what do I do with this being uncomfortable business? I told you about that meeting with the head of the DA's Homicide Bureau. Her bottom line is Dorinda did it. I don't see her—the prosecutor—being corrupt or lazy or anything."

"So she's got ethics?" my grandmother asked.

"I guess. But I wasn't worrying about Eddie Huber's ethics

as much as mine. What do I do? Do I have to do anything? If the cops and the DA's office say that this hooker killed your husband, that they did the investigation and have determined X, Y, and Z is what happened to Jonah, then I told them what was bothering me and they said, 'Okay, but she did it . . .' Isn't that enough? If I still think something feels wrong, even though I could be thinking it because I don't want to admit certain things about Jonah to myself, where do I go with that?"

"You mean, what should you do ethically? I don't know," Grandma Ethel said. "I'm at a loss. Frankly, when people think ethics, the name Ethel O'Shea doesn't usually leap to mind, as you might well imagine. It's a hard thing to think about, that's for sure. But listen, I'll tell you one thing: Don't be put off by authority. Now, call me a taxi and get some sleep or you'll get dark circles. God forbid."

That talk with my grandmother gave me the courage to call Eddie Huber the next morning and ask for a meeting—though I quickly assured her I wasn't bringing my in-laws or their lawyer.

After a long pause, but without any audible sigh, Eddie Huber agreed to my request. Only then did I add, "Oh, I forgot. My elderly grandmother is in from Miami. There's a very slim possibility I might have to bring her along. But she's going to be eighty on her next birthday, so don't worry about her giving you any trouble." Naturally, that conversation—with the word "elderly"—didn't take place in front of Grandma Ethel. I picked her up at her hotel an hour and a half later. By then, she'd had her fill of watching power brokers at the Regency schmoozing and brushing whole-wheat toast crumbs off their ties.

I needed Grandma Ethel along on my visit to the DA not just because her arrival had given me the courage to ask for another meeting, but also as a witness: Had Eddie Huber said what I thought she'd said, or was I misinterpreting? Was she telling the whole truth, a half-truth, or was she full of shit? Was she playing a game with me, and if the answer was yes, what was it?

"Boy, this place stinks like an unwashed twat!" Grandma Ethel announced as we waited to go through the metal detector in the lobby of the DA's office. In the same loud voice, she asked me, "Did I offend your delicate sensibilities or something?"

"A little bit with the volume," I whispered, praying we wouldn't be noticed. Talk about unanswered prayers: An almost-eighty-year-old blonde wearing a pink Chanel suit trimmed in black patent leather and wearing three-inch stiletto heels that showed off still-great legs could not go unnoticed in a hallway filled with lawyers, cops, and assorted shifty-eyed, slobby individuals who might or might not be criminals—especially when she said "twat" loud enough to be heard in all five boroughs. "It doesn't stink *that* much. It's just old."

"I'm old. This stinks. But I'll lower my voice." She did to the point that I could barely hear her. "I'm only here to make you happy," she said.

Of course, the danger of taking Grandma Ethel was that I couldn't predict how she'd behave; I didn't really know her. Having been the professional charmer hosting *Talk of Miami* meant she could be both smooth and savvy, but saying "stinks like an unwashed twat" in front of fifteen or twenty people, including the cop at the security desk, was neither. Still, part of her job had been knowing a little about almost everything; in a potentially hostile environment like the Homicide chief's office, having someone truly savvy and totally on my side was a plus.

Eddie Huber's jaw went momentarily slack at the sight of the "elderly grandmother" in bubblegum-pink Chanel, still a hottie at seventy-nine. Fortunately, she had no cause for complaint about Grandma Ethel's behavior. Neither did I, but it was only a couple of minutes into the meeting.

"I guess this must be a tough part of your job," I told the prosecutor. "Dealing with the families of homicide victims who need a lot of dealing with, when you have so many cases, so much legal work to do." I was trying to be ingratiating.

"This is as much a part of the job as going to court, and just as important to all of us," she said.

I tried to believe her. "Well, I'm very grateful, because I can see how I might be a pain in the neck." Using "ass" wouldn't have felt right. I glanced at Grandma Ethel nervously, grateful for her silence; her legs were crossed, and she was swinging the top one like a metronome, so at least she was occupied.

Eddie Huber was wearing the same bland green sweater she'd worn the time before. I didn't know whether to feel sorry for her or admire her. If someone like me had a second appointment to see me in my office, I would be constitutionally incapable of wearing the same thing. Maybe she genuinely didn't remember what she'd worn, or possibly, she didn't care. Or it could be Eddie Huber's way of sneering at me and my navy Prada pant-suit, which I didn't have on at this second meeting—it was now a white silk shirt and olive gabardine pants, since I'd realized the Manhattan DA's office was a dress-down kind of place.

I noticed I was twirling my wedding ring nervously, so I clasped my hands. "It might help me if I could find out more precisely what happened to Jonah once he got to Dorinda Dillon's." Eddie Huber's eyes moved to Grandma Ethel. "It's fine to speak freely in front of my grandmother," I assured her, just as Grandma Ethel offered her an encouraging smile.

"Can you give me an example of what you'd like to know?" Eddie asked.

"Do you have any idea how long he was there?"

"Difficult to say. When Dorinda was interviewed in Las Vegas, she was asked, and I believe her words were 'I don't know. Not that long.' Beyond that, without witnesses, there isn't enough evidence to make that determination."

"So it's not clear whether 'not that long' is two minutes or, whatever, a half hour or more?"

"We don't know. The natural assumption is that since Dorinda was going to the closet near the front door to get his coat for him, he was leaving after whatever business between them had transpired. What that was and how long it took, we simply don't know. Her interview with our detective and the representatives of the Las Vegas police was cut off after her lawyer arrived."

I took a deep breath. "In the autopsy," I said, "or in the evidence you found, was there anything that showed if . . . whether Jonah had ejaculated?" Out of the corner of my eye, I saw the pointy toe on my grandmother's shoe stop moving.

"It's not that simple," Eddie Huber said. I sat back, deflated. "I assume you mean was there an ejaculation following a sex act?"

"Yes."

"There was semen found on the meatus of the penis. The meatus is the opening of the urethra in the top thing on the end, the glans penis. But besides an ejaculation in a sexual situation, it's also part of what's called the autonomic nervous system. According to the medical examiner, finding semen is common. When someone dies, especially in a sudden, violent death, there is an ejaculation."

"But does that mean he didn't ejaculate before he was stabbed?"

Eddie Huber eyed my grandmother for a second and apparently decided she could handle the subject matter. She looked back to me. "From what I've learned in my experience with homicide cases, there is a little bit of truth in that if there's no ejaculate found, it may mean the man recently ejaculated — before death. But finding semen around the meatus doesn't guarantee Dr. Gersten did not have some sort of sexual experience with Dorinda Dillon. That's especially true in the case of someone being dead for several days at normal room temperature before being autopsied. When there is such a wait between death and autopsy, it usually cannot be determined when the last ejaculation took place. It might have been during a recent marital sex act. It might have been with Dorinda Dillon. An individual can die violently without any ejaculation at all before death and still show no evidence of semen on his glans penis."

I was working so hard trying to keep any thoughts about Jonah close up and impersonal, like cross sections in an anatomy text, that when Grandma Ethel did speak up, I was incredibly grateful. "Susie talked to me about the case in some detail," she said to Eddie Huber. "And on the flight up from Miami, I was reading some press accounts. I forgot where I came across this, but there was a mention about Dorinda getting clunked on the head with an electric broom when she went to get Jonah's coat. That's her alibi, that she was unconscious when Jonah was killed."

"Yes, that's her alibi."

"And you don't believe there's any truth to that?"

"No, we don't believe it. When such a heavy object is used as a weapon, it would have traces of blood and, considering it has bristles, a lot of hair. There was dirt, and I believe a couple of her hairs, which the lab said would be consistent with normal human hair loss. You know, picked up by the electric broom during regular cleaning."

Grandma Ethel rocked her head from side to side as if she were a balance scale weighing what Eddie Huber had said. "What if someone cleaned the blood and hair off the broom after they clopped her?"

Eddie Huber tapped the edge of her desk with her fingertips, either a sign of extreme irritation or a long-suppressed desire to play the bongo drums. "Then the broom would show signs of that cleaning. But there was only normal household dirt on it."

"If Jonah is dead and Dorinda is lying on the floor like a lox," my grandmother said, "would it take a genius to run the electric broom someplace not too obvious, like under a couch or a bed, to get it nice and normally dirty again?"

"It's possible, of course, but not credible. Believable."

"Thank you, but I am functionally literate. I know what

'credible' means." Grandma Ethel kept going, not giving Eddie Huber a microsecond to respond. "Did anyone check her head? If a blow was severe enough to knock someone unconscious, there could be a bruise. Assuming, for a moment, that what Dorinda claimed is true."

Eddie Huber didn't answer immediately. Maybe she was counting to ten. She either did it very fast or stopped at five. "There actually was a bump on the right side of her head, near the crown," she said, giving her own head a light tap to show the precise location. "But—and this is a big but—it could have come from any knock, and she wove it into her story. Prostitutes do sustain quite a few injuries because of the simple fact that a lot of men are abusive to them. On the other hand, the bump could have been self-inflicted."

"It's hard to imagine anyone being able to hit themselves on the head that hard," I said. "I mean, they could think about it, but doing it is something else."

"That is not the case, as it so happens," Eddie Huber said. "Suspects have been known to crack their own skulls to fake an alibi."

Grandma Ethel curled the side of her mouth into a *give me a break* expression, then shook her head slowly, as in *I'm not buying it*. "That must have been one hell of a crack, to still be there when Dorinda was found so long after."

"Or it could have been one hell of a crack sustained when Dorinda Dillon looked out of her motel window, saw she was surrounded by the police, and banged her own head. Let me explain something, Ms.—"

"Just call me Ethel. Everyone does."

"All right," Eddie Huber said cautiously. "What I want to say, Ethel, and to you, Ms. Gersten, is that there is no pristine case. Details crop up. One piece of evidence seems to contradict another piece of evidence, yet both seem solid. What we do, in addition to applying the law in an evenhanded manner, is we rely on the experience and judgment of our law enforcement team, cops, lawyers, forensic experts. It's not that we are ignoring the bump on Dorinda Dillon's head. It's that we've considered it and decided it was just that, a bump. None of her hair or blood was found on the electric broom, so there's nothing to back up her contention that she was knocked out after being assaulted with it. The bump has no meaning to us. It certainly cannot be used to exonerate her. It simply cannot deflect the evidence we have implicating her in the murder of Dr. Gersten."

She was a good lawyer. If Grandma Ethel and I had been on a jury, we would be nodding *Yes, right, I believe her*. Her argument made sense, but sense is what your mind appreciates, not your gut.

"What about her using a pair of scissors?" I asked. "Does that make any sense to you? Why would someone go into a bathroom, open a medicine cabinet, take out something she definitely wouldn't use every day, and choose that as the weapon? Why not go into the kitchen and grab a knife? It's more logical, more normal, in the sense that it's something a person would do. And a knife is easier to stab with than scissors, isn't it? It has a handle. And why stab only twice if she was so angry?"

"I have no idea why she chose a pair of scissors as the weapon. What I do know is that they did come from her medicine cabinet and that her fingerprints are on them. And it's not really relevant that she stabbed only twice."

Eddie Huber wasn't much good at hiding her body language, or maybe she didn't want to. Instead of leaning back in her chair, she sat straight and crossed her arms over her chest. She reminded me of an impatient teacher, annoyed at a disruptive student, waiting for the kid to quiet down.

"One more question," I said anyway. "Why do you think Dorinda called that lawyer she'd used in the past when she supposedly regained consciousness and saw Jonah lying there, dead? Why did she wait an hour for the lawyer to call back?"

"We don't know that she waited," Eddie Huber said. "She said she waited."

"If you can fix the time of the call from the lawyer's voice mail," my grandmother said, "then find out what bus Dorinda took at Port Authority, you might be able to subtract the earlier time from the later time and discover whether she really did hang around for an hour."

"First, even if she did wait an hour, it in no way proves where she waited, or that she didn't murder Dr. Gersten. Staying in her apartment for an hour would, to me, indicate a certain cold-bloodedness. If you came across a dead body, would you stay with it in a tiny one-bedroom apartment? Or would you want out?"

Grandma Ethel didn't take long to admit, "Out."

That was my reaction, too, and I nodded in agreement. Then I said, "Is there any way I could speak with Dorinda Dillon, ask her a few questions?"

I could have done without the recoil on Eddie Huber's part and without her mouthing the word "no."

"It's just that I'd like to know what happened before Jonah—"

"Absolutely not!" She stood and braced herself on her desk. I wasn't totally sure what that meant in body language, but I think she was saying *I am restraining myself from leaping over this crap-covered surface and throttling you, bitch.* "It would taint the entire case. I'm sorry for you, Ms. Gersten. And I admire your wanting to seek the truth. But there is no way I'll let you get in the way of my office doing what needs to be done."

Chapter Twenty-Three

Grandma Ethel's arrival meant trouble: From the moment she and Sparky had walked into the living room that night at the shiva, I'd known it was only minutes until some older cousin would search out a quiet corner to call my mother and whisper, "You won't believe who just came to see Susie!"

The evening following her appearance, my parents had shown up with a shopping bag full of the plastic containers they'd used earlier in the week to bring home a half-ton of smoked salmon, egg salad, and tuna salad from a platter someone had sent over. "Listen," I said as they'd come through the door, "there's something I need to tell you." As they walked through the house, my mother performed her sneezing/coughing/choking number at every vase she happened to notice.

Trailed by my father, she headed for the kitchen. Once there, she pushed up the long sleeves of her mourning apparel, a black T-shirt with an understated World Wildlife Federation logo, and started washing the plastic containers in my sink. As she pumped out enough Dawn direct foam to clean a 747, my father explained that their water in Brooklyn wasn't hot enough. "It's okay," I told him, "I'll put them in the dishwasher." My mother turned from the sink, shook her head, and told me the heat from the drying process would cause the plastic to release toxins that would infect the next food that went into the containers. I offered to take over the washing for her, or have our housekeeper do it first thing in the morning. When she shook her head emphatically, I suggested putting them in the recycle bin, where they could enjoy the company of all their little plastic friends. But she kept saying no, that I had enough on my hands, by which I assumed she meant Jonah's death, not bad smells.

"Mom," I said, resting my back against the side of the sink so she couldn't avoid looking at me, "your mother was here last night." She looked me in the eye, or nearly, and told me she didn't want to hear about it. If I desired a relationship with the woman, I should feel free, but she didn't want to know anything about it. My father chimed in that my mother really meant what she said, then asked me where I kept the dish towels. That was that: end of conversation.

But I knew more discussion was needed and now, having finally deposited Grandma Ethel back at the Regency, my car seemed to go on automatic pilot. It headed for Brooklyn and even found a parking space on Avenue O, around the corner from my parents' building. (If I'd had to go as far as Avenue P, I probably would have chickened out and gone straight back to Long Island.) I called and cut short my father's "By the time you get here, it'll be so late . . ." As I got off the elevator on their floor, I thought that if someone blindfolded me and turned me around a few times, like in Pin the Tail on the Donkey, I would have no problem walking a straight line to the door of their apartment. I'd rely on either the familiarity of having lived in that one place until I was seventeen, or the scent of garlic powder.

After I'd accepted a glass of store-brand seltzer with bubbles the size of my fist, we sat down in the living room. The only photographs were the ones I'd given them framed—our wedding picture and one of the triplets we'd taken when they were eight months and could sit up by themselves. For that one, I'd ordered anti-UV glass, so it was the only thing in the room not faded. The boys' blue, red, and yellow onesies, cute but ordinary, made them look like a riotous circus act in that dead brown room.

"I wanted to talk to you about your mother coming to see me," I told my own mother. Before she could object, I said, "I need to clear the air. Please view it as a favor to me. I'll be as quick as I can, and then I won't bring it up again unless you want to talk about it. Okay?"

"Do you have any idea what kind of person would walk out on, *abandon* her own child?" my father demanded. His voice had double or triple the emotion he normally expressed in his most passionate moments—debunking sciatica cures not sold by My Aching Back. "Do you, Susan?"

"Yes, I do have an idea. She'd be a person with terrible character or who's really disturbed," I said. Turning to my mother, I went on, "In her case, I vote for terrible character."

"Then why did you seek her out that time you went to Florida?" She often sounded angry, but that was everyday bitterness about glass ceilings, polluters, Al Sharpton, or pharmaceutical companies. This was a different anger; while she wasn't at all hoarse, her voice sounded raw. "It was early in your marriage, but I'll bet any amount of money looking for her wasn't Jonah's idea."

"I was curious."

"Curiosity—" my father began, but fortunately, he let it go.

"Your mother has always been the mystery woman," I said, "the subject nobody ever mentioned. I wanted to see for myself. Maybe it was wanting to look into the face of a monster. That visit came around the time everybody was getting into genealogy. It was a chance to see where I came from."

"You came from me!" my mother said. "And him." She

jerked her chin toward my father. "There was no mystery. What in God's name is the matter with you? Why is it a mystery when someone doesn't talk about a person who did them wrong, who put a blight on their whole life?"

"Maybe I wasn't mature enough to understand that." I tried to sound both soothing and sorry.

"Oh, please! A child could understand that. But no, you heard about her, that she was on TV. The big shot: 'Oh, *everybody* in Miami knows Ethel.' What were you doing, looking for a new mother?"

"No—"

"A rich mother who went to the beauty parlor three times a week?"

I had an awful feeling she was going to add "Someone you weren't embarrassed about?" and I would have had to lie and say "Don't be ridiculous." I quickly said, "I already had a mother. You, okay? Why would I have wanted another one?" There were several possible answers, but I kept going. "And of all the people in the world, if I were searching for a mother figure, why would I pick someone who had proved herself to be totally incompetent as a mother? Worse than incompetent: selfish and cruel."

All that was true. Yet walking around Soho with Grandma Ethel after the meeting with Eddie Huber, laughing at lace-sided pants and thousand-dollar military-style boots, then having Japanese beer and sushi and telling her about the weekend I'd moved in with Jonah, had been better for my spirit than any time I had ever spent with my mother.

"Now that she's an old lady, she wants a family?" my father wanted to know. "Don't make me laugh!"

Knowing that was close to impossible, I tried to tell them that Grandma Ethel wanted something or maybe wanted to do something. She was back in town. But my mother didn't give me a chance to talk. "You'll see," she said, "you'll be hearing from her again. She'll call, try to insinuate herself into your life. And then what? You want to know what?"

"She'll drop me like a hot potato," I said.

She nodded. I guess she meant to look wise, but it came off like a bad imitation of Yoda. "That's right! She'll charm the pants off you, then drop you for the pure pleasure of inflicting pain."

"I'll watch out for that," I said quietly.

"Look at the bright side," my father said to my mother. "Maybe she'll drop dead tomorrow and leave you everything."

"Stanley," my mother exhaled. "How can you be so naive? It'll all go to her girlfriend." She shook her head in sadness. "I was always a supporter of gay rights, but to think they can make a will any old way they want and completely cut out the family . . . Not that I ever expected anything." She turned to me. "I don't think I have any memories of her." She tugged at the neckline of her Air America FOR THOSE OF US LEFT . . . sweatshirt. "Is there any resemblance between her and you?" she asked me.

"Yes. It's pretty strong, actually. Same color and shape eyes, same bone structure, body type."

"Funny," she said.

"At least I didn't inherit her character," I said, no doubt fishing for an "Of course not!" All I heard was a grumble from my father's stomach.

Right after the kids left for school the next morning, I went back to sleep. It was one of those awkward situations when, because you don't know the person who's vowing to support you, you don't know if she means what she says. Grandma Ethel's "I'm here for you" might have been the truth; on the other hand, when she mentioned she hadn't been to Barneys in a couple of years, her voice had the wistful tone of someone who had a strong need to scrutinize avant-garde gloves. Still, on the chance she would call, I didn't turn off the phone ringer to avoid the "just calling to check how you're doing" calls, though their number had plummeted in the last couple of weeks anyway. Besides, my mother's warning was still fresh in my ears. It wouldn't have surprised me if my grandmother had simply picked up and gone back to Miami because she wanted to hurt me for the pure pleasure of it. Not that I really believed she would do that, but I couldn't rule it out.

So I was surprised to be wakened at a quarter to twelve when the bedroom door opened and Grandma Ethel, hand on the knob but facing the staircase, shouted, "Thank you, Bernadine sweetheart. I found the room." It was probably the first time in Bernadine's life anyone had called her "sweetheart," and she called back in a sugary voice I'd never heard, "Let me know if you need anything, Mrs. O'Shea."

"You need some more sleep?" my grandmother asked. "I can go read or tiptoe into your closet and try on your clothes. What size are you? An eight?"

"Yes," I said, sitting up and feeling with my feet for my shoes, "but more toward a six than a ten."

"I'm more toward a ten, but I know how to breathe in. You getting up?"

"Yes, but you can still try on my clothes if you want to."

"'Tomorrow is another day.' Know who said that?"

"Scarlett O'Hara."

"Right. So listen, that Eddie Huber? What's with the Eddie? I didn't pick up any signals." Before I could answer, she said, "I'll tell you what bothers me about her. Between you and me and a lamppost, like my uncle Morty used to say, I think she's part of a cover-up."

"Of what?"

I must have gasped "Of what?" because she quickly said, "Calm down. It's no major deal. Let me tell you." She tried to hurry me downstairs immediately. But whenever I woke up, I needed to brush my teeth right away. She followed me into the bathroom, just like the boys did, and talked while I brushed. "I think they all decided that Dorinda was the killer much too fast. That's what I think. What kind of investigation did they do? All they really did was send in a forensics team, do an autopsy—which of course they have to—and then try to track down Dorinda." I spat out the toothpaste, and she asked, "You don't brush your tongue?"

"Yes, I do. Usually my tongue and the roof of my mouth. Under my tongue at night. But we're having a conversation." I rinsed and went on, "But what is Eddie Huber covering up?"

"That the cops and the DA didn't do all that needed doing. They focused right in on Dorinda and said, 'Screw peripheral vision. We don't have to look anyplace else.' I'm not saying they're railroading her. I'm only saying that Eddie is one smart cookie. She's using her legal smarts to fend off any doubts about the case, because they're all committed to it. I admit it's a case that does make sense. And the sense is backed up with evidence. Our Ms. Huber is not going to open it up for more investigation based on your questions, your hunches. She made her argument to convince you, keep you on the reservation, put a million doubts in your mind about what you'd been thinking. But she also made it to convince herself because—it's just possible—some of your doubts sparked doubts in her."

I ran a brush through my hair, then we walked downstairs. "So in making the case to me, she's also working to convince herself how solid it is?"

"Right. She wants to believe their case is solid gold. She wants to show that asking why a call girl would up and kill a nice, paying client with hairdresser's scissors is a stupid question, like all the ones you've been asking. She's convincing herself the victim's wife has gone off the deep end and shouldn't be listened to. Heard out? Definitely, but that's all."

I was going to make a pot of coffee, but Bernadine was still sterilizing the kitchen. She beamed at my grandmother and offered to make us a pot and bring it into the library—a room everyone, including Bernadine, always called the den. She obviously was impressed with Grandma Ethel. I wondered if it was a new crush and if she'd stop watching FOX, waiting for a glimpse of Bill Hemmer.

"Listen, some lawyers do that," my grandmother went on. "They have to convince themselves of the rightness of their cases because that's how they do their best arguing. Sparky isn't like that. She's so cynical about everything. The only thing she believes in is the system. She can argue anything, any side of a case."

"It doesn't bother her when she thinks someone's wrong?"

"Absolutely one hundred percent not. Before she went into public interest law, her civil liberties stuff, she worked in a big law firm representing newspaper publishers, shitheads like you wouldn't believe. She says some of the people she represents now are no better, but it's *justice* she fights for, and these clients can't pay for it, like the newspaper shitheads can. She says everyone who deals with the system has to have someone arguing for them with passion, using everything the law allows. But your Eddie doesn't think like that. She needs to be Good fighting Evil. So when she believes 'Dorinda bad, Dorinda guilty,' she'll stay with it till her dying breath."

"If it turns out, which is a real possibility, that it was Dorinda, then I guess I'm lucky to have Eddie Huber on my side."

"On the case, toots, not on your side."

So where do I go from here? I thought. I looked over at a little settee Jonah and I had bought in Vermont the first time we went away without the kids. It had been pretty much a wasted weekend because we spent it reassuring each other that everything was fine with them, and if there was any trouble, his parents and the au pair we had then would call us. But we'd gone into an antiques store and seen some of those old pieces of furniture made for children, teeny rockers, itty-bitty tea tables. We'd spotted a Federalist settee, as much bench as couch, with a back made of three separate panels. We got it for half the asking price because the store owner said a lovely young couple with triplets deserved a piece like this, and also because sometime between, say, 1810 and 2005, it had been broken, glued, and repegged many times, something Jonah noticed and politely pointed out. I'd been so proud of his classiness that day, that he was direct but low-key and never made anyone feel he was backing them into a corner.

The boys used to love sitting in it together, but now it was becoming a little tight for them, and most of the time they grabbed throw pillows and watched the room's big TV from the floor. Soon it would be a settee for two, then one, then, off in a corner, something they could reminisce about to their friends. "Yeah, believe it or not, we all used to fit in it—with room to spare." Or maybe "Can you believe my mother paid good money for that fucking ugly piece of crap?" Or "That little couch thing was from before my father was murdered."

"Well," I said, "if Eddie Huber is Good versus Evil, and also right, then by the time the boys grow up and graduate from college, Dorinda will still be in jail."

"And I'll be dead," Grandma Ethel said. "Stop! Don't tell me 'You'll still be boogying at a hundred.' Dead. Or demented and tied into my wheelchair with surgical tape. The only attractive part of me will be my dental implants, and that's because they're made of titanium. But let me tell you something about then, Susie. I'll be gone, you'll still be gorgeous—and even if Eddie Huber was absolutely wrong, and Dorinda is telling the truth, she'll still be rotting in jail."

Chapter Twenty-Four

✂───

"What are we looking for?" I asked.

"The truth," Grandma Ethel said. "Or let's call it proof."

We'd finished our coffee in the den and then went into Jonah's study with a plate of uncategorized food Bernadine had put on the tray. The bottom line of the stuff on the plate seemed to be *small,* so maybe it was the Bernadine Pietrowicz version of teatime canapés: string cheese cut into one-inch lengths; half an English muffin with peanut butter sliced like a pie into six pieces, a dab of grape jelly on each; leftover mini–Danish pastries she'd frozen after the shiva, and now had almost defrosted; some almonds.

"Proof of what?"

"Beats the hell out of me," my grandmother said.

I sat in Jonah's chair, and as I tried to think of something, I ate a couple of the canapés. They were an odd combination, but either it was inspired catering or we were starved: The plate was empty in under a minute. "How about . . ." I said very slowly because I had no idea what I was thinking. "Maybe we should see what there is to be seen."

"That means nothing!" my grandmother said. "What are you, a fortune-teller at a carnival, mouthing gobbledygook? 'See what there is to be seen'?"

"No, seriously. Don't be a . . . whatever that word for old and cranky is."

"Curmudgeon?" Grandma Ethel asked.

"No, something else. Forget it. What I want to do is look at the stuff other people already looked at."

"You mean the cops?"

"The cops, but also that investigative agency, Kroll. I hired them when Jonah didn't come home. They only worked on it for a couple of days, but the woman who's like, whatever, my personal private detective or account executive—she gave me a ton of stuff they put on a CD. I've never looked at it."

"Okay," she said cautiously.

"I want to see if, when we look at all the information, we wind up with lots more questions that the cops should have asked, or if it's a collection of unrelated data. Because what you said about them deciding too fast that Dorinda's guilty, that rings true to me." I added, "We can do something else if you'd rather."

"What are you talking about?"

"I mean, if you want to talk, go for a drive, look at stores. There's a really upscale shopping center about fifteen minutes from here, with Van Cleef and Arpels, Bottega Veneta—"

"Stop! There are two things in life, style and substance. Okay? Do you think I'd drop looking into Jonah's death to go see those bronze woven-leather handbags? Well, you might think that. What the hell, I might do it. But not today. Not to you. So for now, I'm all substance."

Everything Jonah had on him when he was killed was still with the police or the DA, being held as evidence. That included his BlackBerry. I knew his password for it, f-a-c-e-s. I turned on his computer but soon realized I could access his office calendar only through the Manhattan Aesthetics website. Except f-a-c-e-s didn't work to enter the site.

Suddenly I had a *ping!* of irrationality, that all I had to do was call Jonah and ask what his password was. He'd tell me. I didn't know whether it was the subconscious or the unconscious popping up with such a thought, but it weirded me out that somewhere in my head a dopey smiley-face of a wish just kept rolling along, no matter how many times it crashed into reality.

After f-a-c-e-s, I tried other word-and-number combos we'd used over the years for our alarm system and ATM accounts: the boys' birth date, the last four digits of our phone number in New Haven, G-i-a-n-t-s because he loved football. I was getting into a sweat that all my tries would kick in a security warning to their webmaster. I'd wind up on a speakerphone call with Gilbert John and Layne saying, "Susie, you simply could have asked us."

Then I remembered before our wedding, when Jonah and I were discussing whether or not monograms were cool, he'd given me a wicked smile and drawn my married name in mock embroidery script with lots of ridiculous curlicues: SBARG, Susan B Anthony Rabinowitz Gersten. Sometimes he'd even e-mail me, "Hey, SBARG . . ." Those initials got me into the website. I brought around another chair so Grandma Ethel could see the monitor. While she went to get her reading glasses, I sat in the quiet room and looked at the calendar for the day he died.

I had no clear memory of our last time together. When I'd woken up and Jonah wasn't lying beside me, I'd gotten so caught up in fear that I'd lost any recollection of our breakfast together on the last day of his life. He said all my breakfasts were the same, that I had zero breakfast imagination—always Cheerios with a quarter cup of trail mix. But Jonah was his own creative breakfast chef. I didn't know why it was important to me to recall whether he'd made scrambled eggs or Irish oatmeal that final morning, but knowing would be a comfort.

I scrolled down to the early evening of his last day. Liz Holbreich had told me that Kroll's computer expert had discovered Dorinda's name and Jonah's appointment with her hadn't been entered until around eleven-thirty that morning; his BlackBerry had been synced earlier, so the Dorinda appointment was missing. Even though I knew it would be on his calendar, I shivered when I saw it: *6:45 pm D.D.* I double-clicked on the entry to see if there was anything under Notes. There wasn't, but I noticed he'd allotted one hour for the appointment, not that he had anything else on the schedule for that evening. I used Search to check the rest of the calendar, but there were no other entries for Dillon, Dorinda, DD, or D.D.

As Grandma Ethel returned with a pair of turquoise reading glasses that looked more old Miami than new, I switched from Day view to Month, as if I needed to minimize Jonah's disloyalty, though I did point out Dorinda's initials to her. As I clicked through each month, starting with the year before his death, I saw that nearly all his early-evening appointments were linked to the practice's patient database. The remainder I either knew about or could figure out. *Mac & Danny-drinks-YC,* YC being Yale Club. *Clean-Eileen,* an appointment with the hygienist in our dentist's office. *See Danny C,* his sports orthopedist, probably for his tennis elbow. Committee meetings, talks—a fair number to the men's groups that basically boiled down to "What to do when your double chin hangs over the knot in your tie." The clinic work he did at Mount Sinai, repairing facial injuries on victims of domestic violence.

"The more I look," I told my grandmother, "the more it confirms that he didn't have a secret life."

"Okay," she said, drawing out the word.

"You mean he may have had a secret life that he didn't put on his calendar."

"That *was* what I was thinking," she said. "But then it hit me that he did put 'D.D.' on it. Of course it was interesting that he only used her initials." Her lipstick had caked on the corners of her mouth, and she kept wiping them with her thumb and index finger. From the repetition, I sensed she was as deep in thought as she got and not doing a quick lipstick fix. "Okay," she finally said, "let's assume Jonah had a clean bill of health marriage-wise—except for Dorinda in the early evening."

"All right," I said. "Then we ought to go through the calendar and see what else he was doing during his days that wasn't linked to patients or something medical-surgical-business. But there are a lot of entries, and it's hard to tell what's what."

"You know what I'm thinking?" my grandmother asked. "I'll tell you. I'm thinking it's hard to interpret the calendar because even though you knew what Jonah did, you probably didn't know the minutiae of plastic surgery, the medical aspect—and the details of a surgical practice's business procedures."

"No. I mean, I have some general knowledge of the flower business just because I'm a partner in Florabella, but Andrea is the super-organized one, so I'm not up on the fine points. And Jonah's practice was so big and complex in comparison."

"I had a private investigator on my show a couple of times. Really easy to talk to, Cuban background, ran her whole operation herself. One of the things that struck me was she tried to learn as much as she could about whatever business she was investigating—wholesale jewelry, outboard motors, gift shops. She said the more she knew, the more comfortable she was in one world or another, the clearer she could see if there was any event or pattern that looked strange."

"That's interesting." *Must have been a riveting show,* I thought as I got busy aligning the keyboard with the edge of the shelf it sat on. "I'd feel awkward calling Gilbert John or Layne or the office manager to tell me about the ins and outs of running a plastic surgery practice. Anyway, Jonah was really unhappy with the office manager not being on top of things, so it would be doubly sticky."

She started working on the sides of her mouth again, even though there were no traces of dried lipstick anymore. When she pulled down, I could see how thin her skin was, how it was so much more loosely attached to her face than a younger woman's would be.

"I still have a little heat on in the house," I said. "It gets dry. Do you want some lip balm?"

"No, don't need it. But you're wasting your money on lip balm. Vaseline. It's the answer to a maiden's prayers. So tell me, what was the trouble with the office manager?"

"Jonah wasn't crazy about him to begin with. The guy's name is Donald Finsterwald. Jonah didn't like the way he sucked up to the doctors but basically didn't care if the rest of the world dropped dead. As far as I knew, he seemed all right at what he did, and he wasn't terrible with the staff. Just patronizing. I really didn't hear that much about him. But Liz—"

"The investigator," my grandmother said.

"Right. She said Jonah thought Donald was doing a lousy job and was really upset. Jonah had e-mailed him about it. With the economy, they needed to do more marketing and PR, but Donald was doing less. And Liz found e-mails from Jonah to Donald about him doing a bad job tracking the practice's financial performance."

I gave her a fast rundown on the personalities: Gilbert John Noakes, the Founding Father, who now expected to pull out major money for traveling to professional conferences and doing pro bono surgery around the world. "Jonah said when Gilbert John took him in, and then Layne, he made a speech about someday wanting to do less for himself and more for the world, but someday came sooner than Jonah anticipated. Gilbert John was doing more for the world, but he never got around to expecting less for himself."

"And the other doctor, Layne, didn't take Jonah's side?" she asked.

"No. She's a good surgeon and a sweetie socially, but she seems violently allergic to confrontation in any form. Jonah used to imitate her in this kind of high-pitched gentle voice: 'Isn't it pleasant to be pleasant?'"

"So," Grandma Ethel said, "you know more about his practice than you thought you did."

"But I didn't get it all from Jonah. I don't know whether he was keeping some of it to himself, so as not to upset me, or because by the time he left the office to come home, he was sick of it."

"The point is, you have some knowledge. It doesn't matter where it comes from. Let's see if anything on his calendar jumps out at us. Print out a set of monthlies so I don't waste what's left of my eyesight on the computer screen."

Jonah had only a couple of pens with dark blue ink, so I hit the boys' art supply basket and came back with a flat box containing a rainbow of thin-tipped markers. We decided to circle any questionable entry on the printed calendar pages. After a couple of minutes, Grandma Ethel found she had too many questionables and insisted I print out another set of calendar pages so we didn't have to share. She wound up finishing ahead of me because as I came to an appointment I couldn't make sense of, I'd switch to Jonah's contacts list and see if I could find something that came close.

I made pretty good progress, although even when there was a listing for the "Jun" who was on his calendar the first week in January at ten-thirty in the morning, it had only a Manhattan phone number. It looked as if Jonah was between surgeries at that hour, but I couldn't get up the courage to pick up the phone. Maybe I was thinking "Jun" was a "We'll gladly come to your office" prostitution ring.

Grandma Ethel reached across me, dialed the number, and

asked for Jun. "Hello. This is an official call," she said. I had no idea what that meant and neither did she, but it sounded important. "We found your name and number in the records of Dr. Jonah Gersten. You've heard . . ." The person on the other side of the line talked, then talked some more. Finally, Grandma Ethel said, "I see. Thank you. We appreciate your cooperation," and hung up.

"Who was it?" I asked.

"The guy who made Jonah's custom shirts. He heard about it, he's really sorry, and he made the shirts but decided not to send them because that might—I forgot his exact words—cause offense or hurt. There's no deposit or refund because Jonah had been a customer for five years. Jun would come to Jonah's office with fabric swatches. He said Jonah stayed the same size, never gained weight or got flabby. That's it in a nutshell."

"What are you not telling me?"

"Aren't you Little Miss Cross-examiner," she said. "What makes you think there's something I'm not telling?" I didn't have time to answer. "Nothing. In fact, it was complimentary in a way. Something to the effect that a fine gentleman like Dr. Gersten should not have to die that way. My first thought was, *If a guy was a redneck slob, he deserved to be stabbed to death?* But like Sidney, my second husband, said once too often, 'Ethel, that remark is beneath you.' Anyway, I wasn't keeping anything from you. I say whatever comes into my head. It's part of my charm. See? I tried to do something unnatural—censor myself— and you picked it up in two seconds flat."

One name started popping up early in November: Marty. The last Marty entry was eleven days before Jonah was killed. I couldn't tell whether the appointments were in or out of the office, but they were all between noon and one in the afternoon. Grandma and I each circled five Martys, which struck us as possibly pertinent, especially when I couldn't find any Marty or Martin in Jonah's personal contacts. There were four Manhattan

Aesthetics patients whose last name was Martin, one with Martin as a first name, and a Martino. Of them, only Brigitte Martin and Denise Martino were Jonah's patients, and I couldn't think of a way to call and ask "Did you have lunch or something else five times with my husband?"

Grandma Ethel was almost as tired as I was, so we called it quits. Bernadine's teatime goodies hadn't been enough, so I made us tuna-fish wraps on whole-wheat tortillas. By the time we were finishing, the boys and the twins had arrived. My grandmother looked from one to the other, not seeming at all appalled, but after being Fun Great-grandmother for fifteen minutes, she had me call a car service to take her back to the city.

As she left, I was on the verge of saying "See you tomorrow," when I realized I might be overstepping my bounds in assuming she'd be around. There probably weren't any such bounds with a sweet old granny you'd known forever. But Ethel O'Shea was not in that category. Besides, she had a life and a lover in another city, and whenever she mentioned Sparky, I could tell she missed her. Maybe I'd soon be on my own in finding the truth about Jonah's murder.

Chapter Twenty-Five

The next morning, since I was stuck in thinking-about-partners mode anyway, I called Gilbert John. I thought both he and Layne would be in on a Thursday morning, operating and seeing patients. I asked if I could come into town and meet with them. Gilbert John said, "Of course!" in his most mellifluous voice, but I could hear he was baffled about why I wanted to stop in. He asked if there were any papers or documents I wanted to look at that they could have ready for me. I was clearly an unscheduled annoyance, though he didn't intimate that. I told him I had no agenda. I wanted to see the two of them, talk with them.

Since Grandma Ethel's habit seemed to be hiring a car and driver to bring her out to Long Island and simply ringing the doorbell, I called her and told her I'd be in the city meeting with Jonah's partners. "Don't ask them directly," she murmured, as if she were cupping the mouthpiece with her hand to avoid being overheard by a crowd of paparazzi just dying to listen in on the conversation of a seventy-nine-year-old.

"Don't ask them what?"

"Don't rush me, I'll work cheaper. What I'm saying is you

shouldn't ask them up-front if there were any serious bad feelings between Jonah and that Donald person. It would only put them on guard. Can you be subtle?"

"I'll give it my best shot." Then I added, "Even if there was genuine hatred, which I can't imagine being the case on Jonah's part, how could that translate into Jonah getting killed at Dorinda's place?"

"Are you having qualms?" my grandmother asked. "You know what I mean. Qualms about questioning the whole rush-to-judgment process." Apparently, being a person with qualms wasn't an asset in my grandmother's book. While she didn't sound pissed at the possibility, her inquiry couldn't be called neutral.

"No, no qualms. I just want to be clear in my head where I'm going."

"Where else would you be clear if not in your head?" I was getting the impression that eight-forty-five A.M. was not Grandma Ethel's finest hour. "All right, I'll tell you what. Call me on my cell when you're finished with them. I'll either be out walking or having my nails done. I'll tell you, I shouldn't have moved from New York. A nail salon on every block, and so cheap compared to Miami."

Moved? I was tempted to ask. Like her leaving was a job transfer or a yen for a warm climate? How about ran from New York, abandoning your child to Lenny the Loser? Yet here I was, hoping this woman who had done something I considered perfectly dreadful wouldn't fly out of my life. As for the woman she'd done the dreadful thing to, who happened to be my mother, I gladly would have given her all my frequent-flyer miles if she'd move someplace else. Arizona, maybe, or some expat town in Mexico for retirees with allergies and personality deficiencies.

"Whenever I'm done," I promised, "I'll call."

Manhattan Aesthetics looked like most other Park Avenue upscale, highly touted plastic surgery practices: modern furniture that went for wood over metal (warmth, genuineness); muted colors, mossy green and cream (tranquil, gender-neutral, conveying confidence that the patients weren't slobs prone to staining furniture); and soft classical music (elegant, calming, as in "Your tummy tuck will be as marvelous as Bach's Air on the G string"). In other words, it was somewhere between chic and inoffensive, but since every plastic surgeon I'd ever met thought he or she was in the ninety-ninth percentile of some Exquisite Taste aptitude test, the only opinion I'd offered was saying "Fabulous!" when their decorator was done.

Gilbert John Noakes and Layne Jiménez must have been buzzed the instant I opened the door because they swept into the waiting room together and gave me a duet of "Susie! Good to see you! Susie! We were so touched you decided to come in!" before I got halfway across the room.

I'd been so focused on talking to the two of them that it hadn't occurred to me how affected I'd be going to the place not just where Jonah had worked five days a week, but to the practice he'd helped sustain and grow. I knew nearly all the staff from holiday parties and from dropping in when I was in the city to meet Jonah, or just to use the bathroom and leave my packages between shopping and a museum. There were kisses, hugs, a gamut of handshakes and "How are you doing?" asked politely or with concern. Because Jonah must have had at least a thousand pictures of the boys and me in his office, everyone asked after them. Mandy, the woman I thought of as the supply/coffee lady although she had some other title, took my hands in hers and said, "There's a hole in my heart." Normally, that sort of comment made me want to stick my index finger in my mouth and mimic retching, but I could only squeeze her hands. If I'd tried to say thank you, I would have broken into sobs.

Since the hallways were big enough for two people walking side by side, or one and a gurney, Gilbert John fell behind and let Layne take me into the conference room. It wasn't really for conferences. The table could seat six and was covered in leather, so in spite of the decorator swearing it was treated, any emphatic gesture near an open can of Diet Coke would probably equal disaster. It was set for lunch with mirrored place mats, octagonal plates I was sure I'd have recognized if my tastes had gone to late-twentieth-century modern, and a platter of sandwiches. I looked at the seven- or nine-grain bread and wondered whether Jonah's death had freed them to give up salads or, if in the less than two months since he'd been gone, there'd been a revolution in Upper East Side lunch thinking.

After my "The boys are doing great, considering" and ten sentences on their spouses plus Layne's children, the conversation began to go slo-mo. Before it could stop totally, leaving us in unbearable silence, I said, "I should be the one giving you lunch, or giving you something. The two of you have been so decent throughout all this. I know it's been an ordeal for you, too, not just because of your professional and business ties to Jonah, but because when you lose someone you really care about at work, there's no kind of formal mourning process that helps you get over it. I just want to thank you for being so strong and so there for me."

Both gave me their version of thank-yous being unnecessary. Layne said a partnership like theirs was another form of family, and members of a family did for one another. Gilbert John quoted a poem, "'No man is an island . . .'" I'd heard it before and, frankly, didn't want to listen to it again. Then he came down to earth a little and said from the first time he'd met Jonah, when Jonah was a resident, he'd known he was superior: not just as a surgeon but as a man. He was gratified that they'd been able to form a special bond. In grievous circumstances like these, he would always hope to be able to reach out and offer help, but the boys and I were a very special case because we were part of what was Jonah.

Just when you thought Gilbert John couldn't go on and on

because he'd used up all the words in the entire universe, he'd stop, giving you hope that there was an invisible THE END sign. As usual, I fell for it, taking a deep breath in preparation for sighing in relief, but then the monologue continued, about Jonah's balance and how he'd fitted the various pieces of his life into a beautiful mosaic.

I tried to tune him out while I had a triangle of turkey and avocado and a bite of a grilled vegetables with hummus wrap that tasted like something you regret buying at an airport. Finally, I set it down, wiped my fingers, and said, "I've spoken with the chief of Homicide at the DA's office a couple of times." The two of them nodded politely. "Mostly, it was because I had some questions."

"About what?" Layne asked. She leaned forward, listening so intently that you'd think she was wishing she could grow another pair of ears to better hear what you were about to say.

"About their case against Dorinda Dillon." I glanced around. Someone, probably Mandy, had forgotten to put out water and soda, and I was thirsty. But I didn't want to ask for anything, because then they'd be upset that she wasn't doing her job. "I have some questions about the investigation, and also about how fast they focused on her being the one who killed Jonah."

They stared at me like I was a foreign movie and the English subtitles had disappeared. I didn't go into a lot of detail. I did mention Dorinda's lack of any history of violence and also the bump on her head that she'd claimed the real murderer had inflicted on her, though I left out the electric broom, as it needed too much explaining.

Without looking at each other, both of them reacted in pretty much the same way: tilting their head to the side and drawing their brows together in an *I don't get it* expression. Gilbert John straightened his head first and said, "I understand your being concerned that the authorities should do a thorough job."

"I feel uncomfortable coming here like this. It's not like me to go on about stuff like justice and ethics, but there are some details of the case that don't seem right."

Layne propped her elbows on the table and rested her chin on top of her entwined fingers. "This must make it even more painful for you," she said compassionately. "Of course you care about justice. You're a good person. That's one of the reasons Jonah loved you so much." She kept going in her lullaby of a voice. I started getting the feeling that Layne was intent on making me feel good because she knew about lots of other call girls in Jonah's life, to say nothing of seventy-five affairs with non-professionals.

When she finally finished, Gilbert John was pulling some excess roast beef from between two triangles of bread. He looked as though he wanted to pop it into his mouth, but he put it on the side of his octagonal plate. "It's impossible not to be touched by your concern, Susie. It does you great credit," he said.

"It was their total focus on Dorinda Dillon," I continued, feeling they needed more of an explanation. "If all they could think about was her, they weren't looking to see if anyone else was involved."

"I see," Layne said softly. "I understand where you're coming from."

"As do I," Gilbert John said. "You should never hold back on questioning authority. However . . ." He hesitated, probably because he was afraid of me reacting with this huge, hysterical fit. But he obviously decided to risk it. "In my opinion, only one person killed your husband. Dorinda Dillon. I'm sorry, Susie."

"I'm not so sure," I said. "I wish I were."

After I left the building, I called Grandma Ethel. She told me I should eat grilled vegetables only in four-star restaurants because lesser places served leftovers soaked in olive oil to revive them. Then she said it sounded like I needed company and to pick her up in front of the Regency in fifteen minutes. When

I did, a bellman was beside her with a huge, impressively aged Vuitton suitcase. "Don't worry," she said to me as the bellman, still thanking her for his tip, closed the car door. "I'll only stay a couple of days. Sparky has meetings in Atlanta, and anyway, you need me. If I get on your nerves, just sic the little tykes on me. Oh, excuse me, before you correct me: my great-grandsons."

While Grandma Ethel unpacked in the guest room, which was as far from the boys' rooms as it could be and still be part of the house, I went into my home office, a room the size of an inadequate walk-in closet, and turned on my computer. There was nothing in my e-mail that made me want to double-click, but I did notice the cursor seemed to be pointing out an emptiness in the Google box. It really was one of those "before I knew it" moments when, the second before, I was wondering if I could still order pizza for dinner, as I'd been planning. Suddenly, there I was, typing *Joel Winters* into the search box.

"Winters," he said. It wasn't necessarily worrisome that a criminal lawyer answered his own phone on the first ring—unless you were a client. The thought went through my mind that his secretary could be out to lunch, though four in the afternoon was a little late for that. Still, I considered she might have gone to the ladies' room and he, busy poring over law books where he would find an old precedent that would save a client from a lifetime behind bars, had been jarred by the phone and grabbed it. But there was something in his "Winters" that sounded both desperate and aggressive.

I hadn't expected him to get on the phone immediately, so my plan for what I was going to say wasn't fully formed. That was like saying a two-week-old embryo wasn't fully formed.

"Joel Winters?" I asked.

"Yeah."

"You're Dorinda Dillon's attorney?"

"Who's this?" I didn't see him showing up on my mother-in-law's guest list, even if she had an opening at the table for someone a little rough around the edges.

"Mr. Winters, my name is . . ." I swallowed, not buying time but because I knew I'd be lying. "Ethel O'Shea. I'm working on an article for *The New York Observer*, and I was wondering—"

"I read it all the time." Compared to his initial "Winters," this response sounded like someone had turned on an eighteen-light Murano chandelier inside him.

"Good, glad to hear it." I said it without too much enthusiasm, since that didn't seem to be a quality a journalist would have or want. "The piece is called 'Dialing for Death.' It's about call girls charged with serious crime."

"You want to ask me about Dorinda?"

I sensed a few of the lights in his chandelier had gone out, so I said, "This is my hook: It's the easy way out for the cops and the prosecutors to target a prostitute for murder. It doesn't require a lot of convincing."

"You know the guy was found in her apartment," he said. I couldn't see a best-selling biography entitled *Joel Winters for the Defense* appearing anytime soon. "But you're right. It doesn't take a lot of convincing. Just say 'The ho did it' and be done with it. Wipe their hands of it. Move on to the next case."

"I'd like to come in and talk to you," I said. "Get a sense of you and your work."

"I'm in the process of moving. My office is a mess."

"I'm not interested in how your office looks. I'm interested in what you have to say about your client."

"Let me see," Joel Winters said. "I've got an opening, a couple of openings actually, early next week."

"Sorry, I've got a deadline. I'd really like to be able to quote you, but it's got to be tomorrow or nothing."

"Okay, tomorrow. What time's good for you?"

Just as I hung up, my grandmother stepped into the room.

"'Dialing for Death'? That is *the* worst name for an article I've ever heard."

"Were you eavesdropping?"

"Were you lying through your teeth and using my name?"

"Yes."

"There you go. Let me tell you something here and now. I don't have many scruples. Three, maybe four, but not when it comes to eavesdropping. Anyway, what does this Joel Winters sound like?"

"Not quite the scum of the earth."

"But close?" Grandma Ethel asked.

"Close as they come."

Chapter Twenty-Six

When the phone rang a little after eleven that night, I tried to sleep through it. Having been married to a plastic surgeon, I'd learned to ignore late-night calls because 99 percent of them were from the answering service about ooze or a patient panicking that once the swelling went down, she would still resemble a duck-billed platypus. But my brain must have been wider awake than I was. It understood *No surgeon in bedroom anymore.* My eyes opened. I glanced toward the caller ID readout, half thinking it must be Sparky calling my grandmother, but it was glowing so brightly I couldn't read it. After a throat-clearing so my "hello" wouldn't sound like a death rattle, I picked up the phone.

"Hey, Susie," I heard. "I know it's late, but we need to talk."

Jonah! I thought.

Of course I knew it couldn't be him. But still, that voice! With a giant *bam!* my heart seemed to explode. Tiny pieces of heart shrapnel shot through my body and, for an instant, filled me with joy. Nevertheless, even while overwhelmed with that euphoria, I was clear enough to ask, "Who is this, please?" Even though Jonah had been murdered, autopsied, and buried, I half expected to hear him answer, "'Who is this?' Susan B Anthony Rabinowitz Gersten, give me a fucking break!"

"It's Theo." I had been sleeping so deeply that I'd missed the big difference between his voice and Jonah's. Theo's perpetual peevishness always emerged within two or three words. Now I heard that touch of whine in his drawn-out "Theee-ooo." In all the years, I had never answered the phone and mistaken one brother for the other. Theo forever sounded like he'd just been given the smaller scoop of ice cream. "Are you okay to talk?" he asked.

"Yes. Sure."

"There's something . . . there's something I want to get some clarity on." Theo sounded agitated, but that was hardly a first. I braced the phone between my ear and shoulder and rubbed my eyes hard to get my depleted tear ducts functioning again. I guessed his issue was a major-major (as opposed to just a big) fight with my in-laws. Or, in descending order, career worries, money problems, women problems, drugs. "Are you all right?" I asked.

"I'm fine," he said brightly, so I knew another sentence was about to emerge to let me know me he wasn't fine. "I've got to tell you. I'm seriously concerned about my mother—her going off the deep end in the DA's office."

I gripped the phone and leaned back on the pillow. "Theo, I don't think you have to worry. Okay, she went off the deep end, but she came back. She offered me a really lovely apology."

"Good. I'm glad about that."

"So am I. I mean, all of us, our nerve endings are so frayed, so it's understandable. But all of us need each other's support to get through this hell."

"You know you always have had my support." It was true that he'd always been decent, never treated me as if any moment I might forget how to handle a knife and fork properly—the way Babs and Clive did—and muddy the name Gersten forever. "I'm on your side. That's part of what I want to talk to you about."

Beyond the built-in touch of petulance in my brother-in-law's voice, I thought I heard something else: strain, maybe anger. This wasn't head-on-pillow talk, so I sat up yoga-style, in a half-lotus position, and elongated my spine. I needed to be ready for whatever was coming, not tensed up.

"My mother's shit-fit outside that Huber woman's office . . ." Theo began. He seemed to be waiting for me to jump in with some comment.

"That's over."

"Look, the last thing in the world I want to do is hurt you, but I think there's a certain need for a reality check when it comes to your behavior." I didn't keep quiet out of any strategy but because I was so taken aback I couldn't think of anything to say. "I hate to say it, Susie, but my mother's mad scene—okay, it was over the top. But it was an appropriate reaction."

It was after eleven o'clock, for God's sake. Did I really have to stay on the phone with him while he worked up his monologue: "A Mother Driven Insane by Grief"? "Theo, you and I have always had a good relationship. We can survive a few bumps, so just tell me straight out what's on your mind."

A reluctant sigh. Theo had had enough acting lessons that it didn't sound theatrical, though I could sense it was a prelude to a rehearsed speech full of naked honesty. Or maybe tough love. I didn't give a damn as long as it was short. I could say "I'm sorry I didn't appreciate the profundity of your mother's anguish" and be asleep by eleven-thirty.

"I've held this in much too long. How could you *possibly* have expected my mother to maintain any semblance of self-control when faced with what you hit her with in Eddie Huber's office? Not just that you'd never given any of us a clue that you had these . . . these beliefs, but the utter irrationality of them. I don't know how to express how worried I am about you and your . . . let me just come out and say it: your delusions. You're seriously considering that the disgusting, cheap whore Jonah went to might not have done it?"

My mouth was open, but I wasn't talking. It was jaw-dropping, not only what he was saying but the harshness. It wasn't just his view of me that was getting me so upset but that he could be so blatantly harsh. I'd always thought of us as allies, the two members of the family his parents didn't approve of.

"Okay, fine," he went on, "maybe my mother shouldn't have been screaming in the halls of justice, or whatever they call that revolting place, but can't you begin to see the double horror of it for her? A murdered son. And then a daughter-in-law—the sole person in custody of her three grandchildren—who's desperately clinging to, quite frankly, an insane theory."

"How about 'a theory my parents and I strongly disagree with'?" I snapped. "And talk about insane: You should keep in mind, Theo, that I wasn't the one who completely lost control in public."

"Listen to me, Susie," he yelped. I may have heard a growl, too, because what popped into my mind as he spoke was our neighborhood psycho-dog, an Airedale that would strain on his leash, bare his teeth, and bark, unable to stop even as his choke collar began to strangle him.

"Calm down," I told him. "Just tell me what the problem is without using the word 'insane.'"

"The problem, Mrs. Gersten, is that with your barrage of questions and your pathological inability to accept the conclusions of more than competent professionals in the DA's office after a thorough investigation—"

"I have doubts about its thoroughness."

"You're jeopardizing the case against Dorinda Dillon!" he barked. "If it weren't for that, trust me, I wouldn't have brought this up. But the cops, the prosecutors, are acutely sensitive to public opinion. To them, you, with your endless questioning of their evidence and competence . . ." He was now so loud I had to hold the phone away from my ear. "You are just a time bomb they're terrified is going to blow up in their faces. And Jonah's killer could go free because of your craziness! You'd better get a grip, Susie. You better get a goddamn grip!" The line went dead as Theo apparently slammed down the phone.

I got so little sleep the rest of the night that the next morning I didn't even consider driving into the city. Though I probably could have found my way to Canal Street in Chinatown, the area of downtown Manhattan around the courthouses was a mystery to me. So I took the Long Island Rail Road and prayed that the subway directions to Joel Winters's office, which I'd gotten from the Internet, were right.

I was a total basket case. First of all, I was carrying my grandmother's old ID card from WPLG in Miami. Aside from the face on the card being decades older and ninety-five shades blonder, there was a resemblance, though not enough to convince any person with half a mind and/or the gift of sight. As the train sped and slowed through Queens and crept into the tunnel into Manhattan, I was dreading Joel Winters would not only ask for identification but actually look at it. Unfortunately, Grandma Ethel had not been very helpful, since her suggestion had been that I become a blonde. She seemed to believe that her picture on her ID and I were practically identical twins, so with me in light hair and bright red lipstick, we could pass for each other.

Right before I left, I'd remembered the Clarins tanning gel I'd bought the summer before and forgotten to use. I slimed it all over myself to get that *I use sunscreen, but hey, I live in Miami* color, but the directions said it took two hours to work. I prayed by the time I got to Joel Winters's office, I'd look like one of those hot bronze goddess statues everyone shleps back from India, not like a walking tangerine. Also, I'd pulled my hair into a ponytail, twisted it, and pinned it up; since all the photos of me in the news were with hair down, shoulder-length, maybe the change would help silence any she-looks-familiar bell.

Riding downtown on the subway, looking at faces, I remembered Jonah had talked about a rare kind of woman, one who was satisfied with how she looked. A plastic surgeon might think she could use several nips and a lot of tucks. That type of woman, though, would have been shocked to hear such a thing. It wasn't that she wanted to age naturally, without intervention. What he was talking about were the confident ones: pretty, plain, or even homely women who thought they were lovely the way they were. My grandma Ethel was one of them. She was truly pretty, but no one would call her dewy. Still, she was one of those who looked in the mirror and, at almost eighty, saw an ageless combination of Snow White, Cinderella, Ariel, and Anne Hathaway.

When I got to Joel Winters's office, I was surprised to find it had a working elevator and granite floors. My image had been so strong, and so Humphrey Bogart detective movie, that I'd been sure I would walk through a door with JOEL WINTERS, ATTY. AT LAW painted on its frosted glass pane: seedy, without the advantage of Humphrey in the role of Joel. Naturally, it wasn't at all like my other picture of a lawyer's office, which was the midtown firm where Jonah and I had made our wills after the triplets came: a forest of lacquered wood, legal pads, ballpoint pens, and mineral water, soda, and bottles of green tea on a credenza beside a stainless-steel bucket overflowing with ice. This place was a disappointment, probably not only to me but to its occupant. The small outer office did have a desk, chair, phone, and cup with a couple of pencils and a ruler, but there was no computer and no secretary.

The inner door opened and Joel Winters said, "Come in, Miss *New York Observer*. You're gonna have to forgive me, but I forgot your name."

"Ethel O'Shea." Here it was, the point he could ask "Can I see some ID?"

"Come in, come in. Sorry, my secretary's out on maternity leave." His office was about the size of the bedroom in our first Manhattan apartment. But that was where the resemblance stopped. With its dark beige carpet, light beige walls, and a medium brown desk, it managed to be unpleasant despite its aggressive neutrality. There were a couple of framed documents with foil seals, but they were hung so high it was hard to see whether they were diplomas or prizes in a pie-eating contest.

Not that he was fat. Winters was skinny—an old-fashioned word, but "thin" gives the picture of someone fit, or at least a person who knows about diet. From his rounded shoulders to his shuffle, Winters gave no impression of having any muscle tone. His walk was old-guy, but my guess was he was, tops, forty.

He gestured to a seat that looked like it had come from some dead relative's dining room set, then he went behind his desk. I pulled out a pen and a spiral notebook I'd bought in Penn Station and said, "Let me get a few particulars about you first."

"You're not taping this?" he asked.

"Oh no." I hadn't even thought to go tape-recorder shopping in Penn Station. "Even the newer ones are unreliable. Sometimes you get back to your desk and you listen and *nothing* . . . The new new thing is that most of the journalism schools have gone anti-digital and are requiring shorthand. Much more accurate." I'd made that up, and it couldn't be true, but Joel Winters was nodding, not only believing me but planning on using it as cocktail-party conversation if he ever got invited to a cocktail party. "I need a little bit of personal background on you," I said. "Age, what law school, how you chose your specialty—that sort of thing."

Obviously, my definition of "a little bit" and his were different. He passed the next five minutes talking about himself without, even for a single second, managing to be interesting. He would have kept going with great "Joel in Court" tales of brilliance and high hilarity, but I cut him off. "How is Dorinda Dillon doing?" I asked.

"You know. Holding her own. Hopes she'll be vindicated at her trial."

"Has there been any talk about a plea deal?" I asked, grateful that the thousand hours I'd spent watching *Law & Order* and *Son of Law & Order* had not gone to waste.

"No." He looked like he was about to add something else, but all he did was scratch behind his ear. It almost seemed like he had an on-off switch.

"What's your defense going to be?"

He gave one of those knowing laughs that sound like "huh." I thought it was supposed to mean *That's easy, and we're going to cream them,* but it just made him sound nervous. Finally, he said, "We're going with the truth."

"Which is?"

"Which is, Ethel O'Shea—great old Irish name, not that you're at all old, so please don't take that the wrong way—that she went to get the doctor's coat and there was somebody in the closet. He picked up the electric broom that was in there—"

"Did Dorinda see who it was? That it was a man?"

"No, actually. What do the politicians say? 'I misspoke.' She opened the closet door, I think got a look at the electric broom, though I'm gonna double-check on that. Then *whomp!* She got hit over the head so hard it knocked her senseless."

"And then?"

"When she came to, she saw the doctor on the floor. Dead. Naturally, she was shocked."

"How come she didn't call 911?"

"Look, Ethel . . . Is it okay if I call you Ethel?"

"Of course. Go right ahead," I said, though not too warmly. Maybe he was a sweetheart, but he had the look of a serious creep, and I didn't want to make him feel too comfortable with me.

"Dorinda may be a really nice girl, woman, but she's a woman who's a hooker and has—I'm not telling you anything here that isn't on the public record—arrests and a conviction on minor drug charges. Cocaine. It's not heroin or anything. Somebody like that isn't so quick to dial 911 about a corpse on her carpet."

I wrote a version of what he was saying in the spiral note-book, to appear reporter-like. When I glanced up, the over-head office light was shining on his hair, which was light brown coated with so much product that it looked like a piece of tinted, molded Plexiglas. "So the defense is that someone knocked her out and then killed the doctor?"

"Not just any doctor. A Park Avenue plastic surgeon." He shook his head sadly, as if this were an added burden he should be charging extra for.

"Does she have any theories who this killer could be?"

"No. None."

"Was there anyone else who had the key to her apartment?"

"The super has keys to everyone's place down in the base-ment but"—he smiled: humor on its way—"the keys are kept under lock and key."

"No one else has one? What about the person who lived in the apartment before she did?"

"Oh no, definitely not. When you're a hooker, you're into privacy big-time. She told me straight out that the first thing she did when she moved in was get a new lock, the really expensive kind. The keys got made on a special machine and had a number. If you wanted to get another one, you had to have the number. So this is not a case of keys floating around."

"It's strange, then, that she has no idea who it could have been."

"What did they used to say? 'Strange but true.'"

"Do you think that will go over with a jury?"

"It'll have to, Ethel. It's true, number one. And number two, off the record . . ." I put down the pen. "We're stuck with it. She talked. Not a lot but enough. In Las Vegas, after her arrest, and they videotaped it: her saying she got knocked out and woke up and there he was, dead."

"Off the record," I said, "if you weren't stuck with that, what would your defense be?"

"She doesn't pay me enough to come up with an alternate defense." Joel Winters had a good laugh about that one, and I joined in with a chuckle to prevent him from having a total ego meltdown. "We could go with the doctor being a real sicko. Self-defense."

I felt my now familiar shock reaction, a wave of nausea. Acid burned my throat, and I hoped I could heave and get it over with. "In what way was he a sicko?" I managed to ask.

"I haven't the foggiest notion," he said. "But if I was going for an alternate defense, I'd spend time with her, probing, maybe finding something we could work with." I nodded. While I now was merely queasy, it was too much to experience that rise of sickness and plunge of spirit, then snap out of it. I couldn't talk. I was desperate to catch my breath—except I was already breathing. "But that's neither here nor there," he went on. "We're stuck with what we have. The truth of the matter is, Dorinda did have a bump on her head when she was arrested. I just have to be convincing enough to the jury that she got it the night he was murdered, that she didn't take a hammer and go *bonk!* to back up her story, which is what the prosecutor is going to argue."

"What kind of sentence would Dorinda get if she saved them the trouble of going to trial and admitted to . . . whatever?"

"Ethel, that's what we in the law call a moot point. She says she didn't kill him, and she's sticking with that story. No matter what. If she pled, I could get her—if the gods were smiling that day?—five to ten if the victim's family would go along. The thing of it is, she just won't plead."

"Makes it tougher for you," I said.

"Hey, if I wanted easy, I would've been . . . I'll tell you what. A Park Avenue plastic surgeon."

Chapter Twenty-Seven

Sparky came into the kitchen while I was chopping a load of rosemary for roast chicken and said, "I'm so glad you convinced Ethel to stay here. I was hating the thought of flying in from Miami to spend two days on the Long Island Expressway, back and forth from the hotel."

"I didn't do any convincing," I said. "I picked her up at the hotel, and the bellman tapped on the window to get me to open the trunk for her suitcase. That was that, and she's here."

"Is she okay with the boys? I mean, is she behaving herself, not waving them away and saying 'Begone, you ghastly creatures!' or some such nonsense?" Sparky sat at the kitchen table, slipped off a loafer, and repositioned her sock. She had a great look: simple. She'd come from the airport in khakis, a white cotton shirt, and a dark blue suede blazer. Her only jewelry was a watch with a brown alligator strap and her giganto diamond stud earrings.

"She's fine. I mean, she's not getting down on the floor and playing with their Hess Oil trucks, but she's amazingly good with their noise. I wouldn't say she's enchanted by them, but she's definitely tolerant."

Sparky gave a small sigh of relief. "She said everything was fine with them and that they adored her. If you haven't noticed, she's given to overstatement."

"In fact, I did notice." I dumped the rosemary into a couple of spoonfuls of olive oil.

"Obviously, I don't have to explain it to you, but she's defensive on the subject of children. It comes out as a stand against a childcentric culture. Or as sarcasm."

"Four-year-olds don't get sarcasm," I said. "They are able to read people, though, even if they don't understand motivations. She's not giving off hostile vibes. I wouldn't go so far as to say they adore her. But she's tall enough to reach the shelf where I keep the cookies, and she doles out one to each of them—makes almost a ceremony out of it. I think they see her as an ally, maybe even a friend."

Grandma Ethel strolled into the kitchen. "Are you talking about me?"

"Yes," Sparky said, "though we were hoping a more interesting subject would come up. Any suggestions?"

"Did Susie bring you up-to-date on her trip to Dorinda's lawyer? She told him she was a journalist. Ethel O'Shea."

Sparky looked from her to me and shook her head in disgust. "Both of you . . . Why didn't you call me before doing something like this? That shmuck is going to be representing Dorinda in court. Do you know what he's going to do when he sees Mrs. Gersten take the stand and Mrs. Gersten is Ethel O'Shea?"

"I pulled my hair straight back," I told her. "Very severe look. Not like Grandma Ethel's photo ID, but I was planning on telling him that I'd let my hair go back to its natural color. He didn't ask for any ID."

"Except—correct me if I'm wrong—he did see you. It's not only that you pretended to be someone else. It's that you visited counsel for the defense under false pretenses."

"Is that a crime?" my grandmother asked. She sat at the kitchen table beside Sparky.

"I don't practice criminal law," Sparky answered.

"That's French for she hasn't a clue," Grandma Ethel told me. "Anyhow, the trial is still not set, most likely months away. Maybe he'll forget you, or you can have your shrink testify that you were acting under some sort of insanity."

Sparky was about to challenge her. I crushed a clove of garlic with the side of a knife and said, "Dorinda insists she didn't do it. She won't go for a plea bargain."

"She's going with the electric-broom story," my grandmother said. "You know, I was thinking. Maybe it was a burglar. It could happen. He knocked Dorinda out. Maybe she saw him, maybe she didn't. But she wasn't the threat. Jonah was, being a man. Maybe the burglar felt threatened, or Jonah could have even tried to stop him, and that's why he got stabbed."

"Eth," Sparky said, "a burglar would probably be armed. And even if he wasn't, why would he get scissors from the bathroom and not a knife from the kitchen? Or some other weapon—the proverbial blunt instrument? Or he could have used the famous electric broom on Jonah as well as on Dorinda."

"I don't think it could have been a burglar," I said. The oven dinged to show it had reached 375. "If it had been, how come he didn't take Jonah's watch? It was a Cartier tank. A burglar would know it or figure out it was worth something. And why didn't he take the money in Jonah's wallet? Dorinda was the one who did that."

"If she'd killed him to rob him," Sparky said slowly, "which would have been completely crazy, it being her apartment . . . But if robbery was her motive, she would have taken the watch. She didn't, which leads me to believe all she wanted to do was get the hell out of there and needed some quick cash."

"She went to her ATM after she left the apartment," I said. "She got another four hundred dollars."

Sparky turned to look at my grandmother. "I don't buy the burglar theory. If a burglar is going to break into an apartment, all he has to do is take one look inside. From what I read and saw on TV, it wasn't a luxurious place. Just the basics, although I think I read something about a carpet in a leopard-skin pattern. But what was there to steal? She didn't seem to go outside wearing a lot of jazzy jewelry. She was a recreational drug user, maybe dealt a little, but she wasn't a dealer with a ton of cash on hand."

I gave the big roasting chicken a rosemary rub and stuck it in the oven. "I'm with Sparky on this," I told Grandma Ethel. "I don't see her having a lot of money. I'm sure her rent wasn't cheap, and there wasn't a line outside the door waiting for the pleasure of her company. She did okay, but I don't know if it was much better than that. She needed to supplement her own clients by freelancing with escort services. And even though she's not using Legal Aid, she can't afford a top lawyer. The guy she's going to couldn't even be called third-rate."

"She would have been much better off with Legal Aid," Sparky said.

Grandma Ethel began, "She would have been much better off . . ." She dropped it, but we all knew she was going to say "not killing Jonah."

I decided to go with roasted sweet potatoes. My grandmother said she'd set the dining room table. She asked, "With Ida and Ingvild, how many? Oh, eight, and you don't have to tell me no wine for the boys."

That was Friday. By Sunday, I was exactly halfway between regretting that Grandma Ethel was leaving with Sparky and rejoicing at having the house to myself—or my version of myself, which included the kids, Ida, and Ingvild. Just as my in-laws arrived on their way back from Water Mill in the Hamptons, exchanging excited hellos and air kisses with my grand-mother and Sparky in the manner of the mutually sophisticated, Grandma Ethel informed me she had canceled the suburban taxi. She was taking my car to drive Sparky to La Guardia, then returning. "You're not ready to be on your own yet," she told me when she pulled the car keys from my hand. I had no idea what kind of a driver she was, but I decided that if Sparky was willing to put her life on the line with my grandmother behind the wheel, it might be okay.

I was tired from a weekend of cooking, so for my in-laws, I'd defrosted a vat of meatballs I'd made in December. I had a brief fantasy of saying "Why don't I go out and you can enjoy the boys' company by themselves?" They'd say "Wonderful!" and I would rush out to Main Street before my grandmother got back and go see a movie, any movie, a Jackie Chan or something sensitive from Hungary, and finish off a giant bucket of popcorn.

When I offered to give them quality time alone with the boys plus meatballs, they asked me please not to go, they really wanted to spend time with me, too. In spite of my fantasy, I'd known that would happen. The older the boys got, the more reluctant most people were to be alone with the three of them. I felt Babs and Clive viewed the triplets as if they were wild horses: beautiful but uncontrollable—rearing up unexpectedly and galloping around stirring up great clouds of dirt.

After dinner and the boys' baths, my in-laws took them off to bed to read to them. I stretched out on the living room couch and prayed that either Sparky's plane would be late taking off or my grandmother was a slow driver. That was the last I recalled until I heard Babs and Clive coming down the stairs, saying "So adorable!" and "What a vocabulary that kid has!" to each other.

I sat up and was smiling expectantly when they came into the living room. I felt like I was giving off waves of charm and totally down-to-earth, nondelusional goodwill.

"We'll only stay a few more minutes," Babs said.

"Please, stay as long as you like."

"That grandmother of yours is a charmer," Clive said. "And I like Sparky, too. What's her real name?"

"Felicia."

"She's much more of a Sparky," Babs said. "Felicia has such a languid sound. So your grandmother's staying on?"

"I guess so. She seems to think I need her, but it may be that Sparky's preparing for a big trial and is working really late every night."

"Maybe she's trying to somehow make up for the fact . . . with your mother." Babs paused, perhaps worrying that her analysis would set me off.

"I think there's a lot to that," I said. "But every time I bring up my mother, just the simple mention of her—not that the two of them should get together or anything—my grandmother changes the subject."

My in-laws nodded their understanding. Then Clive, quite casually, which he wasn't very good at, asked, "Do Ethel and Sparky share a room?" I must have looked at him like he was nuts because he quickly said, "I assume they do. I was just wondering, and you can put it down to my old-fashionedness, if it would have any kind of a negative impact on the boys?"

"You think gay is contagious?" I asked.

Clive smiled—a little. With him, it was hard to tell. Babs didn't smile. "Susie," she said carefully, "it's not that we care one way or another. They are a marvelous couple, which is amazing, because there's such a big age difference. My only concern, our only concern, is the boys. You grandmother is really incidental because she won't be staying that much longer. But with all due respect to you, because you're doing such a magnificent job with them, the boys' lives have changed so drastically. Don't you think they need all the stability they can get?"

"Absolutely." I wanted out of the conversation and was on the verge of offering to make coffee, slice a pineapple, anything to escape them for a few minutes. But I couldn't find a way out. So I sat up absolutely straight, maybe mimicking Andrea's I'm-an-aristocrat/stick-up-the-ass posture, and said, "Tell me what you're thinking about when you're talking about stability."

"To be perfectly honest, we know what a huge job this is for you," Babs said.

"It is pretty huge," I agreed.

"And as a woman who worked all through her children's growing up, I certainly wouldn't ask you to give up the wonderful business you and Andrea have created," she went on.

"Good" was all I could think of to say.

"My question is this: Do you honestly feel that two teenage girls, sweet, lovely girls, I'm not saying they're not, are enough help for you? Enough for the boys? When Jonah and Theo were growing up, we had Margaret. Well, of course. You've met her. When she started with us, she was well into her thirties and had superior credentials. Experienced. Trained. She was a proper nanny. You know, I was talking about this with Jonah—"

"Listen to me." I looked first at her, then at Clive, and sat even straighter. Slumping was a signal of defeat, and I was on the offense. I took a deep breath to calm down, because I didn't want to seem offensive. "I know you spoke about this with Jonah, about us getting a so-called proper nanny. He and I discussed it. And you know what? We rejected it, at least for the time being. But let's put that to the side for a minute." They were about to break in, so I kept talking. "We've all had a loss that's unbearable. Maybe it's bearable, because that's the only way to go on. But you know what I mean." They both looked away from me but not at each other. "The boys are what's left of Jonah. My sons, your grandsons. We can disagree over how I should raise them, and there are going to be times you'll be right and I'll be wrong."

"Susie," Clive said. His mouth, with its upturned smileyness, looked more inappropriate than at any time since the funeral. "It's not a question of right or wrong."

"Fine. But let me be blunt, though you can call it coarse, which apparently is my *spécialité de la maison.* You're concerned about the boys. I know you genuinely love them."

"We do," Babs said.

"But what have you done for them?"

"What would you have us do?" she asked in her cold voice, which, with me, didn't differ too much from her warm one.

"I'd have you spend time with them. If you can't take all three at once, how about one at a time for two or three hours? As for a proper nanny, Ida and Ingvild are two of the finest, most proper people I've ever met. They've worked harder than I would ever dream of asking them to. They are loyal beyond loyal, and they've never once complained. They love the boys, and the boys love them."

"We're not saying—" Clive started.

"Right now I'd rather be the one talking," I told him. "The twins' visas expire in May. I'm already talking to the agency that found them for me. The agency has another set of twins, a brother and a sister, who sound great. So either I'll be getting them or two others like them. If that doesn't sit right with you, if you really, truly feel a proper nanny would be better, then all right." They took a fast glance at each other, then turned back to me. "I'll go along with a proper nanny as long as it's someone who meets my standards, and I'm not just talking background check. I'm talking about someone who will be loving to the boys, strong enough to deal with them, and easy for me to have in the house."

"We wouldn't expect you—" Babs started to say.

"Hold on; that's not all."

"What else?" Clive asked.

"If you want this kind of person, then it will be the two of you who will pay for this kind of person. I'll be glad to contribute, but I'm not going to squander our resources paying for proper."

Clive looked at Babs. She didn't even glance his way. "We'll pay," she said. Then she cleared her throat. "And I *never* called you coarse."

The three of us were in the kitchen having decaf espresso when Grandma Ethel pulled into the driveway. Moments later, there were hugs and more air kisses as she came in and they went out. A half hour later, I was alone, taking off my makeup and feeling something needed doing. I just didn't know what.

The next morning I knew. I called Joel Winters and asked him to put me on Dorinda's visitors list. "That's right. O apostrophe capital s-h-e-a."

Chapter Twenty-Eight

I couldn't believe what I was doing. But I'd asked for it, and now it was happening. In preparation for meeting Dorinda Dillon, or at least getting in to see her, I went to the hairdresser and got the Ethel O'Shea makeover. I saw my hair, light brown with gold highlights, go so light some might call it blond, while gold highlights slid along the precious-metals graph closer to platinum. That was Tuesday morning. Though I'd explained to the boys what I would be doing, I was prepared for an afternoon of hysteria when they saw me as someone other than their light-brown-with-gold-highlights mother. Evan and Dash didn't seem to notice. Mason motioned me to lower my head. I sat on the floor with him. He took a handful of my hair, rubbed it between his fingers, decided it was still hair, and asked for a stick of cheddar cheese.

That night Grandma Ethel asked, "Are you sure you want to go through with this?"

"Listen, I won't use your ID."

"How are you going to get in? Spray mace at them and steal their keys? This is jail you're going to. Use my ID. What do I care about the station anymore? The bastards canceled my show. They should all drop dead."

Despite her protest, I told her that if anyone caught me using her ID, I'd say I'd stolen it from her wallet. "They're not going to arrest me or prosecute me," I said. I hoped I sounded more confident than I felt. "I've been through too much. The worst they'll do is be really, really unpleasant."

"You don't have to say you stole it. I'm a seventy-nine-year-old woman with three gorgeous great-grandsons whose father was brutally murdered. Do you think they're going to arrest me?"

The answer was no, but TV credentials can get you only so far. Other than by committing a crime or being employed by the NYPD or the New York City Department of Correction, it was not easy getting into the Rose M. Singer Center on Rikers Island.

But I'd made two decisions that turned out to be good ones. One was not driving my own car, registered in my name; I took a cab. The second one was leaving my handbag home. I took Grandma Ethel's ID card in one pocket of my jeans; a smaller spiral notebook I'd taken to Joel Winters's office in my other pocket; and two hundred dollars in tens and twenties in my jacket. The only jewelry I wore, since I'd read online that visitors had to put all their belongings, down to their earrings, in a bin that went into a locker secured by the police, was a Swatch with a plastic band that I always wore when we went to the beach.

The guards said in less than trusting voices, "You forgot your wallet?"

I told them I'd intentionally left my handbag at my hotel but forgotten to put the wallet in my jacket. "I'm so sorry," I said. "But what can I tell you? I swear, this is not your usual 'I forgot my wallet' story. I came up from Miami to do background for a big piece, except my plane was late. Once I got to the hotel, I was in such a rush I wasn't thinking."

They weren't buying it. I asked to speak to their supervisor. Though she was wearing a uniform, she reminded me of female guards in concentration-camp movies, big and boxy, with weird, watery, bulgy eyes, as if they were staring out from a fish tank. I wasn't going to win her heart or her mind with a smile. So I didn't smile. I told my story and said I had to catch the four o'clock plane back to Miami, so there wasn't time to go to the hotel and return.

Maybe she caught my exhaustion and frustration, maybe she liked the cut of my True Religion jeans, maybe she was a racist and was giving me points for being light-eyed and white. At least she didn't catch my desperation and near-hysteria. But after a blessedly fast glance at the ID and a check that Ethel O'Shea was on the visitors list, she finally ordered the guards to pat me down, give me my own special tag, and let me through.

I'd been picturing movie scenes with prisoner and visitor sitting opposite each other, separated by bars, and talking into a phone or a stub of a mike. Or another scene where a guard stands blocking the door, legs apart, arms crossed over chest, face like a particularly stupid bulldog's, while prisoner and visitor sit on stools or crummy chairs across the bare room from each other.

I got something else entirely. Teleconferencing. I was so unprepared for being stuck in a tiny room in which someone had recently sneaked more than one cigarette that I almost cried to be let out. The guard turned on a TV monitor and said, "They'll be bringing her into the booth in a minute. Have a seat. If you get any trouble with the audio, bang real hard on the door. This here is soundproof, so even if you yell, I won't hear you. And bang when you're done."

A couple of minutes later, some movement on the screen made me look up. Dorinda Dillon came in, sat, and stared at me. The only thing keeping my heart from rocketing out of my chest was that it didn't seem to be a stare of recognition. Just a dumb stare. Without makeup, her eyes seemed not only less human but even farther apart than in her pictures. Her hair had been cut short since her arrest and was mostly brown except for the bottom couple of inches. At first it looked like she had a rosy glow, but then I saw her face was chapped. Still, she looked . . . not exactly like a little lost pink lamb, but a lost sheep, one who definitely did not look pretty in pink.

"Hello, Ms. Dillon. My name is Ethel O'Shea. Did your attorney explain why I wanted to see you?" I asked.

"I got a message," she said. I don't know what I had expected, but what struck me was that it was such an ordinary voice, not breathy or husky. She just sounded out of town, like an operator at an 800 number.

"Would you like me to explain what my piece is about?" I took out my notebook and pen. She shrugged, so I went into my story about how prosecutors leap to judgment when—I said "someone with your background"—is involved in a serious crime.

"I am not a call girl," she said. "They kept calling me a call girl on TV."

"What do you like to be called?"

"An escort. Right now I don't look my best, but I'm a real escort." Except for a whine, her voice had no emotion. "A guy can take me out and be glad to be seen with me on his arm."

"I understand what you're saying," I said.

"Not that I'm arm candy."

"No, I'm sure you're more than that."

She was wearing a short-sleeved blue coverall, not the orange I'd expected, and once she said "arm," she started rubbing her right arm just above the elbow. "Some bitch pinched me," she said. "Last week, and it's still bruised. Look." She put down her hand and pointed. I thought there might be a black-and-blue mark, but I couldn't be sure. "It still really, really hurts."

"That's too bad."

"Can you see it?" she asked.

I hoped she was too dense to set a trap for me, but I wasn't sure. "Yes. Awful," I told her. She nodded, as in *Awful is right.* "With all this happening, are your friends standing by you?"

"Yeah."

"Have they been visiting?"

"Not yet." It seemed clear that she didn't have friends, but also that she didn't feel terrible about it. She gave her arm another gentle rub to soothe herself. I thought that somebody who complained so much about a several-day-old pinch was a major kvetch. Considering what prostitutes were supposed to do, she probably could take some kinds of pain. But I couldn't imagine her hitting herself hard enough on the head to cause a bump that would last for weeks. "You'd think that shit lawyer Winters would visit, but all I get is messages. He said we'd spend time together when they set a trial date. Like, what the fuck? What am I paying this guy for?"

"Tell me about the bruise on your head. I heard that when they arrested you in Las Vegas, you had a big bump."

"That's because I got hit. I got hit when I opened the closet door. Someone was in there, and they got my electric broom. The next thing you know, I was out cold. And when I came to, the guy was dead."

"Had you ever been with him before?" I asked. My mouth was completely dry. I truly would have given a year's income for a sip of Diet Coke.

"No. He was new. He was a very big plastic surgeon. I guess you know that."

"Yes. He told you he was a plastic surgeon?" I couldn't believe Jonah would give out information about himself like that. He was so discreet about talking about what he did, mostly because people were always asking his opinion on the work they wanted to have done, or whether he thought they needed a certain procedure. He hated being out for an evening and getting cornered by someone displaying arm flab. Also, he said that in most people's minds, plastic surgeons were fabulously rich, and especially when we were out with the boys, he didn't like people thinking of him as wealthy. He said it was simple discretion. I'd always thought he was afraid someone would kidnap the triplets. Possibly even demand a triple ransom.

"Maybe he told me. I forget. I don't think he talked about it, but maybe he said something."

"Did he pay cash?"

"Yeah. Private clients always pay cash. Up-front. With an escort service, they can charge."

She looked more annoyed at her situation than fearful or angry or anything else a person in a blue prison outfit might be feeling. "What did he want done?" I asked.

"He was kind of crazy," Dorinda said. At that moment, I didn't dare ask anything. If she had a train of thought, I wanted her to stay on it. So I kept looking at her. Then I made some scribbles on the pad. "He kept saying he heard I was a miracle worker. A miracle worker? What the fuck? So I asked him what kind of miracle he wanted. And he said something about his hand."

"His hand?" I asked. "What about his hand?"

"I don't know. So I went over, and he started acting funny. I told him not to be scared, to let me help him." She caressed the bruise on her arm again. "Then I brought him into the bedroom and said, 'Why don't you take off your shirt?' So he unbuttoned a couple of buttons."

"And then?"

"He was slow, so I started to help. All of a sudden he got really snotty and shitty and said, 'What the hell are you doing?' I thought it was part of his game, so I slipped out of my dress. Then he said, 'Get me my coat,' like he was the biggest big shot in the world. And he started buttoning his shirt, so I went out to the hall to get his coat."

"And?"

"And then nothing. I got hit. When I came to, when I finally stood up, there he was. Dead. With scissors."

Chapter Twenty-Nine

So Jonah hadn't had sex with Dorinda Dillon. Thank God! The news I'd been hoping for!

Except he was dead.

Every once in a while, like now, waiting in the wholesale flower market later that afternoon while my favorite peony dealer finished haggling with Miss Northern Westchester Floral Design Queen—who was doing everything except carrying a riding crop to show where she was from—I would discover a new way of missing Jonah. This time it was looking at Willie, the exasperated peony guy, sleeves rolled up, punching numbers into his calculator, trying to make the sale and get rid of Miss NWFDQ. It was late for the market, midafternoon, and he'd probably lost most of his patience by nine in the morning.

The hair on his forearms, wet from working with unboxed flowers, looked dark red against his ruddy skin. Seeing it transported me right to our pool. Jonah and I were in the deep end facing each other, our arms crossed and resting on a white float. Just talking. I reached out and smoothed the hair on his arm so it would all go in one direction.

Another punch in the gut. I started crying, not just tears, but with my shoulders going up and down, like I was bouncing. I turned the other way so Willie wouldn't see. Except I was face-to-face with some Dutch bulb mogul I'd seen at a lot of the New York flower events, a young guy with a face full of brown polka dots that looked like age spots. So I turned back and cried facing Willie's face and his customer's horsey ass.

From the beginning, I'd known in my heart that Jonah was what I'd believed he was, loving and true. But along the way, my head had serious doubts. Okay: Not to feel overly guilty, most heads would do the same. Now I knew my heart had been smarter. But aside from feeling so grateful and relieved by my new knowledge, what could I do with it?

"I don't want to hear any explanations," Willie told me once he was free. "You got what to cry about, okay?" He looked around and handed me some green tissue paper to blow my nose in. I probably looked a little too directly into his eyes because I wanted to avoid seeing his arms. "Go ahead, honk away, but don't blame me if you walk out of here with a green nose." Then we did our Florabella business, Willie pushing a dark pink peony, the Edulis Superba, so hard I finally gave in.

Being in the flower market was usually the great joy of my job, in Manhattan in jeans and work boots, sipping coffee that got cold fast from the chill of all the refrigeration. The colors, the smells, the relationships that weren't quite friendships but came close: It all made me feel part of the world where nature and commerce met, maybe what a farmer felt when he hauled his potatoes to market.

But when I stopped crying, the flower market held no charm for me. I could have been in an office with fluorescent lights and no windows. All I could think of was sheepy Dorinda talking in her flat 800-number voice, saying, "He heard I was a miracle worker." And then "something about his hand." Why hadn't anyone asked her about this before? I knew the answer. They had all assumed Jonah was there for sex.

One thing I now was sure of: Dorinda Dillon had not killed Jonah. It simply didn't add up, in either my head or my heart. I believed what she had said. He was a new client. They had hardly gotten beyond the hello stage. She had no reason to kill him. Sparky and I had pretty much demolished Grandma Ethel's burglar theory, but did I have anything to replace it with? A random-intruder theory?

I finished with Willie and a couple of our other dealers and had the flowers and a couple of buckets of the floral preservative we liked loaded into the Florabella truck that I'd parked in a nearby lot before taking the taxi to Rikers Island. It was an old Chevy panel truck we'd bought mostly for its color, a lovely celadon green, a case of foolish business thinking that had actually turned out well. I was heading toward the Midtown Tunnel when I decided to take a look at what I'd been picturing for so long: Dorinda's apartment building. I headed up Third Avenue and turned past her apartment building, a large box with windows, probably badly built in the sixties. As I drove by, I noticed the side entrance about fifty feet from the front door. Just then a doorman walked out in a long gray military-style coat, looking like some character from *The Nutcracker*.

I drove into a garage a block away and talked the guy into taking the truck for fifteen minutes even though he said, "We don't take trucks." Charm and a twenty did it. Walking down the street, I felt at a loss because I was so used to being "done" when I went out: hair, makeup, nails, accessories. My casual was somebody else's wedding day. Jeans, shirt, old quilted vest, hair in a ponytail wasn't the way I dealt with any world except jail or the flower market.

"Hello," I said to the doorman, knowing I couldn't say "Excuse my outfit." "My name is Joan Smith. I'm a social worker from Manhattan Human Services." He didn't look impressed, but on the other hand, he didn't look unsympathetic. "I'm doing some background on Miss Dillon."

"And?"

So he wasn't exactly friendly. I didn't know why, but I got the feeling that his "And?" had zero to do with me and a lot to do with Dorinda Dillon. "All I'm trying to do right now is get a sense of her." I had a flash of worry that he wouldn't believe the Bloomberg administration would be paying for a social worker to get a sense of an accused murderer, but he nodded like he had a parade of social workers dropping by every day looking to get senses. "Did you know her?"

"You might say that," the doorman said. His sleeves were too long. They covered his knuckles, and I wanted to tell him to take his coat to a tailor and ask for a three-inch hem. "I was the guy on duty when the doctor came."

"Do you remember him?"

"Yeah, sure. Well dressed. An East Sixties kind of guy, except I heard he lived on Long Island."

Since the doorman was in a chatty mood, I decided to check out what either Eddie Huber or Lieutenant Paston had told me. "Was he one of her regulars?"

"No. Never saw him before."

I realized I had to start sounding like a social worker, except I wasn't quite sure what one sounded like. "I'm trying to get a picture of her character." He made a face that came close to a smirk but wasn't. I gave him my mega-wattage plastic-surgeons'-convention smile and said, "I'm not asking about deep-down goodness or honor, just what she was like on a day-to-day basis." He seemed a little hesitant, so I added, "Don't worry. I've been at this job over ten years. I stopped getting shocked after three months."

"Bottom line on the character?" he said. "Not so great. Didn't even bother saying hello unless you said it first. Like who did she think she was? A duchess? And another thing: Like you said you've been doing your work over ten years. I've been doing mine for almost thirty." I did the *Omigod! You couldn't be that old* gape, which he seemed to appreciate. "So over the years, in these rental buildings and condos, I run into a fair number of girls who do what she does. Most of them go out of their way to be friendly—friendly in a nice way—because they don't want trouble, they don't want a doorman hassling their johns or even being not polite. And Christmas? They're right at the top of the good-tipper list. You can predict it. Big tip, nice card with a thank-you. You know what I got this year from Dorinda Dillon? Fifty bucks in old crumpled-up bills. The day after Christmas. She hands it to me like it was five hundred in nice crisp bills."

"No card?" I asked.

"No card."

I sighed and shook my head sadly.

"Doesn't that say everything about her character?" he asked.

"Loud and clear," I said. I waited while he let in a tenant with a baby in a stroller, a shopping bag of groceries, and some forsythia branches in cellophane that looked like they had two more days to live. "So how did it work with her clients? Did they just come to the door and ask for her?"

"Right. And I have to ask all the time, 'Who shall I say is calling?' because I have to buzz her. And they all say they're Mr. Johnson, which is what she has them say. And so I let them up."

"Besides the doctor, did anyone else go up there that day?"

"A few hours earlier, the other doorman let in a regular. An old guy. Came and went. And another regular earlier in the day. But nobody else when I was on duty. Not even another girl for a threesome. Maybe I shouldn't say that."

"Please. You should hear some of the things I hear. I'm unshockable."

He smiled. "You must have a tough job."

"Sometimes. I love learning about people, about their lives, so overall, I enjoy the work. You know what the hardest part is?" I asked.

"What?"

"Walking and walking." I lowered my voice. "And if you'll excuse the expression, finding a bathroom."

"Don't I know it. Used to be, you could walk into a bar or restaurant anywhere in the city, do what you had to do, say thank you and goodbye."

"Not these days," I said. "Can I ask? What do you do?"

"Oh. It's no problem. They have a toilet in the basement right by the elevator. They got a buzzer down there. I lock the front door, and if the tenants or someone needs me, they press the button. I'm gone for a minute, but at least it's right here in the building."

"I'm jealous," I told him, and we smiled at each other.

I filled in Grandma Ethel after dinner but begged off her suggestions about researching hand fetishes on the Web or, as her alternate fun-filled evening activity, turning on some station that was having an Audrey Hepburn festival. Instead, I went to bed with a copy of *Vogue,* but I couldn't concentrate on the articles, so I just looked at ads. I must have fallen asleep about nine-thirty because when the phone rang a little after ten, the sound startled me awake. I grabbed it, and my "hello" came out like a chicken's squawk.

"Susie?" Theo. "How's it going?" His bedtime calls were becoming an unpleasant habit.

"Fine."

"I hope I didn't wake you." Without giving me a chance to offer a polite "Oh no, you didn't," which I wasn't going to, he went on, "I spoke to my parents after they dropped by your house on their way home from the Hamptons. They say you're doing so much better."

"It was a nice visit," I said. Clearly, he wasn't going to refer to his last nasty phone call.

"Susie, I know you'll think what I'm about to ask is terrible. But I just want you to understand I really don't mean it in any bad or selfish way."

"Okay," I said. Knowing Theo, I realized a little extra was necessary, so I added, "I wouldn't think that at all."

"Here goes," he said in his smoothest voice. "A while back, Jonah and I were talking. It was around the time you guys asked me if I'd be the guardian for the boys if God forbid you died, and I said yes. Anyway, Jonah said that besides the guardianship thing, he was going to remember me in his will. So I was wondering—you haven't said anything—if he left me any kind of keepsake."

I still hadn't shaken off all the sleep, so I almost said there wasn't any particular keepsake. But I stopped myself, because I realized that when he said "keepsake," he wasn't talking about a memento. He was, as always, talking about money.

"Jonah didn't have anything in particular as a keepsake for you," I told him.

"Oh."

"Is there anything of his you'd like to have?"

"You choose something," he said, like he didn't really care.

"How about his plastic bar mitzvah clock?" I wanted to ask. "Theo, let me think about it, look through his things. I want to choose something that meant a lot to Jonah and will mean a lot to you. I'll get to it over the weekend, I promise you."

Surprisingly, I fell back to sleep almost immediately, probably because my brother-in-law's request was a total nonshock. Jonah and I had debated whether he was needy or greedy or both so many times that we'd finally stopped because we really didn't care. The possibility of his guardianship of the boys had seemed so remote when we'd done our wills. I realized now that we hadn't thought it through. I needed to make a new will. Soon.

My first call the next morning was to the delightful Joel Winters. I told him that I'd had a good interview with Dorinda and, shoveling a little more fertilizer onto his ego, asked what he would do if he could change the criminal justice system. While he talked, I sat in the bathroom in front of a magnifying mirror, holding the phone between my ear and shoulder, and tweezed my eyebrows. When he stopped to take a breath, I said, "I do need one favor from you. I know you can get a message to Dorinda. I really need to find out who referred the doctor, the plastic surgeon who was killed, to her. Unless you know offhand." He didn't. "Was it through one of her own clients? She said he was a private client. I'm a little rushed on this, so I appreciate you getting back to me as soon as you can. And by the way, I know my producer will love what you were just saying about mandatory sentencing."

Since Grandma Ethel was not one of the early risers, I did something I should have done days before: I got out the CD Liz Holbreich had given me with all the materials she and her colleagues had collected during their brief investigation. I loaded it on the computer, but I couldn't figure out how to search through the documents to see if I could find the Marty who'd shown up on Jonah's calendar.

That wanting-to-throw-something rage that comes with computer frustration overtook me, but since I was down in Jonah's study and didn't want to damage anything, I tried to take deep breaths. It worked enough so that actual thinking could take place. I called Lizbeth Holbreich and asked her to help me find Marty.

"I've thought about you so often," she said. "I'm glad you called, because I wasn't sure whether or not to call you. I hope you're doing . . . I suppose I should say 'I hope you're doing as well as can be expected.'"

"I am doing all right. The missing him is much worse than I ever imagined at the beginning, but the day-to-day stuff is coming along."

"And your sons?"

"There are problems, but lots of times they're fine, normal. I just want to strike the right balance between keeping their father as a good memory and not continually poking them and saying 'Hey, don't enjoy yourselves too much because you have a dead father.'"

We talked for a few more minutes, and while I would have loved to get Liz's reading on my whole Dorinda on Rikers Island saga, I asked how to go about finding a name on the CD she'd given me. I made notes that seemed simple enough, but when she said, "Tell me what name you're looking for. I have the information on our server and . . ." I waited under a minute.

"Marty," I said. "The name was first on Jonah's calendar last November, though I only searched back a year. The last time he was on it was eleven days before Jonah was killed."

"No last name, I assume?" Liz asked.

"No last name, no address, no phone numbers. I checked Marty and Martin. There were Martins and a Martino who were patients, but patients were connected with the Manhattan Aesthetics database."

"If you ever give up flowers, you could come and work for us. Give me a moment. Let me see what I can find." This time she took a lot longer than a minute, but I had no desire whatsoever to tweeze my eyebrows. I thought about Theo and why someone with well-off parents, a good education, and an okay career as a casting director would expect his brother to leave him a "keepsake" of money in his will when the brother had a wife and three children. "There's an Anello and Martin, Rare Books and Texts," she said.

"He had started collecting some old medical books," I said.

"And there's a Martin Ruhlmann at a 212 number, no address. Hold on. I'll check him out." It didn't take much longer than a few clicks of Liz's mouse. "Martin Ruhlmann, certified public accountant. A forensic accountant," she said. "But now that I look at the name, it's vaguely familiar. We have forensic accountants here at the agency."

"What do they do?"

"They're auditors, but they bring an investigative mentality to an issue. A good one will have a combination of financial expertise, knowledge of fraud—and fraudsters, too, you might say—and real savvy about how businesses operate. You'd find them working on cases like Enron, or cases where a corporation is involved in a deal it has questions about."

"Why would a plastic surgeon need a forensic accountant?" I asked.

"Any number of reasons, I suppose," Liz said. "But . . . I'm just thinking out loud here. Maybe it was somehow connected to those e-mail exchanges Dr. Gersten was having with his office manager." She must have clicked another couple of times because she said, "Donald Finsterwald. Did you read those e-mails on the CD?"

I hadn't, but I would.

Chapter Thirty

The guard at the security desk in the lobby of Martin Ruhlmann's building smiled at me and Grandma Ethel and said, "You girls must be sisters." I guessed Grandma Ethel was thinking something close to what I was, like *Cut the shit, you creep,* but as he and an elevator were all that was standing between us and the forensic accountant, we smiled with delight.

Martin Ruhlmann and Associates might have been full of accountants, but it wasn't a green-eyeshade sort of place. It had the English-club look, right down to a male receptionist in a suit and tie sitting behind a huge mahogany desk. The walls in the waiting room were covered with antique lithographs of what I thought were drawings of rooms in old English clubs. "You have good eyes," Grandma Ethel told me. "Look. The stuff in the frames hanging on the walls. No, the pictures inside the pictures up there. Are they pictures of more rooms in English clubs? Are you supposed to think, *Hey, maybe it goes on forever.*"

"Maybe."

"Like anyone gives a shit. Oh, I forget to tell you: Sparky says either this Ruhlmann is the one man in New York who hasn't heard about Jonah getting killed, or he's treating whatever information he had about whatever Jonah went to him for as confidential."

"It's possible that the police tracked him down already, and whatever he had to say wasn't important," I suggested.

"Maybe."

A secretary, a woman in one of those dress-for-success suits from the seventies or eighties, except without the stupid little tie, led us into Martin Ruhlmann's office. He stood and, like a proper English gentleman, did not try to shake our hands until we offered ours. Well, mine, because my grandmother was too busy eyeing a grandfather clock in a corner, barely managing not to sneer at it.

We spent the first few minutes on what a fine man Jonah had been. Ruhlmann was unreadable. He might have thought Jonah was terrific, or he might have loathed him, but his words said nothing except every cliché about someone who'd recently died. There wasn't any body language to read, either, unless staying behind a desk with his hands in his lap said everything.

I decided to get to the point. "Could you tell us what the investigation you were doing for my husband was about?"

"This is a fairly complex, technical undertaking," he said.

"Try us," Grandma Ethel told him.

I couldn't get over how his mouth moved when every other part of him remained frozen like a still photo with animated lips. "Essentially, I was asked to look into the use of the practice's surgical suites. The use that was reported did not appear to be in keeping with the gross quarterly revenues."

"Was it Jonah who hired you, or was it the partnership?"

"Just Dr. Gersten."

"Do you want to explain what you mean by the use of the surgical suites?" my grandmother asked.

"I really wouldn't feel comfortable doing that," he said.

"Why not?" I asked.

"Dr. Gersten had a legitimate legal interest in the business of Manhattan Aesthetics."

"And doesn't my granddaughter, who is Dr. Gersten's sole heir, have a legitimate legal interest?" My grandmother, in her pink Chanel once again, looked like she should be wearing storm-cloud gray.

"I would have to look into that," Ruhlmann said. "Or rather, have our attorneys look into it."

"When can you do it?" I asked.

"I can have the answer for you within the week. Possibly a little longer, but I'm sure once they get going on it—"

Grandma Ethel cut him off. "Not good enough."

"I'm afraid, Mrs. O'Shea, that while I can certainly appreciate your interest and your granddaughter's, and your desire to know any details as soon as possible, I have to see that this is looked into in a proper manner as soon as possible."

Grandma Ethel rose in one graceful swoop. "Mr. Ruhlmann, you're obviously a gentleman, and I hope you think we're ladies." He nodded. "Good. Then let me tell you something about dealing with ladies of our caliber. Don't fuck with us."

As we got into the elevator, my grandmother asked me, "Coarse enough for you?"

"Yes," I said. "Thank you very much."

"Susie, I know you're worrying that my behavior might be counterproductive. It might be. But dollars to doughnuts, sweetheart, it'll work. I know how to deal with guys who think they can get away with repro grandfather clocks."

By the end of the week, we still hadn't heard from the forensic accountant. I couldn't believe Jonah had called him Marty or anything less formal than Mr. Ruhlmann. Then it occurred to me that if he hadn't put down an address or a phone number, maybe he'd been concerned that someone might be looking at his calendar. Donald, perhaps? Or someone else at the practice? Late Friday afternoon, I told Grandma Ethel I was going to call and prod Ruhlmann. She said, "Tell him you've got to see him Monday morning, and you'll be there with your lawyer."

"I don't have a lawyer—except the one who did our wills, and her partner, who did the closing on our house. There is no way I can get a lawyer between now and Monday, so I'm not going to give any ultimatums like that."

"Sparky will be here tomorrow morning. She can stay till Monday night or Tuesday, okay? You can't ask for a better lawyer. NYU. *Law Review*. Need I say more?"

At a few minutes after ten on Monday, Sparky Burns was sitting in the chair closest to Martin Ruhlmann's desk, but she leaned in even closer. "I admire prudence," she told him. "But you and I know there is no professional privilege of confidentiality for accountants unless you were working under the direction of an attorney." Ruhlmann cleared his throat, and she said, "What we are asking of you is not imprudent. Dr. Gersten paid you for your services. Mrs. Gersten would like to hear what you found."

"You mean what he hired me to look for," he said. Granted, my grandmother's toughness might have put Ruhlmann off a tad, but even before that, he had been about as aloof as a guy can get without actually being nasty.

Sparky centered the large, round face of her wristwatch on her arm and studied it. "We can have this discussion now. We have no intention of staying for lunch. Or we can come back after an extended period of filings and depositions. You call it." She sat back in the armchair and flashed a look at my grandmother that could not have meant anything but *Keep quiet*. My grandmother, without a word, opened her handbag, rearranged her wallet and compact, and snapped it shut.

Ruhlmann had perhaps hoped to outwait Sparky or give her the silent treatment, but finally, he said, "I have a meeting outside the office at eleven-thirty."

"Shall we begin, then?" Sparky asked.

"A check arrived in the mail at Manhattan Aesthetics made out to Dr. Noakes for thirty-seven thousand dollars. No one could figure out where it came from, because the checking account belonged to something called the GP Fund. Dr. Gersten consulted with his partners, Dr. Noakes, of course, and later, Dr. Jiménez and the office manager, a Mr. Finsterwald. None of them had any idea what the GP Fund was or why it would have sent a check made out to Dr. Noakes. Apparently, the envelope was lost or thrown out, so there was no return address." Ruhlmann took time to adjust the points of the linen handkerchief sticking out of his jacket pocket. "When Dr. Gersten was reported missing, and then found dead, I was still in the process of trying to track down who or what the GP Fund was."

"Why didn't Jonah give the check to the practice's regular accountant to trace?" I asked. For a second I felt uncomfortable, like I had tried to steal Sparky's scene, but she didn't seem to notice.

"I believe he wanted to investigate the matter himself. He was hoping to discover where the check came from and whether its existence was some sort of a mistake, a bookkeeping oversight, or perhaps something—part of something—devious. He was curious about what the GP Fund was. He wanted to see if the check could be the tip of a very unpleasant iceberg."

"So you were hired to explore where this thirty-seven-thousand-dollar check came from?" Sparky asked.

"It wasn't only the check that was troubling him. There seemed to be quite a bit of inventory shrinkage from the surgical suites in the practice's office."

"They did most of their surgery there, not at the hospital," I told Grandma Ethel and Sparky.

"In retail sales, 'inventory shrinkage' can mean shoplifting or employee theft. But in a medical practice, Dr. Gersten was concerned with much more than dollars and cents. What was missing, as I found out, was not at all what he'd expected. It was not easily marketable drugs that had been stolen, but instruments, supplies, anesthesia itself. He couldn't understand why and wanted to know if there was a black market for that sort of thing."

"So no one else in the practice knew that he came to see you?" I asked.

"I don't believe so," he said. "I was to speak only with Dr. Gersten, no one else. My instincts tell me no one else knew, but my instincts don't bat a thousand."

"When you heard about Dr. Gersten's murder, did you contact the police?" Sparky asked. Ruhlmann didn't answer. "Did you get in touch with either of his partners?"

"No," he said.

"I'll tell you what I need from you before we leave," Sparky said. "I need your notes on the inventory shrinkage. I want a copy of the thirty-seven-thousand-dollar check and whatever information you did manage to get on the GP Fund."

"I have very little on the GP Fund."

"I have a suggestion," Sparky said. "You need to get cracking on the person or persons behind GP."

"I'm really not interested in pursuing this matter beyond this meeting," Ruhlmann said.

"You listen to me!" Sparky snapped. Ruhlmann moved. His head snapped back against his leather chair, and his jaw dropped. It was the equivalent of someone else having a major seizure. "There is no excuse—Don't interrupt me with some line your lawyer fed you. There is no excuse whatsoever for your not notifying the police about Jonah Gersten consulting you. Interested or not, you are still on this matter. I might suggest it's your highest priority."

Chapter Thirty-One

When Martin Ruhlmann called that night, it was clear he regretted dropping his jaw. He sounded like he had such a stiff upper lip—to say nothing of his lower one—that I had trouble understanding what he was saying.

"The GP Fund is not an entity of any sort," he said. "It's the bank account of a woman named Phoebe Kingsley. I believe she's a socialite. Her husband is Billy Kingsley."

"Is that a name I'm supposed to know?" I asked, but very politely.

"He owns StarCom. He's considered one of the great figures of the . . ." I couldn't comprehend what he was saying because people don't speak clearly when their jaws are clenched. I asked him to repeat it. "The telecommunications industry. I gather he and Phoebe Kingsley are separated and a divorce is in the works. But that's neither here nor there. Does that conclude our business, Mrs. Gersten?"

"My lawyer will let you know, Mr. Ruhlmann. Thank you for calling." *Phoebe Kingsley?* I thought. I pursed my lips, furrowed my brow, and waited for the name to ring a bell. It didn't.

Grandma Ethel and Sparky passed on pizza and went out

to an Indian restaurant. After I put the boys to sleep, I roamed around the house and wound up in each of their rooms, gazing at them. That peaceful euphoria mothers are encouraged to feel each time they look at their children came to me once in a blue moon, almost always when they were asleep and incapable of shrieking, hurling their Spider-Man accessories, or crayoning a mural on a silk-covered wall.

I walked down the second-floor hallway into my office and Googled Phoebe. There was much to Google. Somehow I'd missed her in those party pictures that appear in the *Times* and all those *Town & Country*–type magazines. Maybe it was because she always showed up in group pictures, never by herself. Billy Kingsley was rich enough to have his wife noticed, but apparently, he didn't care enough to bankroll what it took to be so exquisitely dressed and so philanthropic that reporters and photographers cannot resist coming to your fifty-two-million-dollar home in Southampton to cover your party for the Friends of the South Fork Water Birds Foundation.

But I zoomed in on her again and again, and finally, in one photograph that happened to have an incredible number of pixels, I could see her face clearly. No, I had never met her. Phoebe and I ran in different circles. She was, as Andrea would have said, a type, or at least doing her damnedest to become one. Her hair was coiffed in one of those neo-helmet-head styles socially ambitious women were wearing again, maybe hoping people would take them for the reincarnation of Brooke Astor. She was slim, pretty enough. From the little I could see in the photographs, she wore elegant, safe couture clothes well, and she smiled with every tooth she owned.

What really impressed me was her face. Smooth and unlined. Almost perfectly symmetrical. It was what Jonah called the Gilbert John Noakes signature face-lift. I'd learned to spot one years earlier. Flawless yet natural, except for two slight indentations on the temples near the hairline, less obvious than but a little like the forceps marks you see on some newborns. The dents could definitely be seen; Phoebe Kingsley's helmet hair was full, high, and swept off her face.

I wanted to get her out of my head, not so much because she was upsetting me, but if I could stop thinking about where she fit into the overall picture, maybe something would come to me. To change my mind's subject, I got into bed with an envelope of pictures from a vacation we had taken two summers before, in Chatham, Cape Cod. I'd taken photos of Jonah and the boys on the beach, the best photography I'd ever done. The sunlight had been perfect, illuminating the mist in the air so that all of them—alone or in groups of two, three, or four—looked like they were surrounded by an aura. Better than an aura: more like a head-to-toe halo. I kept going through them, about fifteen photographs, again and again. I didn't cry. Maybe I was melancholy, but I had the feeling you get from looking back on any good time that's gone with no possibility of a do-over. As I drifted off to sleep, I was thinking I could smell the ocean.

I woke up sometime during the night. When didn't I? No dreams startled me awake. No kids were crying. Instead, I recalled an evening Jonah and I had gone out to dinner with Layne and her husband, Mike Robinson, an OB/GYN. Jonah made it a rule never to gossip about one partner when we went out with another. That night, though, Gilbert John was mentioned. Jonah and Layne were deep in conversation about some fat-lasering procedure that Gilbert John had observed and deeply disapproved of. Mike murmured something to me about how he'd hate to have Gilbert John disapprove of anything he did. I'd laughed, partly because it felt like such an illicit conversation for the two spouses to be having about Gilbert John Noakes. I told Mike I didn't know anyone who wasn't intimidated by Gilbert John. He said Layne once had told him that early in her career, when she was assisting Gilbert John during surgery, he'd given her a dirty look for something minor she'd done wrong. Mike said he'd laughed when she described those disapproving eyes glaring over the surgical mask, but Layne was never able to. She'd told him it was like having all the presidents on Mount Rushmore angrily staring down at her.

Mike had been on something of a roll, and he wasn't at all a drinker, so it wasn't alcohol talking. I figured this was a conversation Jonah would rather I not have, so I tried making it a foursome again. But he and Layne were still going on about lasering in the kind of surgeons' shoptalk that gets pretty revolting. Mike hadn't moved on from our conversation, though he'd transitioned to Layne being upset about Gilbert John's lifestyle.

Gilbert John wasn't bringing in anywhere near as much business as he had been. We all knew that, right? Right. So why should Layne and Jonah get stuck subsidizing his house on the ocean in East Hampton and his ski lodge in Steamboat Springs when he was putting less time into the practice and doing more traveling and pro bono work? I kept quiet about Gilbert John's new Bentley convertible, an Azure, which was so big it could almost qualify as a yacht.

Mike was telling me he approved of doctors giving back. He himself was in a program where he was assigned high-risk obstetrics patients who had no insurance and no money. Mike thought Gilbert John's enormous number of good works was a great thing for a plastic surgeon to do toward the end of his career. Layne and Jonah each had their own pro bono causes. But Gilbert John's pro bono time was way out of proportion.

The memory of that dinner with Layne and Mike was still with me the next morning. I was doing busywork, cleaning out the freezer, getting rid of pesto marked *Aug 07* and containers of ancient cookies, when Grandma Ethel and Sparky came downstairs. Sparky asked me if it would be okay if she stayed another day or two.

"You have to ask permission to stay on?" my grandmother demanded. "I'm family, so you're family."

"Grandma Ethel," I said, "if you'd given me one nanosecond more, I could have been the one to tell Sparky that."

"You'd better work on your reflexes. Speaking of which, I heard the phone last night, but you must have grabbed it right away. Any news from the Rialto?"

"It was your boyfriend," I said. "Martin Ruhlmann."

"Eth," Sparky said, "if you want him, I won't stand in your way."

As they took breakfast, I filled them in on Phoebe Kingsley. Then I segued into my waking in the middle of the night, thinking about that dinner with Layne and Mike. I couldn't understand what about the conversation had been so significant that it suddenly came back, considering I'd forgotten it not long after it had occurred. Naturally, I'd mentioned it to Jonah, but he'd come to Gilbert John's defense; it was Gilbert John, after all, who had brought him and Layne into one of the city's most prestigious practices and therefore was entitled to earn a little more than his fair share of the proceeds.

"Maybe it's the connection," my grandmother said. "You know what I mean?"

"Not exactly."

"The connection," she said again, more impatiently, like I was deliberately trying to outdo the dumbest kid in the class.

"I give up," I said. "What connection are you talking about?"

"If I knew, I wouldn't be asking. The connection between Layne and her husband with that Phoebe Kingsley." She reached over to Sparky's plate and helped herself to half her bagel. "You hear from Ruhlmann about Phoebe, then a few hours later, you're remembering that dinner. We'll need to work on why you're tying the two together."

Before I could work on it, the publicity-hungry Joel Winters called my cell. "Dorinda got the client who referred your husband through College Girl Companions," he said. "I gave them a call, but they don't talk to anybody. 'Our business is based on trust.' Can you believe that? Like there's a lawyer-client, priest-penitent, and madam-of-a-whorehouse-john privilege." Joel Winters seemed not just annoyed but upset at not being able to get me the information I'd asked for. I sensed he was worrying that his fifteen minutes of fame would be canceled.

"Who's in charge at College Girl?" I asked.

"Her name is Cleo. Maybe Clea. She's one cold fish. Ice water in her veins. The last thing she wants to do is talk to a reporter, so save yourself some time."

"All right, Mr. Winters, how about this? Let me have your e-mail address. I'm going to send you a photo of someone. I need you to take it to Rikers—"

"Listen, Ethel—"

"This will be a great story. I guarantee it. And it could make you . . . I don't think I have to draw you a picture. You'd be the guy who did what everybody else said couldn't be done—you saved Dorinda Dillon. Okay? Please ask Dorinda if she ever saw the man in this photo. One more thing: I need you to do it fast."

I had to get my grandmother away from Sparky for a few minutes to tell her what I wanted to do next. Sparky was the kind of lawyer who would tell both of us, "Forget it. You absolutely cannot do this." "Grandma Ethel," I said, "I have some lower-heeled Manolo slides that are too narrow for me. Want to look?" She did, of course, and Sparky didn't. When we got upstairs, Grandma Ethel seemed extremely aggravated by my shoe ruse because she'd already entered the Manolos into her "Assets" column. "Please, I needed to get you away from Sparky, because she does the ethics thing twenty-four/seven. Listen, stick with me now. Be with me. I'll give you any pair of shoes in my closet. Two pair."

"Do you think you have to pay me to be with you?" my grandmother asked.

"No. Of course not."

"Good. A couple of years ago, when we came up to New

York and had dinner with you and Jonah, you were wearing a pair of Manolos. Remember? I admired them, and you said you'd gotten them at an outlet. Sling-back, white and taupe stripe, two- or three-inch tapered wood heel. If I didn't have ethics, those are the ones I'd take."

I called back Martin Ruhlmann to get Phoebe Kingsley's number. On my cell, which had caller ID blocked, I reached her in one ring. I held the phone slightly away from my ear so Grandma Ethel could hear.

"My name is Marianne," I said. "I'm the bookkeeper at Manhattan Aesthetics." I heard a big-time tremble in my voice, but my grandmother gave me a smile of approval. "We're having issues about your check to Dr. Noakes." I spotted the striped slingbacks on a high shelf and reached for them. I got only one; the other flew off the shelf, beaned my head, though not too hard, then fell to the floor.

"I sent another check to his home address," Phoebe said, sounding irritated.

"Made out to him personally?" I picked up the shoe and handed the pair to my grandmother.

"Yes," Phoebe said. It came out as pissy hiss. "He was supposed to tear up the other one *personally* and mail it back to me." She took a deep breath. "Can I ask you something, Miss Bookkeeper? How many goddamn face-lifts am I supposed to pay for? I only had one." Phoebe Kingsley didn't sound low-class, but her voice had a raspy hardness, like a diamond nail file. "I can't have my checks floating around where some clerical type could deposit two of them. Listen, I asked for it back. Christ on a crutch! Two times! Do we understand each other?"

"Not completely," I told her. "I'd like to know—"

"That's it," she said. "I am not discussing this anymore!" She slammed down the phone.

I put down my cell and motioned to Grandma Ethel to keep silent because I sensed she was ready to make a noble speech renouncing the slingbacks. I closed my eyes for a moment and chewed on my knuckles. "Okay, let me try this out on you," I said. "It seems to me Phoebe Kingsley's check *was* for Gilbert John. There was no mistake. When Jonah found it, or maybe it was brought to his attention by one of his staff—I don't know— Gilbert John obviously couldn't admit what it was and cash it. So he called Phoebe Kingsley and told her there was a problem with *that* check and she'd have to write another one."

"He told her he'd send back the one made out to him torn into pieces," Grandma Ethel said. She was cradling the shoes in her arms the way someone else would soothe a baby. "But he couldn't because Jonah was probably holding on to it. So, like I used to say on *Talk of Miami*, 'I need to think.'" She smiled into a nonexistent TV camera. "Give me one hundred and twenty seconds, and I'll be back with an answer for you." She walked over to the bergère chair in the bedroom, put the shoes on the floor, then sat, and in under five seconds said, "Okay, tell me if you agree. Phoebe sent Noakes—what the hell kind of stupid name is Noakes?—another check. But she didn't get the torn-up check back. On the other hand, it never got cashed, did it? My guess is she probably forgot about it until just now, when you called. That's what happens when you're in the middle of a divorce. It takes all your energy. I was so grateful when Sidney dropped dead—I couldn't just leave him like I'd left Lenny the Loser, because he was a popular guy and I didn't want to alienate half of Miami. I love Miami. Anyway, if you ask me, and even if you don't, you can safely bet that Phoebe's GP Fund was money she'd socked away for incidentals, like a new face. And probably, when she got closer to going back on the husband market, lipo and new tits." She tried on the slingbacks. They fit.

We went downstairs to tell Sparky that Gilbert John Noakes's pro bono work most likely wasn't so pro bono. If Phoebe Kingsley was any indication, his on-the-sly surgeries were what was causing the inventory shrinkage that had so upset Jonah. We were careful not to let Sparky know how I'd gotten the information.

"The check to Noakes from Phoebe Kingsley's fund shows Gilbert John taking money under the table," Sparky said. "My guess is he's doing side deals with some old patients, friends he trusts, along with their friends. He gets the check made out to him and pockets it. He puts in for the anesthesia and surgical supplies as part of his pro bono work." I must have looked pathetically hopeful because Sparky said, "Susie, if this were reported and substantiated, it probably would be a good case for prosecuting him on tax evasion. But I'm sorry to tell you, this does not prove Gilbert John Noakes committed murder."

Chapter Thirty-Two

"Maybe she'll offer you a job," Andrea said brightly. "Maybe I'll take it." Not so bright.

We'd gone to a luncheon at a private club in Manhattan for a client's fiftieth birthday. Now Andrea was dropping me at a brownstone on West Fiftieth: not one of those pretty places with geraniums in window boxes. Crummy, in fact. College Girl Companions was upstairs. A nail salon a few steps down looked like a place to go if you were interested in taking home a toenail fungus.

The building was not a place that had seen better days ever, though it might have watched its final tolerable ones fly out a dirty window in 1908. Now it was just another sad subdivided space badly in need of a sandblasting it was unlikely to get. This wasn't a block for gentrification. On one side was a locksmith. On the other was an Italian restaurant; its canopy was torn, and the ripped piece flapped crazily in the wind.

College Girl probably needed a midtown address to reassure tourists, but I couldn't imagine many people set foot on the premises. Why would a client want to go to a place like that, much less be seen there? And despite the "College Girl," I couldn't picture a bunch of academic whizzes like Dorinda Dillon sitting around a lounge and reading *Paradise Lost*.

"I'll find a place to park and wait," Andrea said.

"Don't bother. I don't know how long this will take, and you'll wind up getting stuck in rush-hour traffic. I'll grab a cab and get home by train." Our ride into the city, and then being at the same table at the luncheon, had been enough of Andrea for me for one day.

"You are not going home on the train during rush hour." Andrea wrinkled her nose like I'd suggested taking a bath in a vat of pig shit.

"It's okay," I murmured, opening the door of her latest car, a Jaguar convertible.

"It's not okay. I'm going to stay here. You're going to a whorehouse."

"I'm going to the offices of an escort service. What do you think, it's like a dorm and they have cubicles with beds up there? Go on. Go home."

"Susie."

"Andrea." I got out of the car. So did she. "Hey, you're double-parked," I said. "You're holding up traffic."

"I want you to keep your phone on. I'm going to call you in fifteen minutes. If you don't answer, I'm coming in with the police."

"What police? You'll go running to the corner screaming for a cop? You know what will happen? You'll get a ticket for double parking. I'll be fine. And please don't go calling me, because my phone may not work in there, or if I'm talking to someone and getting information, I don't want to be interrupted."

She put her hands on her hips. She'd looked so cool at the luncheon—killer stilettos, a Carolina Herrera dress and coat in gray—but having a snit beside her convertible on this seedy street, she looked bizarre, a deranged rich lady from another neighborhood who'd taken a wrong turn. "Hear me!" she said. "I do not want you to do this."

"Andrea—"

"What? You don't give a rat's ass what I want? Too bad. You can't go."

"Let me explain one last time. I'm trying to get some information so I can have something to push the cops and the DA to reopen the case. The only way I can think of—"

"Forget that I'm your business partner and have a strong financial interest in keeping you alive," she said.

"You can stay here and block traffic if you want." I turned to go upstairs. "I can't worry about you now."

"I don't want you risking your life!" The idea of me risking my life by going to an office was so over-the-top that I wound up smacking myself in the forehead, that *I can't believe it* gesture lusty ethnics do in old movies. But Andrea wouldn't let up. "Susie. You have three children. What if something happens to you? Who are you going to leave them with? Theo, that ridiculous, selfish Munchkin bastard? And if *I'm* calling someone selfish, you can just imagine!" I really couldn't. "Listen to me, Susie."

"I'm listening, and I understand what you're saying. But the only possible danger I can imagine is that they won't let me in. If I thought for one momen—"

"I'm going up there with you," Andrea said.

"No, you're not."

"I swear on all that's holy, I'll behave like the lady I am. I'll even keep my mouth shut."

"No. Anyway, you can't leave your car here."

"Do you think I give a shit about getting a ticket?"

"They'll tow it!" I was shouting as she came around the Jag to stand next to me on the sidewalk.

"So what? Fat Boy will send somebody to get it back. And if it gets dented, I'll get another one. Don't pretend to be appalled. That's the kind of girl I am." She grabbed my upper arm and pulled me toward the brownstone's stairs. "Come on. Let's see if we can make the cut at College Girl."

Once I had seen that College Girl was in a brownstone with a locked door, I'd come up with some sketchy excuses I could use after I pressed the button near the outside door. I needed to be prepared when a voice called out, "Who is it?" The inner door, probably warped, was closed, but the latch hadn't engaged completely. After we read COLLEGE GIRL COMPANIONS and SUITE 3 on the nameplate, we simply hurried up two flights of stairs. Despite our heels, neither of us touched the banister, probably sensing it was coated with decades of secretions from the palms of prostitutes not given to hand washing.

When we knocked on the door, a voice called out, "Who is it?" It was low-pitched, a woman's voice.

"Hi," I called back. "It's Susie."

I heard a chair scraping along a floor. Then the door opened a crack. I did my high school flutter-fingered wave. I must have appeared sufficiently adorable and nonthreatening because she opened the door.

"Hi," I said again. Andrea seemed to be taking her vow of silence seriously; all she did was smile.

The woman holding the door open about four inches was neither a college girl nor an escort anyone but a Boy Scout would touch. She looked like she was past forty and flooring it to forty-five. A fringe of deep vertical scratches radiated from her lip liner, a too thick band of crimson. Her saggy skin seemed to be pulling open her pores. "Are you Cle . . . ?" I asked, dodging the end of the name, not sure if it ended with an O or an A.

"No," she said. "Who are you?" She glanced at Andrea but decided she didn't need an S on "you." Then she looked back at me.

"I was hoping to speak with her for a minute."

"You're who?" she asked.

"I know she's so busy. I won't keep her long."

Without consultation, obviously, Andrea and I broke into our client-winning "You're Never Fully Dressed Without a

Smile" act with so much fervor it would have been impossible for the woman not to smile back. Actually, she began to, but it quickly disappeared into an "Ooh!" of recognition.

"I know who you are," she said to me. "You're his wife. I saw you in the papers. And on TV in an evening gown at some party. With him." Just as it occurred to her that the door would be better off closed—with me and Andrea on the outside of it—I pushed. Not a hostile push, like a break-in. More like a *I know you want me to come in except you're not moving fast enough* push.

"Honestly," I said, "I just want to speak to her for a minute. A quick question and I'm out of here."

"You know, the police thanked Clea for her cooperation on the case." Her voice was soft, a little husky but not a phone-sex voice. More business than pleasure. "Maybe they didn't tell you that, but she cooperated. They made a special call just to thank her."

"They did tell me. I really, really appreciate it. Look, I don't want to make trouble. I swear to you. You know the story: I'm a widow with three little boys. If I make trouble, what's going to happen to them?"

I felt sorry for her. She was overwhelmed. Maybe she'd been coached on how to deal with an obnoxious client, but she clearly didn't know what to do with me and Silent Andrea. "I'm not lying," she said. "Clea's not here. She hardly ever comes in. She monitors the calls sometimes, that's all."

"I'm told you keep records on customers." She was already shaking her head. "I know for a fact that the records are pretty extensive—for Clea's own protection."

"The records aren't here," she said, but ever since that body-language article, I'd watched out for the rampant blinking that signals a lie. *Blink, blink, blink.*

"They are here," I said calmly.

"No, they're not."

I wasn't going to get into a "They are, they're not" game that even the triplets were too sophisticated to play. On the other hand, I couldn't think of what to say next.

Not that I was conscious of it, but I must have been thinking what Grandma Ethel would do in the situation, because what I finally said was so not me: "I want to find out if at some point you might have done business with a certain gentleman. I could give you the gentleman's name, and if you would—" She was shaking her head. "If you can get me that name and show it to me and give me a copy . . . Come on, stop shaking your head. Let me finish. You can make an easy five hundred. We'll leave. Then you'll leave, say, a couple of minutes later. Just tell me which ATM to meet you at, and I'll be there. Bring a copy of whatever record you have with you, watch me withdraw five hundred dollars, and we'll do the exchange right there."

She took a long, quavering breath. She wanted the money. But then she started shaking her head again. "I can't risk it."

That was when Andrea decided not to keep quiet. "Another five hundred from me," she said. The woman barely had time to draw in her lower lip to chew on it in indecision when Andrea added, "Forget the thousand dollars. Within a few minutes, you can have *two* thousand in cash. Or a long afternoon to think of all the things you could have done with two thousand dollars. You decide."

"What's the gentleman's name?" she finally whispered.

"Gilbert John Noakes," I said. "Dr. Gilbert John Noakes."

Chapter Thirty-Three

❧ ───

Andrea and I nearly had twin heart attacks waiting for Ms. College Girl to show at the ATM. When she finally scurried in, head down, obviously avoiding the security cameras as if she were there to rob money rather than receive it, she opened a giant faux–patent leather tote bag that made horrible plastic-on-plastic squeaks. She handed me copies of three MasterCard statements for August, October, and November 2006 with a list of payments to College Girl. Talk about naming names: Noakes, Gilbert John. Twice he had paid five hundred and once seven hundred. I didn't want to know why the price had gone up.

That night, after a dinner featuring brisket I'd found when cleaning out the freezer, frozen after Rosh Hashanah 2008 but that everybody had loved, I put the boys to bed and met Grandma Ethel and Sparky in the den. While they watched me from the couch as if I were a one-woman play, I called Danny Cromer, the orthopedist Jonah had used for his tennis elbow, a guy he'd gone to medical school with; his name had been on Jonah's calendar. I spent a few minutes, too many, thanking him for the beautiful condolence letter he'd written. I sensed he was on the verge of telling me he had an emergency on the other line, so I said, "Danny, the last time Jonah went to see you . . ."

"Yes," he said cautiously, as any doctor in his right mind would.

"It wasn't about the tennis-elbow business, was it?" Counting on all the years of friendliness that would make him reluctant to give me the usual confidentiality speech, I quickly added, "It was the thing with his hand. He told me about it."

"Right." Still cautious.

"I don't want to put you on the spot, but I'd like to be able to reassure his parents. He told us it was nothing to be concerned about, since it wasn't anything like, whatever it's called, that bad-hand thing. But they keep talking about it. It's not exactly rational, but none of us have been lately."

"Rheumatoid arthritis? Is that what they're worrying about? I know his father's a physician. Rheumatoid arthritis can be passed down from parent to child. He's probably worried about your boys. No, this was osteoarthritis. Look, it can be a problem, especially for a surgeon who does the kind of work Jonah did."

"I didn't sense he thought it was affecting his doing surgery." I thought, *I can't believe he didn't tell me,* but then I thought, *I can believe it.* Jonah would want to know the whole picture before letting me in on it. Control. And knowing I was an anxiety queen, he wouldn't want me to agonize unless there was a need to agonize. Also, he'd been so smart about people. Not that we'd ever talked about it, but he would have known I worshiped him a little. Maybe he was afraid to seem vulnerable. Gods didn't get arthritis.

"I didn't find any loss of mobility," Danny Cromer said. "I gave him a shot and some medication for the pain. He was supposed to come back . . . Oh, Susie, I hate to be saying this. He was due to come back. We were going to go over options for treatment. Did he mention anything about how it was feeling after he saw me?"

"He said it was a huge improvement. He was so grateful."

After I thanked Danny and said goodbye, I turned to my audience. "Osteoarthritis," I told Grandma Ethel and Sparky.

"Are you going to call that Eddie back?" my grandmother asked.

"And say what? 'It turns out my husband had arthritis, and that's what he was talking about to Dorinda Dillon when he was complaining about his hand, a conversation I know about because I talked my way into Rikers Island and interviewed her under false pretenses'?"

"So what are you going to do?" Sparky asked.

For a while, all I could think of was picking at the welting on the arm of my chair. Then I went to find my handbag and returned. I searched until I found the card Lieutenant Corky Paston had given me. He answered the phone with "Lieutenant Paston."

"Hi. This is Susie Gersten. I know you probably think I'm crazy, at least if you've been talking to Eddie Huber. But let me tell you what I found out."

He wasn't having any of it. "Mrs. Gersten, you're a really nice woman. No one could have handled the situation you were in any better."

"Thank you, but—"

"To be perfectly honest, I think you need psychological counseling."

"I'm getting it." Then I told him what I'd gotten from College Girl, the copies of printouts with Gilbert John Noakes's name on them.

"Are you crazy?" The way he said it, it wasn't a half-humorous question equivalent to "Are you kidding?" "You actually went there?"

"Who else was going to do it? Now, listen, please, Lieutenant. You seem like a nice person, too. And definitely not crazy. Reasonable. Down-to-earth. So do me one favor." I heard the muffled sound of a phone being covered and him muttering to someone else. "Can't you have someone go back to Dorinda Dillon's building and take the picture of Dr. Noakes from the practice's website? Besides the doorman, there might be a porter or some other building employee who might have seen Gilbert John or dealt with him."

"I'm sorry. I really can't," he said. "The case isn't in my hands anymore."

"It can be your case if you'd just—"

He cut me off. "I honestly wish you well, Mrs. Gersten." At least he sounded regretful. But that was the end of the conversation.

After I related what Paston had said, Sparky got to wondering out loud how to get around him—there had to be a way. Grandma Ethel, on the other hand, took his "I honestly wish you well" to mean "You have my blessing in whatever you do, even though I can't officially condone it."

Fifteen minutes after Sparky's "You're beyond absurd, Eth" rejoinder, she was behind the wheel of my car, driving my grandmother and me into the city. As she pulled into a space beside a fire hydrant one block from Dorinda's apartment, Grandma Ethel told her, "Sit tight, because if you pull into a garage, it'll wind up costing fifty dollars, and it might have security cameras, so there would be proof we were in the neighborhood. Stay in the car, because you don't want to be anywhere near us. In case there's any unpleasantness, Susie and I have a fallback: We can say she's mentally unbalanced and I'm senile. But you could wind up getting disbarred in Florida for pulling a fast one in New York."

My grandmother and I strolled up and down Dorinda's block between the corner and the alleyway with the service door, trying to appear casual when turning midblock to avoid passing the doorman. After ten minutes, it began to get boring. After twenty, when all we'd done was decide the only passerby with any style savvy was an Asian deliveryman with a smartly tied black bandanna riding a bike, we began rethinking our plan. Fortunately, as we were approaching the alleyway for the thousandth time, we saw a guy in a janitor's uniform hauling out a huge can of bottles for recycling.

"Okay, you take him," Grandma Ethel said. "I'll distract the doorman." As she hurried toward the front door, walking as sure-footedly in dagger-heel leather pumps as if she were wearing Nikes, I headed down the alley to meet the porter halfway.

"My name's Ethel O'Shea," I said, and flashed my grandmother's press ID open and shut. Maybe I sounded nasal, because I wasn't breathing through my nose. Though the recyclables were in clear plastic bags, the janitor's hands were in giant leather trash-hauling gloves. I knew all I needed was one whiff of decomposing V-8 juice and I'd gag—not the best way to make friends. "I'm a reporter," I added. He had time to give me only one shake of his head—*No way I'll talk to you*—before I went on, "Sir, I truly want to keep you out of trouble."

"What do you mean?" His eyes moved beyond me toward the street, as if expecting trouble with a capital T to be loitering on the sidewalk. He looked like he was from some unhealthy Eastern European country, heavyset and pasty, with skin dotted by the faded mauve of bygone pimples.

"Look, I found out some of the details about how you let that guy into Dorinda Dillon's apartment. If you tell me the whole story, I won't name names." It occurred to me that he might not have done anything, that there might be some alternate porter or building employee. It didn't help that I couldn't read his expression, because there was nothing yet to read: He appeared to be a majorly slow thinker. "I'm sure whatever help you gave him, you didn't mean any harm by it. You seem like a very decent, honorable man."

"It didn't have nothing to do with the doctor getting killed," he said. He was hard to understand both because he was a natural-born mumbler and because his accent squished words: "Din ha' noth' t' do." "It happened at least a week before that." I nodded sympathetically. "Seven, eight, maybe ten days. And this guy—"

"*This* guy," I said, and showed him the picture of Gilbert John Noakes that I'd downloaded from the Manhattan Aesthetics website. I had a few others in my handbag, photos taken over the years at various conventions and parties, in case the formal portrait drew a blank. I'd made copies for Grandma Ethel, too. But this one was all I needed. The porter was already nodding.

"Yeah, that guy. A hundred-buck haircut if I ever saw one. But I felt sorry for him. He was panicked. He left some important papers up in Dorinda's apartment. I didn't call her Dorinda to her face. I'm just using that with you."

"Right."

"The guy was scared. What if she threw them out? The papers, I mean. What if she tried to sell them to the competition? I felt bad for him, and I said, 'Okay, wait till she goes out for her walk. Tell me where they are, and I'll run up to get them.'"

"Did you?"

"No. He said not to because he didn't know where she could have put them. If he looked, he'd recognize the envelope they were in right away, but I wouldn't, because it didn't have no writing on it. So could he please just get the key, and he'd go in and out fast. He swore if it took longer than three minutes, he'd come back down even if he didn't find them. He said, 'Trust me. I'm very neat. She'll never know I was there.' I did trust him because, you know, he was a really class act. Expensive coat. That's how you tell. Some guys pay a thousand bucks for a suit but buy a crap coat. Not him."

"So he waited there until—"

"No," the porter said. "I told him, 'She goes out every day late afternoon, so get back here at a quarter to four, and you'll be okay.'"

"So he came back?" I asked.

"He came back. Said he might not recognize her if she had clothes on . . . kind of funny, but I understood what he was saying, you know? So I should be on the lookout and signal him when she went out the front door and down the block. He stood across the street, but like right opposite here, because he couldn't go through the front door, past the doorman. He had to use the service entrance. It was better anyway, because I could go right to the room where we keep the apartment keys and give him Dorinda's and then take him up in the service elevator."

"Did you wait for him in the service elevator on her floor while he went in with her key?"

"Strange you should say that. That's what I wanted to do. But give him credit: He was shrewd. He said I should wait outside the service door, right at the end of this alley here, by the sidewalk. That way I could watch the front door, in case she came back early. I told him she never did, but he said, 'You can't be too careful.' Anyway, he gave me his cell number and said I should call him if I saw her."

"Do you still have the number, by any chance?"

He gave a loud "Huh!" like he was reading an instruction: *Insert laugh here.* In case I didn't get the humor, he added, "You gotta be kidding."

"No, I'm not. I even think I could convince my editor to come up with something for it if you do."

He considered the proposition by resting his mouth on the back of his hand—which was covered with the garbage glove. Finally, he said, "No. I threw it out. I mean, the guy came back down in two, three minutes. What did I need it for?"

"Did he find his papers?"

"Yeah. In a plain white envelope, so I wouldn't have found it unless it was the only envelope in her apartment. But he said he knew it right away and it was where he'd left it."

I nodded. "Just out of curiosity, did he give you something

for the trouble you went to?" He didn't say anything. I smiled. "You said he was a class act."

He smiled back. "A little something."

I'd already used a smile, a tossing back of hair as it fell into my eyes: your basic Flirting with Repulsive Guys When You Need to Get Something from Them Fast 101. But now, before the porter lifted the giant can filled with recyclables and started shlepping it toward the street, I had to get beyond the fundamentals to practically graduate-level. That meant a longing gaze that would display the wonders of pale green eyes and long, thick lashes and also would communicate the realization that I was so amazed by his masculinity, I was on the verge of falling in love. Add to that some nibbling of the lower lip to express a mix of hesitancy and embarrassment. It was a feminist mother's worst nightmare.

After the nibbling business, I said, "I don't know how to ask you this."

With something approaching grandeur, the porter said, "Go ahead."

"I've gone totally blank on your name."

"Oh. Pavel. Pavel Ginchev." He even spelled it for me.

Five minutes later, Grandma Ethel and I were walking back to the car. "I got bubkes from the doorman," she announced. She sounded both dispirited and surprised, as in *Life should offer more in the way of excitement*.

"I got a little something," I said. "Like Gilbert John getting the key to Dorinda's apartment and going in there alone."

"Wasn't it one of those special security keys you can't get copied unless . . ." She paused. With a great smile, she added, ". . . unless you're a high-class guy who can intimidate a locksmith—and make him your friend for life with a few hundred bucks. Or a few thou. *That* would get you the key to anywhere you want to go."

Chapter Thirty-Four

✂—————————————————————————————

"Nothing's wrong," I told my cousin Scott Rabinowitz the following night. "I'm healthy. I'm strong. Okay?"

"Okay," he said. Whatever the gene was for drama, he did not have it.

"But I need to ask you a favor . . . with you knowing I'm in really good shape."

"Okay."

"I need to make out a new will."

"Right. You should. Whenever circumstances change—"

"This is a huge thing I'm asking, Scott, so take as much time as you need before answering. You don't need to tell me now."

"Okay."

"Right now, if anything should, God forbid and all that, happen to me, the boys would go to Theo, my brother-in-law. I don't think he's steady enough to take on a responsibility like that."

Scott shrugged. "I don't really know him, but if that's what you think . . . Oh, you mean you're asking me to take the boys?"

"Yes. But I need you to feel free to refuse if you can't see yourself in that role, or if you can't take that kind of responsibility because you have other plans for your life."

"You think I could handle it?"

"Not counting me, you handle them better than anyone." What I left out was that I'd called Liz Holbreich and asked her to look into my cousin's background—and told her the reasons I was asking. When she got back to me, she said she'd found absolutely nothing to rule him out. I went on, "The chances of anything bad happening to me are . . . Well, you're the accountant, so you're better with numbers."

"You're likely to stick around for a while," Scott said.

"Please take time and think about it. And if you say no, I'll find someone else, so don't let that be a concern."

"I'd have to take off a few pounds," he said. "So I don't strain my heart. I couldn't afford to be one of those guys on the D train who drops dead standing up during rush hour because there's no place to fall."

And then he said he was honored that I thought so much of him. He was crazy about the boys. And I should live and be well, but yes, he was willing.

Late that week, I decided I was going to see if Eddie Huber and the forces of justice would take the copies of Gilbert John's MasterCard payments to College Girl seriously enough to check them out. I knew that having told Lieutenant Paston, he wouldn't keep it a secret. He was a pro. He'd want to look into it. So what was going on? Bureaucratic constipation? Being pathologically afraid to commit a mistake? Could Eddie possibly think I was so crazy that I'd made up a story and forged the statements? I needed to do something to get her to move. If not, I would have to hand over my information to my underemployed family press spokesperson, Kimberly Dijkstra, and let her make it public. I had to act.

At some point while driving between Shorehaven and Park Avenue early that Saturday, maybe I came up with a plan. I could have had one before I left. But a few minutes after ten, as I was picking through Jonah's key ring and trying each one on the private entrance into Manhattan Aesthetics' office, I suddenly wondered, *What am I doing here?* It wasn't reassuring that I couldn't come up with an answer. Except for emergencies and treating politicians and celebrities who didn't want to risk being seen within a mile of a plastic surgeon, the offices were closed on Saturdays.

The private door, down the long corridor and around the corner from the official entrance, was for the doctors, so they could avoid walking through the waiting room and getting waylaid. Naturally, it was the exit of choice for bandaged post-op patients who looked like they were starring in *Revenge of the Mummy*; they could be led out without traumatizing prospective surgical candidates.

The keys jingled as if they were trying to get the attention of all New York. Finally, the fourth one I tried not only fit into the lock but turned it. I was in. The buzzing alarm that greeted me was no big deal, because whenever I went into the office with Jonah, he'd mutter 3-3-3-3, his passcode. I'd once said, "You'd think someone would figure out a guy with triplets would use threes." His answer had been tight lips.

Only after the third 3 did it occur to me: *Oh God, what if they deleted Jonah's passcode from the system?* The alarm kept ringing: one second, two seconds, much too long. There I was, in some bizarre fight-or-flight paralysis, when . . . at last, silence. By the time I could breathe again, I had already turned the corner and was walking through the long corridor toward Jonah's office. The usual lights, a gentle, flattering pink, were dimmed to near-darkness, giving the pale peachy-beige walls a spooky glow, as if they were alive.

I didn't know what to expect once I opened Jonah's office door. I was clutching the keys in my fist so they wouldn't jangle, and

I slid out one key with my thumb. As I put it into the lock and grasped the knob, the door opened so fast that I stumbled inside. I ran my hand along the left wall for the light switch, the standard place, but all I felt was a wall sanded to a baby-skin finish appropriate for a plastic surgeon's workspace. The dim light from the corridor didn't shine into the room, but I could see the big things were still there: Jonah's Eames desk with its multicolored panels, chairs, a computer monitor so thin it looked two-dimensional.

I patted and stroked the wall for what seemed like hours until I discovered the light switch, ridiculously low on the right-hand side, as if it had been designed to be reached by preschoolers. As I switched it on and closed the door behind me, I had one of those irrational widow moments when I said to myself, *Don't forget to ask Jonah why the switch is in such a crazy place.*

When I walked over to the desk, I knew immediately that other people had been there. Of course the police would have. The pens in the cylindrical wire cup leaned this way and that; for Jonah, they'd stood at attention. There were papers, too, in reasonably neat piles, though if Jonah had ever left papers on the desk—a dubious proposition—the outer edges of every side of every sheet would have been in perfect alignment. I couldn't make myself sit in his chair, but I stood leaning against the narrow oak rectangle that was the top of the desk and checked out the papers. Nothing unusual: printouts of his notes on patients, a report from a journal about impending thrilling developments in dissolvable sutures. The desk had only one drawer, for files, but even though I looked carefully from A through Z, I found nothing but the alphabetical file dividers themselves.

I'd made up my mind before I got to the office that if Jonah's computer was still there, I wouldn't turn it on. Too big a risk, because there might be some record on the server or network or whatever they called it that would flash an alarm: *Dr. Gersten's computer has been accessed by unauthorized person or persons unknown, but I'll bet you a hundred it's the wife.* I walked around the cool, modern office, angular and spare, so unlike our house, but Jonah always said that his office was like his work, precise and carefully thought out—though he hoped that, unlike his surgery, it wasn't sterile. He said it was great, returning to the warmth, tradition, and layered complexity of the house. I'd laughed and said I'd always dreamed of a husband who could say "layered complexity" and not sound like an ass.

I barely looked at his walls because I didn't like the painting, some streaks of color and scribbles by an artist trying and failing to be an abstract expressionist like Cy Twombly; when I said something diplomatic like "It's pedestrian," Jonah told me he'd already paid for it and told me I was hypercritical and should understand there was a difference between office art and personal art. I'd said something like "bullshit," and that was the end of the discussion.

The only thing left to look at was his narrow built-in closet, a woodworking craftsman's elegant interpretation of a high school locker. I stood before it, I guess looking a little bit like the apes staring at that big black monolith in *2001*. It looked so plain, spare even, yet so scary. There was no knob, but as I reached out to the door's edge to pull it open, my heart was pounding, as if to warn me: *Don't!* Maybe I half expected a dead body to keel over, or a jack-in-the-box with a giant U of a smile painted on his face. When I did pull the door outward, all I found was an umbrella and the pair of black rubber pull-on boots Jonah kept there in case it snowed. God, I hated that he'd died in the winter and never gotten to see the spring.

Just so I wouldn't be angry at myself later, I felt inside the boots. Jonah had been a great one for hiding cash or keys under the orthotics of his sneakers, on the theory that even second-rate burglars wouldn't look in smelly places. The boots were empty. Then I took the umbrella and, turning it right side up, opened it only a little because of the superstition that it was bad luck to open an umbrella indoors. I was thinking, *Yeah, I never opened an umbrella inside in my whole life. Did it bring me lots of luck in the husband-longevity department?* As I started to close it, something floated out: a news clipping from *The Wall Street Journal*. The headline read, REDLEAF CAPITAL'S GRAYSON ASKED TO RESIGN. The dateline was—even I could do the math—six days before Jonah was killed.

It was no big story, just another financial hotshot getting payback for making lousy investments with hundreds of millions of dollars of other people's money, though at one point Redleaf Capital's holdings were "well over $1 billion." As far as I knew, there was no Grayson in Jonah's life. Still, that didn't mean very much, because why would Jonah—if it was indeed Jonah who'd neatly cut out the article—want to hide something like it in an umbrella?

In one of those out-of-the-clear-blue-sky moments, it hit me that when I'd been taking Detective Sergeant Timothy Coleman around the house, I'd looked in the Einstein biography on Jonah's night table. He'd had a list, with razor blades and shoe polish on it and a note, *check red cap.* I'd assumed it meant red capsules.

I pulled out my cell and called Andrea's house. I knew she would be at Florabella, but I didn't care, because I also knew it was the one phone line Fat Boy would answer.

"Hey, Hughie," I said, "it's Susie. Did you ever hear of something called Redleaf Capital?"

I realized I should have said "How are you?" but my lack of graciousness did not appear to be noticed. "Hey, Susie, my wife's working while you're lounging around eating chocolate truffles? How y'doing? Redleaf? Fucking loser hedge fund, one of the greatest of the great Greenwich loser hedge funds. Something in the Connecticut water, maybe. Or all those Irish Catholics and Jews trying too hard to be Wasps up there caused massive brain damage."

"You know how Jonah and you sometimes talked about investments?"

"Sure."

One of the things I liked about Fat Boy was that he made no attempt to think of what he should answer about a guy who'd been murdered. He just said it right out. "Did he ever say anything about investing in Redleaf?"

"No, why would he do such a stupid thing? Anyone who knew shit about money would have the brains to stay away from that stinker. Even when it was good, it was bad. Not that it ever really was good." Fat Boy took a fraction of a second for a diplomatic pause. "He didn't put his money there, did he?"

"No, not that I know of. Not from anything I've seen from the accountants or that Jonah ever mentioned."

"So why are you asking me about a fund that was headed for the crapper two, three years ago and everyone knew it except the fund manager and the investors?"

"Did that guy Grayson do anything criminal?" I asked.

"No. Just dumb, arrogant—the usual stuff. So fucking predictable. Listen, I'd be shocked out of my mind if Jonah—"

I said, "I have to go," because just then the door opened. And there was Gilbert John Noakes.

Even under the best of circumstances, he had a right to be livid about my being there without consent. I, of course, had a right to be scared shitless over what might happen. For too long a moment, nothing did.

Just as he was saying "Susie" and taking a deep breath, I became more alert than I'd ever been in my life. Every cell in my body, simultaneously, was on duty. There was just him and me, which I knew was really he and I, but either way, that added up to only two. His words, all but frozen solid, came out: "Is there any possible explanation for you . . ." I realized two wasn't a good number because it was Gilbert John against me. If he had nothing to do with Jonah's murder other than a history with Dorinda Dillon, then I was destined for more boring, elderly chicken dinners with Coral and him. If all the law-enforcement people were wrong and I was right, I was in major danger.

Something inside me told me I had to up the number from two to three. So I brought in somebody else and talked so fast I might have taken lessons from Fat Boy: "I was talking with the forensic accountant Jonah went to see." That got Gilbert John's attention. It also let him know there was at least one more person in the equation. "He was telling me about a thirty-seven-thousand-dollar check that turned out to be from—"

"Phoebe Kingsley," Gilbert John said. "I would like to discuss that with you."

"Fine."

"Might we go, sit perhaps, someplace else. Unless you would be more comfortable here in Jonah's office. I would understand completely."

On one hand, I was scared that if we walked into the corridor together, he might have a couple of hired goons waiting to do something terrible. He might even hit me over the head with one of his exquisite mosaics that lined the walls. Naturally, my mouth went dry with that dirty-penny taste, even though I couldn't remember ever sucking a penny, so how would I know? On the other hand, could he possibly let anything happen to me if he realized somewhere out there was a forensic accountant who knew about a check made out to him by Phoebe Kingsley? And I did want to get out of Jonah's office. It felt wrong to be in here talking with this man, almost in a religious sense, a desecration, like when you drop the Bible on the floor.

No goons, no Attack of the Mosaics. We wound up in the employees' lunchroom, a small area with a table and chairs, refrigerator, and a soda machine I'd always felt was cheap—Manhattan Aesthetics could offer employees free sodas—but Jonah said they had to charge fifty cents each or . . . I couldn't remember what, just that it had sounded lame.

Gilbert John sat in a not too terrible plastic scoop chair and said, "I have to confess to something."

I nodded and managed to say, "Please, go ahead." I wished more than anything that Grandma Ethel could be sitting beside me, squeezing my hand, signaling, *You're doing fine.*

"The last discussion I ever had with Jonah was an argument about that check. I was sick at heart after it happened, and when Jonah went missing, and then we found out . . ." Gilbert John was pale, that greenish white people turn when they're sick and dizzy. Still, if he had started crying or gotten really emotional, I would have almost laughed. Instead, he said, after swallowing hard and seeming to get a grip on himself, "Jonah was a very balanced individual and a very responsible one. But he was also under a great deal of pressure. Sometimes I felt I was adding to his pressure by not being as active in the practice as I had been. But more and more, Jonah had a tendency to rush to judgment—though fortunately, not when it came to his patients. He was a fine, thorough surgeon."

"What was the argument about? What do you think there could have been about the check that made you think he rushed to judgment? Because I've known him longer and better than you have, I've seen him in every possible situation, and I never once witnessed a rush to judgment."

Maybe I sounded angrier than I meant to sound, because Gilbert John said, "Jonah was an extraordinarily rational man, but if I may contradict you in one small way, you did not see him in much of his professional life, only in its, shall we say, social aspects, in which a spouse is appropriate." I kept looking straight at him; if he'd had half an iota of sense, he'd have realized I was thinking that his spouse, the lovely Coral, was never appropriate. "Jonah was short on time, as well as patience. I believe I might have been traveling when this check arrived. Rather than waiting until I returned, or even phoning me, he took the check that indeed was made out to me to a forensic accountant. This was Jonah Gersten, a man I mentored, brought into my practice, cared for very . . . much."

"But can't you see—"

"No, I really can't. I've tried. Not that it matters anymore, because it was one small incident in a long and deeply felt relationship. But had he asked, I could have told him Phoebe Kingsley was—how best to put it?—a somewhat unbalanced woman. She kept harping, 'People will talk.' Nothing I said could convince her that our nurses, the office staff, are fully aware of the value of silence and of the patient's right to privacy. I explained, in the most conciliatory way possible, that we had dealings with patients far more celebrated than she and that none had any cause for complaint either with the results of their surgery or with our discretion. Mrs. Kingsley was under the distinctly mistaken impression that the way to ensure her surgery being hush-hush was to make out a check to me, to me personally."

"Did you ever explain that to him?" I asked.

"Of course I did. In that last conversation. Alas, Jonah's so-called forensic accountant discovered Phoebe Kingsley had some sort of secret fund, and from there the matter took on a life of its own in Jonah's mind. By the time he came to me for an explanation, he did not want one. All he seemed to want to do was accuse me of dirty dealings." Gilbert John rose from his plastic chair in his elegant fashion, as if from a throne. "All through this talk now," he went on, "I've wanted to say to you, 'Jonah was like a son to me.' I held back because it sounded so fatuous, so histrionic. The truth of the matter is, he was like a son to me." He seemed about to come toward me, but then he turned, nodded goodbye, and hurried from the room as if on the way to an emergency.

What began as a morning head-clearing walk the next day, Sunday, while the boys were at a birthday party, ended with me ringing Andrea's doorbell, the chimes of which would have been appropriate to Westminster Abbey. When I heard the heavy tread coming down the stairs, I almost turned and ran. Either I flaked out for a few seconds, or Fat Boy was faster on his feet than I'd thought.

He opened the door and said, "She's at some hotel, Four Seasons, Ritz-Carlton, in the city because some old ladies from France who embroider things come every year and she has to pick out new linens. What is that, sheets or tablecloths?"

"Probably both," I said.

"Economic stimulus. Who needs the Treasury or the fucking Fed when Andrea Brinckerhoff gets going?" He scratched the gargantuan belly beneath his lavender Polo shirt and invited me in.

We sat upstairs in his office in front of all his TV screens, Fat Boy in his recliner, his bare feet with little curlicues of blond hair on top of each toe hanging over the footrest. I sat a foot away, in a smaller chair that also reclined, although I didn't take advantage.

I filled him in on what had happened with Gilbert John and asked him what he thought. He said, "It's like this with coincidences. One, okay. More than one, a James Bond movie. Get what I'm saying?"

"Not totally," I said.

"Not at all, you mean. So let me explain. The Phoebe check, okay, maybe, could be. But then College Girls and Dorinda? Then add to that Redleaf Capital, because ten minutes after I got off the phone with you, what do I have up on my monitor but a list of Redleaf's investors, past and present. Not to toot my own horn, because I don't have to with you, you knowing I'm . . ." He shrugged.

"What are you going to say?" I asked. "'Aw shucks, well, I'm darn smart'?"

"I was trying to be charming. That well-socialized-modesty

shit. Forget it. I'm brilliant. You know it, I know it. But brilliance is one thing, and getting a confidential list like that in ten minutes on the weekend is fucking off the charts. You've got your dumb look on. You probably lost your train of thought, which people do all the time with me, so this is where I'm at. I looked at the list. Jonah was never a Redleaf investor. No Gersten in the history of the world was ever an investor with them, which speaks well for the family. Now, I'll tell you who was and is an investor in Redleaf Capital: Gilbert John Noakes. Not a high-rolling investor like a lot of the shmucks who sank their money into that fund. But Noakes's original investment of two point five mil has a current value of three hundred thousand and change. With a guy like him, that's real money, a real goddamn fucking hit. And for a guy like me, this information is just another deposit in Gilbert John's ever growing coincidence account. The guy is feeling short of cash. Desperate, maybe."

"But there was something very believable when he said that Jonah was like a son to him."

"Susie, ever hear of filicide?" He didn't give me time to answer, which I might have in an hour or two. "Filicide. The killing of one's child."

Two days later, Eddie Huber finally called to say my copies of Gilbert John's MasterCard payments to College Girl checked out. The last time he had used the service was 2006. But two weeks before Jonah died, Gilbert John had called and said he'd wanted a new girl, someone he hadn't used before. He'd arranged to pay cash. He didn't want anything charged to a credit card, even though it would appear as College Data Research Services.

They got him Dorinda Dillon. A few hours before their scheduled date, Gilbert John called the service to say he couldn't make it. However, there was a 20 percent cancellation fee, so he had a street-level messenger service deliver an envelope with the cash. He hadn't gotten any sex from Dorinda. He hadn't even met her. But he had her name and address.

"We'll keep you advised on the progress of the case," Eddie Huber said to me. Not that I was expecting a thank-you note, but she could have said something like "Good work" or "We would appreciate your not mentioning our little investigatory oversights to CNN."

The life that I was stuck with and blessed with went on. I worked at Florabella, went back to my book group, where, luckily, I'd missed the session on *The Idiot,* interviewed several nannies from what Babs called "the only possible agency" in an effort to replace Ida and Ingvild when they went back to Norway. One nanny seemed really great, but after she met the boys, she said she didn't want to work on Long Island.

After Passover at my in-laws', where Dashiell climbed their bookshelves to toss down a few pre-Columbian statues so the three of them could play a Baby Moses game, I took them and Ida and Ingvild to a hotel in South Beach for the rest of the vacation. We spent half the time at Grandma Ethel and Sparky's. I fantasized, briefly, about opening a Florabella Tropical, but I knew I had to go home. Before I left, I tried and failed to convince my grandmother to have some sort of reconciliation with my mother.

"Fine," she said. "I'll call and say, 'Hello, Sherry, this is your mother. I'm sorry I left you with Lenny. Have a nice life. Goodbye.'"

"Don't you feel—"

"No," she snapped. "I don't feel."

Grandma Ethel came to New York a week later and sat with me in Eddie Huber's office. Gilbert John Noakes had agreed to plead guilty. But as part of the deal, he had to sit with me, face-to-face, and tell me what had happened. The other part of the deal was that during his fifteen to twenty-five years in prison, he would be allowed to do mosaic work for four hours a week, as long as he maintained good behavior.

Grandma Ethel and I were led to chairs across from Eddie Huber. Her desk was bare, and she seemed vulnerable, like a soldier without a weapon. I guessed it was a security precaution. Gilbert John was seated on one side of the room, about eight feet from us. His posture had initially appeared relaxed, close to lounging, especially considering that besides being handcuffed to the arms of the chair and wearing irons on his ankles with a very short chain between them, he had a cop on either side of him, another in front of the window, and a fourth guarding the door. But something in his head must have pinged, *Ladies present!* and his back reflexively straightened.

"I can't tell you how sorry I am about this," he told me in his rich, gentlemanly voice.

"Tell me what happened," I said.

"Where to begin?" Maybe he had an inner voice-over saying, *Everyone leaned forward expectantly,* because when no one reacted, he sighed and said, "It's like this. Over the years, Jonah and I had talked about holding all our tension in our hands." He folded his hands into fists and squeezed them. I had no idea if he was aware of what he was doing. "I saw Jonah rubbing his hand in the offices several times and could see he was in pain."

"Did you know Jonah was suspicious of you?" I asked.

"I wasn't sure. But I pride myself in being perceptive. I knew he was concerned about our inventory shrinkage. And then there was the check from that dreadful Phoebe woman. Do you know what she told me the GP Fund stood for? Gorgeous Phoebe. I knew it would be only a matter of time before . . . I suppose there's no need to go into detail. I realized Jonah was putting it all together, which, as you can imagine, was quite troubling to me. I had no idea he had already begun looking into it in such an organized fashion. In passing, I told him I knew a brilliant massage therapist who had studied in India and did ayurvedic hand massage on the top surgeons of New York. I said I myself had just been to her and that I couldn't stop raving. No one could."

"And then," Grandma Ethel said.

"I bribed the building's porter to get in and get the key. I made an imprint in modeling clay. I knew it would be dangerous to tape a door latch closed. That's how the Watergate burglars were discovered, taping back the locks—a piece of historical trivia. But I did use a high-viscosity skin adhesive to glue the latches of the doors on both the service entrance and the room where they keep the tenants' keys. Marvelous stuff. And it readily cleaned off with a solvent, acetone. However, the debossment of the key in the clay was sufficient, though at the risk of sounding crass, it cost me a fortune to get a copy." He leaned forward to me. It burned me that they had allowed him to put on his own clothes, that they hadn't brought him to the DA's office in a prison jumpsuit. "I know you think I'm terrible. You're right."

"Keep talking," I said.

"I told Jonah I had my secretary make an appointment for him, but I did it myself and entered it on his calendar. I was terribly nervous he might refuse to go, or might not show up. The day before Jonah's appointment with Dorinda, when she went for a walk—the porter told me she went out once a day—I let myself in and looked around."

"Weren't you worried you'd run into the porter?" Grandma Ethel asked.

The small smile that made its appearance and quickly vanished was one I'd seen so often during the years of Jonah's partnership with him: Gilbert John, self-satisfied. "One has to take risks in this sort of enterprise, but risks can be minimized. I called the doorman from my cell phone, taking care to press star-six-seven. That blocks the caller ID, you know. I told him, 'You need to get the porter up to the tenth-floor trash room this minute!' in a very irate manner. I waited three minutes and then took a deep breath and hurried in via the service door. No porter, as I'd expected . . . or at least hoped."

"All right, so you got up there," I said. "Then what?"

"I found her scissors. I sharpened them. The following afternoon, when she went out again, thank goodness, I waited down the street a bit, coat collar up, brim of an old felt fedora lowered so I was not recognized. Finally, I saw the porter. I knew I would eventually. Again a risk, but he was slow-moving, to say nothing of slow-thinking. When he came out the service door with a huge can of recyclables and was setting it on the curb, I rushed down the alleyway, let myself in, and took the service elevator upstairs, taking care to send it back down. I secreted myself in Dorinda's front closet. I'd planned on sneaking up on them, knocking her out with a stun gun, then quickly slitting Jonah's carotid artery with a blade of the scissors." He paused. "I'm awfully sorry to burden you with these details, Susie, but I was told that I had to be completely forthright. What surprised me was that Jonah caught on so soon to what Dorinda actually was. He was so quick-witted. Dorinda came back to the closet incredibly fast to get Jonah's coat. The stun gun fit too tightly in my coat pocket, and I couldn't get it out fast enough. Instead, I knocked her out with the bottom of the electric broom."

"You cleaned off the broom, didn't you?" Grandma Ethel said. "And then vacuumed somewhere it wouldn't show to get the brush dirty again."

"Yes!" He sounded pleased that someone was recognizing his cleverness. "Actually, I dumped out the vacuum's contents and swept them up again." Then his eyes returned to me. "Certainly, I have no expectation that you will approve of me in any way, but I hope someday you recognize that was fast thinking."

"It was fast thinking," I agreed. "But it wasn't good thinking. If it had been good, you wouldn't be in leg irons now, facing four hours a week of mosaics followed by . . . what? Freedom after twenty-five years with no money and jailhouse dentures?

Death." He tried for a nonchalant shrug, but the handcuffs threw off his balance so only one shoulder rose. I went on, "You'll have your art. But most likely, they'll give you cheapo grout."

I sketched that picture, if unconsciously, knowing Gilbert John was at least as visual as I was. He wouldn't be able to resist coloring it and filling in the details: the inferior, gritty grout; the no-deodorant-for-me prison guard coming to take him back to his cell even though he had hardly begun to work.

"Come on," Eddie Huber said to him, "you know the parameters of our agreement. Tell Mrs. Gersten what happened after you struck Dorinda Dillon with the electric broom."

I was annoyed to see Gilbert John's back relax into a slumped C in relief at her interruption. He said, "After hitting the woman, as you might imagine, I was very shaken. Jonah was strong, younger, but he was not prepared. As it turned out, neither was I. I was unable to open the scissors to slit his throat. So I had to stab him. Is there anything else you'd like to know?"

I didn't answer. I just gave him a look I hoped he'd never forget, though I knew he would. I couldn't manage a thank-you to Eddie Huber, but I gave her a nod. Together, Grandma Ethel and I walked out.

Outside, in the bright sun of early spring, I said, "This knowing doesn't make anything better."

"Did you think it would?" my grandmother asked.

"No. But I had to hear it."

"Please, you don't have to explain to me. How could you allow that sociopath in bespoke suiting to get away with murder and not have to face you? Not just you, the wife. You, the person who wanted to know the truth about what happened to Jonah."

"It wasn't so much truth-seeking as I couldn't stand the thought of that repulsive, stupid, useless, innocent hooker rotting in jail . . . not that she'll ever do any good on the outside. But I had to do something."

"I guess that's what ethics are," she said. "Or is it 'what ethics is'?"

"I think it's 'are,'" I said, "but I'm not sure."

"If I still had *Talk of Miami,* I'd have an intern look it up," Grandma Ethel said. She was downcast for an instant, but then she took my arm and smiled. "So, what's the best restaurant around here? I'm talking four stars. I'm paying."

"I don't have much of an appetite," I told her.

"It doesn't mean you don't eat. Life goes on, toots, whether you like the way it goes or not. The best a girl can do is mind her ethics—and eat a nice lunch."

Acknowledgments

True, this is a work of fiction. The novelist needs imagination, the passion to write the story she most wants to read, and talent. Facts, too. Make an avoidable error and some knowledgeable reader will smack palm to forehead in annoyance—and at the same time be pulled out of the universe of the novel. Facts also matter because, as author, the more I know about an aspect of the world I'm creating, the more authentic and authoritative my writing will be. So thanks to the following generous and patient individuals who answered all sorts of questions. However, when their facts did not fit my fiction, I went for the story. The inaccuracies are mine, not theirs.

Joan Smith of Joan Smith Flowers in Port Washington, New York, is a gifted floral designer whose work is gorgeous and sophisticated yet cheery. When I decided to put Susie Gersten in the flower business, I began by asking Joan about her work. Through her generosity, I actually wound up "helping" in the back room of her shop, learning some of the lingo, getting hands-on experience. What fun! I loved the work—plus Joan is a hoot and a half.

I can write short and long fiction, screenplays, op-ed pieces, and book reviews, but I learned I cannot write a clever tabloid headline. After I turned out a series of clunkers, I called Andie Coller—journalist, pundit, and former headline writer—for help. Not only did she do what I could not but she did it expertly and breathtakingly fast.

Jules B. Kroll, founder of the global risk-consulting giant Kroll Inc., told me everything I needed to know about missing persons and private investigative agencies. He was thoughtful, patient, and a charming raconteur. He also was kind enough to introduce me to his former colleague Annie Cheney, who offered me some sound insights.

When my great pal from high school and college, Suzy Sonenberg, told me her son Dan was going to be the father of triplets, I knew his wife, Alex Sax, was someone I needed to ask, well, what it's like to be pregnant with triplets. Alex was informative, knowledgeable, and delightful. (And their three sons are adorable!)

I'm indebted to my friend Adrienne Arsht for reading a draft of my manuscript. She is not only smart about life and art, but about dangling modifiers. And thanks to my pals Victoria Skurnick and Bob Wyatt for prodding me until I came up with this novel's title.

I'm also grateful to Dr. Andrew Jacono for answering my questions about how plastic surgeons work. He is a certified good guy, the national chairman of the Face to Face Committee for the American Academy of Facial Plastic and Reconstructive Surgery, which offers pro bono consultation and surgery to victims of domestic violence. For the past six years, he has chaired About Face: Making Changes, an annual Long Island benefit for survivors of domestic violence.

Also, thank you to Dr. Janice Asher, Dr. Gerard A. Catanese, Samantha Zises Cohen, Susan Lawton, Anthony Lepsis and Brian Whitney of North Hills Garden Design, Lara Zises, and Susan Zises.

The following people made generous donations to charities by "buying" characters' names in this novel: Maureen Ferrari, Lizbeth Holbreich, Gary and Corky Paston, and Chris Pierce (for her mother, Eddie Huber).

I am lucky to have two of the greats of the book business on my side: Nan Graham, my editor, and Susan Moldow, the publisher of Scribner. I'm also indebted to Katherine Monaghan, Paul Whitlatch, and their colleagues. Giga-thanks also to Susanne Kirk; she was a blessing in my life.

I am grateful to the staffs of the Port Washington (New York) Public Library and the Brooklyn Public Library.

My assistant, Ronnie Gavarian, has been a professional caterer, legal assistant, and jewelry maven. In my house we say "Ronnie can do anything." And she does everything, from copyediting to research to cake decorating, brilliantly.

Richard Pine is a super literary agent and a gracious human being. I'm glad he's in my corner.

I keep learning from my wonderful children and in-law children: Elizabeth and Vincent Picciuto; Andy and Leslie Stern Abramowitz.

In ancient days, writers of comedy had Thalia. My muses are Nathan and Molly Abramowitz and Charles and Edmund Picciuto.

And after two score–plus years, my husband, Elkan Abramowitz, remains the best person in the world.

About the Author

Susan Isaacs, novelist, essayist, and screenwriter, was born in Brooklyn and educated at Queens College. Her twelve novels include *Compromising Positions, Close Relations, Almost Paradise, Shining Through,* and *Past Perfect*. A recipient of the Writers for Writers Award and the John Steinbeck Award, Isaacs serves as chairman of the board of Poets & Writers and is a past president of Mystery Writers of America. Her fiction has been translated into thirty languages. She lives on Long Island with her husband.